A History of Modern Chinese Fiction

A History of
MODERN CHINESE FICTION

SECOND EDITION

by C. T. HSIA

NEW HAVEN AND LONDON, YALE UNIVERSITY PRESS

1971

Library of Congress catalog card number: 60–13273
International standard book number: 0–300–01462–7 (cloth) ,
0–300–01461–9 (paper)

Set in Baskerville type.
Printed in the United States of America by
the Carl Purington Rollins Printing-Office of the
Yale University Press, New Haven, Conn.

Distributed in Great Britain, Europe, and Africa by
Yale University Press, Ltd., London; in Canada by
McGill-Queen's University Press, Montreal; in Mexico
by Centro Interamericano de Libros Académicos,
Mexico City; in Central and South America by Kaiman
& Polon, Inc., New York City; in Australasia by
Australia and New Zealand Book Co., Pty., Ltd.,
Artarmon, New South Wales; in India by UBS Publishers'
Distributors Pvt., Ltd., Delhi; in Japan by
John Weatherhill, Inc., Tokyo.

Preface to the Second Edition

IN PREPARING this second edition, I have not revised the main text to the extent of changing its identity as a publication of 1961, though I have corrected to the best of my knowledge all mistakes and misprints to be found in the first edition and added an epilogue and a new appendix to make my account of modern Chinese fiction more up to date and amenable to a theoretical interpretation. I had thought of providing the latest biographical information concerning the authors studied in the book, but since so much of that information has to do with the Cultural Revolution, the added material would have appeared incongruous with the main text, which could not have discussed Communist literature in the context of that revolution. But while I had not anticipated this cataclysmic event, recent literary developments on the mainland have confirmed rather than contradicted my gloomy view of Chinese Communist literature. Now that Mao Tsetung has practically halted all literary production and repudiated all writers of professional standing, few outside mainland China would want to contest my thesis that Mao has been the main cause of the crippling of that literature since the forties.

During the preparation of my book, it looked as though

Mao's cultural deputy, Chou Yang, were equally guilty of the crime of stifling literary expression. But even then I felt justified to speculate that "possibly if he had not early enjoyed great power and the responsibility of enforcing the Maoist line, he might also have ended as a Communist miscreant like Hu Feng, Feng Hsüeh-feng, and his onetime comrade in arms, Hsü Mou-yung. One can never tell." Chou Yang's downfall as a Communist miscreant has since been confirmed. While I see no reason to alter my portrait of him as a detestable henchman of Mao during his enjoyment of power in the forties and fifties, it is also perfectly legitimate to regard him now as the last defender of the leftist tradition who had sooner or later to incur the wrath of Mao. Accordingly, I have so treated Chou Yang in the epilogue to bring out the essential meaning of his disgrace in the context of Mao's fanatic determination to eradicate all leftist influence in the realm of culture.

Big as the first edition was, ideally it ought to have devoted more space to several important leftist novelists receiving only a brief mention in Chapter 13. Now that the leftist tradition has played out its vital role in the development of modern Chinese literature, the task of making a systematic survey of its achievement appears all the more urgent. But clearly such a survey calls for a separate volume and cannot be accommodated in the second edition of my book. Nevertheless, I have provided room in the epilogue for a discussion of one recent novel each by Ai Wu, Chou Li-po, and Ou-yang Shan, all writers schooled in the leftist tradition. I have analyzed these works not only to extend my survey of Communist fiction through the Cultural Revolution (hence the dates 1917–1957 have dropped from the main title) but also to stress the fact that up to that revolution writers of the leftist persuasion had coninued to play a major role in the making of literature on the mainland.

The essay "Obsession with China: The Moral Burden of Modern Chinese Literature," now serving as Appendix 1, is my attempt to define an essential quality of the pre-1949 modern Chinese literature that makes it different from both the traditional literature immediately preceding it and the subsequent Communist literature. I hope its inclusion in the present edition will provide a useful perspective to our understanding of nearly all the authors discussed in Parts I and II. In addition, it serves to round out the chapters on Lao Shê and Shen Ts'ung-wen with a discussion of two further examples of their fiction : *City of Cats* and *Alice in China.* Yang Shuo's *A Thousand Miles of Lovely Land,* also discussed in Appendix 1, complements my account of Communist fiction in Chapter 18 and the epilogue with an important example of soldier fiction.

I have omitted from this edition Tsi-an Hsia's appendix on Taiwan, retaining only my postscript on Chiang Kuei's *The Whirlwind* as Appendix 2. My late brother's essay was full of acute observation and shrewd advice, but it has proudly served its purpose in that, in comparison with the mainland, Taiwan since 1961 has enjoyed a minor literary renascence of genuine promise, even though few Western readers are yet aware of its existence. The best Taiwan writers, including those now residing in America who had studied under my brother, are turning out a fiction and poetry of refined sensibility and careful craftsmanship. But clearly, like the leftist authors of the thirties and forties, these new writers deserve a book-length study and cannot be summarily treated in an appendix. However, I have retained my critique of *The Whirlwind* because, although it does not indicate the new directions of fiction in Taiwan, it has probably remained the most powerful novel ever produced there.

So much has been written about modern Chinese literature since the initial publication of my book that it would not be possible for me to include in the already lengthy bibliography all the new scholarly titles pertaining to my subject. Fortunately, the availability of such new reference works as Tien-yi Li's *Chinese Fiction: A Bibliography of Books and Articles in*

Chinese and English (New Haven, Yale University, Far Eastern Publications, 1968) means that the scholar will know where to look for materials in furtherance of his research interests. For the present edition, therefore, I have added only a number of titles that seem to me most useful to the general reader and the beginning student of modern Chinese fiction.

"Obsession with China: The Moral Burden of Modern Chinese Literature" has earlier appeared in Alona E. Evans, Henry F. Schwarz, and Owen S. Stratton, eds., *China in Perspective* (Wellesley, Mass., Wellesley College, 1967). A longer version of the epilogue, entitled "Literature and Art under Mao Tse-tung," was originally commissioned as a chapter in Frank N. Trager and William Henderson, eds., *Communist China, 1949–1969: A Twenty-Year Appraisal* (New York, New York University Press, 1970). I wish to thank the editors of the respective volumes for granting me permission to reprint my two papers here.

In these pieces I have adopted the standard translations of three Chinese terms ("the Great Leap Forward," "the Writers' Union," "the Yenan Forum on Literature and Art") in place of the ones used in the main text ("the Big Leap Forward," "the Writers' Association," "the Yenan Literary Conference"). I hope the reader will excuse this slight inconsistency, since the latter terms appear too frequently in the main text to warrant change.

Of my several friends who alerted me to mistakes in the first edition, I especially want to thank Professor Liu Ts'un-yan of the Australian National University, who has read it with minute care and spotted errors that would have otherwise escaped me.

C. T. H.

May 1970

Preface

AT A TIME when modern China has become in this
country a subject of intensive study, it is a matter of some
surprise that its literature has been permitted to suffer comparative neglect. Social scientists, in their investigations of
modern Chinese history and culture, have by and large
failed to make use of the literary record, even though they
cannot be unaware of its profound influence on modern
Chinese thought and politics. Possibly, the theory that contemporary Chinese literature is predominantly Communist
in character has become so universally accepted that one
tends to look askance on this literature as an instrument of
political agitation and propaganda and therefore dismisses
it as an unrewarding subject for study. Yet not all of it is
superficial: much bears sensitive and pained witness to the
turmoil and tragedy of the contemporary Chinese scene. A
student of modern America cannot know his subject well
until he has digested the imaginative versions of American
experience shaped by its most significant writers: the same
holds true for the student of modern China. He can ignore
only at his own peril the multiform images of the country
to be seen in its more serious literature. Especially at present,
when so many scholars, it seems to me, are engaged in arid
theorizing about the historical inevitability of the Com-

munist success in the land of Confucius, will the study of its
recent literature serve as a concrete reminder that, all appearances to the contrary, the Chinese are as hopefully and
tragically human as the rest of mankind, with their inescapable burden of follies, fears, and dreams. One incidental
value of this study of modern Chinese fiction should be to
provide a new perspective to the problems and dilemmas
facing the modern Chinese, which specialists have hitherto
pondered in nonliterary contexts.

The present work is not of course designed as an adjunct
to political, sociological, or economic studies. The literary
historian's first task is always the discovery and appraisal of
excellence: he would be forfeiting his usefulness to students
of literature and to scholars in other disciplines as well if
he used the literary material merely as a mirror to reflect the
politics and culture of an age. Although I have been concerned to provide the historical and ideological background
of the period, I have tried mainly to elicit order and pattern
from the chaotic mass of modern Chinese fiction—the most
fruitful and important branch of modern Chinese literature
—and to test this pattern against the Communist idea of the
modern Chinese literary tradition, and against the example
and challenge of the Western tradition, which has informed
its style and direction. In undertaking this latter task, I have
found, regrettably, very little usable criticism in the existing
body of literature on the subject and have turned for guidance, especially in my interpretation of individual authors,
mainly to contemporary American and English critics who
have, in the past twenty years or so, significantly enlarged
our understanding of Western fiction.

On the assumption that most readers do not possess a first-
hand reading knowledge of modern Chinese fiction, I have
included information on plot and character for the tales and
novels that are discussed at length. To offset the tedium of
this procedure, I have, whenever possible, interwoven excerpts in translation with critical commentary so that readers

may sample the flavor of the original and test my judgment. But unfortunately, Chinese being a radically different language from English, even the best translations do not adequately recapture the spirit of the original, and in my attempts to be faithful I have perhaps sinned more than I should against readability. Another method regularly employed to ensure a degree of critical sophistication in my discussion of Chinese writers is to compare them to Western authors, especially to the line of eminent novelists from Cervantes to Faulkner, with whose works most readers are familiar. I am aware that contemporary Japanese and Russian fiction has a great deal in common with contemporary Chinese fiction and would serve better the purposes of comparative study. But for readers I have in mind, to compare these three literatures seems rather pointless, since perhaps only a handful of scholars are equally at home in all of them.

Because I covet readers who know little about modern China but are curious about its literature, I have avoided using special terms that may prove ambiguous. However, I have retained "feudalism" and its cognates because alternatives do not have the same connotation: as used in the book, "feudalism" is little more than a pejorative term descriptive of the backward rural economy of traditional China dominated by the gentry and the scholar-official class. I have also followed the fashion of writers on Communist China in using "cadre" as a singular rather than a collective noun. There are otherwise few English words that call for special definition.

The names of all Chinese persons are Romanized according to the Wade-Giles system, with the exception of a few well-known contemporary figures and one or two ancient sages. For place names I have as a rule followed the conventional postal spelling. I have consistently referred to the great northern city as Peking, even during the years when it was not the national capital; the form "Peiping" is used only when, in discussing or quoting from several works of fiction,

I have to abide by their authors' preference for that designation.

The book was a solitary undertaking in the sense that during the years of its preparation I had regrettably associated with few who were actively interested in my subject. All the more, therefore, I treasure the encouragement and assistance of friends and institutions. My brother, Tsi-an Hsia, who has kindly contributed an essay on the literary milieu of Taiwan, was most generous with his time and advice during the last stages of its preparation. Living far removed from large Chinese collections, I continually relied on his patience to clear up doubtful points in my text, to verify page references to Chinese works, and to check the accuracy of my bibliography. Stephen C. Soong, himself a poet, critic, and translator, supplied me many volumes from Hong Kong which are not easily accessible in America. Ch'eng Tsing-yü, another friend in Hong Kong, has also been assiduous in sending me books. To Tien-yi Li of Yale University I owe hours of delightful conversation on modern Chinese literature. Thanks are also due John H. Davis and Miss Harriet C. Mills of Columbia University for their helpful letters.

To the Rockefeller Foundation, and especially to Dr. Charles B. Fahs, Director of its Humanities Division, I am deeply grateful for the grant-in-aid that enabled me, for three years, to pursue my research without financial worry. To Frederick A. Pottle and Cleanth Brooks, my mentors at Yale, I owe a debt beyond acknowledgment—for their unfailing interest in my work and innumerable kindnesses through the years; Professor Pottle, especially, took the trouble to suggest many stylistic improvements for my completed manuscript. But it is David N. Rowe of Yale University, deeply interested in the project from the very beginning, who gave me courage and self-confidence until it was completed: words, surely, cannot adequately express my appreciation of his loyalty and friendship.

I want also to thank my editor, David Horne, for his ex-

Preface

pert and tactful editing; Howard P. Linton and the staff of the East Asiatic Library of the Columbia University Library for extending me the freedom of using its excellent collection of modern Chinese literature; Norman H. Pearson of Yale for reading the completed manuscript; and Joseph K. Yamagiwa of the University of Michigan and Wilmer K. Trauger of the State University College of Education at Potsdam, for reading portions of the manuscript during earlier stages of its development. Finally, my gratitude goes to my wife for her uncomplaining heroism.

C. T. H.

Potsdam, New York
April 1960

Contents

Contents

PART I

The Early Period (1917-1927)

CHAPTER 1

The Literary Revolution

IN JANUARY 1917 a rather modestly titled article, "Suggestions for a Reform of Literature," appeared in *New Youth*, the leading journal of Chinese intellectuals. Its author, Hu Shih (1891–1962), who was then completing his doctorate in philosophy at Columbia University, had for nearly two years pondered over the necessity of adopting pai-hua or vernacular Chinese as the national medium of communication and had discussed the problem with a number of unsympathetic Chinese friends studying in America. Earlier, in a letter to the editor of *New Youth*, he had introduced the phrase "literary revolution"; in the new essay, however, he refrained from using that explosive term and spoke out for the vitality of pai-hua only under the negative emphasis of "Don't hesitate to use colloquial words and expressions," the last of his eight proposals for reform. Hu Shih did not then suspect that his article would ignite a literary movement of unprecedented scope and importance, radically changing the course and shape of Chinese literature.

Ch'en Tu-hsiu, the editor of *New Youth*, was extremely pleased with his correspondent in America. A veteran revolutionary and dean of the School of Letters at National Peking

University, he was then fired by his enthusiasm for science and democracy and by his ambition to demolish the social and ideological structure of Confucianist China. To him, therefore, a reform of language and literature was but another phase of the battle against the decadent tradition. Warmly endorsing Hu Shih's article, he followed up, in the next number of his monthly, with a pugnacious editorial entitled "For a Literary Revolution." As a piece of fustian interweaving literary ignorance with critical irresponsibility, it departs in spirit almost wholly from Hu Shih's earlier essay, which in the main counsels avoidance of stale sentiments and themes and of outworn diction. Grandiloquently, Ch'en Tu-hsiu calls for the establishment of "a plain and lyrical national literature," "a fresh and sincere realistic literature," and "an intelligible and popular social literature" to replace the time-worn "ornate, adulatory literature of the aristocracy," "stale, bombastic literature of classicism," and "obscure, difficult literature of the hermit and the recluse." [1] The editor gives next a brief, grossly unfair sketch of the Chinese literary tradition as the monopoly of the servile and obscurantist aristocrat, classicist, and hermit, and goes on to invoke the names of six Western authors as example and challenge: "Literary worthies of the nation, dare you promise to become China's Hugo and Zola, Goethe and Hauptmann, Dickens and Wilde?" [2] The enlistment of Oscar Wilde in the cause of a national, realistic, and social literature may be thought appropriately anticlimactic.

Upon his return to China in July 1917 Hu Shih was appointed professor of philosophy and chairman of the English department at Peking University. By that time other faculty members of the University besides Ch'en Tu-hsiu— notably Ch'ien Hsüan-t'ung and Liu Fu—had been convinced of the importance of a literary reform. During the whole year of 1917 and afterward, *New Youth* served as their forum for exchanging views on many theoretical and practical problems relating to the use of pai-hua. If these reformers had anticipated some lively opposition, they were quite disappointed: for the March 1918 number Ch'ien Hsüan-t'ung had to write, under an assumed name, a vigorous letter of protest to the editors, in the hope of stirring up controversy. Among the conservative literati, only Lin Shu, foremost classical stylist and indefatigable translator of Western fiction of his time, had shown from the beginning some alarm, but it was not until March 1919 that he took the trouble of addressing an open letter to Ts'ai Yüan-p'ei, Chancellor of Peking University, deploring his connivance with members of his faculty in the onslaught on Confucian morality and the classical literary tradition. By that time, however, Hu Shih had already written, in his cogently reasoned essay "For a Constructive Literary Revolution" (*New Youth*, April 1918), a solid defense of the pai-hua movement in the perspective of Chinese literary history: Lin Shu's charges of literary subversion therefore sounded rather hollow. In 1920, by the decree of the Ministry of Education, pai-hua was introduced as a medium of instruction into the first and second grades of elementary schools: the work of the reformers had won official recognition.

When Hu Shih began to occupy himself with the idea of a literary reform in the summer of 1915 (he was then a student at Cornell University), he was attacking a problem whose crucial relevance to the task of national reconstruction had been felt by a number of enlightened scholars, journalists, and educators for over thirty years. The accelerated military and economic aggression by foreign powers since the Opium War had entailed an urgent need for more effective communication on all levels: not only had the officials and scholars to arm themselves with a competent knowledge of Western institutions, arts, and sciences, but the populace had also to be alerted to the national danger. The literary language, or wen-yen, with its proverbial difficulty and its pronounced archaic and poetic flavor, was

5

clearly unprepared to fulfill that need. For one thing, it had proved to be an awkward instrument for accurate translation. Yen Fu's elegant rendition of Adam Smith, John Stuart Mill, Thomas Henry Huxley, and Herbert Spencer, is at best a tour de force, unlikely to be duplicated by translators of less literary skill. Lin Shu's popular adaptations from the works of Scott, Dickens, Tolstoy, Conan Doyle, and a host of other serious and popular writers, maintain the integrity of classical prose only by an almost complete disregard for accuracy.[3] For another, wen-yen was found to be equally unsuitable for the task of disseminating modern ideas among a more or less literate public. A group of frustrated reformers, banished from the Manchu court, had turned journalists in order to make their appeals directly to the people, and they were compelled to abandon classical prose and forge a wen-yen style readily intelligible and more hospitable to Western terminology. Liang Ch'i-ch'ao, a prominent member of this group, was especially successful in molding a prose which, while literary, was adequate to the exposition and discussion of ideas and highly effective as an instrument of patriotic propaganda. This style was widely imitated by political writers and revolutionaries of his time, among them Dr. Sun Yat-sen, and persisted as the standard newspaper and bureaucratic Chinese well after World War II.

Vernacular Chinese itself, of course, had been the medium for a number of highly popular novels long before Hu Shih urged its adoption as the national language. Such novels of the late Ch'ing period as *The Travels of Lao Ts'an* and *Bureaucracy Exposed* testify not only to an expanding popular interest in pai-hua literature but to the increasing reliance of writers on pai-hua for satiric exposure of current social and political ills. The development of a modern press at that time also promoted the use of pai-hua in other types of popular edification and entertainment than the novel.

Still other reformers, seeing the impossibility of educating the illiterate masses, advocated the romanization of Mandarin and other Chinese dialects as well as the adoption of a simplified ideographic script. These reformers, prominently Wang Chao and Lao Nai-hsüan, were inspired by the success of Christian missionaries in reaching the peasant population by phonetic rendering of dialects through the use of an alphabet.

Before the time of Hu Shih, the use of pai-hua, a more intelligible wen-yen style, and some alphabetic system of writing, then, was mainly conceived as a political and educational necessity. The early reformers had no thought of encroaching upon the domain of polite letters, and the pai-hua novelists had always regarded themselves as peripheral to the main literary tradition. Hu Shih's distinctive contribution to the pai-hua movement is that while yielding to none in his appreciation of the educational value of the vernacular, he was the first to assert its dignity and importance as a literary medium. To him, the trend of Chinese literature has been its periodic appropriation of subliterary forms of popular entertainment. In his early essays for *New Youth* as well as in his *History of Pai-hua Literature*, Vol. 1, he has demonstrated again and again this principle of growth in the development of Chinese poetry, drama, and fiction.[4] A new pai-hua literature, therefore, far from being a radical departure from the literary tradition, is the only guarantee for its continuing growth and renewal.

In seeking historical sanction for a literary reform, Hu Shih has achieved also a complete reappraisal of the Chinese literary heritage. The task was long overdue. Through the centuries the civil service examination system, which was not abolished until 1905, had willy-nilly perpetuated a narrow canon of prescribed readings: the classics, history, and the poetry and prose of standard authors. With drama and fiction excluded from this canon, the literati aspiring to or holding government positions could afford only a covert interest in these types of literature. As a matter of fact, since the Yüan dynasty the development of drama and fiction has been principally the work of the men who, failing to achieve an official career or early disgusted with it, have written to amuse themselves without any thought of advancing their social position or literary reputation. Even though, by the Ch'ing dynasty, literati and populace alike were showing a growing interest in the novel, and the novelists themselves had gradually assumed a vocational dignity, there were few scholars, with the exception of such heretic spirits as Chin Sheng-t'an, who would openly commit themselves to admiration for the novel as a genre worthy to stand beside poetry or history.

The flourishing of a genre in the teeth of critical indifference or hostility is, of course, nothing unusual in literary history. Few Elizabethan dramatists rated their plays as serious literature, and few English readers in the eighteenth century held Fielding and Richardson in as high esteem as Pope and Milton. Without the reassuring example of Western literary tradition, Hu Shih himself, with all his scholarship and critical daring, could not have brought about a revaluation of Chinese literature. Just as he re-interpreted ancient Chinese thought with the aid of the more precise Western philosophical terminology, he was able to see Chinese literature in a new light by his awareness of the importance of the vernacular element in Western literature since Dante and Chaucer, and of the high critical regard for fiction and drama.

As architect of the literary revolution, Hu Shih saw as his task the bringing about of a heightened appreciation of the historical importance of pai-hua and its unlimited future. He reasoned that if the earlier vernacular literature had produced several masterpieces in the absence of critical guidance or encouragement, the new literature, impregnated with an evolutionary faith in the destiny of pai-hua and responsive to the literary currents of the West, should have immense possibilities. But although eminently sound as a strategist, Hu Shih was not able to provide an example of the new literature through his own writings. His rejection of the wen-yen tradition was for his time and place comparable in revolutionary importance to Wordsworth's rejection of Dryden and Pope, and to the early Eliot's rejection of Romantic and Victorian poets, and was fraught with much greater social and cultural consequences. But unlike Wordsworth and Eliot, Hu Shih did not come upon his critical theory as a justification for urgent personal needs as an imaginative writer. He did produce, dutifully, a pioneer volume of insipid pai-hua verse, called *Experiments* (1920), but only to encourage others to follow his suit in an apparently new field. (One may remark here that Hu Shih's theory of a central pai-hua tradition is least satisfactory in regard to poetry; in his *History of Pai-hua Literature,* he is compelled, quite unfairly I think, by the logic of his thesis to dismiss much important though admittedly erudite and allusive poetry as either academic or spurious.) He also translated a small volume of standard Western short stories, so as to acclimate this genre to the tradition of Chinese fiction.

Primarily and pre-eminently a historian and critic, then, Hu Shih directed attention to a type of humanitarian realism with which he was in personal sympathy. In "For a Constructive Literary Revolution," he rightly deplores the then popular novelists' obsession with the world of bureaucracy, vice, and crime; but characteristically he recommends the following subjects for the new writer: "factory workers of both sexes, ricksha pullers, inland farmers . . . domestic tragedies, marital sorrows, the position of women, the unsuitability of [current] educational practices." [5] An obvious invitation to examine the sad lot of the underprivileged and maltreated, the list betrays Hu Shih's narrow view of literature as an instrument of social criticism.

If Hu Shih was limited in his view of literature, his fellow revolutionaries were downright irresponsible. Ostensibly his supporters, they at heart entertained grave doubts as to the validity or adequacy of his reform program. At times it seems nothing would satisfy them but complete abolition of the Chinese language and culture. Thus Ch'ien Hsüan-t'ung argues:

> To abolish Confucianism and annihilate Taoism, the only way is to store up all the Chinese books in a library and leave them there. Why? Because nine hundred ninety-nine out of every thousand books are either Confucian or Taoist in outlook. The Chinese language has been the language of Confucian morality and Taoist superstition. . . . Such a language is absolutely unfit for the new era of the twentieth century. Let me boldly repeat my manifesto: to the end that China may not perish and may become a civilized nation of the twentieth century, the basic task is to abolish Confucianism and annihilate Taoism. But the destruction of the Chinese written language, which has served as the repository of Confucian morality and Taoist superstition, is a prerequisite for the accomplishment of this task.[6]

Hu Shih must have been made very uncomfortable in the presence of such thoroughgoing radicalism; in reply to Ch'ien Hsüan-t'ung, he could only point to the infeasibility of the proposal and direct Ch'ien's attention to more urgent practical problems. But Hu's prestige was not sufficient to deter all discussion of the subject. Even his favorite student, Fu Ssu-nien—later a distinguished scholar and educator but at that time the editor of the undergraduate magazine, *The Renaissance*—wrote in support of Ch'ien Hsüan-t'ung: "Moreover, the Chinese language has this special defect: its deeply rooted barbaric character. The invention of ideograms being a matter of barbaric antiquity, it cannot be helped that the language has remained barbaric. Can one not be ashamed of its being in continuous use in modern times?"[7] As if the Chinese language were unique in being traceable to barbaric antiquity!

In spite of their apparently successful collaboration,

The Literary Revolution

Hu Shih and his colleagues represent two diametrically opposed intellectual persuasions. Reared upon the rigorous traditions of Ch'ing scholarship, Hu Shih was a Confucian rationalist whose passion for critical inquiry, under John Dewey's personal guidance at Columbia, was early fortified with American pragmatism. He was the realistic optimist who did not flinch from truth, however painful or embarrassing. In his reappraisal of Chinese literature and culture as well as in his commentaries on current Chinese affairs, therefore, he was able to maintain a sense of fact and equanimity of mind, refusing to be overwhelmed by the all too apparent faults and vices he discerned. His colleagues, on the contrary, became involved in a sense of national humiliation; they were eager for radical reform because they were deeply ashamed of China's past. Ch'en Tu-hsiu, Ch'ien Hsüan-t'ung, Li Ta-chao, Lu Hsün—regular contributors to *New Youth*—would have no traffic with tradition. Perhaps in their younger days they had been proud of China, but this pride had turned into a frankly masochistic admission of what they saw as inferiority in every department of endeavor. Disgusted with pigtails, bound feet, and opium—palpable symbols of China's backwardness—they were no less ashamed of her art, literature, philosophy, and folkways. However absurd it may sound today, Ch'ien Hsüan-t'ung's demand for a total repudiation of the Chinese language and culture was made with a seriousness almost morbid in intensity. Positive in their rejections, these intellectuals have been no less dogmatic in their recommendations for curing the nation's ills. It is little wonder that most of them eventually turned to Communism as the answer to their prayers.

In view of the radicalism of Ch'en Tu-hsiu and Ch'ien Hsüan-t'ung, one might think that the pai-hua movement could not have swayed public opinion in its favor, since what was held in question was the very nature of Chinese language and culture. But to the patriotic and restive students of that time who eagerly sought enlightenment from the pages of *New Youth* and *The Renaissance,* the adoption of pai-hua was the first step toward progress and the guarantee for eventual national reformation. Even if some of them shared with the radicals a dissatisfaction with the contemplated language reform, they did not deny themselves the immense advantages of freer self-expression afforded by the use of pai-hua.

To begin with, these students were disgusted with the Peking Government and impatient to exert their influence on the management of national affairs. Their disappointment with the Republican Revolution of 1911–12, which had neither brought about national unity nor averted foreign aggression, finally came to a head over the ignominy of Chinese representatives at the Paris Conference of 1919. On May 4 and the ensuing days, student demonstrations broke out in Peking and the other major cities in protest against government submission to exorbitant Japanese demands for economic and territorial rights in Shantung. Particular grievances against a corrupt and impotent government and its treasonous ministers now swelled into a seething tide of patriotic indignation. It is not without reason, therefore, that this so-called May Fourth Movement has been synonymous in Chinese writings with the new culture movement: it marks the first strong showing of the powerfully articulate class of students and intellectuals determined to effect vast changes in the national life. The May Fourth Movement also assured the initial success of the Literary Revolution: upon its wake, a number of pai-hua magazines, more or less literary, began publication to satisfy the needs of an eager and ever-growing audience.

The conservative literati, indifferent to the theoretical stage of the Literary Revolution, were now alarmed at its nation-wide success. But from Lin Shu to Chang Shih-chao (the Minister of Education in the Peking Government who maintained a belated and foredoomed struggle against the reformers in 1925), even their doughtiest champions produced only a feeble defense of the cultural and literary tradition. With insatiable zest, the best scholars of the day—Wang Kuo-wei, Liang Ch'i-ch'ao, and Hu Shih himself—had taken pains to study Western literature and philosophy so as to breathe fresh life into their Chinese studies. On the other hand, the self-appointed guardians of traditional culture, in their refusal to face up to the Western challenge, were hopelessly lagging behind their time. In their exclusive attack on the supposed vulgarity and cumbersomeness of pai-hua as against the elegance and brevity of wen-yen, moreover, they missed completely the serious danger lurking behind the new culture movement: the confident immaturity and unreasoned dogmatism attendant upon any major cultural reorientation.

It therefore took a group of scholars with an educational background similar to Hu Shih's to lodge some serious protest against the new cultural and literary movement. Mei Kuang-ti, Hu Hsien-su, and Wu Mi, American-educated professors in Nanking, launched in 1922 a *Critical Review* (Hsüeh Heng) to counteract what they regarded as the pernicious tendencies of the movement.[8] While a student of Irving Babbitt at Harvard, Mei Kuang-ti had been one of Hu Shih's friends opposed to his espousal of vernacular; in 1922 he was not so much opposed to pai-hua as to Hu Shih's evolutionary concept that it would necessarily supersede wen-yen. Over and above the issue of pai-hua, the *Critical Review* was mainly concerned with the dangers of ignorance apparent in the naive eagerness with which the new cultural leaders imported foreign ideological and literary fashions. When Karl Marx, John Dewey, and Bertrand Russell—Dewey and Russell were invited to lecture in China respectively in 1919 and 1920 [9]—were worshiped as oracles of truth, when transient literary schools of the present-day West and Japan were blindly imitated to the exclusion of the classical authors, the new cultural leaders could be justly accused of a signal un-

13

awareness of the more abiding literary and philosophical traditions of the West, a shallow delight in innovation and change in apparent disregard for the cultural needs of the country, and a tragic failure to live up to their educational responsibility. Mei Kuang-ti therefore indicts the cultural leaders as "not thinkers, but sophists," "not creators, but imitators," "not scholars, but opportunists," "not educators, but politicians." [10] The indictment is unfair in its failure to make exception of the few serious writers, and of those who, while not original thinkers, ably applied Western ideas to a fresh study of Chinese problems. It is, indeed, malicious in its belittlement of intention, effort, and enthusiasm. Yet, in the long view, Mei Kuang-ti spoke the truth, especially with regard to the radical writers and intellectuals, who, already powerful in 1922, were destined to shape modern China in their own image.

The minority protest of the *Critical Review* had the temporary effect of rallying together the diverse promoters of the new culture. Hu Shih fought alongside his radical colleagues. But once this dissident opinion was silenced, the irreconcilable antagonism of the liberal and radical leaders became apparent. Significantly, Hu Shih and Ch'en Tu-hsiu had earlier reached a parting of ways. The latter had become the founder of the Chinese Communist party in 1920; * for some years he continued to edit in Shanghai and Canton his *New Youth,* now strictly a party organ of dwindling influence. (He was to be divested of his party leadership in 1927 and to die in 1942 a broken man repenting of the Communist folly he had earlier espoused.) Hu Shih, on the other hand, stayed on at Peking University, moving in a circle of more congenial friends who, like himself, were returned students from America or England: Ch'en Yüan, Hsü Chih-mo, Miss

* Although the Chinese Communist party was formally established on July 1, 1921, it had been in existence since May 1920, with Ch'en Tu-hsiu as secretary. See Chow Tse-tsung, *The May Fourth Movement: Intellectual Revolution in Modern China,* p. 248.

Ch'en Heng-chê. He started several magazines to represent his varied interests in historical scholarship and criticism, literature, and government affairs. While he continued to the end to take a paternal interest in the fortunes of the new literature and to proffer sensible, though largely ignored, advice to the National Government, he had found by 1922 his true vocation in historical and literary research. His investigations of the authorship and origins of several classical Chinese novels, especially, are a landmark of Sinology.

With the formation of the Communist party, the radical energies which had been merely destructive during the initial period of the Literary Revolution were now channeled into positive action. In its lack of political affiliation, the liberal camp headed by Hu Shih was clearly at a disadvantage. Moreover, its reformist and pragmatic approach to Chinese problems seemed to be overcautious to the majority of students and young intellectuals who, likewise nurtured on national humiliations, demanded nothing but sweeping changes so as to effect a swift transformation of China into a modern power.

Following the May Fourth student demonstrations, the Peking Government continued to accede to the demands of imperialist Japan and exhibit paralytic unconcern with the task of national reconstruction. In fact, for the greater part of the twenties, the capital was the playground of imbecile warlords intriguing against one another for political supremacy. Meanwhile, the patriotic elements of the nation pinned their hopes on the Nationalist party or Kuomintang which, in the early twenties, was being rapidly transformed in Canton, under its founder Dr. Sun Yat-sen and his able lieutenant Chiang Kai-shek, into a revolutionary army determined to oust the warlords and bring about national unity. (Though the sole revolutionary instrument for toppling the Manchu dynasty, the Kuomintang had gone into an abrupt decline following its compromise with the warlords immediately upon the establishment of the Republic.) But for the reorganization of his party Dr. Sun had accepted Soviet help, partly because the Western powers, which selfishly preferred the status quo of a China in chaos, had turned a deaf ear to his pleas for support and partly because he was naively trustful of the proclaimed good intentions of the Soviet Government. The price of this help was tragic: not only the infiltration of the Kuomintang by a great many Communists and its subsequent ideological split into the right wing and left wing, but the simultaneous unchecked growth of the rival Communist party and the unimpeded success of its propaganda. So when, midway through his trumphant Northern Expedition against the warlords in the spring of 1927, the right-wing leader Chiang Kai-shek finally decided to purge the Communist and leftist elements from within the Kuomintang and outlaw the rival party, his resolute action caused at the same time permanent injury to the reputation and strength of his party. The radical intellectuals and students, who had grown in numbers and influence during the period of Kuomintang-Communist collaboration 1923–27, could never forgive him for his supposed treachery.

A striking illustration of the mass awakening during the middle twenties was the May Thirtieth Movement. On May 30, 1925, following the fatal shooting by a Japanese foreman of a Chinese worker employed at a Japanese cotton mill two weeks earlier, the students and industrial workers of Shanghai held a memorial service for the martyr and proceeded to stage a protest parade in the section of the city policed by the British, the International Settlement. Subsequent police interference resulted in the death of twelve demonstrators and the wounding of seventeen. This event promptly aroused the nation; in all its industrial centers and in Hong Kong, anti-imperialist demonstrations, strikes against foreign factories, and boycotts against foreign, especially British, goods spread like wildfire. The Communist party, which probably had a hand in planning the initial Shanghai rally, reaped huge profits in its subsequent organization of workers and students everywhere.[11] Little wonder that, according to later Communist historians, the event was the first strong showing of a patriotic people fully awakened to the evil of imperialism.

The May Thirtieth Movement, the first mass movement in China of national scope, had immediate important repercussions among writers. With some reservations, one could agree with Communist historians that it marked the end of the period of the initial Literary Revolution and the beginning of the era of Revolutionary Literature. The radical camp of the new culture movement had certainly stolen a march on the liberal camp and emerged in popular imagination as the sole revolutionary vanguard.

The topic of a Communist-directed revolutionary literature will be taken up in due time. For the present, the new cultural and literary movement will be further discussed in terms of its philosophical premises and cultural indebtedness.

For radicals and liberals alike, their sweeping attacks on Chinese institutions during the early Republican period, while intellectually crude, bespeak a kind of moral courage: in history, an alteration of the status quo and a temporary disregard for tradition have always been concomitant signs of a national resurgence of spiritual energy directed toward confident new achievement. In this respect, the optimism and enthusiasm with which the young Chinese greeted the May Fourth Movement are essentially of the kind that enkindled a generation of Romantic poets after the French Revolution. But unlike the Romantic poets, the young Chinese writers were cut off from spiritual resources other than their optimistic vision of a rejuvenated China. While still a student of English literature at Harvard, Liang Shih-ch'iu wrote in 1926 an important paper tracing "The Romantic Tendencies in Modern Chinese Literature," [12] in which he rightly notes an unbridled emotionalism and humanitarianism as its chief characteristics. As a disciple of Irving Babbitt, however, Liang Shih-ch'iu invokes the term romanticism merely to show his utter scorn for the contemporary product, without caring to distinguish between the puerile excesses of many incipient literary movements and the inherent limitations of romanticism. What should be obvious to a later critic is the extremely shallow character of the early romanticism. There was no Coleridge to stress the importance of the imagination, no Wordsworth to testify to an all-embracing higher reality, no Blake to probe man's infinite capacity for both good and evil. The romanticism of early modern Chinese literature is completely secular, philosophically unambitious, and psychologically crude. It is a form of destructive and reformist energy committed to scientific positivism and directed toward the utilitarian goals of a happier life, a better society, and a stronger China. In its failure to explore the deeper reaches of the mind and to give allegiance to a higher transcendental or immanent reality, this romanticism, of necessity, was merely humanitarianism, in its dual form of self-pity and social sympathy, a craving for justice in terms of a more egalitarian distribution of wealth, and at best a regard for nature merely as a solacing agent.

During the initial period of the Literary Revolution, however, one also notices a strong interest in secular humanism, an assertion of man's dignity above and beyond his needs as an animal and citizen. In his famous essay on Ibsenism, Hu Shih championed individualism to combat the debilitating effects of the tradition. The response to this call was tremendous. Ibsen became the earliest Western author to be extensively translated into pai-hua, and the case of Nora was heatedly debated among Chinese youth. [13] Other real or supposed champions of individual freedom from political and social oppression—notably J. S. Mill, Nietzsche, Tolstoy—

were also discussed in the pages of *New Youth*.[14] This belief in human integrity could have had immense literary possibilities, but immediately after World War I, Western individualism was challenged. Such prominent intellectuals as Liang Ch'i-ch'ao and Liang Shu-ming voiced their disillusion over the competitive, warlike Western civilization and pleaded for a return to the Chinese and Buddhist way of life. With a few effective essays, Hu Shih was able to check the growth of this unwarranted pessimism,[15] but even he, of course, could not dissuade the more influential radical intellectuals from admiring the Soviet experiment in Russia at that time, with its promise for a positive advance beyond existing Western and Eastern cultures toward the goal of international peace and brotherhood. Under this Soviet influence, individualism gradually withered, though in the fifties a great number of writers and intellectuals were to discover they were still individualists at heart when they finally became disgusted with the Communist regime on the mainland. Hu Shih, however, had never wavered in his championship of man's inalienable right to freedom; this is the principal reason why, of modern Chinese intellectuals, he has become the symbol of all that is most hateful in the eyes of present-day Chinese Communists.

In view of this stress on human dignity, which is implicit in the new literary movement, Chou Tso-jen's essay on "Humane Literature" (*New Youth,* December 1918) appears as a crucial document. Hu Shih had earlier placed the new literature in a proper historical perspective and suggested its themes: it was left to Chou Tso-jen to define this literature in psychological and moral terms. A returned student from Japan and a faculty member of Peking University, Chou Tso-jen was soon to distinguish himself as a familiar essayist, a Confucian moralist, and an ironic commentator on Chinese mores. But in 1918, apparently engrossed in his study of Western literature and psychology, he was more positivist in temper and less appreciative of the finer aspects of Chinese culture. Both in its scientific and humanistic emphasis, his essay is an excellent distillation of the more constructive thought of the early period.

"Humane Literature" begins with the premise that man is a rational being as well as an animal organism. But the traditional concept of man has tended to oppose reason with instinct, so that two types of literature have largely prevailed, both inadequate to account for the totality of man. The literature of reason is mainly at the service of such religious and political institutions as repress emotions and feelings, whereas the literature of instinct is under the sway of undisciplined appetite, violence, and fantasy. If one examines Chinese literature, especially the vernacular and popular literature, one finds both types in a flourishing state: "slave" literature that sanctions feudal morality, pornographic literature, the superstitious literature of gods and ghosts, the conventionally romantic literature in praise of either glorified robbers and thieves or insipid and idealized lovers, and so forth. In place of this literature, Chou Tso-jen advocates a literature able to uphold man's dignity as a rational animal. While toying with the idea of a Utopian literature which depicts ideal human relationships, he clearly gives his platform of "humane literature" a realistic emphasis. Ibsen, Tolstoy, Turgenev, and Hardy are cited for their ability to foster love, sympathy, and the moral sense in their depiction of ordinary human lives. In the main a restatement of the aims and practices of nineteenth-century realism, the essay registers the strong humanitarian and individualistic temper of its time and bespeaks the search for a new ethic more answerable to the needs of modern man than the Confucian. It serves as an admirable prelude to the finer literary achievement of modern China.

This finer achievement, however, is small in quantity, and it is usually the work of those writers who have been able to withstand to some degree the predominant ideological currents. The basic weakness of modern Chinese literature, as will be made clear in the course of the present study, is its failure to engage in disinterested moral exploration. Even "Humane Literature," admirable as it is, gives the impression that it endorses a literature that is ethically conducive to a happier humanity rather than a literature that, irrespective of its ethical bias, is profoundly moral. Chou Tso-jen takes as the ideal of human excellence the kind of full development of the body and spirit as envisioned in Blake's *Marriage of Heaven and Hell;* but for a student of literature, the logical corollary of this belief is surely not that all literature not in accord with this ethics is automatically to be condemned. Chou apparently thought so: in the essay, therefore, even though he refers admiringly to a specific passage from Homer and calls Dostoevsky "a great humanitarian author," he appears able to take only a historical and anthropological interest in most ancient literature and deplores the irrational perversity of an unnamed Dostoevsky hero because his self-sacrifice seems to have transcended the normal human capacity for emotional and physical suffering. With all his moral seriousness and profound interest in modern psychology—he was apparently the first person to call Chinese attention to Blake and Dostoevsky [16] —Chou Tso-jen, then, was as much dedicated to the task of reforming Chinese society, though not quite in the same fashion, as his fellow intellectuals.

This reformist urge, which accounts for the shallow character of the early romanticism, inevitably leads to a patriotic didacticism. Perhaps even without the massive influence of Communist practice and ideology, the moral exploration of the mind would still remain an expendable luxury to most writers who, in their earnest effort to transform China into a modern nation, took upon themselves primarily the task of educating their benighted countrymen. Several early writers, notably Lu Hsün and Kuo Mo-jo, have testified that they chose literature as their career because they believed it to be a more effective weapon than science or politics to fight lethargy, cowardice, and ignorance. Behind their seemingly diverse artistic credos is inescapably the didactic and patriotic motive.

This didactic concern engenders by and large an attitude of indifference toward art. While exposed to a wealth of literary influences unfelt by their forebears, modern Chinese writers were apparently drawn more to the ideology than to the artistic achievement of foreign authors. Moreover, even in the case of the exceptionally intelligent, like Hu Shih and Chou Tso-jen, their understanding of Western culture was of necessity partial and fragmentary. As the more influential writers were nearly always returned students, the ideas and prejudices that happened to be in vogue in the countries where they had studied invariably colored their literary and cultural endeavor. Indeed, without much distortion of history, one could regard the struggle between liberals and radicals as a struggle between Anglo-American-returned and Japanese-returned students. (There are prominent exceptions, of course: Chou Tso-jen was more responsive to certain vital currents in modern Western thought than most writers who had studied in the West. His essays on religion, folklore, and sexual mores show the decisive influence of Frazer, Freud, and Havelock Ellis.) Japan, the United States, and England were the major centers of foreign study, even though a number of Chinese went to France and the Soviet Union. The latter, with a few exceptions, tended to support the radical cause.

Japan had undergone a literary revolution about three decades earlier, during the reign of Meiji. Even prior to the fall of the Ch'ing dynasty, therefore, Chinese who studied there—such future intellectual leaders as Ch'en Tu-hsiu and Lu Hsün—could not help being influenced by this literary movement and the Western ideological and literary forces that had prompted it. Because of the literary bias of their earlier education, these students as a rule read avidly in contemporary Japanese literature and such Western authors as were then esteemed in Japan. Among the latter the Russian novelists occupied a pre-eminent position, and later the same enthusiasm was transplanted to China. For intellectuals of these two countries, chafing under the shackles of tradition and striving to bring about national reform and social justice, the impact of Russian fiction could be nothing short of exhilarating in its vast social sympathy, its nihilistic defiance of custom and authority, its earnest seeking for the meaning of life, and its sardonic but unshakable faith in the greatness of the mother country. During the first decade of the twentieth century, romanticism was highly popular in Japan; later, the Creation Society, a literary clique of Japanese-returned students, duly imported this enthusiasm. By the early twenties Marxism had become fashionable in Japan; even though Ch'en Tu-hsiu and Li Ta-chao had independently shown a similar interest, it was again the infectious Japanese example that gave impetus to the Communist literary movement in China.

In contrast, the literary scene in England and the United States during the first two decades of the century was more placid. The experimental writers, like T. S. Eliot and James Joyce, were not yet established to the extent of influencing academic thinking. Chinese students taking liberal arts courses in the two countries were inescapably under the spell of Romantic and Victorian literature. They were of course at the same time attracted to the intellectual and literary currents of the time: the Imagist school of poetry, which served as a direct stimulus to the pai-hua movement and early attempts in pai-hua poetry; [17] the pragmatic thinking of Dewey, Russell, and G. Lowes Dickinson; the problem plays of Ibsen, Shaw, and Galsworthy; and, slightly later, the Humanism of Babbitt and More. But these influences were of less moment compared with the enthusiasms imported from Japan. Except during the initial period of the Literary Revolution, the Anglo-American group found themselves, upon their return to China, already in a minority position, out of sympathy with the literary and ideological fashions firmly established by the Japanese-returned students. They gradually retreated into a defensive position, excelling in constructive criticism on all phases of Chinese life and combating the radical and leftist influence as best they could. As college professors, however, they fostered an academic climate of free inquiry and serious literary study, enabling a good number of talented young writers to withstand the insidious lure of Communist rhetoric.

One cannot evaluate the literature of a period solely by the poverty or wealth of its indebtedness, of course. Relative Chinese indifference to the Anglo-American tradition must be accounted for by the remoteness of that tradition to the burning issues then gripping the intellectuals. Even if the returned students from England and the United States had exercised a greater influence, it was highly probable that the Anglo-American tradition would be so interpreted as to yield a revolutionary and leftist emphasis. Paradoxically, the most influential and popular American writers in China, Whitman and Upton Sinclair, were championed by Japanese-returned students. In an underdeveloped country where tradition was on the point of being discredited, the genuine elite whose concern with culture took serious forms of necessity fought a losing battle against the half-baked intellectuals and writers who could rally the masses to their support precisely because they pursued a few half-understood ideas with self-righteous zeal but a singular lack of wisdom and patience. The predominance of this latter group is a fact of primary importance in our understanding of modern Chinese literature.

The present study is mainly concerned with the development of fiction from the period of the Literary Revolution to its present moribund state under the Communist regime, although, as I have done in this chapter, I will continue to trace the ideological debate among writers in the same period

—the achievement and failure of fiction can be fully illuminated only against this intellectual background. The course of development in poetry, drama, and the essay will also be touched upon, so as to provide a more rounded picture for those readers little acquainted with modern Chinese literature. This so-called modern literature, of course, is not the only type of literature produced in modern China. Under the educational policy of the National Government, students are still required to read some classical Chinese literature and to write passably in the wen-yen style, though only a dwindling number of old-style literati have been cultivating the traditional styles of prose and poetry to any extent. Peking opera and other varieties of traditional drama were in a more or less flourishing state; new plays, often representing a compromise with modern taste, were constantly added to their repertoire. Until the fall of the mainland, contemporary novels in the old style were avidly read by a large audience seeking primarily escapist entertainment. Ranging from sentimental romance to incredible adventure, these novels stemmed from the earlier vernacular tradition and have little in common with the new fiction except for their use of pai-hua. Though contemptuously dismissed by the partisans of the new literature for its unconcern with social issues and its unawareness of the Western tradition, this fiction actually boasts several practitioners who are in narrative skill much superior to their more ideologically enlightened fellow craftsmen.[18] It should be instructive to attempt a serious study of this fiction, if not to discover literary merit, at least to analyze the kinds of daydream and fantasy to which a large section of the reading public yielded during the Republican period.

Following Hu shih's lead, many advocates of pai-hua wrote poems in the vernacular, and with expectedly little success. Whereas the long tradition of vernacular fiction had made the assimilation of Western techniques a relatively easy task for the new story-writers, there was very little in the Chinese poetic tradition to help the pai-hua poet. It is quite true that, when recited, a great many favorites in standard anthologies could prove perfectly intelligible to an unlettered person, but even these deceptively easy poems are molded upon a strict prosody which had evolved, during the pre-T'ang period, in accordance with the special genius of the Chinese language. Moreover, because poetic composition was an essential part of traditional education, there had developed an elaborate set of rhetorical rules governing diction and imagery, and a number of time-honored themes and sentiments to which the unambitious poets usually conform. The modern pai-hua poet has either to defy these principles and conventions completely or so to adapt them as to meet the demands of a necessarily more colloquial rhythm and diction. In the presence of the varied and splendid achievements of the old tradition, both courses are admittedly arduous.

Especially, the modern poets are perplexed over the problem of rhythm. The prosodic system of traditional poetry is built upon the matching tonal qualities of individual words. Insofar as spoken Chinese is no longer monosyllabic, this system has perforce to be abandoned. During the early experimental period, most poets followed the vogue for *vers libre* to write a poetry of no apparent rhythm and optional rhyme: the American Imagists, Whitman, Tagore, and the Japanese *haiku* poets all encouraged the tendency toward relaxation and anarchy. Slightly later, the returned students from England and America adopted the English stress system. Prominently, Hsü Chih-mo and Wen I-to, both lovers of English Romantic poetry, were able to impose some kind of order in their use of many kinds of stanzaic structures. At about the same time, some others began to imitate French symbolist poets. The adaptation of Western meters, however, brings with it a music too faint to please ears accustomed to the sonority of traditional Chinese verse; but in the absence of other alternatives, few contemporary poets have been able to dispense with the stress system. The shallow clarity of imagist and romantic poetry as well as the dazzling obscurity of much symbolist poetry indicates also the absence of personal feelings powerful enough to elevate language into a condition of pregnant tension. The search for a poetic style has still a long way to go.[19]

Likewise, during the first ten years after 1917, experiments in Western-style drama were none too successful. Accustomed to the operatic Chinese theater, the public was not ready to tolerate endless talk on stage, even though it found in the cinema an immediately acceptable medium of entertainment. Unlike the few serious poets who were dedicated to their art in spite of their manifest inability to surmount technical difficulties, nearly all the early playwrights yielded too readily to the temptation of using the stage as pulpit, which further repelled the public. Amid the antifeudal and anti-imperialist rantings of Hung Shen, T'ien Han, and Kuo Mo-jo, the one-act plays of Ting Hsi-lin offer the welcome relief of parlor comedy. But their studied air of comic contrivance is superficial in the extreme.[20]

The short story, however, was immediately established as a genre of great promise: the publication in 1918 of Lu Hsün's "The Diary of a Madman," in its complete departure from traditional storytelling as well as its brilliant use of Western techniques, marks the first appearance of the modern short story in Chinese. The strong tradition of colloquial fiction had understandably removed both language difficulty and audience hostility in regard to the making of a new pai-hua fiction, though few early writers were ready for the novel. Among the many predictably bad and immature story-writers, a few have met the test of time and are responsible for the positive achievement of the period. In the following chapters these writers—Lu Hsün, Yeh Shao-chün, Ping Hsin, Ling Shu-hua, Lo Hua-sheng, Yü Ta-fu—will be discussed.

CHAPTER 2

Lu Hsün (1881-1936)

THE EARLIEST practitioner of Western-style fiction,
Lu Hsün has also been generally regarded as the greatest
modern Chinese writer. During the last six years of his life he
was the prominent cultural hero to a large public nurtured on
leftist opinions; since his death in 1936, his fame has turned
positively legendary. The immediate posthumous publication of his twenty-volume *Complete Works* was an unprecedented literary event in modern China, but even more impressive has been the unabated growth of a Lu Hsün
literature: memoirs and biographies, studies of his works
and ideas, and countless magazine articles commemorating
the anniversary of his death for over the past two decades.[1]
No other modern Chinese writer has received comparable
adulation.

This adulation, of course, was a Communist enterprise.
During the period of the Communist struggle for power, Lu
Hsün was immensely useful as the beloved spokesman for
the cause of antigovernment patriotism. Even Mao Tse-tung,
rarely generous in his appraisal of his Chinese contemporaries, felt justified in paying this author the highest tribute,
in *The New Democracy* (1940):

Since the May Fourth Movement, China had produced an entirely new and vigorous cultural force: it is the Communist ideology as guided by the Chinese Communist party; it is the Communist world view and its theory of socialist revolution. . . . And Lu Hsün was the greatest and bravest standard-bearer of this new cultural army. As commander of the cultural revolution, Lu Hsün was not only a great writer, but a great thinker and revolutionary as well. Lu Hsün's bones were the hardest; there was in him not the slightest trace of subservience and sycophancy. This rectitude was indeed the most valuable trait which a colonial and semicolonial people could possess. In the cultural battle front, Lu Hsün was the representative of the large majority of the nation and the most correct, courageous, resolute, loyal, and sincere fighter against the enemy, indeed an unprecedented national hero. The direction of Lu Hsün is the direction of the new Chinese culture.[2]

Lu Hsün was, of course, a highly acclaimed writer even before the Communists made him their own hero; they could not have fabricated his myth without the foundation of his appeal and prestige. As a matter of historical fact it should also be noted that it was such liberal critics as Hu Shih and Ch'en Yüan who spoke out from the first in behalf of Lu Hsün's talent, whereas the Communist critics remained uniformly virulent until his conversion to their cause in 1929.[3] The Lu Hsün myth was particularly beneficial to the Communists during the thirties and forties, when they could use his writings to reinforce the impression of Kuomintang decadence and corruption. Today this myth has more or less outlived its function, though it is apparently still to the advantage of the Communist regime to perpetuate his fame as a national hero while actively discouraging any attempts to imitate his satiric style.

Lu Hsün (his real name was Chou Shu-jen) was born in

29

1881 in Shaohsing, Chekiang, the eldest son of a somewhat impoverished family which had nevertheless retained the tradition of learning. Both he and his younger brother, Chou Tso-jen, went to Japan to study on government scholarships, after spending some time at the Naval Academy in Nanking. For his field of study Lu Hsün now chose medicine, believing it could do the most to help his countrymen. Laboriously studying for his medical career in preparatory school and college, he was at the same time much drawn to Western literature and philosophy, which he could now read in Japanese and German. He read Nietzsche, Darwin, and such Russian writers of fiction as Gogol, Chekhov, and Andreyev, all of whom remained the most vital influences on his career as writer and thinker.

Lu Hsün finally chose writing as his profession, after seeing a news slide of the humiliations of his countrymen during the Russo-Japanese War of 1904–05. On the screen a Chinese, caught by the Japanese as a Russian spy, was about to be decapitated; meanwhile a group of Chinese were watching the event with curious interest, insensible of the shame involved. Many years later, Lu Hsün was to refer to this incident in the preface to his first story collection, *The Outcry* (1923):

> From that moment I felt medicine was not the important thing I had thought it was. The people of a weak, backward country, even though they may enjoy sturdy health, can only serve as the senseless material and audience for public executions. In comparison, to die of diseases is not necessarily so unfortunate. Our first task was surely to transform their spirit, and I thought at that time that literature could best meet the task of spiritual transformation. I then began to think about promoting literary activities.[4]

Lu Hsün duly made an abortive attempt to launch a magazine in Tokyo and wrote a series of didactic essays in the wen-yen style, urging the Chinese to heed the Darwinian lesson of the survival of the fittest and to accept the Nietzschean call for heroic endeavor. These essays were later included in the volume called *Tomb*. Lu Hsün also translated three stories (two by Andreyev and one by Garshin) for his brother's two-volume anthology of foreign fiction. Only about twenty copies of each volume were sold in Tokyo.

Discouraged with his literary ventures, Lu Hsün returned to China in 1909 and taught biology for three years in the middle schools of Hangchow and Shaohsing. Upon the establishment of the Republican Government in 1912 he accepted a counselorship in the Ministry of Education and moved to Peking. During his first years at the capital Lu Hsün was still playing the recluse, busying himself with antiquarian research in Chinese literature. But his literary ambition revived with the Literary Revolution. At the request of Ch'ien Hsüan-t'ung, who had known him in Japan, Lu Hsün contributed some poems to the May 1918 number of *New Youth,* as well as a story called "The Diary of a Madman." In the following months he wrote for the magazine a number of short essays, commentaries and reflections on the current Chinese scene, which would eventually receive the appellation of *tsa-kan* (random thoughts) or *tsa-wen* (random essays). In 1919 he contributed two more stories: "K'ung I-chi" and "Medicine." In the winter of 1919–20, famous as a writer and financially secure with his income from the government sinecure and his newly appointed lectureship of Chinese literature at National Peking University, Lu Hsün went to his native city to sell the old house there and move his mother to Peking. This visit proved to be a most opportune event at this point of his writing career.

If his first three stories, unmistakably set in Shaohsing, were any indication, Lu Hsün's home town was the principal source of his inspiration. After his return from Japan, he had taught there for a short period, and that many years ago, when the town was still under the Manchu rule. Now, during his second visit, he saw that nothing had apparently changed much in spite of the nominal success of the Republican Revolution. His nostalgic love for his birthplace was therefore transmuted into a kind of compassion, with the attendant feelings of sorrow and anger. Lu Hsün was, moreover, a man approaching forty who had enjoyed a youth of comparative silence and had kept his emotional strength relatively untapped. The result, in such stories as "My Native Place," "Benediction," and "In the Restaurant," which unmistakably allude to his visit home, was a more complex mode of fiction than was practiced by the immature young writers at that time. One may indeed compare the best stories of Lu Hsün to *Dubliners*. Shaken by the sloth, superstition, cruelty, and hypocrisy of the rural and town people, whom new ideas could not change, Lu Hsün repudiates his home town and, symbolically, the old Chinese way of life; yet, as in the case of Joyce, this town and these people remain the stuff and substance of his creation.

Lu Hsün's best stories are contained in two volumes: the aforementioned *Outcry* and a second collection, *Hesitation* (1926). Along with many volumes of essays and a book of prose poems, *Wild Grass*, these were composed during his residence in Peking in a period of apparent creative felicity. Lu Hsün was never to be the same again after his departure from the city in August 1926, when it had become a stronghold of reaction under the control of a powerful warlord. In view of this dramatic change in his career, it seems appropriate to comment on his best stories, in the chronological order of their appearance, before resuming the biographical narrative.

The first story in *The Outcry,* "The Diary of a Madman," conveys most succinctly the author's attitude toward the Chinese tradition. Suffering from a persecution complex, the madman thinks that all those around him, including his immediate family, are going to kill and eat him. To confirm

left in January 1927 for Canton, to serve as dean and chairman of the literature department at Sun Yat-sen University. Earlier, members of the Creation Society, a Communist literary group, had taught at the University and made it a hotbed for revolution. Still very much an individualist, Lu Hsün was sickened by the unbridled revolutionary enthusiasm of the students there and spoke out, in many lectures and speeches, against the kind of revolutionary literature then in vogue among them. To him, literature shouldn't be an adjunct to patriotic propaganda and students genuinely eager to embrace the revolutionary cause should accept more arduous duties than purveying revolutionary literature. In April of the same year, however, Chiang Kai-shek had decisively launched an anti-Communist campaign in Shanghai. Lu Hsün was further distressed to see the subsequent persecution of Communist students in Canton, and for a while he again buried his head in research. In October 1927, he left for Shanghai, where, except for a brief trip to Peking, he stayed until his death.

The years 1927–28 were crucial to Lu Hsün's intellectual and emotional development. The mood of despondency and pessimism characteristic of *Hesitation* and *Wild Grass* had taken a stronger hold on him as the result of his encounter with revolutionary and counterrevolutionary activities in Canton. As an independent patriotic writer, he had from the first despised the Anglo-American group of writers, who seemed to him apologists for a capitalist culture; now he also began to distrust the revolutionary writers whose manufacture of a puerile proletarian literature was causing a steady deterioration of literary standards. Neither right nor left, Lu Hsün stood virtually alone.

In 1928 two major Communist groups, the Creation Society and the Sun Society, started a concerted attack on Lu Hsün in retaliation for his jeering attitude toward revolutionary literature. In the forensic article "The Age of Ah Q Is Dead," Ch'ien Hsing-ts'un, the leading Sun critic, declares Lu Hsün an anachronism. He argues as follows: Most of Lu Hsün's characters, like Ah Q and K'ung I-chi, are drawn from the period of the downfall of the Ch'ing dynasty: lazy, shiftless, feudal-minded, they bear no resemblance whatever to the enlightened peasants and workers of the present day. Far from realizing the outdated nature of his fiction, their creator is still entrenched in the petty-bourgeois individualism of the May Fourth Movement and refuses to keep step with the new age. His reactionary character is amply exposed in his ridicule of the promoters of revolutionary literature. He is already somewhat advanced in age, and unless he joins the revolutionary ranks now, the final warning goes, he will be doomed to immediate oblivion.

To attacks like this Lu Hsün replied with his customary sarcasm and self-possession, but at heart he was troubled and not so sure of himself. He had always regarded himself as a guide to youth, but now the students were deserting his leadership and embarking on a course which, however foolish in his eyes, seemed to promise more tangible results. Could it be that his individualist philosophy was no longer adequate to meet the needs of his time? Even while he was attacking his detractors with great verve and force, Lu Hsün began to read in Japanese about Marxism, and about the literature of Soviet Russia. To all intents and purposes, this reading had only the slightest effect upon his personality and thought: the essays he wrote after his capitulation to the Communist camp in 1929, except for a superficial gloss of Marxist dialectic, deviate little from the ideas and prejudices of his earlier writings. But as if to convince himself of the importance of Soviet literature, he took time to translate such works as Lunacharsky's treatise *On Art* and Fadeyev's novel *The Nineteen*. Years later, in the preface to his collection of essays called *Triple Leisure* (1932), Lu Hsün consoles himself with the observation that he was the first Chinese to conscientiously translate Soviet literary theory and criticism, in contrast to his opponents, who had launched revolutionary literature with little scholarly preparation.

Lu Hsün's struggle with the Communist writers in the late twenties will be again touched upon in a later chapter. Suffice it to say here that after his capitulation, the writing of short essays became with him even more of a consuming passion, in compensation for his creative sterility. Lu Hsün must have been painfully aware of his inability to write more stories in the early manner and confided on many occasions to one of his younger friends, the later prominent Communist critic Feng Hsüeh-feng, his passionate longing to revisit Shaohsing, the seat of his nostalgic inspiration.[18] Although he contemplated many ambitious projects, including a satiric novel on modern Chinese intellectuals, he could never summon enough courage to commit them to paper. Instead, he disguised his loss of creative powers in the bustle of an endless series of personal and nonpersonal quarrels. As the nominal leader of Communist writers (though prudently he never became a party member), Lu Hsün attacked, among other subjects, the National Government and the Nationalist writers; the adverse critics of Soviet Russia and leftist literary programs; the defectors from the leftist camp; the Anglo-American school of writers; and all lovers of traditional Chinese art and culture.[19] Only on a few occasions, as when he wrote in memory of the young Communist writers executed by the Nationalist police, did he speak out again with a genuine touch of personal emotion.

Lu Hsün, moreover, was quite ill with pulmonary tuberculosis during the last two or three years of his life. Every day, even when he was confined to a sick bed, he would spend hours reading newspapers and magazines, in search of stupidities in the literary and political scene; from this perusal, he would obtain the necessary ideas for a short essay. (For a time Lu Hsün was almost a daily contributor to the Liberty Page of *Shen Pao*.) To placate his conscience over his creative barrenness, he would set aside a few hours each day for the task of translation (he translated some twenty books by

Japanese, Russian, and other European authors; with the exception of Gogol's *Dead Souls,* over which he toiled during the last years of his life, they all seem to be second-rate items). For his recreation, he either browsed in his favorite Japanese bookstore or played with his hobby of collecting and printing woodcuts. As one reconstructs Lu Hsün's daily life in Shanghai, one cannot help noticing a spiritual and intellectual shallowness in his roles as polemic journalist, plodding translator, and amateur connoisseur of art.[20]

Lu Hsün's essays are extremely entertaining as a satiric survey of the foibles and fashions of the Republican period for over two decades. But because his basic ideas are few even if they are often trenchantly applied, the over-all impression of his fifteen volumes of *tsa-wen* is that of a quarrelsome garrulity. A more fundamental criticism will be that, as a satiric commentator on passing events, Lu Hsün is not free from the sentimental bias of his age. Not to mention his later essays where an adulatory attitude toward Soviet Russia often vitiates his patriotic integrity, he displays throughout his writing career an indulgent attitude toward the young and the poor, especially the young, which is the more insidious form of sentimentality. Most of his poorer stories are infected with this spirit. In "The Solitary," the hero indulges in characteristic wishful thinking:

> "Children are always good. They are all so innocent," he said to me one day as if he had detected my impatience with children.
>
> "That is not necessarily true," I said, indifferently.
>
> "Children do not have the bad traits that grown-ups have. If they become bad later on—the kind of badness that you attack—it is because of their environment. They are not bad to start with; they are innocent . . . I think the only hope for China lies in that."
>
> "I disagree. If children do not have the seed of badness in them, how can they bear bad flowers and fruit

when they grow up? It is only because a seed carries within it the embryo of leaves, flowers, and fruit that it sends forth these things later on. How could it be otherwise?" [21]

The analogy voiced by the first-person narrator represents a truth accepted by Lu Hsün as a Darwinist and satirist but deliberately suppressed in his writings. His general attitude is clinched by the phrase in "The Diary of a Madman": "Save these children." An open letter he wrote in 1928 discloses his acute awareness of his intellectual inconsistency:

> I do entertain the hope that China will soon see some reform, some change. Although it has been said by some that I am a writer with a "venomous pen" and without any prospects (what prospects? To become a *chuang-yüan?*), I believe that I have never deliberately smeared everything. I have always thought that the lower classes are superior to the upper and that the younger generation is superior to the older; so I have never sprayed the lower classes and the younger generation with the blood from my pen. I also know that, once they are motivated by self-interest, they may become as bad as the older generation and the upper classes; but this is quite inevitable under the present social setup. However, there are plenty of people attacking them; so why should I abet this persecution? The vices I uncover may be only one-sided, but this is not done with the intention of deceiving my young readers.[22]

This is a piece of poignant confession: Lu Hsün hopes against his better knowledge that the lower classes and the younger generation will turn out to be better and less selfish. His defense of the young, especially, has made him an idol among students. In the long perspective, therefore, while Lu Hsün is capable of true indignation and can be truculently self-assertive when aroused—this spirit of defiance is perhaps the most valuable legacy he has left among his many disciples who have to live in an age of increasing intellectual conformity—his self-imposed sentimentality disqualifies him from joining the ranks of true satirists from Horace to Ben Jonson to Aldous Huxley, who have no compunction in lashing alike the vices of old and young, rich and poor. Inasmuch as Lu Hsün focuses his attention upon the apparent faults of the tradition and connives at, and later in his career, actively encourages the operation of the raw and irrational forces, which in the long run have proven to be more destructive of civilization than mere stagnation and decadence, he appears to be largely the victim of his age rather than its self-appointed teacher and satirist.

CHAPTER 3

The Literary Association

FROM 1917 to 1920, while the groundwork for a new literature was being laid, creative expression in the pai-hua idiom was limited to a few short stories and a body of puerile verse appearing in *New Youth* and *The Renaissance*. By 1921, however, the impact of the May Fourth Movement had begun to be felt on a national scale. A growing number of young writers were making themselves heard in new literary magazines, which were often launched at their own expense. Among the latter, the most durable and important was *The Short Story* Magazine (Hsiao-shuo Yüeh-pao), which for a dozen years was the unchallenged pacemaker for modern Chinese literature.

In November 1920 Chou Tso-jen, Shen Yen-ping, Cheng Chen-to, Keng Chi-chih, Yeh Shao-chün, Hsü Ti-shan, Wang T'ung-chao, and five other aspiring writers and scholars in Peking and Shanghai formed the Literary Association (Wen-hsüeh yen-chiu hui) [1] for the express purpose of creating a new literature, appraising traditional literature, and introducing Western literature. To facilitate this task, they persuaded the Commercial Press, the largest publishing house in China, to give them editorial control over *The Short*

Story, which had been for eleven years a vehicle for old-style belles-lettres. Under the editorship of Shen Yen-ping, the first issue of the renovated monthly came out in January 1921; it immediately set a standard for later journals of literary importance.

In spite of its title, *The Short Story* was a general literary miscellany: poetry, criticism, translations, essays, and novels as well as short stories were admitted in its pages. While original stories were the central attraction in each issue, this predominance was due not so much to editorial policy as to the predilection of its contributors, who found in the short story form the easiest means of self-expression. The first respectable modern Chinese novel didn't arrive until 1928 and the first modern play to enjoy critical and popular success came belatedly in 1934, but meanwhile, during the period 1921–28, *The Short Story* was instrumental in developing several important short-story writers, and in fostering a realistic tradition, which has remained the only fruitful tradition in modern Chinese fiction.

Unlike most of the later, politically slanted cliques, the Literary Association was by and large a scholarly group seriously interested in literature. In its early manifestoes the founding members affirmed the humane importance of literature and the literary profession and expressed a partiality for the kind of realism exemplified in nineteenth-century Western fiction. This is substantially the stand of Chou Tso-jen's "Humane Literature." Though Chou Tso-jen maintained only a tenuous relationship with the Association, the critic Shen Yen-ping, the story-writers Yeh Shao-chün and Hsü Ti-shan, the literary historian Cheng Chen-to, the translator of Russian fiction Keng Chi-chih—to name the members whose contributions seem especially important— all carried forward the realistic and humane tradition.

The Literary Association also advocated from the first the translation of Western literature. It was its conviction that modern Chinese literature would remain necessarily immature until it was informed with the spirit and practice of modern Western literature. Throughout its career *The Short Story* devoted ample space to the introduction and translation of Western writers of the nineteenth and the present century. Russian fiction from Turgenev and Tolstoy to Andreyev and Artzybashev received the major attention. The literature of Poland, Hungary, Czechoslovakia, and other small European nations was also stressed, out of the mistaken belief that China belonged with these oppressed nations and could profit from their trial and courage.[2]

While in its early phase *The Short Story* had only about a dozen regular contributors, by 1928 it had attracted every distinguished name in fiction up to that time: Mao Tun (pen name of Shen Yen-ping), Lao Shê, Shih Chih-ts'un, Shen Ts'ung-wen, Pa Chin, and Ting Ling, most of whom became famous after they had first published in that magazine. *The Short Story* was thriving as usual when, during the Sino-Japanese engagement in Shanghai in 1932, the Commercial Press Building was destroyed by enemy bombing. In consequence, the magazine folded, and with its demise the Literary Association, always a rather loose organization, may be said to have terminated its career.

In this chapter we shall study three writers whose pre-1927 contributions to *The Short Story* as well as whose subsequent careers have significantly enriched modern Chinese fiction: Yeh Shao-chün, Ping Hsin, and Lo Hua-sheng (pen name of Hsü Ti-shan). For convenience, a writer unconnected with the Literary Association—Ling Shu-hua—will be discussed in the same section with Ping Hsin.

YEH SHAO-CHÜN (1893–)

Of all the early story-writers for *The Short Story*, Yeh Shao-chün (since World War II he has preferred to appear in print as Yeh Sheng-t'ao) has best stood the test of time. None of his works hit the contemporary public with the shattering impact of "The Diary of a Madman" or "The True Story of Ah Q" nor can they claim the same kind of pivotal importance in literary history. But whereas Lu Hsün has achieved his classical status by virtue of only a handful of stories, Yeh Shao-chün, in his quiet and methodical way, has maintained in over half a dozen collections a standard of competence which few of his contemporaries could rival. Along with his sure craftsmanship, he has also evinced a civilized sensibility which, while nourished upon the prevalent attitudes of his time, remains nearly always invulnerable to cant and pretentiousness. These two qualities alone should have earned him a higher critical esteem than he seems to have enjoyed among Chinese readers.

Born in 1893, Yeh Shao-chün was for ten years after his graduation from high school an elementary school teacher in his native city of Soochow, Kiangsu. He devoted himself to literary studies at the same time, and with the encouragement of his high school classmate, Ku Chieh-kang, then a rising historian in Peking,[3] he published his first stories in *The Renaissance*. By 1921 Yeh Shao-chün had become a founding member of the Literary Association and moved to Shanghai. He taught Chinese at various high schools and colleges and served as editor of *Women's Magazine* and *The Short Story*. In the early thirties he joined the Kaiming Press as co-editor of the influential magazine for adolescent readers, *The Middle School Student*. In collaboration with the essayists Hsia Mien-tsun and Chu Tzu-ch'ing, he compiled several textbooks of Chinese literature and also wrote a number of introductory studies in Chinese literature and rhetoric, which were quite popular with high school students. But for the period 1921–37, of course, his chief output lies in the field of fiction: six story collections (*The Barrier, Fire, Under the Line, In the City, Without Satiety, At Forty-three*) and two volumes of children's tales (*The Scarecrow* and *The Statue of an Ancient Hero*). After the outbreak of the Sino-Japanese War he moved with the Kaiming Press to the interior and wrote very little besides a volume of essays called *West of Szechwan*. As a cultural official of some importance, he has written occasional pieces during the early years of the People's Republic.

Writing in 1951, in a preface to his *Selected Works*, Yeh Shao-chün takes only a modest view of his abilities and achievement. Possibly to account for his failure to tackle the more revolutionary themes of his time, he tells the present-day Communist public:

> In retrospect, I seem never to have written about anything of which I had only vague or hazy knowledge. In other words, I cannot write anything by merely imagining it, though I do not wish to banish the element of fancy. I lived in the cities, towns, and villages, and I wrote what I had observed there. As a teacher, I knew something about life in educational circles and I wrote about that. In a rather elementary and superficial way I watched the gradual development of the Chinese Revolution and I wrote about that too. Nearly all the characters in my fiction are intellectuals and small citizens, because I did not have a personal knowledge of the peasant and worker classes or of the rich merchants and high officials, and was only slightly better acquainted with the intellectuals and small citizens.[4]

This self-criticism actually reads like a sly rebuke to the trends in writing today, which Yeh Shao-chün could not openly deplore: the inescapable duty of every writer to write about peasants and workers at the complete disregard of his personal experience and background and of his predilections as to theme and subject. In the same preface Yeh Shao-chün goes on to defend the writer's inalienable right to do the best of which he is capable. Viewed against the present Communist emphasis on depersonalized writing in the service of propaganda, this assertion of the importance of language takes on the aspect of a positive act of courage:

59

So, whenever I hear people say that language is a small matter and content is all-important, I cannot agree, though I have not written any articles to refute this. I am not disagreeing as to the importance of content. . . . But to say that language is a small matter—is this not equivalent to saying that language is negligible? That slipshod language can serve as the vehicle for a worthy content, this argument I cannot really figure out. According to my stupid way of thinking, a worthy content can only reveal its worth in a worthy language. In the term "language" as I use it here, I include the single phrase and the single sentence as well as the discourse of some thousand, ten thousand, or hundred thousand words. In other words, a worthy language is the concrete expression of a worthy content. I don't pretend to know what that thing "content" is when detached from language; anyway, it can no longer be literature.[5]

This argument is rather elementary, though in itself a piece of crucial criticism against the whole Communist approach to literature. For a writer unacquainted with modern Western criticism, as Yeh Shao-chün apparently is (he has learned some English and Japanese, but not to the point of reading the languages with ease), it also indicates a remarkable intelligence able to work out the Jamesian theory of fiction on its own. In his own practice he has also apparently grasped the implications of his theory, for his best stories represent an admirable fusion of content and language, idea and style.

Most of Yeh Shao-chün's early stories deal with school children and teachers. They embody his passionate concerns as a dedicated teacher—traditional indifference to child psychology and welfare, and the apathy of society toward modern education. In stories with the latter emphasis, zealous and idealistic educators usually encounter difficulty and frustration. In "The Principal" the hero is thwarted in his attempt to dismiss three undesirable teachers; in "Struggle" the teacher who agitates for higher pay is expelled from school when his cowardly colleagues fail to support his move to the end; in yet another story, called "In the City," a group of conscientious young educators meet with tough opposition from the city fathers and elder teachers when they propose to open a new school on modern educational principles. All these stories point to one basic Chinese problem: the failure of reformist energy and zeal to overcome the powerful forces of custom, self-interest, and ignorance.

The stories about school children possess decidedly greater interest and merit. Yeh Shao-chün shows in these a playful tenderness and a serious pedagogic concern, as well as an astonishing command of the juvenile mind. The result is a more complex mode of fiction. In such an apparently simple story as "One Lesson" there is an expert use of interior monologue to body forth the inattention and reverie of a child in classroom. In "Yi-erh" Yeh Shao-chün traces the crippling effect of home and school on a twelve-year-old boy with an irrepressible inclination toward the visual arts. The indictment as such, however, is couched in comic terms. In their failure to understand the boy's urge for creative expression and in their employment of threats and cajolery to force him to attend to his regular class work, his elders are shown to be blind rather than cruel; the distraught mother, a widow pinning all her hopes on her only son, is especially affectionate and solicitous of his welfare. The resultant tug-of-war between the stubborn boy and his good-willed guardians is a brilliant comedy with tragic overtones.

The use of comic irony is seen to even better advantage in "Rice." It is the story of a poor teacher and of a village threatened by famine. The teacher has under his care a group of urchins who, with their still undiminished animal spirits, are apparently not much concerned about the famine. To them, "death is like sleep, hazy and dark. When it covers you, you cannot eat, you cannot play, and you cannot make a single move, as if something had tied you down. And when will this tie ever be loosened?" [6] But for a moment they are oblivious even of this hazy image of death in their huge enjoyment of their teacher's distress. The point of the story is the children's final comprehension of the menace of famine and death as something involving not only their teacher but their parents and themselves as well.

As the children noisily assemble in their classroom, Mr. Wu is late as usual. It is his invariable habit to buy his groceries for the day before coming to class. But today the school inspector has arrived. A cheat who regularly pockets a portion of the monthly salary due the pitifully underpaid teacher, he is not above putting on a stern face over the latter's delinquency. He asks the students the whereabouts of Mr. Wu, and they, in happy anticipation of a dramatic scene, are only too eager to respond:

> The boys heard the school inspector's question; three or four replied in their noisy manner, "He is out buying groceries, buying bean curds and scallions." A few tittered.
>
> "This is quite irregular, not to come to class at this time," the inspector murmured to himself. After a pause he asked, "Is he like that every day?"
>
> "He is like that every day; he has to eat," a boy with a big pigtail answered.
>
> Another boy said, "My mother sometimes buys groceries for him."
>
> "Don't listen to him, but—"
>
> The sturdy boy with the silver earrings had not yet finished his sentence when Mr. Wu came in, his hands empty. He had probably deposited his groceries near the pots and stove. Seeing the school inspector standing angrily beside the blackboard, he didn't know what to do. He swayed his body right and left, folded his hands and bowed his head in salutation.

Making a slight nod, the school inspector said coldly, "Class has started some while ago, and you have just arrived."

Mr. Wu wanted very much to reply in suitable words but couldn't find them. His embarrassed manner made the boys giggle. Knowing that it would be futile to make any excuses, he mumbled out the truth in a trembling manner, "I was out buying groceries and didn't expect I would be late."

"Buying groceries!" The inspector raised his voice to a high pitch. "Class has started, the students are all here, and they have to wait till you finish shopping!"

"Then I shall not buy groceries from now on," Mr. Wu said involuntarily. The boys burst out laughing. Pointing at him, they mumbled excitedly among themselves, "Teacher won't eat from now on, teacher won't eat from now on!" [7]

Even in the incomplete context of this quotation one can appreciate the ironic function of the students' chant, "Teacher won't eat from now on." But what appears very funny gradually takes on a serious aspect. As the teacher apologizes for his behavior and haggles timidly for the remainder of his salary, the fear of hunger dawns upon the boys and implicates them in the general plight:

Pulling his clothes, the boy with the big pigtail whispered to the boy in front of him, "Did you hear? Teacher's family are expecting him to feed them; otherwise they would be dying of hunger."

Disbelieving, the boy with the silver earrings contradicted him, "Teacher is far richer than we. When our bones rot, his belly would be still full. Don't talk nonsense!"

"Must we die of hunger and must our bones rot?" A little boy eagerly asked, his eyes filled with apprehension.

"You will have no rice to eat when you go home today. Tomorrow you will die of hunger, and day after tomorrow your bones will begin to rot and rot until they become a mess of wet earth." Very pleased with himself, the boy with the silver earrings replied.

The little boy dared no longer ask any questions; he was wrapped in some fantasy of mystery and fear.[8]

Yeh Shao-chün's preoccupation with educational problems finally led him to write in 1928 a novel which is more or less autobiographical, *Ni Huan-chih*. By that time he had been living and teaching in Shanghai for some years, had shared with most other writers the enthusiasm over the May Thirtieth Movement and the disillusionment with the failure of Kuomintang-Communist collaboration. The novel therefore also incorporates the author's responses to the larger political issues. A high school graduate and teacher in a village elementary school, Ni Huan-chih enjoys the trust of the principal and the love of the girl whom he later marries. Responding enthusiastically to the May Fourth Movement, he embarks on a few reforms in school, only to be met with indifference and hostility; he is further distressed to find that his wife, once a partner of his vision, now contentedly busies herself with only her domestic duties. He leaves the village to teach in Shanghai and at the same time to engage in social work. As an active participant in the May Thirtieth demonstrations, he feels a renewal of hope. But his disillusion returns with the massacre of Communists in April 1927. Ni Huan-chih drowns his sorrow in drink and is eventually stricken with typhoid fever. As he lies dying, he murmurs to himself: "Ay, so let it be death! Feeble ability and unstable emotions, they are useless, completely useless! One hope after another came within my grasp and then fled; if I had thirty more years to live, it would be still the same!"[9]

Ni Huan-chih does not come off very well as a novel, though for its time, when good novels were just beginning to appear, it was a notable achievement. Despite its apparent honesty, the sympathetic bond between author and hero is too personally close to generate the kind of ironic objectivity which distinguishes Yeh Shao-chün's better short stories. The slow movement, the stylized language, and the pervasive cast of melancholy remind one, oddly enough, of Johnson's *Rasselas*. In a later story called "The English Professor" (1936) Yeh Shao-chün tries to distill the tragic essence of *Ni Huan-chih*. The hero, Tung Wu-kou, is a good man, almost a saint. When he returns from Harvard, he is for some years a conscientious professor of psychology at a college in Shanghai. A dutiful son, he goes to his home town every week end to be with his mother, and in time he gets married and lives happily with his mother and wife in his insulated world of domestic tranquillity and scholarly pursuits. The May Thirtieth Movement, however, rudely awakens him to the suffering of the Chinese. From then on, he works tirelessly for the revolutionary cause, until with the massacre of Communists in 1927 he suffers a nervous breakdown and turns to Buddhism for solace. In the course of years he is bereaved of both mother and wife and lives his life of meditation in increasing poverty. A friend, seeing his distress, finally reinstates him as a college teacher. Having outgrown his interest in Western psychology, Tung Wu-kou agrees to teach only a course of freshman English. Every morning he worships in his room, unperturbed by the curiosity of the students over his odd habits. He maintains his unequivocal stand on pacifism when asked by some of the students if China should arm herself to meet Japanese aggression.

One has no doubt that in the author's attitude toward Tung Wu-kou there is a strong element of animus: "He crawls in a corner of the college like a mouse underneath the floor; one sees only the floor and not the mouse underneath." [10] This is a derogatory image intended to sum up the hero's impotence and futility in his renunciation of the patriotic task and espousal of Buddhism. But this image jars upon the gently ironic and largely sympathetic texture of

the story. In view of Yeh Shao-chün's strong personal interest
in Buddhism (he was a great admirer of the celebrated
Buddhist monk Hung I, under whom his good friend the
artist and essayist Feng Tzu-k'ai served as a disciple), one
is quite convinced that "The English Professor" is, like
Ni Huan-chih, a mortifying essay in self-criticism. It gives
the impression that its author would like very much to be
with the vanguard of leftist and patriotic writers but that,
with his early loss of courage following the political events
of 1927 and with his constitutional incapacity for the life of
action, he is merely filled with self-reproach. The unresolved
tension between satire and tragedy in "The English Professor" is poignantly symptomatic of Yeh Shao-chün's personal dilemma.

Because of the strong note of self-reproach, *Ni Huan-chih,*
"The English Professor," and other stories about educational
reformers do not present Yeh Shao-chün at his happiest. His
imagination cannot have free play when it is under the constant necessity of measuring personal failure against the
dictates of ideological fashion. It is only when he ponders
the destinies of people quite unlike himself that he appears
as the assured storyteller, blending sympathy with irony
much in the manner of Chekhov. Stories about the gray
lives of small citizens are invariably among his best.

"Solitude" (1923) is a study of a lonely old man. A famous
winebibber in his prime, he now lives in a rented room in
a state of helpless decrepitude. He has only hot water for
supper and gets up in the morning with the greatest difficulty. He usually spends his day in a teahouse; occasionally
he buys some fruit for the landlady's little daughter so as
to obtain from her a reluctant greeting. One wintry day he
pays a rare visit to his niece and her husband, but their
perfunctory reception makes him completely ill at ease. In
the same vein as "K'ung I-chi," "Solitude" is a more ambitious psychological study evoking a quiet sense of desolation.

In "Autumn" we have another study in loneliness. The heroine, an unsuccessful obstetrician in her late thirties, returns from Shanghai to her home town to attend the annual family reunion on the occasion of sweeping the ancestral graves. As a professional woman in competition with quacks and old-style midwives, she is tainted with their disrepute and faces almost certain spinsterhood. When her sister-in-law tentatively inquires if she would consider marrying a widower over fifty years of age, she cannot help feeling great humiliation. The next day, as she sails in the boat with her kinsfolk toward the cemetery, she recalls the gaiety of similar trips a dozen years before, when her parents were still alive and she herself was happy and carefree. She feels the world is caving in upon her.

Yeh Shao-chün captures with remarkable psychological precision the heroine's somber mood during her short visit home. The brief first paragraph, descriptive of her entrance into her room in the old house, immediately sets the tone of the story: "She unlocked the door and pushed it open: a musty smell. In the gloom of a late autumn afternoon, the obscure furniture looked hardly recognizable after her long absence. She opened two windows and saw that everything was covered with a layer of dust." [11] The mood is maintained throughout the story, except during her reminiscent pause on the boat:

> In comparison with similar excursions ten or more years ago, the present trip was much too quiet and dispiriting. In those days the different branches of the family were living in the same house; on the morning of the day set for sweeping the graves they would all be assembled in the main hall and make a joyous scene. Young mistresses, married and unmarried, would appear in new dresses made according to their own design: this dress was embroidered with butterflies and that with peonies, and there would be on view all kinds of

laces and patterns. The fragrance of rouge and powder emanated from every face and every arm, slightly intoxicating those around them with an ineffable joy. Children romped in and out, urging immediate departure: this one would drag his uncle and that one pull his father. When everyone had arrived, the journey would begin. There would be three boats; and when they were rowed toward the broader section of the river, they would glide on, side by side. Tea and fruit, all kinds of desserts and sweets, were spread on tables, and flutes and recorders played in unison. Laughter darted back and forth from boat to boat. It was indeed a picnic for the whole family.[12]

This scene not only defines the heroine's present loneliness but brings to the reader's attention the social changes that have made her what she is: the disintegration of the big family, the passing of the old amenities, and by implication the hard lot of working women longing nostalgically for the parental roof. Yeh Shao-chün explores these changes in the context of the woman's life and admirably refrains from making any kind of explicit commentary.

In "Richer by Three or Five Pecks" (1933), one of his few stories about the peasants, Yeh Shao-chün depicts with unsurpassed success for his time the plight of the Chinese village. In tackling such a subject most story-writers would impose upon it an economic-political interpretation; while Yeh Shao-chün appends at the end of his story a brief didactic commentary, the main body of his narrative has a concrete presence of humanity which is touching because of its restrained note of sympathy and indignation. In the story a group of peasants have rowed their boats to town to sell their new rice. The harvest has been excellent, but the wholesale price has proportionately dropped. Reluctantly the peasants sell their produce with little or no profit, though they have come to town with high hopes that they would get enough cash to buy some sorely needed goods:

> Each of these fellows in old coarse felt caps had come to town today with great plans. As there was no more soap at home, he had to buy eight or ten cakes. He had also to buy a few boxes of matches. Since to buy kerosene from the village peddler was too costly—ten coppers for one small ladle—it would be much cheaper if he and his friends could buy a whole tin jointly. The pretty-colored cotton piece goods, he heard, sold for only eight and a half cents a yard. His woman had been tempted for a long time. This morning she was quite determined to accompany him on his trip to unload the rice: a few yards for herself, a few for the big child, and a few for the second—this was all in her plans. Some women planned, furthermore, to buy an oval foreign-style mirror, a snow-white towel, or a pretty woolen baby bonnet. With Heaven's blessing this year, so hard to expect, each *mou* had yielded three or five more pecks, and who is to say it isn't right that the hand, usually so tightfisted, should feel freer to spend? There would be enough money to pay rent, debts, and lottery dues, and perhaps even a little to put aside. In this mood some even aspired to a thermos bottle. This thing is really wonderful: it doesn't need fuel. You put in hot water and it will stay hot when you pour it out some time afterward. Compared with the teapot cozy made of rice straw, this is infinitely better.[13]

Few Chinese writers specializing in peasant life could produce a passage like this, so concretely vivid and so faithful to the sensibility of the peasants. Yeh Shao-chün has invested their poverty with dignity by viewing the necessities through their own eyes as objects of great aesthetic and practical value. The story continues with a few more pages of

69

this type of intimate and precise realism. When it is time for the peasants to return to their boats, they have bought only a few out of the many items they wanted. Yet they are not so sore as to begrudge themselves a little fun on the return trip:

> The country folk also bought a little wine, and a little meat from the vendor of cooked meat, and returned to their boats, which were fastened against the pier of the Wan-Sheng Rice Warehouse. They took out a few dishes like pickled cabbage and bean curd soup from the stern of their boats and began to drink wine at the bow. Their women were cooking rice at the stern. In a short while, one boat after another began to smoke, irritating all eyes to the point of tears. The children were either tumbling and fighting in the empty and uncovered holds or playing with slimy matter caught on the surface of the river. Only *they* were unspeakably happy.[14]

The three stories just discussed stand high in the central tradition of modern Chinese fiction as carefully wrought vignettes of ordinary life informed with an unobtrusive sympathy. As editor of and regular contributor to *The Short Story,* Yeh Shao-chün is generally regarded as an exponent of the school of art for life's sake. This phrase is quite meaningless if it is merely intended to contrast the Literary Association with its chief rival, The Creation Society, with its vaunted pursuit of art for art's sake (see below, pp. 93 ff.). What should be emphasized is that Yeh Shao-chün and a few other story-writers for *The Short Story* have evinced a far stronger sense of artistic vocation and responsibility in their striving for truth as they personally knew it. Yeh Shao-chün's hatred for the ugly aspects of Chinese life and his despondency over the course of events since 1927 are shared by the more doctrinaire writers; but with him at least, these feelings are generally kept in place under a comprehensive view of humanity with all its courage and weakness, its decency and isolation.

As a writer of children's tales, Yeh Shao-chün is often unwarrantably didactic. His best-known tales, like "The Scarecrow" and "The Emperor's New Clothes," are all in imitation of Andersen. As an essayist, he employs the same cool and well-mannered style of his fiction. It is not gaudy and ornate, as with those who mistakenly pursue an "aesthetic style," nor aggressively familiar, as with those who imitate the late Ming essayists. Its strength lies in observation. In a famous essay, "Two Buddhist Priests," Yeh Shao-chün records his impressions of two equally celebrated figures: Abbot Yin Kuang and the aforementioned Hung I. Yet under his scrutiny the latter emerges as a truly humble practitioner of his religion, while the former shows himself as a moralist and almost a charlatan, still under the sway of pride and anger.

PING HSIN AND LING SHU-HUA

A regular contributor to *The Short Story,* Ping Hsin (1902–) enjoyed tremendous popularity in the early twenties, though with the establishment of a revolutionary orthodoxy since 1928 it has been the critical fashion to dismiss her as somewhat passé. For a modern Chinese author her output is small: the standard edition of her collected works, first published in 1932, comprises only three volumes respectively of her short stories, poetry, and prose. In the subsequent years, there have been a few stories, a translation of Kahlil Gibran's *The Prophet,* and a volume of essays *On Women,* written during the War of Resistance, to add to the corpus. Her most significant work was produced from 1919 to about 1925.

Ping Hsin represents the sentimental tradition in Chinese literature. If there had been no Literary Revolution, she would still have emerged as a poet and prose writer of some importance; most probably, she would have been much happier and more productive under the old dispensation. Her study of Western culture has only encouraged a didactic tendency, which is destructive of her sensibility; her fondness for Tagore and Gibran has fostered a pseudo-mystical regard for nature, which would have been held in check if she were exposed only to Chinese poetry. Neither sentimental preaching nor pantheistic worship, of course, represents Ping Hsin's real strength, which is grounded in a concrete knowledge of a limited range of feelings.

A native of Foochow, Fukien, Ping Hsin (her real name is Hsieh Wan-ying) was brought up in a comfortable home in Chefoo, on the seacoast of Shantung. She was a precocious child and had read most of the Chinese novels and romances by the age of eleven. When not reading, she loved to roam on the beach and watch the sea and stars, which to her are proofs of a benignant cosmic order as certain as the love she enjoyed in the company of her mother and brothers. At the age of ten she was taught Chinese poetry by one of her scholarly uncles; for the next few years she read and composed verses continually. She moved with her family to Peking in 1914 and studied for the next six years at a missionary girls' school. Her literary interest, which had temporarily waned, revived under the stimulus of the Literary Revolution. During her last years at high school she had already contributed to the Literary Supplement of the Peking *Morning Gazette,* and as a student at Yenching University (1920–23) she continued to write stories, poems, and essays for that paper and for *The Short Story.* Upon graduation she went to Wellesley College for advanced study and wrote of her life in America in a series of *Letters to My Little Readers,* which proved to be a great success with the younger audience. Ping Hsin returned to China in 1926 to teach at Yenching University; three years later she married the sociologist Wu Wen-tsao. Today she lives on the mainland, a member of the Writers' Association specializing in juvenile propaganda.

Ping Hsin wrote at first mainly problem stories, tracing the dilemmas of the younger generation in a period of agonizing transition. During her stay in America she elaborated her philosophy of love in a number of tales, notably "The Superman" and "Awakening," which met wide acclaim at the time of their publication. But profuse with rhapsodic apostrophes to the moon and stars and to mother love, these stories are unabashedly sentimental in their ambition to idealize the world in the image of the author's own childhood happiness. It is only when Ping Hsin is content to desist from philosophizing and to focus her attention on the simple joys and sorrows of children and adolescents that she emerges as a writer of remarkable sensitivity within her narrow range. Her best stories, mostly written when she was still in college, all attest to this unpretentious sensitivity.

In "Loneliness" (1922), Hsiao-hsiao, a boy about seven years old, hurries home from his last final examinations at school to see his younger cousin, Mei-mei, who is expected to arrive with her mother on that day. Having recently lost a son, the latter is invited to spend a few days with Hsiao-hsiao's mother. The two children spend two wonderful days together, telling stories, playing games, and fishing for crabs. On the third day Hsiao-hsiao has to go to school to attend an art exhibition; by the time he returns home, Mei-mei and her mother have already left. The boy is filled with a wistful sadness, which appears the more real because of the earlier vivid evocation of childhood happiness. Cast in the author's simple and lucid prose, the story is an almost faultless idyl, except for a brief scene in which one feels the intrusion of a didactic concern with mother love. In that scene Ping Hsin has Hsiao-hsiao listen to a lecture by his mother: "Auntie liked the style of that little straw hat I bought you and she wanted to buy a similar one for Hsüan-ko. Then she suddenly remembered that Hsüan-ko is dead and she cried again. So we left the place—you see how intense is a mother's love for her son!" [15]

In "A Year Away from Home," Ping Hsin applies the theme of loneliness to older children. A thirteen-year-old boy leaves his parents and sister, who is one year older, for school in another city. At first, separation is unbearable for both brother and sister, but gradually the boy becomes accustomed to his new life and even learns to enjoy it. When he returns home after the spring semester, he is a somewhat more mature person. Like "Loneliness," the story is concretely evocative of a small range of familiar feelings.

"Since Her Departure" plays yet another variation on the theme of solitude. The hero, a thirteen-year-old orphan living at his uncle's home, has just seen his elder sister leave by train in the morning to become a bride in another city. Feeling very desolate, he accepts a wealthy classmate's invitation to spend the afternoon with him. While he has passed Yung-ming's house every day on his way to and from school, this is the first time he has been privileged to go inside. He has never seen such comfort and elegance: Yung-ming's many sisters and girl cousins, especially, strike him as creatures of sheer enchantment. He particularly adores Yung-ming's second sister, a beautiful girl in a light purple dress, so different in every way from his own sister. The orphan passes the afternoon very agreeably helping the girls cut up paper ribbons in preparation for the New Year festivities and listening to their easy and lively conversation. Soon after supper, however, the boy has to go home and leave the world of warmth and gaiety behind him. As a parting present, Yung-ming gives him two packages of fruit.

Staying that night in his own room with the servant Wang Ma, who is making soles by pasting together many layers of rags, the boy tries to write a letter to his sister. Inadvertently his brush slips into the phrase, "My sister in purple":

At that moment he suddenly remembered that his sister had never worn a purple dress. Dejectedly he threw down his brush. Before his eyes emerged the sallow and thin face of his sister, with its high cheekbones and expressionless myopic eyes. Before her departure she had been for two or three months working on her wedding wardrobe, like a professional seamstress, neither vexed nor happy. Her deportment suggested a floating spirit in a dream. Aloof with people and rather apathetic toward him, she seldom took his hands to inquire after his health. This morning in the train, she just stared at him with those dazed and wooden eyes of hers as if she didn't grasp the meaning of separation or think ahead of her future fate . . .

He was in a stupor; rolling his eyes, he saw the girl in the purple dress. White arms, radiant dimples, warm and loving eyes, clear and deep as water . . . this sister in purple was not his; she was Yung-ming's! . . .

Slowly he placed his brush against the top of the ink box. As he peered dully at the flame of the kerosene lamp with his moist eyes, the halo appeared blurred and the flame flickered unceasingly. Finally tear drops fell upon the paper.

Wang Ma, who was putting the rags together, looked up and said, "You're thinking of your sister. Don't be so sad. Go to bed now or else find something to amuse yourself with." He shook his head and sighed, then stood up and crumpled that sheet of letter paper and dried his tears with it. After standing listlessly for a while, he saw the bowl of paste on the desk and suddenly wanted to paste up some paper ribbons and festoon his room with them. He thought perhaps his aunt would give him some money to buy color paper, and he walked out of his room.

No sooner had he approached the upper room than he heard the voice of his aunt scolding his two cousins:

"Whence is so much money to buy this and that? All you can think of the whole day is to play and eat." Following this was the cousins' indistinct murmur of disappointment. He paused there for a while and then returned to his room, bowing his head dejectedly.

Seeing the two packages on the chair, he quietly went over to them and in a minute he had removed the two sheets of wrapping paper. He returned to his desk and cut them into thin strips with Wang Ma's scissors. He pasted up these strips, red alternate with green, to form a cord.

There was no more paper when the cord reached the length of about three feet. He took it in his hands and surveyed his room. After some deliberation he hung it up between the hooks of his bed curtains. Then he slowly reclined on his bed.

Paying him no attention, Wang Ma was still straining her tired eyes to paste together the layers of the sole. Half sitting up on his pillow and cupping his chin with his right hand, he cast a long look at the thin, long, and unappreciated paper cord hung near the soiled, old, and graying bed curtain. It seemed to him as if he were enjoying himself in spite of his desolation.[16]

A proper appreciation of this passage demands the context of the happy afternoon which the hero spends at the home of his friend. But even detached from the rest of the story, this concluding section with its admittedly overfeminine touches testifies to Ping Hsin's delicate realism and her ability to conjure up the feeling of youthful melancholy. "Since Her Departure" is the most ambitious example of the author's art and stands high among the early short stories.

After her return to China, Ping Hsin tried with little success to write of adult life. In "The West Wind" (1936), however, she achieves a sensitive psychological study comparable to her best early stories. But the theme this time is again loneliness, indicating her inability to develop further. The plot also conforms more to a sentimental formula. Aboard a ship sailing from Tientsin to Shanghai, the heroine meets with a friend who has proposed to her ten years ago in America. At that time she has refused him, intent on her studies and confident of her future. Now a lonely career woman shorn of her youth, she is very much ill at ease in his company. She shies away from him when he disembarks to meet his wife and children waiting on the pier. A reluctant witness to the happy scene of family reunion, she remains on the pier until they have left, feeling quite chilly and lonely as a gust of west wind blows up the litter of waste paper and dried leaves. In this admittedly woman's story, Ping Hsin tests her heroine against a series of difficult situations with restrained feminine sympathy.

Despite her slim body of work, Ping Hsin is rightly entitled to a place of distinction among writers of the first period. Her poems and essays tend to sentimentalize in the absence of a realistic framework, but in a few of her stories she speaks out with an individual accent and evinces a refined sensibility above the heat and fury of the modern temper.

Along with Ping Hsin several other women writers made some impression in this period: Huang Lu-yin, a very mediocre story-writer and novelist and frequent contributor to *The Short Story;* Ch'en Heng-chê, an essayist and critic in the circle of Hu Shih; Feng Yüan-chün, author of intimate and daring love stories and sister of the well-known professor of Chinese philosophy, Feng Yu-lan; Su Hsüeh-lin, a French-returned student and Catholic who published in 1929 an autobiographical novel called *The Bitter Heart* but achieved later a more solid reputation for her criticism and research in Chinese literature.[17] In creative talent, however, none of these approached the skill and brilliance of Ling Shu-hua who, like Ping Hsin, wrote short stories about women and children. But unlike Ping Hsin, she early manifested a more adult sensibility and psychological acumen, which promised greater achievement. Her infrequent publications in the thirties unfortunately did little to confirm that promise.

A native of Kwangtung, Ling Shu-hua came to Peking in the early twenties to study English literature at Yenching University. Ch'en Yüan (courtesy name: Hsi-ying; 1896–1970), Professor of English at National Peking University and a prominent member of the Anglo-American group, was early impressed with her talent and published her first stories in his weekly, *Contemporary Review*. Later they were married, and during the second half of the twenties they were justly famous as a literary couple. As author of *The Causeries of Hsi-ying*, brilliant commentaries on politics and literature culled from *Contemporary Review*, Ch'en Yüan was at the height of his critical influence and Ling Shu-hua was producing her most significant fiction. Unfortunately, embroiled in a bitter quarrel with Lu Hsün over a petty issue, Ch'en Yüan soon grew disgusted and relinquished his post as urbane critic and liberal spokesman on Chinese affairs (in the thirties only occasional writings and translations appear over his name in magazines) and his wife seems to have followed his example in writing less. After World War II they lived in London, and Ch'en Yüan was for many years China's chief delegate to UNESCO.

Ling Shu-hua's first book, *The Temple of Flowers* (1928), comprising her stories of the period 1924–26, possesses a remarkable thematic unity. Quite ably it probes into the anxiety and fear of slightly old-fashioned girls caught in a period of changing manners. Brought up in the style of traditional propriety and decorum, these girls lack the necessary courage and cunning to compete with their more Westernized rivals in the love game and suffer consequently in quiet desperation. The heroine of "The Tea Party" misconstrues a returned student's Western style of courtesy as a sign of his positive interest; she is later mortified to receive the news of his engagement to another girl. Anticipating Ping Hsin's "The West Wind," "The Second Encounter" depicts the abasement of an unmarried schoolteacher on meeting a classmate of hers who has become a prosperous official. In "After the Tea Party," two sisters discuss the dresses, manners, and flirtations of their wealthier friends at the party until, in a moment of pause, they both realize how slim their marital chances are in that world of inviting gaiety.

"Embroidered Pillows" registers with especial power the plight of the old-fashioned girl. One sultry day the daughter of an impoverished genteel family is embroidering away at a pair of cushions. Tomorrow her father will present her handiwork as a birthday gift to a high official who, if impressed with her artistry, may consider her as a match for his second son. The girl apparently accepts her father's reasoning and is extremely nervous on the last day of her work. After months of unremitting toil she has great difficulty in keeping the cushions from being soiled by her perspiration and in discriminating between many subtle shades of colored threads to be used. The daughter of the amah, a girl in her early teens, excited over this stunning handiwork, tries to have a closer view of it; her mother, however, shoos her away for fear of her soiling the cushions.

Two years later the young mistress is still not married. One day the amah's daughter excitedly shows her a pair of soiled but still exquisite pillow cases which have come into her possession. She tells her mistress that they used to be cushion covers at a certain rich home; that, on the day of their arrival, one of the cushions was vomited upon by a guest at the house and the other was thrown onto the floor and used as a footstool; that consequently they were immediately turned over to the servants' quarters. Upon viewing the pillow cases, the young mistress recognizes them as her handiwork upon which she has pinned such hope and expended so much industry.

79

Ling Shu-hua suffuses the two parallel scenes of her story with an imagery which is of an unparalleled richness for its time. In the first scene the gorgeous cushions are contrasted with the sweltering heat, which is symbolic of the heroine's drudgery; in the second, the cushion covers themselves have become a symbol of the girl. As she listens to the story of their degradation, she realizes it is herself rather than her handiwork that was so exquisitely prepared, so contemptuously received, so rudely vomited and trampled upon. Despite its brevity, "Embroidered Pillows" was the first modern Chinese short story to be sustained on the dramatic irony of a pervading symbolism. And this symbolism, in its minor way, is of the order of Desdemona's handkerchief in *Othello*.

The most powerful piece in *The Temple of Flowers*, however, is "The Eve of the Mid-Autumn Festival," which gives a grim portrait of a pathetic and narrow-minded woman of the old order. Ching-jen and his wife are just sitting down for their first festival dinner together; both are of the small-town, shop-owning class unacquainted with modern ideas and manners. For the occasion the wife has prepared the customary "harmony duck" to symbolize her happy union with her husband. But just when they are about to start eating, a telephone call urges Ching-jen's immediate presence at his stepsister's dying bed. Rather stubborn in her superstitious ways, the wife is unwilling to have him leave until after the end of the meal and insists that he at least take a piece of duck. He takes a bite, but as it is too greasy, he spits it out.

Upon his return home at midnight, Ching-jen regrets that, had it not been for his wife's urging him to eat part of the dinner, he could at least have been with his stepsister before she died. In her own way, the wife is sulking under this unlucky interruption of their important dinner. In the ensuing quarrel Ching-jen smashes a vase, one of his wife's cherished objects, and she breaks out crying.

his suspicions, he one evening delves into a book of Chinese history: "This history recorded no dates, but over every page were scrawled the words 'benevolence, righteousness, truth, virtue.' Since I couldn't go to sleep anyway, I made a close scrutiny of this book, until by midnight I discovered all over it a succession of two words between the lines: 'Eat men!' " [5] In spite of the Chinese profession of benevolence and righteousness, therefore, traditional life consists of cannibalism. At the end of the story, the madman makes a plea which has become proverbial with Chinese readers: "Perhaps there are still some children who have not yet become cannibalistic? Save these children . . ." [6]

Despite its obvious moral seriousness, the indictment that Chinese life is hypocritical and cruel is presented in an ingenious manner which is more indicative of the author's erudition than his satiric ability. In his failure to provide a realistic plot for the madman's fantasies (no one apparently is trying to eat him), Lu Hsün merely garnishes his story with miscellaneous items relating to the practice of cannibalism in China and fails to present his case in dramatic terms. As the very first story composed in the Western manner, however (both the title and form are indebted to a story by Gogol), "The Diary of a Madman" evinces a remarkable technical virtuosity as well as a good deal of irony. The introductory section says of the madman that "after his recovery, he has gone to a certain district to await official appointment"; [7] the price of sanity, then, is collaboration in the old game of cannibalism.

"K'ung I-chi" was Lu Hsün's first story in the lyrical mode: a touching if sketchy portrait of a marginal member of the literati who has turned thief. The only long-gowned customer associating with the poorer folk at the tavern, K'ung I-chi uses a bookish style of language to expound the distinctions between mere stealing and stealing books, for the benefit and amusement of his teasing audience. As a book thief, he is regularly beaten black and blue by the gentry until he finally dies nobody knows when or where. His pathos lies in his clinging to the genteel ways when he should have had more self-knowledge as to his status in traditional society. As told by the boy whose job is to warm the drinks at the tavern, the story has an economy and restraint characteristic of some of Hemingway's Nick Adams stories.

"Medicine" is a much more ambitious performance than either of its predecessors. At once a realistic exposé of the traditional way of life, a symbolic parable on revolution, and a touching tale of parents' grief over their children, dead in their prime, it has, as the author puts it, "the calculated cruelty of Andreyev." [8] A young man named Hsia has just been decapitated for his part in the revolutionary conspiracy against the Ch'ing Government. Meanwhile, in the same town, another youth by the name of Hua is dying of consumption. Hua's aged father, clutching at the straw of superstition, buys from the executioner a roll of bread soaked with the dead revolutionary's blood in the vain belief that this blood will give his son a new lease of life. Hua gobbles the bread down, but he dies nevertheless.

The two young men have died differently: one as the martyr of a hopeful cause and the other the victim of crass ignorance and a national scourge. But to their mothers, who care little what kills them, each death is a crushing and incomprehensible blow to be absorbed and forgotten in the sad rhythm of Chinese feudal life. One cold morning in early spring, as the mothers repair to the adjacent graves to mourn their dead, they face each other in the kinship of sorrow.

Lu Hsün has attempted in the story a complex structure of meanings. As indicated by their names (the phrase *hua-hsia* being a poetic synonym for China), the two young men represent the hopeful and the doomed mode of Chinese existence. Hua's failure to survive even after he has drunk Hsia's blood symbolizes the death of the feudal order, unlikely to be resuscitated in the event of a revolutionary change. The death of Hsia indicates Lu Hsün's gloomy view of the revolutionary cause in China. But in spite of his pessimism, he lodges a memorable protest over Hsia's unjust execution. In visiting his grave, his mother is utterly puzzled to find on the mound a Western-style wreath of red and white flowers, possibly placed there by his comrades. She fancies it could be a miraculous sign from her son to indicate his unpacified soul:

> The old woman moved a few steps nearer, gave it minute scrutiny, and then muttered to herself: "The flowers have no roots; they couldn't have bloomed there of themselves! Who could have placed them there? Children don't play here, and my relatives have long stopped visiting this place—what does it mean?" She thought for a while and then, her tears coursing down, she shouted: "Yü-erh, they have wronged you and you can't forget. Are you so unhappy that you have especially given me a sign to let me know?" She looked around and saw only a crow perched on the branch of a leafless tree; so she continued: "I understand. Yü-erh, they have cruelly murdered you, but Heaven sees and they will receive their retribution. You just close your eyes and rest in peace.—If you are really here and can hear me, then let this crow fly over the top of your grave before my eyes."
>
> The breeze had stopped earlier; the withered blades of grass stood there like copper bristles. The thin, trembling voice became more and more rarefied until it vanished into the air, and the rest was dead silence. The two women stood among the stalks of withered grass and looked up at the crow. The crow, his head drawn back, perched among the straight boughs as if it were cast in iron.[9]

This bleak scene, in which a mother's cry, wrung from her despair and her desperate belief in Heaven's justice, becomes a symbolic questioning over the meaning and future of the revolution, is one of the imaginative heights in modern Chinese fiction, with its dramatic irony of the crow, perching there motionless, utterly unresponsive in its sphinxlike silence to the mother's cry.

In "My Native Place" Lu Hsün further attacks the inexorable sway of traditional social laws. On his return trip to his home town the author meets with Jun-t'u, once his boyhood companion and now a weather-beaten man burdened with family care. The author recalls the happy hours he has spent in his company when they were both boys, but now Jun-t'u is just another peasant, respectfully aware of the economic and social distance between himself and his erstwhile friend. To the latter's affectionate salute, "Brother Jun-t'u," he can only reply "My lord (*lao-yeh*)." Meanwhile, the author's nephew and Jun-t'u's son have struck up a friendship. As Lu Hsün leaves the town, he wistfully ponders if this new friendship will last, if the younger generation will enjoy a new kind of life:

> When I realized what I was hoping, I suddenly became afraid. When Jun-t'u asked me to give him the censer and candlesticks, I had laughed to myself, thinking that he was always worshiping idols and would not for a moment leave them alone. But what was this so-called hope of mine if not also an idol fashioned by my own hands? Only his wishes were concerned with the more immediate things, while mine were not even remotely feasible.[10]

In this passage Lu Hsün reveals a strain of honesty characteristic of his best stories. Much as he wishes to change the social order, he also recognizes the naiveté of refashioning reality in order to satisfy his didactic impulse. "My Native Place," in its gentle lyricism, approaches the reminiscent personal essay. There are, indeed, a few items in *The Outcry* that cannot be called short stories at all: "The Country

Theater," especially, is a charming narrative about the author's childhood.

The major work in *The Outcry* is, of course, "The True Story of Ah Q," the only modern Chinese story to have attained an international reputation. But as a work of art it has surely been overpraised: it is mechanical in structure and facetious in tone. The circumstances of its composition may help explain these defects. Lu Hsün had agreed to write a humor serial for the literary supplement of the Peking *Morning Gazette* (Ch'en Pao), providing in each issue a comic episode illustrative of the character of Ah Q. When eventually the assignment proved irksome, Lu Hsün changed his original plan and thrust upon his hero a tragic destiny. But he apparently never bothered to correct the resultant incongruity of tone in his story.

The immense success of "The True Story of Ah Q" with the Chinese public was mainly due to its recognition of the hero as the embodiment of a national disease. Ah Quei (the name was shortened to Ah Q after the author facetiously confessed to his inability to determine which Chinese character should be adopted to designate the sound "quei") is a village lout of the lowest economic status living at the time when the Ch'ing dynasty is about to topple. Repeated humiliations have taught him to pretend to "spiritual victory" when bullied, and to bully the physically weaker whenever they come across his path. But since most villagers are better off and stronger, Ah Q has perforce to live in a slaphappy world of self-deception. He cheers himself up under whatever distressing circumstances and assumes an air of superiority in the face of manifest defeat. To Chinese readers this trait of character, reminiscent of recent history, gave a fresh satiric perspective to their country's pathetic stance among the bullying and more powerful nations.

"The True Story of Ah Q" is an acute commentary on recent Chinese history in yet another fashion. At the end, Ah Q is punished with death for his eagerness to join the revolution. After he has antagonized the chief family in the village, he drifts into the city among a gang of thieves and hears rumors about the anti-Manchu revolution. Whenever he returns to the village to sell his stolen goods, he brags about the revolution as if he were personally involved in it. He does this partly to show off and rebuild his prestige and partly to frighten the gentry who have maltreated him. He pretends to being a revolutionary because he is vaguely aware that revolutions create new privileges and settle old scores. But ironically, when the revolutionary forces finally enter the village, they join hands with the local gentry to try Ah Q for his supposed part in a robbery. Innocent, the bewildered hero can only confess to his envy for the revolutionaries, who have allied themselves with the gentry and refused to admit him as one of their own. Lu Hsün implicates his hero's death, therefore, in the failure of the Republican Revolution, which has done nothing to improve the lot of the poor. He accuses his readers of being accomplices in the crime, and suggests what the Ah Q's of the world, fully awakened, will accomplish or destroy. In this regard the hero represents not only a national vice but the crude awakening to the need for better justice with which modern Chinese literature has been vitally concerned.

Hesitation comprises eleven stories written during 1924–25. On the whole a finer volume than *The Outcry*, it has received less lavish praise because of its dominant mood of despondency. The author himself, however, is aware of its superiority; quite ironically he once commented on its comparative neglect: "Later on, in such stories as 'Soap' and 'Divorce,' while I have outgrown the influence of foreign authors and while my technique has become more mature and my depiction of reality more incisive, a diminution of passion has at the same time taken place, so that readers have paid them scant attention." [11] Precisely because of the subdued presence of such personal passions as anger and sorrow, one is almost tempted to rejoin, the four best stories in the collection—"Benediction," "In the Restaurant," "Soap," and "Divorce"—are among the most profound studies of Chinese society in fiction.

"Benediction" is the tragic tale of Hsiang-lin Sao, a peasant woman hounded to death by feudalism and superstition. Unlike most writers, however, Lu Hsün is not content merely to illustrate the horrors of the two traditional evils; he defines, first of all, the life of the heroine in the actuality of her ethos, which prescribes conduct and a world view as explicitly as any religion or philosophy of greater sophistication. The primitive peasant society to which she belongs, therefore, emerges from the story no less strangely and terrifyingly credible than the heroic society of Greek tragedy. Instead of being derogatory terms in the arsenal of antitraditional propaganda, "feudalism" and "superstition" take on here flesh and body.

Upon the untimely death of her first husband, Hsiang-lin Sao puts up a desperate struggle against her mother-in-law, who wants to sell her to some other man as wife. Determined to preserve her chaste widowhood, she finally flees to Lu-chen (Lu Hsün's fictitious name for his home town) to serve as a maid. But her mother-in-law finally tracks her down and forcibly marries her to another peasant in the hills. Two years later her husband dies of a fever and her child is devoured by a wolf. Hsiang-lin Sao has no choice but to return to Lu-chen and reinstate herself as maid with the same family.

Unhappy as she is, Hsiang-lin Sao is made even more miserable because she is regarded now as an unlucky woman and is forbidden by her mistress to assist at ceremonies of religious worship. As a result she becomes daily more preoccupied with her own supposed vileness and is pessimistic over her future fate. A maidservant in the same household comments on the perilous state of her soul:

"Hsiang-lin Sao, you've got for yourself a really bad bargain," Liu Ma said slyly. "If you had only resisted a little longer or knocked your head off, it would have been much better. But now? You lived with your second husband for only two years and you've committed a great crime. Just think, when you get down to the Court in Hell and the ghosts of your two husbands fight to get you, how would you propose to give yourself to both? The great King Yama could only saw you in two and divide you between them. I think this is really . . ."

Panic came to her face: this was something she had never heard of in the hills.

"I think you'd better atone for your crime while there is still time. Donate a doorsill to the T'u-ti temple. Let it be your substitute as thousands of men step on it and go across it. This will atone for your sin and you might then escape the tortures in store for you." [12]

The religious world envisaged here is compounded of gross superstitions; but because the author has taken this world seriously, it appears nonetheless real for all its strangeness and cruelty.

"Benediction" begins rather leisurely amid the busy festival preparations for the new year. Lu Hsün has just returned to his home town and he has an odd conversation with Hsiang-lin Sao, now a beggar, about the future life. This conversation, ironically, fortifies her will to kill herself. Lu Hsün's subsequent regret over and sorrow for the woman's fate reinforce his own loneliness in a town which is no longer a part of himself. These personal touches add a lyrical warmth to the otherwise stark tragedy of feudal existence.

"In the Restaurant" is another story imprinted with the author's personal experience during his sojourn in Shaohsing in the winter of 1919–20. Sipping wine alone in a restaurant, Lu Hsün meets an old schoolmate and former colleague at the Shaohsing middle school whom he hasn't seen for many years. Lü Wei-fu now bears little resemblance to that energetic youth of reformist zeal that he once was. He has been teaching school in a far-away province and is now visiting his home town to do errands for his mother. She has been distressed that the grave of her younger son, who died many years ago at the age of three, has been invaded by water and she has asked Lü Wei-fu to remove his brother's corpse to another location. Although no remains of his brother could be found, to please his mother he "wrapped up in a piece of cloth some earth where his body had been, put the bundle in a new coffin, and had it carried to my father's tomb and buried by its side." [13] Lü Wei-fu tells further that, again at his mother's request, he has come back to give some artficial flowers made of velvet to a fisherman's daughter, of whom he himself has retained some fond recollections. The girl is now dead, and he has given the flowers to her younger sister instead. But upon his return to the province, he will tell his mother that the gift has been properly disposed of. What does lying matter if it can make someone a little happier?

Lü Wei-fu confides his story to Lu Hsün in rather shamefaced fashion, fully aware that he would not have been so sentimentally filial if he had retained his faith in the new culture. There is little doubt that it was also Lu Hsün's explicit intention to depict his friend as a wreck of a man who has lost his nerve and compromised with the old society. Yet, as actually realized in the story, the kindness and piety of Lü Wei-fu, however pathetic, also demonstrate the positive strength of the traditional mode of life, toward which the author must have been nostalgically attracted in spite of his contrary intellectual conviction. For Lu Hsün "In the Restaurant" is a lyrical confession of his own uncertainty and hesitation. He is rather like Matthew Arnold, "wandering between two worlds, One dead, the other powerless to be born." The lines from the great poet Ch'ü Yüan, which Lu Hsün has adopted as the epigraph for *Hesitation,* fully confirm this mood.

Unlike the two preceding stories, "Soap" is a brilliant satire which dispenses completely with nostalgia and doubt; it is also Lu Hsün's only successful story whose setting is Peking rather than Shaohsing. The hero, a latter-day Confucian moralist paying lip service to traditional virtues, is a popular butt of Chinese satire; but as Lu Hsün presents him, he stands revealed almost as a universal hypocrite.

One evening Ssu-ming comes home and solemnly gives his wife a cake of scented toilet soap, an article of luxury for which she is rather unprepared. While he accepts her thanks with his customary composure, he is apparently perturbed by the events of the day. First of all, he cannot understand the English profanity thrown at him by students while he was comparing several brands of soap at the pharmacy. The attending clerk was irritated by his fussiness, and the students, in calling him an "old fool" (for this was the supposed profanity), were merely giving vent to that feeling. Ssu-ming now demands that his son, a high school student, translate the words for him, giving him a rough phonetic approximation to work on. As the latter fails to identify the English expression, Ssu-ming breaks out into a tirade against modern education, which breeds only ignoramuses with bad manners. The traditional Confucian education is much to be preferred. Yes, even today, before he was exposed to the contempt at the store, he had witnessed a touching example of traditional piety in the person of a beggar girl ministering to her decrepit and blind grandmother. The times have surely changed. Instead of showing proper respect and benevolence, Ssu-ming goes on to tell his family, the passers-by on the street regarded the pair with only amused indifference. One rascal went as far as to remark salaciously of the girl to his companion: "A-fa, don't belittle this baggage just because she happens to be dirty. All you have to do is to buy two cakes of soap and, *k-ch'ee, k-ch'ee,* give her a thorough scrubbing, and she will be as nice a piece as you'll ever find." [14]

Ssu-ming's wife has been quite grateful for the soap and rather ashamed of herself because it reminds her of the accumulated dirt on her neck. But taking in her husband's long speech, she perceives an obvious connection between his praise of the beggar girl and his purchase of soap. During the dinner, while Ssu-ming continues to scold his son, she flares up:

> "How could he learn since he cannot even read your mind? If he could read what's on your mind, he would have lit the lantern long ago, sought out the filial maid, and brought her to you. Fortunately, you have already bought one cake of soap for her; all you have to do now is to buy another—"

> "Nonsense, that's what the rascal said."

> "I'm not so sure of that. All you have to do is to buy another cake, and *k-ch'ee, k-ch'ee*, give her a thorough scrubbing, and set her up on an altar, and peace will again reign in the world."

> "What are you talking about? What has that got to do with it? It was only because I happened to remember you wanted soap—"

> "What has that got to do with it? You bought the soap especially for the filial maid. You go and give her, *k-ch'ee, k-ch'ee*, a good scrubbing yourself. I am not worthy of it, and I don't want it. I don't want anything that was intended for the filial maid."

> "What words are these? You women . . . ." Ssu-ming parried. His face was oozing with an oily sweat, just like [his son] Hsüeh-ch'eng's after he had finished his *pa-kua-ch'üan* exercises, although the sweat could have been only due to the hot meal.

> "What about us women? We women are better than you men. You men are either cursing teen-age girl stu-

dents or praising teen-age girl beggars. You haven't got a decent thought in your heads. *K-ch'ee, k-ch'ee,* this is shameless!" [15]

The next morning, however, Ssu-ming's wife rises early and dutifully washes her face and neck with the scented soap. "The lather rose behind her ears, as foamy as bubbles forming over the mouths of large crabs." [16] She takes a new interest in her daintiness because she knows that, in buying the soap, her husband has transferred his lascivious thoughts from the beggar girl to herself. The quarrel over the dinner table is almost forgotten.

Technically, "Soap" is Lu Hsün's greatest success; no other story evinces so fully his keen ironic intelligence, which attends to Ssu-ming's every gesture, speech, and thought. Moreover, the satire of the story is sustained by a shrewd symbolism. The beggar girl, in her dirty rags as well as in her imagined state of freshly scrubbed nudity, stands at once for the shabby Confucianism which Ssu-ming ostensibly upholds and for the libidinous daydream to which he actually yields. And Ssu-ming himself, with his lascivious turn of mind and pretension to moral rectitude, stands convicted as the average respectable man of middle age, in nearly every society and culture.

"Divorce," the last story in *Hesitation,* is a tragedy of the Chinese village, told with dramatic objectivity. Ai-ku, who has been living for three years with her father, is fighting hard to be reinstated in her husband's home. Although the latter was maltreating her and carrying on with another woman at the time when she left him in a huff, Ai-ku feels that her subsequent rejection by her husband's family is a defamation harder to be borne than the fate of being an unloved wife. She and her father, therefore, argue her case before the squire Ch'i Ta-jen and put up vehement remonstrations. But Ch'i Ta-jen (Lu Hsün has great fun with him as a pseudo-antiquary, ecstatically smelling an anus-stopper

supposedly of the Han period) finally cows her into accepting the terms of divorce dictated by her husband's family.
The pathos of Ai-ku lies in the unreasonable discrepancy
between her actual distaste for her husband and her desperate
struggle to maintain her married status: she would rather be
unhappy than dishonored. By dramatically presenting the
quarrel and refraining from taking sides, Lu Hsün reveals
the feudal system in all its moral turpitude.

The nine stories we have just considered, from "The Diary
of a Madman" to "Divorce," constitute the finest body of
fiction of the first period and place their author in the forefront as a story-writer. Though mainly descriptive of village
and small-town life in a period of transition, they possess
enough power and variety to command the interest of posterity. But even during this period of happy creativity,
1918–26, Lu Hsün's taste is none too sure (stories like "A
Little Incident," "The Story of Hair," "The Happy Family," "The Solitary," and "Remorse" show him very much
at the mercy of a sentimental didacticism) and his incapacity
to draw creative sustenance from other experiences than
those rooted in his native town also indicates a real limita-
tion. No doubt Lu Hsün could have continued to draw from
his reservoir of memory and written stories in the vein of
The Outcry and *Hesitation,* but his unsettled and unhappy
life in Amoy and Canton following his departure from
Peking in 1926 and his subsequent quarrel with Communist
writers distracted him from fiction. Following his conversion
to Communism in 1929, he gloried in his role as cultural
hero with an immense following and could no longer summon the kind of honesty requisite for the writing of his best
stories without also dragging to light the extreme superficiality of his new political allegiance. Lu Hsün settled for
emotional sterility in the interests of ideological consistency.

While he was writing the stories that were eventually to
be collected in *Hesitation,* Lu Hsün also happily applied his
talent in other directions: the aforementioned book of

45

somber prose poetry, *Wild Grass,* and *Morning Flowers Picked in Evening,* a delightful volume of childhood reminiscences. After 1926, all Lu Hsün produced as a writer of fiction was gathered in one volume entitled *Old Legends Retold* (1935), which combines topical satire with malicious caricature of ancient Chinese sages and mythological heroes. Confucius, Lao Tzu, and Chuang Tzu parade before us in the guise of clowns, mouthing equal portions of modern colloquial speech and their recorded aphorisms. In his fear of searching his own mind and disclosing thereby his pessimistic and somber view of China at complete variance with his professed Communist faith, Lu Hsün could only repress his deep-seated personal emotions in the service of political satire. The resulting levity and chaos in *Old Legends Retold* mark the sad degeneration of a distinguished if narrow talent for fiction.

It must be remembered that Lu Hsün's primary ambition as a writer was to serve his country as a spiritual physician. In his best stories, however, he is content to probe the disease without prescribing a cure: he has too high a respect for the art of fiction to present other than the unadorned truth. But during the period 1918–26 Lu Hsün also satisfied his didactic impulse as a satiric essayist, castigating all manner of Chinese vices in a humorous and often rude fashion. By the criteria of Darwinian evolution and Nietzschean energy, Lu Hsün believes, the Chinese race was doomed to extinction unless it girded itself for a tough struggle. He is therefore most piercing as an essayist when he is needling popular assumptions of national superiority and puncturing the dormant state of mind induced by centuries of cultural insularity. As early as 1918 he pokes fun at national complacency, for example:

> Unfortunately, this form of self-conceit has been perversely present in China. Since everything the an-

cients said and did was good, how can we speak of
reform when we have hardly time to follow their precepts and emulate their actions? The attitude of this
self-conceited patriot takes several slightly different
forms, though its underlying motive is the same. We
may roughly list four types:

A says: "China has vast territory and enormous material wealth; its culture was the earliest and enjoys unrivaled moral superiority in the world." This is self-
conceit pure and simple.

B says: "Although the material civilization of foreign
countries is superior, the Chinese spiritual civilization
is much better."

C says: "The discoveries and inventions of foreign
countries are nothing new: China once had them all.
This branch of science, for example, can be exactly
traced back to the writings of that particular ancient
philosopher." These two opinions have all flowed from
the "ancient vs. modern and Chinese vs. foreign" school
of thought; they subscribe to the maxim of Chang Chih-
tung: "Chinese learning for the fundamental principles,
Western learning for practical application."

D says: "Foreign countries also have beggars, (or)
slums, prostitutes, bedbugs." This is negative protest.

E says: "Chinese are barbarians, so what?" And he
adds: "You claim Chinese thought is muddled, but this
is precisely the achievement of our nation. Our ancestors have muddled through and so will our descendants; we have muddled through in the past and so
shall we in the future. . . . (We are four hundred million strong) and do you think we shall perish from the
face of the earth?" E has gone a step farther than D;
he is not content to pull other peoples to our level, but
takes pride in parading our ugly and sinister features before them. His swagger is as truculent as that of Niu
Erh in *Water Margin.*[17]

Lu Hsün goes on to analyze the attitude of E from the viewpoint of heredity and evolution. What is still of interest today is not the applied ideas but the ironic and vivid manner with which he tells the unpleasant truths about China: his disconcerting art of deflating the national ego.

The early essays, in *Tomb* and *Hot Wind* (1925), are more general and therefore more important. In attacking backwardness, ignorance, and misgovernment, Lu Hsün forcibly presents his case for spiritual rejuvenation, an emphasis also to be discerned in the early essays of Chou Tso-jen. Generally regarded as the greatest prose stylists of their age, the two brothers for a time wonderfully complemented each other with their contributions to their joint magazine *Yü Ssu:* incisive and lively essays on every aspect of Chinese society and culture. But even during the second half of the twenties, Chou Tso-jen was more inclined toward the personal and familiar essay while Lu Hsün chose to be more topical and polemic. In his short essays written during the period 1925–27, for example, Lu Hsün attacks Chang Shih-chao and other members of warlord governments; Ch'en Yüan and other members of the Anglo-American group; young writers like Kao Ch'ang-hung who, once his disciples and protégés, had now dared to break away from him. These *tsa-wen* contain vivid homespun imagery and illustration, occasionally brilliant epigrams, much sardonic humor and venom. But on the whole they leave the impression of trivial self-assertion. Lu Hsün was so vain that he was quite incapable of admitting error or fault. The more important social and cultural criticisms in these essays are inseparable from the element of sophistry, as Lu Hsün relentlessly hounds his enemies and vindicates his infallibility at the expense of logic and fact.

Along with many other intellectuals, Lu Hsün left Peking in 1926, resigning from his government and teaching posts to accept a professorship of Chinese at the University of Amoy in southern Fukien. He was quite unhappy there and

While his wife was replacing her facial towel after wiping away her tears with it, he saw that her red and swollen nose was uncommonly large. Because rouge had been erased from her usually lovely lips, he saw only a purplish and flat mouth ready to assume the position of crying. Her eyes had not been pretty to begin with, but as he was in love, he had not been aware of any defect. Now he noticed that the outer corners of her eyes were slanted very high and he suddenly remembered his mother's saying, "Slant-eyed women are hardest to deal with." For the first time since his marriage, he felt that his woman was ugly.[18]

That night the quarrel is not patched up. Ching-jen stays awake in bed thinking of his deceased stepsister:

He recalled how seven years ago, when he was stricken with malaria, she had helped his mother nurse him back to health, and how, when he had refused to take quinine pills, she had restrained her tears and cajoled him into taking them. Mouthful by mouthful, he had sipped sugar water from a glass held by her hand as he took those pills. At the last mouthful, his lips had touched her smooth and powder-scented hand, and his heart had felt an indescribably delicious sensation. He couldn't help kissing it violently. Her cheeks had been flushed with crimson, and he had settled back on his bed with a smile. Afterward, although she looked somewhat embarrassed whenever she saw him, she had appeared to be even more solicitous of his welfare.[19]

The next morning the wife leaves her home to stay with her mother. In the company of his bad friends, Ching-jen now frequents theaters and brothels. The next year the wife becomes even uglier after a miscarriage, and her mother-in-law complains of her inability to keep her husband home. In the third year, following another miscarriage, the doctor examines the foetus and finds it to be syphilitic. In the fourth year the husband has squandered most of his money and is ready to sell his own house. The wife has a confiding talk with her mother, who remarks that no one could have thought that her husband's family should go downhill so fast. Her daughter replies:

> "Who could have thought of . . . But, mother, this is because my fate has pre-ordained me to suffer." She cleared her nose and continued to sob. "During the first eve of the August festival after our marriage we had a quarrel. He took one mouthful of the harmony duck and spat it out. I felt very chagrined. Later on that night, when he kicked to pieces a vase that had seen service in the worship of gods, I was even more certain that things were taking a bad turn." [20]

Her mother asks her to submit to her fate and hope for a better life during her next incarnation.

To the end, the wife persists in her superstitious interpretation of the events. But the reader views them differently, in the author's psychological and even naturalistic perspective. The wife is pitiful as the victim of her husband's hostility and libertinism, but in his fond remembrance of his stepsister, he shows himself to be not incapable of affection: it is the wife's antipathy toward the dying woman in the first place that precipitates the quarrel and hastens him on his downward path. "The Eve of the Mid-Autumn Festival" is comparable to Lu Hsün's "Benediction," with its grim revelation of certain senseless aspects of traditional life.

In his foreword to *The Temple of Flowers* Ch'en Yüan promises that his wife's next collection will reveal significant new facets of her talent. Unfortunately, most of the eight stories in *Women* (1930) are quite undistinguished, and the best of the lot, "Little Liu," shows its author at her characteristic game of chronicling a woman's defeat. Unmerciful in her youthful freedom, the pretty and vivacious Little Liu

obtains the aid of her high school classmates to put to shame
a fat and pregnant fellow student, who hobbles on her bound
feet. A dozen years later, Little Liu herself is revealed as the
battered victim of the traditional mode of life, the sallow
and sickly mother of three girls and one utterly spoiled and
unmannered boy. Briefly in another story, "Schoolmistress
Li," Ling Shu-hua reveals her special insight into the character of Chinese women behind their facade of obedience
and decorum. Now an old maid, the schoolmistress recalls
her past as she checks out the girl students for the week end:

> When she was seventeen or eighteen, a relative came to
> her home to arrange a match: the prospective bride-
> groom was a cousin on her father's side, quite capable
> and good-looking. Both families seemed to be agreed
> on the match, but before leaving, the matchmaker said
> to her mother with a smile that the groom's family de-
> sired the removal of the mole under *hsiao-chieh's* eye,
> as it augured bad luck. The next day, when her mother
> was taking her out to have the mole removed, her second
> brother made a few facetious remarks, which turned
> her embarrassment into anger. She resolutely refused
> to have her mole removed and announced further that
> she would never marry.[21]

Ling Shu-hua's third collection, *Little Brothers* (1935),
reflects her new experiences as a mother and as a resident in
Japan during the early thirties. Mainly about children, these
thirteen stories are sensitive and intelligent but lack enough
substance and power to rank with her best. In "Akiko" a
Japanese child shows a prattling and winsome charm as she
celebrates her second birthday with her parents in the park.
In "Chiyoko," an ironic study of the evil of patriotic propaganda, another Japanese girl discovers by herself the truth
about Chinese people, which is in violent contrast to the
myth of Chinese barbarism which she has learned at home
and school.

One of Ling Shu-hua's later stories, "On a Journey" (first published in *Wen-chi Yüeh-k'an*, June 1936), attests, however, to her continued fascination with the decadent and cruel aspects of Chinese life. Compelled to share a compartment on the train with a frowzy woman and her two malformed children, the first-person narrator later elicits from the elder boy the gruesome tale of a syphilitic family. Utterly ignorant of the nature of his disease, he lays bare the profligacy of his father and the brutalized existence of his mother. The narrator's feminine squeamishness accentuates the horror, not untempered by a feeling of compassion for the helpless participants in this tragedy.

Prized by a discriminating public, Ling Shu-hua has never won wide public recognition, and by the thirties her small output had been dwarfed by the productivity of the greater writers of fiction who had appeared on the literary scene. But as a keen observer of the frustrations and tragedies of Chinese women in a transitional period, she holds her own with any other writer; her achievement on the whole is superior to Ping Hsin's.

Lo Hua-sheng (1893–1941)

What distinguished Lo Hua-sheng from his contemporaries was his religious preoccupation. Ping Hsin extols mother love and pantheism, but her philosophy, erected primarily upon her childhood happiness, is little implicated in the deeper religious issues. Lo Hua-sheng, on the other hand, was mainly concerned with the basic religious experience of charity or love and attempted in nearly all his stories to demonstrate its ubiquitous presence in human lives. Though his success is largely unimpressive and his influence on other writers minimal, his almost unique endeavor to recover spiritual values for his time entitles this author to our respect and a place in this history.

Lo Hua-sheng was early exposed to diverse religious influences. Born of Buddhist parents in Changhua, Taiwan, and brought up in Lungki, Fukien, he seems also to have acquainted himself during his youth with the ways of Christian missionaries, both native and foreign, who traveled over South China to preach the gospel. Later, as a student at Yenching University, he was further exposed to the missionary influence and developed a personal as well as scholarly interest in the world's religions.

While still in college, Lo Hua-sheng became a founding member of the Literary Association and contributed regularly to *The Short Story*. From 1923 to 1926 he studied at Columbia and Oxford. Upon his return to China he became more of a scholar with a wide range of interests than a professional writer (among his books are a *History of Taoism*, a manual of Indian literature, and a study of diplomatic relations between China and Great Britain during the Ch'ing dynasty), but he continued to write stories intermittently. In 1933 he published a volume of stories called *The Liberator*, which showed considerable technical improvement over his earlier collections: *The Vain Labors of a Spider* (1925) and *Letters That Couldn't Be Sent Anywhere* (1928). During the last ten years of his life (1931–41), Lo Hua-sheng was a professor at the University of Hong Kong and published little fiction. But his long story "Yü-kuan," first published in a posthumous volume [22] which in the main reprints *The Liberator*, came as a powerful surprise and compels a new appraisal of his achievement.

By temperament Lo Hua-sheng was a writer of romances. Most of his early pieces, barely suggestive of the disciplines of the modern short story, have an affinity with popular Buddhist tales and medieval Christian legends. The most ambitious of these, "The Vain Labors of a Spider," conforms clumsily to the pattern of forgiveness and reconciliation of Shakespeare's last plays. The heroine, a Chinese Christian living in the South Seas, is almost a saint, persevering in her path of charity and accepting misfortune with the uttermost indifference. Falsely accused of infidelity by her jealous husband, Shang-chieh relinquishes her portion of their joint property and accepts employment as a secretary on another island. She also spreads the Christian gospel among pearl divers in her spare time. Three years later her husband sends word through a friend that he is now penitent and wishes a reunion. "Shang-chieh received the word with no special expression of pleasure on her face and said only, 'I have never intended to make my actions public so as to receive from people either commiseration or praise. I am always resigned to the way people treat me. Since I have always forgiven those who hurt me, how much more wouldn't I do for him?' " [23] By the time she reaches home, however, her husband, feeling too ashamed to face her, has left the place to seek further penitence. Shang-chieh takes this calmly, too: "For love? To leave me for love? It is only natural, since love is a sharp ax employed more often in hewing down one's fortunes than in mending them. He has already set his course of action; so why should I waste time to look for him? I never make up my mind beforehand; I submit to events as they come." [24]

Toward the end of the story Shang-chieh spells out her life in a parable on religious patience:

> I am like a spider and the web is my fortune. The spider eats all kinds of poisonous and nonpoisonous insects and then spins his web. The first time he emits his filament, he doesn't know how far the breeze will carry it. But once it is attached to something, his web will be formed.
>
> He doesn't know when or how his web will be broken; but once it is broken, he retires temporarily until he has another chance to spin a better one.
>
> Meanwhile the broken web remains on the tip of a tree branch. When the sun shines upon it, its thin filaments are refulgent with the colors of a rainbow; if by chance there are dewdrops upon it, it will appear even more resplendent and lovely.

> Wherein is the difference between the destiny of a
> spider and the destiny of man? One weaves one's own
> pattern; whether it is broken or remains whole, one can
> only leave it to nature.[25]

Though the story fails to incorporate this insight with any
degree of dramatic effectiveness, the religious paradox of
action and suffering contained in the parable is beyond the
intellectual capacity of most contemporary Chinese writers.

In his later stories Lo Hua-sheng continues to decipher
the meanings of love and patience. In contrast to the early
gaudy style of "The Vain Labors of a Spider," they are set
in a disciplined and spare prose, which makes them more
readable; but the author's romantic propensity for intricate
plots continues to be characteristic. In "Ch'un-t'ao" the title
heroine makes her living by collecting and selling rags and
waste paper. Her husband was pressed into military service
some years ago and hasn't been heard of since; meanwhile
the woman has been living rather happily with her male
partner. One day she accidentally meets with her husband,
now a crippled beggar. Even though she loves her present
partner, she takes him home and cares for him. She soothes
the mutual jealousy of the two men and manages to persuade
them to live with her under the same roof. In "Mr. Tung-
yeh" the hero is a retiring and mild-mannered schoolteacher
who lives placidly with his adopted child, the son of some
revolutionary martyr. His peace is disturbed when his wife
returns to him after a ten-year stay in Europe. Tung-yeh
has to regain her affections while at the same time trying
to track down the whereabouts of the deceased revolutionary's other survivors. He succeeds in both tasks after a
rather trying time. Good and kind, Tung-yeh is something
of a Mr. Pickwick, but he never becomes fully alive under
the weight of an extraneous plot about revolutionaries,
which is highly contrived and lacking in moral substance.

Without "Yü-kuan" it could be said that Lo Hua-sheng's
quest for a perfect fable to embody his vision of the good

life had ended in failure: Shang-chieh, Ch'un-t'ao, Tung Yeh, and others like them, with all their charity and virtue, are allegorical characters rather than dramatic. Since, in the history of fiction, there have been very few saintly characters who are at the same time alive and interesting, Lo Hua-sheng's failure would still have deserved commendation for his single-minded determination to attempt the supremely arduous task. But in "Yü-kuan" he did achieve a small masterpiece, a rare spiritual testament in an age of crude ideology and rampant materialism. For once the author has the conviction of his romance material: he ignores completely the conventions of the modern short story and unashamedly lards his story with coincidences and mistaken identities of a kind that would always look out of place in a piece of realistic fiction. To give his story the freedom of romance, he even shuns the use of dialogue. The result, notwithstanding, is a moving narrative of about fifty pages in length, in which all the characters and incidents are suffused with life and the heroine, especially, stands out against a Providential background with all her unforgettable humanity.

Yü-kuan is a young woman of South Fukien whose husband has died in action in the Sino-Japanese War of 1894. She lives entirely for her infant son and hopes that someday he will become an official and erect an arch in honor of her virtuous widowhood. After repeated molestations from her brother-in-law, who is something of a blackguard, she obtains work as a domestic in the home of a foreign missionary and becomes gradually interested in missionary work. She soon becomes a Bible woman herself, following the example of her best friend, Hsing-kuan. To all appearances Yü-kuan is a zealous Christian worker, though she retains her Confucian scruples as to the propriety of neglecting ancestor worship and other traditional rituals, to which she has been accustomed. Characteristically, she carries a copy of the *Book of Changes* along with the Bible whenever she travels.

On many of her field trips she meets with a peddler named Ch'en Lien, with whom she gradually falls in love. Now that her son is growing up and well on his way to completing his free education at the local missionary school, she feels the need of a new life and wants very much to marry the peddler. But she gives up the idea when she learns that he is really the husband of Hsing-kuan and that he has just returned to the neighborhood without his wife's knowledge. It appears that, many years ago, Ch'en Lien left home to avoid arrest after he had assaulted a Christian convert for wantonly smashing his idols.

Yü-kuan's son in time marries Hsing-kuan's daughter. Yü-kuan feels very lonely, and quite jealous of their intimacy. Soon afterward her son goes to America to study for a religious career and his wife dies in giving birth to a son. Yü-kuan takes care of her grandson and continues with her missionary work. She suffers many humiliations during the Communist occupation of South Fukien. But she doesn't come to serious harm and is even in a position to help her fellow victims of Communist terror, largely because her brother-in-law, now a Communist officer, affords some protection.

Her troubles are far from over, however. Soon after the evacuation of the Communists, her grandson suffers a serious fall and becomes a permanent cripple; and Ch'en Lien is again leaving for the South Seas. In her misery, Yü-kuan is excited to learn that her son is finally returning to China after a protracted stay in America of eight or nine years. In the meantime the latter has repudiated his missionary upbringing; he goes directly to Nanking to accept a government post and marry a rich and spoiled girl whom he has courted in America. (This girl is actually Hsing-kuan's other daughter, kidnapped in infancy by Yü-kuan's rascally brother-in-law and eventually adopted by a wealthy family in Shanghai.)

Yü-kuan goes to Nanking to live with her son. Much to

her dismay, she finds her new life almost intolerable. A total stranger to their Westernized bourgeois ways, she cannot get along at all with her son and daughter-in-law. Her new unhappiness prompts her to review her past life:

> She sat at home musing. She recalled that all her actions since her widowhood, though preparing for her son's success, were at bottom selfish. Like a peddler in chinaware who uses at home only mended bowls, she had not at all benefited by religious teachings during the decades of her missionary life. The moment she realized this, she stood up suddenly, as if she had found an invaluable lesson from her life. She felt that the words with which her brother-in-law had taunted her when she had been a recent widow were after all right. She felt that her persistence in widowhood had been dictated by vanity, that her missionary work had been almost a form of hypocrisy, and that her present suffering was the natural consequence of her past actions. She wanted now to return to her villages to really engage in missionary work. But first she had to offer penitence. She had at least to render one good deed for some other person; in her mind she made a resolution.[26]

In spite of her advanced age, Yü-kuan returns to Fukien and works tirelessly for the next two or three years in the villages. To commemorate her fortieth year in missionary service, the villagers, many of whom have received succor from her during the period of Communist terror, now wish to present her a concrete testimonial of their love and esteem. Yü-kuan, who had dreamed of a widow's arch in her younger days, is completely uninterested. Finally the villagers win her permission to build a concrete bridge. Upon its completion they give a party in her honor and even her son and daughter-in-law come back for the occasion. Yü-kuan is deeply moved. A few days later she embarks for Borneo to bring back Ch'en Lien for her lifelong friend Hsing-kuan.

This is the one good deed which she has earlier pledged herself.

The foregoing synopsis is probably more than useless in suggesting the many virtues of the story or the winsome, complex personality of its heroine. With all her virtues, ambitions, and weaknesses, Yü-kuan is an excellent specimen of traditional Chinese womanhood; even before her final awakening, she would be regarded as a very good person indeed by any ethical code. The religious criterion of conduct, by which her life is rigorously tested as a search for disinterested goodness, in no way supersedes the everyday moral criterion: the employment of this double perspective is the only means for fully establishing her fallible yet astounding humanity. Yü-kuan is in many ways reminiscent of Félicité, the heroine of Flaubert's *A Simple Heart;* but instead of shriveling inside herself, the goodness of the Chinese woman extends outward into the practical world of love and work.

Most contemporary Chinese writers reserve their sympathies for the poor and downtrodden; the idea that any person, irrespective of class and position, is a fit object for compassionate understanding is alien to them. This failure of sympathy accounts for the moral shallowness of the bulk of modern Chinese literature: in its preoccupation with national and ideological issues it is little disposed to examine individual destinies in the spirit of charity. In this respect, "Yü-kuan" is a triumphant exception. To most Chinese intellectuals, with their scorn for religion and their hostility to the Christian Church in particular, the story perhaps would appear as an unjustifiably sentimental eulogy of its missionaries. But "Yü-kuan" is not exactly a Christian apology: its heroine is stubbornly Chinese and lacks the intellectual capacity for grasping the central Christian dogmas. The important consideration is that in this story Lo Huasheng has successfully incorporated the religious mode of understanding, which transcends the prevalent attitudes of humanitarianism and indignation. Among his younger contemporaries, Shen Ts'ung-wen alone evinces the same kind of religious awareness. But unlike Yü-kuan, most of his characters live on the instinctive level of innocence and animal grace, pastoral creatures not fully committed to the struggle of good against evil.

In the absence of a fully translated text, it is futile to comment on the skillful projection of the heroine's struggle with herself, in her arduous pursuit of goodness, through many a wonderful scene: her fear in a haunted temple, her passion for Ch'en Lien, her quarrels with Hsing-kuan, her bitterness toward her two daughters-in-law, and her profound disappointment in her son. Nor is it of any use to direct attention to the rich panorama of Chinese history with which her adult life is intricately interwoven: the Sino-Japanese War of 1894, the Boxers' Movement, the spread of Christianity, and the rise of Communism. But the story possesses much more than psychological and historical interest: in it Lo Hua-sheng has upheld what Allen Tate has admirably defined as the responsibility of the man of letters in the modern world: "He must recreate for his age the image of man, and he must propagate standards by which other men may test that image, and distinguish the false from the true." "Yü-kuan," therefore, belongs with those works of literature which are "the recurrent discovery of the human communion as *experience,* in a definite place and at a definite time." [27]

CHAPTER 4

The Creation Society

THE CREATION SOCIETY (Ch'uang-tsao shê) was
formed by a group of Chinese students in Japan in the summer of 1921. From the beginning a clique of close personal
friends, it became even more of a militant band of dedicated
revolutionary propagandists following its espousal of Communism some years later. In view of its meager literary
achievement, its power over the minds of youth was extraor-
dinary; even after its dissolution in 1929 by government
order, the Creationist spirit continued as a predominant
force in the shaping of modern Chinese literature. Unlike
the Literary Association, with its serious study and translation of foreign literature and its tolerance of a diversity of
opinion, the Creation Society was pedantic, dogmatic, and
bellicose, in its early romantic as well as in its later Marxist
phase. It was largely instrumental in bringing about a Communist orthodoxy in Chinese letters.

The history of this society is best told in the career of its
dynamic and ambitious leader Kuo Mo-jo (1892–). On the
surface, it is a story of spectacular success. As Director of the
Academy of Sciences and President of the All-China Federation of Literary and Art Workers, Kuo Mo-jo is nominally

in charge of all research and creative activities on the mainland and as one-time Vice Premier of the Peking Government (1949–54), he has retained a political prestige unrivaled among literary men. Yet properly understood, his career only underscores the more dramatically the tragedy of a generation of intellectuals who began in romantic revolt and ended in subservience to a despotism which they themselves had helped to create.

Kuo Mo-jo has written over the years a long series of autobiographies, gathered in Volumes 6–9 of his collected *Works* (1959). From these we know that he was something of a rebel even in his childhood. Born into a gentry family in Loshan, Szechwan, he early chafed under parental and school authority. Even though he was an excellent student with a predilection for Chinese literature, he was once expelled from school for insubordination. When he came of age, his parents constrained him to marry a complete stranger, who appeared to him utterly repulsive. This distasteful experience soon precipitated his decision to leave home and study in Japan.

For reasons similar to those that had impelled Lu Hsün, Kuo Mo-jo chose medicine as his field of study, in spite of his defective hearing. While studying methodically for his medical degree, he also read a great deal of literature, especially in the German and English romantic poets. His life in Japan was on the whole happy and exciting. He in time married a Japanese girl and managed to support a growing family on his meager income derived mainly from a government scholarship. With the success of the pai-hua movement in China, Kuo Mo-jo seriously contemplated a literary career and made friends with those Chinese students in Japan known to have active literary interests: Yü Ta-fu, Chang Tzu-p'ing, Ch'eng Fang-wu, T'ien Han. With these kindred spirits he founded the Creation Society.

In the same year (1921), the T'ai Tung Book Company in Shanghai published the first three books by members of the

Society: Yü Ta-fu's *Sinking,* a collection of short stories; Kuo Mo-jo's volume of poetry entitled *Goddesses;* and his translation of Goethe's *Werther.* All three met an enthusiastic reception. In May 1922 *Creation Quarterly* was launched; by that time most Creationists had completed their studies and returned to China, although Kuo Mo-jo was to visit Japan frequently afterward.

Creation Quarterly was planned deliberately as a challenge to *The Short Story* Magazine. It professed romanticism and art for art's sake in opposition to the latter's espousal of a realistic and humane literature. It vaunted its creative energy and ridiculed the latter's emphasis on translation and the occasional mistranslations to be found in its pages.[1] As a matter of historical fact, of course, both groups of writers shared essentially the same humanitarian and patriotic preoccupations; only with the Creationists a maudlin sentimentality was operative under the guise of romanticism, so that their writings are completely deficient in restraint and objectivity. Their asestheticism amounts to little more than art for the sake of emotional dissipation.

Creation Quarterly suspended publication after only six issues; it was succeeded by *Creation Daily* and *Creation Weekly,* both of which were short-lived. In 1925 the Creation Society published a fortnightly called *The Deluge,* in which a shift from aestheticism to Marxism began to be visible; in the next year it launched *Creation Monthly,* which unambiguously announced its new Marxist stand in such editorials as Kuo Mo-jo's "Revolution and Literature" and Ch'eng Fang-wu's "From Literary Revolution to a Revolutionary Literature."[2] To account for this dramatic change, we have to resume our story of Kuo Mo-jo.

Kuo Mo-jo was a prolific and indefatigable writer. For the period 1921–49 he wrote a large quantity of poetry, drama, fiction, autobiography, and diverse kinds of prose ranging from personal essays to political journalism; he also turned out several volumes of Marxist studies in ancient

Chinese history and thought, in addition to an immense amount of translation, including the early novels of Upton Sinclair; *Faust,* Parts I and II;[3] and *War and Peace.**[4] (Since the establishment of the Communist regime, his writings have been confined to addresses and reports delivered at literary and cultural meetings and poetry of an occasional character. A sampling of the latter, *Odes to New China* contains grossly adulatory verse in praise of Stalin and Mao Tse-tung.) While his translations still await critical scrutiny as to accuracy and style, and while his interpretations of ancient China are of debatable value at best, his creative output, upon which his literary reputation must primarily rest, is of a very mediocre quality indeed. Of all the acknowledged leading writers of modern China, Kuo Mo-jo possesses least enduring merit. He must be eventually remembered as a colorful personality of his period, who played a leading role in many literary and political enterprises.

What immediately captured public attention upon the publication of *Goddesses* was Kuo Mo-jo's daring style, which broke away completely from the tepid imagism of earlier pai-hua poets. In such ambitious performances as "The Hound of Heaven," "The Nirvana of the Phoenixes," and "Earth, My Mother," he resorts at once to Western and Chinese mythology and a modern scientific vocabulary to simulate Shelley and Whitman. With equal fervor he sings the unity of the cosmos, the chaos of modern city life, the imminent collapse of the present society, and the rhapsodic vision of future humanity. This medley of romantic techniques and attitudes could not fail to dazzle the untrained readers of the time. Actually, of course, the seeming vitality of this verse is not nourished by any inner wealth of feeling: both its mechanic rhythm and its overuse of exclamatory sentences betray a lack of poetic sensitivity. The more subdued nature poems of the early period, apparently written in imitation of Goethe and Tagore, possess in contrast an authentic, if

* Kao Ti, co-translator.

slight, lyrical note. Kuo Mo-jo's best poetry consists of a few songs interspersed in his historical plays of the forties, which make able use of traditional rhythm and sentiment.[5]

The early rhetorical verse represents the author's attempt to reach the state of self-intoxication: it bears little integral relationship to his stories and essays of that time, which reveal a personalism as pronounced as the writings of the other major Creationists. Like Yü Ta-fu and Chang Tzu-p'ing, Kuo Mo-jo is perennially bewailing his poverty, his harassed domestic life, and the injustice and cruelty of the world. Occasionally he counters this gloom with a superficial optimism of social protest. In possibly his feeblest work, a trio of historical plays known as *Three Rebellious Women* (1925), this note of protest, asserted in complete disregard of the social reality of ancient and medieval China, becomes a positive source of unintended comedy.[6]

In his early writings, therefore, Kuo Mo-jo reveals himself as alternately despondent and defiant, the self-confessed failure and weakling as well as the optimistic singer of a new society. Overwhelmed by personal and national problems, he could not order his mind in any meaningful direction, but fundamentally a man of action, he could not rest content with emotional dissipation either. In 1924, when Marxism had already become a fashion among radical intellectuals and when the political climate was positively favoring the expansion of Communism, Kuo Mo-jo declared himself a Marxist. In April of that year he sailed to Japan to visit his wife and children; he took along two books which he intended to translate: a German version of Turgenev's *Virgin Soil* and a treatise on *Social Organization and the Socialist Revolution* by the noted Japanese political scientist Kawakami Hajime. As he read the latter book, probably his first scholarly introduction to Marxism, he became converted. In a letter to Ch'eng Fang-wu, he imparts his new enthusiasm:

Fang-wu, we are living in a most meaningful age, the age of the great revolution for mankind and civilization!

97

I am now thoroughly converted to Marxism. . . . Fang-wu, I have now come to the realization that the melancholy and fatigue which we share and which, I am afraid, the whole younger generation shares with us are due to the fact that we are not fortunate enough to achieve self-realization and at the same time to lead the way for the free development of the masses. Our inner demands do not square with the external conditions; as a result, we lose track of our directions and sink into nihilism. We become melancholy and world-weary and wander about aimlessly; we even contemplate suicide. Fang-wu, now that I have come to this realization, I have completely shaken off my old way of thinking, which was deeply ingrained with individualism. . . . Although this awakening began to rouse my spirit two or three years ago, I have lain in my bed in a state of semislumber. Now I am wide awake, Fang-wu, wide awake. I am now able to impose order on all the ideas which I could not reconcile; I have found the key to all the problems which appeared to me self-contradictory and insoluble. It cannot be helped if this means the death of my poetry; I only hope that it would sooner die.

Kuo Mo-jo goes on to discuss the present role of literature in the light of his conversion:

I have now completely changed my views about literature. I have come to feel the triviality of any theory based on technique or style; what matters is [an awareness of] the literature of yesterday, the literature of today, and the literature of tomorrow. The literature of yesterday was the unself-conscious and superior enjoyment of aristocrats, who enjoyed all the prerogatives in life. For instance, even if Tagore in his poetry and Tolstoy in his fiction preach benevolence and love, I feel that they are just administering charity to the famished.

The literature of today is a literature embarking on a revolutionary path: the outcry of the oppressed, the yell of the desperate, the imprecation of the fighting will, the anticipated joy of the revolution. The literature of today is a revolutionary literature; I think this is a transitional but unavoidable phenomenon. What will be the literature of tomorrow? It will be what you once referred to as the literature that transcends its age and environment. But it will not come to pass until after the realization of socialism. With the realization of socialism, the great literary geniuses will have complete freedom for development because at that time there will be no social classes and all the frets and sorrow in life, except those pertaining to our physiological constitution, will be eliminated. Man will be restored to his original state and literature will have as its subject pure and real human nature. Then there will be a genuine pure literature. At present we can only seek the material for a pure literature in the amorous dreams of the young, the warm creature-comforts of the rich, the euphoria of the morphine addicts, the inebriety of the alcoholics, and the hallucinations of those famished to the point of death. Fang-wu, we are men on the revolutionary path, and our literature can only be a revolutionary literature. The literature of today can only justify its existence by its ability to hasten the realization of socialist revolution; only that literature which promotes socialist revolution can be called the literature of today. Otherwise it is only the rank odor of meat and drink and the aroma of narcotics, and what does that signify? Real life points to only one road; and as literature is the reflection of life, there can be only one type that is authentic. Fang-wu, this is my firmest conviction; in reaching this conviction, I have been able to form a clearer view of literature and to recover my faith in it. This is the age of propaganda and literature

is the trenchant weapon for propaganda; my tendency
toward indecision and uncertainty has stopped.[7]

The preceding excerpts from Kuo Mo-jo's letter have been
given instead of some comparable passages from his more
formal writings because the provisional character of this discourse reveals with greater clarity the working of his mind
toward the acceptance of Communism and of the Communist concept of literature. The early advocates and practitioners of pai-hua literature would have disagreed violently
with Kuo Mo-jo's formulation of the function of present-
day letters. Hu Shih had envisaged a literary renaissance.
The Literary Association, while stressing the social uses of
literature, did not question its autonomy as art. The Creation Society went further in affirming art for art's sake and
the afflatus of the artist. But at the same time it was quite
apparent that the renaissance was not forthcoming: the
imagination, tethered to patriotic, humanitarian, and reformist ideals, could not encompass the higher levels of
achievement. Under these circumstances, it was quite natural
for the more politically minded writers to blame their failure
on the environment and to engage more and more in social
reform. Kuo Mo-jo's letter traces the plight of the modern
Chinese writer to his lack of "self-realization" as well as to
his failure to promote "the free development of the masses."
The Marxist program of action was welcome, therefore, not
only because it promised the achievement of the twin goals
but because it salved the artistic conscience by postulating
a millennium of literary greatness in the socialist future.
The key sentence in the letter is Kuo Mo-jo's frank admission that "this is the age of propaganda and literature is the
trenchant weapon for propaganda." In a moment of candor
he lays bare the doctrinal core of what was to become known
as revolutionary or proletarian literature, without the usual
embellishment of Communist jargon.

It is a commonplace to observe that writers achieve what

they can despite their personal frustrations and their consciousness of the corruption and vulgarity of their times. These conditions are nearly always concomitant to serious artistic endeavor. Only those writers who are not seriously committed to art in the first place would readily abnegate their craft at the supposedly urgent dictates of social and political reform. Kuo Mo-jo, however, had apparently little difficulty in persuading himself and most of his colleagues to adopt the Marxist and propagandist approach to literature. Chang Tzu-p'ing, who was by that time a highly popular and commercial writer of romantic fiction, dissociated himself from the Creation Society, and so did Yü Ta-fu, after a period of perfunctory cooperation. But their defection was more than compensated for by the recruitment of students newly returned from Japan: the so-called junior Creationists. Led by Kuo Mo-jo and Ch'eng Fang-wu, the Creation Society bravely entered the Communist phase of its career.

The times were rosy for Communism. The May Thirtieth Movement of 1925 proved a spectacular success with the public, especially students, writers, and industrial workers. The anti-imperialist sentiments seeped through nearly all strata of Chinese society. To Communist historians this movement was the second pivotal event in the development of modern Chinese literature, denoting the increased collective revolutionary consciousness of the times as against the more liberal and individualist patriotism of the May Fourth Movement. At about the same time the Kuomintang, in its bid to regain power and oust the warlords, was in close cooperation with the Communist party. Communist intellectuals were taking over important educational and propaganda functions within the Kuomintang apparatus. In 1925 Kuo Mo-jo, Ch'eng Fang-wu, and other Creationists left Shanghai for Canton to direct the liberal arts college of Sun Yat-sen University. In the next year, with the launching of the Northern Expedition, Kuo Mo-jo became an important propagandist in the Political Department of the

Revolutionary Army Headquarters; many other Creationists and Communist writers also joined the expedition. They looked forward hopefully to a political career: it was only after the forcible expulsion of Communists from the Kuomintang Government in 1927 that they returned to their literary profession with the avowed purpose of converting the reading public to Communism.

The later history of the Creation Society from 1927 on will be introduced in due course. In its early romantic phase its popularity solely rests upon the writings of three members: Kuo Mo-jo, Chang Tzu-p'ing, and Yü Ta-fu. Kuo Mo-jo's early poetry still possesses a technical interest, and his autobiographies are an important document in Chinese intellectual history. The early sentimental stories of Chang Tzu-p'ing are not without psychological truth, though his later triangular romances, designed to titillate the student audience, have long passed into oblivion. But it is Yü Ta-fu who is responsible for the unique contributions of the Creation Society. While nearly all the early Creationists subscribed to a subjective romanticism, Yü Ta-fu alone has appropriated the individual psyche as a moral theme for literature. Admittedly personal, maudlin, and decadent, he has the courage to push to its farthest limit the quest for individual freedom implicit in the May Fourth Movement.

YÜ TA-FU (1896–1945)

Strikingly dissimilar to anything written by Lu Hsün, Yeh Shao-chün, and other early fiction writers, Yü Ta-fu's first publication, *Sinking* (comprising three stories: "Sinking," "Moving South," "Silvergray Death"), had an immediate impact upon the contemporary audience. Its daring and originality at once captivated the younger audience and enraged the moralists, who found its decadence highly corruptive. No less a critic than Chou Tso-jen himself came unsolicitedly to its defense, praising its moral seriousness.

Placed in its proper literary contexts, *Sinking,* of course, is neither very daring nor very original: it stems from the Japanese and European decadent writers as well as those Chinese poets and essayists who have habitually bewailed their loneliness and poverty as outcasts from philistine officialdom. Even though Yü Ta-fu's preoccupation with sexual fantasies has obscured his equally characteristic struggle against vulgarity, he was no less a seeker of self-knowledge and damnation than a hermit recoiling from the modern age. For his time, this combination rightly exercised a peculiar fascination.

Like many other eminent contemporary writers, Yü Ta-fu was brought up in an impoverished genteel family in northern Chekiang, where a strong literary tradition had apparently persisted. He had read a great deal in traditional fiction and drama before embarking for Japan at the age of seventeen. During his first four years at a Japanese preparatory school he read, according to his own estimate, about a thousand titles in European and Japanese fiction; the great Russian novelists particularly delighted him. Later, as a student of economics at Tokyo Imperial University, he not only continued with his reading of fiction but ventured into the bohemian life of wine and women. Yü Ta-fu later recalls: "Every day, if I was not reading novels, I was most often seen in cafés, seeking girl companions to drink wine with me. No one was studying hard, no one would have thought that I would now earn my living by writing fiction." [8] In the absence of Confucian restraints, the future author responded with characteristic adolescent intensity to sensual pleasures. But at the same time he felt sad and guilty after each debauchery, lonely in an alien country and self-reproachful in not being able to lead a constructive and useful life. Out of the matrix of such feelings came his first attempts in fiction.

"Sinking" is a mawkish tale of adolescent frustration and guilt. It opens on a pastoral landscape in which a Chinese student in Japan is reading Wordsworth aloud to himself. Though a great lover of nature and poetry, he obtains only a momentary relief from his unrest because he is ruled by a strong sexual compulsion, mainly taking the form of voyeurism. (In the course of the story, he will have occasion to fortify himself with Heine, Gissing, and Chinese poetry, but with equal futility.) He lives in an inn, apart from other Chinese students, and indulges in nightly masturbation. One evening, carried away by an irresistible impulse, this youth sneaks downstairs to peep at the innkeeper's daughter taking a bath. He is overly excited by this scene and hurries back to his room to contemplate his guilt. The next day he moves into an isolated house on a wooded hill. For a while he is able to curb his lust and attain a degree of tranquillity in his new retreat. But he becomes a complete nervous wreck when, wandering in a field, he accidentally overhears a Japanese couple making love among the bushes. Around four o'clock that afternoon he takes the trolley to the city, and emboldened by the flaunting presence of heavily painted waitresses at its entrance, he ventures into a brothel-restaurant and orders a meal. But understandably as a Chinese, he receives only brusque attention from the girl waiting on him. He is now infuriated at his own degradation; he recites poetry to himself and gets progressively more drunk until he falls asleep. At eight-thirty that evening he wakes up to find himself lying in bed in a perfumed room. He pays his bill and walks toward the nearby seashore. After a long apostrophe to China, whose shame has fallen upon him, he has the sudden impulse to end his life and walks slowly into the water.

Even in this bare summary a high-strung emotionalism is apparent. A Wertherian self-pity exaggerates alike the hero's love for nature and the ache in his heart; it, moreover, fails to account for his death in adequate terms. As he paces the seashore, the hero addresses his shadow: "O my poor shadow, you have followed me for twenty-one years and now this great sea is going to bury you. Though my body has been insulted and injured, I should not have let you grow so thin and emaciated. Shadow, O shadow, please forgive me!" [9] Here the style exhibits the worst sentimental affectation; but precisely because of the utter discrepancy between the excessive emotion and the trivial action, "Sinking" has generated a kind of nervous intensity which transcends its manifest sentimentalism.

To its contemporary student readers, moreover, the story represents the discovery of sex as a serious concern. Through sex the hero has come to realize his personal failure as well as the national shame; impelled by the call to freedom and yet thwarted at every turn by traditional forces, the students shared more or less the same kind of frustration. Understandably, they responded with keen sympathy to Yü Ta-fu's portrayal of a lonely and patriotic youth bent on self-destruction.

Though a third-person narrative, "Sinking" is unabashedly autobiographical. The familial and educational backgrounds of author and hero are almost identical, and the story is told in an intimate fashion. In that sense, the whole body of Yü Ta-fu's fiction, with the few exceptions in the proletarian mode, constitute a Rousseauist confession. In one of his essays Yü Ta-fu declares that all literature is autobiographical, but characteristically he fails to emphasize the kinds of subtle transformation to which a great writer invariably subjects his personal experience. His own practice testifies to the predominance of a literal imagination fascinated by the narrow world of his private sensations and feelings.

The subjective hero is not without social significance, however: he is the impotent patriot, the harassed family man, the artist alienated from society. At times he is even the proud genius conscious of his superiority and scornful of the world's inattention. In "Ts'ai Shih Chi" (1922), a story about the distinguished Ch'ing poet Huang Chung-tsê,

Yü Ta-fu gives a magnificent if idealized self-portrait. Arrogant, lonely, and extremely sensitive, the poet pits himself against the famed scholar and philosopher Tai Tung-yüan (one of Hu Shih's great heroes) and regards him as merely a member of the official establishment and therefore a pseudo-Confucianist. The poet himself patterns his life after Li Po, the genius of poetic spontaneity. In the story, Huang Chung-tsê sulks and falls ill, recalls the past love of his early youth and weeps at the tomb of Li Po, laments his fate, and above all composes verse. By inserting a good many of the poems in the biographical contexts of their composition, Yü Ta-fu restores to the emaciated poet all his feverish intensity.

Yü Ta-fu's autobiographical hero has also been generally regarded as a decadent character. Yet this decadence is only superficial, far from incompatible with a scrupulous moral sensibility. In "One Intoxicating Spring Evening" (1923), the first-person hero is a struggling author down on his fortunes. Evicted from a cheap hotel, he moves to a flat in a slum district in Shanghai; in the same flat lives a girl who works in a cigarette factory. She suspects the writer to be a thief, since he never goes out to work in the daytime but takes frequent strolls at night. The girl, however, is sympathetic and friendly, and once invites him over to share some food with her. One day the writer receives a five-dollar pay check; he goes out to take a bath and buy some clothing, and to repay the girl's kindness buys some fruit and dessert. That night at ten o'clock the two enjoy a snack together. In her candor, the girl asks him not to smoke so much and not to associate with thieves. Deeply touched by her solicitude, the writer restrains his impulse to embrace her and bids her good night with a promise of reform. Mainly of humanitarian interest in its depiction of two people in the clutches of poverty, the story also asserts the paralysis of lust in the face of innocence. Similarly, in "Late-blooming Osmanthus" (1932), the first-person hero restrains his concupiscence toward a lovely young widow because her purity and animal grace have inspired him with a brotherly love. In both stories one notices a kindness and ultimate decency on the part of the autobiographical hero, staying well within the bounds of Confucian propriety.

The most adult manifestation of this postdecadent decency is found in the story "The Past" (1927). The first-person hero once lived in the same residential terrace in Shanghai with four not very respectable sisters. The eldest was a banker's concubine, and the other three were also financially dependent on him. The hero was madly in love with the second sister, from whom he suffered many masochistic humiliations. When she finally got married to another man, he took Lao San, the third sister, on a trip to Soochow, where they spent a night together in a hotel. Because he was still thinking of the second sister, they did not consummate their passion that night, even though he knew Lao San was deeply in love with him. The story opens three years later with the hero recuperating from a pulmonary disease at Macao. One rainy day he accidentally runs into Lao San, now a widow and much sadder and thinner after a marriage without love. They renew their friendship and see each other daily. The hero is now consumed with the passion to possess her; one evening he stages a dinner for her at a good restaurant and later half drags and half persuades her to spend the night with him in a hotel:

> The night thickened and the wind was whistling outside. The 50-watt light bulb, which had turned much brighter after midnight, illumined the unusual loneliness in my heart. The room was also getting colder. Still with her clothes on, she was lying in bed, wrapped in a blanket and facing the wall. I threw myself over her several times and each time I was pushed away. At my last attempt she burst out crying. And she talked incoherently while sobbing:

"Mr. Li, our—our affair was finished a long—long time ago. That year, if that year—you could—you could have loved me as you love me now, I would—would have been spared all that suffering. I—I—you know—how during the last two or three years I—"

At this point she sobbed even more hysterically; she covered her head with the blanket so as to allow for uninterrupted crying. I thought of her earlier life and her present state, of her tenderness toward me in the past and still more of the already misspent half of my own futile life, and I became deeply touched by her sobbing. Even though I couldn't cry, I was seized with spasm after spasm of remorse. For half an hour while she was crying, I sat in bed in silence and felt that my lust was being washed away by her tears and that my mind was becoming again clean and undistracted.[10]

After she has stopped crying, the hero leans over to her side to beg her pardon. In a speech which is too full of bathos to merit quotation here, he confesses that even tonight his intentions have been despicable and asks her to turn her head toward him if she forgives.

Prone on the edge of her pillow, I waited in silence for a while upon finishing what I had to say. Her head was still toward the wall and her body was motionless. Then she turned her head and looked at me, her tearful eyes filled as it were with both commiseration and resentment. I felt more grateful for this stare than when the convict, sentenced to die, suddenly receives his pardon. She then turned her head to the other side and I also reclined outside her blanket. Lying there, we both didn't go to sleep; but relaxed and happy, I stayed quietly that way till dawn.[11]

In style and structure "The Past" is much too faulty to deserve comparison with Joyce's "The Dead." Yet like Conroy, the Chinese hero does reach a condition of self-knowledge which enables him to realize the difference between love and lust. In spite of his habitual sentimentality, Yü Ta-fu presents in the story a memorable epiphany, the shamefaced and happy awakening of a rake to the fact of human sorrow and integrity.

If the decadence of Baudelaire is explicable only in terms of a Christian faith, then, likewise, the guilt and remorse of Yü Ta-fu is to be understood in the framework of a Confucian ethic, which had conditioned his upbringing. Even when engaged in casual amorous pursuits, Yü Ta-fu or his fictional alter ego always suffers from the acute awareness of his truancy as son, husband, and father. A recurrent theme in his work is that of returning home. In the diary "A Trip Home," in the thinly disguised autobiographical stories, "Smoke Silhouettes" and "In the Cold Wind," Yü Ta-fu goes home deliberately to hear the taunts of his angry mother or to share the misery of his tearful wife and sickly children. One doesn't need biographical corroboration to feel the force of his emotional predicament.

Yü Ta-fu was a writer of unique importance in the first period because he alone dared to expose all his personal weaknesses in print and, in so doing, extended the psychological and moral frontiers of modern Chinese fiction. It is regrettable that none of his followers, while parading their eroticism and decadence, possessed his kind of honesty and seriousness and that with the ascendancy of the leftist movement by 1928 his type of fiction should have gone so soon out of fashion. It is also unfortunate that Yü Ta-fu shares with the other Creationists a sentimental and careless style which blemishes all his stories. This indifference to art in turn vitiates his task of self-exploration. One at times has the feeling that in spite of his candor, Yü Ta-fu is also something of a poseur who has pilfered from psychological manuals to supplement his genuine insights. By turns voyeur, fetishist, homosexual, masochist, and kleptomaniac, his autobiographical hero is much too versatile.

Yü Ta-fu lost both self-confidence and friendly support

when the Creation Society marched forward as the avant-garde of revolutionary literature. He went along with Kuo Mo-jo and Ch'eng Fang-wu to teach at Sun Yat-sen University and played half-heartedly with the new line. Soon disgusted, he returned to Shanghai to take charge of the branch office of the Creation Society there and had many unpleasant quarrels with the junior Creationists. In 1927 he wrote a satiric article in *The Deluge* exposing the revolutionary antics of teachers and students at Canton, an article which highly incensed Kuo Mo-jo and led to the eventual estrangement of the two friends. In 1928 Yü Ta-fu quit the Creation Society to join forces temporarily with Lu Hsün as a co-editor of the magazine *Pen Liu.* A year later, however, he again yielded to leftist pressure and became editor of *Mass Literature.* In 1930 he was a founding member of the League of Left-wing Writers. But chafing under group pressure and propaganda duties, he soon left the organization [12] to join the circle of Lin Yutang and Chou Tso-jen, who were then promoting a nonpolitical personal literature.

During the period of vacillation Yü Ta-fu had turned out a series of bad books: *Nine Diaries* (1927), a trivial day-by-day record of his life in Canton and Shanghai during the period 1926–27; *The Stray Sheep,* a maudlin novelette about a college graduate and a small-town actress; *She Was a Weak Woman* (another title: *Forgive Her!*), a naturalistic tale of sex and violence. But moving in the circle of Lin Yutang, Yü Ta-fu apparently regained his peace of mind. From 1932 to 1937, even though he contributed occasional stories to leftist publications, he wrote mainly essays and diaries for Lin Yutang's magazines. No longer the morbid explorer of his own soul, he appears in these a Taoist recluse drawing a quiet satisfaction from his readings and travels. Among his later books, *Footprints Here and There* especially shows a strong affinity with the older travel literature and reasserts his literary importance.

At the time of the outbreak of the Sino-Japanese War,

Yü Ta-fu was a small official in the Fukien Provincial Government. In 1938 he became a newspaper editor in Singapore. When the latter city fell into Japanese hands in 1942, he fled to Sumatra, living there under a different name for the remainder of the war; but soon after the victory, the Japanese police tracked him down and killed him. For a writer who was neither a Communist nor very patriotic, this was surely an ironic end.[13]

PART II

A Decade of Growth (1928–1937)

CHAPTER 5

Leftists and Independents

IN POLITICAL history the decade 1928–37 begins
with the establishment of the Kuomintang-controlled National Government and ends with the nominal resumption
of Kuomintang-Communist collaboration to face the war of
resistance against Japan. On the surface, it is a decade of
impressive achievement for the National Government, and
a decade of defeats and setbacks for the Communists. After
a series of abortive uprisings in various parts of the country,
the Communists, under the shrewd leadership of Mao Tse-
tung, managed to consolidate their strength in their self-
styled Soviet Republic in Kiangsi in 1931. But repeated government campaigns to subdue the region finally forced them
to abandon their strongholds and undertake their grueling
Long March in 1934. One year later they arrived at Paoan,
Shensi,* considerably shattered in morale and armed strength.
During the period, the government leader Chiang Kai-shek
also brought many warlords and dissident politicians under

* Yenan was not captured by the Communists until December 1936,
immediately following the Sian Incident. In March 1937 the Shensi-
Kansu-Ningsia Soviet Government was formally established, with Yenan
as capital.

control, though some of them continued to make intermittent disturbances. In spite of the great odds against him, therefore, Chiang Kai-shek was able to establish a degree of peace and unity which China had not enjoyed since the Republican Revolution; he could have accomplished a good deal more if he had not been at the same time harassed by the steady expansion of Japanese aggression.

Early in the decade Japan conquered Manchuria and obtained special economic rights in North China. Even though he reluctantly allowed a brief period of armed resistance in the Shanghai area in 1932, Chiang Kai-shek could not afford a firm opposition to Japanese aggression, for the obvious reason that the nation was not adequately prepared for a protracted war. He sought public support for his policy of achieving internal unity as the prerequisite for meeting foreign aggression. He reasoned that, until the Communists were quelled, there would be little sense in engaging the country in foredoomed resistance. But as early as 1933, while they were sorely beset by government forces, the Communists were clamoring for the creation of a United Front to fight Japan.* As this clamor met increasing popular approval, Chiang Kai-shek was finally compelled to abandon his own policy and adopt the ruinous course of action which precipitated the whole country into an ill-prepared war against a vastly superior enemy and gave the Communists a much-needed respite to rebuild their strength.

* It should be noted, however, that the early United Front policy called for all patriotic elements to subvert the Kuomintang as well as combat Japanese aggression. It was only following the proclamation of a global united front against fascism at the World Congress of the Comintern in Moscow in August 1935 that the Chinese Communist leadership was compelled against its will to accept collaboration with the National Government for united resistance. For a detailed study see James C. Thomson, Jr., "Communist Policy and the United Front in China, 1935–1936," in *Papers on China*, Vol. 11 (December 1957), duplicated for private distribuiton by the Center for East Asian Studies, Harvard University.

Leftists and Independents

It was quite inevitable that the Communist line of the United Front should appeal to Chinese intellectuals. The whole course of modern Chinese history with its long catalogue of humiliations had prepared for, and the May Fourth and May Thirtieth movements had only too recently demonstrated, a high-strung, patriotic state of mind which could brook no further insult to the nation and heed no long-range plans for preparation and unification. By cleverly exploiting this sentiment, the Communists easily imposed upon the public the myth of their being cruelly persecuted patriots whose only crime was the demand for an all-out offensive against Japan. The whole nation exulted when, after the Sian Incident of 1936, the Communist party agreed to cooperate with the Government and nominally relinquish its control over the Red Army in the interests of national defense.

During this decade, the National Government did much to develop commerce and industry and to improve the livelihood of its people, especially in provinces directly under its control. But on this record alone it could neither command . respect nor check discontent. Its failure to obtain popular support for its anti-Communist policy indicates finally a more serious weakness: the lack of an intelligent ideological platform with which to combat Communism and win back the intellectuals.[1] A great many intellectuals and writers who had become disaffected with the Kuomintang after its persecution of Communists in 1927 remained so throughout the period. And it was they who were responsible for generating a climate of public opinion favorable to the growth of Communism.

During its initial period of cooperation with the Communists, the Kuomintang had done its share in demolishing the traditional cultural structure. After it had emerged into a dominant position, it had no constructive doctrine or philosophy to turn to except the writings of Sun Yat-sen, especially his *San Min Chu I*, which was duly made a com-

117

pulsory subject of study from grade school to college. Dr. Sun's unsophisticated presentation of the Western concepts of nationalism, democracy, and socialism, however, was not designed to woo the more intelligent students. Although he tried to interpret these concepts in the light of the Confucian tradition, Dr. Sun was a typical modern liberal in his naiveté, good will, and lack of wisdom. He had great difficulty in dissociating his principle of People's Livelihood from Marxist socialism because he couldn't bring himself to repudiate the latter entirely. The compulsory study of *San Min Chu I* under teachers ill-trained in political philosophy, as was the practice in most schools, could conceivably turn disgusted students toward the more attractive logic of Communism.

Chiang Kai-shek does not have the Western learning or the liberal mind of Sun Yat-sen; on the contrary, he has an immense respect for the Chinese moral tradition and models his personal life upon that of the Confucian statesman, Tseng Kuo-fan. In time he reversed the radical trend of the Kuomintang and re-emphasized in the school curriculum the study of Confucian ethics and the classical language. In 1934 he launched the New Life Movement to impress upon the people the importance of good manners, righteousness, integrity, and self-respect. Seeing the accelerated recovery of Germany under Hitler, Chiang Kai-shek also made much of the cult of the leader to enforce discipline and unity. Military training was introduced for male students in high schools and colleges.

In introducing his reforms, Chiang Kai-shek was fired by an earnest ambition to mold a unified and stronger China. While some of these reforms were admirable, his whole program was vitiated at the start by the incompetence and provinciality of the personnel entrusted with the tasks of moral discipline and ideological persuasion. They were men of little learning and less culture, incapable of fighting Communism on the dialectic level. Even such leading propa-

118

gandists as Ch'en Li-fu and Chou Fo-hai could only embellish and gloss over the confused teachings of Sun Yat-sen.
In a decade of political frustration and military defeats, the
Communists therefore gained ground steadily on the cultural
front, where the Nationalist forces were shabby and ill-
equipped.

The year of the Communist setback, 1927, saw the determined efforts of Communist writers to seize leadership in the
world of letters. Ousted from direct participation in politics,
these veterans of the Northern Expedition returned to their
earlier profession with the fanaticism born of defeat and
frustration. While Kuo Mo-jo had to flee to Japan in 1928,
he and his lieutenant Ch'eng Fang-wu continued to direct
the Creation Society vigorously. Its ranks were now swelled
with such new writers as Li Ch'u-li, Feng Nai-ch'ao, P'eng
K'ang, and Chu Ching-wo, who, having just returned from
Japan where a proletarian literary movement was in full
swing, were confident that a like movement would soon
sweep over China. In the same year Chiang Kuang-tz'u and
Ch'ien Hsing-ts'un formed the Sun Society and launched the
Sun Monthly. Living in relative safety in the foreign concessions in Shanghai, members of these two societies and
other smaller affiliated groups boldly proclaimed the era of
revolutionary literature. Like the then Communist political
leaders who sought to obtain control of China by engineer-
ing a few insurrections and uprisings in cities and villages,
these literary agitators thought they could easily prevail by
forcing upon the public a sufficiently large quantity of revolutionary literature and by attacking and discrediting all
writers of importance who refused to fall in line. Vehement
polemics ensued.

Recent Communist studies in this period have fostered
the impression that the revolutionary camp represented a
compact majority of writers. Actually, its numerical strength
was not so formidable nor were its ranks so closed. Not only

did individual groups compete with each other for power
and prestige; more important, they were torn by political
conflicts. Just as Trotsky debated with Stalin over the miscarriage of the Chinese Revolution, so among revolutionary
writers Trotskyites, while admittedly a small minority, contended with Stalinists. An important member of the Creation
Society, Wang Tu-ch'ing, was a French-returned student of
fine arts and author of several volumes of poetry and a play
called *The Death of Yang Kuei-fei*. He went to Canton with
the other Creationists and served as dean of the liberal arts
college of Sun Yat-sen University after Kuo Mo-jo had left
the post to participate in the Northern Expedition. Later in
Shanghai he was dean of another Communist school, the
Shanghai College of Fine Arts. After the disbanding of the
Creation Society, however, Wang Tu-ch'ing published in his
own magazine, *Chan K'ai* (September 1930), a controversial
article entitled "The Creation Society: A Final Appraisal
and an Account of My Role in Its History." Speaking as a
Trotskyite, he accuses the other Creationists, and especially
Kuo Mo-jo, of being lackeys of Stalin and betrayers of the
Revolution. Kuo Mo-jo promptly wrote an equally virulent
rejoinder to answer the charges, and the other former
Creationists also joined in the fray.[2] This debate, while failing to provide completely reliable historical data, establishes
beyond a doubt the existence of internal dissensions within
the revolutionary camp and, incidentally but more importantly, the subservience of the Creation Society to the Comintern. After Stalin had established his power, of course, the
Trotskyite writers gradually dwindled into insignificance.

Whatever its internal rivalry and dissension, the revolutionary camp put up a united front in attacking its enemies.
After a target had been chosen, denunciatory articles would
appear simultaneously in such magazines as the *Sun Monthly*,
Creation Monthly, and *Cultural Critique* (another Creationist publication). These repetitive articles by the same authors
appearing under a variety of pseudonyms gave the impres-

sion of a solid majority. As a matter of fact, of course, the revolutionary camp was then only a minority, viewed with distress and alarm by all the more serious writers who cared for the development of modern Chinese literature. The Literary Association was represented by *The Short Story Magazine*, still the outstanding and most influential journal of its time. In 1928 Hu Shih, Hsü Chih-mo, and Liang Shih-ch'iu launched *Crescent Moon* to succeed the now defunct *Contemporary Review*. In opposition to the propaganda emphasis of revolutionary literature, this group tried to reassert the standards of health and dignity. Another powerful literary magazine was *Yü Ssu:* its guiding spirits, Chou Tso-jen and Lu Hsün, stood for uncompromising individualism.[3] Lin Yutang, a regular contributor to *Yü Ssu,* also began to attract notice.

These three groups, each in its own way conserving and carrying forward the finer creative and critical traditions of the Literary Revolution, could not, however, make a united stand against the demagogues of the revolutionary camp. The *Crescent Moon* group, as the supposed spokesmen for capitalism, were especially isolated: not only the revolutionary writers but Lu Hsün and his followers were continually attacking them. The revolutionary camp thrived in this state of disunity.

The revolutionary writers opened fire on, and in turn provoked, two prominent writers of respectively the *Yü Ssu* group and the Literary Association: Lu Hsün and Mao Tun. Unlike the *Crescent Moon* group, these two were writers of commanding influence and represented, each in his own fashion, certain strands of the revolutionary tradition. It was a matter of urgent necessity, therefore, for the revolutionary camp to force them to follow the orthodox Communist line in literature or else destroy their reputations in case they remained stubbornly uncompromising. In the chapter on Lu Hsün we have summarized the kind of attack to which he was subjected. In reply to attack, Lu Hsün showed himself to be a master of contempt. But over and above his jeering attitude was his serious concern over the menace of the revolutionary writers. While agreeing with them on Upton Sinclair's dictum in *Mammonart* that art is propaganda,[4] Lu Hsün would not for a moment allow the cynical exploitation of art in the supposed interests of the Revolution. In his address given at the Whampoa Military Academy on April 8, 1927, he gives perhaps his most succinct statement regarding the relations between literature and revolution:

> But the writers at this revolutionary base, I am afraid, are inclined to stress a close bond between literature and revolution in the understanding that literature should be employed to propagandize, to promote, to incite, and to help fulfill the Revolution. But I think writing of this kind will be very ineffective because good literary works have never been composed in accordance with other people's orders; rather, they are disinterested and an expression of the natural or spontaneous outpourings of the heart. If you have first entertained a thesis and then tried to illustrate it accordingly, your writing will be no different from the eight-legged essay. It will have no literary value, nor any effect upon the readers. So, for the sake of the revolution, let's have more workers for the revolution and not be overworried about "revolutionary literature." [5]

In his quarrel with the revolutionary writers Lu Hsün maintained this stand throughout.

As author of the trilogy *The Eclipse,* Mao Tun (Shen Yen-ping) emerged in 1928 as the first major novelist on the contemporary literary scene. Though long affiliated with the Literary Association, he had been for some time an active supporter of the Communist party. Like Kuo Mo-jo, he had served in the Political Department of the Revolutionary Army Headquarters during the Northern Expedition. Precisely because his Communist faith was of tougher intellectual caliber, however, he recorded in *The Eclipse* the failure of the revolution with imaginative objectivity. To the revolutionary critics who wanted only an optimistic propagandist literature, this was an unpardonable offense. They had no choice but to attack Mao Tun as the pessimistic spokesman of petty-bourgeois decadence.

In his reply to this attack—the long essays "From Kuling to Tokyo" and "On Reading *Ni Huan-chih*"—Mao Tun draws some elementary observations for the benefit of his critics, namely that a writer has an inalienable right to his own vision of reality and that the emotional and ideological postures of the characters in a literary work may not be naively identified with those of the author. However, Mao Tun admits to his petty-bourgeois bias and builds his defense upon it. He argues that the revolutionary writer should at present write for the petty-bourgeois audience because this is the only audience he possesses. In view of the tremendous revolutionary potential of this audience, it is surely unrealistic and foolish in the extreme to cater to the proletarian classes, who are illiterate and therefore beyond the reach of literary communication. The hopes and aspirations of the petty bourgeoisie should be served first.

In substantial agreement with his critics, Mao Tun proposed in effect only a change of emphasis. With greater sagacity he called for a Communist literature that would not be easily discredited and ridiculed but would effect a lasting hold on the reading public. Instead of the stereotyped formulas of proletarian fiction, would it not be better to observe the problems of the students, shop apprentices, and white-collar workers, who were equally disaffected with the National Government? However, at the time of the debate the revolutionary writers failed to grasp the essential similarity between Mao Tun's approach and theirs.

Communist literary critics have generally regarded the quarrels of 1928 and 1929 as a necessary but regrettable episode in the history of Communist ascendancy. Necessary because, without the hue and cry of the Creation and Sun societies, a militant Communist orthodoxy could not be so speedily achieved; regrettable because the quarrels involved on the defensive side Lu Hsün and Mao Tun, who were to become the leading Communist writers. In the light of their later prominence, it has been the practice of these critics to prove that Lu Hsün and Mao Tun had always been revolutionary writers and to chide somewhat the Creationists and their affiliated groups for their erroneous judgment and excessive harshness. It is relatively easy to trace Mao Tun's Communist background, but Lu Hsün's intransigence implies such a deep-seated personal contempt for the Creationists (to his dying day he will bear a grudge against them) that the available biographical evidence offers little satisfactory explanation for his capitulation to the Communist camp. While we know that Feng Hsüeh-feng was most instrumental in bringing about that event, we do not have the precise details of the secret negotiations entered into by the Communist underground leaders and Lu Hsün to compel the latter's surrender.

The literary battles had become futile by 1929. In attacking others, the revolutionary camp had become itself exposed to ridicule and abuse; moreover, the National Government, which earlier that year had disbanded the Creation Society, was beginning to be watchful over the subversive activities of Communist writers. The Communist leaders in Shanghai, who had counted on the Creation and Sun societies to achieve a literary dictatorship, now saw the need to adopt a less radical and more flexible line in literature so as to rally more writers. In February 1930, with the prominent support of Lu Hsün and Mao Tun, the League of Chinese Left-wing Writers was formed; its Manifesto bore the signatures of some fifty writers, most of whom were members of now-defunct Communist literary societies. Though the Manifesto maintained a firm stand on "the liberation struggle for the proletariat," the choice of the key term "left-wing" was intended to disguise the overt Communist character of the League and to attract writers with merely an anti-feudal, anti-imperialist, and anti-Kuomintang bias. It proved to be a wise choice: upon the formation of the League, Communist dominance of Chinese letters became a reality.

The Left-wing League was a militant organization, incorporating a powerful executive committee and several other committees assigned to cultural, social, and propaganda tasks. It was in close touch with affiliated Communist organizations among students, workers, and peasants, and it was well supplied with funds, possibly from Comintern sources, to ensure publication of a large and steady output of books and periodicals. In its first two years, for example, the following magazines were published: *World Culture, Sprout, The Pathfinder, The Big Dipper, Modern Fiction, Mass Literature, Literature Monthly,* and *Literary News.* Though most of these sooner or later ceased publication because of censorship difficulties, new magazines would immediately replace them. From 1933 to 1937, the leftist magazine with the greatest prestige and popularity was *Wen Hsüeh* or *Literature.*[6]

The League exercised, as expected, formidable sway over a large number of young writers who, fashionably conditioned by leftist attitudes and eager to publish, could not help availing themselves of the large number of League-sponsored magazines. Especially after 1932 was leftism in fashion. On the one hand, the increasing severity of government censorship of Communist literature since that date had necessitated a retreat from the outspokenly revolutionary line of propaganda. On the other, the League was responding to the tactical changes in Soviet literary policy. In the same year of 1932 the Russian Association of Proletarian Writers was replaced by the somewhat more liberal Union of Soviet Writers, and the principle of Socialist

Realism was enthroned in conscious repudiation of the earlier, exclusively proletarian approach to literature. While Socialist Realism still insists on the positive depiction of optimistic revolutionary reality, it does permit a greater degree of latitude in the choice of technique and subject matter. (In actual practice, of course, Socialist Realism is a deliberately ambiguous and flexible term used by Soviet critics to designate any piece of writing that enjoys party approval.) In adopting this critical principle the League seems to have encouraged a literature of collective action that differs little in principle from the earlier proletarian literature; but on the other hand, perhaps more in concession to government censorship than to the Soviet example of greater tolerance for individual diversity, it also allowed a leftist literature with a negative emphasis on the decadent aspects of Chinese society. This new freedom enabled a few gifted writers, notably Chang T'ien-i and Wu Tsu-hsiang, to achieve a satiric fiction of great power and subtlety; in fact, nearly all leftist literature which achieves realistic integrity, in contrast to the orthodox revolutionary and optimistic Communist literature, stems from the satiric tradition.

The League lost no time in launching a series of campaigns for the suppression of dissident opinion. It conducted these campaigns with the same ruthlessness and scurrilousness that distinguished the Creation Society, but unlike the latter, it was now able to strike with an overwhelming force. Shortly after the League had come into existence, a group of writers in Nanking, possibly subsidized by the National Government, launched a nationalist literary movement to counteract Communism. Led by Lu Hsün, the leftist critics immediately quelled this movement by insinuating that its anti-Soviet propaganda was designed merely to divert public attention from the Government's weak stand on Japan.

In 1932 Hu Ch'iu-yüan, a self-styled liberal well versed in Marxist aesthetics, ridiculed the puerile harshness of League critics and demanded greater literary freedom. Rallying to his support, Su Wen (or Tu Heng), co-editor of the influential literary magazine *Les Contemporains,* called ironic attention to the plight of "the third group"—of writers who wished to pursue their craft seriously but were no longer able to do so during the present struggle for dominance between liberal and leftist doctrinaires. In pleading for the writer's independence, Su Wen was merely restating Lu Hsün's position in 1928 in slightly different terms. But this time Lu Hsün and other League writers atacked him in unison to stamp out the heresy that a writer could remain neutral in the struggle for the supremacy of the proletariat. Toward the conclusion of this long debate, the League placated Su Wen and Hu Ch'iu-yüan to some extent by admitting the unreasoned dogmatism of some of its members, but this temporary gesture at a compromise did nothing, of course, to alter its actual policy of stamping out dissident opinion.

To all appearances the most assiduous persecutor of non-leftist opinion was Lu Hsün, but he was hardly the guiding spirit of the League; for three years that role fell upon the shoulders of the Communist leader Ch'ü Ch'iu-pai, who returned to Shanghai in 1931 after a period of exile in Russia. He had gone there once earlier in 1920 at the age of twenty; upon his return in 1923 he was elected a member of the Central Committee of the Chinese Communist party. He became Secretary of the party following the expulsion of Ch'en Tu-hsiu from that post in 1927. Though shorn of much of his political power after he himself was expelled from the same position, he was apparently entrusted, upon his second return to China, with the vital task of cultural and ideological subversion outside Communist areas. According to Feng Hsüeh-feng, he was not officially appointed as director of the League: "It was not the decision of the Party but rather his own zeal which led Comrade Ch'iu-pai to participate in and guide the work of the Left-wing League; at the same time, his poor health and the white terror of the period were also accountable for his intimate association with the Left-wing League." [7] This may well be true, but there was no one at the League who could rival his eminence as a party leader. Lu Hsün became the nominal spokesman for the League mainly because of his backing. For the period 1931–33, therefore, Ch'ü Ch'iu-pai was the policy-maker of the League. In January 1934 he left for the Soviet Republic in Kiangsi to accept the post of minister of education; captured by government forces in February 1935, he was executed the following June. [8]

As one of the few Chinese writers who knew Russian well, Ch'ü Ch'iu-pai translated a good deal from Soviet writings, but he made the most effective use of his pen in a series of short polemic essays in the style of Lu Hsün, in which he enunciated party policies and mapped out lines of attack with regard to particular issues. The large number of pseudonyms he had to use for these essays (he lived in hiding throughout his stay in Shanghai) obscured his prominence in the public eye, but for his primary audience, the Communist and fellow-traveling writers, his authority was unmistakable. The posthumous publication of these essays, in a volume entitled *Random Plunking*, [9] offers conclusive evidence of his leadership over the League.

Ch'ü Ch'iu-pai was once an important contributor to *Chinese Youth* (1923–27), organ of the Communist Youth League. In that magazine the editor Yün Tai-ying as well as Teng Chung-hsia (both of them early Communist leaders) and Ch'ü himself frequently pronounced on the importance of the proletarian and revolutionary line in literature. [10] Since then, Ch'ü had remained apparently unwavered in this conviction; as the policy-maker of the League, therefore, he was chiefly concerned with the reform of the existing language and literature. To him both the language and the literature were too Westernized and difficult for the masses, much too steeped in petty-bourgeois sensibility to reflect the true revolutionary spirit. Since the aim of literature is propaganda, and since the objective of propaganda is to reach as large an audience as possible, Ch'ü was willing to reverse the trend of Western-slanted pai-hua literature toward a popular mode of writing making able use of the many forms of folk entertainment. Following his initial discussion of the problem the year earlier, he agitated in 1932 for a *ta-chung wen-i* or literature for the masses:

> The revolutionary vanguard must not detach itself from the masses to indulge in its conceit that it could accomplish singly "its heroic and sublime enterprises." To maintain in general that new content calls for new forms, that it is up to the masses to raise their level of art appreciation but not up to the writer to lower his standards to meet the masses, is to assume the arrogance of a "great writer"! The revolutionary literature for the masses must begin with the utilization of the advantages of the old forms—the kinds of fiction, poetry, and drama to which the masses are accustomed—and then gradually introduce new elements, so that, as the masses are getting used to this new art, the art level of both writers and readers will be raised. In its formal aspects the old folk art has two advantages: its close alliance with the oral literary tradition and its simple and plain methods of narration and exposition. The revolutionary literature for the masses should heed the importance of these two advantages.[11]

It would be advisable, Ch'ü Ch'iu-pai goes on to say, for the writer to appropriate the techniques of comic strip artists and teahouse storytellers, to experiment in the varied forms of traditional regional drama. (In the subsequent debate on ta-chung wen-i, Su Wen observed caustically that no writer could hope to become a Tolstoy or Flaubert by drawing comic strips; with complete self-possession, Lu Hsün retorted that comic strip art may not produce a Tolstoy or Flaubert, but it contains the possibilities of a Michelangelo or da Vinci.)

The creation of a ta-chung wen-i clearly calls for language reform. To Ch'ü Ch'iu-pai, the current pai-hua is as bad as wen-yen: riddled with Europeanized vocabulary and syntax, it has become the vehicle of capitalist ideas and sentiments and the monopoly of the new intellectuals. (One must remember in this connection that Ch'ien Hsüan-t'ung had objected only to the Confucian and Taoist connotations of the Chinese language.) Ch'ü therefore speaks hopefully of *p'u-t'ung-hua* or common vernacular (the kind of debased Mandarin intelligible to large segments of the population) as the medium for the mass literature. To those who objected to p'u-t'ung-hua as at best a linguistic fiction, in view of the multiplicity of Chinese dialects, Ch'ü was also equipped with an answer. During his second stay in Russia, he had attended the conferences of Soviet linguists engaged in devising an alphabetized script for Chinese residents in Siberia. When he returned to China, he brought back with him the Soviet system of Latinizing Chinese, known as Latinxua.[12] In his essays on ta-chung wen-i, therefore, Ch'ü Ch'iu-pai dropped many hints as to the ultimate necessity of discarding the Chinese script in favor of Latinxua so as to enable the masses to read without going through the long and painful process of learning the characters:

> I grant that to record the common vernacular in Chinese characters will be still "a big mess," but the easy way out is surely to discard the Chinese script and to record this genuine vernacular—the speech of living men—by means of a Latin alphabet.

> As to the language of regional literature, this problem cannot be thoroughly solved until after the adoption of Latinization. We should also direct our endeavors in this direction.[13]

Ch'ü Ch'iu-pai precipitated a lively discussion among leftist writers about the importance and necessity of a literature for the masses in 1932, but he had already left for Kiangsi when the League finally promoted Latinxua in real earnest. In 1934, in response to the Nationalist educator Wang Mou-tsu's renewed advocacy of wen-yen, a group of League writers discussed the best possible way to counteract this baleful influence and, no doubt remembering the currency of the phrase *ta-chung wen-i,* hit upon the idea of promoting *ta-chung-yü* or language for and of the masses.[14] Soon the mass language movement was in full swing, and in its wake came the agitation for Sin Wenz or a new script recorded in Latinxua. Quite a number of competent linguists and liberal leaders lent their prestige to these movements. But however fervent the discussion, few writers were able to write in ta-chung-yü simply because the pai-hua then in use of necessity represented popular speech on a more literate level, and yet fewer were foolhardy enough to adopt Sin Wenz on even a moderate scale (only the covers of leftist magazines flaunted large-type Latinized words purporting to be transliterations of their Chinese titles). Besides, with the National Government still in effective control of the country, the time was not yet ripe for such grandiose enterprises. Years later Mao Tse-tung was to push Ch'ü Ch'iu-pai's programs—the manufacture of a simple literature for the masses, the utilization of folk art forms and folk speech—with much greater success. As for language reform, a simplified script has been adopted in Communist China since 1955, even though the Latinization of the script remains only a distant goal.[15]

In the face of leftist domination, many writers wisely refused to engage in quarrels with the League, in which they knew they would surely be worsted. Oppressed by both Communist and Nationalist cant, these writers were not so much interested in the making of a serious modern literature as in the maintenance of honest opinion. They adopted humor, satire, and a generally playful attitude to assert their individuality. In 1932 Lin Yutang, the leader of this group, launched a magazine of humor, *The Analects,* which proved to be an instant success. In 1934 and 1935 he published two similar magazines to promote the familiar essay and other types of personal writing: *This Human World* and *The Cosmic Wind.* These magazines constituted a sizable setback for the League insofar as they enjoyed a wide popularity even among progressive student circles. When its concerted attack on these magazines proved of little avail to curb the fashion, the League had to put out a personal magazine of its own, *T'ai Pai,* to counteract Lin Yutang's influence.[16]

In the context of Chinese literary history, the ascendancy of the familiar essay means primarily the reassertion of traditional sensibility. Despite the great popularity of fiction, the familiar essay had always had its practitioners since the Literary Revolution: the Chou brothers prominently, and also Chu Tzu-ch'ing, Yü P'ing-po, Yü Ta-fu, Kuo Mo-jo, Ping Hsin. Not only was this genre practically an offshoot of the indigenous tradition, but it answered such personal needs of writers and readers as the experimental fiction, poetry, and drama had left unsatisfied. A writer may easily embrace a new faith or philosophy in conscious defiance of his traditional upbringing, but he cannot alter his sensibility by a sheer act of the will. One therefore often detects the odd persistence of traditional moral feelings and aesthetic preferences in modern Chinese writers otherwise intellectually and even emotionally committed to a new ideology. Even with such progressive writers as Kuo Mo-jo and Pa Chin, one finds, especially in their incidental and personal writings, a nostalgia for home and childhood, a fondness for flowers and pets, and a deep-seated Confucian or Taoist piety, which are completely alien presences in their world of revolutionary action. At a period when traditional sensibility remained suppressed in its more serious literature, the writing of familiar essays was for many authors a personal necessity.

In the circle of Lin Yutang the foremost essayist was Chou Tso-jen, who had by the middle thirties chastened his voracious appetite for Western learning to become the spokesman for a refined and skeptical Confucianism. He styled himself now the Old Man of the Knowledge Studio, to indicate his great fondness for the Confucian saying: "Knowledge consists in knowing what one knows and what one doesn't know." His essays of this period, invariably commentaries and reflections on rare Chinese books which had aroused his curiosity or interest, appeal primarily to an audience learned in folklore and bibliography. They touch only indirectly on contemporary life. But they do have the modesty and humaneness of a lover of wisdom who knows his own limitations and is finally intolerant only of barbarity and dogmatism. Chou Tso-jen attracted many imitators at that time, but few equaled him in philosophical breadth and urbanity.

As a literary critic, Chou Tso-jen abides by the traditional dichotomy of *tsai-tao* (didacticism) and *yen-chih* (self-expression) only to declare his unreserved preference for the latter.[17] Lin Yutang, whose critical thinking was influenced by Croce and Spingarn, independently reached the same position. Later, they both invoked the familiar essayists of the late Ming period as patron saints of contemporary writing not only because these essayists exemplified the yen-chih tradition but because they cultivated *hsing-ling*, the unbridled human spirit. Between them Chou and Lin initiated a minor revolution in literary taste to counteract the prevalent didacticism of their times.

Didacticism is certainly the cardinal vice with leftist writers, but "self-expression," as understood by Chou and Lin, is no constructive proposal for modern Chinese literature either. With them and their disciples, it is nothing but a cult of personalism, which eschews high seriousness and prizes the essay almost to the exclusion of the more complex literary forms. If one examines Lin Yutang's Chinese writings of this period, one finds that, while his pointed, paradoxical epigrams are often brilliant, his essays written in the British familiar style are only studiedly whimsical without ever attaining the higher reaches of hsing-ling. In buttressing his position against leftist critics, Lin Yutang of course draws upon the Western heritage. But instead of serious literary or intellectual standards, he invokes only an assortment of unrelated personal enthusiasms: humor, academic freedom at Oxford University, pipe-smoking, Bernard Shaw, the factual and candid quality of articles in popular American magazines. As channels of self-expression, Lin Yutang's magazines became finally the haven of those writers who reported on personal and historical trivia and who sought only mental relaxation in their study of Chinese and Western literature. Lin Yutang did more than any other writer of his time to alienate readers from Communism, but he ended in the blind alley of hedonism, unable to provide the necessary critical incentive for the disinterested pursuit of art. Soon after the publication of his highly successful book, *My Country and My People,* in 1935, he moved to America and became a less active influence among Chinese writers.

During the period 1932–37 there were other literary magazines that were opposed to the Communist stand on literature. Often at first glance they looked deceptively leftist, because they not only drew upon leftist contributors but shared to a greater or lesser extent the same attitudes of discontent and disgust with Chinese society and the National Government. Nevertheless, their editorial policy was to foster a serious new literature rather than to engage in political propaganda.

Upon the demise of *The Short Story* in 1932, a literary monthly appeared in Shanghai which seemed likely to become its worthy successor. *Hsien Tai* or *Les Contemporains* was able to attract all the leading writers of fiction of the time: Chang T'ien-i, Mao Tun, Shen Ts'ung-wen, Lao Shê, Pa Chin, Wang Lu-yen, and others. It also published a few fairly respectable poets: Tai Wang-shu, a French-returned student, is especially remarkable for his adaptation of the metrics and imagery of the French symbolists. Its chief editor, Shih Chih-ts'un, was himself a distinguished story-writer who had developed, in such stories as "The General's Head" and "Shih Hsiu," a penchant for Freudian studies in the sexual compulsions and frustrations of famous historical and legendary characters. Under his wise critical guidance, *Les Contemporains,* while eclectic in its choice of contributors, promoted a serious and politically independent literature. Persistent Communist attacks, however, finally forced its suspension in 1934. Afterward, Shih Chih-ts'un edited two short-lived magazines, which catered more to the growing demand for the familiar essay. By that time he himself had become more of a conventional writer depicting contemporary life in the usual modes of pathos and satire than a Freudian romanticist exploring the realm of the unconscious. It is a pity that Shih Chih-ts'un never lived up to his great promise: since 1937 he seems to have withdrawn from an active literary career.

In January 1934 another important magazine, *Literature Quarterly,* appeared under the joint editorship of Cheng Chen-to and Chin I. Cheng Chen-to was a former editor of *The Short Story* and founding member of the Literary Association, and Chin I was a rising writer of fiction: between them they lined up an impressive roster of contributors ranging from such veterans as Yeh Shao-chün, Ping Hsin, and Ling Shu-hua to such promising new writers as the playwright Ts'ao Yü, the poets Pien Chih-lin and Ho Ch'i-fang, and the story-writer Wu Tsu-hsiang. From 1936 to the outbreak of the Sino-Japanese War this magazine appeared monthly as *Wen-chi Yüeh-k'an,* with Pa Chin and Chin I as editors. It continued to draw upon the same panel of writers; while the leftist note was unavoidable, it gave serious encouragement to a middle literature, steering clear of both left-wing dogmatism and right-wing levity.

Literature Quarterly was published in Peking; its younger contributors were nearly all faculty members of the universities of Peking and Tientsin: Peking, Tsing Hua, Yenching, and Nankai. In 1934 one could speak of a renascence of letters in Peking after its long eclipse by Shanghai as the center of literary activities. During the first half of the third decade, whereas writers in Shanghai were inescapably under the dominance of the Left-wing League, writers in Peking were relatively free from leftist influence. Moreover, as academics they were aware of the challenge and example of the serious modern Western writers and attempted to incorporate the more advanced techniques and strategies into their own writing. The poet Pien Chih-lin, for example, wrote a most allusive and obscure poetry making extensive use of the stream-of-consciousness method. Though largely unsuccessful, this attempt to encompass the wit and density of the best modern Western poetry deserved praise for its single-minded courage.

In 1934 the veteran story-writer Shen Ts'ung-wen emerged as a prominent leader of the Peking school by becoming editor of the Literary Supplement to the *Ta Kung Pao* of Tientsin and Shanghai. Under his guidance, this weekly publication became a serious critical journal, anti-Communist as well as avant-garde. It published some of the best prose and poetry of the new Peking writers: Pien Chih-lin, Ho Ch'i-fang, Hsiao Ch'ien, Lu Fen, Li Ni. In 1935 Hsiao Ch'ien succeeded Shen Ts'ung-wen as editor and maintained the same high standards for poetry and prose.

In Communist criticism Shen Ts'ung-wen was often vilified, in company with his friend Chu Kuang-ch'ien, an aesthetician and critic. He had studied at Edinburgh and Strasbourg; upon his return to China, he wrote several popular books on the appreciation of poetry and art. The Communist critics attacked these volumes harshly because of their absolute indifference to Marxist literary concerns and values. Actually Chu Kuang-ch'ien was only a middling aesthetician of the school of Croce, though a quite astute commentator on the contemporary literary scene. In 1937 he became editor of *Wen-hsüeh Tsa-chih* or *Literary Magazine*,[18] which, like the *Ta Kung Pao* Literary Supplement, was devoted to fostering a serious literature and criticism and was supported by the Peking writers. In the first number of the monthly Chu Kuang-ch'ien announced his critical position in an editorial called "My Hopes for This Magazine." He began by observing the parallel symptoms of "didacticism" and "withdrawal from life" in contemporary literary expression and went on to diagnose the nature of the disease as an ill-considered drive for cultural and ideological conformity. He concluded:

As for literature, we hold the same attitude as for culture and thought. The new Chinese literature is also in its tender sprouting stage; it also needs harmonious diversity and unhampered growth. We advocate more exploration and experimentation, and we do not wish a particular mode or style of writing to become the "orthodoxy." This is the experimental age of our new literature. During this experimental period we have to stand a certain amount of waste and sacrifice. We have to walk the crooked and wrong paths and we cannot expect any immediate astonishing success. But when more seeds are sown, a richer harvest will result. When different approaches and styles have received parallel development, we will be able to profitably and judiciously study and correct one another's writings. In the field of literature, for ourselves as well as for the others, clear-headed and impartial criticism is the best medicine for preserving health. Ulteriorly motivated wanton attacks and mutual praises are symptoms of a feeble artistic conscience. Without this artistic conscience it is impossible to have real artistic achievement. The approaches and styles of the others may be diametrically different from ours, but if their intention is sincere and serious, we should still show them due respect. The directions of our endeavors may differ, but all roads lead to Rome. If we earnestly strive forward, we may ultimately by our different ways build a glorious future for modern Chinese literature.[19]

Chu Kuang-ch'ien made no attempt to assail the leftist and Communist writers because he knew this would probably be unsuccessful. He pleaded with friend and foe alike to develop a mutual forbearance, so that the new literature might improve and prosper. In 1937, with such magazines as *Wen-hsüeh Tsa-chih, Wen-chi Yüeh-k'an,* and *The Cosmic Wind* competing for attention with leftist periodicals, it looked as though Chu Kuang-ch'ien's prayer might be possible of fulfillment. But, rather shortsightedly, he did not foresee the war of resistance and the opportunity it afforded the Communists to exploit literature, in the name of patriotism, for their own ends. Modern Chinese literature suffered a precipitate decline during the war years.

The decade 1928–37 began in confusion, with the Communist writers bidding recklessly for literary dictatorship. The formation of the Left-wing League signaled a major victory for them, but it also marked their willingness to temporize in a politically unfavorable hour. They attacked their opponents and launched many radical campaigns, but in the main they were content with a leftist product less openly agitational, so as to comply with censorship requirements. Meanwhile, a few groups of independent writers struggled to maintain their ground and make serious contributions to literature. As a result, this decade represents the richest literary period in modern China; fiction, especially, made big strides forward. In comparison with Lu Hsün, Yeh Shao-chün, Yü Ta-fu, and other early writers, the new writers of fiction—Mao Tun, Lao Shê, Shen Ts'ung-wen, Chang T'ien-i—are far more copious and resourceful. The majority of fictionists, of course, were too much ridden by leftist attitudes to achieve individual distinction, but the very facts that there were so many of them and that they were so uniformly industrious bespeak the vitality of the period. In the following chapters the most significant writers as well as a few representative Communist propagandists will be discussed.

CHAPTER 6

Mao Tun (1896-)

ALTHOUGH, as editor of *The Short Story*, Shen Yen-ping had served modern Chinese letters in an important capacity since 1921, he did not emerge into prominence until he published serially in that magazine in 1927–28, under the pen name of Mao Tun, his trilogy of short novels: *Disillusion, Vacillation, Pursuit.* Unlike most of his contemporaries, therefore, he seems to have taken pains to learn his craft and enlarge his experience before venturing into a career as a novelist. A native of T'ung-hsiang, Chekiang, and a graduate from a Hangchow middle school, Mao Tun studied at National Peking University for three years before financial difficulties compelled him to accept a position as proofreader at the Commercial Press in Shanghai. But he soon assumed heavier editorial responsibilities at the firm. During this formative period he read widely, especially in such authors as Dickens, Zola, Maupassant, Tolstoy, and Chekhov, and later as editor of *The Short Story* he had further opportunity to extend his knowledge of Western literature.[1] Besides a regular monthly summary of foreign literary news, he wrote a number of introductory articles on modern authors, indicating in most instances his strong interest in the literature of Poland, Hungary, Norway, Sweden, and other small European nations. He also wrote for the magazine several critical essays on the Chinese literary scene, showing an incisive if narrowly naturalistic viewpoint.

In 1923 Mao Tun resigned from the editorial board of *The Short Story* to engage in political action. Then already a staunch supporter of the insurgent Communist movement (though, like Kuo Mo-jo, he seems never to have joined the party),[2] he taught for a while in Shanghai College, a center of Marxist training staffed by noted Communist leaders. During the Northern Expedition he served as a propagandist in the Political Department of the expeditionary forces; following the capture of Hankow he became editor of the *National Daily* (Min-kuo Jih-pao) in that city. He retired from politics following the Kuomintang-Communist split in the spring of 1927 and vacationed in Kuling, a famous resort in Kiangsi, to recuperate from an illness. For the next half year or so, beginning in August, he lived in seclusion in Shanghai to write his trilogy, drawing upon his personal experiences during and after the Northern Expedition. Later published under the collective title *The Eclipse,* this work was of such scope and honesty that it cast into utter insignificance the few novels of the first period by such authors as Wang T'ung-chao, Chang Tzu-p'ing, and Chiang Kuang-tz'u. While Mao Tun was vacationing in Japan in the latter half of 1928, he found himself acclaimed in China as the foremost novelist of his time.

Following the success of *The Eclipse,* Mao Tun wrote five studies of young women caught in the conflict of old and new, later collected under the title *The Wild Roses.* In 1929 he published serially in *The Short Story* another outstanding novel, *Rainbow,* which despite its obvious Communist dialectic reveals a new psychological depth. Two negligible and strongly Communist-colored novelettes about student life followed in 1931 and 1932: *Three Men* and *The Road.*

His next major novel, *The Twilight* (1933), is a monumental, often powerful but frequently boring, piece of naturalistic fiction; it has been generally regarded by Communist critics as his masterpiece. On a much smaller scale, *Polygonal Relations* (1935) depicts the financial panic in 1934 as it affects a small city near Shanghai. From 1928 to 1937, Mao Tun wrote also three volumes of stories besides *The Wild Roses;* most of them were later included in his *Collected Short Stories,* published in two volumes by the Kaiming Press. The present chapter will mainly discuss *The Eclipse, Rainbow, The Twilight,* and a few of the more important short stories; a later chapter will deal with Mao Tun's career after the outbreak of the Sino-Japanese War.

The Eclipse spans the turbulent years of 1926–28. In *Disillusion,* the slightest of the three, Mao Tun introduces his characteristic technique of evaluating experience through the contrasting sensibilities of virginal idealism and cynical sophistication. The heroine Ching, a girl of small-town gentility studying in a Shanghai college, is eager to achieve good but readily discouraged in her contact with the uglier aspects of life, while her friend Hui, who has studied in France and seen the world, can be regarded as the same person a few years hence, a woman who has been hurt by life but assumes a nonchalant gaiety to disguise her basic anxiety and thwarted idealism.

On the first anniversary of the May Thirtieth Incident, the two girls are escorted to a movie by Pao-su, Ching's classmate and persistent suitor. Finding in Hui an apparently easier prey and more amiable companion, Pao-su now shifts his attention to her, though she only trifles with him. Feeling sorry for his new condition, Ching foolishly yields to his importunate demands and discovers too late that he is not only a philanderer but a government agent. Delirious with sorrow and anger, Ching seeks a rest cure in a hospital, only to be stricken with scarlet fever. During her convalescence, she enjoys the visits of her college friends, who all exhibit boundless enthusiasm over the initial successes of the Northern Expedition. She soon joins them in Wuhan, the revolutionary capital.

Despite the fervor and excitement which she has witnessed at the initiation of the second Northern Expedition at Nanhu (April 20, 1927), she is appalled by the general irresponsibility and frivolity of her co-workers and unable to immerse herself in the revolutionary task. With the supplanting of the traditional ethic by a foreign ideology, a false gaiety has informed the life between the sexes and this, in turn, has engendered corruption in the political life. As her friend Hui amusedly adjusts herself to this environment, Ching changes from job to job, unhappy and filled with self-reproach over her inability to follow the accepted pattern of behavior. She finally installs herself as a nurse in the officers' hospital in Kiukiang and falls ecstatically in love with a patient, Ch'iang Meng. As a futurist, Ch'iang represents a perversion of the revolutionary ideal: he lives for excitement only. Nevertheless, upon his recovery the couple have a brief, delicious interlude of happiness in Kuling, oblivious of the war and corruption. But Ch'iang Meng is soon afterward recalled to military duty and Ching again faces a period of vacuity.

Disillusion registers only peripherally the revolutionary experience. Nevertheless, what Ching stands for is the discrepancy between individual effort, which avails little, and the general prevalence of anarchy. In Mao Tun's scheme, the young participants in the Northern Expedition are fired by the dual ideal of personal emancipation and patriotic service. Ching's failure to realize either is partly a matter of sensibility; but more important, it is also the inescapable reaction to a state of affairs that are a caricature of purposeful action.

In *Vacillation,* Mao Tun explores further the chasm between revolutionary ardor and revolutionary reality. In

January 1927, the Kuomintang-Communist forces have captured a Hupeh *hsien* on the bank of the Yangtze, a small town of gentry and shopkeepers. Feeling insecure under the new government, Hu Kuo-kuang, an unscrupulous member of the reactionary gentry, shrewdly obtains the support of his friends and relatives to win election as a member of the newly formed trade union. He pretends to be an ardent revolutionary and stirs hatred and fear among the apprentices and neighboring peasants by his advocacy of extreme reforms. The local Kuomintang representative, Fang Lo-lan, can do nothing to cope with this growing menace. A man of tortured conscience, he is further paralyzed by his wife's silent reproach of and increasing alienation from him under the suspicion that he has formed a liaison with his co-worker Sun Wu-yang. Obsessed with his marital crisis, Fang Lo-lan is utterly powerless to prevent the demagogues both within and outside the Kuomintang from turning the proposed reforms topsy-turvy.

A party inspector from the provincial capital fails to detect Hu Kuo-kuang's duplicity. As a result he grows even bolder and turns the town into a complete chaos by liberating all nuns, widows, and concubines from their religious and marital bondage. When another inspector finally unmasks him, it is too late. By May 1927 the right-wing Kuomintang forces have begun to purge Communist and radical elements in the party. Hu Kuo-kuang now shrewdly allies himself with the ascendant group and unleashes the fury of terrorism among the townspeople. Many party workers are brutally mutilated or killed, while Fang Lo-lan, his wife Mei-li, and Sun Wu-yang barely make their escape to a nearby decrepit convent.

Hu Kuo-kuang is not merely a demagogue and voluptuary; he is the power-driven man bent on self-aggrandizement, a frequent protagonist in naturalistic fiction. But vital as his presence in the novel is, it is his antagonist Fang Lo-lan who exemplifies the title theme *tung-yao,* vacillation. In both his

private and his political life he is the frustrated liberal idealist unable to cope with strong tradition and unreasoned radicalism. Mao Tun ably mirrors his futility in his marital
crisis: Mei-li, bitterly unhappy in her inability to adjust to
the present and step boldly into the unknown future, stands
for tradition, while, like Hui, Sun Wu-yang is the modern
nihilist who, having shed traditional manners and pieties,
is merely carried into the vortex of the Revolution. In this
symbolic scheme, the decrepit convent in which Fang Lo-
lan and the two women finally seek refuge stands for an
old and decayed China. At the very end of the novel Mei-li
has a nightmarish vision of the fall of this structure, whose
crash stamps out any sign of resurgent life underneath.

In the political sphere Fang Lo-lan is caught between the
reactionary demagoguery of a Hu Kuo-kuang and the impotence and blundering of the party personnel who have
likewise abetted tyranny in the name of reform. On the eve
of the massacre Fang listens to his conscience accusing himself and his colleagues:

What has been done since January needs a final reckon-
ing! You have deprived people of their livelihood and
provoked their hatred; now is the time for your retribu-
tion. You have resorted to so much oppression that
out of sheer desperation people have no choice but to
fight back. Didn't you know that animals at bay still
fight? You have created countless new enemies out of
the so-called village despots and bad squires; you have
driven out the old-style village despots only to replace
them with new-style land ruffians who thrive under the
revolutionary flag; you wanted freedom, and get only
despotism. More severe measures of repression, even if
they succeed, could only create another kind of despotism, beyond your control. Let me tell you, be mag-
nanimous, be moderate! Only magnanimity and modera-
tion can prevent this dreaded vengeance and killing.

What good would it do to shoot five or six men? It could only lead to vengeance and killing on a much larger scale.[3]

It is passages like the above, ringing with the accents of disturbing honesty and compassion, that make *Vacillation,* for Chinese mainlanders today more than ever, a work of crucial political importance. In spite of his intellectual repudiation of Fang Lo-lan as a weakling, Mao Tun has presented in his hero's agonizing debates with his conscience a case against tyranny which is finally irrefutable. Although one cannot be sure whether, at the time of the composition of the trilogy, Mao Tun has consciously followed the axioms that the will is a necessarily corrupting agent and that politics directed toward the achievement of an abstract good can only turn out to be evil if it provides no safeguards against evil passions, the pessimism of *The Eclipse* does seem to be imbued with an imaginative apprehension of these truths. The frustration, despondency, and nihilism of many college youths in *Disillusion,* and especially in *Vacillation,* attest not only to the evils of the old order but to the woeful inadequacy of radical politics when not guided by charity and intelligence. It is little wonder that the Communist critics chose to attack the trilogy upon its publication, for its thesis undermines the very foundation of Communism. But apparently Mao Tun, a fellow Communist, wrote better than he knew: in his defense he can only reiterate that his ideological orthodoxy should never be questioned insofar as his trilogy is merely an objective chronicle of its times.

Pursuit begins with a reunion scene of the disillusioned veterans of the Revolution at their alumni club in Shanghai. Saddened at the full establishment of the "counterrevolution," these men and women still cling to the hope of achieving something constructive for themselves and for society. With quite a number, of course, this desire is at odds with a decadent nihilism. A prominent representative of this group is Miss Chang Ch'iu-liu, who re-enacts the roles of Hui and Sun Wu-yang with even greater bitterness. At the party, she takes a fancy to her old classmate Shih Hsün, who has changed beyond recognition since his college days. He is now a physical ruin and a suicidal maniac. Shortly after the reunion he attempts to take his own life, but Chang Ch'iu-liu nurses him back to a semblance of health. Together they live wildly, and at a beach party he finally dies a ghastly death due to excessive sexual and alcoholic indulgence. Chang Ch'iu-liu, meanwhile, has contracted syphilis from him and becomes even more psychotic. But she is not alone in her misery: quite a number of her friends have either been shot or have degenerated into streetwalkers.

At the reunion party is also Chang Man-ch'ing, who used to be Chang Ch'iu-liu's admirer in college days. Now he is a changed man, cautious and narrow in vision, pinning his happiness on being a good high school teacher and on his impending marriage to Chu Chin-ju, a fellow teacher. The latter, who seems to him all pliant sweetness, turns out after their marriage to be an impossible shrew. She is so limited in her interests and so concerned with security that her husband cannot maintain even a semblance of his earlier idealism.

Still another classmate, Wang Chung-chao, who attends on the same day the wild beach party and Chang Man-ch'ing's wedding, has reason to congratulate himself. After all, the misfortunes he has witnessed could not likely overtake him. Having recently won permission, after a bitter fight with the chief editor, to run his local news page with a free hand, he looks forward to an exciting newspaper career, and besides, he is soon to marry a charming and understanding girl who is not at all like Chu Chin-ju. But a few days later a telegram reaches him with the disconcerting news that his fiancée has met with a car accident that will disfigure her permanently.

This ending, coming as it does upon a train of disasters,

is admittedly a melodramatic trick, and the novel is in this respect pretentious. But Mao Tun encompasses the theme of futility at the same time with a richness of psychological understanding that redeems somewhat the more obvious faults. The story of Chang Man-ch'ing and Chu Chin-ju, especially, is a miniature drama of marital tension and frustrated idealism that suggests, however faintly, the story of Lydgate and Rosamond in *Middlemarch.* In the trilogy as a whole, and especially in *Pursuit,* Mao Tun presents a vision of nihilism akin in spirit to the early novels of Hemingway, Huxley, and Waugh. Just as the latter writers scrutinized the amoral consequences of World War I and a belated liberation from Victorianism, Mao Tun, in his more naturalistic fashion, makes a similar inquiry into the effects upon Chinese youth of the miscarriage of the Kuomintang-Communist coalition, and of the decline of Confucian authority in the realm of conduct. Despite its florid colors and its occasional lapses in taste, *The Eclipse* was the first work in modern Chinese fiction to interpret contemporary history and to apprehend reality in terms that transcend the simple formulas of sentimental didacticism. It is a work fraught with an awareness of fundamental human limitations.

Rainbow, Mao Tun's next novel, is in many respects his finest. Even though the novelist, as a result of his debate with his critics in 1928, has become a more orthodox Communist and adopted the more conventional Marxist critique of Chinese society, he demonstrates here an even surer skill in his rendition of psychological reality. For the new work he again adopts the feminine angle of observation; but unlike Ching in *Disillusion* the heroine of *Rainbow* is a complex character: she is, in fact, the author's most ambitious and fascinating creation. Basically a girl of traditional sensibility, Mei is less easily repulsed by reality, greedier for experience, and more serious in her search for the meaning of life. The story chronicles her quest for meaning between the significant dates of May 4, 1919, and May 30, 1925.

The novel consists of a prologue and three parts. In Part I Mei, a high school girl in Chengtu, Szechwan, is trying to liberate herself from the shackles of tradition. Disappointed in her weakling lover Wei-yü, she finally agrees to marry her cousin Liang Yü-ch'un, at the insistence of her father, who is beholden to him for financial help. A shopowner without the benefit of modern education, Liang tries his best to please his bride but only succeeds in alienating her affections completely. Mei finally leaves her husband to look for Wei-yü in another city. But he proves as disappointing as ever.

In Part II, Mei strikes out for independence as a teacher in a progressive grammar school in Luchow, Szechwan. Much against her will, she finds herself steadily drawn into a life of intrigue and frivolity among her fellow teachers. She is disgusted with herself, but at the same time she cannot help enjoying a new sense of power in her manifest popularity with a large train of suitors and sycophants. She finally excites the interest of a division commander, a typical Republican general who talks reforms but retains at home a harem of concubines. He installs Mei in the decorous and highly compromising position of tutor to his children.

In Part III, Mei embarks upon a new life in Shanghai. She meets there some of her old friends who have become Communists. Among them she feels the inadequacy of her individualism, which hasn't brought her any genuine happiness through the years. She feels especially piqued and inferior in the presence of Liang Kang-fu, a Communist leader among factory workers. For the first time in her life she has met a man who is apparently indifferent to her charms, and yet he is such a dedicated worker for his cause that he compels her admiration. For a time Mei hesitates to commit herself to Communism, but in the general excitement over the Communist-instigated May Thirtieth demonstrations, she emerges as a new person, haranguing in streets and defying the police.

In Part I of his novel Mao Tun seems to have caught once for all the conflict, animosity, and disgust implicit in many family-arranged marriages. In comparison, all the subsequent novels on this theme appear maudlin and superfluous: they all too patently invoke the tear-jerking formula of anti-feudalism. Their characters are predictably stereotyped: the heroine who has married against her will and languishes in sorrow, the tyrannical father, the sentimental and ineffectual lover, the inconsiderate and often moronic husband. But surely, even in the case of the worst-matched couples under the Chinese marital system, there must be matters of positive human interest to engage the attention of a serious novelist. The psychological tensions existing between a newly married couple who have been practically strangers should, I think, challenge him to uncover a new realm of sensibility and emotion practically untouched by traditional Chinese novelists. *Rainbow* is a pointer in the right direction.

A faithful reader of *New Youth* Magazine, Mei knows *A Doll's House* by heart. As she contemplates her impending marriage, she sees herself in the guise of Christine Linde, to her a woman of much greater courage than Nora. Unafraid of new experience, Mei is confident that she will not be enslaved by her marital bond. Yet when she finds herself surprisingly weak and yielding in the arms of her husband, she can only reproach her inferior will power. The only way to save her pride, under this humiliating circumstance, is to detest her husband. She soon finds cause enough in his jealousy of Wei-yü and in her discovery of his prenuptial dalliance with prostitutes.

A product of his upbringing and environment, Liang Yü-ch'un is a rather coarse person, but as Mao Tun depicts him, he is not at all unsympathetic, tragic even in his determination to win back his wife. During their separation, he pleads with her in a speech of touching eloquence:

You have your reason and I'm not saying you are wrong. But look, can you put the blame on me? At thirteen, I worked at the Hung Yüan pawnshop as an apprentice, I never had a warm coat or a full meal, I swept the floor, fetched water and emptied toilet bowls, I was abused and beaten: what hardships have I not endured! Like a simmering pot I was waiting and waiting; waiting for what? I thought I was also a human being, having the same nose, eyes, ears, hands, and feet as any other man, and was entitled to some happiness. I thought then I could do hard work with my hands and see with my eyes, and why should I be an apprentice all my life, poor all my life? In those days I suffered beatings and scoldings in the daytime, but at night I would dream that I also had a shop of my own and that I had a good woman for wife and enjoyed life like any other man. Now with naked hands I have established something for myself; the shop I now own is bigger than Hung Yüan and it means every drop of blood and sweat I've shed. I have no parents, brothers, or sisters; when I had some money, I wanted only a good woman, because my heart was lonely. I wanted only a good woman to share happiness with me. When I saw you I was very pleased, and I thought it wasn't for nothing that I had struggled for half of my life. But now all this looks like a dream. My heart is also flesh, and do you honestly think I can't suffer? Other people have what they want; I am also a man, and am I really asking too much? Yes, I whored and gambled, but what man doesn't whore and gamble? Why should I be singled out for such severe punishment? Even if someone had committed an enormous crime, he would be given a chance to repent; why should I be denied the chance to repent and mend myself? You think your life is ruined, but what about me? Do you think I am happy? Look, you are a reasonable person and can you put all the blame on me? [4]

This impassioned materialistic argument jolts Mei's self-righteous idealism. As Liang Yü-ch'un persists in his post-marital courtship, Mei feels in danger of yielding to his power:

Every evening when he came home, he would always bring a big bag of fruit or delicacies to old Dr. Mei's room; another small package he would bring to Mei herself. He would quietly place it on the desk and then walk away. Sometimes he would also sit down to talk a little, usually about something inconsequential. He also frequently bought books for Mei; he would buy every book and magazine whose title bore the character "new." Thus *A New Talk on Hygiene, A New Way to Play Baseball,* or even *A New Discourse on Sexual Intercourse* would be thrown in the heap with copies of *New Youth* and *New Tide* (Renaissance) magazines, which often made Mei laugh without ceasing. Probably he had seen Mei subscribe to a magazine called *The Student Tide;* once he bought all the books published by the Commercial Press and the Chung Hua Book Company bearing on their titles the character "tide," and packed them in a large rush-bag. His brow covered with sweat, he held it up with both hands and walked over to Mei and said:

"Look, it's quite a load of books here; there must be some you'll love to read."

Of this kind of solicitude from Liang Yü-ch'un, Mei was more afraid than if he had applied high-handed measures out of anger. Especially when she realized that Liang Yü-ch'un was to some extent genuinely sincere and wasn't trying to fool her, she was plunged into a quandary. She felt as if invisible threads, soft but strong, were insidiously tying up her heart. Her heart wanted to break away from these ties, but she had no way of loosening them. She was a woman and she had the traditional feminine weakness of being touched by emotion.[5]

In delineating the marital tensions between Mei and Liang Yü-ch'un, Mao Tun achieves his best writing, about a hundred pages of sustained psychological drama.

Rainbow is by design an allegory of recent Chinese intellectual history. In Part I, which encompasses the initial period of the cultural revolution, Mei represents the finest type of Ibsenian individualism pulling away from the fascinating hold of tradition, in the person of Liang Yü-ch'un. Her lover Wei-yü represents, oddly enough, Tolstoyan defeatism. (*New Youth*, while introducing many Western thinkers and writers, inevitably distorts them to suit its own intellectual scheme; thus the later philosophy of Tolstoy is supposed to be that of abnegation, and is accordingly deplored.) Part II of the novel dramatizes the second intellectual phase: the supposed bankruptcy of individualism in the early twenties, and its degeneration into libertinism and irresponsibility. The progressive school where Mei is situated is a microcosm of transitional China; her fellow teachers constitute a variant of the lost generation, abusing their newly earned liberty in every kind of frivolous pursuit and political intrigue. The division commander, cloaking his ambition and sensuality under reformist guise, is representative of the vested power groups fishing in the muddy water of confusion. Partially contaminated by these people, Mei is still able to sum them up:

> These people, the parvenus buoyed upon the new ideological tide, how are they fit to reform education and change society? They get their bowl of rice by shouting "Down with the old morality," just as their predecessors got theirs by quoting Confucius and the

> *Book of Poetry,* or just as the division commander, "duly aware of my responsibility in promoting, etc.," gets his by doing the job of a warlord.[6]

As a record of Mei's involvement with a particular phase of decadence, Part II is a much less arresting drama than Part I, but it is still the same kind of fiction dictated by the author's painfully honest search for truth as he knows it. By contrast Part III, which depicts China's readiness to embrace the Marxist faith, is altogether inferior. In rejecting feudalism and individualism for Communism, Mei is representative of a significant segment of Chinese youth of the time, and there is no reason why her conversion to the more persuasive rhetoric of Marxism should not prove as exciting a subject for study as her previous ideological entanglements. But in this section of the novel an insidious propagandist note has crept in and the texture of reality is much altered for the worse.

With reference to the problem of belief, T. S. Eliot once asserted the primacy of rational assent over emotional acceptance. Because of the shallow intellectual basis of Communism, it has been the invariable strategy of the Communist novelists to substitute a sentimental appeal to their readers for the search of truth, especially an appeal to the feeling of guilt among the bourgeoisie. Although elementary Communist dialectic plays a part in the conversations of Part III, the transformation of Mei into a dedicated Communist takes place primarily under the influence of Liang Kang-fu. The latter is a well-nigh perfect instrument of Marxist action, but as a character of fiction he does not inhabit the same world with Mei or Liang Yü-ch'un. He is the stereotype hero who has dominated Chinese revolutionary fiction since Chiang Kuang-tz'u: a man of iron will and perfect psychological economy, absolutely imperturbable to either feminine guile or enemy threat. By literary genealogy he is the descendant of the Byronic hero, with his mystery, solitude, and defiance of society; he accounts for much of the shabby romanticism in Communist fiction. *Rainbow* fails in the end, therefore, not because Mao Tun plays advocate to the Communist cause but because he has failed to present his defense in the psychological and realistic manner of the earlier portion of the novel. The ring of intellectual and emotional honesty is no longer there.

In *The Twilight,* Mao Tun continues with his chronicle of modern China. A most ambitious portrayal of China in the year 1930, the novel is a work of tremendous research, impeccable in documentation, larded with allusions to topical figures, and crammed with political and economic facts. But all this adds up to a work that is quite often irritating and boring; insofar as it is still a work of some tragic insight, it evinces no technical advancement beyond *The Eclipse* and *Rainbow.* One observes a marked reduction in the range of sympathy and the predominance of the naturalistic methods of caricature and sensationalist description. In the two earlier novels, the notes of caricature and eroticism are on the whole consonant with the nihilistic mood. In *The Twilight,* one feels, even the sensitive and cynical types of female characters, by which Mao Tun has done so well, have degenerated into caricature: the sensibility of the novelist has definitely coarsened.

With the expulsion of the Communists in 1927 the right-wing Kuomintang Government could never again rally intellectuals to its support, nor could it for a long time cope effectively with dissident power groups. In 1930 the Kuomintang politician Wang Ching-wei, in alliance with the warlord Feng Yü-hsiang, was in armed revolt against the Government in North China; Communists were brewing trouble everywhere, instigating petty peasant uprisings as well as strikes among workers in industrial cities. In July the Communist forces under General P'eng Tê-huai occupied Changsha, the capital of Hunan. It is against this turbulent background that the drama of *The Twilight* is unfolded in Shanghai, where native industry suffers a severe recession and the stock market characteristically responds to national turmoil with an upsurge in wild speculation. Wu Sun-fu, the hero of the novel, is a powerful industrialist with a strong faith in national capitalism. He has been doing well by his silk factory and his investments in his home town in Chekiang, which, under his patronage, is becoming modernized. But as the story opens, a Communist uprising in his home town has virtually wiped out his revenues from that quarter, and his silk factory is limping along under the pressure of recession. Wu is nevertheless far from being pessimistic: the insolvency of many smaller mills has given him the rare chance to annex them at minimal cost and thereby consolidate his silk empire. He doesn't realize, however, that it takes more cash than he can command to start these factories, and they soon prove to be a huge liability.

Wu now plunges into speculation on the stock market. His initial ventures are successful, but they offer little solace in view of the protracted nature of Communist-organized strikes at his factory, which he is no longer able to break. Moreover, Chao Po-t'ao, a sensualist and financier amply backed by foreign capital, is clearly the dominant figure at the stock exchange; as a national capitalist, Wu is hardly his rival. But after Chao has insulted him with an offer to buy out his interests and make him a subordinate, Wu, always contemptuous of compradorism, is determined to challenge Chao's supremacy. In the final contest at the stock exchange, he pours in all his resources to sell short as against the bullish practice of his opponent; he could have won the day but for the fact that his trusted partner and brother-in-law, Tu Chu-chai, has without his knowledge thrown in his resources on Chao's side. Wu goes bankrupt.

A fuller account of the novel would have to attend to a welter of subplots: the Communist uprising at the home town and the resultant panic of the Kuomintang personnel, the strikes at the factory and Wu's repeated attempts to break them, the antics of the upper-bourgeois youth and the comic tribulations of the feudal-minded older generation stranded in Shanghai. But Wu Sun-fu, of course, is the central figure; an attempt to assess his character and appraise its meaning will go a long way toward clarifying Mao Tun's attitude toward his material and the structure of the novel.

On one level, Wu is the conventional tragic hero defeated by overpowering fate or circumstance, a familiar figure in the naturalistic fiction of Zola, Norris, and Dreiser. But on another level, as a man fired with the zeal to industrialize China by use of native capital, Wu is a pathetic, blind Oedipus, unredeemed even after his decline and fall because he has never heard or heeded the Marxian oracle. His personal tragedy is embedded in his larger failure to perceive certain historical forces, whose eventual assertion alone is the guarantee of China's salvation. Insofar as rampant feudalism and imperialism foredoom any attempt to develop national capital, Wu's grandiose gesture is utterly futile in his unawareness of the necessity for a complete overhaul of Chinese economy and politics.

In the degree that the other characters acquiesce in Wu's kind of blindness but lack his nobility of purpose, they are subject to caricature. Insofar as caricature is a legitimate literary technique, one should not condemn its use outright merely for the suspicion that it subserves, as in the present instance, the aims of Communist propaganda. Barring its intrusion upon the tragic realm, there is little reason why a Marxist satire of bourgeois life should not be as good as a satire written from a Christian or Confucian viewpoint: what matters is the perspicacity of observation and the genuineness of the attendant feelings of hatred or scorn. Mao Tun is precluded, however, from any degree of satiric success, because one feels his supercilious attitude toward the bourgeoisie lacks the accent of passion or conviction. The self-tormenting honesty of *The Eclipse* and *Rainbow* stems from the fact that Mao Tun at once clings to and rejects the middle class. In *The Twilight* he tries merely to be aloof and superior, with the disastrous result that most of his bourgeois characters are only puppets, now and again occupying the stage with their expected patter and lovemaking. Li Yü-t'ing alone, with his continual jeremiad, attains a certain degree of pathos as the spokesman for the doomed bourgeois intellectual. But the poetaster Fan Po-wen, the returned student Tu Hsin-t'o, the sensualist Miss Chang Su-su, the young wife of Wu Sun-fu with her romantic notions inculcated in missionary schools, and the others of the younger set merely parade through the novel without attaining comic individuality.

Mao Tun is more successful in his caricature of feudal-minded characters. Possibly because of a genuine abhorrence, he draws them in firm, bold outlines and often achieves the effect of grotesquerie. The small-town squire, Tseng Ts'ang-hai, is especially well drawn: his joy in welcoming his rascally son as a newly elected member of the Kuomintang and his subsequent panic at discovering that his young grandson has sacrilegiously urinated upon the new heirloom, a copy of the *San Min Chu I*, are uproarious bits of malicious comedy. The provincial squire Feng Yün-ch'ing, who has converted his land into cash in order to dabble in speculation in Shanghai, is also a sound caricature. A slave to his ninth concubine, he nevertheless has no compunction in sending his only daughter to bed with Chao Po-t'ao so as to obtain a tip from the latter about the stock market, but the daughter is so stupid that her information serves only to ruin her father completely.

A more telling symbol of the feudal order is Wu Sun-fu's old father, who expires at the end of the first chapter, upon reaching his son's Shanghai mansion. In fear of the impending trouble in his home town, Wu has moved his father and younger sister to the big city. A complete stranger to the capitalistic way of life, the old man clings desperately to his copy of the Taoist bible *T'ai-shang Kan-ying P'ien* (commonly known in English as the *Book of Punishments and Rewards*) as he experiences his first ride in an automobile through the nocturnal glitter of the metropolis. But the strong perfume of his daughters and daughters-in-law proves too much for him and he suffocates in the car. In pointing up the abysmal contrast between feudalist and capitalist China, the death of the old man is grotesque but justified. And the copy of the Taoist bible runs through the novel as a feudal motif in Mao Tun's dissection of capitalist society. Wu's country sister, Hui-fang, alternately hugs and spurns it. Unlike the other women characters in the novel, she retains the sensitivity of Mao Tun's earlier heroines; a product of strict feminine upbringing, she feels at once fascination and revulsion toward the gay life of her city cousins. Finally, in a fit of depression, she shuts herself up in her room, chanting from the Taoist bible and inhaling the aroma of incense sticks. But she is presently dragged away to a picnic, and irrevocably to the frivolous life of amorous dalliance. She is still enjoying herself at the picnic when a sudden shower dashes through the windows of her room and drowns out her earlier existence:

> Around five o'clock it began to rain; it was a slanting type of rain. At Wu's residence the men and women servants hurriedly closed the windows facing east. The pair of windows in the fourth *hsiao-chieh's* room also admitted rain, but somehow nobody came around to shut them. The downpour was now heavier; driven by the east wind, the rain darted through the windows and made the *sa-sa-sa* sound. That precious *Book of Punishments and Rewards* was on the desk against the windows and it was now soaked with water. The red rulings on the pages of fine Hsüan-ch'eng paper began to blur out. Water overflowed from the Hsüan-tê censer [made during the reign of the Ming Emperor Hsüan-tê] onto

the desk, soaking that bunch of precious incense sticks. The incense sticks also began to melt, turning into a wax-colored, thin, and fragrant paste trickling near the *Book of Punishments and Rewards.*[7]

The concrete imagery, the symbolic embodiment of the end of an old order in the desecration of its tools of worship, indicates a novelist of considerable craftsmanship and imagination. *The Twilight,* however, with its pronounced naturalistic bias, offers few glimpses of Mao Tun as the impassioned artist; he is primarily the sociological painter of his times. One is continually under the impression that characters are drawn merely to fit the stereotypes of Marxist vilification: even Wu Sun-fu, a rather coarse man, lacks the moral dimension of Fang Lo-lan or Mei. And one may say of the whole novel that, in spite of its panoramic coverage of people and events, it is little kindled with moral insight. The socio-economic material, like any other material for fiction, is inert in itself; it becomes alive only when the creative imagination orders it into an organic whole. Mao Tun has in the novel substituted orthodox Communist criticism for personal vision.

In view of the scarcity of good fiction, *The Twilight* still ranks among major contemporary Chinese novels. It is only in terms of what Mao Tun could have achieved that one pronounces it a big failure. The misdirected ambition to attempt a thorough investigation of Chinese society indicates its author's obsession with scientism, Marxist as well as naturalistic, from which he can no longer, except in rare interludes of creative felicity, free himself.

As a prominent man of letters, Mao Tun has written besides fiction a large body of essays, criticism, and literary and political journalism. The personal essays collected in such volumes as *Sketches and Notes* and *Impressions, Reflections, and Reminiscences* seem to have been dashed off in a hurry;

they cannot compare for style and wit with those of Chou Tso-jen and Lu Hsün. But as a literary critic, Mao Tun showed from the first a serious concern with modern Chinese writing: a representative early piece, "Naturalism and Modern Chinese Fiction," contains sober criticism of the degeneracy of traditional fiction as well as the sentimental excesses of the new. The two eloquent essays in self-defense, "From Kuling to Tokyo" and "On Reading *Ni Huan-chih*," as has been earlier noted, bespeak an impatience with proletarian cant and a preference for petty-bourgeois subject matter, even though they follow in the main the Communist line of argument. Since the early thirties, Mao Tun has followed rather faithfully the party line in criticism, but until the outbreak of the Sino-Japanese War he still maintained his standing as a discerning critic of his contemporaries. His studies of the members of the Literary Association are especially noted for their intelligence and personal warmth.[8]

As a short-story writer, Mao Tun has touched on practically every phase of contemporary Chinese life. Rather similar in tone to *The Eclipse*, *The Wild Roses* studies the vacillation and exasperation of the younger generation as it grapples with ugly reality. The heroine of "Creation" feels compelled to leave her husband and mentor because she has advanced beyond his noncommittal intellectual dilettantism to a positive socialist position. In contrast, the heroine of "Suicide" has to kill herself after she has been made pregnant by a revolutionary youth; an old-fashioned girl, she has not advanced intellectually far enough to defy social ostracism. In "A Girl," a small-town beauty finds that, after her family has suffered several reverses, her once abject suitors now snub her. Her earlier disgust with men consequently turns into pronounced misanthropy. All these stories in the volume, while rather conventional in theme and ideology for their period, share the languorous feeling and ornate style characteristic of Mao Tun's early novels.

With the enthronement of Socialist Realism among leftist

writers in the early thirties, Mao Tun turns his attention to the peasants and small shopkeepers under Kuomintang oppression. He wrote during that period a handful of proletarian stories which are considerably better than similar stories by less competent hands; but they, too, fail to transcend the perplexing problem with which proletarian fiction is saddled: how to explore the enormity of oppression and destitution without reducing human beings into mere pawns of callous fortune. The social evil depicted in proletarian fiction is usually of such weight and magnitude that the characters caught under it cannot possibly counteract it in any human manner; hence no tragedy. Unless he resorts to the formulas of mass uprising and revolt, the proletarian writer can only expose and protest. He cannot encompass any significant human action. In the long story "Lin's Store," for example, Mao Tun does his level best to chronicle the tribulations of a family under oppression, but he is unable to present at the same time any matter of serious moral interest. It is to Mao Tun's credit that the Lins, victims of Kuomintang rapacity, appear as likable, decent people, but the meaning of their tale is predictably shallow.

The one story which comes nearest to transcending the inherent limitations of the proletarian genre is "Spring Silkworms," Mao Tun's best story and perhaps the outstanding achievement in Chinese proletarian fiction. During a typical silkworm-raising season, the old peasant Lao T'ung-pao and his family strain their every effort to care for the worms and to provide them with enough mulberry leaves. As a result, they reap an abundant crop of cocoons. But before they can rejoice, they learn to their dismay that most silk factories have shut down as a consequence of armed conflict between Chinese and Japanese in the Shanghai area (the January Twenty-eighth Incident of 1932) and there is no demand for cocoons. Lao T'ung-pao's family sell the crop at a great loss and are much the worse off for their season's worry and work.

As a Communist commentary on the Chinese scene, "Spring Silkworms" shows the bankruptcy of the peasantry under the dual pressure of imperialist aggression and traditional usury, and as such the story is usually praised. Yet this standard interpretation hardly explains its strength and appeal: almost in spite of himself, one feels that Mao Tun is celebrating in his tale the dignity of labor. Raising silkworms in the traditional Chinese manner is a primitive but exacting form of endeavor that calls for love, patience, and the favor of the Deity; it is almost a form of religious ritual. Mao Tun is able to recapture this religious spirit and to invest the family, and especially the old man T'ung-pao, with the kind of unquestioned piety habitual with Chinese peasants with their unsparing diligence and unfaltering trust in a beneficent Heaven. Although it is Mao Tun's articulate intention to discredit this kind of feudal mentality, his loving portrayal of good peasants at their customary tasks transforms the supposed Communist tract into a testament of human dignity.

As if dissatisfied with the ambiguity of "Spring Silkworms," Mao Tun wrote a sequel entitled "Autumn Harvest" to drive home his Marxist message. Following the silkworm season, Lao T'ung-pao has a siege of illness which leaves him much weakened. But he still believes in moral rectitude and honest work in spite of his increasing poverty. He is much horrified when he discovers that his younger son, To-to-t'ou, has joined the other peasants in looting the granaries. Comes summer and he again rallies his family to the task of planting rice. In spite of a threatened drought and the contraction of more debts, the crop is good. But, expectedly, the price for rice has dropped and a summer's work brings the family nearer starvation. "The bitter experience with spring silkworms had given Lao T'ung-pao a long bout of illness; the bitter experience with autumn harvest now cost him his life. He was dying: his tongue was already too rigid to form speech but his eyes were still very bright. They glanced toward To-to-t'ou, as if saying, 'Strange! I would never have thought you could be right.' " [9]

In "Autumn Harvest," as in *The Twilight* and his other fiction since *Rainbow,* one sees Mao Tun's conscientious Marxist approach to Chinese problems. Lao T'ung-pao, the eternal Chinese peasant, repudiates his way of life on his deathbed and yields his place to To-to-t'ou, the new enlightened rebel in possession of a more advanced class consciousness. The triumph of this generation of rebels is the prophetic message, reiterated over and over by leftist writers, and Mao Tun proves no exception. But in command of a more acute awareness of fact and history, he is much less facile and seemingly incapable of overindulgence in revolutionary optimism. Even though a later chapter will show (with the exception of one novel) the steady deterioration of a powerful imagination in the service of propaganda, Mao Tun is without doubt the greatest Communist novelist in modern China and ranks among the other great writers of the period.

CHAPTER 7

Lao Shê (1899-1966)

LAO SHÊ and Mao Tun, the two major novelists of the second decade, offer in many ways an interesting contrast. Mao Tun uses an ornate literary vocabulary; Lao Shê at his best writes a pure Peking vernacular. Using the time-honored test of Northern and Southern literary sensibilities, we may say that Lao Shê represents the North, individualist, forthright, humorous, and Mao Tun, the more feminine South, romantic, sensuous, melancholic. Mao Tun is distinguished for his gallery of heroines; Lao Shê's protagonists are nearly always men; whenever possible, he eschews romantic subject matter. Mao Tun records the passive feminine response to the chaotic events of contemporary Chinese history; more concerned with individual destinies than social forces, Lao Shê shows his heroes in action. While Mao Tun very early turned to Communism as the only solution for China's problems, Lao Shê remains until his novel *Camel Hsiang-tzu* (1937) the staunch believer in a simpler patriotic injunction that each Chinese should perform his chosen duty to the best of his ability in order to rid China of her stagnation and corruption.

Mao Tun is schooled in Russian and French fiction; by

temperament and training, Lao Shê takes to the English novelists. It was perhaps a lucky accident that during the years 1924–30, while Mao Tun was actively engaged in political work, Lao Shê was in London, writing his first novels and carrying on a program of study and research little dictated by intellectual fashions in China at that time. In a book of random comments on his literary career, *The Rickety Ox-cart,* Lao Shê regrets that he did not personally participate in the May Fourth Movement and that he missed all the stirring events taking place in China during the second half of the twenties. But had he stayed in China during that period, it is most probable that he would have been engulfed in the revolutionary tide and have assimilated all the political and literary creeds of the radical camp. Under these circumstances, it is hard to conceive that he could have cultivated his individualistic brand of fiction.

A native of Peking, Lao Shê (pen name of Shu Ch'ing-ch'un) was born of Manchu parents in 1899. Early bereaved of his father, he had to support his mother upon graduation from a normal school at the age of sixteen. He managed to study for a short period in his spare time at Yenching University and became in 1923 an instructor of Chinese at the Nankai Middle School. In the next year he sailed for England to teach Chinese on a meager salary at the University of London's School of Oriental Studies. Once abroad, he took to reading English novels, primarily to improve his English. Dickens so appealed to him that he wrote in imitation of *Nicholas Nickelby* a comic novel entitled *The Philosophy of Lao Chang.* Upon the recommendation of Lo Hua-sheng, then studying in England, it was serialized in *The Short Story* in 1926. Lao Shê followed this with another comic novel called *Chao Tzu-yüeh;* still under the influence of Dickens, it showed considerable technical improvement over the former. *The Two Mas,* a novel about Anglo-Chinese relations, was the last Lao Shê wrote during his sojourn in London as a Chinese instructor.

In 1930, after a summer's vacation in Europe, Lao Shê sailed for China. On his return voyage he was stranded for some time in Singapore, where he wrote a fantasy for children called *Hsiao P'o's Birthday* and witnessed for the first time Communist agitations in the Orient, which much disturbed him.[1] Back in China in 1931, he taught for three years at Cheloo University, Tsinan, and continued to teach at other universities until 1937. Always harassed by magazine editors for contributions, he often had to write in a hurry, so that, in his own estimation, some of his later stories and novels did not come off too well. Among his failures he listed *City of Cats* (discussed in Appendix 1), a Martian fable which, if somewhat crude as fiction, contains his most savage indictment of the Chinese nation, and the *Biography of Niu T'ien-tz'u*, a comic novel. *Ta-ming Lake* (a novel upon which the author set a high value, never saw publication, its plates being destroyed when the Commercial Press Building in Shanghai suffered a direct hit by an enemy bomb during the Sino-Japanese engagement in 1932. But *Divorce* (1933) and *Camel Hsiang-tzu* continue to testify to his steady progress as a novelist.

The Philosophy of Lao Chang, which the author dismisses as a trifle, is the story of a villainous schoolteacher and grocer. Almost a total failure in its attempt to be at once funny and indignant, the novel does anticipate, however, Lao Shê's later fiction in its heroic approach to the fact of injustice. *Chao Tzu-yüeh*, a much funnier and better-constructed novel, could have been subtitled "A Study of the Degeneration of the Heroic Ideal." Generous, reckless with money, naively trustful, and a *bon vivant,* the titular hero is the corrupt embodiment of that ideal. With all his affable qualities, he tries to acquire the trappings of fame as understood among the corrupt bureaucracy of Peking in the early Republican period: wine, women, song, and, most important, an official title. Chao Tzu-yüeh is not ambitious or avaricious: his humiliation is that, without an official post, he cannot lay claim to gentlemanly distinction. Neither is he in any way lecherous: if he never goes home to his country wife out of the mistaken pride that her bound feet will shame him, he as vainly pursues the college student, Miss Wang, solely for the consideration that a gentleman is entitled to a beautiful and accomplished wife.

As the story opens, Chao Tzu-yüeh is seen carousing with his select college buddies: the playboy Ou-yang T'ien-feng, the chubby-faced Mo Ta-nien, the politician Wu Tuan, and the poetaster Chou Shao-lien. They are planning to stir up a riot at their college. As author of a book on mahjong and another on Peking opera, Chao is already a person of some note, but he thinks that, as a college student, he has to distinguish himself as an athlete and strike leader as well. He feels only somewhat uncomfortable in the company of Li Ching-shun, his true but distant friend who disapproves of his ways. But he soon loses his qualms in his pursuit of glory on the soccer field and as a riot leader. For the latter offense he is duly dismissed from school.

With the same kind of gullible zest, Chao now pursues a government post. He first goes to Tientsin to look up Chou Shao-lien, who is now safely enrolled in the College of Sacred Changes, after being expelled from the first college. (In a chapter of grotesque satire, Lao Shê describes the curriculum of that anachronistic institution: freshmen and sophomores devote their time to the study of the *Book of Changes;* for juniors and seniors, the president himself chooses their field of concentration by resort to divination.) Not getting much help from his poet friend, Chao finally agrees to serve as tutor to the son of a general, in the hope that the latter may reward him with a government post. When the promised job doesn't materialize, Chao returns to Peking. His friends now devise a strategy whereby he could gain solid control of the Society for the Promotion of Women's Rights. At much personal cost, Chao gives a benefit opera performance for the Society. He gains some newspaper notices and a few sponging friends, but nothing that furthers his official career.

Chao's funds are running low, and his friends no longer gather at his apartment every night. Wu Tuan has obtained a post in the Peking municipal government; Mo Ta-nien is working as a bank clerk; Li Ching-shun is concentrating on his studies. Only the playboy Ou-yang T'ien-feng is still around, instigating him to woo Miss Wang even harder. In the belief that a good wife is a prerequisite for officialdom, Chao heeds Ou-yang's advice and tries futilely to have a tryst with the girl. By now the novel has become increasingly melodramatic; Ou-yang emerges as a typical Dickensian villain with some sinister power over Miss Wang, which is duly explained in the last chapter. In time Chao sees through Ou-yang's duplicity.

Chao had always thought of himself as an important personage; but because his courtship of Miss Wang is none too successful and his talents and schemes lead him nowhere, he comes to the humiliating conclusion that he has been a dupe of all his false friends. He returns to his "conscience," Li Ching-shun, who gives him this piece of advice: "Now there are only two roads to go: bury your head among books and after finishing your studies work for the people so as to slowly rebuild the national character and spirit, or dare your life to kill the bad ones." [2] Chao decides on the latter course, and as his first intended victim he chooses Wu Tuan, who has been for some time negotiating with a foreign government for the sale of the Temple of Heaven. Chao is determined to stop him, to kill him if necessary. But in the meantime Li Ching-shun has been arrested for his attempted assassination of some corrupt official; in the impending execution of this noble friend, Wu Tuan repents of his nefarious scheme and undergoes a patriotic awakening. Unlike Chao, he chooses the path of study.

The first serious comic novel in modern Chinese literature, *Chao Tzu-yüeh* has remained one of the few delightful creations in that genre. Despite its melodramatic lapses at the end, its spirit of comic abandon, of burlesque even, has made possible a trenchant study of national corruption without undue patriotic solemnity. In the absurd adventures of the hero, Lao Shê has presented a way of life which is the direct antithesis of the heroic: the selfish and unrealistic pursuit of glory and honor at the total disregard of the needs of the Chinese people. In his want of solid learning and constructive usefulness, the reawakened Chao can only abide by terrorism, a caricature of the ideal of *hsia* (its nearest English equivalent would be knight-errantry), so celebrated in popular Chinese fiction. But in the modern age, this could only be a desperate remedy, the assertion of personal courage and integrity in one's despair of finding something more useful to do. Repeatedly Lao Shê stresses the importance of conscientious study and work as the only road to national reconstruction.

Because of his ingenuousness and latent patriotism, Chao Tzu-yüeh is treated in terms of a broad satire which is kindly in intention. But the novel as a whole is informed with an intensely personal disgust toward all politicians, students, and soldiers who have failed the common people. In the following passage the students and soldiers are lashed for their cowardice:

> There are two great forces in the new society: soldiers and students. Except that they won't fight foreigners, soldiers give everybody three lashes. Except that they won't fight soldiers, students beat everybody with their canes. Consequently, these two great forces march on in unison, giving people some idea of the "new militarism." If the soldiers who daren't fight foreigners did not oppress and maltreat the people, they would forfeit their title to soldiers; if the students who daren't fight soldiers did not beat the presidents, deans, and teachers, they would forfeit their right to be called righteous youth.[3]

A mock-heroic description of the aftermath of a student riot vents a strong animus against mob irresponsibility and cruelty:

> Outside the President's office lay a broken strand of rope: the President had been tied up and beaten. In the hallway were five or six satin slippers: the teachers had escaped barefoot. Pinned against the door-frame of an office by a three-inch-long nail was an ear with its blood already congealed: it had been lopped off the head of a faithful, prudent (his crime!) supply clerk of twenty years' standing. On the green near the hothouse was a patch of blood that had turned black-purple: it had poured forth from the nostrils of a gardener whose income was ten dollars per month.
>
> In the aquarium the goldfish were floating in the tank on the surface of water, their white bellies gleaming: whole boxes of chalk, dumped into the bottom of the tank, were giving forth bubbles, frying the undeparted souls of the little fry. In the laboratory the eyeballs of the frogs were stuck on bricks; the frogs had forfeited their little lives otherwise dedicated to experimental purposes. For a whole day the sun, hid behind black clouds, did not show his face. In the dark, the overhappy rats were nibbling away at the dead frogs' legs.[4]

In *Chao Tzu-yüeh* the chief fault of the students is that they ape the ways of officialdom: the era of Communist-directed student movements has not yet begun. In our examination of his later novels we shall see that Lao Shê is also unsparing in his use of withering satire against the new breed of Marxist student-politicians.

In his next novel Lao Shê curbs his tendency toward broad comedy and restates his patriotic message in more or less tragic terms. Whereas *Chao Tzu-yüeh* is Dickensian in quality, *The Two Mas* is more reminiscent of a number of late Victorian and Edwardian novels which depict the conflicts between father and son. As a study of Anglo-Chinese relations, the novel also clearly invites comparison with *A Passage to India*. But keenly aware of the humiliations of Chinese abroad, Lao Shê cannot afford Forster's complete ironic detachment: the accents of sorrow and indignation too often muffle the undertones of irony. There are also in *The Two Mas* a number of didactic passages touching on China's future, which serve the function of chorus to the main dramatic action.

Ma Tsê-jen, a Cantonese whose long years of residence in Peking in expectation of an official post have infected him with the typical vices of the old-style gentry, sails with his son, Ma Wei, to London to take over his late brother's curio shop. A clergyman by the name of Evans, who has known the Mas in China, befriends them and finds for them a flat in the house of Mrs. Wendell, a widow.[5] At first both Mrs. Wendell and her daughter Mary, who are subject to popular misconceptions about Chinese, are highly inconvenienced by their lodgers, but gradually they find them to be very considerate and kind people. Mrs. Wendell, especially, is quite taken by the elder Ma and intends to marry him, even though she is keenly aware of social disapproval. One day, as they are shopping for an engagement ring, she sees Mr. Ma treated with open contempt by the store clerk, and this makes her call off the marriage.

Meanwhile Ma Wei is doting on Mary who, trying pathetically to secure a husband of her own color, reciprocates his kindness only once, in a moment of drunken despondency. Ma Wei sets up a strenuous program of work and gymnastics for himself in order to forget about Mary. But he apparently cannot shake off his obsession, even though he obtains occasional consolation in the company of Catherine, the clergyman's understanding daughter.

Lethargic and contemptuous of business, the elder Ma hardly works at the curio shop, but with the help of his friend, Li Tzu-jung, Ma Wei manages to keep the store in a flourishing state. Trouble is brewing, however. The elder Ma has, without his son's knowledge, played the part of a Chinese villain in a movie and this action has stirred up much resentment against him among the Chinese working class in London; Ma Wei himself has antagonized some Chinese students. When the rumor reaches him that a mob is about to attack the store, Li Tzu-jung sees an excellent chance to capitalize on the event and expand the store's volume of business. But the elder Ma, afraid, sells out and retires. Disgusted with his father, himself, and his passion for Mary, Ma Wei bids farewell to Li Tzu-jung and leaves London.

In the novel the elder Ma is a pathetic and comic creature; unlike the much-maligned older members of the gentry in most Chinese fiction, he is a caricature only in the sense that Micawber is one. His eagerness to save face, his generosity with money—which serves too often merely to mitigate a strong inferiority complex, his lack of common sense and contempt for what he terms vulgarity, and even his selfishness and indolence are all touching, if slightly ridiculous. And with his daydreams and solicitude for sympathy and kindness, the elder Ma is also something of a Leopold Bloom. In this context, his son is the counterpart of Stephen Dedalus, forging the conscience of a new China in exile.

Ma Wei is principally bothered by the open contempt or condescending kindness shown by the British toward the Chinese. Why are the Japanese and Chinese treated differently, even though they have the same color of skin? To his sensitive nature, the answer can lie only in the ludicrous posture of China among the nations. He is further irritated by his father's apparent acquiescence in the kind of ill-treatment he frequently receives in London and by his childish joy whenever some of his English friends speak up for

China. Inured to a life of ease and consumed with a life-long dream for officialdom, the elder Ma hasn't begun to acquire the kind of national consciousness which stamps the younger generation. To Ma Wei, his father is the embodiment of national shame.

The sensitive and romantic Ma Wei is contrasted with his methodical and realistic friend, Li Tzu-jung. The latter is working his way through college by accepting any job that comes along; much to Ma Wei's surprise, he even accepts his engagement to a barely educated girl back home with hardly a protest. To him, the forfeiture of personal comfort and happiness is the inescapable price one has to pay for China's progress. But much as Ma Wei admires his friend, he cannot bring himself to work methodically for self-improvement and, indirectly, for national welfare. His personal problems are too real and too pressing to await solution until such time as China has become a strong nation. The thought of his father's unworthiness stings; the image of Mary haunts his waking hours. If Lao Shê upholds Li Tzu-jung as an ideal, he also shows in the case of Ma Wei the tragic dilemma facing every patriotic Chinese youth. Li is a stoic by choice as well as by virtue of his defective sensibility. But to the extent that China needs men of Li's dedication is the tragedy of Ma Wei—with his shame and passion, his divided allegiance to self and country—poignant.

In *The Two Mas* the patriotic theme, of course, is embedded not only in the father-son struggle but also in situations involving British and Chinese in social intercourse. Particularly impressive is Lao Shê's staging of three dinner scenes to point out the larger ironies implicit in Anglo-Chinese relations. At the first dinner, given by Mr. and Mrs. Evans for the Mas and Wendells, we see the coarseness of Alexander, Mrs. Evans' brother, who has earned his fortune in China and is now continually telling jokes at the expense of the Chinese; and the guarded kindness of the Evanses, whose missionary experience has not eradicated their basic dislike for the heathens. For dessert, Mrs. Evans serves rice pudding. Prepared on the assumption that all Chinese like rice, this unpalatable concoction is symbolic of the missionary attitude toward the Chinese, compounded of ignorance and patronage.

The second dinner treats the Anglo-Chinese theme at a more intimate level. At the Christmas party the Mas are Mrs. Wendell's only guests, her other friends having scorned to come on account of her Chinese lodgers. There is an attempt at cheerfulness at the party, however, until Mary announces her engagement to her friend Washington. Ma Wei swallows his bitterness in silence, and Mrs. Wendell suddenly realizes that she will be unbearably lonely after her daughter marries. Impulsively, she kisses the elder Ma and decides to marry him.

The third dinner, with Ma Wei in the company of Catherine at a Chinese restaurant, is really the climax of the novel. Lao Shê has a penchant for satirizing Chinese students, but in no other novel has he displayed such virulence as in his portrayal of the chauvinistic and ill-bred student leader, Mao. Also at the restaurant, the latter regards Ma Wei's dining out with a white girl as a personal affront. He remarks loudly in English to his table companion: "Foreign whores are only to sleep with. If you have money, sleep with them, but coffee-shops and restaurants are not the place for them. To tell you the truth, old Ts'ao, I'm not against whoring and I've whored many times. But I detest most of all young boys showing off their whores in public. Bring a whore to a Chinese dinner! Hum!" [6] Turning pale at these words, Catherine is ready to leave; but Ma Wei detains her and walks up to Mao to demand an apology. When the student leader refuses, Ma Wei slaps him on both cheeks. This brawl, in turn, angers Paul, Catherine's brother, who is dining in the outer room. To Paul, with his militant pride and conservatism, it is an insult that his sister should date a Chinese in the first place. He hits Ma Wei and a fight ensues, from which Ma Wei emerges the victor.

Colonialism, in its assertion of the superiority of the white race, has given rise to two myths which used to be prevalent in pulp fiction and cheap movies with an Oriental setting, namely that the nonwhite man secretly lusts after the white woman and that a nonwhite man will not fight a white man in self-defense. *A Passage to India* takes up all the implications of the first myth: the fright of a white girl alone in a dark cave with an Indian. Lao Shê stages the fight between Ma Wei and Paul not merely to explode the myth of the supposed cowardliness of the Chinese but also to emphasize the typical British and Chinese reactions to the event. Duly outraged is Mrs. Evans, whose long residence in China has led her to believe that it is the duty of the Chinese to obey the white man and accept his Christian religion. And the elder Ma, with the fear of the white man in his heart, expectedly hurries to the Evans' home to apologize for his son.

The three dinner scenes, in their exploration of Anglo-Chinese relations, underscore Lao Shê's command of his complex material and his refusal to commit himself to a simple patriotism. His British types, while conventionally simple, are fairly realistic, and the elder Ma and the student leader Mao are sufficiently disgraceful as representatives of their country. In the dilemmas of Ma Wei and in the humiliations of Chinese abroad, Lao Shê has uncovered facets of the problem of national reconstruction which remained obscure in *Chao Tzu-yüeh*.

Divorce [7] is a continuation of Lao Shê's two earlier novels, in the sense that it explores further in a different setting the weaknesses of the Chinese character and the sickness of the Chinese society. Still opposed to the Communist writers with their economic and political analysis of the Chinese decadence, Lao Shê maintains that the intolerable situation in China is directly due to the slackened moral fiber of the people: the country is weak because the people, especially the upper and middle classes, are cowardly and compromising and have lost the nerve to act. They persist in the old ways as long as they can keep their rice bowl full. As we have seen in the terrorism of Li Ching-shun and the frustrated romanticism of Ma Wei, there is more than a hint of violence in Lao Shê: he demands that the gangrene be cut from the body politic. Even though the task of national reconstruction demands arduous work and study, to dare one's life is at least preferable to cowardice. In *Divorce,* ironically, it is Ting Erh-yeh, the dispossessed man, who kills the villain Hsiao Chao: he has little to lose except his own life. The hero Lao Li cannot act so decisively because he is hopelessly committed to his family, job, and social routine.

As in the earlier novels, the shallow student and intellectual also figures importantly as an object of satire. In T'ien-chen (meaning "naive") Lao Shê presents a sound caricature of the college man of the coastal cities, living at once in the dream worlds of Hollywood and the Marxist utopia. He never studies, squanders money, addresses his long-suffering father, Old Brother Chang, as an "old capitalist," and yet has enough casual acquaintance with leftist politics to become the victim of a trumped-up charge of Communist conspiracy. Ma K'o-t'ung, another comic figure, is the devastating caricature of a romantic revolutionary. "He liked to consider himself the younger brother of Marx [*Ma K'o Ssu* in Chinese], but his revolutionary thought and behavior were dictated by considerations for his own success." [8] "He always thought that a revolutionary should only move about in cars, make speeches, and drink a large quantity of beer, and then he would become a comrade, high above the multitude." [9] He also thinks women the best ally for his advancement and attaches great value to his conquests, though eventually he blames his failure on his women.

The principal satiric target in *Divorce,* of course, is not the opportunistic intellectual but the small family man and bureaucrat who grinds out his existence in fear and conformity. Lao Li, Old Brother Chang, and their colleagues are all more or less resigned to family unhappiness and drudgery. The title *Divorce* is therefore symbolic of an act of courage which these characters fail to achieve, because they are content with "marriage," or cowardly submission to an intolerable status quo. The Lis, the Ch'ius, and the Wus all have cause enough to wish to dissolve their marital bonds, but no one dares to make the first move at the risk of insecurity and social disapproval.

The hero, Lao Li, is an older and more subdued Ma Wei in that, despite his drab existence, he still cherishes the romantic dream of a world with poetry and meaning. Upon the advice of Old Brother Chang, he reluctantly moves his wife and two children to Peiping so as to mitigate his unhappiness. At first humiliated by his wife's rustic ways, he very soon becomes infuriated over the bourgeois manners she has acquired in the company of his colleagues' wives. She shops frequently, nags, and spies on him. The only consolation Lao Li has against this perpetual harassment is his silent adoration of the discarded wife of Ma K'o-t'ung, a beautiful and lonely woman who lives in another quarter of the same building. At the deep level of his being, Lao Li wishes to quit his government position, leave his family, and flee with Mrs. Ma to some tropic island. He is all excited, therefore, when the news reaches him that Ma K'o-t'ung is returning home. Will his wife finally break with him? What will *he* do once she is free? But when Ma returns from Shanghai with his comrade-mistress, Mrs. Ma is soon reconciled to his brazen neglect and impudence. To Lao Li, this is unbelievable: her behavior is beyond all the acts of compromise and cowardice he has perpetrated as husband and civil servant:

When night came, his heart went completely numb. Comrade Ma had gone to sleep in the eastern room [Mrs. Ma's bedroom]! The world of Lao Li was shattered like a piece of old pottery crashing down from mid air. "Poetic sense?" There is no such thing in this world. Beauty and grace and independence: all these terms are now void of meaning. Life is only compromise, *fu-yen*, and dragging along without ideals. Other people may do so, but she, she is also like that! Perhaps in her eyes Comrade Ma was attractive. But why? Jealousy often prompts people to ask such silly questions.[10]

As a last gesture of defiance, Lao Li quits his job and goes back to his country home. But as Old Brother Chang predicts at the end of the novel, "Lao Li will soon return, just wait and see. Do you think he can forget Peiping?" [11]

Divorce reveals new facets of Lao Shê's comic talent: satiric representation of the manners of the small bureaucracy; clever manipulation of dialogue; and witty juxtaposition of incongruent ideas in many a polished sentence. And like *The Two Mas*, it is a serious novel, though possessing less fire and passion. Just as Ma Wei rejects his father in the end, Lao Li, temporarily at least, rejects his family, position, and friends. He prefers to stay in the country with Ting Erh-yeh, the man who dares to kill. In *Divorce*, Lao Shê pleads that a little courage will go a long way. He repudiates the opportunists in both the traditional and the Marxist camp; he also repudiates, though with more sadness, the little men and women circumscribed by the meaningless routine of their cowardly existence.

Before tackling Lao Shê's next major novel, *Camel Hsiang-tzu*, we should devote some attention to *The Biography of Niu T'ien-tz'u*.[12] In spite of its slight literary merit, the latter is symptomatic of a change of attitude, which becomes quite pronounced in *Camel Hsiang-tzu*. Both novels are attempts to answer the question: what makes a man what he is? In a humorous vein, *Niu T'ien-tz'u* traces "the education of a little hero of the petty-bourgeois class"; [13] in a tragic vein, *Camel Hsiang-tzu* depicts the unavailing struggles of a good member of the proletariat. In both looms large the factor of environment which frustrates natural good impulses as well as the striving for personal integrity. In *Divorce*, Lao Shê was still very much the individualist, castigating the Chinese people for their cowardice and admonishing them toward greater heroic endeavor. In *Niu T'ien-tz'u*, however, the doubt is entertained whether individual heroism could be of any use in a generally corrupt society; in *Camel Hsiang-tzu*, there is positive affirmation for the necessity of collective action. Without documentary evidence one cannot say for sure whether Lao Shê reached this conclusion of his own accord or under leftist pressure. In the thirties he was a highly acclaimed and popular writer, on equally good terms with the Left-wing League, the Lin Yutang group, and other middle groups. Both *Niu T'ien-tz'u* and *Camel Hsiang-tzu* were initially serialized in Lin Yutang's magazines, but it is equally significant that, upon the outbreak of the Sino-Japanese War, Lao Shê was elected, with the unanimous support of the leftist and Communist groups, to the presidency of the Chinese Writers' Anti-aggression Association.

Niu T'ien-tz'u is in many striking ways modeled upon *Tom Jones*. The hero is a foundling; his foster parents, his nurse, his amah, his boyhood friend Ssu Hu-tzu, and his tutors all have their comic counterparts in Fielding's novel. There is the same leisurely pace of narration, the same good-natured caricature, and predilection for essay-like discourses. Toward the end, when the hero is in deep distress, again as in *Tom Jones*, good fortune in the unexpected person of the old tutor intervenes. But *Niu T'ien-tz'u* ends with the twenty-year-old hero, with many assurances of success, embarking for the great city Peiping, so that it contains no comparable picaresque action of Tom Jones' journey to London.

Consciously identifying himself with the virtues of the gentry, Fielding allows in his novel the triumphant vindication of a good and generous heart. More satirical toward the small landowning class of which his hero is a typical product, Lao Shê tries to prove how Niu T'ien-tz'u's generous impulses are gradually deadened in the home, school, and small-town environment, until what remains is channeled into greed and a desire for social conformity. Niu T'ien-tz'u is sympathetic toward the poor peasants and invariably enjoys a sense of expansive freedom in the company of his plebeian friends, but he is nevertheless steadily drawn to the flippant and callous ways of his own class. He adopts in turn all the social and literary fashions, old as well as modern, of the upper stratum of his community. Especially, he never forgets his stepmother's dying injunction that he become an official. In the bankruptcy and death of his stepfather, he finally realizes the supreme importance of money. Bereaved and poor, "he cried until his eyes were pained with the exhaustion of tears. Now he knew: money is everything; the whole civilization is built upon it. Everybody is a huckster, including the people of the Cloud Society [a poetry club]. Everybody is a huckster, trying to get money in an easy way, hypocritical, scheming, and cheating." [14] Shorn of his earlier follies, determined to make money, and handsomely equipped by his tutor for a college education, the chastened young hero has every prospect for success. But his success is also his failure: the atrophy of good impulses in the pursuit of worldly goods by worldly methods.

The Biography of Niu T'ien-tz'u is an amusing novel, informed with a sane, satirical view of humanity. But its pace is too slack and its humor too pedestrian to indicate other than the author's indifferent emotional involvement with his subject. *Camel Hsiang-tzu,* on the contrary, is a deeply personal novel, in which Lao Shê tries to embody his newly felt belief in the futility of individual effort. Whereas Niu T'ien-tz'u feels only a slight twinge of conscience in his submission to environmental forces, Camel Hsiang-tzu keeps up a good struggle for an honest and independent living until his final moral and physical exhaustion. In this respect, the new novel reveals a close emotional affinity with Hardy's fiction, especially *The Mayor of Casterbridge*. The influence of the English novelist is also felt in the tight architectonic structure of its plot.

An honest, taciturn, and sturdy Northern lad, Hsiang-tzu is a ricksha puller in the streets of Peiping. His one ambition is to save enough money to buy a ricksha of his own. But no sooner has he fulfilled his dream than he is inadvertently drafted into the army as a coolie and his ricksha taken away from him. One night, he escapes from the barracks, taking along with him three army camels, which he sells cheaply in a hurry for only thirty-five dollars. He excuses the theft on the ground that he has been unjustly deprived of his ricksha, but it nevertheless represents the first step in his downfall, because his integrity has suffered.

Spurred by his ambition to own another ricksha, Hsiang-tzu now works twice as hard and takes prospective customers from even the aged ricksha pullers, with whom he formerly disdained to compete. As before, he enjoys the confidence of the proprietor of the ricksha rental shed, Liu Ssu-yeh, and sleeps at his place every night after he has turned in his ricksha. Tiger, Liu's ugly and imperious daughter, seduces him. Hsiang-tzu's succumbing to this temptation means another compromise: he has always intended, when he has enough money, to marry a clean, strong-bodied country girl. Ashamed of himself, he leaves Liu's place to accept employment as a private ricksha puller for Professor Ts'ao. Hsiang-tzu could have regained his purity under the kind care of his new employer, who is a mild-mannered socialist, but Tiger comes repeatedly to molest him, pretending to be pregnant.

During a police raid of Professor Ts'ao's home on the alleged charge of his conspiratorial activities, Hsiang-tzu forfeits all his savings to an unscrupulous detective. He has now no choice but to return to Liu's ricksha shed. Liu regards him askance because of his daughter's unaltered intention to marry a penniless coolie rather than a person of higher economic status. The animosity between father and daughter finally comes to a head on Liu's sixty-ninth birthday. During the ensuing quarrel, Hsiang-tzu is bound by decency to side with Tiger: in spite of his aversion to her, he is infuriated over her father's unjust accusations of his mercenary character. He and Tiger get married and move to a slum district.

Counting on her father's eventual forgiveness, Tiger lives an easy life on her savings. Thoroughly hurt at being tricked into this marriage, Hsiang-tzu asserts his independence by pulling his ricksha harder than ever. One extremely hot day, wet by heavy showers, he comes home with a fever, and stays bedridden for two months. His health remains impaired, and his wife's continual taunts about his foolish independence subject him to even greater misery. Hsiang-tzu, however, obtains some solace in the company of a neighboring girl who supports her drunken father and younger brothers on her meager income as a prostitute. After Tiger has died of a difficult childbirth, Hsiang-tzu wants very much to marry this unhappy and kindly girl Hsiao Fu-tzu. But the prospect of supporting her large family is too frightening, and he moves out of the neighborhood without even bidding her good-by.

In low spirits Hsiang-tzu begins to smoke and drink, and to associate with the shiftless ricksha pullers whom he formerly despised. He even contracts gonorrhea from the mistress of the house where he is temporarily employed. Under this last humiliation he pulls himself together: he wants to marry Hsiao Fu-tzu and seek employment again from his former benefactor, Professor Ts'ao. The latter is glad to have him back, but first he has to find the whereabouts of the girl he has left behind. After a desperate search, he learns that Hsiao Fu-tzu has hanged herself after working for a period among the lowest prostitutes. Now Hsiang-tzu's will is completely shattered; he doesn't go back to work for Ts'ao because to do so would mean to keep up the Sisyphean struggle for decency, for which he has no longer the necessary courage and fortitude. Delighting in small gains as a petty thief and occasional informer, he becomes every day dirtier, lazier, and more shiftless. He ends up as a mean-spirited loafer, parading for a small pittance in Peiping's endless wedding and funeral processions.

This synopsis supports the impression that Hsiang-tzu's praiseworthy attempt to work toward a decent living deserves all our sympathies, and as a matter of fact, readers of the once-popular English translation of this novel, *Rickshaw Boy*, will surely remember that the hero is finally reunited with his girl and rewarded with happiness.[15] But Lao Shê regards him rather differently. The tragedy of Hsiang-tzu is not merely due to the conspiracy of circumstances that combine to thwart him; the implied meaning is that even if the hero had surmounted all the difficulties enumerated in the novel, he would surely have encountered another set which would have defeated him. In the absence of a healthy environment, the kind of individualistic striving in which Hsiang-tzu is engaged is not only of no avail—it is finally destructive of one's body and soul. Primarily an object of compassionate study, the character of Hsiang-tzu also bears, toward the end of the novel, the burden of a parable on individualism. In the account of his final degeneration, one feels the intrusive presence of satire, which is incongruent with the sympathetic texture of the main body of the novel. The emphatic sentence that closes the novel is fraught with the author's undisguised contempt for his hero: "The once respectable, ambitious, dreamy, self-centered, individualistic, strong-bodied, and great Hsiang-tzu paraded in these funeral processions for heaven knows how many times; he didn't know when or where he would bury himself, bury that degenerate, selfish, and unfortunate product of a sick society, that ghost of an individualist pushed to the wall!" [16]

From a writer who has espoused heroic action in the service of society, the last quotation is surprisingly leftist in its point of view. Lao Shê has apparently come to the conclusion that, in a sick society, it requires some form of collective action to improve the lot of the proletariat, and that any member of that class, in trying to better himself by his own effort, merely hastens his own ruin. In the novel the mouthpiece for this viewpoint is an old ricksha puller who enters into Hsiang-tzu's life twice briefly, each time precipitating a decision that represents a shrinking of his pride and self-confidence. The first time, Hsiang-tzu sees the old man staggering into a teahouse with his grandson and helps him to a seat; in the subsequent conversation, Hsiang-tzu learns that this relic of a man, now reduced to extreme poverty, was once an independent ricksha puller, with a ricksha of his own. Fear begins to haunt Hsiang-tzu: can owning a ricksha save him from pauperdom—and what is so bad about marrying Tiger?

> Thinking in this way, he felt there was no need to struggle against Tiger's threat; anyway he himself couldn't jump out of the net, so what difference did it make what kind of woman he was going to take? Not to say that she would bring him many rickshas: why not enjoy life while you still can? Once you see through yourself, you don't have to despise the others; so let it be Tiger—what more is there to say? [17]

Toward the end of the novel, when Hsiang-tzu is looking everywhere for Hsiao Fu-tzu in an effort to reform himself, he again by accident meets the old pauper in the teahouse. The latter, whose grandson has in the meantime died, confides to Hsiang-tzu:

> For a coolie to gain a competent living by his own effort is harder than to enter heaven. How can he always stay resilient? Have you ever watched a grasshopper? Alone by himself, he can jump quite far, but once caught by a boy and tied with a thread, he can't even fly off the ground. But let him join a swarm of other grasshoppers and go forth in battle array. *Heng!* In one sweep they will destroy acres of crop and who can stop them! Tell me, am I right or wrong? My heart is good, but I can't even keep one boy. He got sick; I had no money to buy medicine and watched him die in my arms. There's no use talking about it! Get your tea here! Who will drink a cup of hot tea? [18]

Hsiang-tzu takes this lesson hard; later, when he finds out about Hsiao Fu-tzu's death, he accepts defeat without any more struggle. In the old ricksha puller he has seen the futility of striving.

There is no doubt that Lao Shê intends this social criticism as an integral part of his novel. Fortunately, it gets in the way of the tragic logic of the hero's life only infrequently, and the main body of the narrative is exciting precisely because of its unswerving dramatic focus on the fact of struggle. In the depiction of the hero's repeated desperate efforts to keep his body and soul together, Lao Shê displays an astonishing moral and psychological acumen. Particularly brilliant is the delineation of tensions existing between Hsiang-tzu and Tiger before and after their marriage: here, surely—as in Mao Tun's study of Mei's married life with Liang Yü-ch'un in *Rainbow*—the reader scales a high peak of modern Chinese literature to look down on naked human experience in all its horror and fury, without any attendant sentimentality, didacticism, or melodrama. The following scene, which depicts the quarrel of the couple soon after their marriage, may serve as an illustration:

"All right, tell me what's on your mind." She moved a stool over and sat down beside the stove.

"How much money have you got?" he asked.

"So I'm right after all. I knew you were going to ask me just that. You didn't marry a wife, you married that little bit of money, didn't you?"

It was as if Hsiang-tzu had been caught in a sudden gust of wind and knocked breathless. He gasped. Old Man Liu and the ricksha men at the Human Harmony Ricksha Shed all thought it was because he was covetous of her money that he had seduced Tiger. Now she herself had put that same suspicion into words. Without cause or reason he had lost his own ricksha and then later his own money, and now he was to be crushed beneath a few dollars of his old woman's. It was as if the very food he ate had to go down his backbone! He wished he could clench his two hands around her throat and choke her and choke her until the whites of her eyes showed. He would choke everybody to death and then cut his own throat. They weren't people, they should die. He himself wasn't a man either—he should also die. Nobody should hope to live! [19]

Written on the eve of the Sino-Japanese War, *Camel Hsiang-tzu* may be taken as the finest modern Chinese novel up to that time. The other important novelist, Mao Tun, was writing more and more to the tune of Communist propaganda; even though his mind was wavering from his earlier stand of individualism, Lao Shê was apparently still an independent writer, and what he has achieved in *Camel Hsiang-tzu* is, all criticisms considered, essentially an impassioned and tightly constructed novel of realistic integrity. Its crisp and racy language catches the very accent and flavor of the Peking vernacular; its principal characters are all memorably human. In dramatic power and narrative skill the novel is superior to all of the author's previous works, even though *Chao Tzu-yüeh, The Two Mas,* and *Divorce* each possess points of excellence which it does not claim. And it towers above Lao Shê's later works, of the war years and after. The mind conceiving *Camel Hsiang-tzu* is seeking a new synthesis: on the one hand, it continues to air its disgust with the unprincipled student-intellectual-politician in the character Yüan Ming (the person whom Hsiang-tzu betrays to the police); on the other, it expresses a dissatisfaction with the patriotic formula of heroic individual endeavor. It is not fully committed to a leftist program, but is critical of liberal individualism.

Under the stress of the war years Lao Shê reaffirmed heroic action in the cause of anti-Japanese patriotism—but only on a propaganda level and without his earlier insights into the needs and faults of China.

CHAPTER 8

Shen Ts'ung-wen (1902-)

In the tenth chapter of *Feng Tzu*, a long narrative by Shen Ts'ung-wen, the Chinese visitor, after witnessing the religious ceremonies of an aboriginal tribe, confesses to its chieftain with obvious emotion:

Day before yesterday you told me God is indispensable here; I had my doubts then, but now I know. I have always regarded myself as a modern man, one who respects reason and rejects superstition. I cared little for monks and temples, and regarded these as well as the crowd who go to the temples to worship and solicit favors from their idols as beneath my contempt. I thought that, as a philosophical concept, the term God, in spite of its historical function in relation to human life, has become debased by urban civilization and that the existence of God is no longer justifiable or possible. In the cities, God may be regarded as the symbol of falsehood: he sanctions man's stupidity, cloaks his cruelty, and enhances his ugliness. But from the ceremonies I have just witnessed, I realize that God exists now as in earlier times. But his majesty and beauty are only apparent under a certain condition: namely, the plain honesty of human emotions, the simple purity of thought, and the presence of a pastoral environment. Only when this condition is fulfilled can God exist and can he increase the beauty of human life. Lacking this condition, God perishes. What I have just witnessed was not the ritual of paying homage or giving thanks to God, but rather a play wholly magnificent, a play indescribable and indefinable. And in this play is the source of poetry and drama and music as well as the substance of God. Sounds and colors, lights and shadows were woven into a pageant of glory, and God exists in that whole. In that vision I almost believed that I saw your God; I thought to myself what a miracle that was! Now I understand why God is always on your lips; you have your reason. Now I understand why two thousand years ago China had produced a Ch'ü Yüan, author of such beautiful and fabulous poetry: he was merely a recorder of the scenes of this region. Ch'ü Yüan has been dead for two thousand years, but the *Nine Songs* still exists in its pristine glory. If one were willing to try, I think one could still draw fresh, transparent water from this old well! [1]

As a modern Chinese author's religious testament, the foregoing passage, however theologically naive, possesses a quality of wisdom which is in surprising contrast to the utilitarian materialism of his time. Shen Ts'ung-wen posits no supernatural order but affirms the primacy of the mythical imagination, which alone is able to reinstate the wholeness of life in modern society. In this respect, his creative concern is akin to Yeats': to stress, in the teeth of a materialist civilization, the virtues of an ordered existence in rhythmic keeping with nature and the gods, filled with animal grace and pride and yet without cunning and greed. While sharing their positive distaste for the frivolity and decadence of bourgeois life, Shen Ts'ung-wen is unlike most of his fellow writers in that he also abhors the shallow day-dream of a Marxist utopia whose success would mean the total eclipse of God from human society. With a piety unique in his time he places his faith in the old China, the shrinking area of rural and "feudal" economy little touched by mercan-tilism and still less by modern ideological influences, and uncovers beneath its dirty and often bizarre surface the life-giving stream of emotional integrity and instinctive hon-esty. But Shen Ts'ung-wen is not a primitivist, much less a sentimentalist purveying the supposed charms of a bygone era and futilely protesting against modern tendencies. Though much of it can be labeled pastoral, his extremely variegated fiction is shot through with a comprehensive awareness of the contemporary situation and a firm conviction that, unless certain pieties and attitudes persist, China and, by extension, the rest of the world will become increasingly brutalized. The pastoralism of Shen Ts'ung-wen therefore is on the same moral plane and speaks with the same urgency to modern man as that of Wordsworth, Yeats, and Faulkner.

To account for his dissimilarity from his fellow writers, Shen Ts'ung-wen is in the habit of stressing his rural back-ground as opposed to their urban education. "I am a coun-tryman," he writes in one of his prefaces, "and I say this without pride or modesty. A countryman has as a rule his deep-seated stubborn rustic ways and conforms to a pattern of loves, hatreds, sorrows, and joys entirely different from that of the man of the city. A countryman is conservative; he is obstinate; he loves the earth; he does not lack wit but is incapable of cunning. He is as a rule serious about every-thing, perhaps in the eyes of the world too serious, so that he even appears to be foolish." [2] Shen Ts'ung-wen, like many another modern Chinese writer the product of genteel pov-erty, was of course no peasant. But his self-description as a countryman is not merely a disarming way of rebuking the others for being uprooted from the Chinese tradition and too easily impressed by newfangled ideological fashions. It is his way of calling attention to an intellectual incorruptibility resulting from his abiding loyalty to humble farmers, soldiers, boathands, and small traders in the Chinese interior, among whom he moved during his formative years.

Until his twentieth year, when he was seized with the ambition to study in Peking and to prepare for a writing career, Shen Ts'ung-wen was practically untouched by that aspect of China which was shaped materially and intellectually under the Western influence. Born in 1902 in the small town of Fenghwang, on the western border of Hunan province touching Szechwan and Kweichow, he was brought up in a family of official standing. His grandfather had made a name for himself as Governor of Kweichow; with less success, his father and uncles pursued military careers. Because his father was stationed in Peking during the greater part of his childhood, Shen Ts'ung-wen had little strict family discipline; rather, he was a regular truant from school, watching all manner of natural and human phenomena in his home town with unchecked enthusiasm. "All day long I roamed in the mountains and orange orchards, watching, listening, smelling," he writes in his *Autobiography*, which serves as a Wordsworthian prelude to his fiction. "The smell of dead snakes and rotting straw, the body odor of butchers, and then the scent arising from the kilns after rain—I could not then describe these olfactory sensations in words, but could detect them instantly. The squeak of a bat, the sigh of the cow as the butcher's knife pierces its throat, the rattle of yellow-necked snakes hidden in fields and caves, the faint sound of fish jumping in the dark—because these sounds were then registered in their uniqueness, even now I can recall them distinctly." [3]

At the age of thirteen, in accordance with family tradition, Shen Ts'ung-wen was sent to a military school. He learned little about military science there but developed an intense

admiration for an old-style coach who, almost a hero out
of the pages of popular Chinese historical fiction, was adept
in the use of broadswords and spears. Two years later Shen
Ts'ung-wen was assigned to a regiment stationed first at
Yuanling and then at Hwaihwa; in the latter place, in the
space of sixteen months, he witnessed about 700 decapita-
tions. Subsequently he wandered with different regiments to
various places in Hunan, Szechwan, Kweichow. Still later he
also served as police clerk, revenue collector, and employee
in a newspaper office.

During this period of peregrination on land and water (he
was a frequent passenger on ships sailing up and down the
Yüan River in West Hunan) Shen Ts'ung-wen met all kinds
of people: officers, bandits, prostitutes, and boathands. An
adolescent in the adult world of passion, depravity, and
heroism, he was indelibly impressed with the perverse but
often beautiful manifestations of the human spirit. Later,
in his *Autobiography* as well as in a large number of stories,
he records the incidents and characters that have haunted his
imagination most. One such example (in the story "Three
Men and a Girl") is the youthful proprietor of a bean-curd
store who spends three days and nights in a cave with the
corpse of a girl who was the object of his secret passion; upon
being discovered, he accepts his death sentence cheerfully.
Another (in the story "Ta Wang") is a reformed bandit who
has dispatched 200 people in his time and who is treacher-
ously executed by the military commander under whom he
has served as bodyguard.[4]

This period of wandering was of crucial importance to the
future writer, not only because it supplied a rich variety
of sensation and experience but, more important, because it
fostered in him a sense of fact and of history from which he
would never swerve under the insidious pressure toward
leftist conformity. He has seen the lives of Chinese people
in all their intertwined ugliness and beauty; he is therefore

able to reject from the beginning the Communist cant that explains Chinese society in such convenient terms of half-truth as feudalism and imperialism.

During his years of wandering, Shen Ts'ung-wen was not without his share of lucky accidents and opportune friends, all of which helped enkindle his literary ambition. A set of Dickens translated into elegant Chinese by the great wen-yen stylist Lin Shu would transport him for months on end under the spell of a kindred imagination; copies of Shanghai newspapers he accidentally ran into would open his eyes to a new China of which he had little personal knowledge. While with the newspaper firm prior to his journey to Peking in 1922, he made friends with a compositor who introduced him to the new magazines and books which had appeared since the May Fourth Movement. Shen Ts'ung-wen had assiduously practiced calligraphy, studied rather methodically the contents of a large dictionary, *Tz'u Yüan,* and read in traditional poetry and prose during his years in the army and on the river, but this was the first time he had come into contact with the new thought and the new literature. Utterly fascinated, he spent four days in meditation before disclosing to his employers his intention to study in Peking. They honored his decision and even helped him financially. Thus begins one of the most fecund and distinguished careers in modern Chinese letters, which comes to a precipitate end only with the Communist usurpation of the mainland in 1949.

After two years of struggle in Peking, Shen Ts'ung-wen began to receive attention. He came under the protection of the Anglo-American wing of writers—Hu Shih, Hsü Chih-mo, Ch'en Yüan—and published regularly after 1924 in their organs: the Literary Supplement to the Peking *Morning Gazette, Contemporary Review,* and *Crescent Moon.* On the surface there would seem to be little in common between these professors and expounders of Western culture and their protégé, a young "countryman" who couldn't speak a word of English. Ting Ling, a good friend of Shen Ts'ung-wen's at that time and years later a prominent Communist writer, writes in 1950: "Shen Ts'ung-wen frequently vacillated: while opposed to the ruling classes (in his youth he really shared somewhat of this passion), he at the same time hoped to gain for himself a position in the upper society. . . . Because of his friendship with the writers of *Crescent Moon* and *Contemporary Review,* he always admired the gentlemanly class." [5] This observation is widely off the mark, of course: the bond between Shen Ts'ung-wen and the professorial writers was one of intellectual affinity. By 1924 the radical tide was gathering momentum, and Hu Shih and his friends were already on the defensive against the pernicious influence of the new writing. With all their critical erudition and talent for poetry, they had in their ranks, with the exception of Ling Shu-hua, no distinguished practitioner of fiction to compete with, say, the Creationists. They were impressed not only by Shen Ts'ung-wen's facility with his pen but by his innate conservatism and his genuine faith in China's destiny built upon a realistic apprehension of her virtues and vices. They felt that, like their own critical liberalism, this realistic conservatism was corrective of the hasty revolutionary temper of the times. Their faith was to become amply rewarded: Hu Shih devoted himself more and more to historical research and politics, Hsü Chih-mo met a tragic death (in 1931) in an airplane crash, and Ch'en Yüan more or less retired from the literary scene; Shen Ts'ung-wen was to remain the sole major example of artistic sanity and intellectual incorruptibility.

A diligent story-writer striving for self-improvement, Shen Ts'ung-wen was at first perhaps little aware of the critical responsibilities the writing of fiction would entail upon him. Experimenting with a variety of themes and styles, he turned out an endless succession of stories, good, bad, and indifferent, and the Communist critics, noticing his odd persistence, his avoidance of topical issues, and his gradual mastery of a personal prose style, were content to dismiss him merely as a prolific and ideologically naive stylist. But with the years he increasingly gained in stature. When he assumed editorship of the Literary Supplement to the *Ta Kung Pao* in 1934, he was already in the eyes of leftist writers a center of rightist reaction. From then on, throughout the war years and afterward, he was an object of constant Communist vilification. He was supposed to be an exponent of "Kuomintang agent literature," a literature abetting the tyranny of the ruling clique and the landlords, whereas the ironic truth was that he didn't get along with the Government too well in the forties and his writings were often censored. Brushing aside the unwarranted attacks with aristocratic disdain, the later Shen Ts'ung-wen reveals himself as a true artist with a serene faith in his own creation. As early as 1936, he writes proudly in reference to his supposed backwardness: "Two thousand years ago, it looked as though Chuang Tzu were lagging behind many of his contemporaries. These people were all dead now, but when you and I read 'Autumn Floods' and 'Horses' Hoofs' [two chapters in *Chuang Tzu*], we seem to meet face to face with that man who had been behind his times." [6]

The evolution of Shen Ts'ung-wen's art was at first painfully slow. When he began to write, he was a novice, little acquainted with the Western traditions of fiction. Yet during the years 1924–28, when he should have been learning his craft, he was compelled by financial necessity to dissipate his copious imagination in a regrettably large output of fiction. He appeared the inexhaustible storyteller, spinning with equal ease yarns about his personal life, about student, bourgeois, and proletarian life in the coastal cities, about the picturesque customs of West Hunan, and about the handsome youths and pining maidens of the aboriginal tribes. In spite of their sensitivity to a remarkable range of experience, perhaps few stories of that period were not marred to some degree by structural and stylistic defects. Unaware of the formal properties of the modern short story, Shen Ts'ung-wen told his tales in the traditional fashion and adorned them often, under the sway of his undisciplined fancy, with passages of superfluous description and essay-like discourse. In his innocence of modern Western fiction he appropriated such models as were available to him: *Alice in China** is a satire in the vein of Lewis Carroll, *Under Moonlight,* a series of Buddhist tales assembled in the manner of *The Decameron.* Even during his early period, of course, Shen Ts'ung-wen could write simply and elegantly; but possibly to compensate for his ignorance of Western tongues, he affected then the long-winded sentence, the English periodic structure. For the early stories, the strictures of the critic, Miss Su Hsüeh-lin, are apt:

> Though in choice of diction and in the arrangement of his sentences he tries to achieve terseness, his descriptions are still verbose and cumbersome. Sometimes, several hundred words fail to yield the "central idea." Reading him, we are reminded of a crone's prolix and redundant gossip which, in spite of its length, fails to convey what she is driving at, and of soft punches directed at a fat person which are unable to hit where it really hurts. We can abbreviate a thousand-word passage into a hundred words without losing the original import. For this reason his language cannot pierce a reader's heart like a rapier; however pathetic or tragic his stories are, they cannot stay in the reader's mind as an ineradicable memory.[7]

The stories most vulnerable to the preceding criticisms are those dealing with the Miao tribes. Though Shen Ts'ung-wen hasn't written much in that vein since 1932, he is apparently very fond of them, judging from the fact that he has chosen three such stories, "Under the Moonlight," "The

---

* Discussed in Appendix 1.

White Kid," and "Lung Chu," for the English anthology of his fiction, *The Chinese Earth,* prepared by Ching Ti and Robert Payne. As a great traveler in Hunan, Kweichow, and Szechwan, Shen Ts'ung-wen has undoubtedly firsthand knowledge of the Miao tribes, who inhabit mostly the mountainous areas of that region. But such knowledge, unaccompanied by anthropological research or genuine understanding, tends only to spread a haze of glamor over the aborigines. In depicting the ecstasy and death of young lovers in his Miao stories, Shen Ts'ung-wen succumbs utterly to the idealizing tendency, and the result is a specious product with little correspondence with reality. The language shows also the irresponsibility of pastoral indulgence. In the following passage, he introduces his favorite hero, Lung Chu:

> Among the Miaos, the White Ear tribe was famous for its handsome youths. It looked as though the parents of that district had all participated in the task of carving a statue of the God Apollo, and so handed down to their sons a model of beauty. Lung Chu, the son of the chieftain, was seventeen years old, and he was the most handsome of all the handsome sons of the tribe. As beautiful and strong as a lion and as gentle and meek as a lamb, he was the archetype for man; he was authority, strength, light. Because of his beauty, he deserved all these similes. As with beauty, he was gifted also with moral virtues, which far surpassed the share for ordinary men.[8]

If the English is ludicrous, the original is not less so. The second sentence, particularly, hardly makes sense; the inappropriate mention of Apollo indicates ostentation of literary knowledge. (In the subsequent revised version of the story, "the God Apollo" is replaced by the phrase "Buddha the Heavenly King," which is only slightly less preposterous.) All the generic adjectives are banal.

The passage, of course, is exceptional even for the bad

stories. But the fact that its author could perpetrate this kind of writing is an emphatic reminder of his slow endeavor to reach maturity and command the full exercise of his imagination. Not until he joined the teaching profession was he relieved of the necessity of writing continually under pressure. In 1929, after the failure of his two magazines, *Jen Chien* and *Red and Black,* he became a teacher of Chinese at Woosung China Institute in Shanghai, where Hu Shih was then president. The next year he taught for a term at National Wuhan University; from 1931 to 1934 he was Professor of Chinese at Tsingtao University. From 1934 on to the postwar years, he was Professor of Chinese at National Peking University, the Southwest Associated University, and then again Peking University. The emergence of a distinguished supple prose in his writings of the early and middle thirties is directly traceable to his continual exploration of varieties of Chinese prose as professor of Chinese. These years were also the happiest years in his personal life: a long courtship had terminated in a felicitous marriage and given new dimensions to his sensibility; frequent travel and a few extended trips into his native region renewed his bonds of sympathy with the common people. The result for the period 1930-37 was a long string of fine short stories (collected under such titles as *Ju Jui Chi, The Floating World, Eight Steeds, New and Old, The Housewife*); a novelette entitled *The Border Town;* two distinguished volumes of prose, his *Autobiography* and *Random Sketches on a Trip to Hunan;* and many critical and biographical studies of lesser importance.

The ample volume and range of Shen Ts'ung-wen's fiction call for clarification of his general attitude toward life before we can profitably discuss his individual stories. On the primary level, the writer stresses the importance of animal innocence as the prerequisite for attainment of higher human virtues. He ascribes to the romantic and Taoist view that without a highly developed intellect and emotional capacity one may nevertheless attain instinctive happiness and unconscious wisdom. In "Hui Ming," an early story not without a trace of jocular verbosity, the title hero is an army cook who has passed his prime but lives cheerfully in expectation of no improvement of his present lot. His one vague ambition is to live someday on the Western frontier amid the immense forests, a dream planted in his mind some ten years ago by the speech of a general urging the reclamation of the West. Though often made fun of for his harmlessness, Hui Ming is happy, smoking his pipe and dreaming about his forests. When some rival warlords prepare for renewed hostilities, the cook moves along with his regiment to the front. He wishes the fighting to take place soon, because by summertime the stink of the corpses will be offensive. Meanwhile, there is no fighting and Hui Ming chats with the villagers from whom he buys the provisions. They in turn give him a hen. Feeding and caring for the hen becomes with him a new source of pleasure, and in time twenty little chickens are hatched. Fussing over them makes him so happy that he even forgets about his frontier dream. War is soon averted, and the cook returns with the regiment to their old station.

> At the front Hui Ming had been a cook; he remained a cook when he returned to his old post. With no war going on, he felt that the chances for his being stationed in the big forest and seeing his banner waving over the garrison were rather remote. But he fed his chickens, tended them with great care; he had enough tobacco leaves to last him forty days, and he was very happy. June had come and gone, and none of the troops in his company had died and rotted. As Hui Ming looked at them, he smiled, but the meaning of his smile was not apparent to them.[9]

In this simple story one sees the affirmation of simple Taoist virtues in the cook's spontaneous affection for and joy over the chickens. A Wordsworthian hero, Hui Ming is also the perennial Chinaman abiding by the wisdom of the earth and enjoying a realistic sense of contentment which redeems his animal existence. In another story, "Hsiao-hsiao" (first composed in 1929, revised in 1935), one observes the even more subtle manifestations of the powers of innocence and spontaneity. In the poorer regions of the interior provinces it is customary for a girl to marry a boy considerably her junior in order to be able to assist in the household and farm work until such time as they become properly man and wife. An orphan girl, Hsiao-hsiao is married into a peasant family at the age of twelve; her husband is only three years old. She tends him and carries him with her wherever she goes. At fourteen, Hsiao-hsiao becomes quite a comely girl; a hired man easily seduces her with ballads and promises. Months later he leaves her when her pregnant condition is becoming obvious. Hsiao-hsiao, now wholly desperate, attempts to cause an abortion by drinking copiously from the stream and by swallowing incense powder at the temple. As none of these methods proves to be of any avail, her condition is finally noticed. Her husband's grandfather invites her uncle over to discuss whether, in accordance with custom, she should be drowned or sold as a concubine. The latter course is decided on, and Hsiao-hsiao is to stay with the family until someone proposes to buy her.

> Tranquillity was restored. At first the small husband was not allowed to be near Hsiao-hsiao. But soon they lived again as brother and sister in a normal and not unpleasant life.
>
> The little boy vaguely understood what was inside his wife and why she was to be married to someone else. But he was not willing to let Hsiao-hsiao go, and she did not want to leave the place either.
>
> In this strange atmosphere the family waited for somebody who might be willing to have Hsiao-hsiao, but by December nobody had appeared. In February

Hsiao-hsiao sat on a straw mattress and gave birth to a boy, with a round head, big eyes, and a deep voice. Both mother and son were well taken care of. According to custom, the mother was fed chicken broth and rice wine to improve her blood, and paper offerings were burnt to thank the gods. The whole family was fond of the baby.

As it was a boy, Hsiao-hsiao didn't have to be married into another family.

By the time Hsiao-hsiao was formally wedded to her husband, her son was ten years old, a useful member of the family able to look after cows and cut grass. He addressed Hsiao-hsiao's husband as Big Uncle and Big Uncle would answer to that, far from displeased.

The son was called Ox Boy, and at the age of twelve, Ox Boy himself was married to a girl six years older. An older daughter-in-law could do more work and be a real help to the family. As the sound of reed pipes approached the door, the bride was weeping inside her sedan chair. The great-grandfather and grandfather had quite a busy time.

That day, Hsiao-hsiao held her newly born son Yüeh Mao-mao in her arms as she had held her husband ten years before, and watched the bustle from the fence near the tree.[10]

Hsiao-hsiao reminds one forcibly of Lena Grove in *Light in August:* both simple farm girls seduced by hired men yet utterly inviolable in the strength of their animal purity. It is not at all coincidental that Shen Ts'ung-wen and Faulkner have evinced a similar interest in this kind of innocence and have often tested it against the absurd or cruel codes of society: in their loyalty to the earth and to the common man, they both regard it as the foundation for the more difficult virtues of charity, gallantry, and courage. Hsiao-hsiao is situated in a primitive society in which a kind of corrupted Confucian ethic still governs, but her temporary fear of family disapproval and censure leaves no marks of injury on her being. The reader leaves the story refreshed with a sense of the fitness of all things in the natural scheme.

The trustful, innocent maiden is a recurring figure in Shen Ts'ung-wen's fiction. In "San-san," the title heroine feels a wistful sadness over the death of a consumptive young man from the city who for some time has occupied all her thoughts; in *The Border Town* the heroine Ts'ui-ts'ui, daughter of an old ferryman, waits patiently for the return of her sulking lover, whose nocturnal serenade has for a brief time filled her heart with unforgettable ecstasy. Unlike Hsiao-hsiao, whose self-consciousness remains dormant, these country girls are the embodiments of first love, tremulous with longing and hope and yet immobilized in their eternal purity because their affections will never meet adult fulfillment.

If this Lucy figure stands at one pole of Shen Ts'ung-wen's world, at the other stands the Wordsworthian old man who has drunk life to its dregs and reached a stage of tranquillity beyond joy and despair. In the story "Living" (1933), a sixty-year-old puppeteer tries to attract customers at the plebeian amusement center to his act, which consists simply of two puppets, named Wang Chiu and Chao Ssu, knocking against each other. The old man also has some trouble in evading the policeman, who is trying to make him pay his overdue booth tax. Against a background of bustling activity, the story is in the undistinguished realistic, humanitarian manner; but suddenly, in the last two paragraphs, it is lifted to a high level of poetry:

> He then squatted on the ground like the puppets, counting the coins and smiling at the white-faced puppet Wang Chiu and repeating to himself the jokes which he had used earlier and which had provoked laughter from the audience at his own expense. The words he

A Decade of Growth

addressed to Wang Chiu were very intimate and gentle.
He wouldn't let people know that Wang Chiu was
named after his deceased son; he wouldn't even explain
that his son's death was the result of a fight he had with
Chao Ssu. He never mentioned these things. He only
let people see that when the puppet Wang Chiu and
the puppet Chao Ssu were wrestling, even though
Wang Chiu was at first always at a disadvantage and
Chao Ssu always took the offensive, the final victory
invariably went to Wang Chiu.

Wang Chiu had been dead for ten years; for ten
years inside and outside the city walls of Peking, the
old man had been playing Wang Chiu's fight with
Chao Ssu. The real Chao Ssu had also died of jaundice
in the city of Paoting five years ago.[11]

This passage, almost Dantesque in its pregnant terseness,
reaches back and invests the whole story with a larger meaning. In his perpetual re-enactment of his son's last fight the
puppeteer shares a lonely grandeur with Michael and the
Leech Gatherer.

In "Night," Shen Ts'ung-wen recounts rather leisurely
how once he and his four companions on a military mission
lost their way and took shelter at an old man's house. As the
soldiers spend the night swapping stories, the old man listens
quietly and seems profoundly engaged in thought. When
pressed to contribute to the session, he says he has no story
to tell.

It was getting light and cocks began to crow in the
distance. My comrades were dozing as I finished my
story. I was wide-awake, however, and begged the old
man persistently to tell me a story. The latter looked
at the fire and then at my dozing comrades. "I want to
go to my room and take a look," he said at last. "If you
insist on having my story, you can come with me." I
followed with a palpitating heart. I had passed all the

tests and at last he was going to show me his treasures and reveal to me his secrets.

At first I could only discern the usual jars and baskets for storing provisions. When I turned my gaze to the bed which I had seen only dimly from outside, however, I was shocked to find in it a woman's corpse, yellow as wax, dried and shriveled up like a potato overexposed to the air.

"What?" I exclaimed. "You have a dead person in the house!"

The old man did not lose his strange calm. He only looked at me with his sad eyes and sighed softly.

"This is my story," he said. "The dead one was my wife. I have lived with her in this lonely spot for sixteen years. She died last night at supper time. If you had not come, I would have had to sit by her all by myself for the night. I myself am going to die very soon. I have no story to tell except this. It is getting to be broad daylight. Heat the water yourself. I do not want to live any longer than I have to, but I must first go and dig a place for her . . . so that she can wait down there for me in peace."

When the author and his friends leave, "I heard, to the left of the house, the sound of digging as the spade fell slowly and weakly upon the damp earth." [12]

With its loose structure allowing for a number of unrelated tales, "Night" is definitely among the author's weaker stories. But the haunting image of the old man in the final section again represents human truth of a high order: the firm grasp of a stoic dignity and an irreducible human decency that transcend the Yeatsian rage at decrepitude and the nihilistic insomnia of the old man in Hemingway's "A Clean, Well-lighted Place."

The young girl on the threshold of adult experience and the old man affirming life even in sorrow and despair—these are Shen Ts'ung-wen's primary symbols of emotional integrity, of an uncompromising beauty in defiance of the world. But the world, with all its ugliness and depravity, is also part and parcel of his fiction: one does not begin to appreciate his pastoralism until one is aware of his satiric anger, his hatred for emotional and intellectual flippancy. Apropos of the charge that he is a mere entertainer and stylist, Shen Ts'ung-wen coolly reproves his left-slanted critics and readers: "You could enjoy the fresh quality of my stories, but as a rule neglect the passion seething underneath; you could enjoy the plain sincerity of my style, but as a rule disregard the note of latent sorrow in my writings." [13] Shen Ts'ung-wen's affirmation of innocence and integrity has made possible a critique of Chinese society which is the more valuable precisely because of its insistence on smugness and flippancy as a major disease. The same sane vision informs the pastoral world in its wholesomeness and dignity as well as the world of the modern man with his alienation from the earth and common affections, his sloth and cowardice, his pursuit of false values.

Of Shen Ts'ung-wen's stories about modern urban experience, the more explicitly satiric are often the less successful, owing to the intrusion of a too self-conscious didacticism. But in a few good ones the writer presents a powerful vision of modern China in her diseased state. "Big and Small Yüan" (1937), a study of two types of futility, is such a story. Big Yüan, cautious and mildly hedonistic, persists in the ways of the old-style gentry and ends comfortably as dean of his alma mater; Small Yüan, impetuous and opportunistic, seeks the life of danger in the supposed interests of the Revolution and dies finally in a prison. In pondering the latter's "martyrdom," Shen Ts'ung-wen avoids alike the partisan attitudes of praise and disapproval; rather, he formulates his indictment of the revolutionary youth in China in almost the identical terms of Arnold's censure of the romantic poets: with all their enthusiasm and valor, they don't know enough.

The literary importance of Shen Ts'ung-wen, of course, is not primarily dependent upon his contributions as critic, satirist, or even advocate of the simple and heroic life. His criticism of modern Chinese life and letters is always judicious and pertinent, his affirmation of the human spirit nearly invaluable, but what constitutes his major distinction is his copious imagination and his dedication to his craft. When one compares the early stories with those of the thirties or with their revised later versions (Shen Ts'ung-wen is the only modern Chinese writer with a passion for revision), one is astonished not only at his progress as a writer but at his spirit of dedication. In his maturity he has at his command not one but several styles: the limpid pastoral prose with its concrete evocation of landscape, for which he is especially noted and whose most finished example is perhaps *The Border Town;* the terse narrative style strongly under the influence of early Chinese redactions of Buddhist tales; the elaborate periods encompassing fluid mental impressions of the characters under description and representing a triumphant adoption of the European syntactic structure for Chinese prose. The last achievement is particularly remarkable when one remembers the writer's crude attempts in this direction in his apprenticeship years. In a story like "The Housewife" (1936), which discloses the mind of a happily married woman in a reminiscent mood of morning lassitude, the prose is as distinguished and elaborate in its way as that of Proust or Mann. (Unfortunately, Shen Ts'ung-wen defies translation. While irreproachable as to accuracy, *The Chinese Earth* retains little of the flavor of the original.)

The style and the pastoral vision are, of course, finally inseparable: they bespeak a high order of intelligence, the type of mind abundantly gifted with "negative capability." To capture the form and shape of a blossoming tree in its unique loveliness as well as to enter the heart and mind of a boat-hand and his girl in all their uncouth talk and animal integrity denotes in the end the same talent for rendering actuality. Even though he is bound by his moral convictions to rehearse examples of pastoral humanity, Shen Ts'ung-wen is at his happiest, in my opinion, when he is merely recording scenes and events of no apparent design, drawn from the reservoir of his capacious and retentive memory. He is the greatest impressionist in modern Chinese literature: no one equals him in his effortless capturing of the essence of a landscape, much in the manner of the best Chinese poets and painters, or in his rich evocation of the subtle nuances of feeling. In "The Day before He Ran Away" a young soldier registers with lingering affection the sights and sounds of the little town in which he is stationed; in "On the Mountain Path" three men, traveling from Yunnan to Kweiyang in the summer heat, pause at noontime at a narrow path to enjoy the most delicious scenery and caressing breeze. In many other stories, as well as in countless passages in his longer fiction, Shen Ts'ung-wen displays the same consummate impressionistic skill.

As a last example of his fiction I propose to discuss the story "Quiet," because it seems to me to have distilled in a few pages the art of Shen Ts'ung-wen in all its complexity—impressionistic rendition of scenes and feelings as well as a pastoral regard for human dignity in the teeth of ironic awareness of the chaos and sorrow of a war-torn China. In the story a much-harassed family, refugees from a war zone, are temporarily stalled in a small town, unable to make the next move without news from their menfolk. The mother, seriously ill with a pulmonary hemorrhage, is confined to her bed while her elder daughter and daughter-in-law have gone out to consult a fortuneteller. The maid is doing the washing. In this long spring day, therefore, the only members of the family less immediately concerned with their plight and enjoying comparative freedom are the teen-age daughter Yo-min and the five-year-old son of her elder sister, Pei-sheng, and it is upon these two that Shen Ts'ung-wen builds his story of considerable beauty and poignancy.

As the story opens, Yo-min is standing on the drying terrace watching the kites; soon afterward, Pei-sheng joins her there. The wide expanse of view from the terrace affords the youngsters a glimpse of spring, conspicuously unnoticeable in the dingy rooms downstairs, with the sick old woman and the worry and waiting. Pei-sheng is happily excited when he spies several horses grazing near a small river.

> Besides, there were three white horses and two brown horses, unattended, grazing at their ease or pacing gently.
>
> Seeing two of the horses running, the boy cried out in glee, "Little auntie, little auntie, look!" Little auntie gave him a look and pointed her finger downstairs. The boy understood; afraid that he might disturb the people downstairs, he hurriedly covered his mouth with his palm and shook his little head, as if saying, "Don't talk, don't talk, don't let them know." [14]

But it is Yo-min herself who needs most the sunshine, the breeze, the green meadow, and the limpid little river. In the subsequent oppressive silence she contemplates her own problems, particularly her desire to study in Shanghai. She watches a nun coming out of her convent and going to the riverside to wash clothes and vegetables, and for a while she is completely happy. But again the oppressive quiet returns. She goes downstairs to inquire after her mother:

> "How is your coughing?"
> "Better now, it's not important and doesn't really hurt me. This morning I was not careful and ate some fish and my throat got scratchy. It's not important."
>
> After the exchange of conversation, the girl thought

of going over to inspect the contents of the small spittoon near the pillow. Knowing what she intended to do, the patient said, "There's nothing." And then: "Min-min, stand there and don't move. Let me see, you have again grown taller this month. Almost a full-grown person now!"

Yo-min smiled shyly, "I'm not like a bamboo, mama, am I? I am afraid it's not pretty to be so tall at the age of fifteen. People will laugh at a tall girl." [15]

The elder daughter and daughter-in-law return later in the day and conversation is renewed. In the evening, Yo-min again goes up to the terrace to watch the view: smoke from the chimneys and a bride being ferried over the river. When she goes downstairs, her mother, sister, and sister-in-law are already in bed. The boy is dozing beside a toy dog, and the maid is whitening her face with tooth powder in the kitchen. Yo-min is startled to hear someone knocking on the door of a neighboring house; for a moment she thinks it might be her father and elder brother coming here to join the family. Then the evening again is quiet: the girl doesn't know that her father, a military officer, has died in action.

In a brief postscript, Shen Ts'ung-wen states that the story was written in memory of his sister's deceased son, Pei-sheng. So presumably all the characters were modeled upon people dear to the author, and one can sense the presence of a subdued but strong personal emotion. But for a proper appreciation of the story the biographical consideration is not pertinent. What Shen Ts'ung-wen has accomplished is the feeling of quietness, a mood of poignant sadness completely objectified in the helplessness of all the characters in their automatic motions of work and play, in the small-talk which fails to dispel gloom, and especially in the contrasting views of the dingy house and the loveliness of spring outside. The precise details observed from the vantage-point of the terrace —the river and meadow, the kites and horses, the nun and the bride—become each a symbol of liberty and joy beyond the reach of the family. In the thirties no Chinese writer other than Shen Ts'ung-wen could have quite encompassed within a story this rich structure of symbol and feeling.

CHAPTER 9

Chang T'ien-i (1907-)

CHANG T'IEN-I is the most brilliant short-story writer of the decade. When his first stories appeared in 1929, even his adverse critics could not deny the new writer's exceptionally keen ear and eye and his comic exuberance. With a minimum of description and exposition, Chang T'ien-i catches every salient feature of his characters in action, in a style that is dramatic and rapid. He does away with ornate language, discards the lengthy paragraphic structure, renders the speech habits of every social class with comic or dramatic precision. No other modern Chinese writer has surpassed him in the accuracy and range of his dialectal representation. In relation to the fiction of his time, Chang T'ien-i has operated with the surgical daring of a Hemingway in his ruthless excision of journalese, verbosity, and imprecision from the pai-hua idiom.

Yet this taut realism is not merely external; it has a serious moral interest. In view of Chang T'ien-i's unquestioned adherence to the leftist cause, this moral engagement is the much more remarkable achievement. One is almost tempted to see in him a Shakespearian creator who takes the predominant ideology of his age for granted and yet is able to use it as a vehicle for his superior moral intuitions. In a great number of his stories his satire of the upper and middle classes along prescribed Communist lines transcends the propagandist level to arrive at an ironic revelation of the basic human abjectness and cruelty. This moral vision, while amenable to Communist interpretation, is essentially the testimonial to a highly individual talent.

The least autobiographical of contemporary Chinese authors, Chang T'ien-i almost never adopts the first-person mode of narration. Yet his life in many ways sheds interesting light on his work. His grandfather, a native of Hsiang-hsiang, Hunan, served under the great statesman Tseng Kuo-fan during the time of the T'ai-p'ing Rebellion and established himself as a distinguished member of the landowning gentry in the province. His five sons all held the high rank of *chü-jen* and their children were accordingly reared for government careers. Born in Nanking in 1907, Chang T'ien-i was the fifteenth and youngest child; by that time his father had fallen from affluence and had to move about a great deal in order to earn a living. Chang T'ien-i was therefore exposed from early childhood to a great variety of dialects and to people of varied social backgrounds with whom his father associated for business or pleasure. After completing his high school education at the age of eighteen, Chang T'ien-i moved to Peking and began to study Marxism and prepare for a literary career. During the next few years he took such odd jobs as came along and was in turn government clerk, minor officer in the army, newspaper reporter, and school teacher. While his brothers, sisters, and cousins all moved in the higher governmental and educational circles, Chang T'ien-i stuck doggedly to his nonconformist path and gathered a rich store of variegated material for his fiction.[1]

Chang T'ien-i published his first story, "A Dream of Three and a Half Days," in 1928 in the magazine *Pen Liu* when he was twenty-one. Its editor, Lu Hsün no less, was greatly impressed by this new talent. From then on, Chang T'ien-i published in the space of ten years a rapid succession of stories, collected under such titles as *From Vacuity to Fullness, Little Peter, The Honeybee, Moving About, Counterattack, Spring Festival, Pursuit, Fellow Villagers,* as well as four satiric novels: *A Journal of Hell, One Year, The Strange Knight of Shanghai,* and *In the City.* With such a prolific output faults are to be expected. In many stories Chang T'ien-i duplicates themes and situations already used and comes perilously close to self-parody; in others he indulges his bent for a gratuitous form of low humor as he exaggerates the repulsive mannerisms of his characters. Some stories are told at unwarranted length and lack the author's customary power and restraint. But considering the fate of Chinese writers at that time, financially insecure and constantly harassed by magazine editors for contributions, Chang T'ien-i did remarkably well. If we except roughly a third of his stories as standard proletarian exercises in the manner of Socialist Realism, the remaining bulk testifies not only to his fertile abundance but to the consistently high level of achievement. Of his contemporaries, only Shen Ts'eng-wen closely matches him for the quality and quantity of his short stories, but Shen lacks his biting power and savage wit.

We may divide Chang T'ien-i's stories into three categories: agitational, ideological, and satiric. In the agitational stories, as has been just mentioned, we have the familiar situation of a revolt or uprising, the standard cliché of Socialist Realism. A group of peasants or soldiers, reduced to the last extremity, are incited to take desperate action against their oppressors. Contrary to the author's habitual presentation of sharply defined characters, the stage of such proletarian dramas as "Twenty-one," "The Bread Line," and "The Failure of Lord Snake" is usurped by a band of little-differentiated men shouting the same slogans and profanity. The action is predictably simple and uninteresting.

The ideological stories come under another category of leftist fiction which has as its main theme the hesitation or cowardice of a bourgeois intellectual when confronted with revolutionary experience. The titular hero of "Mr. Ching-yeh" is such a person; after momentarily regaining courage from the harrowing experience of the torture and death of his revolutionary friend, he relapses eventually into his old decadent habits. "The Sorrows of Pig-guts" deals with another such, resigned to bourgeois conformity and yet sad with the knowledge of the inevitable victory of the proletarian cause. In "Mutation" (included in the anthology *Living China*), the heroine, after a trying period of revolutionary work during which she has witnessed the death and torture of many of her dear friends, settles for a life of outward luxury and inner unrest as wife of a rich merchant. These stories, with their denser psychological texture, are in some ways superior to similar efforts by Mao Tun, Ting Ling, and Pa Chin, but they again afford Chang T'ien-i little chance to display his satiric ability or tragic discernment. Only in one story of this type, "After Her Departure" (discussed below), does the ideological conflict reach the status of a fascinating moral drama.

The best stories fall under the category of satire. In these Chang T'ien-i makes little exception of class and individual: gentry, bourgeoisie, and proletariat are alike grist to his mill. Doubtless with these stories in mind, the Marxist critic Hu Feng once labeled Chang T'ien-i a "plain materialist"—that is, an author who refuses to complement his realistic observation of society with the required dialectic of Communist optimism.[2] And yet in this refusal to discriminate between the good and bad, the hopeful and decadent, lies precisely our author's satiric strength. The world of Chang T'ien-i is largely the old world in its decadence, a cruel world of sadists and masochists, snobs and ambitious underdogs, betrayers and betrayed. In the following pages we shall study a few of the best stories in order to arrive at a clearer view of this world.

"The Bulwark" depicts with robust humor the bogy of

modern Chinese literature—the old-style, hypocritical Confucian gentleman. As applied to the hero, the Chinese title *ti chu*—a proverbial metaphorical expression for an upholder of orthodoxy and morals in a depraved age—is clearly ironical. Huang Yi-an is nothing of the sort, but rather, like Ssu-ming in Lu Hsün's "Soap," a hypocrite with a lascivious turn of mind, pretending to moral rectitude and complacently disapproving of modern tendencies. He is also a sadist. The undertones of cruelty in the story are characteristically Chang T'ien-i's own.

On a voyage upon the Yangtze, Huang Yi-an is escorting his sixteen-year-old daughter to another city to be looked over by a high-ranking official; he is hopeful that the latter may take a fancy to her and agree to a match with his son. Though handling her future in this callous manner in order to improve his own prospects, Huang Yi-an nevertheless jealously guards Chen Mei-tzu against corruptive influences on the crowded ship. Having spied her in the company of a woman breast-feeding her baby on the deck, he peremptorily summons her back to the cabin and gives her a stern lecture. While he is talking, he smells the aroma of opium and overhears fragments of a lewd conversation wafted over from the next cabin. He becomes increasingly fascinated but at the same time alarmed that his daughter may also be listening. Chen Mei-tzu, to whom the lingo is hardly comprehensible, keeps on knitting.

> He glanced at the wall for a while, then again turned his gaze on Chen Mei-tzu.
>
> She sat near the window and he could see only her stooping silhouette. But he felt that her face was flushed with crimson and her eyes were glistening—they were so moist and bright!
>
> *"Heh-heng!"* He loudly cleared his throat and pulled a long face.

Chen Mei-tzu was startled; a tremor went through her body.

Now he was sure she was guilty. The old man felt something was choking him inside and he couldn't even breathe properly. His eyes were almost popping out of their sockets, glaring with baleful fire at Chen Mei-tzu. He resolved to give her a sound lecture, a sound scolding, but his tongue was tied:

"Chen Mei-tzu! . . . you . . . *heng,* damnation . . . I'm telling you . . . understand that one, one . . ."

His mouth failed to produce any sound in spite of its violent motion; his sparse mustache also twitched. Then again he cleared his throat and words exploded from his mouth:

"One shouldn't listen to the improper! . . ."

The other stared at him with wide-open eyes and a mouth ajar.

"Don't just look at me!" The old man loudly hissed his words from between the teeth. "One should constantly examine oneself whether one has done anything improper . . . One . . . one . . . if one listens to improper language, then one oneself becomes improper! Now you understand!"

Chen Mei-tzu was dumfounded:

"How? What have I listened to?"

"What have you listened to? Next room . . . next room . . . I see you are . . ."

The father glared at her for a while, then heaved a long, disappointed sigh. He looked at his own feet, at the ceiling, then again in spite of himself, at his daughter.

She was still staring at him; he fumed as if highly offended:

"So you haven't listened! If one has faults, one should try to correct them; if one hasn't, one should strive

217

> hard to become even more virtuous . . . So there, why
> don't you return to the work you were doing . . ." [3]

In the original the passage is uproarious: the girl's dumb
innocence serves as the perfect comic foil to her father's over-
wrought indignation as well as to his mortifying discovery
of having made a complete fool of himself. He just can't understand his daughter's unfathomable stupidity.

Increasingly engrossed in the conversation in the next
room, Huang Yi-an becomes every minute more restive; his
excited manner even makes Chen Mei-tzu somewhat sus-
picious. Finally he feels he has to stop the talk. As he walks
into the next room, a fellow Confucian gentleman recognizes his identity, compliments him on his amatory prowess,
and presses him to tell before the group the juiciest episodes
in his life. Aware of his awkward position, Huang returns
to his own cabin to order his daughter to go up on the deck
and then rejoins the congenial company.

"The Bulwark," first of all, is a vivid account of life on
the ship as seen through the eyes of the hero. Huang Yi-an
evaluates every person and incident in accordance with his
dirty frame of mind and distorts its significance accordingly.
A woman breast-feeding her baby becomes a cause of libidinous disturbance as well as an object of moral reprehension.
Behind the comic surface of the story, however, lurks the
drama of a father who is going to sell his daughter. The
stupid girl is perhaps unaware of the mission of her trip; if
she knows, she betrays no sign of protest. Her quiet and unobtrusive presence in the midst of bustle and conviviality
underscores the mercenary cruelty of her father as well as
the comic gusto of the story.

To turn to another story, "On the Journey" again depicts
an everyday occurrence in China. A village bully by the
name of Chi reluctantly consents to travel aboard a cargo
train instead of the expected passenger coach. Vastly inconvenienced by the presence of two peasants in the same car,

he is further piqued when they won't allow him to use their bundle of clothes as a cushion. He is also very thirsty and it maddens him to see that the louts have brought with them a thermos bottle. He drinks from the bottle anyway and then again settles back to his manner of injured superiority.

While the train is about to start, a bald man with a gray beard comes aboard with his servant. Chi feels relieved at the prospect: here at last is someone socially his equal with whom he can converse. But the bald man doesn't pay him the slightest attention. Sulking angrily, Chi comforts himself with the thought that maybe the bald man is not so important as he looks; he aggressively places his left foot on the latter's trousers to test his reaction. After a brief period of forbearance, the bald man is thoroughly incensed. He proclaims his identity as a rich and retired general who once tried to prosecute Chi for his part in a famine relief swindle. As the general berates him for the rest of the journey, Chi listens in cowed silence in the mortifying presence of the two peasants. Once the general leaves the train, Chi can no longer contain his anger and humiliation and shouts to himself:

"What a jerk! . . . How did you get hold of your two millions, you beast! . . . You think your father is afraid of you, you beast! There will be one day when I shall . . . Whose bundle is this?"

His feet tripped over the gray bundle and forthwith he gave it a vehement kick.

Greatly startled, the two peasants apprehensively lifted their faces.

The big shot from Ma-p'o rushed before them, brandishing his two fists in the air. He shouted until his face turned purple:

"Why do you keep staring at me . . . You want a fight with me, don't you! . . . You blockheads, pigs! . . ."

He gave vent to his wrath by kicking Long Face; but
as he was bowlegged, his kick only brushed against the
other.

"Kicking me?" Long Face flashed his eyes like lightning.

"I kicked you, so what? . . . What were you snicker-
ing at then? What were you making faces for? You both
ought to be shot. You are bandits, beasts!" [4]

The three enjoy some respite of silence until they all get
down at the same station. Chi runs over to Long Face to slap
his mouth. As the latter dare not retaliate, Chi finally feels
relieved and resumes his leisurely style of walking. His light
blue gown sways on both sides, gleaming under the afternoon sun.

In the story the despicable character of the village rascal
is completely dramatized against the setting of a train journey. The smoldering anger of the peasants who can obtain
vicarious relief only when the general berates the rascal is
of course amenable to a Communist interpretation, but the
fact that the rascal also suffers humiliation in the hands of
the general, who presumably is a bigger scoundrel because
he is far richer and more powerful, makes "On the Journey" a comedy about a special brand of Chinese snobbery
which equates social prestige with the ability and power
to inflict pain upon one's inferiors. In this regard the village
rascal becomes a memorable embodiment of that ubiquitous
and perverse Chinese disease.

Another dramatic illustration of the theme of insult is the
story "The Mid-Autumn Festival," which is almost without a
parallel in contemporary Chinese fiction for its haunting
evocation of cruelty and abjectness. The village squire K'uei
Ta-yeh, with his wife and eight-year-old son, is going to
partake of their festival dinner at noon. Invited for the occasion at the wife's insistence is her poor brother, who otherwise would have no place to go on that important day. The

dishes have been laid out on the table for some time, but K'uei makes no motion to have the family seated. He detains in conversation his brother-in-law, who tries to be pleasant in spite of his extreme hunger. The impatient young son goes over to the table to snatch a bite. His father slaps his face, reproves him harshly, and then continues with his jeremiad on the ingratitude of relatives: "Other people have relatives, too—can count on them for help. But as for me, *heng*, every relative wants to use my money, to rub off my grease. I really can't understand, I really can't understand." [5] The wife remonstrates feebly to stop K'uei from continuing with his cruel game. Meanwhile, the dishes are getting cold.

A peasant-tenant walks in to present to K'uei a live capon as a festival tribute. When the latter shows evident displeasure at the size of the capon, the peasant has enough courage to retort and walk out with the gift. During this scene the poor relative has for a moment the warming sensation that the peasant is speaking for him too; but bound by his ingrained gentility he soon grows indignant at the peasant and even totters to the door to catch him. When he returns, K'uei repays his good office by another tirade on ingratitude. To save him from further humiliations, the wife finally asks her brother to leave. As he walks into the courtyard, he faints away out of sheer mortification and hunger.

The story can be interpreted in Communist terms insofar as the poor relative is a contemptible coward unable to take a firm stand with the peasant against the landlord; but again, as in "On the Journey," Chang T'ien-i takes full command of the dramatic situation and squeezes from it every possible drop of irony without yielding to the obtrusive gestures of protest and overt sympathy. K'uei Ta-yeh is a positive character in his own right, whose cruelty requires no explanation in terms of class struggle. Likewise, the poor relative is pathetic not because he has not received the Marxist revelation but because he is inescapably conditioned by his upbringing, by his unreflective and shabby gentility.

With the same unflinching realism, Chang T'ien-i portrays in "Lu Pao-t'ien" a character opposite to the poor relative, a small man trying desperately hard to improve his social status. The titular hero is a small government clerk so grotesquely spurred by his ambition to get ahead as to become completely blind to reality. Generally regarded as a harmless fool, he nevertheless prides himself on his cunning: he pokes his nose into factional politics and even plays the informer against his colleagues as a way of currying favor with the department head. Debilitated by a serious tubercular condition, he carries official letters from the office and copies them well into the night. Though pinched for money, he dares to join his superiors at a social occasion. He drinks and smokes until he is almost choked to death; he loses heavily at the mahjong table. Still undaunted, he later joins the company at horseback riding. He suffers a fall and blood spurts from his mouth.

He is now confined to his bed. Weeks later a fellow clerk comes to see him, trying to break the difficult news that he is fired. Though almost dying, Lu Pao-t'ien confides to his visitor: "Though I am on sick leave, in fact I can still handle secretarial work for Secretary Fei here at home. Old Lin, what do you think? I think this can be arranged." [6]

The pathos of Lu Pao-t'ien has a macabre quality. With a savagery characteristic of Elizabethan drama in its treatment of fools and lunatics, Chang T'ien-i subjects his little man to a continuous round of punishment. But he is not only the victim of cruel jokes; in his self-centered calculations for advancement, in his love of conspiracy and intrigue and masochistic enjoyment of drudgery and teasing, he is also the obstinate man blind even to the all too apparent deterioration of his body. The result is a tragic farce providing a horrifying look at the social struggle for survival.

As the last three stories would indicate, Chang T'ien-i is a highly class-conscious writer depicting the tensions, snobberies, and struggles between members of the same or different social classes. The ultimate moral is Marxist in its implication that a more egalitarian and humanitarian society will eliminate the terrible farce of insult and injury; but in his portrayal of the class lineaments of his characters, Chang T'ien-i abides with the integrity of a Ben Jonson by the realistically observed manners and conventions, refusing, except in his standard proletarian pieces, to distort and simplify life in accordance with some prescribed formula. Few of his contemporaries have grasped so clearheadedly and dispassionately his satiric and tragic view of man's fundamental perversity and his disposition for evil. The best stories of this author therefore possess a breadth of human truth uncommon in an age of humanitarian didacticism.

Chang T'ien-i's art is so rich that further examples from his short fiction are necessary to do him justice. The following three stories—"Spring Breeze," "Little Peter," and "After Her Departure"—are designed to suggest more fully his versatility and originality.

In the long story "Spring Breeze" Chang T'ien-i examines an artificial society cemented by the bonds of hatred and contempt. The title designates a free elementary school open to the children of all employees of the Provincial Highway Bureau; as Principal T'ung expounds it, it is symbolic of democratic education, blessing rich and poor equally, like the breath of a zephyr. Actually, of course, the class origins of students are rigidly observed by the principal and teachers, who, doomed to live on a miserable salary with no future prospects, vent their anger and resentment mainly on the great majority of dirty and ill-clad students, the children of road workers. The teachers, who also quarrel among themselves, only unbend in the presence of the neat students, whom they pamper and flatter. Conscious of their advantages, the children of the well-to-do employees of the Bureau are hopelessly arrogant and vicious. Chang T'ien-i has written many animated comic stories about student life, and in this one he exhibits, with more than his usual moral clairvoyance, the depravity and corruption among his assorted teachers and students. The following passage shows how Teacher Ting conducts his class; a jovial school physician with a humorous approach, he is only superficially unlike his sadistic colleague, Chin:

> In the classroom of Teacher Ting, there were frequent outbursts of laughter.
>
> At these times, Teacher Ting would appear even more animated than usual and his eyes and eyebrows would dance with joy.
>
> "Do you know—what is cleanliness?" Teacher Ting raised his book on high and asked the familiar question.
>
> As usual, the whole class answered satisfactorily: "Cleanliness is hygiene."
>
> Teacher Ting slightly inclined his head.
>
> "Correct, hygiene. Hygiene is very important and takes such forms as inoculation and vaccination. If one hasn't been vaccinated—is this right or wrong?"
>
> "Wrong!"
>
> "Yes, wrong. One who isn't vaccinated will become pockmarked like Liao Wen-pin . . . Liao Wen-pin, why didn't you have vaccination?"
>
> "I don't know." Liao Wen-pin was ready to cry and wiped his mouth with his sleeve.
>
> Pointing his finger at Liao Wen-pin's face, Teacher Ting forthwith gave a long lecture as if the little urchin had committed some serious misdemeanor and deserved a major demerit. He now shrugged his shoulders and now raised his eyebrows. Finally he punched his face with his fingers and made a wry mouth:
>
> "Hi, hi, hi, all the pockmarks, all the pockmarks! *Aya*, how ugly, how ugly, *aya, aya!* . . ."
>
> The class roared with laughter. Some even clapped their hands and stamped their feet.
>
> But Liao Wen-pin burst out crying.

The one on the platform imitated this with a loud "Wa!" Then with some difficulty he restrained his guffaw, puckered his mouth, and asked with a malicious twinkle in his eye:

"Why should you cry? Whom could you blame for being pockmarked?"

Another uproar of laughter. Unable to stop it with his waving hands, Teacher Ting stood there waiting for a while. His belly stuck out and his face shone.

"Yu Fu-lin," he finally shouted. "Are you fit to laugh at others? You yourself have a scabby head. It is as ugly as a pockmarked face. Hi, hi, how dirty, how dirty . . ."

He took a piece of gauze from his pocket to protect his mouth and giggled to himself until everyone else had quieted down. Then he put on a serious face and asked the usual question: Who was the cleanest in the class?

Every student knew what was on Teacher Ting's mind.

"Lin Wen-hou!"

Then—everyone glanced in the direction of Lin Wen-hou.

This paragon of neatness hurriedly assumed a dignified air, shutting his mouth tight. Though his eyes were roving left and right, he sat most properly: his chest stuck out so much that his back assumed a concave shape. He looked like a piece of ill-shapen sculpture.

Teacher Ting was blowing his nose with his piece of gauze. As he was on the point of resuming talking, Lin Wen-hou suddenly shouted:

"Sir, Chiang Jih-hsin is making eyes at me!"

The teacher stared at Chiang Jih-hsin, protruded his lower lip and shook his head in a warning manner.

After a while, Lin Wen-hou again shouted:

"Sir, Chiang Jih-hsin's dirty clothes have touched my person—they are so dirty!"

Many students stared at Chiang Jih-hsin and then at

Teacher Ting. Some faces wore a peculiar expression, in keen anticipation of something about to take place. One student loudly smacked his lips.

"Now, Chiang Jih-hsin, are you again asking to be beaten?" Teacher Ting merrily rolled up his sleeves and made a face to excite laughter.

In spite of the defense put up by the dirty boy, he talked on.

"Now you set the penalty: How many strokes . . . What? I don't care whether you did it intentionally or unintentionally; even if you did it unintentionally, you have to be beaten . . . Tell me quick how many strokes . . . two strokes? . . . Hi, hi, hi, don't you think that will be too few? . . ."

He set the penalty at fifteen strokes and then started using his blackboard eraser. Shrugging his shoulders and twitching his nose, he uttered another witticism:

"This will serve as a kind of vitamin for the little scamp." [7]

The passage reminds one of the scene in Mr. Gradgrind's school at the beginning of Dickens' *Hard Times,* so expertly analyzed by F. R. Leavis in *The Great Tradition.* Teacher Ting's boisterous clowning, compounded of malice and condescension, is not only ironical in that it wins over the students; it is indicative of a deep-seated inhumanity which describes all the other teachers as well and makes life in Spring Breeze School a virtual hell for the poor and dirty students. As Aldous Huxley has reminded us in his essay "Hyperion to a Satyr," there is nothing that separates humanity as effectively as filth and unclean disease; in "Spring Breeze" as in his other stories about children, Chang T'ien-i makes a universal symbol of unwanted humanity out of the dirty Chinese child in his manifold guises—scabby head, pockmarked face, running nose, shiny sleeves. In this context Teacher Ting's emphasis on hygiene, his ridicule of the unvaccinated and uninoculated children, and his use of a piece of gauze as a disinfectant are themselves shrewdly observed symptoms of his failure to love and care.

The hero of "Spring Breeze," Teacher Ch'iu, is somewhat better than his colleagues by virtue of his deep dissatisfaction with his present lot and his ambition to quit the place and enter college. But he is equally ridiculous, equally impatient with and contemptuous of the poor children. He again is the small man who has taken on the evil quality of his environment because he hates it and is unable to leave it. The wealth of Dickensian comedy in "Spring Breeze" is rooted in the sardonic perception of how one doomed class on a slightly higher economic level may positively hate another on a lower. The story is another masterly study in cruelty and snobbery.

"Little Peter" is sardonic in another fashion. The title refers to a pet dog owned by a manufacturer who pampers it with beef, milk, and chocolate and allows it to run freely about his factory. The workers and clerks in the factory hate the dog because it is a symbol of luxury and a part of their master which they can hurt. Whenever convenient, they throw stones at it and molest it in other ways. The manufacturer becomes quite incensed and keeps Little Peter indoors. But one day the dog is again at large and it is caught by seven or eight workers and clerks. They kill it and make a delicious meal out of it. "They felt elated. But on their way home, none was inclined to talk: the sense of elation was felt to be quite hollow and at odds with some unnamed disquietude." [8]

On its appearance in 1931 Lu Hsün and the other Communist critics pronounced the story frivolous: the nasty business of killing and eating a dog seemed uncalled for if the author's primary intention were to inculcate hatred for the manufacturer. But precisely here Chang T'ien-i, with his superior moral intuitions, parts company with his critics: he sees beyond the required clichés to arrive at a disturbing commentary on the perversity of the human will. He bowed before this criticism, however, and hasn't written again about the industrial proletariat in quite the same fashion. "Little Peter" has remained therefore an isolated example of what its author could do with this material; it still stands unchallenged as the most ironic study of capital-labor relations by a Chinese writer.

"After Her Departure," as already mentioned, is Chang T'ien-i's only ideological story that attains the status of moral drama. Like the author's other stories about intellectuals, it suffers from too much ideological disquisition as well as a style of dialogue which, in contrast to the richly idiomatic speech of his village and small-town characters, appears abstract. But it nonetheless conveys in concrete human terms the philosophical dilemma of idealism vs. reality. A small-town girl brought up in impoverished circumstances has been tutored in Communist ideology by her seventh uncle prior to her marriage to the wealthy manufacturer, Ho Po-chün. Living a life of ease in Shanghai, she takes everything for granted and develops qualms over her husband's unjust dealings with factory workers. Acting on an impulse of righteous indignation, Mrs. Ho suddenly returns home as the story begins, and tells her stupefied parents that she is going to obtain a divorce. Her father, who has just quit his ill-paid job in expectation of a more comfortable life, now becomes alarmed that he may again face a bleak future. Contemptuous of her parents' fear and anxiety, Mrs. Ho tries to obtain moral support from her seventh uncle; the latter, a prudent and cowardly man who only professes Marxism, can give her little comfort either, however. Pacing in her old bedroom, our heroine begins to take in her shabby and dingy surroundings and see the helplessness of her parents and the monotony of her former existence:

> Her mother and old Wang Ma were in another room looking for a pair of scissors; they were mumbling as if

blaming each other. From the living room came the noise of her father inhaling his pipe. It sounded so listless and monotonous, as if the world were made only for pipe-smoking and as if he were waiting with resignation for old age and death.

All this of course was familiar to *ku-t'ai-t'ai*. She felt as if she had never left home, never met Ho Po-chün, never married. As if she had just returned from school.

But there was some difference: at the earlier time she had been wearing a shabby cotton-padded jacket and, on top of it, a blue dress that had been darned and redarned. She was shod in a pair of India rubber shoes: in summer her feet were steaming with perspiration and in winter cold as ice.

"Eh, that life!"

What kind of life was that—no vivacity, no fun, no happiness!

For twenty years days had mechanically succeeded one another. Home from his government office, father would complain about poverty and put on a sour face. He would play his set of dominoes and calculate at what year he would be able to shuffle off his bad luck. He would then mumble to himself and heave a long sigh, complaining that he was making life hard for his children and his children were making life hard for him. Then mother would have her nervous fits and start to cry; she wouldn't cease until old Wang Ma asked her how to prepare bean curd.

Ku-t'ai-t'ai at that time had no idea that a family could have joy and laughter. Though she didn't have a hand in the management of the house, her heart was filled with an unnamable melancholy. At dusk and before the lamps were lit she would listen to father's sighing and puffing at his pipe, the bickerings between mother and old Wang Ma, the cluckings of the hens in the yard, the wind in the sky, the distant bugle calls from the barracks, and then a sadness would seize her and she would often cry without cause or reason.

Only her seventh uncle gave her comfort—those books, those ideas. It was also he who introduced her to Po-chün.

But now her seventh uncle was also like that, telling her that life is but . . .

Her heart sank. Tired of continuously pacing in her room, she wished she could recline on a brass bed with a thick, resilient mattress: but there was only that old and rickety Ningpo bed.

She didn't sit down, however, only stared at the housetop with no ceiling to speak of and the paper-covered lattice windows. It suddenly appeared incredible that she could have been brought up in this damp and dingy house. She felt creepy, as if little gnats that batten upon garbage were stinging her body all over.[9]

Now she begins to be horror-struck at what she had done: suppose her husband doesn't care and doesn't entreat her to return! How could she endure to live in this place the rest of her life and take care of her parents and younger brothers and sisters besides? She cries convulsively. But a telegram from her husband soon averts her crisis.

A typical leftist writer would have developed the story differently. He would see to it that the heroine's moral courage stays firm to the end; most probably the story would end rather than begin with her departure from her husband's home—using the familiar formula of *A Doll's House*. But in the present story the moral interest centers upon the aftermath of the heroine's impulsive action, the shattering of her schoolgirlish idealism in her reluctant submission to the dictates of reality. There is little doubt that Chang T'ien-i holds the seventh uncle in contempt and regards his heroine's eventual prudence as an act of cowardice; but at the same time he is the profound psychologist transforming her mental conflict into a parable of universal ironic significance.

Chang T'ien-i is a master of the short story, as his choice pieces from "The Bulwark" to "After Her Departure" have made abundantly clear. As a novelist, however, he appears rather at a disadvantage. His clipped style, which lends vigor to the short stories, tends to be monotonous when maintained over the length of two or three hundred pages; his knack of broadly defining a character in terms of a few recurrent traits becomes stultifying in a longer narrative, for it precludes psychological development. *In the City,* for instance, a workmanlike novel of 500 pages, is crowded with dozens of scheming and quarrelsome small-town characters. Each is crafty in his own way, but the concatenation of intrigue fails to generate even a modicum of excitement. Only toward the end, when the principal villain, T'ang Lao-erh, and his mother wrangle over money and disclose their greed and mutual hatred hitherto hypocritically masked, does the novel attain a moment of dramatic animation. This scene is so brilliant that by its standard the rest of the novel is merely a pedestrian and superficial study of small-town manners. *One Year,* a satiric novel about government clerks, shares the plodding quality of *In the City.*

In *The Strange Knight of Shanghai,* however, Chang T'ien-i achieves a very delightful comic novel. Like *Chao Tzu-yüeh,* it is a farcical account of the decline of heroism and chivalry and owes a great deal to *Don Quixote* and popular Chinese adventure fiction for its conception of the gullible man as hero. Its theme is likewise patriotism. But whereas Lao Shê shows an insistent didactic concern over the fate of China, Chang T'ien-i is merely content to expose the frauds and delusions stemming from the commercialization of and unrealistic obsession with patriotism. In literary form, his novel is more obviously a burlesque, but in possession nevertheless of satiric brilliance and unusual comic verve.

By the early thirties China is awake to the threat of Japanese aggression. The Government invariably appeals to the popular patriotic sentiment to sell its programs: the New Life Movement, the building of an air force, or even the sale of air force lottery tickets is supposed to "save the nation." Businessmen, industrialists, and educators follow this lead in peddling their wares in the name of patriotism. Thus an old-style educator would demand a return to the study of the Confucian classics as indispensable for national salvation; an owner of a cabaret would impudently advertise the patriotic virtues of social dancing. It is against this background of the commercial deluge of patriotic goods and ideas that *The Strange Knight of Shanghai* has its satiric relevance. Even its hero, though a complete fool, is primarily bent on saving his country by means of Taoist magic and gymnastics. In the novel a character reads a wall poster:

ONLY THERMOS BOTTLES CAN SAVE THE COUNTRY! ??? !!!
In the Northeast it is bitter cold. So when the brave volunteers are fighting the Japanese enemy, each soldier always carries with him a Moonlight Brand thermos bottle, because Moonlight Brand thermos bottles are quality products at a low price and are guaranteed to keep water hot for 72 hours. All patriotic people love to use them. So let's say:

ONLY THERMOS BOTTLES CAN SAVE THE COUNTRY! ? !!!
Don't lose this chance to become patriotic! ?? [10]

But even this bit of nonsense is not gratuitous humor; it is consonant with the satiric theme of the novel.

The story begins with the Shih family, in fear of the impending Japanese occupation of North China, moving by train from Peiping to Shanghai. On the way, Shih Po-hsiang, a prey to fortunetellers, and his scatterbrained second wife confide to a fellow passenger that his younger son, Chao-wu, is destined to become a division commander at the age of fifteen. Now already fourteen and very much pampered, the latter therefore completely outshines his elder half-brother Chao-ch'ang, who hasn't achieved anything yet even though in his middle twenties. Sitting glumly in his seat, Chao-ch'ang, however, is contemplating his far more illustrious destiny. An addict to adventure fiction and conscientious student of Taoist exercises, he is confident that he will soon achieve the magic powers with which to rout the Japanese.

Once in Shanghai, Chao-ch'ang meets with a rascal, Hu Ken-pao, who introduces him to his fellow Hunanese swindlers, the holy man T'ai-chi Chen-jen and his disciple Half Dust. Duly impressed by his supposed feats of super-human power, Chao-ch'ang becomes a disciple of the holy man and agrees to donate four thousand dollars to defray the cost of building an Alchemic Altar at the Kunlun Mountains, the legendary resort of Taoist celestials.

In his more mundane home environment, Chao-ch'ang associates with some wealthy citizens who are organizing a Society to Promote Abstention from Food by All Prominent Citizens as a Means of Saving the Country. These prominent citizens abstain from rice only to indulge in all kinds of delicacies. Another group of enterprising people, with whom our hero is only casually connected, organizes a Committee for Donations to the Cause of Conquering the Barbarous Enemy. Huge sums contributed by the overseas Chinese go to the pockets of the committee members.

Our hero is a romantic, and he is thrilled one day to watch Mary Ho starring as "The Female Patriotic Knight" in a musical staged by the Modern Patriotic Song-and-Dance Troupe. Since all heroes have their ladies fair, Chao-ch'ang is convinced that this female patriotic knight is his destined partner in the task of vanquishing the Japanese. Again making free with his money, he wins some token favors from Mary Ho, only to beat a hasty retreat when he discovers her in the lap of another lover.

Chao-ch'ang is now persuaded by his Taoist friends to seek his mate from among the plebeian class. After watching a street acrobatic performance, he thinks he has found the end of his search in the young female acrobat. He is, however, unceremoniously rebuffed by the girl's father.

The Sino-Japanese Incident of 1932 begins in Shanghai. Our hero, in a fit of delirium, dashes out into the streets, mumbling his Taoist spells, brandishing a sword (actually a pocketknife) and sucking in his mouth the magic pills given him by his Taoist friends (actually hard candies). Heedless of the bombing overhead, he is immediately wounded in the shoulder and sent to the hospital by an acquaintance. Meanwhile, living safely in the foreign concession, Mrs. Shih is playing mahjong and, as always, praising her own son, supposedly soon to become a division commander.

The foregoing paragraphs give only as much idea about the novel as textbook synopses of *The Alchemist* and *Bartholomew Fair* give of Jonson's great comedies. Until the last chapter, which gives due prominence to the element of fantasy in the hero's encounter with reality, *The Strange Knight of Shanghai* moves in the satiric open, crowded with impostors, swindlers, and frauds of every description. The hero's misadventures are generally hilarious, especially in scenes with the Taoist rascals or Mary Ho. With a flair for verbal comedy approaching Dickens,[11] Chang T'ien-i renders with apparently effortless skill the Hunan dialect of the Taoists and the peculiar imitation-Mandarin of Mary Ho. As a sheer robust farce, *The Strange Knight of Shanghai* has no equal in contemporary Chinese fiction.

The novel, of course, is not a great book. The Marxist critique of Chinese social types, which the author implicitly follows, restricts satire to mere ridicule. Though patterned after Don Quixote, Shih Chao-ch'ang is not intended to breathe in the tragic element. As a character, he is to be taken even less seriously than Chao Tzu-yüeh, who is shown in the end capable of some regeneration. A victim of chauvinism and adventure fiction, Chao-ch'ang is also a typical product of his genteel environment. He abuses the cook, scorns the poor, and once provokes a quarrel with factory hands on strike. Though easily duped, he is cunning with money in his own fashion and tries repeatedly to pass on a false coin. Chang T'ien-i, while indulging himself in the broadest farce, never lets his reader forget for a moment the class implications of his hero. The other characters—Chao-ch'ang's parents and half-brother, the Taoist crooks, Mary Ho, the prominent citizens turned swindlers—are also what they are because they represent the decadence and corruption of feudalist and capitalist China.

In spite of its Marxist bias, *The Strange Knight* emerges as a sound study of the people who exploit the patriotic sentiment for their private gains. The hero, though symptomatic of a deep-seated atavism in his aping of the ways of the Boxers, is at least not rapacious: his delusion and naiveté contrast powerfully with the more sinister implications of the other characters. The satiric picture is comprehensive enough, though one could have wished that the author had castigated also the patriotic pretensions of the leftist students and writers.

Chang T'ien-i kept up his prolific pace until after the outbreak of the Sino-Japanese War. During the first few years he busied himself with patriotic and propaganda work of various kinds, first in Changsha and then in Szechwan, and published *Three Sketches,* a satiric study of undesirable types of intellectuals thriving under the chaotic conditions of the war.[12] This has proven to be his last significant contribution to fiction, for soon afterward he found out that he was seriously afflicted with pulmonary tuberculosis and had to recuperate in retirement. His pen remained idle for almost a dozen years.

In the early fifties one again comes across Chang T'ien-i's writings in the leading literary journals, such as *People's Literature.* These are mostly tales and one-act plays about children designed for juvenile readers.[13] In view of his remarkable command of the juvenile mind (as is evidenced in "Spring Breeze") and the great success of his earlier children's tales (such as "A Strange Place" and "The Kingdom of the Golden Duck"), the Communist cultural leadership, apparently, has asked Chang T'ien-i to specialize in juvenile literature. This is no mean assignment when one realizes the extreme importance accorded by the Communists to the ideological conditioning of young minds. Chang T'ien-i has remained a figure of some importance in the literary hierarchy; in fact, since December 1957 he has been editor-in-chief of *People's Literature*. His new juvenile creations are expectedly full of Communist clichés, but as the short-story writer and novelist who has asserted the sturdiest independence of leftist tradition while staying well within it, Chang T'ien-i is already a part of Chinese literary history.

CHAPTER 10

Pa Chin (1904-)

PA CHIN is one of the most popular and voluminous writers of this period, but he is not one of the most
important. Despite the high critical and popular esteem he
has enjoyed, one fails to find in his work of this period (he
gradually improved as an artist during the war years) the
striving for excellence that has distinguished such diverse
writers as Mao Tun, Shen Ts'ung-wen, and Chang T'ien-i. A
man of intense moral, even religious, fervor, Pa Chin professes to serve an ideal higher than art. "I am not an artist,"
he confides in a preface to one of his story collections. "People say that life is short and art is long. But I think there is
something which has a more perennial value than art. That
thing enthralls me. For it I am willing to forsake art without any compunction. What is art if it cannot bring some
light to the masses and strike a blow at darkness?" [1] To the
few critics who censured his style and craftsmanship, he replies in effect that his novels and stories are the product of
inspired, automatic dictation, to which conventional artistic
criteria are irrelevant:

> I lack the temperament of an artist; I cannot compose
> a novel as if it were a work of art. When I write, I for-

237

get myself and become practically an instrument: I have really neither the leisure nor the detachment to choose my subject and form. As I said in my preface to *Light*, at the time of writing I myself no longer exist. Before my eyes looms a dark shadow, and it expands until it becomes a series of pathetic pictures. My heart becomes as it were whipped by a lash; it palpitates, and my hand moves rapidly along the paper, beyond my control. Many, many people are taking hold of my pen to express their sorrows . . . Do you think I can still pay attention to form, plot, perspective, and other such trivial matters? I am almost beside myself. A power drives me on, forcing me to find satisfaction in "mass production"; I have no way of resisting it and it has become a habit with me.[2]

Pa Chin seriously believes in his daemonic possession, and apparently the student readers of the thirties and forties shared that belief. More than any other writer, he was their hero; his noble revolutionary humanitarianism spoke directly to their hearts.

If his writings of this period are any indication, Pa Chin himself never outgrew his own adolescence. As a child, he was extremely sensitive to pain and suffering; in his *Reminiscences* (1936), he recounts many of his early encounters with sorrow and death, which seem to have left open wounds in his adult life. Born into a large, landowning family in Chengtu, Szechwan, Li Fei-kan (the pen name Pa Chin was formed of syllables from the names of two anarchists, *Ba*kunin and Kropot*kin*) was showered with affection, especially from his mother. But even love could not ward off the unpleasant aspects of life which unavoidably accompany the process of growing up. As a boy of five or six, Pa Chin was very fond of poultry in the courtyard. A pied rooster, which he particularly loved, was one day killed for a feast. As the boy came to its rescue, its throat was just being cut:

"The big pied rooster was flapping its wings on the ground and was moving slowly. There were some splashes of blood on its pine-green feathers. I came near it and cried, 'Big pied rooster.' It closed its eyes and hung its head. It was flapping and its body rubbed against the dirt. There was a big gash on its throat and blood was oozing out." [3] For Pa Chin, this experience was traumatic; characteristically, he restaged the scene in his first novel, *Destruction*.

Soon after the incident, his nurse Yang Sao died. She had remained with the family as a servant and had fallen critically ill. Pa Chin went to see her. "There was no sound in the gloomy and dark room. There was only stench. The stumpy bed was half hidden by the blue-cloth curtain. An old cotton quilt covered the lower half of her body. She was sleeping . . . I couldn't think of a word to say and only wetted her hands with my tears. 'You are crying! You have a good heart. Don't cry. I'll get over this sickness.' " [4] This experience is later movingly embodied in the death scene of the maidservant Ch'ien-erh in the novel *Autumn*.

Pa Chin was to suffer more important bereavements. In 1914, when he was only ten, his mother died. Soon afterward his second elder sister passed away, and also a maidservant who had been his dear playmate. In 1917 death claimed his father. Many years later, in the spring of 1931 when Pa Chin was already an established writer, came the shattering news of the suicide of his eldest brother in Chengtu. Only two months earlier Pa Chin had received from him a twenty-page letter, recounting his woes as a victim of the big family system.

If the youthful Pa Chin was continually preoccupied with the facts of death and suffering, he was also, to a lesser extent, seized with hatred and indignation. His loving and sensitive nature reacted with anger and disgust to the inevitable quarrels between different households living together under the rule of his grandfather; the occasional cruelty and lewdness of his father and uncles; the sad lot of servants; the utter inefficacy of Chinese herb medicine to check the prevalence of disease. As he grew older and saw more of the misery and injustice in the outside world, he began to seize upon the new ideas then propagated in *New Youth* and other progressive magazines. His need for love and his vast humanitarian sympathy determined his course of reading, and in time he was to become the pre-eminent advocate of anarchism as well as the greatest authority on the revolutionary and anarchistic literature of the West among modern Chinese writers. But this reading arrested rather than broadened or altered the outlook of a fifteen-year-old boy who found in a tract by Kropotkin entitled *An Address to Youth,* and a play by the Polish author Leopold Kampf, *Le Grand Soir,** all he needed in the way of intellectual guidance and spiritual revelation. Years later, in the preface to his own translation of this play, Pa Chin tells of its impact upon himself:

> It is probably ten years ago that a fifteen-year-old child was reading this little book. At that time he had just embraced the ideal of loving mankind and loving the world; he had the childlike illusion that a new society

* Born in Austrian Poland, Leopold Kampf suffered persecution as a patriot and revolutionary and emigrated to Germany as a young man. He wrote there in German the play that was to have such a profound influence on Pa Chin. Because he couldn't get his play produced there, he eventually left for America. When the play was finally presented in German in a New York theater, it caught the attention of a visiting French producer. In 1907(?) the French version of the play was presented in Paris, and it was, according to contemporary reviewers, a resounding success. The French text of the play by Robert d'Humières, entitled *Le Grand Soir,* was published in *L'Illustration Théatrale,* No. 81 (February 8, 1908), with an introductory note on Leopold Kampf by Gaston Sorbets. According to Sorbets, Kampf was 32 years old in 1908.

Pa Chin Wen-chi (The Works of Pa Chin), Vol. 5, gives the following brief informtaion on the play: "*Le Grand Soir,* a three-act play by the Pole Leopold Kampf (1881–?), was produced in Paris in 1907. A Chinese translation was published by the World Society (Shih-chieh shê), Paris, in 1908; it was pirated in Shanghai in 1920" (p. 382).

in which everybody shares happiness would rise with tomorrow's sun and that all evils would instantly vanish. Reading the little book in this frame of mind, he was indescribably stirred. That book opened for him a new vista and let him see the great tragedy of a generation of youth in another country striving for the liberty and happiness of the people. In that book the fifteen-year-old child found for the first time the hero in his dreams, found moreover his life career. As a precious jewel, he introduced that book to his friends. They even copied it down word by word, and because it was a play, they played it on stage several times. This child was myself, and that book was the Chinese translation of *Le Grand Soir*.[5]

For most serious readers, a favorite book at the age of fifteen will usually be outgrown by the age of twenty-five, or else approached with a new understanding of its intellectual and literary qualities. The case with many Chinese writers (and here Pa Chin stands only as an extreme example) is that books prized in their untutored adolescence remain throughout their writing careers as fountains of inspiration and guides to action. Their mediocrity as writers is partly traceable to their failure to advance beyond their adolescent literary taste and intellectual understanding. In his reading the young Pa Chin came across many writers with whom he felt a spiritual affinity and to whom he has given his unswerving loyalty. One such discovery was Emma Goldman, the eccentric anarchist and author of *My Disillusion with Russia* and a two-volume autobiography, *Living My Life*. Pa Chin acknowledged her as his "spiritual mother" and, later in his life, carried on a desultory correspondence with her.

Though his reading sustained his faith in a better humanity and though, as editor of a school magazine, he had the chance to propagate his ideas to a circle of congenial friends, Pa Chin was becoming increasingly disgusted with his feudal existence at home. In 1923, he left Chengtu for Shanghai and went on to Nanking to complete his high school education. He returned to Shanghai in 1925 to recuperate and prepare for a literary career. He translated a book by Kropotkin and launched a little-known magazine. In January 1927, at the age of twenty-three, he went to France, where he stayed mostly in Paris. He applied himself diligently to the study of French, began his translation of Kropotkin's *Ethics*, and completed a novel entitled *Destruction* (or *La Pareo*, in Esperanto). The latter was published serially in *The Short Story* Magazine, and when Pa Chin returned to China in 1929, he found himself, somewhat to his surprise, already an acclaimed writer.

From then until the outbreak of the Sino-Japanese War Pa Chin wrote and translated prolifically. He composed some dozen novels and novelettes, in addition to four collections of short stories. From December 1933 to July 1935 he lived in Japan. Returning to China, he became a founder of the Culture and Life Press and co-editor of *Wen-chi Yüeh-k'an*. In both capacities he encouraged many new talents of the period.

Destruction is a romantic tale about love and hatred: in anarchistic fervor it excels quite a number of Pa Chin's later novels, which are essentially variations on the same theme. Like the author himself, the hero Tu Ta-hsin (Tu Big Heart) is a sensitive child who cries over dead chickens and is early bereaved of his mother. In a season of famine, he sees human misery in all its grimness: "In the fields outside of the city huge pits were dug. Those who died of starvation were tossed pell-mell into the pits, like so many maggots." [6] As he grows older, Big Heart falls in love with a girl cousin who, submissive to parental authority, finally marries someone else. Some years later, after he has moved to Shanghai to engage in revolutionary activities, he again meets this girl. Now an unhappy widow, she entreats his forgiveness and love, but Big Heart is too embittered to care. With a flourish he dismisses her: "No, I can no longer love you. I no longer have that heart of love. This heart is no longer capable of loving or being loved." [7]

Far from being unable to love, of course, Big Heart is now dedicated to the love of the suffering masses. He is poet, pamphleteer, leader of a labor union, and editor of its magazine. He lives by the proposition that "whoever builds his own happiness on the suffering of other people shall be destroyed." [8] One day, drawn to an automobile accident (a recurring motif in Pa Chin's fiction), he strikes up a friendship with Li Leng and his sister Li Ching-shu. Despite their bourgeois upbringing, the latter are soon endued with Big Heart's revolutionary spirit. What's more, Li Ching-shu falls passionately in love with him.

Big Heart has a close friend who works for the labor union; he is arrested by the police and soon afterward decapitated. Big Heart now resolves to assassinate the chief of police. Ching-shu tries to dissuade him, in one of the more moving speeches in the novel: "We all are victims of the modern social system. . . . No one has the right to kill. Who was not born of the blood and flesh of his parents? Who doesn't have parents, brothers, and sisters like us? What crimes have these people committed? . . . Big Heart, let's not re-enact the tragedy of revenge, in the spirit of tooth for tooth and eye for eye. Have we not seen too many examples of this type of tragedy?" [9] Even though he loves her dearly, Big Heart remains implacable. As he embarks on his abortive attempt to kill the chief of police, he leaves behind a valedictory poem: "Whoever wants to strike the first blow against oppression shall be visited with destruction: I know this full well but my fate is already sealed. Tell me, at what time and in what place can liberty conquer the field without sacrifice? For my best-loved fellow men under oppression, I will to perish: I know I can and I will do so." [10]

The novel ends with a surprising passage of savage satire, the like of which is rarely seen in Pa Chin's early works:

> The chief of police didn't die; after a few days his health was completely restored. He was in a rage and locked up the chairman of the trade union on the charge that the latter had suborned his enemies to kill him. As a result, the chairman of the trade union had to contribute half a million dollars toward the provision of the army to buy back his freedom.
>
> The chief of police didn't die: he congratulated himself that because of Tu Big Heart's bullet he had acquired half a million dollars and his several concubines had acquired new jewelry. But Tu Big Heart's head, put on display in a cagelike structure on top of a streetlamp pole, had already turned into a leaking bag of stinking water, which made passers-by cover their nose.[11]

Ching-shu and her brother, however, are determined to carry on Big Heart's work. Five years later they are among the instigators of the May Thirtieth Movement in the sequel *New Life* (1932).

What is one to make of Pa Chin's first novel? In the context of modern Chinese fiction, it is surely superior to the early revolutionary fiction of Chiang Kuang-t'zu and the Creationists: Pa Chin's anger occasionally animates his flat and wooden style, and his reasoned anarchistic position is more philosophically interesting than the stereotyped Communist approach. Yet until toward the latter end of his career, Pa Chin differs from the average leftist writer only in degree rather than in kind because of his manifest inability to give the illusion of life to his characters and scenes. Already in *Destruction,* with all the freshness and daring of a first novel, one sees a palpable reliance on shabby literary props, a pronounced bias to simplify life in an abstract and theatrical fashion. Big Heart is but the Byronic hero in proletarian dress: somber, brooding, and defying God in the guise of a cruel social order. Ching-shu and her brother are the awakened bourgeois, ready to offer self-sacrifice but still unwilling to relinquish the comfort of personal love. Big Heart's rejected cousin is a weakling unable to extricate herself from the toils of the tradition. All these stereotypes have appeared elsewhere and are to recur in Pa Chin's later works.

If it can be said that the serious modern novel has taken over the role of poetic tragedy of earlier times, then the species of revolutionary fiction which *Destruction* represents is surely the recrudescence of heroic drama—with its representation of abstract passions and ideas, of the unambiguous conflicts between good and evil. In the novels and novelettes following *Destruction,* Pa Chin abandons himself to this type of theatrical reality, manipulating a predictable set of characters and situations in a make-believe world of unvaried intellectual debates, romantic entanglements, and revolutionary conspiracies. The *Love Trilogy,* which is his longest work in this genre, may be taken as fully representative.

The trilogy consists of three novelettes—*Fog, Rain,* and *Lightning*—together with a short interlude called *Thunder,* which precedes *Lightning. Fog* is the story of a weakling named Chou Ju-shui, who has just completed his studies in Japan and is spending the summer in a seaside hotel near Shanghai. His friends, especially Ch'en Chen and Wu Jen-min, come to see him frequently, and they discuss together the revolutionary prospects for China. A zealous revolutionary, Ch'en Chen scorns the attention of his female co-workers, whom he contemptuously dubs "petty-bourgeois women." Chou Ju-shui, however, soon falls in love with one of these, Miss Chang Jo-lan. As a married man, he is diffident of success and finally forfeits the love which Miss Chang is ready to offer him with the selfless generosity of a Turgenev heroine. The belated news that his wife in interior China has died over a year before only makes him more disconsolate.

In *Fog* we are introduced to two contrasting types of characters: Ch'en Chen, the man of dedication, and Chou Ju-shui, the irresolute coward. In *Rain* they yield the stage to Wu Jen-min: impetuous and romantic, he is the man of contradictions, ridden with bourgeois guilt but capable of violent outbursts of energy. Early in the novel Ch'en Chen is crushed to death in an automobile accident, though Chou Ju-shui lives on for some time as the inept lover of Li P'ei-chu. He lends her many revolutionary tracts, but this very reading opens her eyes and makes it impossible for her to accept his love. Contemptuous in the manner of Sanin,[12] Wu Jen-min finally tells the despondent lover to "jump into the Hwangpoo River, to end your life in a minute, lest your meaningless existence shame humanity." [13] Chou duly drowns himself. (One is reminded here of a similar episode in Waugh's *The Loved One,* but the death of Chou is merely illustrative of the consequences of cowardice, and is not supposed to be comic.)

In *Rain* Wu Jen-min is not yet capable of decisive action, though he is at times acutely aware of the suffering of his fellow revolutionaries. Once he tells a friend of his a horrible dream:

> Chih-yüan, I have traveled to Hell in my dream. I saw many young people. Some of them had their bellies ripped open and their hearts pulled out. Some of them were being shot or beheaded. Some of them were suffering inquisition and torture in prison. I realized they were also made of flesh and blood and I saw the weeping and lamentation of their parents and wives. I asked someone why they were so treated. He answered that they had committed the crime of free thought. I was on the point of saying, "Truly, these young people deserve their fate," when everything disappeared. Before my eyes was just a pool of evil-smelling blood. Startled, I began to cry. Then I woke up. I found that I am still

living the life of a petty bourgeois in a foreign-style house, that I am a revolutionist who only talks revolution in a comfortable home. Chih-yüan, I am frightened, frightened of myself in that dream.[14]

A recent widower, Wu Jen-min is, however, too much engrossed in carrying on two love affairs at once to pursue any other course than talk. One of the girls is married to a powerful bureaucrat and finally commits suicide; the other, so the plot goes, has no choice but to marry the same bureaucrat and leave her lover to the consolation of his revolutionary task. She is a consumptive in the last stage of her disease and will die in a half year or so anyway, but Wu Jen-min tries desperately to save her from her fate. One of his revolutionary friends now sternly warns him against this foolish course: "Jen-min, I feel you have no more reason to look for her. None of us has the right to wantonly destroy his own life. We should use our lives to fight our real enemy. This is the system and not the individuals. Our enemy is the system. That man is only your love rival. You have no right to sacrifice your life for love; your friends are expecting great things from you." [15] Leaving this friend's house, Wu Jen-min walks into a torrent of rain, which purges him of his personal unhappiness and rededicates him to the revolutionary cause.

In *Lightning* Wu Jen-min, Li P'ei-chu, and their comrades have left Shanghai to fight tyranny in Fukien. Pa Chin, who has had no personal revolutionary experience, shows extreme clumsiness in his handling of mass scenes in this work. Many of the comrades suffer arrest or death, but their martyrdom hardly excites a flicker of interest. In fact, one is never aware of the positive presence of any evil with which the comrades are supposedly contending: their enemy, a bandit turned warlord, never once shows his face. Instead, one is invited to ponder time and again the persistent problem of revolutionary fiction: love vs. duty. Dying, a callow youth in love with a girl comrade implores Wu Jen-min for an answer: "I want to ask you, among us can love . . . I mean can we love like other people? Do we have this right? They say that love can hurt work and interfere with the revolutionary task. Don't laugh at me . . . I still cannot . . . solve this problem . . . for a long time I have been wanting to ask you." [16] Wu Jen-min, who has found new happiness with Li P'ei-chu, can afford to be smug in his answer: "Why should you doubt? One's personal happiness is not necessarily in conflict with the happiness of the masses. Love is not a crime. On this point we cannot be much different from other people." [17] This conversation, intended to be a scene of edifying pathos, is fairly representative of the intellectual and dramatic level of *Lightning,* which supposedly strikes the note of affirmation after the cowardly hesitation and passionate conflict of *Fog* and *Rain.*

More than *Destruction,* the *Love Trilogy* exhibits Pa Chin as a bookish writer who chooses to depict a generalized world of love and revolution without any recognizable reality. Even though its characters and locales bear Chinese names, there is little else in the work to suggest the concrete presence of any particular Chinese manners and scenery. In *The Eclipse,* Mao Tun deals also with the world of love and revolution; yet his trilogy not only spans a particular historical period but is alive with the feelings and sensations of real people contaminated with a real evil. Pa Chin's imagination is utterly unnourished by the senses; it merely plays with clichés. For the youthful audience of the time, however, the dilemma of love vs. duty is no doubt exciting. On the one hand, it seems so noble to relinquish romantic love, that last infirmity of the bourgeois mind, for the pursuit of a more arduous ideal; on the other, it is perhaps even more thrilling to find the solace and beauty of love in the very context of revolution. What could bring greater personal satisfaction than to face the firing squad with the girl one loves and to die together for the sacred cause? In depicting these alternatives, one doesn't feel that Pa Chin is writing down to his audience; he appears seriously concerned.

Perhaps even more damaging to the quality of his fiction is Pa Chin's conviction that "the system" is alone responsible for the existence of evil. This is the cardinal tenet of all naturalistic writers. But Pa Chin is no naturalist; he is not primarily interested in tracing a character's life against his heredity and environment. His fiction rehearses the elementary struggle between good and evil, and his characters are either heroes or weaklings: the former defying and the latter submitting to the evil of the system. Defiance and cowardice presuppose free will, however, and Pa Chin's refusal to account for evil in terms of individual responsibility therefore undercuts the ground of reality from his fiction. Evil characters are presented, but time and again the author absolves them of that evil so as to maintain his theory that the system alone is to blame. This discrepancy between feeling and theory, uncomfortable in *Love,* becomes even more pronounced in the first two volumes of his next ambitious trilogy, *The Torrent,* whose central concern is the ills of traditional Chinese society.

Seemingly weary of his colorless revolutionaries even while he was completing the *Love Trilogy,* Pa Chin turned to autobiographical experience for a renewal of inspiration. In 1931 he contemplated a new trilogy drawing upon his family life in Chengtu during his adolescent years; but the news of his eldest brother's suicide so shocked him that he had to plan it anew, placing in the center of focus a similar victim of feudal oppression. The first volume, *Family,* was published in book form in 1933, and its sequels, *Spring* and *Autumn,* were completed respectively in 1938 and 1940. For Pa Chin, while he turned out in the interim many volumes of translations, essays, and short stories, the trilogy was apparently a labor of love, written with the full conviction of its truth. It was, until the postwar publication of Lao Shê's novel, *Four Generations under One Roof,* the longest and most ambitious piece of modern Chinese fiction. The mental anguish underlying its composition is apparent in the author's preface to *Autumn:*

> The last few months I have been in the worst state of mind; the writing of *Autumn* was not at all a pleasant task. (In a letter to a friend I wrote: "Last night as I was writing *Autumn* I cried . . . This book is tormenting me so that I shall be deprived of one or two years from my span of life on its account.") I said that I was engaged in the task of "digging up human hearts" (pardon me for using these four words in such a mad manner). I made the dead live and again sent the living to their graves. I entered into another world to see how the men and women there laugh and cry. I used the knife to slash my own heart. My nights were terrible. Every night I bent over my desk until three or four o'clock, then climbed to bed with my eyes full of the vision of dead spirits.[18]

Victims of the Chinese family system, these dead spirits relive their unhappy lives in the pages of the trilogy.

Family (497 pages), *Spring* (547), and *Autumn* (705) chronicle the tribulations of the Kao clan in Chengtu and the attempts of a few of its younger members to defy tradition and live a new life. These youths are the protagonists of the trilogy: the Kao brothers, Chüeh-hsin, Chüeh-min, Chüeh-hui; their younger sister, Shu-hua; and their girl cousins, Ch'in and Shu-ying. Most of the other younger members, however, are unable to oppose the blind cruelty of their feudal-minded elders and merely suffer and die. With complete disregard for monotony, Pa Chin traces, one by one, the tragedies of these weaklings: every family-arranged marriage ends ruinously, and every unhappy youth loves in vain and either commits suicide or dies of some horrible wasting disease.

In *Family* Chüeh-hsin, who is modeled upon the author's

eldest brother, bears the main brunt of the suffering. He is a good-hearted and sentimental man who lets his elders run his life and tries in vain to patch up the many inevitable family quarrels and contentions. While he watches helplessly, his cousin Mei, with whom he has been in love since childhood, pines away in sorrow and finally dies of tuberculosis. In deference to the wishes of the scheming members of the family, he subjects his wife during her second pregnancy to a cruel superstitious custom that ruins her health. She dies in childbed, and Chüeh-hsin becomes a lonely and sad man, pinning his hope on his first-born son, Hai-ch'en.

The second brother, Chüeh-min, fares much better. Because he is brave enough to show a certain amount of defiance to his grandfather, his romance with his cousin Ch'in survives family interference. The third brother, Chüeh-hui, who is the author's self-portrait, is the most resolute and enlightened youth in the family, though he emerges from the novel a truly insufferable bore. At school he is the agitator and pamphleteer; at home he is rather disrespectful toward his elders and often harshly reproves his elder brothers for their cowardice. But engrossed in his studies and extracurricular activities, he seems to be completely oblivious of the plight of the pretty maidservant Ming-feng, who is to be sold as a concubine to an old roué. She adores Chüeh-hui and timidly seeks his help on the eve before her wedding. When she sees him apparently preoccupied with his work, she drowns herself instead in the pond. (To many sentimentalists, the death of Ming-feng is the most affecting scene in modern Chinese literature.) Upon her death, Chüeh-hui's anger is thoroughly aroused; he leaves home after the death of his grandfather to engage in further study and revolutionary work in Shanghai.

Spring is almost an exact duplicate of *Family* in the main outline of its plot and in its perpetuation of the same sentimental clichés. Chüeh-min continues in love with Ch'in and not much happens to obstruct their happiness. He has become a more determined revolutionary, having taken over the role vacated by his younger brother as a student leader engaged in pamphleteering and dramatics. A very lonely soul after Hai-ch'en dies of an infectious disease, Chüeh-hsin becomes in time sentimentally attached to another of his cousins, Hui, who is forced to marry a very disagreeable person against her will; sorrowfully he watches her maltreatment in the hands of her husband's family, her final illness, and her death. Yet another cousin, Shu-ying, is fated to marry a wretch. She is a courageous girl, however, and with the assistance of Chüeh-min and Ch'in she escapes from home to join Chüeh-hui in Shanghai. On the journey she is escorted by her abject and consumptive lover, who dies upon reaching the big city. Shu-ying's positive action makes Ch'in murmur in admiration, "Spring is ours!"

After the lugubrious happenings in *Family* and *Spring*, *Autumn* comes as a powerful surprise. Pa Chin here refrains from overplaying the themes of sentimental cousin love and amateur revolutionary activities and depicts instead the family squabbles and degenerative diseases to their last gruesome detail. In *Autumn,* moreover, one feels that the author has encompassed a more mature understanding of evil because he no longer cares to draw at every point the moral that the system alone is to blame. Age as a criterion of good and evil no longer matters. Even in *Family* and *Spring,* of course, in spite of his thesis that all those entrenched in power in the family are bad or wicked, Pa Chin has to portray a few sympathetic characters among the elders, such as Ch'in's mother and the grandfather who, despite his autocratic ways, maintains something of the Confucian rectitude. In *Autumn* the author further enlists on the side of good the third uncle and aunt and the magnificent Grandmother Chou, who continually berates her son Chou Po-t'ao, a good-for-nothing squire, with the utmost heat and scorn. These characters are good and at times noble, not because they have imbibed the new ideas but because they are sensible and charitable in the traditional Confucian manner. On the other hand, the evil ways of the fourth and fifth uncles have been visited upon their sons, Chüeh-ying and Chüeh-ch'ün, who turn out to be completely corrupt. In attempting to build an artificial pattern of good and evil to accommodate his theory, Pa Chin has succeeded in being unredeemedly sentimental in his two earlier novels; the new alignment of the opposing forces, while undercutting this theory, gives *Autumn* a new human dimension. Pa Chin is finally about the business of a novelist; the evil he uncovers in the fourth and fifth uncles and their wives, and in the grandfather's concubine, Mistress Ch'en, neither proves nor disproves the wickedness of the Chinese family system; it shows only that human beings are capable of such malevolence that no systems and institutions are safe from it.

Autumn begins with Chüeh-hsin befriending Young Squire Mei, younger brother of Hui and the most gruesome wreck of all consumptive characters in modern Chinese literature. He is pushed into a marriage by his father Chou Po-t'ao, soon grows much worse, and dies an agonizing death. In showing the worst possible mental and physical degeneration under the feudal system, Pa Chin is no longer content to rest in his lachrymose manner but evinces a new macabre and grotesque effectiveness. Cherishing the memory of Hui, Chüeh-hsin further befriends the Chou family by repeatedly demanding that her husband's family give her a decent burial. He achieves this end finally with the help of his more forceful brother. While still a nonentity in chapters devoted to his romantic and revolutionary pursuits, Chüeh-min has grown steadily more mature in his dealings with the hostile relatives. And his long-suffering brother, continually pushed around by his elders and answerable for the defiant acts of his brothers and sisters, also gains tragic stature as a man of infinite patience. He finally obtains solace in the love and devotion of the maidservant Ts'ui-huan.

In *Autumn* the Kao family finally breaks up. The fourth

and fifth uncles set up separate apartments for their concubines and seek the company of disreputable opera singers. Meanwhile, their unhappy wives quarrel continually with Mistress Ch'en. The fifth aunt abuses her own daughter most unconscionably until the latter drowns herself. Ch'ien-erh, a maidservant in the fourth aunt's employ, dies unattended in her dingy room of a wasting disease. The third uncle, who has been very severe with his daughter Shu-ying in *Spring*, emerges now as a benign Confucian, sorrowing over the impending dissolution of the family. Upon his death, the separate households wrangle over the common property and decide to sell their old house.

All these incidents, in a way, serve only as the background for the recurring scenes of quarrel involving on one side Chüeh-min and his younger sister Shu-hua, and on the other their disreputable elders. Shu-hua has been too young to figure importantly in *Family* and *Spring*, but now she is a quick-tongued girl lashing out unafraid at her aunts. During these quarrels, brother and sister draw upon the whole range of tragedies and scandals in the family, so that one feels the emotional weight of the entire trilogy behind their eloquence. Not that Pa Chin has created memorable characters out of Chüeh-min and Shu-hua; it is only when the paroxysms of anger seize them that they become transfigured out of recognition from their usual youthful selves. Whereas in *Family* and *Spring* the oppressed have only two alternatives, escape (Chüeh-hui and Shu-ying) and submission (Chüeh-hsin and Hui), in *Autumn* Chüeh-min, Shu-hua, and even Chüeh-hsin in his fashion stand their ground, seeing evil eye-to-eye and actually attacking their depraved elders, during those heated sessions, in terms of the Confucian morality they have set at naught. And the result is moral drama, as distinguished from the allegorical and ideological drama of *Family* and *Spring*.

Autumn should be ranked among the major novels in modern Chinese literature. It demonstrates that in spite of a flat style and a psychology that ignores the subtler aspects of character, something powerful could still be achieved by staying true to one s feelings. In *Family* and *Spring,* Pa Chin's powerful feelings are at the service of a theory which stultifies them; the triumph of *Autumn* is finally the assertion of the emotional integrity of the novelist over the didacticism of the shallow philosopher and revolutionary. The didactic notes are still in the novel, in its references to Turgenev, Emma Goldman, and the Russian revolutionary Sophia Perovskaia, in its description of the journalistic activities of Chüeh-min, in its explicit denunciation of the system; but they assume now only a decorative function in relation to the main body of the novel.

Autumn was first published in 1940; by that time Pa Chin had written most of his fiction in the vein of revolutionary romanticism. He had become a wiser and more disinterested writer, though for the remainder of the war period he did not produce any work comparable to the novel. It is only with the postwar publication of the novel *Cold Nights* that Pa Chin demonstrates briefly (for the Communists would soon run China and reduce all arts to the level of propaganda) his full maturity as a novelist.

Though best known for his novels, Pa Chin is also a respected short-story writer. His stories range from personal reminiscences to revolutionary legends culled from French or Russian history. In *Destruction,* the inset tales about a seventeenth-century Russian peasant-hero and of a Chinese student's estrangement from a French girl give readers a first taste of Pa Chin's exoticism. His stay in France and Japan has given him a first-hand knowledge of these countries; but more important, his voracious reading in the revolutionary literature of the West has enabled him to reconstruct episodes from foreign history. The French Revolution and the Decembrist Revolution in Czarist Russia seem to have exerted particular fascination on him.

Pa Chin's stories about contemporary China share the sentimental excesses of his novels and novelettes. In some exceptional cases, however, a grim realistic note is introduced: the long story "The Antimony Miners," telling of trapped slaves working without pay and without hope under primitive conditions in the interior, is a surprising departure for the author. "Dog," perhaps Pa Chin's most famous story (included in *Living China*), has the simplicity of a parable. The hero, a young pauper, daily roams in the streets of Shanghai and watches with envy sleek and pampered dogs walking beside their foreign mistresses. Every night he repairs to a decrepit temple and prays to the idol that he, too, might become a dog to enjoy the love and protection of a white woman. This fine theme—the dispossessed man in his last extremity—fails to receive tragic illumination, however, in a story overladen with anti-imperialist propaganda of the most transparent kind.

Unlike most Chinese writers whose translations of foreign authors represent passing vogues and a miscellaneous, uninformed personal taste, Pa Chin as a translator is dedicated to the propagation of his liberal and revolutionary anarchism. Kropotkin, Pushkin, Herzen, Turgenev, the early Gorky, Alexei Tolstoy (*The Death of Danton*), and Vera Figner are among the authors he has translated. It is regrettable that his translations of Kropotkin's *Ethics* and *Memoirs of a Revolutionist* have never reached any degree of popularity.

CHAPTER 11

Communist Fiction, I

MAO TUN and Chang T'ien-i were the greatest Communist writers of the decade, but precisely for that reason they were not the most typical. Pa Chin's revolutionary novels have much in common with Communist fiction, but then Pa Chin was an anarchist and his romanticism, though much imitated by Communist writers, was frowned upon by orthodox Marxist critics. To define the literary quality, as well as to illustrate the propaganda themes, of Communist fiction of this period, we shall study in this chapter three popular and representative authors: Chiang Kuang-tz'u, Ting Ling, and Hsiao Chün. The trio exemplify the trends of Communist fiction in the years 1926–37: proletarian, romantic-revolutionary, neorealist, anti-Japanese.

In 1929 the Communist critic Ch'ien Hsing-ts'un published his highly controversial Volume 1 of *Contemporary Chinese Writers,* consisting of four earlier published articles on Lu Hsün, Yü Ta-fu, Kuo Mo-jo, and Chiang Kuang-tz'u. Subjecting Lu Hsün to harsh censure but according praise to the last three in a crescendo of critical extravagance, the book was apparently designed to enthrone Chiang Kuang-tz'u, the author's good friend, as the leading writer of his time. But obvious even to the more discriminating readers of that time was the critic's complete wrongheadedness: he judged the four in the reverse order of their literary importance. Lu Hsün is the finest writer of the group, Yü Ta-fu a writer of honesty, and even Kuo Mo-jo is to be preferred to Chiang Kuang-tz'u because, while they were equally bad writers of fiction, the former did break some ground for modern poetry. But in ignoring these elementary discriminations, Ch'ien Hsing-ts'un is not merely satisfying his personal whims; he is also applying a yardstick of correctness. Chiang is the greatest writer because he is the most correct. Without a trace of irony, the critic characterizes his friend as one who takes up his pen to supply what the masses need: "His writings all have an important mission: propaganda!" [1]

While never regarded as the greatest modern Chinese writer except by his partisan friends, Chiang Kuang-tz'u (1901–31) was certainly the earliest professional Communist writer as well as the most prolific for his period. Among the first Chinese to study in Soviet Russia, he returned to China in 1923 to agitate vigorously for a revolutionary literature, in such articles as "Proletarian Revolution and Culture" (*New Youth*, 1924) and "The Present-day Chinese Society and Revolutionary Literature" (*Awakening*, 1925). In 1925 he published two volumes of poetry entitled *The New Dream* and *Lament for China;* these were followed by a rapid succession of works, mainly of fiction. At the same time he taught at Shanghai College, a Communist center of training staffed at one time or another by such Marxist intellectuals as Ch'en Tu-hsiu, Li Ta, Shao Li-tzu, Ch'ü Ch'iu-pai, and Mao Tun.

Though he did not participate in the Northern Expedition, Chiang Kuang-tz'u affected, like the Creationists, a boundless enthusiasm for propaganda work following the debacle of Nationalist-Communist collaboration. In 1928 he formed the Sun Society with Ch'ien Hsing-ts'un and Yang

Ts'un-jen and launched *The Sun Monthly* to dispute the supremacy of the Creation Society in the guidance and promotion of revolutionary literature. This attempt to hoist himself as the leading writer of his time made him suspect among Communist groups, for the Creation Society apparently enjoyed stronger party backing and greater numerical strength and the later Communist critics invariably sided with it to denigrate Chiang as a figure of negligible importance. When *The Sun* folded, he published in 1929 *The New Current Monthly*, which proved also to be short-lived. In the next year he started another foredoomed journal, *The Pathfinder*, but by that time his health had deteriorated and his importance as an effective Communist propagandist had dwindled. He was expelled from the party in October 1930 and died of tuberculosis the following June.[2] In the same month the Communist leader Ch'ü Ch'iu-pai dismissed him rather contemptuously in an article called "Long Live the Literary Dictators!"[3]

Chiang Kuang-tz'u left behind him about a dozen volumes of fiction. His first novelette, *The Youthful Tramp* (1926), deserves attention not only because it was the first example of proletarian fiction of that length (125 pages) but because it managed to embody most of the themes that later became standard in Communist fiction. As propaganda, *The Youthful Tramp* is also interesting as a rare example of the early party line, in ostensible support of the Kuomintang-Communist collaboration. Unlike post-1927 Communist fiction, the book is friendly to the Nationalists.

Supposedly a long letter addressed to the author in October 1924, the novelette traces the life of the hero, Wang Chung, from 1915 on. In that year his parents, small tenant farmers, met death in the hands of a cruel landlord, and our bereaved hero, then only fifteen or sixteen years old, thought at first to turn bandit to expedite his task of revenge. But he was prevented from doing so by a long siege of illness. Upon his recovery he became a vagrant and came across an old-style tutor, who took him as a servant. When the tutor approached him as a pederast, Wang Chung again took to the road.

A few months later he was befriended by a shopkeeper and made an apprentice. Despite the usual hardships of this mode of life, he was quite happy in his love for the shopkeeper's daughter. But her father naturally tried to put a stop to this kind of nonsense, and the girl, in consequence, fell sick. On the day Wang Chung was dismissed, after two years of hard work at the store, she died. Wang Chung now accepted a position as junior clerk in a store in another city; by this time he had acquired a few modern ideas, after a course of self-study, and realized the importance of boycotting Japanese goods. When he saw that his store was one of the principal targets of student demonstrations against Japanese goods, and that the storekeeper was going to beat up the student leaders, he managed to notify them of this villainy and was consequently dismissed.

Wang Chung sailed for Hankow. After serving as a waiter in a hotel for a brief period, he became a worker at a British-owned textile mill. He was again dismissed, after agitating with other workers for higher wages and fewer working hours. At that time—January 1923—the workers on the Peking-Hankow railroad were on strike against the warlord Wu P'ei-fu and the foreign powers; Wang Chung joined the railroad workers' union and witnessed the martyrdom of the Communist labor leader Lin Hsiang-ch'ien (a historical figure). After a period of imprisonment, our hero turns up in Shanghai, as a union leader among the textile workers there. Disgusted with the despotic ways of foreign capitalists, he writes this letter and sends it to the novelist on the eve of his departure for Canton to enroll in the Whampoa Military Academy. In a postscript, Chiang Kuang-tz'u adds that Wang Chung has fallen in action against the rebellious forces of Ch'en Chiung-ming. He dies happily with a slogan on his lips: "Down with the warlords, down with imperialism!"

In its utter naiveté, *The Youthful Tramp* reads like a travesty of the more ambitious Communist fiction to come. Its author should be given credit, however, for being able to exhibit in a short space all the clichés: the evils of feudalism, the crimes of warlords and foreign imperialists, the strikes and demonstrations of enlightened workers and students, the insurgence of a revolutionary army. As the son of an oppressed tenant farmer, the overworked apprentice, the unhappy lover, the enlightened factory worker, the union leader, and the dedicated soldier for the cause of revolution, the youthful tramp is virtually all revolutionary and proletarian heroes rolled into one. One should also note the propaganda value of the four cunningly spaced death scenes: the hero's parents die of landlord oppression; his love dies of feudal inhumanity; the labor leader Lin Hsiang-ch'ien dies of combined warlord-imperialist tyranny; and the hero himself perishes as a willing sacrifice in the cause of freedom.

As an example of Chiang Kuang-tz'u's later fiction, we may turn to *The Moon Emerging from the Clouds* (1930), his most popular novel. As with a number of novels following the debacle of the so-called Great Revolution, it adheres to the superficial formula of revolutionary optimism despite its predominant tone of romantic nihilism. The novel opens with Wang Man-ying taking under her protection a pathetic young prostitute, A-lien. Herself a streetwalker for some time, Man-ying is chastened and ashamed in the presence of her innocent protégée. She recalls that, only a few years back, she was studying in a political training school with revolutionary zeal and that soon afterward she was marching along with the soldiers of the Northern Expedition. But when the reaction set in, she escaped to Shanghai to become a misanthrope, "an extreme nihilist using her body to revenge herself on mankind." [4] She has been doing nothing but enticing and humiliating all kinds of men who lust after her flesh.

Still more disconcerting is her chance meeting, some time

later, with her old comrade, Li Shang-chih, who even now is carrying on his revolutionary work. Man-ying justifies her indolence, however, on the ground that she has become syphilitic: since she can be of no use to the revolution anyway, what better work could she do than to infect all her corrupt customers? But when Li Shang-chih takes A-lien away from her for her supposed unfitness to be a guardian, Man-ying feels that the last human tie has been broken. She tries to commit suicide, but is persuaded to become a factory worker, to share the joys and sorrows of the proletariat. Properly reconditioned, she regains her faith in the revolutionary cause and discovers, furthermore, that she doesn't have syphilis after all. She now joins Li Shang-chih and A-lien and lives happily with them.

As a hollow exercise in the romantic-revolutionary vein, this novel hardly needs commentary. We have seen the world-weary, sensual women and the dedicated revolutionary workers in the pages of Mao Tun, and Man-ying and Li Shang-chih are clearly unintentional caricatures of them. Although Chiang Kuang-tz'u has written some novels like *Sans-culotte* (1928) in the outspokenly proletarian manner, his predilection for romantic subject matter must have eventually cost him his ranking position among Communist writers.

For a conscientious proletarian writer who has been until very recently a pillar of Communist literature, we turn next to Ting Ling (1907–). Unlike Chiang Kuang-tz'u, Ting Ling began her career as a highly personal author rather than a dedicated propagandist. In her first phase (1926–29) she was primarily interested in probing the meaning of life in unabashedly feminine and autobiographical terms: the stories in her first collection, *In the Darkness* (1928), notably "Meng K'o" and "The Diary of Miss Sophia," all flaunt the sexual restiveness and impotent fury of a warm-hearted girl in the sinister powers of the city. Apparently lonely and confused,

Ting Ling pours all her resentments and exasperations in the diary mold of her fiction. Her next work, *Wei Hu* (1930), a long story noted for its frank descriptions of sex, is an exercise in the romantic-revolutionary manner: its theme is the incompatibility of a couple when one member advances beyond the other in revolutionary behavior and outlook. In two companion pieces, "Shanghai, Spring 1930," Parts I and II, Ting Ling continues with her probing of the dilemmas of a bourgeois intellectual when confronted with proletarian experience.

In 1931 Ting Ling joined the Communist party and turned resolutely into a proletarian writer. "The T'ien Village," a transitional piece, depicts a city-bred Communist working among Hunan peasants; the long story *Water* describes a peasant uprising under the provocation of famine. From that story on, even though she returned briefly to her despondent, nihilistic mood when she could no longer hide her disgust with the Communist regime at Yenan in the early forties, Ting Ling has written about little else but peasants, soldiers, and Communist cadres, with this work culminating in her novel about land reform, *Sun over the Sangkan River* (1949).

In view of her colorful life, Ting Ling's early fame or notoriety is easy to understand. Daughter of a well-to-do landowning family in Liling, Hunan, with a distinguished record of government service under the Manchus, Ting Ling (her real name: Chiang Ping-chih) early rebelled against her gentility and left for Shanghai in her late teens. She attended there the Communist-directed P'ing-min Girls' School, and later Shanghai College. Known for its Marxist indoctrination, this college was equally notorious for its sexual license. According to one reliable source, one Miss Wang, a rich Szechwan girl who had come to Shanghai with Ting Ling, openly cohabited with Professor Ch'ü Ch'iu-pai, and Ting Ling herself was on very intimate terms with Ch'ü's younger brother.[5] Then she went to Peking, trying

futilely to enter Peking University. With her good looks
and literary ambition, however, she soon attracted a group
of admirers, among them Shen Ts'ung-wen and a struggling
author and ex-navy cadet from Fukien by name of Hu Yeh-
p'in. Ting Ling lived with the latter as his common-law wife,
giddily happy and writing for *The Short Story*. In 1928 this
couple and Shen Ts'ung-wen moved to Shanghai, launching
in succession two short-lived monthlies, *Jen Chien* and *Red
and Black*. In financial straits, Hu Yeh-p'in went with his
wife to Tsinan to teach school for the year 1929–30.

Returning to Shanghai in the summer of 1930, the couple
soon joined the League of Left-wing Writers. Their life during the subsequent half year tells so much of the conspiratorial activities of the League that it deserves closest attention. Hu Yeh-p'in, appointed a member of the Executive
Committee of the League and chairman of the Committee
for Worker, Peasant, and Soldier Literature, was consequently very busy and seldom at home. In her recent memoir
of her husband, Ting Ling gives a fascinating account of a
secret meeting which he had to attend:

> It was probably in the month of August. Yeh-p'in at-
> tended a meeting without even telling me about it. He
> only said he wouldn't be home for the evening, and I
> didn't ask him any questions. He returned after two
> days and handed me a letter written by Comrade Ch'ü
> Ch'iu-pai to myself. After I had guessed what he had
> been doing during the last two days and known that
> they [her husband and Ch'ü] had met, he told me that
> he had really attended a meeting. The Communist lead-
> ers from all over China were there and he described for
> me the place of the meeting. This conference was held
> in utter secrecy. He said that it took place in a swank
> foreign-style house and that the ground floor was en-
> tirely furnished in the manner of a rich private home.
> Regularly ladies came and left; they played mahjong

and turned on the phonograph. The representatives from other cities went in one by one; once they were in, they were confined on the third floor. The windows on the third floor were as a rule never open. The comrades in Shanghai went in last; after they were in, the meeting commenced. The conference room was hung all over with sickles, hammers, and red flags; it was very solemn. After the meeting was over, the representatives from other cities left first. As to what went on at the conference, Yeh-p'in didn't tell me a thing; so even today I am still not very clear about the nature of this meeting. But I saw then that this meeting enhanced Yeh-p'in's already strong interest in politics.[6]

During the next few months Hu Yeh-p'in, though busy with other work, managed to complete a novel entitled *A Bright Future Lies Ahead of Us*. On November 8 Ting Ling gave birth to a son in hospital; the same evening her husband attended another meeting of the Left-wing League. At this meeting he was elected a representative for the First Conference of Soviet Representatives to be held in Kiangsi and made his formal application for party membership. After he became a member (Ting Ling joined some months later), small cell meetings frequently took place at his home. As chairman of the Committee for Worker, Peasant, and Soldier Literature, he also made friends with Communist factory workers.

But Hu Yeh-p'in's heart was set on Kiangsi. He frequently consulted with the Preparatory Committee for the First Conference of the Soviet Representatives. On January 17, 1931, he left home in the morning to attend a meeting of the Executive Committee of the League. Later in the day he was arrested by the Nationalist police along with four other young authors and Communist members—Chao P'ing-fu (pen name: Jou Shih), Li Wei-sen, Yin Fu (alternate pen name: Pai Mang), and Miss Feng K'eng—at the secret office of the Preparatory Committee. On February 7 these five writers plus eighteen other young Communists were executed at Lunghwa, near Shanghai. The event caused a great stir in China. The Left-wing League relayed the news to Communist writers' organizations throughout the world, and the sympathetic journalists Agnes Smedley, Edgar Snow, and Nym Wales wrote about the atrocity for the English-reading public. But actually these five little-known authors were not executed for the crime of writing in behalf of Communism: more influential writers of known Communist affiliations were at large then and afterward. Along with the others, these five were presumably sentenced to death as Communist conspirators planning to join the red forces in Kiangsi.

Ting Ling was very unhappy after the event. Shen Ts'ung-wen, who had done his best to save Hu Yeh-p'in's life (he had asked Ts'ai Yüan-p'ei and Hu Shih to intercede with government authorities), now accompanied her to Hunan, where she deposited her son in the care of her mother. Upon her return to Shanghai, she cohabited with another young man and edited a magazine called *The Big Dipper*, which was soon suppressed. On May 4, 1933, Ting Ling herself was arrested in Shanghai; for the next two or three years she was confined in Nanking under the surveillance of the National-ist secret police. Then, presumably released, she made her way to Peking, and from there to Sian, where she stayed until it was possible for her to join the newly arrived Communist forces at Yenan.

The above biographical sketch is partly taken from Ting Ling's memoir of her husband, "The Life of an Upright Man," and partly from Shen Ts'ung-wen's two-volume biography *About Ting Ling* and *More about Ting Ling*. The latter was written with evident affection in 1933, at a time when Ting Ling was missing and presumed dead. She emerges from these pages as a sincere, loving, and courageous person, but for all their friendship Shen Ts'ung-wen is not one to minimize her faults and limitations. To him both she and her husband were deluded victims of Communist propaganda. Meeting them again in the winter of 1930–31, after they had been converted to Communism, Shen Ts'ung-wen felt both happy and sad:

> I was happy because in a half year's time both had changed and were now under the spell of a new ideal, sad because what they knew of the conditions in China was so narrow and little. A new kind of life, of course, had made them both strong, simple, pure, and hence very lovable, but that certain element of dogmatic ignorance had now conditioned their attitude toward life. . . . If they really wanted to do something about the social order, should they not first form a clearer view of all the phenomena under this order? For intellectuals revolutionary work entails more understanding than emotion. The faith of both was built upon what they could see and hear in the foreign concessions and upon the hard-to-believe reports, statistics, and documents issued from a certain quarter. This made me feel not only very sorry for them but that they were rather pitiful.[7]

Shen Ts'ung-wen notes further that, after their conversion, both Ting Ling and her husband were impatient with the pen, as if they thought they could accomplish something much greater the moment they were engaged in actual politics. And not only this couple but the host of other young writers in Shanghai were so eager for action, so taken up with the propagandist role of literature, as to neglect completely the necessary training of their craft and imagination. Shen Ts'ung-wen sums them up: "I further pointed out how writers in foreign concessions, ignorant of history and the times, were really wasting their energies to no apparent purpose when they discussed the function of various types of literature designed for the masses, and the importance of conveying a certain ideology through that literature for the benefit of the youth in the provinces. And the farsighted Communist party should alter those directives which, formulated in blindness to reality, merely tended to confuse and mislead the young and obstruct the natural progress of society." [8]

The reputation of Ting Ling during the thirties was mainly sustained by her early stories, which are supposedly "modern" in their attitude toward sex and therefore superior to the more decorous fiction of Ping Hsin and Ling Shu-hua. When Ting Ling turns to proletarian fiction in 1931, she is stripped of even that youthful nihilistic candor, revealing her essential triteness as a propagandist. *Water,* generally regarded as one of the proudest exhibits of Communist fiction, may serve as an example. Though in style and intent it differs little from the earlier proletarian stories, it can be taken as a forerunner of socialist-realist fiction. In his comments on the story-writer Sha T'ing, the critic Han Shih-heng has given an excellent description of this genre:

> There is little doubt that this author writes in accordance with the theory of neorealism. He attempts to depict collective life; hence there are not only no individual heroes in his works but no characters with any individuality. He also makes no use of the ordinary techniques of fiction, such as developing a plot from one central situation or incident; he only observes the social surfaces.
>
> The characters in his stories always constitute a gang or crowd: a troop of soldiers or refugees, a gathering of petty tradesmen or peasants, a group of oppressors or oppressed. They come and go before us like riders on a merry-go-round; we cannot remember them or catch hold of their individual qualities. Although they engage in actions and conversations which have a realistic basis, they do not act or talk like individualized characters. They are examples of the "collective, depersonalized uniformity"; their actions and conversations do not add up to a coherent work of art. This writer knows how

in general circumstances peasants act and talk, but he cannot realize the particularity of a speech or action of a particular peasant under particular circumstances; in other words, he cannot properly imagine it. So the reader cannot remember which actions are Chang San's and which Li Ssu's; even the author himself would be hard put to it to differentiate them. So all his characters receive the following sort of appellation: Tall Fellow A, Shorty B, Fatso C, Thin Man D, Pockmarked E, Malarial F. This descriptive method is puerile and cannot create a deep impression.[9]

In both its collective emphasis and its narrative method *Water* fully conforms to this formula. It is a confusing tale put together with extreme ineptitude. In view of the author's high reputation even among nonleftist quarters, one could only wonder about the taste of the age that could have accepted such a fraud. As a story-writer, Ting Ling is much worse than Chiang Kuang-tz'u or Kuo Mo-jo, who at least wrote lucidly in spite of their great shallowness; she belongs with such early women writers as Huang Lu-yin, who could not write one decent paragraph in Chinese. The style of *Water* shows at once a clumsy handling of the pai-hua idiom and an attempt to assimilate the Western syntax, a defective ear for peasant speech and a striving after descriptive elegance. The result is stilted language of the worst kind.

In the story Ting Ling tells of the impact of the flood upon the political consciousness of a group of peasants. At one particular village the peasants have tried their best to prevent the flood from crossing over the dyke, but to no avail. Eventually those who have survived the water have to flee toward a town, like refugees from other villages which have been earlier inundated. They wait outside the town gates in patience and silence, expecting food and succor from the local and provincial governments, from philanthropists and rich landlords. They wait in vain, and many die of starvation. Finally, after many days of passive suffering, the surviving peasants realize the perfidy of the gentry and the government and are ready to march to the town to rob the granaries. Their leader is a half-naked, dark-faced peasant who is energetic enough, despite his long starvation, to climb up a tree to give a long talk, whose effect upon his fellow-victims is instantaneous:

> "Right, what he said is right! . . ."
> "Second sister, it's exactly as he said. We are too pitiful . . ."
> The land was seething, and there was shouting heard:
> "Let's think it over! . . ."
> A man on the opposite tree also shouted:
> "Why shouldn't we think it over and what's the use just talking? The present is our immediate concern. Many of us have died, and those of us who have remained alive are famished. Even if we eat the corpses, we won't stay alive for long! Our bones are hard and our heart is human and you won't expect us to eat live people! . . ."
> "Your mother's! You go and eat live people! . . ."
> "Eat live people, what's so strange about that?" that half-naked man again said. "Aren't we daily devoured by people? Just think, those who sit in the *yamen* to collect taxes, those who sit in tall houses to collect grain, what have they got to eat if not our own labor and blood! You bastards! We have been eaten so thin and how can we be still so muddle-headed as to regard them as good people and to expect them to help us! *Heng!* Wait until you are so famished that even your intestines come out, and do you suppose they would then send us some rice? Let me tell you, there are so many of us that even if thousands upon ten thousands die they don't have to worry because some of us will remain to serve as their slaves! . . ."

"*Aya!* That's really frightening, the way we are being eaten . . ."

"What's there to be afraid of? Arise, let's fight back, the worst is death . . ."

"Right, the worst is death . . ." [10]

The exchange of opinions goes on for some while (the whole story consists mainly of a series of exclamations by anonymous peasants shouting at the top of their voices) until the peasants are ready to march into the town. "Therefore, when the dawn was just breaking," Ting Ling ends her story with a typical flourish, "this troop of people, this troop of hungry slaves, yelling their lust for life as the men walked ahead with the women running closely after them, pushed on toward the town with a fury surpassing the flood's." [11] One should remember, of course, that this militant band of peasants has been starved for a week or more (Ting Ling doesn't specify the number of days but one receives the general impression that they have been famished for a much longer time) and have been talking and yelling all this time; it is a truly Marxian miracle that their shouting and marching could still surpass the fury of a flood. The men, however, are apparently doing much better than the women, for the latter, with all their running, fall behind.

I have poked fun at Ting Ling not out of malice but because her story, certainly better than most less acclaimed proletarian or neorealist fiction, warrants some attention. There is nothing wrong with the basic situation depicted in *Water*. Chinese peasants have time and again suffered from famine and received no succor from the well-to-do and government agencies. The theme is of crucial human importance, and properly handled, the story should become a moving tragedy, irrespective of the point of view of the author. But intent on illustrating her Marxist thesis and beautifying her language, Ting Ling has apparently forgotten the all too apparent physiological reality of people under famine. This blindness to physical reality, and to psychological and social reality, constitutes the one fundamental weakness of Communist writers, though ideally there is no reason why they should be so unobservant. Perhaps the type of mind which takes to the oversimplifying formulas of Marxism is naturally of an abstract order, incapable of much interest in the fascinating concrete phenomena pertaining to human existence. Nearly all proletarian stories by Communist writers of this period are duplications of *Water* against little-changed village, factory, and army settings. Such exceptions as Mao Tun's "Spring Silkworms" are the product of an entirely different creative impulse, in that they have achieved a degree of felt life.

In his excellent article "Proletarian Literature: A Political Autopsy," Philip Rahv has correctly defined this species of writing as "an internationally uniform literature . . . whose main service was the carrying out of party assignments." [12] While remaining uniform in intent and quality, proletarian literature in China has time and again responded to changes in party assignments. The Japanese invasion of the Northeast and the subsequent establishment of Manchukuo had alerted Communist leaders to the importance of anti-Japanese propaganda. The Sino-Japanese engagement in the Shanghai area prompted the first essays in this direction. "Total Retreat" (1932), a story by the woman writer Ko Ch'in, indicts the defeatism of the National Government in its conduct of the Shanghai Incident. But it was a group of Northeastern writers, refugees from Manchukuo, who gained for the Communist party a large public receptive to its demand for a United Front to combat the Japanese. With the possible exception of Tuan-mu Hung-liang, these refugees —Hsiao Chün and his wife Hsiao Hung, Li Hui-ying,[13] Lo Feng, Shu Ch'ün—were all slipshod writers untrained in the craft of fiction. But because they were all undeviatingly Communist in their demand for an all-out war with

Japan, and because they all wrote about the conditions in Manchuria with which the Chinese public was then keenly concerned, they became the darlings of the Left-wing League. Lu Hsün himself launched at personal cost a "Slave Series" to accommodate their creative output, and wrote prefaces for many of their books. One of these was *Village in August,* the first novel by Hsiao Chün or T'ien Chün (1908–). Upon its publication in 1935 it became an immediate sensation and remained a best-seller for many years.

This novel also enjoyed the distinction of being the first contemporary Chinese novel to be published in English. It was launched by its American publishers in 1942 as "China's Great War Novel" with a warm endorsement by Edgar Snow; the translation was by Evan King, who did a fairly accurate job except for his deliberate editing of a few passages whose connotations of international Communism might have shocked the American public. Thus when the heroine Anna, a Korean patriot, says in the Chinese, "Only when the revolution of the proletariat of the whole world breaks into the open can our own country be saved!" the English version tones it down to a merely patriotic message, "When once the whole Chinese people arise against Japan, our own country can be saved!" [14]

The first nationally successful Communist novel to embody the theme of anti-Japanese resistance, *Village in August* is in method and technique a descendant of the earlier proletarian and romantic-revolutionary fiction. The novel is a highly episodic narrative about a roving band of guerrillas in Manchuria; it tells, among other things, of a couple of peasant lovers suffering extreme indignities in the hands of the Japanese, the shooting of a pro-Japanese landowner and the recruitment of a few of his tenant farmers to the guerrilla band. But its main plot concerns a romantic triangle: Captain Hsiao Ming, Anna, and their immediate superior and commander of the guerrillas, Ch'en Chu. Hsiao Ming and Anna are very much in love. Ch'en Chu watches this romantic attachment with great displeasure, and when the time comes for his band to join the other guerrillas elsewhere, he takes Anna along but leaves Hsiao Ming behind with a small detachment to take care of the sick and wounded. The lovers part sadly and reluctantly. For a moment even Anna, a dedicated revolutionary and patriot, wavers from her duty. Being of bourgeois origins, Hsiao Ming takes the deprivation of his personal happiness much more seriously. Dispirited, he resigns himself to the scorn and ridicule of his men, though at the very end he seems to have outgrown his despondent phase.

A careful reading of the novel fails to disclose whether Ch'en Chu is in love with Anna himself or whether his decision to separate her from Hsiao Ming is purely a matter of principle. In any case, as we have seen in the novels of Pa Chin, the conflict between romantic love and revolutionary duty is a literary convention that can be traced back to Turgenev or earlier. In Hsiao Ming's final entreaty to Anna after she has agreed to abide by Ch'en Chu's decision, we are given a revealing glimpse of the literary character of the lover's perplexity:

> I want to ask you, Anna! Have you really given our love the death sentence? I didn't know that love could have so impaired our will power. How can you explain it? I have read many novels dealing with the conflicts of love and revolutionary duty. In most, love is sacrificed for revolution, but in some, love conquers the revolutionary will and the hero goes down the path of suicide. Anna, I really don't know what would happen to us.[15]

In *Village in August*, of course, this romantic-revolutionary idyl serves as a framework for the proletarian epic of national resistance. Instead of the famished peasants, the collective hero is now the guerrillas. In accordance with the method of Socialist Realism, each of these soldiers is given a staggering gift for billingsgate and some marked physical or mental characteristic to remember him by. But in making the guerrillas the collective hero, even though he was apparently influenced by the Soviet war novels,[16] Hsiao Chün also initiated a line of anti-Japanese fiction. Just as Chiang Kuang-tz'u, Pa Chin, Ting Ling, and others had contributed to the plot and structure of *Village in August,* so in turn Hsiao Chün bequeathed a legacy of formulas for guerrilla fiction: the coarse language of the peasant soldiers, the patriotic songs to be sung at regular intervals, the incidental pastoralism of landscape painting, and the frank descriptions of sex and violence in the supposed interests of uncovering Japanese atrocities. With this novel we are entering the extremely uncomfortable period of wartime patriotic propaganda.

A zealous Communist, Hsiao Chün has not exactly planned his novel according to the Comintern line laid down for the period of the United Front. It preaches class struggle and the revolution of the proletariat with undue vehemence, and it blames the Kuomintang for all the evils committed by the warlords, the local despots and bad gentry. The important episode of the shooting of the landlord Wang Lao-san, furthermore, anticipates the novels of the land reform period. In all these respects the author proved himself a naive patriot deluded by Communist propaganda.

Following the success of *Village in August,* Hsiao Chün turned out another novel, *The Third Generation* (1937), and two story collections, *The Sheep* and *On the River.* During the first two years of the war he served as editor of the literary page of the Chengtu newspaper *Hsin Min Pao.* Then he went to Yenan.

Since the names of Hsiao Chün and Ting Ling were eventually to be linked together as infamous Communist renegades, what little we know of their lives in Yenan is of particular value in enabling us to trace the gradual disillusionment of many writers and intellectuals whose naive idealism had led them to espouse Communism with an unquestioning faith. Ting Ling, who had reached Yenan much earlier than Hsiao Chün, was at first undoubtedly treated as a celebrity; she was on friendly terms with Mao Tse-tung and for some time romantically involved with General P'eng Tê-huai. But the hypocrisy and cruelty of the Yenan regime made her restive, and by early 1942 she had become apparently disillusioned, along with Hsiao Chün and many others: the poet Ai Ch'ing, the Manchurian author Lo Feng, and two writers subsequently exposed as Trotskyites, Wang Shih-wei and Li Yu-jan. (In Communist literary history, the arch-Trotskyite Wang Tu-ch'ing was eventually to be regarded as the earliest renegade among Communist authors.) While hardly a clique, these writers wrote regularly for the literary supplement of the Yenan *Liberation Daily,* edited by Ting Ling and Ch'en Ch'i-hsia.

Though a bad writer, Ting Ling was apparently a warm-hearted woman who couldn't abide the callousness with which the Communist regime treated its subjects; the fate of women, supposedly emancipated but actually subject to worse contempt and misery than under the Kuomintang rule, especially obsessed her. In 1941 she wrote a story entitled "In the Hospital," published in a Yenan magazine and subsequently reprinted in the Chungking journal *Wen-i Chen-ti.* In this story she returned to her nihilistic mood, exposing the corruption and bleak poverty of Yenan life and showering her sympathy upon her sensitive and suffering heroine—the young obstetrician Lu P'ing—whose attempt to correct medical abuses has only brought upon her head undeserved censure and calumny.[17] On March 9, 1942 —March 8 being the women's day—Ting Ling wrote an editorial in the literary page of the *Liberation Daily* called "Thoughts on March 8," lamenting the fate of women under Communist rule. (In this as in her earlier story, however, she refrained from outright criticism but ended on a note of cautious optimism.) Following this editorial was a spate of articles in the *Liberation Daily* which, though mild in tone, voiced an undisguised discontent with the regime: notably, Ai Ch'ing's "Understand Authors, Respect Authors," Lo Feng's "This Is Still the Age for *Tsa-wen*," Wang Shih-wei's "The Wild Lily" (published in two installments on March 13 and 23), and slightly later, Hsiao Chün's " 'Love' and 'Patience' among Comrades." These articles immediately prompted Mao Tse-tung to call a literary conference to correct the unorthodox tendencies of Yenan authors (of which see below, Chapter 13). But for the time being, though Ting Ling was censured, this outburst of criticism was not regarded as an antiparty plot. Wang Shih-wei was made the scapegoat, not only because "The Wild Lily" and his other articles of the time contain the most outspoken criticism of the regime but because he could be easily convicted as a Trotskyite. Apparently only lightly punished, Ting Ling and the other writers became quite docile for their remaining years at Yenan. For a long time this episode of dissidence was known only as the Wang Shih-wei case.

Hsiao Chün was the first to become openly defiant. In September 1946 he was assigned to Harbin as editor of the newspaper *Cultural Gazette* (Wen-hua Pao), which published every five days. A patriot at heart, he was embittered to see the newly liberated Manchuria under a worse tyranny than during the puppet regime. During the second half of 1947 he began to attack in a series of articles and editorials the arrogance of Russian officers and advisers, the pointless tragedy of the civil war then raging in Manchuria, and the unprecedented cruelty of Communist cadres in their enforcement of land reform. (In an editorial greeting the new year of 1948 he castigated the Communists as worse than Li Tzu-ch'eng and Chang Hsien-chung, two infamous Ming bandits hitherto unsurpassed in Chinese history for their record of wanton killing and pillage.) [18] The Communist authorities were finally alerted to this heretic impudence, and by March 1948 all leading Communist writers, Ting

Ling among them, were appearing in print to denounce Hsiao Chün. For the remainder of the year the "problem of Hsiao Chün" became the central issue in Communist literary circles. Relieved of his editorship, the persecuted author was sentenced to hard labor at the Fushun coal mines in Manchuria.

In November 1954 Hsiao Chün emerged from his long obscurity with a novel entitled *Coal Mines in May;* to be allowed to do so, he must have given proof of complete ideological reform. Published by the Writers' Press and released through the Hsin Hua Book Co., this work should be free of gross faults; in fact, it is a routine piece of propaganda showing the bravery and patriotism of the miners under the guidance of the party. To support the southward march of the Liberation Army in 1948, these miners show unbounded zeal and capacity for self-sacrifice; they increase production in the Stakhanovite manner and overcome every obstacle in their way, including the blundering and bureaucratism of some of the party cadres (to expose the faults of minor officials is a permissible, even standard, theme in recent Communist literature). At first the book received no hostile criticism. But the literary hierarchy eventually decided to attack the work of a notorious apostate rather than to praise it. About a year later, two rather obscure writers, apparently with party approval, raised an alarm over the "poison" of the novel in the leading critical journal, the *Literary Gazette* (Wen-i Pao):

> After reading this book, we could feel only extreme indignation. We believe that, through his use of revolutionary clichés and a gaudy vocabulary and through his affectation of zeal, Hsiao Chün has tried to camouflage his seriously intended caricature and calumny of socialist enterprises, of the working classes and their political party. The facts prove that, in *Coal Mines in May*, Hsiao Chün has not only failed to show the

grandeur of our new life but has persisted in, nay developed further, those reactionary ideas of his which
were subjected to censure at the time of the Liberation
War.[19]

Other attacks soon followed; Hsiao Chün's attempt to vindicate his new orthodoxy had only boomeranged.

By 1957, of course, the fate of Hsiao Chün had become
inseparable from that of his Yenan associates: Ting Ling,
Ch'en Ch'i-hsia, Ai Ch'ing, Lo Feng, Li Yu-jan. (Wang Shih-
wei has dropped from view almost completely since 1942.)[20]
Ting and Ch'en had been suspect since 1954; by 1957 they
and their associates were "exposed" as antiparty rightists of
the blackest dye. His intention to prove himself a docile
writer notwithstanding, Hsiao Chün was also drawn into
the vortex of persecution. In January 1958 the *Literary
Gazette* reprinted Ting Ling's "In the Hospital" and the
offensive *Liberation Daily* articles of sixteen years ago and
assigned them a new sinister significance: it was to the advantage of the party leadership to prove that, so far as the
Ting-Ch'en clique was concerned, the rightist movement was
not spontaneous but the well-planned plot of a group of
ambitious conspirators whose dissidence could be detected as
early as 1942. This whole rightist movement is treated in
greater detail in Chapter 13.

In this chapter I have chosen Chiang Kuang-tz'u, Ting
Ling, and Hsiao Chün to illustrate the various modes of prewar Communist fiction. Whatever their labeled differences,
*The Youthful Tramp, The Moon Emerging from the Clouds,
Water, Village in August,* and other works of the same
caliber are essentially exercises in propaganda clichés. In
retrospect, therefore, the lives of these authors seem to possess greater historical significance than their works. Hsiao
Chün and Ting Ling especially are typical of the many
patriotic and idealistic writers who finally saw through the

cruel hoax of Communism and dared to defy tyranny. Their attempt to reassert their integrity deserves all our sympathy and admiration, but there is no reason why we should condone their earlier works as other than crude propaganda. With all the apparent nobility of some of these writers, their gullibility in accepting the Communist doctrine in the first place betrays a want of intelligence, the kind of intelligence essential to the creation of a mature literature.

CHAPTER 12

Wu Tsu-hsiang (1908-)

By THE middle thirties the leftist attitudes had become predominant and the new writers of fiction shared almost without exception a hatred of the old order, a discontent with the National Government, and a certain degree of personal commitment to the Communist cause. With the majority the conflicting claims of art and propaganda never became an issue because they had no personal vision other than the picture of Chinese society as drawn by Communist critics. Even for the best younger writers the problem was not so much conscious repudiation of the Communist critique—because they thought they passionately agreed with it—as the successful incorporation of their moral and psychological intuitions within the framework of that critique. The writer who tackled this problem with the greatest success was Wu Tsu-hsiang, who rose to fame in 1934 with his first distinguished book of stories, *West Willow*.

Wu was brought up in a landowning family in Chinghsien, Anhwei. A married man even while a student of Chinese literature at Tsing Hua University, he avoided from the beginning the romantic-revolutionary subject matter, choosing instead the people he knew best, the gentry and peasants of his native province. One of his earliest stories, "Kuan-kuan's Tonic" (1932), shows unmistakably his unsentimental, powerfully ironic approach to rural life. Kuan-kuan is the pet name for the first-person narrator, the spoiled son of a rich landlord. The horror of the story lies in his total unawareness of the amount of suffering that goes into the making of his amusing anecdotes, which he tells with relish. Kuan-kuan sustained serious injuries after his car crashed during a reckless drive in Shanghai with a taxi dancer, who died on the spot. His own life was saved after several blood transfusions; the donor of blood is an ex-tenant on his farm who has come to Shanghai to look for employment. When Kuan-kuan returns to his village to recuperate, his mother, following a local superstition, hires a peasant woman, the wife of the blood donor, to provide two bowls of her milk each day as a tonic for her son. As the peasant is squeezing milk from her breasts, Kuan-kuan "looked on from a distance, very much amused. This woman looked stupid as a cow, but after all she was more clever. The cow can't sell her milk; she has to be milked and she can only put her head into the trough to feed on fodder; this wet nurse, this cow, on the contrary, could squeeze milk with her own hands, could sell this milk to feed her family and herself. I think man is after all more clever than a cow!" [1]

Wu Tsu-hsiang makes use in the story of a bold symbolism: Kuan-kuan, the playboy and landlord's son, literally supports his life on the blood and milk of peasants. Against a Swiftian narrative this symbolism works rather powerfully. Toward the end, the peasant woman's husband, while engaged in an abortive uprising with other villagers, is caught as a bandit and killed without a trial. Kuan-kuan's uncle remarks over the corpse, "This turtle's blood isn't worth half a penny now; last year it sold for five dollars a quart." [2] The element of grudge in this laconic remark bares a meanness of spirit among the gentry who have completely abdicated their humanity. This savage irony is essentially the author's own; it owes little of its strength to the formula of peasant uprising which is perfunctorily introduced in the story.

Wu Tsu-hsiang's major piece in *West Willow*, "Eighteen Hundred Piculs," illustrates even more clearly this juxtaposition of moral substance and proletarian convention. This long story of over a hundred pages, first published in *Literature Quarterly* (January 1934), is a work of considerable technical brilliance. Subtitled "A Sketch of a Meeting at the Ancestral Temple of the Sung Clan, July 15," it reports the conversations and events of a few hours' duration as the numerous representatives of the clan wait in the hall for the important conference which never comes off. This clan, which runs into 2,000 separate households, has seen better days in the last decades of the Ch'ing dynasty, when several members were top mandarins. Now generally impoverished, the clan gathers to debate the disposal of the 1800 piculs of rice and of the jointly owned ancestral land, both of which are entrusted to the management of Sung Po-t'ang. Many suspect that Po-t'ang, in alliance with another powerful member of the clan, Yüeh-chai, is hoarding the rice for selfish purposes, and they demand an investigation. Not a few wish to divide up the ancestral land among the separate branches of the clan, while some, sentimentally abiding by the wishes of their ancestors, want to keep it intact as a source of revenue to meet educational and relief expenses.

Wu Tsu-hsiang gives at least a dozen deft sketches of the family members assembled at the hall: the chairman of a small-town trade union, the proprietor of a bean-curd store, a high school teacher, an ex-official, a small-town politician, an old-style lawyer, an herb doctor, a fortuneteller, a grammar school principal, an old-style tutor whose son has turned Communist and disappeared. As these characters discuss the disposal of the land, the drought, and various other matters, and as Po-t'ang keeps postponing the meeting on the excuse that Yüeh-chai has not yet arrived, tempers run high and the discursive drama inches toward the anticipated climax: the great family quarrel. But the author suddenly shirks his task and resorts to the *deus ex machina* of proletarian fiction: the peasants, already famished under the drought, have arisen and are marching toward the ancestral hall to plunder the 1800 piculs of rice. The assembled clan members are seized with panic.

The peasant uprising is surely a cheap trick, thrown in almost as an afterthought in compliance with fashion; it is a sad falling off from the sustained social and psychological drama of the main body of the narrative. The clan members at the assembly are all real people, talking a real language and pondering real problems from points of view that represent subtly different shades of middle-class and lower middle-class opinion. This achievement indicates a talent of high order: even the crowd scenes in Mao Tun and Chang T'ien-i seldom attain a complete avoidance of stereotyped representation.

Following *West Willow,* Wu Tsu-hsiang published in 1935 a collection mainly of essays and reminiscences entitled *After-dinner Pieces.* Nearly all are of some interest: the essay on dreams, especially, throws much light on the author. But the most important item is the sixty-page story called "Fan Village," which is Wu Tsu-hsiang's masterpiece.

The story tells of a poor peasant couple, Hsien-tzu Sao and her husband. To earn supplementary income they put up a tea booth along the road, for wayfarers. But business at the booth is none too good, and Hsien-tzu's husband is finally persuaded to join a bandit group. He is caught, however, after his initial robbery of a nunnery. To ensure his fair treatment at prison and his eventual release, Hsien-tzu Sao has to raise a large sum of money to bribe the jailors and the petty officers involved in the case. For help she turns to her mother, who has served in genteel families for a number of years and is believed to be relatively well off even though she has her own large family to feed. One evening, as her mother stays overnight in her hut, Hsien-tzu Sao attempts to steal from her fifty dollars' worth of bank notes. Upon being discovered, she kills her mother with a candlestick. That same night the bandits have raided the nearby town and liberated her husband from prison.

According to a so far uncontested Communist appraisal, " 'Fan Village' depicts the unavoidable upheaval following the bankruptcy of the rural economy, which compels a virtuous peasant to turn into a robber and a good peasant woman to kill her own mother for the sake of fifty dollars."[3] But with all its obvious proletarian touches, the story is not so much concerned with economic necessity as with a theme of more absorbing moral interest: Hsien-tzu Sao's hatred for her mother. As the author masterfully unfolds her character, the mother, though pathetic in her own way as a peasant woman implicated in the general plight of rural China, is seen as a positive presence of evil in the story—the type of snobbish and mean-spirited person who through long habituation to town life has adopted her employers' attitude of contempt toward her own folk, especially those deviating from their path of honest poverty, and who, in the atrophy of her good impulses, has clung to money as her very life. "Fan Village" begins with a squabble between Hsien-tzu Sao and her mother, who is stopping by the booth to return home since her employers have left for Shanghai. Before she resumes her journey, she chats with a Buddhist nun, also resting at the booth. These two have a lot in common and the author ably discloses through their conversation their miserliness, their horror for banditry, their fulsome respect for their social betters, and their undisguised scorn for the improvident poor. About a month later, on her way back from the town where she has just received fifty dollars as a member of a credit union, the mother again stops by Hsien-tzu Sao's hut. She refuses to part with any of the money to help her daughter.

As Hsien-tzu Sao premeditates on theft and goes on to commit murder, she is not so much provoked by her dire need as by the ugly manifestation of her mother's evil spirit, which she has to destroy in order to preserve her own moral sanity. For a while, therefore, the story moves steadily in the rarefied region of high tragedy.

In the years prior to the outbreak of the war, Wu Tsu-hsiang ranks as the foremost practitioner of peasant fiction among leftist writers. He does not have the abundance and range of Chang T'ien-i but shares with him the same kind of disgust toward the parasites in Chinese society who batten on the peasants. In "A Certain Day," which Wu Tsu-hsiang contributed to that excellent anthology of short stories *A Decade*,[4] he explores the fascinating situation of a shabby-genteel rascal who comes to the village to vent his pretended indignation over the death of his daughter, who, when alive, has been a constant source of irritation to her peasant husband. The rascal had literally forced his daughter, who was blind in one eye, on the industrious peasant because none of his genteel connections would have wanted her. The peasant didn't mind so much her ugliness as her corrupt, arrogant, and spendthrift ways and her bad influence on their son. A slothful glutton during her second pregnancy, she finally dies in childbed. Now her father, pretending ignorance of her death, tries to blackmail her husband for negligence or possible murder. Faced with these trumped-up charges, the peasant unleashes all his pent-up resentment. His friends in the village join him in threatening the rascal with physical violence if he dares to return. Again in this story the author develops a theme of absorbing moral interest in the antagonism of the peasant and the rascal, and again he sidesteps it toward the end in compliance with proletarian fashion.

In contemplation of "A Certain Day" and "Kuan-kuan's Tonic," and especially of "Eighteen Hundred Piculs" and "Fan Village"—two long stories of consummate skill and power, and only slightly marred by the intrusion of proletarian formulas—one is led to wonder if Wu Tsu-hsiang would have emerged as a truly great story-writer if he had lived under a different ideological climate. Still, his moral perceptions are keen and sound, his picture of village life is unsentimentally realistic, and his prose precise and clear, free of literary mannerisms and of the deliberately uncouth colloquialisms of most peasant fiction. The virtues of his style are especially in evidence in his rendition of peasant and gentry dialogue.

After the outbreak of the war, Wu Tsu-hsiang moved to the interior. In 1942 he wrote *Duck Bill Fall* (later retitled *Mountain Torrent*), considered by many critics the finest patriotic novel of the war period.[5] Yet with all his skill in portraying vividly the peasants of his native province, this novel about guerrilla warfare in Anhwei is still no more than a patriotic novel, circumscribed by its propaganda requirements. Wu Tsu-hsiang seems to have written very few stories during the war, and these few have not been collected in book form. It is a genuine loss to modern Chinese literature that this brilliant talent had such a promising but small output. In 1946 he came to the United States as the personal secretary of General Feng Yü-hsiang. He has been a Professor of Chinese at Peking University since 1949, specializing in literary research.

PART III

The War Period and After
(1937-1957)

CHAPTER 13

Conformity, Defiance,
and Achievement

THE LEAGUE of Left-wing Writers was dissolved in the spring of 1936. In view of the mounting pressure of Japanese aggression, it was clearly to the advantage of Communist writers to abandon overt leftism and initiate a more inclusive and elastic organization under the banner of patriotism. It was not until March 1938, however, that the Chinese Writers' Anti-aggression Association was formally organized under Communist leadership; meanwhile, for the remainder of the year following the dissolution of the League, one witnessed the vociferous Battle of Slogans, in which nearly all the important Communist writers were engaged.

In June 1936, over 120 Communist and leftist writers, styling themselves the Chinese Writers' Association, proclaimed the slogan "Literature for National Defense." Not all the former members of the League joined this organization, however, and the name of Lu Hsün was conspicuously absent from its manifesto. Slightly later, Lu Hsün and sixty-six self-styled Chinese Literary Workers issued a rival declaration, in which the proposed catchphrase for the United Front period was "People's Literature for the National Revolutionary Struggle." The manifestoes of the two groups are alike in their patriotic grandiloquence; but why two separate slogans and organizations? The answer is that Lu Hsün and his group, loyal in their fashion to the Communist party, were disappointed and angry with the United Front policy.

As has been mentioned, Lu Hsün was the nominal leader of the League, but he was not a member of the party, nor did he ever seek membership. Especially after the departure of Ch'ü Ch'iu-pai from Shanghai, he enjoyed little power in the League and had no hand in the making of its vital policy decisions. Real power resided in the hands of the younger Communist writers, such as Chou Yang, Hsia Yen, and Feng Hsüeh-feng, who maintained connections with party leaders in the interior. Feng Hsüeh-feng, especially, enjoyed the distinction of being a participator in the Communist Long March. When he returned to Shanghai from Shensi in April 1936, he found Lu Hsün in a state of gloom, partly due to his failing health, partly to his concern over the divisive tendencies among leftist writers, but mainly because of the disregard for his authority in the sudden policy shift calling for the dissolution of the League and cooperation with nonleftist elements to support the United Front. Feng Hsüeh-feng, who was partial to Lu Hsün's position, later recalls: "He was really skeptical of the policy of the National United Front, because no one had given him a correct explanation; moreover, he did not even participate in the discussions leading to the dissolution of the Left-wing League; at that time, his feelings could not be straightened out." [1]

For a writer subject to gross Communist adulation today, this belated disclosure that, during the last years of his life, Lu Hsün enjoyed little power and trust among party workers constitutes a strange kind of compliment indeed. In the light of this revelation, Lu Hsün's refusal to subscribe to the slogan agreed on by the majority and his vigorous sponsorship of a rival phrase in league with such prominent writers as Mao

Tun and Feng Hsüeh-feng can only be construed as deliberate acts of insubordination, dictated by wounded pride and a mistaken zeal to serve the party. For in comparison with the innocuous "Literature for National Defense" the unwieldy "People's Literature for the National Revolutionary Struggle" carries more of a specific Communist message: it points to the Communist struggle for ultimate victory in China rather than to the impending war with Japan. This connotation was clearly something not wanted by framers of the United Front policy. In view of Lu Hsün's commanding position among readers, however, the orthodox Communist writers had little choice but to fight him in the open. For over four months the rival camps carried on a silly and vehement debate over the relative merits of the two slogans.

When the debate seemed interminable, Lu Hsün was again subjected to intimidation, as he had been earlier during his quarrel with the Creationists. On August 1 Hsü Mou-yung, a member of the orthodox group and probably already then a Communist, wrote him a letter calling for his immediate obedience. Hsü was assigned the task probably because, alone among the orthodox group, he was Lu Hsün's good friend and frequent correspondent. (According to the *Letters* of Lu Hsün, Hsü received forty-three letters from November 1933 to February 1936; only Lu Hsün's mother and five other friends, Hsiao Chün and his wife among them, corresponded more often.) But apparently dressed in party authority for the occasion, Hsü barely disguises his censure with his careful observance of epistolary courtesy: "At present I cannot help feeling that your words and actions for the past half year have been unwittingly strengthening the vicious tendencies." [2] In extenuation, he attributes this fault to the influence of certain deviationist writers: the critic Hu Feng, the translator Huang Yüan, and the novelist Pa Chin: "You have failed to observe minutely the unscrupulous character of Hu Feng or the sycophancy of Huang Yüan; you have become instead their permanent tool, dazzling and perverting the public like an idol. Hence it has been impossible to put a stop to their deviationist movement, which is dictated by ambition . . . I can understand your original motive very well. You were afraid that the comrade writers who have joined the United Front would relinquish their original position, and seeing that Hu Feng and the others are so attractively leftist, you agreed with them." [3] Despite this mitigating circumstance, Hsü warns Lu Hsün in no uncertain terms:

> May I remind you, sir, all this is due to your lack of comprehension of the present basic policy. . . . At present, to raise leftist slogans in support of the United Front is wrong, is in fact endangering the United Front. In your most recently published "Replies to an Interviewer during Illness," therefore, you are in the wrong to have said that "People's Literature for the National Revolutionary Struggle" is the latest phase of proletarian literature and ought to be employed as the general slogan for the United Front. [4]

Seriously ill, and thoroughly incensed by the effrontery of a writer so inferior in rank, and a personal friend to boot, Lu Hsün published Hsü Mou-yung's letter without asking for his permission and appended a six-thousand-word reply which rocked the literary world with its unceremonious disclosure of mean factional struggles within the leftist ranks and its passionate denunciation of the unscrupulous, browbeating tactics employed by the dominant Communist group to quash opposition. "From my own experience," writes Lu Hsün as he compares in his own mind his present opponents with the Creationists of the late twenties, "those who wear the face of 'revolution' for all to see and won't hesitate to wrongly accuse others of being 'secret agents,' 'counterrevolutionaries,' 'Trotskyites' or even 'traitors' are mostly questionable characters. As they cleverly hamstring the national revolutionary strength and seek personal gain in the name of revolution and at the expense of the revolutionary interests of the masses, frankly I even doubt if they were not sent over by our enemy." [5]

In October the quarrel was finally patched up, and a Literary Workers' Manifesto on the United Resistance and on Freedom of Speech was proclaimed to signalize the achievement of a new unity. Lu Hsün, Mao Tun, Kuo Mo-jo, Lin Yutang, Pa Chin, Chang T'ien-i, and a dozen other leftist, liberal, and old-style writers undersigned the document. Soon afterward, on the nineteenth of the same month, Lu Hsün died, and his last act of defiance was generously reinterpreted by Communists as an instance of his personal rectitude and courageous leadership.

In their discreet treatment of this intraparty struggle, Communist critics have tended to whitewash Lu Hsün of any taint of intransigence and unorthodoxy. The anti-Communist critics, on the contrary, are inclined to see in the defiant writer a genuine patriot awakening to the fact of Communist conspiracy which subverts patriotism for its own ends. But the truth, as has been already suggested, is much simpler. Lu Hsün, who had gone along wholeheartedly with Communists in their persecution of nationalist and liberal writers, could not have been the dupe the anti-Communist critics have supposed. In assailing the supporters of the slogan "Literature for National Defense," he was principally dictated by his blind loyalty and wounded pride. He could not see why Communist writers should stoop so low as to seek a coalition with liberal and old-style writers; and a literary dictator in his own conceit, he could not brook a dictatorship that had neglected to honor him with at least the external gestures of deference.

In retrospect, however, the Battle of Slogans is significant not merely for Lu Hsün's splendid act of self-assertion; it brings to the fore a number of new personalities who were to play crucial roles in the continuing ideological struggle among writers in the war years and after, prominently Hu Feng and Chou Yang. In 1936 Kuo Mo-jo was still in Tokyo; he was to return to China on the eve of the War of Resistance;

for the time being, Chou Yang (his real name: Chou Ch'i-ying) was the chief spokesman for the majority group who followed blindly the Comintern and the Paoan leadership. It was he who was given the signal honor of introducing the slogan "Literature for National Defense," in his article "Literature at the Present Juncture." A native of Hunan, Chou Yang stayed in Japan for some time after his graduation from the Great China University in Shanghai. He became a translator of leftist books upon his return to Shanghai but soon wormed his way into the inner Communist literary circle. He first attracted general notice early in 1936 over his debate with Hu Feng on the issue of "typical characters" in literary creation. Dogmatic, insensitive to literature, and blindly loyal to the party, he was dubbed by Feng Hsüeh-feng during the Battle of Slogans as "a junior Ch'ien Hsing-ts'un." [6]

(It was surely lucky for Chou Yang that Hsü Mou-yung was assigned the thankless task of writing that harsh letter to Lu Hsün; Hsü fought alongside Chou Yang and the leading Marxist dialectician Ai Ssu-ch'i over the slogans and moved with them to Yenan upon the outbreak of the war. But whereas both Chou and Ai were immediately rewarded with top positions in the Yenan cultural hierarchy, the opprobrium Hsü had suffered from the pen of Lu Hsün prevented him from rising as high. He was finally purged in 1957 along with many other so-called rightist intellectuals: part of his crime was his impudence in having written that letter to Lu Hsün.)

On the other hand, the phrase "People's Literature for the National Revolutionary Struggle" was introduced by Hu Feng, at Lu Hsün's behest, in his article "What Do the Masses Want from Literature?" A native of Hupeh, Hu Feng (his real name: Chang Ku-fei) had been a member of the Communist Youth League until, frightened of warlord persecution in Peking, he resigned from the organization in 1925. He was briefly a political worker stationed with Chiang Kai-shek's Communist-fighting troops in Kiangsi. Then, like

Chou Yang, after staying for some time in Japan he returned to Shanghai to become an important member of the Left-wing League. The above information, publicized in the most authoritative party organ, the *People's Daily* (Jen-min Jih-pao) to smear Hu Feng's character on the eve of his final denigration, is not entirely reliable, however: according to the author's own biographical sketch he was in Japan from 1928 to 1933 and joined the Left-wing League in 1934 so that it would have been physically impossible for him to have joined Chiang's expeditionary forces in Kiangsi.[7] But even in the thirties, the whispers went among his enemies that Hu Feng was a Kuomintang spy. Arrogant, individualistic, and a sophisticated Marxist, Hu Feng was not one to ingratiate himself with the Communist literary hierarchy, but apparently many people were drawn to him because of his loyalty and personal magnetism. During the last year of his life, Lu Hsün was constantly with him; to those who were trying to compel Lu Hsün to obey the party leadership, this was another black mark against him. In his letter to Hsü Mou-yung, Lu Hsün discloses an underhanded plot to alienate him from Hu Feng:

> Next, as to my relationship with Hu Feng, Pa Chin, and Huang Yüan. I have known them for only a short time, in connection with our literary work; though not confidants, they can be called my friends. To accuse my friends of being "spies" or "despicable" without producing any factual proof is an act that calls for my correction: not merely in consideration of our friendship, but in consideration of the whole situation. Hsü Mou-yung's accusation that I am partial to friends but blind to reality is a libel: it is only because I have been aware of the real situation that I can easily place people like Hsü Mou-yung. One day last year (at that time I did not know Hu Feng too well), a very important person asked me to have an appointment with him at his

place. On arriving there, I saw hopping from a car four men: T'ien Han, Chou Ch'i-ying, and two others. Sharply dressed in foreign suits, they all looked very smart and cocky. Their specific task was to inform me that Hu Feng was a spy sent over by the Government. When I demanded proof, they replied that they had got the word from the turncoat writer Mu Mu-t'ien [also purged in the 1957 anti-rightist campaign]. I was quite stunned that the word of a turncoat could be taken as gospel truth by the Left-wing League. After a few more rounds of interrogation, my answer was "I don't believe this: the evidence is too feeble." We parted in a far from amicable mood, but since then I have not heard people mention Hu Feng as a "spy."

But the strange thing is that, whenever the mosquito papers attack me or Hu Feng, they always link our names together. The latest gossip concerned my views [on the two slogans] as reported by O.V. in *Realistic Literature:* the *Social Daily* maintained that O.V. is none other than Hu Feng and that his report does not agree with my original views. . . . Last winter or perhaps this spring the same paper carried a piece of news framed with fancy margins to underscore its importance: that I was ready to surrender to Nanking and that the most active intermediary was Hu Feng who, depending on his skill, would sooner or later bring about this event.

I have also observed events not immediately concerning me. Is there not a youth who, having been dubbed a "spy" and consequently shunned by all his friends, wandered homeless in streets until he was finally caught and tortured? Is there not another youth who, equally maligned as a "spy," is now languishing in a Soochow prison for his participation in the heroic struggle, and nobody knows if he is still alive or already dead? These two youths are factual proof that they have not written

any splendid recantations like Mu Mu-t'ien or put on
a big show in Nanking like T'ien Han [T'ien Han is
a playwright; the language here is deliberately ambig-
uous]. At the same time I have also observed people.
Even if Hu Feng is not reliable, I can at least trust
myself, and I have not negotiated with Nanking through
Hu Feng. Therefore I can only come to the conclusion
that Hu Feng is truthful precisely because his blunt
honesty has made him an object of dislike and resentment. On the other hand, I have my doubts about, and
even detest, such youths as Chou Ch'i-ying who slander
others without compunction. Of course, Chou Ch'i-ying
may have some good qualities; he may change and become in time a real revolutionary. Hu Feng has also
his weak points: his nervous temperament, his excessive
regard for detail, his doctrinaire tendency, his refusal
to popularize his style of writing; but all considered, he
is undeniably a promising youth who has never joined
any movement hindering anti-Japanese patriotism or
obstructing the United Front. Even if people like Hsü
Mou-yung try their best to smear it, his record stands
clear.[8]

I have quoted at some length because Lu Hsün's evaluation
of the characters of Chou Yang and Hu Feng will prepare us
to enjoy more keenly the irony of the subsequent struggle
between the rival critics. The Battle of Slogans, a silly quarrel
in itself, is, finally, important in outlining sharply the struggle between two factions of Communist and leftist writers:
Lu Hsün, Mao Tun, Feng Hsüeh-feng, Hu Feng, and their
friends on the one hand, and the orthodox group headed by
Kuo Mo-jo and Chou Yang on the other. Though, as in 1928,
the latter group again yielded ground in 1936, they soon regained their overbearing manner in the confusions of the
succeeding war. (By 1957 nearly all of Lu Hsün's followers
—Hsiao Chün, Hu Feng, Feng Hsüeh-feng, Huang Yüan,

and others—had been purged.) Under the convenient guise of patriots, they again brazenly dictated literary fashions and agitated over slogans and issues which are completely extraneous to the promotion of contemporary writing on a serious level. With the death of Lu Hsün and in the absence of effective opposition from among the anti-Communists, they fostered a spurious propaganda product which marks a decided setback from the relative brilliance of the literature of the middle thirties. In the Nationalist interior the only persistent harasser of the predominant Communist policy-makers remained Hu Feng, who, having inherited the mantle of Lu Hsün, fought them with relative impunity, though even he was of little consequence in actually raising the literary standards of the time.

(Feng Hsüeh-feng, as Lu Hsün's most intimate friend, should have been his legitimate successor, but immediately upon the outbreak of the war he registered his sharp disagreement with Communist literary policy by retiring to his home town in Chekiang. Subsequently he was imprisoned in the Nationalist concentration camp at Shangjao, Kiangsi, for 1941–43, so that, although he shared Hu Feng's critical position, he remained inactive during most of the war years. Mao Tun seems to have returned to the orthodox Communist fold soon after the Battle of Slogans.)

Although it is not entirely beyond the realm of possibility that Hu Feng was a paid agent of the Kuomintang (the crime of which he was finally convicted in 1955), this supposition would credit the Nationalists with a sophistication and cunning totally unfelt in their habitually clumsy struggle against Communism, and contradict completely the critical record of Hu Feng, who never said a good word about the National Government. While it is true (as his late persecutors have charged) that throughout his extensive critical publications Hu Feng wasted little space denouncing the Government, this was because he took it for granted that his readers were disaffected already. Hu Feng's criticism bespeaks rather a man so passionately concerned with the welfare of modern Chinese literature that he could not brook any deliberate injury to its growth. And because the injurers were consistently Communists rather than Nationalists, who took little paternal interest in literary activities, the former became the main target of Hu Feng's attack. In maintaining this attack, however, Hu Feng had eventually to contend with a man so much more politically powerful that his failure was foredoomed. The man was Mao Tse-tung himself.

In the prewar years the Communist power in China did not exercise a direct control over literary and cultural expression in the country. It supervised, of course, the propaganda programs in its own regions, but the management of revolutionary and leftist literary movements in Shanghai was left in the hands of its agents, who appeared at times as much the henchmen of the Comintern as of the native Communist leadership. This was so because the latter had not developed a positive cultural program for China as a whole other than that devised by the Kremlin: the clamor for a United Front during the middle thirties, for instance, was heard in all democratic countries where the Comintern was permitted to operate. With the outbreak of the Sino-Japanese War, however, the Chinese Communists became more of an autonomous power and their leader Mao Tse-tung concerned himself more and more with the cultural direction of the nation as a whole. In his 1938 speech entitled "The Position of the Chinese Communist Party in the National Struggle," Mao issued one of his first cultural directives that, while apparently echoing Stalin,[9] was to change drastically the literary scene, and the national scene as a whole:

> To make Marxism concretely Chinese, to ensure that its every expression manifest Chinese characteristics—that is to say, to apply Marxism with due regard for Chinese qualities—this is the urgent problem which

the whole party should try to understand and solve. Foreign-slanted pedantry and obscurantism must be abolished, hollow and abstract clichés must be discouraged, and dogmatism must be arrested so that a fresh and vivid Chinese style and manner, of which the Chinese masses are fond, may take their place. To separate international content from national forms is to betray one's ignorance of internationalism; we must weld the two closely together.[10]

In enjoining upon all party cadres the importance of remaining Chinese while practicing their Marxism, the passage itself, if one may quibble, is a tissue of hollow, abstract, and obscurantist clichés (it is hard to tell what is meant, for example, by "national forms"). But in the literary context the meaning is quite unambiguous: "national forms" can only mean the kinds of indigenous literary and art forms which Ch'ü Ch'iu-pai had already praised while promoting his "literature for the masses." By the same token, "foreign-slanted pedantry and obscurantism," "hollow and abstract clichés," and "dogmatism" can only mean the theory and practice of Western-slanted modern Chinese literature which Ch'ü had also abhorred. In insisting on "a fresh and vivid Chinese style and manner," therefore, Mao is merely carrying forward Ch'ü's striving for a literature completely alienated from the West.

Mao Tse-tung attacks Chinese feudalism and decadence no less strongly than Ch'en Tu-hsiu and Ch'ü Ch'iu-pai; he is unlike them in his more unequivocal assertion of a revolutionary tradition in Chinese literature and thought. In the late thirties he was ready to initiate his program of New Democracy, to glorify the Chinese past and the revolutionary contributions of Sun Yat-sen, and in so doing establish a rapport between Chinese history and the Chinese Communist party: the devil to be exorcised in this new alignment of forces was the bourgeois and petty-bourgeois consciousness with its liberal and revolutionary ambitions anchored in the Western tradition. Completely untenable as history, Mao's revolutionary thesis was calculated to impress his dialectically minded followers and the nation at large, insofar as it represented a new synthesis of thought transcending at once the flat despair of Ch'en Tu-hsiu and the empirical reformism of Hu Shih. It was also designed to flatter the patriotic pride of the wartime people and to undermine their fear and distrust of Communism.

In repudiating the Western tradition in modern Chinese literature, Mao Tse-tung has by fiat reversed the course of that literature and killed its potential for further experimentation and development. It would be salutary if by "national forms" he had meant the central traditions of poetry, drama, and fiction: after twenty years of assimilating the Western lesson, it was time for writers to learn from their forebears, to enrich their sensibility and imagination. But when Mao extolled the revolutionary tradition in Chinese literature, he probably had in mind only such popular novels as *Water Margin,* which he read with pleasure as a schoolboy and which he had found to be continually instructive during his years as a harassed military leader. And as Chou Yang and other Yenan critics expound Mao's term, one sees further that "national forms" are to be identified not so much with classical vernacular literature as with those marginal, semi-literate, and regionally diversified forms of entertainment which still enjoyed a diminishing popularity among the less educated strata of society. It frequently happens that a poet or school of poets could alter expression and sensibility through a renewed contact with folk literature. But such a renewal or change could not take place without a concomitant attempt to make use of certain elements of the poetic tradition currently dormant. In ignoring this tradition, the appropriators of "national forms" can only turn into facile entertainers and propagandists.

Mao's injunction that writers utilize "national forms"

added further to the confusion existing among writers during the first years of the war. The upshot of the Battle of Slogans had been an inundation of patriotic sentiment among diverse groups of writers in upholding their immediate duty as fabricators of anti-Japanese propaganda. Upon its formation in 1938 the Chinese Writers' Anti-aggression Association immediately adopted the twin slogans of "Let Writers Go to the Villages" and "Let Writers Serve the Armed Forces." Few authors saw active combat duty, but many units of literary and theatrical workers frequented the front and entertained the troops. With the evacuation of the Government from the coastal provinces, this type of propaganda activity probably exercised a salutary influence on the morale of the soldiers and of the ill-prepared population in the interior, and if the aims of propaganda and serious writing were kept distinct, writers could have ideally performed their patriotic duties without relinquishing their more serious professional pursuits. But for many writers, who had few artistic scruples to begin with, the necessity of reaching a large and unsophisticated audience served only as a plausible excuse to manufacture an unashamedly crude propaganda literature. Mao's decree further strengthened this trend. In both Nationalist and Communist areas, writers turned out a large quantity of ephemeral writing: stories in the style of cheap historical romances, poems to be recited in the manner of popular ballads, skits and plays improvised in accordance with the varied conventions of regional drama. The art of realism was imperiled.

This patriotic craze provoked Hu Feng, who has little use for the Chinese tradition and regards the new literature as a complete break from that tradition. He was alarmed that the attempt to distort and minimize the significance and contributions of this literature, implicit in Mao's denigration of the Western influence, went unchallenged, that the Western realistic tradition, which had shaped the best modern writers, was now to be discarded in favor of a mythical, at best largely

unself-conscious, native revolutionary tradition. In this concern Hu Feng was one not only with Lu Hsün, who scorned
classical Chinese literature, but with Hu Shih, who as a
strong advocate of the Western tradition is at times bluntly
critical of classical literature in spite of his passionate scholarly interest in the field. (During the persecution of Hu
Feng in 1955, the names of Hu Feng and Hu Shih were
bracketed together not only for their supposed counterrevolutionary stand but for their denigration of classical Chinese
literature.) Soon after Mao Tse-tung's views on "national
forms" were publicized in the Nationalist interior, Hu Feng
spoke out, in essay after essay, against the Maoist apologists.
In 1940 Hu Feng summarized his views in a small book called
On the Problem of National Forms, which is an eloquent plea
for the continued vitality of the realistic tradition in modern
Chinese literature. Largely because of his prestigious friendship with the late Lu Hsün and the lack of strong opponents
(his powerful enemies being in Yenan), Hu Feng commanded
a wide hearing. Moreover, many writers in the Nationalist
interior were by that time tired of their masquerade as folk
artists, and with the gradual subsiding of the patriotic fervor
they returned, whether under Hu Feng's influence or not, to
the beaten paths of the modern tradition.

As the critic who has done most to counter the baleful influence of Maoist orthodoxy in the war years and after, Hu
Feng deserves our sympathetic attention. There is no doubt
he is a Marxist; he quotes Marx and Stalin left and right to
confound his enemies and to buttress his somewhat heretical
position. In his first volume, *Literary Essays* (1936), he appeared a socialist-realist critic, reproving, as we have noticed,
even Chang T'ien-i for his failure to provide an optimistic
vision. (This volume also established his reputation as a
Marxist critic of unmatched erudition and sophistication.)
But in his succeeding volume of essays written during the
Battle of Slogans, *The Gathering Clouds: The Manners of a
Period,* he began to weary of cant. Upon the outbreak of the

war Hu Feng launched a magazine called *July,* to serve as a vehicle for himself and his friends. Increasingly bold, he wrote in 1938 an essay on "The Cultural Movement under a Protracted War of Resistance," in which he deplores the fashion of writers to visit or cover the front, and the deluge of writings about the war. One of Hu Feng's favorite expressions is "Life is everywhere and literary material is everywhere"; one doesn't have to go out of one's way to seek signif :ant experience. For those patriotic and Communist writers docilely following fashion and decree, Hu Feng reserves the contemptuous term *shih k'uai,* meaning opportunists, mercenaries, and Philistines. In addition to *The Problem of National Forms,* he wrote in the forties such critical volumes as *The National War and Literature, In A Muddle,* and *Stemming the Adverse Current,* in which he continued to clarify his own theory of literature and attack the opportunists.

Hu Feng agrees with the conventional Marxist critique of Chinese society, but he also believes that a writer, if he is endowed with genuine literary talent, can and should grasp these truths of his own accord, feel them with his own pulse. To mechanically follow the Marxian precepts for writing is worse than useless: it indicates the lack or atrophy of the requisite creative talent. To Hu Feng, therefore, a genuine piece of literature is at once objective and subjective in character, a happy fusion of the author's objective recognition and subjective apprehension of historical reality. Against the formulas and recipes for correct writing Hu Feng raises the standard of "the subjective fighting will." Since the central social and individual experience is the fact of struggle between the forces of light and darkness, the duty of every serious, every realistic writer is to celebrate that struggle against darkness, to unfold the primitive terror and animal savagery inherent in the struggle, to attest to man's inviolable dignity and his desire for light. Especially is it the writer's duty to assert the defiant will of the individual hero, even in apparent defeat and death. Realistic integrity consists in "the writer's dedication [to truth], his love and compassion, his naked vision of life as it is, his complete abhorrence of dishonesty, of any attempt to deceive himself or others." [11] To be faithful to reality in this fashion is the only guarantee of a writer's being faithful to his art. Thus Hu Feng never fails to stress the writer's sincerity, character, and humanity.

It is apparent that there is a good deal of romanticism in Hu Feng's conception of realism. One has the impression that his theory grew out of his fondness for a type of modern literature, and of modern Chinese literature in particular, which depicts the perennially unavailing but heroic struggle against darkness. Quite unmistakable is the note of Dionysiac masochism, which permits the critic to glory in the blood and tears of the defeated and oppressed. (As a noted poet, Hu Feng practices what he preaches by resort to violent imagery and rhapsodic exclamation.) But what emerges as truly admirable is his insistence on the subjective element, the personal honesty of the writer, without which all writing is in vain. Prudently Hu Feng never attempted to solve the crux: what if a writer's honesty leads him into conflict with the Marxist revelation? The answer is never given, but the logic of Hu Feng's critical position should entail, I think, the writer's relinquishment of the luxury of Marxian dogma in order to stay truthful to his own vision.

In hewing to the individual vision, Hu Feng serves notice of the central malady of modern Chinese literature as the later Lu Hsün could not do with his self-distrustful eagerness to follow the Soviet lead, his blind deference to Ch'ü Ch'iu-pai. With Lu Hsün, finally, the nation comes first, and in the interests of national welfare he is willing to subordinate the freedom of the writer. Hu Feng, on the contrary, maintains that the writer's primary loyalty is to himself and that he can only serve the nation by staying honest: those critics and writers who sanction and practice fraudulent writing in the name of national welfare are themselves the primary exhibits of a sick society. In his important 1943 article "Realism Today," Hu Feng diagnoses the prevalence of antiliterary criticism:

> First there is the fact staring in one's eye that literature is not wanted, and then there will be the "theory" to justify this doing away with literature. . . . I call this situation a crisis, and I want to plead for the continuing health of literature: don't compel writers to lie, don't "do dirt" [the Laurentian expression is adopted here for its appositeness to the Chinese phrase] on life! [12]

Though unidentified, the "theory" referred to can be none other than that of Mao Tse-tung, and in 1943 Hu Feng is finding his battle against his principal adversary increasingly arduous. The year earlier, the Communist leader had launched a *cheng-feng* movement to rectify the unorthodox tendencies among his cadres. With the migration of a large number of writers and intellectuals to Yenan following the outbreak of the war, Mao was faced with a serious disciplinary problem. It seemed that many of these intellectuals, used to the unregimented petty-bourgeois life in Shanghai or Peking, continued to think and behave in a non-Communist fashion. The rectification movement was designed to make these intellectuals and other recalcitrant party elements repent of their petty-bourgeois ways and fall in line with Mao's own ideas about Communism and proper Communist behavior. Specifically, in response to the hostile criticism voiced by Wang Shih-wei, Ting Ling, and their friends, Mao called in May a conference of literary and art workers to expound the objectives of Communist literature and art and outline the methods for their implementation. His inaugural and concluding speeches at the meetings, immediately published in pamphlet form as *Talks at the Yenan Literary Conference*, became the new oracle for all literary and art workers in Communist areas.

Mao Tse-tung denies that the writer is entitled to his individual vision of truth; the latter can only be a petty-bourgeois illusion. Ignorant of foreign languages and nurtured on an old-fashioned education, Mao betrays in these talks a strong personal antipathy toward what little he has read in modern Chinese literature. Even though, for tactical reasons, he has earlier praised Lu Hsün to the skies, the kind of prideful self-assertion which Lu Hsün at his best invariably maintains can only be anathema to him. At the conference, therefore, he reproves those Communist-area writers who, following Lu Hsün, are too fond of exposing the dark side of society and reluctant to celebrate the bright: it is time for these writers to refrain from the satiric Lu Hsün style and take notice of the positive achievement of the party. Mao speaks heatedly against the reformist idealism of petty-bourgeois Communists: "Through various ways and means, including literary and art means, the intellectuals of petty-bourgeois origins have always tried stubbornly to express themselves and spread their own opinions; they have always demanded that the party and the world be remolded in their image." [13]

Mao goes on to rebuke and ridicule the many kinds of petty-bourgeois self-indulgence. Of the so-called subjective writers who have retained illusions about love, for example, he has this much to say: "Now how about love? In a class society there is only class love. Yet these comrades want to look for some kind of super-love which transcends classes: they seek an abstract love, as well as abstract freedom, abstract truth, abstract human nature, etc. This clearly indicates that these comrades have been deeply influenced by the bourgeoisie." [14]

In lieu of a literature that serves truth and goodness, embraces all humanity, and attacks all institutions of cruelty for the greater dignity of the human individual—in other words, the kind of literature envisioned by Hu Feng—Mao Tse-tung endorses a literature that is merely the subservient instrument of the Communist party. Since all the existing contemporary Chinese literature is infected with the petty-bourgeois spirit, Mao cannot point to concrete examples of the kind of literature he wants; this literature is yet to be created. To guarantee its arrival, Mao exhorts the writer to measure himself against five yardsticks: standpoint, attitude, audience, work, and study. Does the writer stand for the people—primarily, the workers, peasants, and soldiers—and their party? Are the attitudes reflected in his writing concretely representative of the specific aims and goals of the party at the time of its composition? Does he write primarily for the people, or does he still cherish petty-bourgeois illusions and write for the petty bourgeoisie? If he retains petty-bourgeois illusions, does he try to improve himself by "work"—that is, by participating in the labors of the workers, peasants, and soldiers so as to correctly assimilate their idiom, feelings, and aspirations? Is he able at the same time, while shedding his petty-bourgeois illusions through actual participation in the people's work, to help himself to the food of Marxism-Leninism so as to remain intellectually incorruptible in his service to the people?

Unlike Marx and Lenin who occasionally dabble in critical appraisals of capitalist writers, Mao Tse-tung merely lays down a program of authorial discipline to ensure the appearance of a correct literature. The program is so narrow as to constitute a plank rather than a platform, and the writer who walks on it is always in danger of losing his balance and plunging into the sea of petty-bourgeois and reactionary heresy underneath. But by leaving the fulfillment of his literary idea to the writers themselves, Mao Tse-tung himself has always remained infallible and beyond criticism. His program is inviolable because any one of the five yardsticks can be used as a cudgel to beat the erring or complaining author with. If a writer is incorrect, then obviously he should mind his standpoint and attitude, his study and work habits. What if a writer, after conscientiously remolding himself, still cannot turn out satisfactory work? Then, equally obviously, his petty-bourgeois mentality must be, unknown to himself, causing mischief, and he should study and work even harder to rid himself of the demon. What if the general level of writing, in the opinion of the reigning party critics, remains mediocre and luckluster in spite of the writers' conscientious attempt to remold themselves—if there is a frequent eruption of unorthodox ideas and sentiments among writers in spite of the vigilance of party supervision and censorship? Then it is time to punish with ritualistic fanfare all the major offenders and to urge the rest of the writers to undergo another protracted period of self-remolding. By resorting to these strategies, Mao Tse-tung has by and large maintained during the last fifteen years the inflexible harshness of his literary line.

In his *Talks* Mao Tse-tung further addresses himself to a problem of much practical import for his largely illiterate region: whether the literary cadres should aim at the achievement of a higher literary culture or a broader literary dissemination. He admits the primacy of popularization but sees the two tasks as interrelated: "Popularization should proceed on the principle of elevation; elevation should build on the foundation of popularization." [15] Unaware that the elevation of literary quality should properly call for the writer's disengagement from his propaganda task, Mao regards the advanced literary product as merely a stylistic and rhetorical refinement of the simpler. Until the people have developed a greater aptitude for literary appreciation, such refinement is patently unnecessary. Artistic standards are, after all, subordinate to political, and the correct message is all that counts. Mao shrewdly observes: "So far as the political content of a work of art is pernicious, the more artistically successful it is the more pernicious it becomes." [16]

In his formulation of a worker, peasant, soldier literature innocent of the ideology and techniques of Western writers and expressly designed for popular consumption, as well as in his earlier endorsement of national literary and art forms, Mao is clearly carrying forward the unfinished task of Ch'ü Ch'iu-pai (see above, Chapter 5). In spite of the allegation by fawning critics that Mao manifests unprecedented critical originality and genius in his formulation of literary policies, the *Talks* can be seen, in the perspective of Chinese literary history, to be only a restatement of the extremist Communist literary opinion of the two preceding decades. As early as 1923 the *Chinese Youth* had formulated the worker, peasant, soldier direction of Communist literature.[17] In his representative article "Revolution and Literature" (1926), Kuo Mo-jo had admonished youth to "ascertain the main literary current, and go among the soldiers and people, go into factories and the storm-centers of the revolution." [18] Mao Tse-tung himself had outlined in 1929 a program of literary, theatrical, and art propaganda among Communist troops, which was later implemented by Ch'ü Ch'iu-pai during his brief tenure as Minister of Education in the Kiangsi Soviet Government.[19] The propaganda activities at Yenan had conformed to this simple pattern. As a blueprint of Communist literature and art, the *Talks* is little more than Mao's sanction of the kinds of propaganda already in existence in Communist areas.

Yet for writers at large the *Talks* was a thunderbolt from the blue, a new beginning. Chou Yang correctly hailed it as the greatest literary event since the initial Literary Revolution, as, in fact, "the second, and even more sweeping and profound, Literary Revolution." [20] The history of literary debate in modern China has been a series of altercations between doctrinaire radicals and Communists who manipulate literature and literary opinion for ulterior ends and the majority of writers who, whatever their political sympathy, prefer to work in freedom and care to some degree about art. Because the doctrinaires had hitherto failed to establish an absolute dictatorship, serious writing could still be produced, though under admittedly distracting and distressing circumstances. With Mao's entry into the national literary scene, however, the doctrinaires, vested with delegated authority, have become undisputed legislators of literary expression. By 1949 even Hu Feng, who had been fighting the doctrinaires in the open, had to exercise extreme caution in order to maintain his struggle. But during the war and the first postwar years, Mao's authority did not extend effectively beyond his own territory: a semblance of freedom of debate was still possible and serious writing projects could still be entertained in areas beyond his control.

Mao Tse-tung's talks at the Yenan conference were intended primarily for Communist-area writers; they did not create so much stir in the Nationalist interior as one would have expected, though following the debate on "national forms" Communist critics in Chungking or Kweilin had continued to voice their support of policies and directives issued in Yenan. But by and large, Communist writers in Nationalist areas, and in Hong Kong and Shanghai until Pearl Harbor, were entrusted with the more important task of discrediting the National Government in the eyes of the people, especially the student and petty-bourgeois elements, of airing Communist complaints about the conduct of the war, of demanding unlimited freedom for the pursuance of these propaganda objectives. The key word now was democracy.[21] Just as Chou En-lai, the Yenan representative in Chungking, was in the eyes of many gullible American officials and reporters a charming spokesman for democracy, so were Communist writers, to progressive and gullible elements of the population, gallant fighters for freedom. During the heyday of the Left-wing League these same writers had been leftists; during the coalition period of the United Front they had been patriots concerned with the cultural defense of the nation; so, following Mao's promulgation of New Democracy in 1940, they became democratic cultural leaders fighting tyranny and oppression in their own country. During the honeymoon period of Nationalist-Communist coalition the literary product had been a chaotic profusion of war propaganda. Following 1940 the patriotic gesture was still observed, to maintain the myth of heroic Communist resistance, but more and more the leading critics and writers were concerned with the real enemy to Communist advancement—the National Government under Chiang Kai-shek. This new approach won over to the Communist side many college students and professors who were genuinely unhappy about the Government, especially for its failure to stem increasing poverty and corruption and for its reliance on the secret police to fight Communist subversion. The most celebrated convert was Wen I-to, a professor of Chinese and an early poet of the Crescent Moon school; he took under his wing many fledgling Communist poets and spoke out loudly against Kuomintang fascism. In 1946 he was assassinated in Kunming by the secret police; in Communist and progressive circles his fame ranked for a while almost as high as Lu Hsün's in their eagerness to exploit his martyrdom.

The literary scene in the Nationalist interior is extremely hard to assess because so many of the shabbily printed wartime publications, books as well as magazines, have not been preserved, certainly not in Taiwan, Hong Kong, or the United States. For another thing, many prewar cultural leaders have left the scene: Lu Hsün is dead; Hu Shih and Lin Yutang are in America, the one as Ambassador to Washington and the other as a best-selling author purveying the charms of old China and reporting on the heroism of the new; Chou Tso-jen, too much in love with the culture of Peking to undertake the long trek to the interior, is content to remain as minister of education in the puppet government of North China. Of the prewar anti-Communist critics, Shen Ts'ung-wen, Chu Kuang-ch'ien, and Liang Shih-ch'iu did move to the interior, and they made intermittent attempts to air their dissent from Communist literary opinion. Even the Communist writers themselves are split by geographical divisions. Though travel is possible (after Pearl Harbor many writers stationed in Hong Kong escaped to the interior, and writers in the Nationalist and Communist interior frequently exchanged visits) and the Anti-aggression Association serves as the transmitter of Communist literary policy, there is clearly no acknowledged cultural center in which the majority of writers are gathered and the ideological battles fought, as is the case with Shanghai during the prewar decade.

Wartime fiction in the Nationalist interior nevertheless presents a coherent picture insofar as nearly all the major novelists and story-writers of the preceding decade stayed within government territory for the duration of the war. Pa Chin, Shen Ts'ung-wen, and Mao Tun (he stayed in Hong Kong in 1938, and again in 1941; shortly after Pearl Harbor, he returned to the Nationalist interior) were still producing significant work, and Pa Chin especially showed steady progress during the eight years. As has been mentioned, Chang T'ien-i was stricken with tuberculosis after turning out three satiric sketches, and Wu Tsu-hsiang didn't write much after his patriotic novel *Duck Bill Fall*. As head of the Chinese Writers' Anti-aggression Association, Lao Shê was a conspicuous example of unstinted patriotic service.[22] He turned out many propaganda plays and a great quantity of verse in the folk style, but he found time to write only one novel, and a routine exercise in patriotic propaganda at that.

Of the other writers whose fiction made some mark during this period, Ai Wu, Sha T'ing, Tuan-mu Hung-liang, and Lu Ling deserve mention.[23] The most prolific of the four, Ai Wu, wrote of the war, the peasants in the interior, and his varied personal experiences in Southwest China and Indo-China in his many volumes of short stories, novels, and autobiographies. Though not a talent of the first order, he was deservedly given high praise during and immediately after the war.

A good friend of Ai Wu's, Sha T'ing was known as early as 1932 for his first collection of stories, *Voyage beyond the Law*, but it was only during the war that his fiction showed satiric skill. A native of Szechwan, Sha T'ing was thoroughly familiar with the dialect and manners of the province; the impingement of the Chungking Government upon the lives of the Szechwan people gave him ample opportunity to exercise his talent. His writings for the war period and immediately after include a collection of short stories, *The Sowers;* a novelette, *Storming the Gate;* and three novels, *Prospecting for Gold, Beasts at Bay,* and *The Return of the Native.* But even in his most acclaimed novel, *Prospecting for Gold,* his satire never fully realizes its tragic possibilities. The novel has a promising theme in the greed of two rival rascals trying to buy a burial plot, supposedly the site of a gold mine, from a hard-dealing but powerless widow. But no sooner has one of them acquired the land than the Jonsonian satire is abandoned. For the last third of the novel Sha T'ing substitutes for it a much shallower social commentary to the effect that, because inflation is so rampant and hoarding so profitable in wartime Szechwan, the rascal received no financial support at all for his gold mine and is compelled to abandon his project. In spite of his satiric command of the superficies of life, Sha T'ing can only depict a world simplified enough to meet Communist propaganda requirements.

In point of language, Tuan-mu Hung-liang was the most resourceful writer in unoccupied China. A native of the Northeast, he shows in his novels of this period—*The Khorchin Grasslands, The Sea of Earth, The Great River*—not only a passionate attachment to the mountains and ravines, the peasants and hunters of Manchuria, but an intimate sensuous awareness of the scenes and inhabitants of other parts of China as well. In these chaotic works the characters are earthy and primitive, the action is simple and often incomplete, and the ideology an uneasy blend of Marxism with the traditional ethic; but the style has a Wolfe-like exuberance, richly evocative of sensations of every kind. In *The Great River* the geographical account of the Yangtze in the first chapter and the description of wounded soldiers in search of water in a parched area in the sixth are pyrotechnic examples of rhetoric and imagery the like of which has never been attempted by any other modern Chinese writer. But until he has mastered the other essentials of fiction, Tuan-mu Hung-liang can only be regarded as an exceptionally gifted nature lyricist.

Lu Ling was a protégé of Hu Feng's. As editor of *July* Hu Feng, himself a poet, sponsored many new poets, notably I Men (better known later as A Lung), Lu Yüan, and Chia Chi-fang. But of the new writers of fiction whom Hu Feng had encouraged, only Lu Ling was after his own heart for his celebration of primitive and defiant energy battling against darkness. Like the heroine of the novelette *The Hungry Kuo Su-o,* and Chiang Shun-tsu the hero of the novel *The Children of the Rich,* Lu Ling's protagonists are either downtrodden peasants and tramps or proud intellectuals who fight alone and die tragically without enlisting the collective strength of their fellow sufferers. Despite the reservations of orthodox Communist critics who deplore this despondent heroism, Lu Ling was generally praised during the war and after, and not merely by the Hu Feng group.[25]

Notwithstanding the veteran and comparatively new writers just instanced, the fiction in the Nationalist interior generally lacks excitement and distinction. Mao Tun's *Maple Leaves as Red as February Flowers,* Shen Ts'ung-wen's *The Long River,* and a few other titles compose a literature quantitatively much smaller than the best fiction of the prewar decade. The stereotypes of guerrilla warfare and student romance and the ubiquitous note of patriotic propaganda mar most of the wartime novels. Discounting this poverty in fiction, however, most critics would cite the immense popularity of Western-style drama as evidence of the continuing vitality of modern literature in the war period.[26] To them the latter was veritably the golden period for the theater.

In the middle thirties the Western-style drama had finally achieved commercial standing with the middle classes in the coastal cities, after the repeated failures of pioneer playwrights to create a modern theater that would vie in interest with traditional opera and the movies. This is largely the success story of one man, Ts'ao Yü, whose three sensational prewar plays, *The Thunderstorm, Sunrise,* and *The Wilderness,* caught public enthusiasm wherever they were played. On the strength of this success a few theatrical companies were established and many other authors turned playwrights. Without this burgeoning interest the wartime public, in the interior as well as in occupied Shanghai, could not have responded so readily and favorably to the modern theater.

A graduate of the Western languages department of Tsing Hua University, Ts'ao Yü was a conscientious playwright very much at the mercy of the prevalent attitudes of his time. Even though borrowing liberally from Ibsen and O'Neill and echoing familiar situations in Greek tragedy, his three early plays are essentially of the order of the well-made melodrama. They capitalize on the stock bourgeois responses to certain decadent and corrupt aspects of Chinese society and vaunt a superficial leftist point of view, of which only the most rigorous Marxist critic could disapprove. A serious artist in his own conceit, Ts'ao Yü complained in his postscript to *Sunrise* that, much as he was attracted to Chekhov, in the absence of a more mature audience he could not experiment in the Chekhovian manner. His plays supply contrary evidence, however: that the bad taste is inherent in his manifest inability to represent life in mature and unpretentious terms. Ts'ao Yü solemnly invokes fate, heredity, jungle law, and the class struggle to illuminate and ennoble the melodramatic action of his plays, but this syncretism only underscores his lack of a personal tragic vision.

During the war Ts'ao Yü wrote a rousing patriotic play, *Metamorphosis;* a tragedy of feudal decadence, *Peking Man;* and adaptations of *Romeo and Juliet* and Pa Chin's *Family.* All these were commercial and critical successes; but only in *Peking Man,* his finest play, despite his use of the ape man as the crude symbol of the inevitable forward march of evolution, does Ts'ao Yü achieve a quality of compassion in his portrayal of abject weaklings caught in the toils of a moribund genteel tradition.

Insofar as Ts'ao Yü is much more competent than any other playwright of this period, the common assumption that the war years saw the flowering of modern drama should be radically revised. As a matter of fact, very little mature drama was produced. The plays that were the biggest hits—Ts'ao Yü's *Metamorphosis*, Lao Shê and Sung Chih-ti's *The State above All*, Hsia Yen's *The Fascist Bacillus*, Wu Tsu-kuang's *Song of Righteousness*, Kuo Mo-jo's *Ch'ü Yüan*, and many others—on rereading today all prove to be shallow patriotic propaganda or the more insidious and deceptively patriotic Communist propaganda.

Many factors contributed to the theater boom in the war years: the craving for patriotic titillation, the need for escapist entertainment at a time of drab austerity, and the financial incentive for the writers. But the most important cause surely was the shrewd and determined exploitation of the medium by Communists, under favorable as well as adverse circumstances. Immediately following the outbreak of the war, small leftist theatrical troupes were set up to perform in various parts of the country. In 1938, in line with the coalition policy, Kuo Mo-jo was again entrusted with an important government function. As head of the Third Department in the Political Training Board of the National Military Council, he was virtually the director of national propaganda, and under his guidance Communist theatrical activities increased in influence and volume. By 1940 the relations between Nationalists and Communists had worsened and the Third Department was consequently reorganized. Kuo Mo-jo now became chairman of the Cultural Work Committee, nominally still in charge of propaganda but enjoying much less power. In January 1941 Nationalists and Communists renewed hostilities over the so-called New Fourth Army Incident. After this event the Chungking Government enforced a more vigilant censorship of Communist propaganda and the period of unhampered Communist activities in the theater was brought to a close.

To circumvent censorship, Kuo Mo-jo dashed off in the space of three months (December 1941 to February 1942) three historical plays, *The Devoted Siblings,** *Ch'ü Yüan,* and *Hu Fu,* in which characters and events of the ancient Warring States period are freely distorted to make room for antigovernment and pro-Communist propaganda.[27] (In his prefaces to these plays Kuo Mo-jo boasts of his speed of composition— he completed *Hu Fu* in nine days without curtailing his busy official and social schedule—and compares himself to Shakespeare, but the plays suggest more of a degenerate Schiller working out his patriotic bombast in prose.) Among Communist playwrights historical drama soon became the trend: it enabled them to sidestep censorship regulations and still make oblique comments on contemporary events. The theatergoing public also liked the formula: it provided costume and pageantry and recalled heroic deeds of long ago. When patriotic sentiment finally waned toward the end of the war and the public seemed to prefer light comedy, the Communist playwrights again changed their line and turned out a number of comedies satirizing the corruption of high officials and war profiteers. One somber exception is Mao Tun's *Before and after the Spring Festival* (1945), which harshly chastises the industrialists, speculators, and politicians thriving under the Chungking Government.

The propaganda note, which vitiates the fiction and drama of the period, was also dominant in poetry. The promising poets of the middle thirties went into an abrupt decline. Early during the war the lyrical poet Ho Ch'i-fang went to Yenan for a visit and stayed there as a professor in the Lu Hsün Institute of Arts and a rising member of the cultural hierarchy. His friend Pien Chih-lin, who had written some of the most obscure and daring poetry of the middle thirties, also followed

---

* *The Devoted Siblings* is in the main a revision of two earlier works of the author's: a verse play of the same title and a prose drama called *Nieh Jung,* which was included in *Three Rebellious Women.* The heroic legend of Nieh Jung and her brother Nieh Cheng had claimed Kuo Mo-jo's dramatic attention as early as 1920, when he was a student in Japan.

the leftist fashion for a while. Under the circumstances Communist poets were thrust upon public attention. Ai Ch'ing, T'ien Chien, and Tsang K'o-chia were especially acclaimed. Of these, only Ai Ch'ing, a French-returned student, attained an unpretentious simplicity of statement, and then only occasionally, as in his poem "The Second Time He Died" (1939). After both Ai Ch'ing and T'ien Chien left for Yenan to rally to Mao's call for a worker, peasant, soldier literature, Yüan Shui-p'o eclipsed Tsang K'o-chia as the leading Communist poet in the Nationalist interior with his three volumes of satiric *Mountain Ballads,* which affect a folk style. Lao Shê and the Hu Feng group, as earlier noted, also contributed patriotic poetry.

The Western influence was not completely dormant, however. In the Western languages department of the Southwest Associated University, the veteran poet Feng Chih turned out a volume of *Sonnets* to vindicate further his reputation as a follower of Rilke, and a few young poets wrote under the influence of Eliot and especially of Auden, who toured China briefly during the war with Isherwood. Two alumni of the same University, Mu Tan and Tu Yün-hsieh, later served in the Burma theater of war and embodied their war experiences in a lyrical poetry of remarkable dense imagery and sophisticated wit.[28] This Auden school constitutes one promising line of development which is uncontaminated with the propagandist spirit of the period.

The foregoing brief account of the fiction, drama, and poetry of the Nationalist interior is not the whole story of wartime literature, however. Until the Japanese attack on Pearl Harbor, Hong Kong and to a lesser extent Shanghai were still centers of literary activity, where many Communist and leftist writers had remained to carry on their propaganda work. Even after Pearl Harbor many plays, imported from the interior, met enthusiastic reception in Shanghai. And as a reflection of growing Communist power and confidence,

Yenan in time also became a cultural center, with a corps of writers faithfully doing the bidding of Mao Tse-tung and turning out a new literature which in style and intent was markedly different from Communist literature produced in the Nationalist interior.

It would seem paradoxical to assert that the most important new talents of the war period were fostered in Shanghai rather than in Chungking or Yenan. Few writers in the Nationalist interior could break away from the formulas of patriotic propaganda; in the Communist areas, the literary dictatorship of Mao Tse-tung left writers no choice but to be purveyors of the official Communist myth. In Shanghai, on the contrary, the noncollaborationist writer was under much less pressure to conform and was able to explore himself and the world around him with comparatively greater freedom.

It could be just an accident, of course, that a few serious writers were staying in Shanghai at that time. The city during the early years of the war certainly had its share of leftist playwrights; under the puppet Nanking regime it also developed a corps of writers whose job was to praise Japan and her policy of military and economic conquest in Eastern Asia. But so thoroughly discredited was Japanese imperialism that even its apologists were just mercenary hacks incapable of much enthusiasm, and most writers in Shanghai eschewed politics to write innocuous essays and stories and escapist plays. The leading writer in occupied China was Chou Tso-jen who lent prestige to the Japanese cause but who, characteristically, continued to write his own kind of essays, mostly erudite marginal notes on Chinese culture and books. He was sentenced to ten years' imprisonment after the victory.

The most talented writer to appear in Shanghai was Chang Ai-ling or Eileen Chang, known to American readers for her novel *The Rice-sprout Song*. She may well prove to be the greatest Chinese writer since the May Fourth Movement. Utterly uncontaminated by the leftist influence, her stories of this period are concerned with modes of existence in Shanghai and Hong Kong, ranging from traditional opulence of the official families to the cosmopolitanism of the smart set. For technical brilliance and psychological penetration, these stories are well-nigh unequaled in modern Chinese literature.

A prodigious scholar, Ch'ien Chung-shu returned to Shanghai from the interior during the latter half of the war to devote himself to the composition of a novel entitled *The Besieged City*. When published after the victory, it immediately became a new landmark in Chinese fiction. There has been no other Chinese novel so delightful for its satiric verve and comic spirit. The works of Eileen Chang and Ch'ien Chung-shu, though they represent the finest creative achievement of this period, receive of course no mention in standard Communist literary manuals.

A lesser talent, Shih T'o, who had written stories and essays before the war, also matured in Shanghai during the Occupation. He wrote in his postwar novel *Marriage* a brilliant and devastating study of corruption in Shanghai. In this connection we might mention the poet Wu Hsing-hua who resided in Peking during the war and after. A graduate of Yenching University, he studied intensively nearly all the important poets in Chinese and the major Western languages. In his own practice he attempted to create a metrics and idiom that would retain the characteristic strengths of traditional Chinese verse while assimilating important lessons from Western poetry. He often achieved startlingly good results and would have become a major poet if he could have continued to experiment after 1949.[29]

It was surely a hopeful sign for the future of Chinese literature that, at the end of the war, despite the predominant Communist influence among writers and critics, there were writers of fiction as disinterested and good as Pa Chin, Shen Ts'ung-wen, Eileen Chang, and Ch'ien Chung-shu and poets as dedicated and resourceful as Wu Hsing-hua, Mu Tan, and Tu Yün-hsieh. In their literary erudition and passionate study of Western and traditional Chinese literature, Wu Hsing-hua, Ch'ien Chung-shu, and Eileen Chang especially represent a new generation, far maturer than that which shaped the Literary Revolution. Intent on creating a new literature, they have profited from the faults and excesses of their predecessors and reacquired the sense of tradition. They would unhesitatingly subscribe to T. S. Eliot's dictum on tradition: "It cannot be inherited, and if you want it you must obtain it by great labor." In addition to their painstaking study of Western and Chinese traditions, these writers also evince a keen interest in language and an unshaken loyalty to their own sensibility and imagination. Altogether a new breed, they are independent of literary fashions and unashamedly serious in their pursuit of art.

The brief postwar period, which saw the rise of a new serious literature, came to an abrupt end with the Communist conquest of the mainland. In July 1949, a Conference for the Representatives of Chinese Literary and Art Workers was convened in Peking with Kuo Mo-jo as chairman and Mao Tun and Chou Yang as deputy chairmen. Some 650 writers, artists, actors, and musicians listened to addresses by Mao Tse-tung, Chu Teh, and Chou En-lai and resolved to perform their tasks in strict adherence to the cultural policy of Mao Tse-tung. A new era of Communist literature was formally ushered in on a national scale.

The new era turns for guidance almost solely to Mao's *Talks*. Immediately following the Yenan literary conference, Communist-area writers confessed with great alacrity their petty-bourgeois errors and, somewhat more slowly, turned to the task of manufacturing a Mao Tse-tung literature. Ho Ch'i-fang, head of the literature department of the Lu Hsün Institute of Arts, was a decidedly Western-slanted, petty-bourgeois poet and writer; his confession to the erroneous policy he and his colleagues had adopted at the school is therefore particularly revealing:

Our error at that time was to separate mechanically elevation and popularization and to regard elevation as our primary and even our only task. In the department of literature we uncritically emphasized the study of Western classical authors, disproportionately emphasized technique, inappropriately emphasized "writing what you know about intimately and saying what's in your heart." Since all of us had only recently begun to participate in the new life, undue emphasis on familiar subjects created a predilection for writing about past experiences and old-type characters and a disinclination to realize constructively and to treat boldly the new life and the new characters. Since all of us were petty-bourgeois intellectuals and had not undergone a proletarian transformation, undue emphasis on saying what's in your heart tended only to confirm the unsound thoughts and feelings and to neglect or even to fail to understand the importance of self-remolding. . . .

As to the task of assimilating the literary heritage, we uncritically stressed the study of foreign classics of capitalist realism, ignored the Chinese literature of the past, especially the folk literature, not knowing that, while some of this literature is feudalist, some of it belongs to the people, and also not knowing that, while feudalist literature is admittedly antiquated, capitalist-realist literature is not quite new either. In the study of literary works, furthermore, primary importance was attached to the artistic rather than to the political criteria, and at the same time an abstract and unchanging standard of artistic excellence had been erected which was based on the famous works of the capitalist-realist tradition. All the errors in the same category resulted from one fundamental confusion: our inability to give proper intellectual solution to the problem of art *vis-à-vis* the masses, and our failure to relate this problem to all the other art problems from the viewpoint of the masses.[30]

This confession tells us directly about the damage Mao Tse-tung has done to the study of literature and indirectly about the kind of literature to be written under his surveillance. Except for his spurious interest in traditional Chinese literature (lately many classical Chinese authors, from Ch'ü Yüan to Ts'ao Hsüeh-ch'in, author of *Dream of the Red Chamber,* have been resuscitated by the Chinese Communists for their supposed contributions to the revolutionary tradition), Mao Tse-tung has nothing of positive interest to offer to the writer. Ho Ch'i-fang correctly guesses that the new writer has to consider his memory and desire as dangerous aids to creation, has to ignore the nonrevolutionary classics, has to repudiate the absolute standard of artistic excellence as incompatible with political expediency. In other words, the new writer can be only a party propagandist.

Ho Ch'i-fang's confession is of further interest to the literary historian because it reveals the prevalence of the literary sentiments of which Hu Feng was now the chief spokesman. In his scorn for traditional Chinese literature, in his high regard for the Western tradition of realism, in his emphasis on subjective experience and "the heart's desire," Ho Ch'i-fang was in complete agreement with Hu Feng. But in 1944, as Yenan's cultural delegates, Ho Ch'i-fang and Liu Pai-yü (a noted reporter and story-writer) were to visit Hu Feng to compel the latter to follow the Maoist line in literature.[31] There is little doubt that during the war Hu Feng and his group were regarded by the orthodox Communists as heretical allies rather than enemies beyond redemption. It was only when victory was in sight that the orthodox Communists finally despaired of their conversion and attacked them in the open. But Hu Feng appeared so formidable and his surrender so valuable that they chose his friends as their chief targets rather than Hu Feng himself, so that the latter, when he did fall in line, would not have lost much face in the process.

In January 1945 Shu Wu published in Hu Feng's new magazine *Hope* a long article "On the Subjective," which immediately drew fire from the Communist critics residing in Chungking. The debate was kept open in the following years, until in 1948 a new wave of attack was launched by a group of writers in Hong Kong connected with the Communist journal *Miscellany of Mass Literature* (Shao Ch'üan-lin, Lin Mo-han, Ch'iao Kuan-hua, Hu Sheng). (With the Western powers' surrender of territorial rights in Shanghai, Hong Kong supplanted Shanghai as the postwar center of uninhibited Communist propaganda; such leading writers as Kuo Mo-jo and Mao Tun all resided there.) The Hu Feng group, however, fought back unperturbed. Earlier in his preface to *Stemming the Adverse Current* (1947), Hu Feng had declared that his task was to rout "the menacing advance of that great adverse current that had been gathering in strength since the publication of the *Talks at the Yenan Literary Conference.*" [32] To answer his critics, he now wrote a short book *On the Path of Realism* (1948) to reaffirm his literary principles. In a letter he reassured Shu Wu: "Our task is to topple the ruling hierarchy of the mechanical theorists of the last twenty years; it is imperative that we exert all our strength." [33]

The picture completely changed with the Communist seizure of the mainland. For one thing, writers and publication facilities, including newspapers and magazines, were rigidly organized to further the interests of the party, and no intransigent writer could dare to publish. For a while, therefore, Hu Feng had to simulate joy over the Communist success; he wrote a long poem called "Time Has Now Begun!" to celebrate the event; in 1950 he tried with great difficulty to launch *The Starting Point,* a magazine that soon folded. But Hu Feng was determined to assault the cultural hierarchy; in 1951, apropos of his poem (which the critics were to find completely heretical and defiant in spirit), he confided his ambition to a friend, employing somewhat mixed metaphors: "To have this poem published while the vampires are ruling the literary stage makes me feel rather miserable. . . . I am sharpening my sword and exploring the directions; when the time is ripe, I am willing to cut off my head and hurl it against that stinking wall of iron so as to shatter it." [34]

For the next few years Hu Feng couldn't do much except sharpen his sword. In 1950 A Lung's articles, "On Positive and Negative Characters" and "On Tendentiousness," had been subject to attack. This event immediately recalled the earlier debate on subjectivism. By the middle of 1951, moreover, Mao Tse-tung was launching another rectification movement among literary and art workers. This movement was prompted by the notorious case of the film *The Life of Wu Hsün* and many other minor instances of unorthodoxy. It demanded that all writers exercise self-criticism and repent in public. Under the circumstances Shu Wu broke down; in 1952 he submitted to the *People's Daily* a long recantation entitled "I Must Study Anew the *Talks at the Yenan Literary Conference.*" In publishing this, the editor supplied a head-note officially designating the Hu Feng clique as dangerous upholders of bourgeois and petty-bourgeois individualism. Soon afterward Shu Wu published in the *Literary Gazette* an open letter to Lu Ling, urging him to repent. Public discussions of the ideology of the Hu Feng clique followed.

Hu Feng hated Shu Wu's treachery; from then on he never again mentioned his name in his letters but called him Shameless (Wu Ch'ih). It was a remarkable tribute to Hu Feng's sincerity and leadership, however, that none of his other corresponding friends—numbering about twenty—turned against him, as they could easily have done during the difficult period following Shu Wu's defection. In early 1953 two prominent Communist critics, Ho Ch'i-fang and Lin Mo-han, wrote further articles attacking Hu Feng.

Though biding his time, Hu Feng had not been entirely idle. He urged his friends to stay in good spirits, to apply for party membership, to infiltrate Communist organizations if they could. Two of his friends, Lü Yüan and Lu Tien, did become party members, and a few others were successfully placed in the Shanghai New Literature Press, an organization headed by Liu Hsüeh-wei, a veteran Communist critic and Hu Feng's friend. In 1952, simulating a readiness to discuss his ideological errors, Hu Feng, who had been mainly stationed in Shanghai since the Communist victory, asked authorities to assign him work in Peking. His petition was granted, and by late 1953 his position was somewhat improved: he was made a representative for Shanghai in the National Assembly and appointed to the editorial board of *People's Literature*. But he remained powerless to initiate any effective countermove.

In March 1954 Lu Ling published in *People's Literature* a story about the Korean War called "The Battle on the Marsh." [35] It was immediately criticized in the *Literary Gazette* for its subjective heroism. The magazine itself was then in trouble, and its editors saw fit to punish a vulnerable person to redeem their earlier delinquency. The Hu Feng group was again subjected to harsh criticism.

After this last humbling experience Hu Feng was finally ready to make a counterattack. In July he sent to the Central Committee of the party a 300,000-word memorandum—which he had been long in writing during his years of enforced silence—embodying his views on literature and the necessary reforms to be undertaken. With reckless abandon he deplored the major emphases of the Maoist literary program as "five daggers" plunged into the skulls of writers: the arbitrary imposition upon all authors of the Marxist world view as interpreted by the literary hierarchy; the worker, peasant, soldier direction of literature; the remolding campaigns; the utilization of national forms; the subservience of literature to politics. Though he deferred to Mao Tse-tung and attacked only the literary establishment, he tore Mao's *Talks* to pieces and went on to lament the present state of Chinese literature. Since the Communist seizure of the mainland, Hu Feng wrote, our literature "has not only shed no luster, it has to bow its head in shame before the masses of the Chinese people and the peoples of the world . . . Writers or the so-called literary cadres have been wasting their lives [in manufacturing propaganda] and at the same time have been encountering everywhere reprimand and sarcastic criticism . . . so that many promising authors have begun to wither and the party-directed people's literature, which should have been fulfilling its functions with less shame, is grossly neglected." After being subject to criticism, writers "are not permitted to or dare not defend themselves; as a result, a great many literary cadres think of changing their profession, others have put down their pen and stopped writing, and still others dare not seek publication for what they have already written . . . Among the masses there have been dissatisfaction and bewilderment, and among writers there has been general distress . . . The vital force of the new literature accumulated during its thirty years of participation in the revolutionary struggle has now spent itself in fighting off suffocation." [36] Following this long jeremiad, Hu Feng proposed the establishment of seven or eight semi-autonomous writers' organizations with full authority to supervise their own publications. This free competition in the absence of rigid party controls, Hu contended, would immeasurably promote the health of literature.

Judging from this memorandum, one could only say that Hu Feng's zeal for literature was equaled by his blindness: his letters at the time suggest that he seriously believed a frontal assault of this type would lead to a radical reform of literature. His utter disgust with the present literary establishment had apparently got the better of his prudence, and his appeal to the Central Committee can be viewed only as a reckless gesture of hurling his head against "that stinking wall of iron." Later in the year, at the joint conference of the All-China Federation of Literary and Art Workers and the Writers' Association to punish the editors of the *Literary Gazette,* Hu Feng threw all caution aside and further denounced the literary hierarchy in the open. He was instantly made the new target of attack at the conference.

To properly understand this renewed persecution of Hu

Feng calls for an examination of the *Literary Gazette* affair itself. During the 1951–52 cheng-feng movement this leading critical journal, along with many other magazines, was found to be in grave error, and its editorial board was consequently reshuffled. Ting Ling, who had been editor-in-chief, yielded the position to Feng Hsüeh-feng. Ch'en Ch'i-hsia, who had worked closely with Ting Ling in Yenan, was permitted to retain the post of associate editor. But this slight change in personnel did not affect the policy of the magazine; it was still in the hands of those resentful of Chou Yang's increasing encroachments upon their domain. Ting Ling and Feng Hsüeh-feng especially were good friends, and they were both veteran Communists who had done meritorious service for the party long before Chou Yang's rise to prominence.

As Deputy Director of Propaganda in the Central Committee of the party (under Lu Ting-i) and as one-time Vice Minister of Culture in the Peking Government and Vice President of the Writers' Association (in both capacities under Mao Tun), Chou Yang apparently enjoyed, and still enjoys, the absolute trust of the party leadership. He was a ruthlessly ambitious man, constantly exhorting writers to follow the Mao Tse-tung line in literature and periodically initiating attacks on unorthodox writings and writers. To make his position impregnable he worked closely with such party faithfuls as Ho Ch'i-fang, Yüan Shui-p'o, Shao Ch'üan-lin, and Lin Mo-han and patronized such writers as Chao Shu-li, K'ang Cho, Hou Chin-ching, and Ch'in Chao-yang, the Yenan talent he had fostered as new artists fully committed to the worker, peasant, soldier literature. His men were placed in nearly all the regional organizations of the Writers' Association. To Chou Yang, therefore, the *Literary Gazette* was an uncomfortable reminder that his power was not yet absolute.

In alliance with Hu Ch'iao-mu, editor of the *People's Daily* and likewise Deputy Director of Propaganda, Chou Yang soon found his chance to humble the *Literary Gazette*. In 1952 Yü P'ing-po, a noted essayist, scholar, and authority on the classical novel *Dream of the Red Chamber,* was commissioned by a research organization to produce a book on the novel, to prove its revolutionary thesis of class struggle. Yü did nothing of the sort, however; he merely refurbished his earlier book on the novel and published it under the new title *Studies in Dream of the Red Chamber.* Possibly because of its avoidance of Marxist jargon (actually, of course, Yü has little understanding of the art of the novel and his appreciation of *Dream* is personal and naive in alarming ways),[37] the book was well received. Feng Hsüeh-feng, then editor-in-chief of the *Literary Gazette,* praised it in his pages. Riding on the crest of success, Yü wrote a few more magazine articles on the novel.

Finally the unorthodoxy of Yü's approach caught the attention of the party leadership, and Chou Yang and Hu Ch'iao-mu began to instigate young writers to write articles to discredit the scholar. The attack became national in scope when the *People's Daily* published in October 1954 a formal denunciation of Yü's interpretation of the novel. Yü P'ing-po was duly summoned to defend himself during eight sessions of the joint congress of the Federation of Literary and Art Workers and the Writers' Association, lasting from October 31 to December 8. At these sessions Yü got off somewhat lightly with an acknowledgment of error and a promise to reform. He was not severely punished, mainly because Chou Yang and his clique were using him as an excuse to lead up to persecutions that would give them greater personal satisfaction. The case of Yü P'ing-po served to show the prevalence of the liberal, capitalist ideology of Hu Shih—subsequently the target of renewed vituperation—among writers, and Feng Hsüeh-feng, in praising Yü, was shamelessly perpetrating this heresy. Abjectly, he had to confess his errors. It was a great triumph for Chou Yang, who, after eighteen long years, had finally the satisfaction of seeing one of his great adversaries at the Battle of Slogans prostrate himself before his feet. Feng Hsüeh-feng was consequently relieved of his editorship of the *Literary Gazette,* though he was retained as a member of the editorial board. K'ang Cho, Hou Chin-ching, and Ch'in Chao-yang, all Chou Yang's men, were now appointed executive editors.

Hu Feng was invited to attend these meetings. As Merle Goldman has brilliantly guessed,[38] this invitation was a trap set by Chou Yang and his cohorts, who had read Hu Feng's memorandum, to bring about his downfall. But Hu Feng was not a complete dupe. While he was hopeful that the censure of the *Literary Gazette* could be a prelude to genuine literary reform, he was also apprehensive that his long report would provoke only the wrath of the literary establishment. Before Chou Yang had gained complete control over writers, Hu Feng apparently thought, it would be best for him to appeal directly to the literary workers present, to enlist their sympathy in his cause, to expose once and for all the sinister dictatorship of Chou Yang and his associates: there was a bare chance for the overthrow of this hated clique. Accordingly, on November 7 and 11, Hu Feng delivered two speeches which, while ostensibly attacking the *Literary Gazette,* constitute a serious indictment of the literary establishment itself. Characteristically, he expresses a profound regret over the delinquencies of "our old comrade" Feng Hsüeh-feng because there are so few "old comrades" left among us, but makes no similar reservations in his biting remarks on Chou Yang and Ho Ch'i-fang and his blunt criticism of Yüan Shui-p'o, editor of the literary page of the *People's Daily.* By dwelling upon the case of A Lung, who had been treated most shabbily by the editors of the *Literary Gazette* and the *People's Daily,* Hu Feng accomplishes the remarkable feat of equating the magazine under attack with the sacrosanct party organ—and by implication the whole party-directed literary hierarchy—for their surrender to capitalist ideology, their blind worship of authority, their adherence to "scholastic" Marxism and consequent persecution of all progressive young writers whose depiction of reality shows a firm grasp of "empiric" Marxism. Toward the end of his second speech,

Hu Feng dramatically discloses the existence of a secret news-letter which the editors of the *Literary Gazette,* apparently with the connivance or approval of the ruling hierarchy,[39] regularly circulated among a network of correspondents, enabling the latter to write letters to the magazine in support of whatever policies and persecutions pleased the editors and thereby maintaining a spurious uniformity of public opinion. One can imagine that Hu Feng held his audiences, most of whom probably had no knowledge of his memorandum, under the spell of his outspoken courage.

Actually, in their published form the speeches cannot be construed as a reckless diatribe (with belated prudence, Hu Feng had deleted or rephrased some of his more intemperate accusations before allowing the *Literary Gazette* to print them). But for the ruling clique they were provocation enough. Yüan Shui-p'o, Chou Yang, and their allies rose as one man to defend the party and attack Hu Feng. Though the meetings had been held primarily to combat Yü P'ing-po and the editors of the *Literary Gazette,* Hu Feng emerged as the principal villain in Chou Yang's concluding address at the conference, subsequently reprinted as "We Must Fight." From then on, Hu Feng was doomed. After his memorandum was published as a supplement to the January 1955 number of the *Literary Gazette,* it became a convenient source to dip into for all literary and art workers who now had to write articles against his heresy. Denunciations began to appear in magazines and newspapers.

In the same month (January), realizing the utter futility of his protest, Hu Feng wrote a recantation in the expected manner of self-abasement and submitted it to the *People's Daily,* the usual channel for such publications. But the editor of the paper not only demanded revision and expansion, as was expected; he held up the publication of the revised confession until more damaging evidence had been gathered to prove its utter hypocrisy. When it was finally printed, in the May 13 issue, the *People's Daily* concurrently published a whole series of excerpts from Hu Feng's letters to Shu Wu written over a long period of time to document the thesis that Hu Feng and his clique were counterrevolutionaries because they were the paid agents of the Kuomintang. The editorial headnote, which bluntly asserted the charge, also demanded Hu Feng and his friends to hand over all their private correspondence, as Shu Wu had done. In a short while the editor got hold of all the correspondence of the clique (including letters to Hu Feng's wife) and published two more articles reinforcing the thesis that they were Kuomintang agents. In all these compilations, actually, there is no evidence even remotely relevant to the charge. In addition to the undocumented biographical information about Hu Feng (given earlier in the chapter) and A Lung (he was once a Nationalist army officer in the service of the anti-Communist general Hu Tsung-nan), the only positive evidence purporting to link the Hu Feng group with the Kuomintang secret police apparatus consists of, so far as I can judge, two items: (1) in 1947 Hu Feng asked A Lung in a letter to intercede with one Ch'en Ch'o for the release of Hu Feng's friend Chia Chi-fang, who had been imprisoned by government authorities (according to a note supplied by the editor, Ch'en Ch'o was a member of the Nationalist secret police); (2) in 1944 Lü Yüan informed Hu Feng in a letter that he was now working at a Sino-American government organization (which, again according to an editorial note, was the training center for the cadres of the secret police).[40] But these same excerpts, however immaterial as documents in support of the counterrevolutionary allegation, give fascinating glimpses of the group's utter disgust with Mao's cultural policy and the Communist cultural hierarchy, their despair over the state of letters, their determination to do what little they could to destroy the monolithic structure and breathe some new life into literature. They are also shown as merry fighters with a gift for derision. Over the years (the letters cover 1944–55), they had developed a terminology of extreme sarcasm to indicate their scorn for the ruling hierarchy: Hu Feng invariably refers to Kuo Mo-jo, Chou Yang, and the like as "lordings," "ambassadors," "officials," "opportunists," or "maggots." Together, these three compilations constitute the most spirited and important literary document ever published in Communist China; one could only wish for the ungarbled publication of the entire correspondence in a more auspicious time.

Until May 1955 the attack on Hu Feng, however fierce, covered only his subjective idealism, his liberal, petty-bourgeois intransigence, his contempt for the Chinese people and Chinese literature, his anti-Mao attitude. He was not accused of conspiring against the party. Now, with the publication of excerpts from his correspondence, another wave of attack was mounted to support the charge that he and his clique were counterrevolutionary agents. In the same month Hu Feng was placed under arrest and deprived of his rights as a citizen.

During 1955, it was estimated, 2,131 articles of varied lengths appeared in periodicals and newspapers in support of the anti-Hu Feng campaign, not counting readers' letters, news articles, and minutes of conferences.[41] Riding on the crest of success, Chou Yang was now determined to eliminate all rival power groups, especially the Ting Ling–Ch'en Ch'i-hsia clique. While the battle against Hu Feng was still raging in the press, the party nucleus (*tang-tsu*) of the Writers' Association held sixteen meetings in August and September to combat Ting and Ch'en for their supposed crimes of rejecting party guidance and disrupting party unity, of fostering cliquism and promoting capitalist-individualist thought. Under duress both confessed their "errors." The censure was upheld; but possibly because of Ting Ling's prominence in the public eye, the case was not publicized.

By 1956, the year that marked China's total conversion to socialism, writers were completely broken in spirit. Not only did the novelists, playwrights, and poets write in accordance with the safest formulas, but the critics also, when confronted with a new piece of work, did not know what to do: they had to await their cues from the Propaganda Department of the Central Committee. But if neither praise nor blame was forthcoming in regard to a particular work, they could only practice a lukewarm kind of criticism, mildly commending it and then qualifying the praise with an enumeration of faults, so that, by the end of the review, nothing had really been said. Everybody was playing safe. It had been planned that the year would be a big one for the theater, during which the Western-style spoken drama would be reactivated. But theater audiences were dismally small. New movies, books, and magazines, in all probability, didn't fare much better.

The public's great indifference to manufactured propaganda and the mechanical conformity of the writers and artists themselves finally became a matter of some concern to the party leaders. In an unpublished address to the Supreme State Conference on May 2, therefore, Mao Tse-tung proclaimed the slogan "Let a Hundred Flowers Bloom, Let a Hundred Schools of Thought Contend" to spur the prosperity of cultural and intellectual enterprises within the confines of strict socialist discipline. Soon afterward, in a speech subsequently reprinted in the *People's Daily* (June 13), Lu Ting-i made the first public airing of this policy. He made it clear, however, that the newly promised freedom to bloom and contend had to be used with discretion, in furtherance of stated Communist objectives.

"Let a Hundred Flowers Bloom" was not a new Communist slogan; for some years the reformers of the Chinese theater had carried on their work under the banner of "Let a Hundred Flowers Bloom; Utilize the Old so as to Create the New." Translated into plain prose, this slogan means that all schools of regional drama shall flourish and by due revision of all acceptable plays in the old repertory a splendid new drama shall be born. But in actual practice, the reformers had proscribed the great majority of the plays available and changed the acceptable plays beyond all recognition, and in the process all but completely alienating the great masses of theatergoers. In early 1956, however, a *k'un-ch'ü* opera, *Fifteen Strings of Cash*, was revived and met enthusiastic reception in the big cities. The reason for this success was quite obvious: first, being far more literary and refined than other regional drama, k'un-ch'ü was seldom heard even under the National Government; secondly, the revived play was perhaps not much changed in text and spirit from the original. The shock of this discovery—that the public preferred the genuine old theater to the reformed propagandist theater—prompted the party leaders to reconsider the total propaganda program and concede greater freedom not only to theatrical workers but to all writers, artists, and intellectuals.

Following Mao Tse-tung and Lu Ting-i, Mao Tun gave an important speech in his capacity as Minister of Culture, openly airing his dissatisfaction with the existing literature and drama and affirming the importance of creative and critical diversity:

> During the first half of this year theater attendance was generally low. Why? Because there was a lack of new productions of good plays. For this qualitative and quantitative poverty, what is the main reason? Audiences and readers have unanimously answered with these words of reproof, "Too dry, every piece alike." This dryness surely stems from the general adherence to stereotyped concepts; this uniform monotony from formulism, from arbitrary confinement to a narrow range of themes and ideas. . . .
>
> In accordance with the policy of "Let a Hundred Schools Contend," we should *tolerate different schools of literature and art* [Italics in the original] and let them engage in free debate and mutual competition so that their survival value may be tested.
>
> What the mass audiences are weary of is not the too frequent embodiment of weighty social events in literary

works, but the monotonous uniformity of subject matter
and technique. . . . Since ancient times, our people
have created a literature which has been never monotonous and uniform, never stiff and unlively, but inclusive
of all aspects of life, full of colors and graces. We have
only the responsibility to develop this tradition to even
greater glory, not the right to destroy it.

"The Contending of a Hundred Schools" in literary
theory and research will further encourage "the Blossoming of a Hundred Flowers" among writers and artists.[42]

One might observe here that, in admitting the sterility of the
current literature, Mao Tun was almost repeating the earlier
criticism of Hu Feng. In denouncing formulism and mechanical uniformity, the many writers who wrote in Mao
Tun's wake also echoed Hu Feng's sentiments.

At first, of course, writers were hesitant to assert their new
freedom. They were compelled to praise the new policy and
venture some criticism of the existing literature, just as,
earlier, they had been compelled to denounce the Hu Feng
clique. Gradually, however, criticism grew more outspoken.
The Lu Hsün type of tsa-wen became established as a regular
feature in nearly all literary magazines and the literary pages
of all leading newspapers, including the *People's Daily*. Nonparty members were invited to serve on the editorial boards
of important magazines: the well-known liberal writer and
journalist Hsiao Ch'ien, for example, became an editor of
the *Literary Gazette*. Most writers, however, were content to
air their grievances in short essays, poems, and sketches against
the tyrannic harshness (*ts'u-pao*) of official criticism, the
stupidity and blundering of the bureaucrats in charge of
literary and theatrical enterprises,* the poverty of writing in

* Since in tracing the ideological struggles in Communist China, I
have been concentrating on the major issues and personalities, it is
pertinent to mention the plight of obscure literary and art workers in
the inland provinces, under the callous mismanagement of the Com-

339

general; they didn't have time to embody their new sentiments in serious fiction or drama. But bold constructive proposals were raised. As early as September 1956 Huang Ch'iuyün, an admirer and translator of Romain Rolland, asked writers not to avert their gaze from the real conditions in Communist China: "Today, in our country, there are still floods and droughts, still famine and unemployment, still infectious diseases and the rampant oppression of bureaucratism, plus yet other unpleasant and unjustifiable phenomena. An artist in possession of an upright conscience and a clear head ought not to complacently shut his eyes and remain silent in the face of real life, of the sufferings of the people." [43] The uprising of the Hungarian people against their Communist rulers later that year further emboldened Chinese writers; by the end of 1956 not a few daring souls

---

munist cadres. The following excerpt, about provincial theatrical troupes, is from an unsigned news article titled "Look after Artists, Respect Artists," which appears on p. 41 of the *Literary Gazette*, No. 17 (September 15, 1956):

The Huang-kang Han Opera Troupe regularly travel on foot one thousand and several hundred *li* a year among villages and hills to give four to five hundred performances. But for several months each year since 1952 they have received no wages, and this year they have received no wages for five consecutive months. They work hard for months and years on end, don't have enough to eat, and can't get warm clothing; the health of the actors is undermined by exhaustion. Eighty per cent of the troupe are sick. Some fainted on the stage when performing; some had no money to treat their diseases and died. One actor, whose wife had died of disease, was compelled by hunger to leave the troupe: he has become a shoeblack in the day and a teahouse singer at night. The Lin-ts'ang Theatrical Troupe of West Yunnan regularly give performances in the evenings and chop wood in the hills in the day. There is no artistic creativeness to speak of, since they toil the whole day in order to survive. Actresses, eight or nine months pregnant or even on the day of parturition, have to perform and sing on the stage; consequently there are frequent miscarriages. One actress has miscarried five times in succession. Old actors are abandoned without care; the Loyang Opera Troupe discharged two old actors in this manner.

were already demanding less interference from the ruling cultural hierarchy for the radical improvement of literature and art.

In spite of audible opposition from some party leaders,[44] Mao Tse-tung renewed his pledge of flower-blossoming freedom in his famous address of February 27, 1957, "On the Correct Handling of Contradictions among the People." Probably, in view of the Hungarian revolt and its strong impact on Chinese intellectuals, Mao had little choice but to grant them an extended period of grace so as to avert a similar national uprising. Possibly Mao truly believed that inimical contradictions between party and people had really disappeared and that free discussions and friendly debate would be from now on the best means for furthering socialism. But it was more likely that, in view of the widespread discontent already in evidence, Mao was simply using his speech to entice all antiparty elements to declare their intransigence, so as to effectively purge them later on.

Mao's speech received immediate enthusiastic support through all official channels of communication so that, during the ensuing three months, and especially May, a great many people fearlessly spoke out against the party. Leading the attack were the politicians and intellectuals of the Democratic League, a minor political party headed by Chang Po-chün and Lo Lung-chi; their organ, the Shanghai *Wen Hui Pao*, became virtually the standard-bearer of what subsequently became known as the rightist movement. College students and professors in Peking were staging a new May Fourth Movement to usher in an era of freedom; other intellectual and professional groups besides writers and artists were swelling the chorus of dissidence. By June, when this movement had truly got out of hand, the Government dramatically reversed its policy of limited license and launched a nation-wide campaign against the "rightist" and "revisionist" defamers of the party. But grown heady with their new freedom, quite a few writers continued to shout their defiance during the month of June.[45]

341

When the rightist dust had somewhat settled, it was seen that the scope of dissidence had gone beyond the calculations of the party leaders. According to one careful student of the event, among writers and artists alone at least 1,000 people were subject to subsequent rectification for the imprudence with which they had written earlier.[46] This figure is not at all fantastic if one takes into consideration all the miscellaneous articles published during the spring of 1957 in all the magazines and newspapers in China, for the rightist movement affected not only the major cities but even such remote areas as Szechwan and Sinkiang. Not to mention the veteran writers who spoke out after a long silence only to be immediately subject to punishment again—Ch'en Meng-chia, Hsü Chieh, Huang Yüan, Mu Mu-t'ien, Shih Chih-ts'un, Sun Ta-yü, Yao Hsüeh-yin, and countless others—the major offenders among those closely connected with Communist literary and cultural enterprises were Hsiao Ch'ien, Huang Ch'iu-yün, Wu Tsu-kuang (for his criticism on drama), Chung Tien-fei (cinema), Chiang Feng (art), Ch'en Yung, Liu Pin-yen, Wang Jo-wang, Huang Yao-mien, Hsü Mou-yung, Ch'in Chao-yang, and Liu Shao-t'ang (not to be confused with Liu Shau-tong, author of *Out of Red China*). With the exception of the first three, the others on the list were nearly all Communist members in charge of important functions, and some of them quite young. Prior to their declared intransigence, Ch'in Chao-yang and Liu Shao-t'ang especially were the darlings of the literary hierarchy, the former an associate editor of *People's Literature* generally praised for his peasant fiction, the latter the youngest author to rise on the literary scene, a party member at seventeen and only twenty-two in 1957, a story-writer nurtured under the Communist system and ideally incapable of disaffection. But prominently in their serious critical articles—Ch'in's "Realism—the Broad Path" (*People's Literature,* September 1956), Liu's "The Development of Realism in the Socialist Age" (*Peking Literature,* April 1957) and "My Views on the Current Literary Problem" (*Literary Study,* No.

5, 1957)—these two authors advocated the replacement of the formulistic and mechanical socialist realism by the Hu Feng type of realism. Liu Shao-t'ang particularly went all the way with Hu Feng to declare the total failure of party-directed literature since the promulgation of Mao's *Talks* in 1942. The recrudescence of Hu Feng's thought among nearly all the rightist and revisionist critics—so soon after the purge of the hated heretic—was particularly disturbing to the party leaders. Liu Shao-t'ang was later subject to vitriolic persecution at combat meetings sponsored by three different party organizations.

But the chief victims of the antirightist persecution were, of course, the Ting-Ch'en clique: Ting Ling and her husband Ch'en Ming, Feng Hsüeh-feng, Ch'en Ch'i-hsia, and all those with whom Ting and Ch'en were associated during the Wang Shih-wei case of 1942: Ai Ch'ing, Li Yu-jan, Lo Feng and his wife Pai Lang—only a few years ago she had been officially praised for her novel *For a Happier Tomorrow*—and Hsiao Chün (who was subject to renewed attack in 1958, though he hardly wrote anything during the flower-blossoming period). Unlike the many rightists and revisionists who had exercised their right to criticism, as it were, by official order, these veteran Communists had shown signs of dissidence since 1942 or earlier and could be legitimately regarded by Chou Yang and his cohorts as antiparty conspirators of long standing. From June 6 to September 17 the party nucleus of the Writers' Association held twenty-seven meetings to combat the clique, with Shao Ch'üan-lin, *tang-tsu* secretary and Chou Yang's principal henchman, presiding. Regularly, over 200 people attended these meetings, but for the last two sessions over 1,350 literary and art workers were invited to hear the speeches of Lu Ting-i, Chou Yang, Kuo Mo-jo, Mao Tun, and other dignitaries.[47] Pronounced completely guilty of the antiparty crimes charged against them, the Ting-Ch'en clique were duly expelled from the party and deprived of their rights as authors and citizens.[48]

Since the speeches made by the defendants at the meetings were never disclosed to the public, one can reconstruct the case only by the testimony of the numerous speeches for the prosecution, which did receive extensive publication. It seems that at the first three sessions Ting Ling was able to sway the audience in her favor, but after the fourth meeting she didn't have a chance and members of her group were eventually brought to heel. Actually, their conspiracy during the flower-blossoming period amounted to very little. The main charges ran as follows:

1. Ting Ling and Ch'en Ch'i-hsia tried to exonerate themselves from the official censure of 1955. In collusion with *Wen Hui Pao* and the rightist elements at the *Literary Gazette,* they attempted a public airing of their case, thereby embarrassing the party authorities.

2. Ting Ling, Ch'en Ch'i-hsia, Feng Hsüeh-feng, and their rightist friends tried to build an "independent kingdom" among the literary ranks. They planned to launch a magazine to rival the *Literary Gazette.* As director of the People's Literature Press, Feng Hsüeh-feng supported rightist activities. (Actually, Feng had been only a figurehead since 1955; the deputy director Pa Jen—pen name of Wang Jen-shu—was in virtual control of the publishing company.)

3. It was revealed that Ting and Ch'en had planned to split the literary ranks wide open at the proposed October conference of All-China Literary and Art Workers. If they didn't succeed in their aim, they were to publicly announce their resignation from the Writers' Association.

On the strength of these charges—though there was no documentary evidence of any kind to support the second and third—the prosecuting officers of the Writers' Association inferred a monstrous antiparty group in operation through the years. Had not Feng Hsüeh-feng been a good friend of Hu Feng's since the thirties? Had not Ting Ling occasionally reprinted Hu Feng's articles in the literary page of the Yenan *Liberation Daily?* Had not Ting Ling, Ch'en Ch'i-hsia, and

Feng Hsüeh-feng been in active collusion since the early fifties? Therefore, the intransigence of Ting Ling, Wang Shih-wei, and their kind in 1942, the defiance of Hsiao Chün in 1947–48, the conspiracy of the Hu Feng clique in 1954, and the rightist plot of the Ting-Ch'en clique in 1957 were not isolated instances of rebellion but four tidal waves, each stronger than the last, of one major "adverse current" beating in vain against the towering edifice of monolithic Communism. Moreover, were not Ting Ling and Feng Hsüeh-feng also Kuomintang agents like Hu Feng? Caught as a Communist, didn't Ting Ling confess her sins to the Nanking secret police in 1933 and proceed to live on parole for almost three years as the wife of a member of the secret police? Why did she wait until 1943 to tell her story of infamy to the Communist authorities, and then give only a garbled version of it? Likewise, didn't Feng Hsüeh-feng obtain his release from the Shangjao concentration camp in 1943 only after he had signed a recantation? Duly brainwashed by the Nationalist secret police and sent back to the Communist fold, both had failed to make a clean breast of their ignominy but had behaved like counterrevolutionary black sheep, which indeed they were. (The inference was that, if Chou Yang had been caught by the Nationalist police, he would rather have died under torture than make a routine confession in order to regain his freedom and make good use of it in the cause of Communism.) [49]

The trial of the Ting-Ch'en clique was characterized by extreme vilification rather than serious ideological debate. Their nebulous plot, if their rightist promptings could be called a plot, was doubtless motivated by their animosity toward the ruling hierarchy and their ambition to regain prestige and power. But not exclusively: insofar as they wanted to bring about a genuine literary reform (though Ch'en Ch'i-hsia seemed more of an ambitious careerist than anything else), they, too, were repudiating the literature of the recent past and demanding the removal of party control over literary

345

enterprises. Feng Hsüeh-feng and Hu Feng especially were much alike as literary critics. Not only did they fight together against Chou Yang and Kuo Mo-jo during the Battle of Slogans, but Feng Hsüeh-feng later supported Hu Feng over the issues of "national forms" and "the subjective." In his 1946 book *The Literary Movement of the Democratic Revolution* Feng Hsüeh-feng interpreted modern Chinese literature in much the same fashion as Hu Feng, and he, too, demurred at the platform of Mao's *Talks,* though as a ranking Communist critic he could not speak out aloud. As a matter of indisputable fact, these two critics, along with Lu Hsün and Mao Tun, represented the moderate wing of Communist intellectuals still seriously concerned with literary and humane values. To uphold the orthodoxy of Mao Tse-tung and Chou Yang was therefore also to repudiate Lu Hsün and Mao Tun. And Mao Tun did criticize bureaucratism and formulism quite freely until he furled his rightist sails in time to resume his conformist stagnancy.[50]

In his final summary of the antirightist persecution entitled "The Great Debate on the Literary Front"—based on his speech given at the penultimate session of the Ting-Ch'en trial and published in the March 11, 1958, issue of the *Literary Gazette* and other journals at about the same time— Chou Yang devoted the bulk of space to vilifying the clique. But of course even he could not seriously entertain the theory of rightist treason. In the same long article, therefore, he traced the evolution of the Chinese intellectual since the May Fourth Movement to show why so many veteran Communists fell by the wayside just when they were marching nearer and nearer the Communist goal of total national reconstruction. He recalled that once upon a time all revolutionary writers in China were much alike, sharing the same dreams and aspirations:

> Let's review the path most of us have traversed. Many
> of us came from families of feudal landlords and other

exploiting classes, then already waning in influence and fortune. By nurture and world outlook we were basically capitalist intellectuals. The May Fourth New Culture Movement brought us science and democracy, exposed us to the intellectual currents of socialism. At that time we were eager to absorb all new knowledge from abroad, hardly differentiating anarchism from socialism, individualism from collectivism. Nietzsche, Kropotkin, and Marx at that time equally fascinated us. Later on we began to recognize Marxism-Leninism as the only truth and the only weapon to be used for the liberation of mankind. We threw ourselves into the task of liberating the proletariat, but basically the capitalist-individualist thoughts, sentiments, and habits we had acquired didn't change. We had an abstract Communist faith, but our actions frequently followed the impulses of individualistic heroism. We weren't united with the workers and peasants, didn't even closely approach them. The democratic revolution was our urgent personal demand, but the socialist revolution remained only an ideal. At that time, it could be said that many of us belonged to the petty-bourgeois democratic revolutionary camp rather than to the proletarian revolutionary camp. We couldn't liberate ourselves from the hold of individualism. It may be recalled that in those days individualism was closely identified with such concepts as "the liberation of personality" and "the independence of character" and spurred us to oppose feudalist oppression, to fight for freedom. The masterpieces of nineteenth-century European literature habitually described the conflicts between individual and society, the anarchistic rebellion of isolated, defiant individuals against the detested society; this had left a strong impression upon our brain. We once fervently welcomed Ibsen, took to heart his famous saying "The strongest man upon earth is he who stands most alone." Many of us embarked on the revolutionary path via the individualistic detour, and joined the revolution with the individualistic knapsack upon our back.[51]

Chou Yang goes on to say that many eventually threw away this knapsack, but many could not. Like Mr. Christian who has to remove his burden of sins before he can make his journey to the Celestial City, the Communist has to discard the knapsack of individualism before marching onward to the Communist earthly paradise. One may push the analogy even further by saying that many writers and intellectuals apparently thought they had thrown away the knapsack, and it was only after they had lived under Communism for some time that they discovered that the invisible bag still weighed heavily upon them. One feels almost a wistful note in Chou Yang's recall of the heady days of the Literary Revolution: possibly if he had not early enjoyed great power and the responsibility of enforcing the Maoist line, he might also have ended as a Communist miscreant like Hu Feng, Feng Hsüeh-feng, and his onetime comrade in arms, Hsü Mou-yung. One can never tell.

Chou Yang's analysis of the modern Chinese intellectual evolution further supports Mao Tse-tung's thesis that "intellectuals of petty-bourgeois origins have always tried stubbornly to express themselves and spread their own opinions; they have always demanded that the party and the world be remolded in their image." Early deluded by Communist promises, the Chinese writers and intellectuals, by and large, did not awaken from their dogmatic slumber as a great many American and European leftist intellectuals apparently did under the shock of the Hitler-Stalin pact. They went along with the Communists and found out too late that they, too, hankered after freedom. Whatever the labels—liberal, capitalist, rightist, antiparty, counterrevolutionary—thrown at the dissident writers of the fifties, Chou Yang has surely chosen the right word to define their crime—individualism.

The rightist movement is sufficient demonstration of the scope and magnitude of the tragedy of a great many Chinese writers—their voluntary relinquishment of individual freedom and their belated desperate attempt to recover it.

CHAPTER 14

The Veteran Writers

As HAS BEEN mentioned in the last chapter, a major portion of the serious fiction of the war period and after continued to be written by established writers. Mao Tun, Shen Ts'ung-wen, Lao Shê, and Pa Chin, each in his own fashion responding to the demands and trials of the times, produced work of varying importance. Increasingly preoccupied with propaganda, Mao Tun wrote at least one novel that compares with his best. His artistic integrity still very much intact, Shen Ts'ung-wen combined his love for his native region with a serious concern over China's fate to produce in *The Long River* his maturest piece of fiction. Lao Shê ruined himself with propaganda work and proved eventually, when his monumental novel, *Four Generations under One Roof,* was completed, his inability to recover his old brilliance. Pa Chin, on the contrary, became during the war a much more chastened and less pretentious novelist. His postwar novel, *Cold Nights,* is for compassion and honesty a rare achievement in modern Chinese fiction.

MAO TUN

During the war, Mao Tun was the leading Communist writer by a comfortable margin. He maintained this position mainly because, residing in Hong Kong and the Nationalist interior, he could afford to ignore the directives from Yenan and continued to practice his petty-bourgeois brand of fiction designed to entrap the petty-bourgeois conscience. His wartime novels were all written before the end of 1942: *Story of the First Stage of the War, Putrefaction,* and *Maple Leaves as Red as February Flowers.* After he moved from Kweilin to Chungking in the late fall of that year, he served on the Cultural Work Committee under Kuo Mo-jo for the remainder of the war and did little serious creative work—with the exception of one play, *Before and after the Spring Festival.*[1]

Story of the First Stage is a slight performance modeled on *The Twilight* and peopled with almost an identical set of characters: a national industrialist, a big speculator on the stock market, a pro-American professor bemoaning the fate of China, an anachronistic feudalist, and an assortment of young men and women of bourgeois and petty-bourgeois backgrounds displaying varying degrees of frivolity and patriotism. Told against the background of the heroic Chinese resistance in Shanghai during the summer of 1937, the story was written in accordance with the United Front policy of celebrating the national awakening in the face of Japanese aggression. But the Communist messages are nevertheless explicit: upon the evacuation of Chinese troops from Shanghai one group of patriotic youths decide to trek to the Communist interior in North Shensi, and another group of recently released Communist prisoners map plans for underground work in their various native provinces. A whole chapter is devoted to the unmasking of Trotskyites, who were then supposed to be a menace to the war effort.

Characteristically, however, Mao Tun achieves his best effects in scenes depicting the weakness of bourgeois youth after a brief flirtation with patriotism. The heroine P'an Hsüeh-li, daughter of the big speculator, has until the outbreak of the war lived the life of thoughtless gaiety; during the three months of fighting in Shanghai she volunteers as a nurse of wounded soldiers and enjoys the thrill of patriotic service. Upon the evacuation of the troops she feels anew the crushing weight of an empty life:

> Miss P'an stood at the corner of the street for a while, looking around aimlessly. The weather was humid, the place was quiet, and there was no sound of artillery or airplanes. Had not the familiar sound of artillery and airplanes become in the space of three months almost a part of her life? But now it was gone; Miss P'an felt that something had been taken away from her life. She stood there depressed, ruminating over the sensation of solitude.
>
> Suddenly two or three British military trucks passed by in a row. As if tired from overwork for days on end, the British soldiers just squatted in the trucks, bowing their heads and resting their rifles obliquely against their shoulders.
>
> Miss P'an watched the trucks go by and thought that, maybe in a matter of days, work would start on the removal of sandbags and barbed wires from the streets of the International Settlement and the French Concession. The lonely feeling she had as a child when she saw lamps and festoons being taken down after weddings and celebrations again surged back into Miss P'an's heart.[2]

In passages like this Mao Tun shows his competence as a prober of bourgeois guilt. But the over-all effect of the novel is almost unredeemed dullness.

In *Putrefaction,* a novel highly acclaimed by Communist critics for its exposure of Kuomintang corruption, Mao Tun reverts to his favorite method of mirroring evil through a feminine perspective. The heroine, Chao Hui-ming, is an agent for the Kuomintang secret police in Chungking; still pretty at twenty-four, she has tasted much sorrow and seen a great deal of the world's ugliness. From her earlier idealism, therefore, she has retreated almost to a position of nihilistic acceptance of the status quo, though in the company of her disgusting colleagues her old anger still burns. She frequently blames herself for not being "sufficiently despicable, shameless, and unscrupulous." Writing in her diary at night, she often thinks of her first true lover and of her child abandoned as a baby many years ago, the fruit of an affair with a perfidious man. Her conscience awakens when she is assigned the task of pumping information from a Communist prisoner who turns out to be her first lover. He refuses to give the names and addresses of his comrades and is put to death.

Hui-ming is now assigned to work among college students. She befriends a college girl, also on the payroll of the secret police. Hating to see this inexperienced agent repeat her own mistakes, Hui-ming helps her escape beyond the reach of the secret police, but in doing so she herself is presumably killed. Her diary, which constitutes the novel, abruptly stops at this point.

Putrefaction is a poorly written book. Its style is uneven and its diary form handled ineptly. Neither the heroine's personal reminiscences nor her daily entries of often trivial happenings generate much interest. To saturate the novel with the air of corruption, Mao Tun makes frequent mention of venomous insects, rapacious beasts, and baleful demons and goblins, but the imagery remains superficial, a matter of propagandistic emphasis. A good passage showing the habitual mood of the heroine and the animal imagery follows:

January 11 [1941]

Yesterday I went into "the City"; I sensed a peculiar smell in the air, faint and yet palpable—the stench of something in the process of putrefaction, also with the odor of blood and of newly cut flesh. If I had to find a fitting term, I think that the two words "corpse stink" would do.

353

I won't admit to the charge that my senses are confused. Then I might be accused of being hypersensitive. Of course, if a woman has suffered many vicissitudes in this world and has lived for so long among ox-demons and snake-spirits, she will naturally have keen faculties. She may not be able to tell what plots people are hatching, but she can smell the air and tell vaguely whence the wind is blowing. Eight or nine cases out of ten, she will be right.

Before a big storm the weather is always sultry. All kinds of venomous mosquitoes, gold-headed and disease-carrying flies, spiders poised on their webs in dark corners, lizards crouching in the dingy nooks of a house—they either hum and fly all over the sky or crawl and hiss with laughter. They advance together; the world is theirs.

But what secretly frightens me is my attitude of cold indifference. It seems as though I were no longer a part of this world and had no connection with anything. Recently I have been like this. Perhaps this is not right? Well, who says it is? Only I dare ask: what is there still left for me in this world? [3]

In reading this passage, one wonders if the heroine's premonition of evil has special reference to the events of her time. The date of the entry—January 11, 1941—is the key clue. At about that time the New Fourth Army under the command of the Communist general Yeh T'ing was being trapped and disbanded by Nationalist forces in Anhwei. The smell of putrefaction refers to Kuomintang corruption and treachery in general, and the odor of blood and flesh alludes specifically to the Communist catastrophe. "Before a big storm the weather is always sultry." The storm is the total Communist revolution in China; the mosquitoes, flies, spiders, and lizards that dance and laugh before the coming storm are of course all the elements that support and thrive under the Kuomintang Government. In this respect *Putrefaction* is at once a lament for the tragedy of the New Fourth Army Incident and a prophecy of ultimate Communist success.

Though actual references to the Incident are few because of censorship difficulties, there is little doubt that the novel was conceived as a protest against supposed Kuomintang treachery. In the heroine's association with agents sent over to Chungking from the puppet Nanking regime, one grasps, furthermore, Mao Tun's innuendo that the disbanding of the New Fourth Army was the joint work of the Chungking and Nanking governments.

To modern man the secret police represents the worst form of totalitarian tyranny—witness the astonishing relevance to the contemporary scene of such novels as *Darkness At Noon* and *Nineteen Eighty-Four*. In *Putrefaction* Mao Tun shrewdly exploits the aspect of Kuomintang power that was most vulnerable to criticism: increasing resort to methods of the secret police during the war period to combat Communism. No one should extenuate the enormity and political folly of such practices, but an impartial novelist genuinely concerned with the welfare of China could not ignore the even more efficient and sinister methods employed by the Communist party, including all the paraphernalia of secret police and thought control, to mold public opinion, sabotage the war effort, and eventually obtain control of the mainland. During the war, understandably, *Putrefaction* enjoyed wide popularity among the students and intellectuals who were disaffected toward the National Government. If the novel had been better written, it could have been a triumphant tour de force to confound the aims of Communism with the aspirations of humanity.

To turn from *Putrefaction* to *Maple Leaves as Red as February Flowers* is to enjoy the fresh breeze from a vernal scene after a close session with partisan politics. For *Maple Leaves,* Part I of a projected trilogy, takes place in 1926 in a small city, where "Communism" was still unheard of. No doubt the completed trilogy would have inevitably placed the novel in an altered perspective: the political sympathies of its author give us little ground to doubt that Communist intellectuals and agitators were to play a prominent role in the second and third parts. Even the title, which is an intentional misquotation of a famous line by the T'ang poet Tu Mu,[4] holds such a promise. According to Mao Tun's postscript to the new edition of the novel,[5] the red flowers of the earliest spring (February by the lunar calendar) symbolize the true revolutionaries, and frosted leaves (maple leaves under the frost) the false revolutionaries who have become disillusioned or reactionary following the events of 1927. The unwritten portions of the trilogy will demonstrate that, while under the frost of the counterrevolution the maple leaves will look apparently as red as February flowers, the true flowering youth of Communism will eventually bear fruit.

In the scheme of the trilogy the first volume traces the clashes between liberal idealism and traditional feudalism, between incipient national capitalism and a stagnant landlord economy. In the novel the Communist leader Ch'en Tu-hsiu is referred to by one of the characters as Ch'en Tu-hsieh or Ch'en the Venomous Scorpion, but the full impact of his teachings is not yet felt. While relevant to the Chinese scene in the forties, the issues in *Maple Leaves* are hardly urgent with reference to the Communist struggle for power. Mao Tun can therefore afford to break away from the self-imposed limitations of overt propaganda and develop incidents and characters in the concrete manner of the best portions of *The Eclipse* and *Rainbow.* The resulting novel shows a surprising recrudescence of the old power. If Mao Tun could proceed to complete the trilogy in the same spirit of compassionate detachment, with what hints we have in *Maple Leaves* of the small-town situation, the thwarted idealism and reformist zeal of some of the heroes, and the tensions between a few mismated couples, the whole work might have become a modern Chinese equivalent of *Middlemarch*. But, of course, with the changed literary climate in Communist China, Mao Tun would be foolish to continue with the second and third volumes, and *Maple Leaves* will always remain a splendid fragment.

In a small community whose members are all more or less related by blood, two men wield the greatest economic power: Chao Shou-i, the biggest landowner of the place, and Wang Po-shen, the new capitalist who owns a steamboat line. These two and their families often clash because they represent two opposing ways of life: agrarian and mercantile. The greater part of the novel, however, traces the fortunes of several younger members of the scholarly but poorer Chang family. Chang Hsün-ju is an intelligent man with a touch of weakness to his character. Married to an extremely understanding and pliant woman, he nevertheless cherishes a strong affection for his younger cousin Hsü Ching-ying and borrows money from his sister Wan-ch'ing to help her enroll in a school at the provincial capital. A clever and capable woman, Wan-ch'ing is unhappily married to Huang Ho-kuang, who bitterly laments his own sexual impotence and addiction to opium. Another of Chang Hsün-ju's cousins is Ch'ien Liang-ts'ai, a widower with a young daughter under his care and an idealist who tries to check the rapacity of the steamboat company and teach the peasants to protect their own interests. There is a possibility that some day he may take Ching-ying to wife.

As the work stands in its incomplete form, a number of delicate domestic situations are not given proper dramatic solution. What we know of the relations between Hsün-ju and his wife, between Hsün-ju and his sister, and between Wan-ch'ing and her husband is highly intriguing, but we are not in command of enough facts to predict the outcome of these various entanglements. In the latter part of the book Ch'ien

Liang-ts'ai emerges as the hero, though it is reasonable to presume that all his cousins will play equally important roles in the sequels. Taking advantage of a flood, Wang Po-shen has let his steamboats run over the rice fields and break the dykes. Ch'ien Liang-ts'ai takes it upon himself not only to stop Wang in his course of villainy but to organize the peasants to repair the dykes and save what remains of the rice crop. What exasperates him is the indifference of the community and the ignorance of the peasants, who have little idea of what they are fighting against. There is no joy in his work, but he perseveres, mindful of his late stepfather's injunction that "a gentleman walks the straight path; he seeks only the peace of his conscience and ignores what people think of him." [6] As a zealous reformer encountering difficulty at every turn, Ch'ien Liang-ts'ai compels as much interest for his humanity and courage as Lydgate in *Middlemarch*. Also admirable is the novelist's skill in depicting the peasants as intractable in their stupidity without making them appear either too ridiculous or sympathetic. This sense of realism, which informs all the other episodes as well, makes *Maple Leaves* a truthful book, however incomplete. It offers a searching and intimate glimpse into the intricacies of the Chinese family system and nostalgically relives the vital issues and struggles of some thirty years ago, now completely superseded by the success of Communism.

Since the war Mao Tun hasn't written much fiction. A few installments of his new novel *Discipline* appeared for a brief time in a Hong Kong newspaper, and a new collection, *Grievances*, reprints five stories written during the last years of the war. In 1946 he made a tour of the Soviet Union. Upon his return he settled in Hong Kong and edited a new magazine called *Fiction Monthly*. Since 1949 he has been Minister of Culture in the Peking Government, president of the Chinese Writers' Association, and vice president, under Kuo Mo-jo, of the All-China Federation of Literary and Art Workers; in addition he holds many other semi-official and honorary posts.

Until 1953 the editor-in-chief of *People's Literature,* he is also the editor of *Chinese Literature,* an English journal devoted to the translation of modern and classical Chinese authors as well as recent Communist literature and criticism.

Mao Tun has turned out many articles and addresses to reiterate the importance of the Mao Tse-tung line in literature, but has cautiously refrained from writing any fiction himself. In a preface to his *Selected Writings,* published in 1951, he admits to the rueful inadequacies of his major novels by the Maoist standard; along with "Spring Silkworms," "Lin's Store" and some other stories, he reprints there only two travel accounts of little literary value: the story of his escape from Hong Kong after Pearl Harbor and his impressions of the Soviet Union.

SHEN TS'UNG-WEN

As Professor of Chinese at the Southwest Associated University, Shen Ts'ung-wen stayed mostly in Kunming during the war and didn't write many new books, though he took great care to revise and polish his many early writings. A number of titles published by the Kaiming Press during and after the war contain mostly revised stories that had seen pre-war publication: the most important is *Black Phoenix* (1943), which contains "Quiet" and the equally exquisite "Daytime." In addition to *The Long River* his new writings include *West Hunan, Watching Clouds in Yunnan,* and *Winter Scene in Kunming.*

By the outbreak of the war Shen Ts'ung-wen had unequivocally chosen his native region of West Hunan as the major concern of his imagination. In the winter of 1934, after an absence of eighteen years, he revisited the region and afterward wrote *The Border Town* and *Random Sketches on a Trip to Hunan* to register his mixed emotions over the changed texture of life there despite the persistence of a certain degree of pastoral nobility. In his preface to *The Long River* he recalls his feelings during that trip:

As I entered the region of the Ch'en River, I found everything had changed. On the surface every aspect of life showed quite naturally a great deal of improvement, but upon closer examination, I discerned a decadent tendency in this change. What was most apparent was the all but complete usurpation of the honest and plain human integrity, characteristic of a rural society, by the practical, selfish, and vulgar attitude toward life, nurtured in the last twenty years in a pragmatic environment. Common sense had naturally destroyed superstition involving a reverence for gods and spirits and a fear of Providence, but at the same time it had deadened the human instinct to prefer righteousness above self-interest, to discriminate right from wrong.[7]

In the winter of 1937 Shen Ts'ung-wen again stayed in West Hunan for over four months. While he saw a hopeful sign in the eagerness of the young officers to defend their country, the larger volume of government exploitation of the region in the supposed interests of national resistance only confirmed his earlier gloom. Accordingly, he wrote two complementary volumes of fact and fiction, *West Hunan* and *The Long River,* to sound anew his fears and his faith.

The Long River is the best of Shen Ts'ung-wen's longer works because it is the most richly inclusive of the many facets of his talent. Pastoral, comedy, and social criticism are expertly blended in this book of uncommon distinction. Even though it is the first volume of a contemplated trilogy which, under the present circumstances, will never be completed, *The Long River* can be regarded as a self-sufficient novel because its episodic chapters are built upon a central theme, permanence versus change. In the book the scenery and rituals are as much an integral part of the action as the temporal sequence of events. The autumnal beauty of orange orchards on the banks of the Ch'en River, the boisterous ceremony of picking oranges, and the rustic gaiety of a thanksgiving festival are depicted with the same evident affection as the spontaneous and indestructible humanity of the principal characters: the orange-grower T'eng Ch'ang-shun, the vivacious and winsome fifteen-year-old girl Yao-yao among his many children, and his best friend, the Old Sailor. The permanence of this scenery, these people, and their age-old customs, however, is pitted against the relentless changes toward a brutal new social order. By Chinese standards T'eng Ch'ang-shun is a fairly prosperous farmer, but even he finds it trying to meet all the taxes and levies and bear up under the continual bullying of the militia and petty officials. The captain of the militia, for instance, demands a free boatload of oranges, and schemes to make Yao-yao his wife. In keeping with the pastoral mode, both crises are averted in the end; yet the reader is left with a bitter taste in his mouth, indignant over all the injustices and indignities that Chinese farmers are subject to. Shen Ts'ung-wen avoids exaggeration and melodrama, and the innocence and gaiety of his village characters stand out in sharp and poignant relief against the brutality of a parasitic ruling class.

The Long River is a comedy by virtue of its author's implicit faith that love, friendship, work, and ritual will survive tyranny and rapacity. The rich quality of humor, however, is hard to define, being so fraught with social criticism and so nearly allied to awareness of tragedy. As a small example of the book's comic manner, we may quote a passage from chapter 2. The Old Sailor, who serves as a steward for the ancestral temple, watches the peasants who pause there for refreshment and conversation before they resume their journey:

> The woman interrupted the conversation, saying: "Big brother, let me ask you, the 'New Life' is coming soon, is it not? I heard Captain Sung of the militia at T'ai-p'ing Ch'i mention this and he is a cousin of my maternal aunt's."

361

A man answered her in an irresponsible and exaggerated manner: "Who says it's not so? Some people have already seen it with their own eyes. At our place, the Communists have just gone and the 'New Life' is now upon us. Even though the crops are good this year, the world is in a pretty bad shape. We are all doomed and there will be no escape. It is said that even the Heavenly King Bodhisattva at Chiang-k'ou, who has always been efficacious, won't be able to save us now, though we kill pigs and sheep and make vows before him!"

This woman, who had been wondering about the "New Life" for some time, could only recall that five years ago the Communists had come and gone and that later the Central troops had come and gone; she didn't know if the "New Life" would also conscript and kill people. She had put this question to many people and they couldn't figure it out either. Now that she heard this man say that some people had already seen the "New Life," she supposed this must be true. If so, then when the "New Life" did come, very likely villages everywhere would again be in a state of confusion. Troops and horses would be huddled together; men would be conscripted and foodstuffs levied, and no family could escape from hardships. Everyday someone would strike the gong to announce that a meeting was to be held at three o'clock in the village. Men and women would all have to go, so that there would be a big crowd to watch the shootings. All would have to shout at the top of their voice, "Down with local rascals; liquidate the reactionaries!" After one group of men and horses had gone, another group would come and again there would be more levying of men and food from every family, more meetings, more killings. So when she heard that the "New Life" would come soon, she became very much depressed. Although the two little pigs in her bamboo cage had given her some happy dreams, that "New Life," like a hammer, had shattered these dreams into pieces.

She wanted to know about the "New Life," and again asked the villager who pretended to be an expert: "Big brother, then have you heard if they will be passing through here? And how many troops and horses do they have?"

Seeing that the woman was genuinely worried, the man put on a very grave face and said: "Who said they are not passing through here? When they want to come, they come, and when they want to leave, they leave. A man from the Kao Village told me that, as his boat was reaching Ch'en-chou Fu, he personally saw the "New Life" going aboard the ships from the bank of the river, and what a huge number of men and horses! Machine guns, howitzers, six-shooters, seven-shooters, thirteen princes,* they've got everything! The Chairman-Commander sat on a big white horse, crossing his hands and addressing the people (here the man mimics the style of official oratory), "Brethren and comrades, fathers and elders, brothers and sisters, I am the 'New Life.' I am the Commander. I must struggle. . . .''

The woman was now completely taken in, so without waiting for him to finish, she asked, "Will the Central troops chase them from behind?"

"That I wouldn't know. However, once he even chased the Central troops! But the Generalissimo will surely know how to handle him. He will send troops and horses after them, but they will be slower on the way because there will be too many men and guns."

* I am not sure that six-shooters and seven-shooters are the right translation for the terms *liu-tzu lien* and *ch'i-tzu chen,* but they are weapons of some sort. The villager apparently has very limited knowledge of modern weapons, and so to make his list more impressive, he names two more or less antiquated firearms. The numerals 6 and 7 suggest "thirteen princes": in popular Chinese fiction and drama, many a tribal chieftain on the Chinese frontier has thirteen princes, some his own sons and some adopted, who are known for their fighting ability.

The woman asked, "Will they go down to Yunnan?"

"Of course, they'll go down to Yunnan. The saying goes, 'Go down to Yunnan and thrash the Melon Spirit.' The saying is now fulfilled. They'll go down to Yunnan to thrash the Melon Spirit."

Having asked these questions, the woman was very much frightened. Her simple heart told her that the "New Life" now must come. She thought of the twenty-four silver dollars she had buried beneath the brick floor under her bed and she became very uneasy. She thought she must do something about it because the situation looked very unsafe. So she hoisted her pig cage to her back and went hurriedly on her way. The two little pigs, probably also indirectly frightened, were squealing all the time as she went down the slope.[8]

This passage is more than good-natured rustic humor. As the reader will recall, the New Life Movement was launched in 1934 by the National Government to rectify the morals of the people and encourage hygiene and civic-mindedness. It was an innocuous movement, though a big bother to policemen entrusted with the task of enforcing many new regulations and to the poorer classes who continually violated them. In 1936 (the novel takes place in that year) this movement has just got around to the remote corners of West Hunan; and to the peasants there who have no idea what it is all about, any governmental innovation or program is a scare, for from past experience they know that such regulations always interfere with their natural rhythm of work and play and impose new sacrifices in terms of food, money, and man power. The comedy of the peasant woman linking up the incomprehensible term "New Life" with her vivid experiences with recent Communist and government tyranny is therefore at the same time an astute piece of social commentary. The woman is happy with her two squealing pigs and her twenty-four silver dollars: they represent possibly all her wealth and they are in her eyes real, tangible, and aesthetic objects, in contrast to which all wars, revolutions, and regulations are nightmarish abstractions. Even the Old Sailor, who is something of a village philosopher, becomes quite agitated upon overhearing this rumor of the "New Life" and goes about to discuss it with his friends. All the episodes in *The Long River* disclose the same basic fear of government, insofar as it is identifiable with empty form, superfluous regulation, and intentional cruelty, not to say war and killing, in the bosom of every farmer in China and perhaps in any other country. In eliciting this profound piece of Taoist wisdom, *The Long River* emerges as much superior to the author's earlier story *The Border Town,* which remains for the most part an idyllic exercise, and to most modern Chinese rural fiction, which offers pathos and violence without any comparable sage vision.

After the war, Shen Ts'ung-wen returned to Peking as Professor of Chinese at Peking University. In Chu Kuang-ch'ien's *Wen-hsüeh Tsa-chih,* which resumed publication in 1947, and some other journals he began to publish installments of a long romance about hot-headed passions and blood feuds of the village clansmen of West Hunan. It bids fair to become a massive imaginative reconstruction of life in that region during the Republican period: the extant chapters [9] constitute a narrative of sustained brilliance, fraught with a compassionate understanding of man's folly and heroism. When the Communists came into power on the mainland, of course, Shen Ts'ung-wen was silenced and his ambitious project perforce abandoned. With his long record as an anti-Communist critic and with his supposed affiliations with the Kuomintang (though the National Government had harshly censored his books during the war), he became the natural target of concerted attack by the Communist press. For a time Shen Ts'ung-wen suffered severe mental shock in his enforced isolation, and even attempted suicide.[10] He has remained silent, though by 1957 he had apparently become a member of the Writers' Association and a volume of his selected fiction had been published by the People's Literature Press.

LAO SHÊ

Lao Shê left North China for Hankow in 1937. Upon the formation of the Chinese Writers' Anti-aggression Association on March 27, 1938, he was chosen its president, and throughout the war years he remained its principal administrator.[11] That Lao Shê, who during the prewar period had studiedly avoided all literary politics, agreed to head the dominantly leftist organization should come as a surprise. But, for one thing, Lao Shê was a genuine patriot who sincerely believed that the Association could unite writers of all shades of opinion to work for the common cause of national resistance. For another, the Communists needed a writer of Lao Shê's stature and independence to serve as a front, to lure other politically uncommitted writers to join their ranks, and to exact greater freedoms from the Government in the name of patriotic necessity. Especially during the early period prior to the New Fourth Army Incident, Lao Shê counted as an important factor in the expansion of Communist propaganda.

During the war Lao Shê was himself a touching example of selfless service. As head of the Association he directed the work of its many branches in the interior and edited, with Yao P'eng-tzu, its chief organ, *Literature for National Resistance* (K'ang-chan Wen-i), the most durable of the wartime literary journals. In compliance with fashion he wrote much poetry designed to be read aloud: the forty-thousand-word poem *North of Chienmenkwan* (Chien Pei P'ien), for example, was composed in the style of *ta-ku,* a popular ballad form in North China. He also wrote and collaborated on many plays, such as *The State above All, The Dispersed Fog, The Problem of Face,* and *Chang Tzu-chung* (a famous Nationalist general who scored a few victories during the first stage of the war). They were all superficial, designed to arouse patriotic sentiment.

When Lao Shê was finally persuaded to write a novel in 1943 after his many stints for the theater, the result was distinctly unsatisfactory. In his candid preface to *Cremation* (1944), he apologizes that "in prewar times I would have destroyed the manuscript, but now economic necessity enforced its publication." [12] He goes on to enumerate the many difficulties facing the patriotic novelist:

> Literature for national resistance—it is not easy!
>
> What a stupendous phenomenon is war! Where should the writers start? They don't know about the mechanics of war, the military life, the tactics and weapons used for attack and defense, for transportation and control; probably they don't even have a too clear idea about the state of preparedness, the regulations and rules in the interior. What should they write? How can they write? [13]

What apparently didn't occur to Lao Shê was why he and his fellow writers should labor under this difficulty when they could have chosen areas of experience with which they were more familiar. Lao Shê didn't question the major assumption —and the reason why most wartime patriotic literature was fatuous—that, since literature is an adjunct to the war effort, writers should preferably write about the war and convey such experiences as will be most conducive to a patriotic frame of mind. He was only more honest than the others in admitting the difficulty of even covering the war on the factual level.

Cremation is about traitors and patriots in a fictitious northern city named Wen Ch'eng. Mr. Wang, a locally respected scholar known by his academic title *chü-jen,* has finally agreed to serve under the Japanese and restore order in the city. He is merely the front, however, because real power goes into the hands of the despicable collaborator, Liu Erhkou (Second Dog Liu), who is also the suitor of Mr. Wang's daughter, Meng-lien. The latter, whose real lover has earlier joined the Nationalist Army, abhors Liu's attention.

Presently Meng-lien's lover, Ting I-shan, sneaks into the city on a tour of reconnaissance; he has just returned to the area as the second in command of a small guerrilla force. Second Dog hears of his movements and has him killed. Now the guerrillas under Captain Shih enter the city, enlist the help of the populace, and set parts of the town on fire. In the ensuing struggle about 150 Japanese are killed, along with Mr. Wang, Second Dog, and the other traitors. His mission accomplished, Captain Shih immolates himself in the conflagration. Assisted by her trusted friend, a sturdy old tenant farmer called Uncle Sung, Meng-lien departs from the city to join the Nationalist forces.

Cremation suffers, as the author was the first to admit, from a kind of guerrilla romanticism; its depiction of the occupied city and of guerrilla warfare in general is altogether unrealistic. But the more damaging fault of the book is its naive patriotism. Patriotism is not an unworthy theme for fiction: Lao Shê's earlier novels—*Chao Tzu-yüeh, The Two Mas, Divorce*—have seriously and successfully explored its possibilities. But years of propaganda work have impaired the novelist's critical faculty—he has sacrificed intelligence to the myth of national heroism. Lao Shê, of course, is still on firm ground when he maintains, in *Cremation* as in his earlier novels, that China stands in need of moral courage in order to rid herself of cowardice and stagnation. But in *Cremation* the depiction of courage versus cowardice, principle versus opportunism is altogether superficial. The names of the good characters in the novel contain such Chinese characters as *shan* (mountain), *shih* (rock), *sung* (pine), *lien* (lotus)—all traditional symbols of strength and purity. The chief puppet and opportunist, on the other hand, is Second Dog. He looks like a "huge eel"; in imitation of the Japanese, "he cultivated a small mustache over his upper lip; where the mustache was not thick enough, he applied some shoe polish." [14] This last detail could be of some account in a genuine satire, but in the novel it is just one more item in a pile of grotesque and disgusting characteristics indicating the man's utter villainy.

Immediately after the war Lao Shê announced his most ambitious project, entitled *Four Generations under One Roof*. It was to be a novel of a million words, and to be published in three parts as *Bewilderment, Ignominy,* and *Famine*. Critics greeted this announcement with expected enthusiasm and predicted that the novel would be his greatest achievement.

Bewilderment and *Ignominy* were published respectively in July and November of 1946 (in April of that year Lao Shê, along with Ts'ao Yü, had arrived in the United States for a year's visit at the invitation of the State Department); *Famine* did not begin serial publication until May 1950, in *Fiction Monthly*. These three volumes, which are available in a much-abridged English version by Ida Pruitt entitled *The Yellow Storm* (New York, 1951), fall considerably short of the high expectations and must be rated as a major disappointment.

Clearly Lao Shê never recovered from the drug of patriotic propaganda. The vision of *Four Generations under One Roof* is so conventionally patriotic (with only a touch of liberal internationalism toward the end) as to make one wonder what sustained the novelist in his detailed tracing of the fortunes of several families, his panoramic coverage of the Peiping scene, his diligent research into the occupation period when all he maintains is the sharp opposition between principle and opportunism, courage and cowardice, heroism and villainy. Lao Shê is traditional in the sense that this moral dichotomy is inherent in Chinese folk literature and drama. But in a genuine novel any moral truth should be grasped as it were for the first time, caught in the inexorable logic of its pattern of events. As one reads on from *Bewilderment* to *Famine,* one becomes increasingly embarrassed by the mechanical application of the principle of punishment, the meting out of sudden disaster and ignominious death to all the traitors and collaborators in the book. Such naive patriotism and detestation of evil make the novel unreal.

Four Generations is the history of a residential lane in

Peiping during the eight years of Japanese occupation. Among the families living in that lane, the Ch'is and Kuans receive the major attention. Four generations of the Ch'i family are still alive: Old Man Ch'i, seventy-five in the year 1937, traditionally well-mannered and kind, cautious and afraid of trouble, who built his house with hard-earned savings; his son T'ien-yu, the manager of a cotton goods store who commits suicide after suffering disgrace in Japanese hands in *Ignominy;* the eldest grandson Jui-hsüan, a gentle and cultured schoolteacher who works for some time at the British Consulate and who, until his participation in the patriotic underground work in *Famine,* suffers from an uneasy conscience living under the Japanese; the second grandson Jui-feng; the third, Jui-ch'üan, a college student who early in *Bewilderment* joins the Chinese forces and disappears from the scene until his return as an underground worker in *Famine;* a son and daughter by Jui-hsüan and his wife. The daughter dies of malnutrition and appendicitis on the eve of victory at the end of the novel.

The second grandson, Jui-feng, is the bad one in the family. Abetted by his plump, selfish, and luxury-loving wife Chrysanthemum, he seeks a lucrative post in the puppet government. He makes friends with other opportunists, especially the Kuans in the same lane.

Kuan Hsiao-ho and his loud and vulgar wife, dubbed Big Red Melon throughout the novel, are shunned by most inhabitants of the lane because of their servility toward the Japanese. To get ahead as collaborators, they even inform against their neighbor Ch'ien Mo-yin after the latter's younger son has deliberately overturned a truckload of Japanese soldiers, causing their death. The Kuans have two daughters: the plain and good-hearted Kao-ti and the pretty and evil Chao-ti, who later serves as a member of the Japanese secret police. Kuan Hsiao-ho also has a concubine, who is much victimized by Big Red Melon but dies a patriotic martyr.

The residential lane, called the Little Sheepfold and intended as a microcosm of Peiping, is also the home of diverse characters whose fortunes are delineated more or less fully in the novel: a furniture mover and his good-hearted wife, a waiter in the British Consulate who professes to be a Christian and worships the British, a foreign-educated professor who later turns collaborator, a ricksha puller later mistakenly executed by the Japanese, a barber, a policeman, an old widow and her moronic grandson who grinds a music box on the streets, a loving couple of aristocratic Manchu descent who make scanty living as part-time opera singers. But the hero of the novel is the proud and lonely Ch'ien Mo-yin, who is severely punished by the Japanese after the Kuans have informed against him. An unobtrusive poet and connoisseur of wine and art in times of peace, he has embraced since childhood the moral precepts of the Confucian tradition and displays great spiritual courage when being alternately wheedled and tortured by the Japanese. He escapes from prison a dedicated man, severing ties with family and friends and going underground to fight traitors and Japanese militarists. It is significant that Lao Shê has chosen this middle-aged traditional poet as his primary example of patriotism rather than the younger and less mature third grandson of the Ch'is, Jui-ch'üan; by doing so, the novelist stresses the continuity of Chinese history and culture. In *Bewilderment* Ch'ien Mo-yin towers above the other characters and injects some excitement into an otherwise pedestrian narrative.

Through officiousness and treachery Red Melon is finally awarded the lucrative post of director of the Bureau for the Inspection of Prostitutes. Her husband, who adopts a more refined style in entertaining the puppet and Japanese officials, ironically gets nowhere. Lao Shê apparently means to show that, in the struggle for power among the collaborators, even the common rules of courtesy are brushed aside and the more unscrupulous a person, the better his chances for getting ahead. Red Melon and her prosperous associates are all painted in the most repulsive colors. Among the associates are Jui-feng and Chrysanthemum, a military officer who used to be a petty warlord, and a schoolteacher and scribbler by name of Lan Tung-yang (a pun on "Rotten Japanese").

The intrigues and rivalries among these collaborators finally lead to their downfall. At the conclusion of *Ignominy*, Jui-feng and the small warlord have been removed from their posts and Red Melon has been arrested by the Japanese gendarmes and her house confiscated. Only Lan Tung-yang, the most despicable of the lot, is still forging ahead. "This is the age of Lan Tung-yang. He is ugly, he is dirty, he is shameless, he is cruel, he is a disgrace to humanity but a darling to the Japanese. He rides in a car. He is busy with his work for the New People's party, busy writing, busy organizing the Literary Association and other societies, busy spying and getting information, busy in love. He is the busiest man in Peiping." [15] But in *Famine* even this character gets his due punishment. Threatened by underground patriots, he seeks sanctuary in Japan only to die in the atomic holocaust at Hiroshima. By that time the other traitors have long met their end: Red Melon dies insane in prison, her husband is buried alive by the Japanese as the supposed carrier of an infectious disease, her daughter Chao-ti is strangled by her early lover Jui-ch'üan, Jui-feng is killed upon the instructions of Lan Tung-yang, and Chrysanthemum is rotting as a third-class prostitute in Tientsin. This insistent melodrama of crime and punishment is ludicrous in a novel supposedly tracing the rebirth of China under the trial of enemy aggression. About the only characters credibly human (the hero Ch'ien Mo-yin becomes romanticized in proportion as the traitors are caricatured) are the members of the Ch'i family who try to preserve their patriotic integrity under the most humiliating circumstances.

Like most other novels by Lao Shê, *Four Generations under One Roof* is a study of the Chinese character. Its major thesis is that, under the cataclysm of national resistance, its finer elements have been preserved and strengthened while its baser elements, embodied in the traitors, are once and for all discarded. On the one hand, Jui-hsüan "saw the real strength of the genuine Chinese culture because he had seen a bar of gold. No, no, he would never think of returning to the past. Only he had found in the person of Old Man Ch'ien the indubitable proof of Chinese culture. Only with this proof could the Chinese have self-confidence, and only with this self-confidence could they start on the path of reform. A pine tree, when its growth has been guided into a straight position, can be made into pillars, but what is the use of an ailanthus, even if it has been guided erect? He had always regarded himself as a new Chinese . . . He had maintained that one must eradicate the old to plant the new. Today he began to realize that the old as exemplified in Mr. Ch'ien is really the basis for any reform or renewal." [16] On the other hand, Ch'ien Mo-yin tells Jui-hsüan:

> This war of resistance ought to be a big house-cleaning for the Chinese nation, not only to oust the enemy but to sweep away our own rubbish. Our traditional maxim of "climbing up the official ladder and making a fortune," our feudalistic thinking, which encourages one to become a high official but at the same time to remain a contented slave, our family system, our educational methods, and our habit of seeking shameful security at whatever cost —all these are hereditary national diseases. During times of peace these diseases have made our history colorless and dull; time crawled on like an old cow and we can boast of very few inventions and contributions which have illumined the world. But when our nation faces a danger or crisis, these diseases break loose like tertiary syphilis and cause putrefaction all around. Red Melon and her like are not people, they are syphilitic sores and malignant boils which ought to be removed with a scalpel! Don't think they are just some purblind and in-

373

consequential insects and let them alone. They are maggots. And maggots will turn into flies, carrying infectious diseases. Today, their crimes are already as numerous and enormous as those of the Japanese. So, they also ought to be killed! [17]

These complementary insights, reiterated by Lao Shê since his earliest novels, constitute a sounder guide to the task of national reconstruction than any ideological planning which repudiates the past and ignores the symptoms of decadence in the present, and the reader can only admire the novelist's passionate insistence, in a period of almost unchecked Communist expansion, on the necessity of spiritual preparation. But in reading over the massive novel, one also feels the complete irrelevance of its sanguine thesis to the facts of history as one knows them. Did the protracted war against Japan perform any such cathartic and restorative functions as are maintained in the novel? After the initial period of patriotic enthusiasm, the Chinese people, in the interior as well as in the occupied areas, by and large suffered patiently and awaited only favorable developments in the outer theaters of the war to bring about their deliverance from the enemy. Increasingly in the clutches of poverty, they sank into despondency, if not downright despair, and lost touch with the spiritual values which had sustained China in all her historical crises. They naturally blamed all their troubles on the inefficient and corrupt government and allowed themselves to be seduced, often against their best convictions, by the propagandist wiles of the Communist party. This connivance with Communism, whatever the nature of the exigencies and the amount of ignorance and gullibility involved, bespeaks that loss of self-confidence in Chinese culture of which Ch'ien Mo-yin is such a proud symbol. For surely the gravest consequence of the war for China, already apparent in the war years, was the spread of spiritual and physical exhaustion, the sapping of the Chinese tradition, making possible the eventual conquest of the mainland by Communism. Yet Lao Shê was so preoccupied with the evil of Japanese aggression and the crime of treasonous collaboration that he completely ignored this reality; as a result the moral atmosphere of his novel is altogether too sanguine and unreal.

By resort to egregious flattery Lao Shê stayed near the top of the literary hierarchy after the establishment of the People's Republic, and unlike most major writers who have either abandoned their creative responsibility or undergone a protracted period of agonizing silence before venturing to write again, he remained amazingly active during the fifties, apparently little bothered by artistic scruples. *Fang Chen-chu, Dragon-beard Ditch, Spring Flowers and Autumn Fruit,* and *Look Westward to Ch'ang-an* are among the many plays he wrote, celebrating the transformation of the Chinese people and land under Communism. Of these, *Dragon-beard Ditch,* about the reclamation of a slum district in Peking, had enjoyed the greatest critical and popular success, earning its author the title of people's artist. For a long period of time, therefore, Lao Shê appeared happily adjusted to a busy but hollow existence under the Communist regime, unaware that he was going to forfeit his life with the coming of the Great Cultural Revolution.

PA CHIN

Pa Chin emerged as an important novelist with the publication of *Autumn* in 1940, but during the first years of the war he was still a propagandist. In 1938, while engaged in the writing of *Autumn,* he began another trilogy to embody the patriotic experiences of the first years of national resistance. Part I of *Fire* was published in December 1940, and Part II in January 1941. In Part I two girl students, Feng Wen-shu and Chu Su-chen, and their friends are seen as anti-Japanese propagandists in Shanghai during the first stage of the war. With the fall of Shanghai this student group is driven under-

375

ground. While Liu Po, Chu Su-chen's lover, chooses to stay in Shanghai, other members of the group eventually leave for the interior. Their further adventures as cultural workers at the front and as guerrillas are depicted in the second volume.

Of Part I of *Fire* Pa Chin says in a postscript: "In writing this novel, I wanted not only to communicate my fervor and indignation but to stimulate other people's courage and strengthen their faith. I also wanted them to see from the activities of these simple youths the hope for a new China. Frankly I wanted to write a work of propaganda. But after I completed these eighteen chapters, I realized that I have failed in my task." [18] Pa Chin apologizes for Part II in a similar tone: "This is a book of propaganda, but a failure at that. For the sake of propaganda, I dare not hide my own deficiencies; I allowed this book to be published so that it may receive proper criticism and correction." [19] Although Pa Chin was a sincere patriot, it is plain from these admissions that he wrote propaganda out of a sense of duty and without much personal satisfaction. Pedestrian narratives as they are, the first two parts of *Fire* are actually superior to the *Love Trilogy* in their greater independence of the romantic-revolutionary clichés.

Part III of *Fire*, completed in 1943 but not published until 1945, can and should be considered as an independent novel. True, the heroines of the preceding volumes, Feng Wen-shu and Chu Su-chen, reappear, and Chu Su-chen finally decides to go to Shanghai to carry on Liu Po's unfinished work after his murder by the secret police. But domiciled in Kunming and far from the battle fronts, these two girls are for the duration of the novel not active patriotic workers; they serve mainly as witnesses to the happiness and tragedy of the T'ien family. T'ien Hui-shih, an exemplary Christian beloved by his wife and three children, is the hero of the book. Grief-stricken over the death of his second son during an air raid, this usually cheerful and apparently healthy man is finally laid low with a high temperature. A heavy dosage of wrong medicine aggravates his belatedly discovered tubercular condition and hastens his death. While occasionally sentimental, this simple story of a good man is not without its moments of moving pathos.

Aware of the low opinion of Chinese intellectuals for Christianity, Pa Chin asserts in his postscript to the novel, "The reader of this book may possibly entertain the idea that I am a Christian; this will be the height of absurdity." [20] But the very fact that he has chosen an exemplary Christian as his hero underscores his mature approach to human problems. (In a prewar story called "Ghost" Pa Chin portrays a devout Japanese Buddhist as a pathetic escapist who has repudiated his earlier socialist and revolutionary views out of fear and cowardice.) In the novel T'ien Hui-shih often clumsily argues with the atheist Feng Wen-shu over the doctrinal points of Christianity. Before his death, however, he asks her to take over his Christian and patriotic magazine; when she declines on the ground of belief, he replies, "What's the difference? Christians and non-Christians are all alike. If only you believe in love and believe in truth, if only you are willing to sow the seeds of life and to encourage people to seek life, then what is the difference between you and me?" [21] This, then, is Pa Chin's new position.

Insofar as he has always stood for love and truth, wherein does the new Pa Chin differ from the old? The difference lies in his deeper understanding of the meaning of love, in his more concrete and realistic view of the human condition. Growing older and more serene during the war years, Pa Chin has apparently become disenchanted with his earlier revolutionary enthusiasms and his utopian faith that a change in social and political structure could bring about a millennium. He was married in May 1944 at the age of forty: his interest in concrete marital problems rather than in abstract romantic issues, evident in his subsequent fiction, is traceable to that change in his life. Since 1944 Pa Chin has retained his humanitarian impulse toward anarchism—that the world always stands in need of a little more sympathy, love, and mutual aid—but he has discarded the violent political paraphernalia of anarchism. Still no profound novelist because of the inherent limitations of his talent, he has become a civilized, and in the context of modern Chinese fiction, a distinguished one.

With his changed mode of perception, Pa Chin turned away from revolutionary themes to write about *Little People and Little Events,* a collection of stories (1945); but the title also aptly describes his three novels since *Fire,* namely *Leisure Garden, Ward No. 4,* and *Cold Nights.* In all these works there is abundant evidence of sharpened observation of the vexations, sorrows, and tragedies which beset inland Chinese during the war. For example, in "Chickens and a Pig," one of the items in his story collection, Pa Chin tells of a widow trying to raise a pig and several chickens in her courtyard as a supplementary source of income. A neighboring boy often molests them, and her landlady demands higher rent as a condition for her keeping them. The widow refuses to pay and her landlady orders her servant to kick the pig. It dies, and at the end of the month, with only one chicken left, the widow moves away. In this simple story Pa Chin gives us a memorable portrait of a lonely and defeated woman, in all her pettiness and sorrow.

Leisure Garden (1944) is the least successful of Pa Chin's last three novels. Though it shows a new maturity, its style is still flat and its tragic theme isn't adequately developed. The story makes use of a double plot linking the fates of the present and past residents in a house named "Leisure Garden." Mr. Yao, its present owner, lives there with his second young wife and his son by his deceased first wife. A woman of delicate sensibility, the second Mrs. Yao faces an acute problem in the intractability of her stepson, who is in his early teens. She cannot apply disciplinary measures without appearing as a hard stepmother; meanwhile the boy's maternal grandmother, who bears an unreasoned grudge against the wife, daily spoils him. Her husband, a rather weak character, is not much help to her either. Finally the boy is drowned, and Mr. Yao sees his own punishment in this irreparable loss and discovers a new love for his wife.

The tragedy about the former owner of the house is much more interesting. A typical wastrel brought up in an affluent family, Mr. Yang dies as a beggar and thief attended only by his devoted second son. In the most moving section of the novel the latter recounts the story of his father's disgrace. After squandering his inheritance, Mr. Yang shamelessly uses his wife's money to support a concubine and periodically returns to Leisure Garden only to quarrel with his wife and appropriate more of her jewelry. The elder son, siding with his mother, develops a deep hatred for his father, and when he becomes the breadwinner he refuses to admit his father to the house. Destitute and sick, the repentant father dares not ask for forgiveness and eventually dies in a decrepit temple.

In the development of the second plot a new tenderness is apparent. Unlike the bad uncles in *Spring* and *Autumn,* the prodigal father is not subject to malevolent caricature; if anything, his pathos is rather sentimentalized. In contrast to Pa Chin's hearty endorsement of the rebellion of the Kao brothers against their elders, his attitude toward the righteous elder son is now one of implicit judgment for his lack of charity. But the humanitarian novelist is still not a moral dramatist: when one remembers Lawrence's subtle explorations of the relations between a rejected father and a self-righteous son siding with his mother in *Sons and Lovers,* one instantly sees that Pa Chin has done scant justice to his tragic material.

Ward No. 4, written in 1945 and published one year later, is an unflinching contemplation of the facts of physical pain and suffering, though unlike Chekhov's *Ward No. 6,* it does not probe the issue of moral and philosophical complacency. In this work, Pa Chin, the erstwhile novelist of bookish inspiration, has turned into a keen observer of the world around him, scrupulously attending to significant detail and effort-

lessly recording a variety of dialects in the speech of his characters. The setting of the novel is the third-class ward for male
patients in a poorly equipped hospital in the interior. The
narrator, who occupies one of the twelve beds in that room,
records in a diary what he sees there during his three-week
hospitalization. The room is filled with the odor of urine and
other smells, and patients needing simple surgery lie beside
victims of infectious diseases. A patient suffering from severe
burns dies untreated because the company he works for refuses to pay the medical expenses. An old vegetarian, rotten
with syphilis, dies after a short stay. A twenty-two-year-old
peasant, who has come to the city for work and has been
hospitalized for a broken arm, suffers a delirious death from
typhus contracted during his brief stay in another hospital.

From the foregoing account one would gather that the
novel is an indictment of malpractice in wartime hospitals
and of the callousness of those concerned with the welfare of
the sick and injured. It is nothing of the sort. Patients suffer
and die because they are poor and the hospital is poor. With
the best intentions in the world, the doctors and interns cannot save them unless they have the means of buying the right
medicines, of which the hospital has no stock. The protagonist
of the novel is the woman intern, Dr. Yang, who takes a sympathetic interest in all her patients. At parting, she gives the
diarist a book about Gandhi and says, "I like this book. It
gives such a wonderful portrait of Gandhi. He is so good
and so humane, he is like a kind mother. Really great men
should be like this. If you read this book frequently, you'll
feel as if you were by the side of Gandhi, and that would make
you a little better, purer, or perhaps a little more useful to
others." [22] The reader closes the book, as the diarist leaves the
hospital, impressed with the goodness of that woman.

Ward No. 4 inevitably calls to mind Ts'ao Yü's famous play
of the early war period, *Metamorphosis.* It too is about a selfless woman doctor, and about a corrupt and inefficient hospital which, under her influence, becomes good and clean.

The play was much admired because the contemporary audience saw in the transformation of the hospital a parable for China and in Dr. Ting an exemplary patriot who gives everything, including her son, to her country. Yet the play is patent propaganda: Dr. Ting is grossly idealized and the hospital has no correspondence with the realities of wartime China. Dr. Yang in *Ward No. 4,* on the contrary, is real, and so is the hospital with its staff of more or less competent doctors who can do little to alleviate suffering, the squeamish but good-hearted nurses, the janitors inured to pain and callous to death, the hopeful, dejected, merry, or cynical patients who cry in agony, shout for a bedpan, or pass jokes around. In the novel Pa Chin captures all the unpleasant realities of suffering humanity; more important, he is able to convey that note of compassion which illuminates every action, cruel or kind, taking place amid the squalor of the ward.

In *Leisure Garden* and *Ward No. 4* Pa Chin records the tragedies of the common man, but his predominant sympathy precludes a search for the whole truth. He is content to show that people suffer and die and that love and kindness will prevail, but he evinces neither the ability nor the interest to depict the naked human condition of suffering and love with anything approaching a psychological fullness. Even after *Autumn* and the other commendable novels, therefore, *Cold Nights* comes as a happy surprise, for in that work Pa Chin fully vindicates himself as a serious novelist.

He began *Cold Nights* in the winter of 1944–45 and completed it two years later. It was serialized in the outstanding postwar magazine *Literary Renaissance* (Volume 2, Numbers 1–6, August 1946 to January 1947) and came out as a book in March 1947. It was apparently a work of love, one upon which the author had spent a good deal of thought and care. Pa Chin has always prided himself as the explorer of the human heart (*chüeh-fa jen-hsin,* his favorite phrase); in *Cold Nights* the heart has finally yielded its secrets.

The novel tackles a familiar situation in such families as

have not entirely broken ties with the traditional pattern of life. The hero is an unexceptional man, to be met with in every Chinese city before, during, and after the war: a college graduate who has failed to make the grade in society and supports his family on a small salary. His problem is not so much poverty or discontent as a lack of tranquillity resulting from bitter antagonism between his mother and wife, who love him but hate each other. The mother-in-law has become a proverbial American joke; yet to the young Chinese wife, who, as a rule, has to live under the same roof with her husband's mother, the latter is anything but comic. She is the jealous, overseeing intruder, a source of daily irritation and often of irreparable tragedy. In *Cold Nights* Pa Chin weaves a poignant drama out of these three everyday characters.

Wang Wen-hsüan, thirty-four years old, lives with his mother and wife in an upstairs apartment in wartime Chungking and works as a proofreader in a semigovernmental publishing company. He has a thirteen-year-old son, who lives at school. To his family and associates, Wen-hsüan is a *lao-hao-jen* ("a good old fellow"), meaning a good and dutiful nonentity in the world of competition and hypocrisy. Because of this characteristic weakness, he can compose the differences between his mother and wife only by an appeal to their pity. In many ways he is the new version of Kao Chüeh-hsin, the patient and suffering man. But almost until the end of the trilogy Chüeh-hsin lives in the world of shadows, forfeiting our sympathy because he resigns himself to his fate without much struggle. In contrast, Wang Wen-hsüan has the selfless perseverance of a meek man, and therefore something of the tragic quality of the hero of *The Idiot;* he tries, despite his failures, to mold the world around him for the better. Even the tragic dilemma is the same: can the two women who love him most love each other for his sake? The Chinese hero does not have the complete candor or the prophetic wisdom of Prince Myshkin, for his disease is not epilepsy but pulmonary tuberculosis, which does not flood one's consciousness with a mystical light;

nonetheless, it envelops its victim in a world of love and death and enables him to perceive meaning in the commonest daily occurrence. Pa Chin does ample justice to this aspect of the hero's character, both in his awareness of his rapid physical deterioration and in his hypersensitivity to the bickerings around him.

As the story opens, Wen-hsüan is walking home one cold autumn night after the sirens have sounded the call that the enemy planes won't visit Chungking tonight. Wen-hsüan is ruminating over his wife's abrupt departure from home the evening before. At thirty-four, Shu-sheng is still youthful-looking. During the first years of their marriage, they lived in Shanghai and enjoyed some material domestic comfort. Conditions have considerably worsened since they moved to Chungking, and this year, 1944, is really the worst. Soon the Japanese will launch a renewed offensive, sweep over Hunan and Kwangsi, and threaten even the safety of Chungking. Shu-sheng works as a secretary at a bank, earning a higher salary and enjoying a more active social life than he. She cannot be blamed, however, because she needs the fun and gaiety which he cannot provide and because, with the continual taunting from his mother, her own home is not really tolerable.

Last evening, for example, Shu-sheng walked out because she refused to tell, at his mother's insistence, the name of the person who wrote her what looked suspiciously like a love letter. His mother resents Shu-sheng's social life; besides, in her eyes, he and his wife are not even properly married because they had neglected to fulfill the traditional wedding ceremonies. It is understandable, of course, that his mother, a widow for many years, should show such protective and jealous love for her only son and should be hostile toward any woman who enjoys physical intimacy with him. Wen-hsüan ruminates over the past as he walks home; he doesn't know what to do except to ask his mother and wife to exercise mutual forbearance.

That same night he has a nightmare. It seems that the enemy troops are finally attacking Chungking and that he, his wife, and his son are joining the long exodus of refugees. His mother, however, has been separated from them; she lies prostrate by the roadside, blocked from them by a mountain of traffic. Wen-hsüan tries to succor her, but his wife presses for time and wants to leave her where she is. As he goes toward his mother, Shu-sheng carries out her threat by walking ahead with their son. Wen-hsüan tries to catch up with them; and then he wakes up.

The first two chapters, freely paraphrased in the three preceding paragraphs, have stated the theme of the novel, and the remaining twenty-nine chapters proceed to develop it with a series of subtly delineated incidents. In charting this tragedy, Pa Chin steadily keeps his eye on the three main characters and offers few distracting episodes. A friend of Wen-hsüan's, crazed over the death of his bride, seeks consolation nightly in a tavern and meets his end in a truck accident. Another friend, who works for the same publishing company, catches cholera and dies immediately in a makeshift hospital crowded with unattended patients. But even these two episodes are not introduced for gratuitous pathos: they are parallel examples of disintegration, physical and emotional, that in the end engulfs Wen-hsüan. They also serve to accentuate the prevalent gloom and sickness of the people in the interior during the last years of the war: the poverty, the contempt for individual life, and finally the utterly meaningless and accidental character of the victory. For Wen-hsüan dies ironically a few days after the formal proclamation of peace.

Shu-sheng returns home the next day after listening to her husband's pleadings. Her problem, as Pa Chin poses it, is more conventionally romantic. She is young and still eager for life. Her immediate superior at the bank intends to marry her; while she doesn't care for him much personally, to all appearances he will give her a fuller and less complicated life.

When he is to be transferred to Lanchow, Kansu (at a time when Chungking is threatened with imminent Japanese attack), he offers to take her along. After many excruciating days and nights, she finally agrees to go, partly because her income there will help her husband to get along now that his worsening health has made him unfit for work. Insofar as it conforms to the stereotype of wifely duty versus romantic dream, Shu-sheng's individual drama is rather sentimental. And her final letter sent from Lanchow requesting her husband to release her from conjugal bonds ("I am not selfish, I only want to live, and to live joyfully. I want freedom") [23] is rather banal. But in spite of her romantic ratiocinations, as an actual presence in the novel she also moves in the circle of charity. She loves Wen-hsüan and loves her son, who is rather indifferent toward her. At times she tries hard to ignore her mother-in-law's continual and deliberate taunts. She would have stayed with Wen-hsüan to the end if he had been more assertive in character. She is pliant femininity, to be molded into complete loyalty only by a firmer masculine hand. Her tragedy is that, though her husband loves her and wants her desperately, his unselfish goodness leaves her too free in the realm of moral choice. If he could have asserted his will or made a more moving display of his need, she would have clung to him in spite of his mother. As it is, she leaves her dying husband in vain pursuit of her romantic illusion; when she comes back to Chungking to revisit her home a few months later (she didn't marry her superior after all), Wen-hsüan is dead and his mother and son have moved away.

So far in our analysis of the novel, the mother has been presented as a kind of villain, which she is not. She is narrow and ignorant but she is a good woman and a loving mother. Having lived over fifty years in the traditional manner of self-abnegation expected of Chinese women, she doesn't need freedom (because her happiness is completely bound up with the welfare of her son and grandson) and cannot understand that craving for freedom in her daughter-in-law. Therefore she resents Shu-sheng's social life, which represents an allegiance other than home and husband, and detests her superior education, which has given her strange ideas in the first place. She cannot conceive of a wife for her son who is not exactly like herself. Vainly she tries to fill the wife's place, during Shu-sheng's absence, to comfort his son, to minister to his needs, to bolster up hope. She serves him chicken broth, she asks after his health, and she is in every other way solicitous. But because she cannot assuage his spiritual suffering, the many sessions when mother and son are together, talking quietly and comforting each other, are among the most affecting scenes in the novel.

Cold Nights is firmly grounded in physical and everyday reality. To watch the gradual but inevitable disintegration of the hero's body is in itself a shattering experience. All the tender and pathetic scenes establish their immediate authority by virtue of their almost unbearable closeness to ordinary Chinese family life. With this novel Pa Chin has become a psychological realist of great distinction. And because he is solely concerned with the presentation of truth as he knows it and makes no bid for ambitious philosophical meanings, he also succeeds to a remarkable degree in giving his novel symbolic dimensions: the fate of the three principal characters is not only a parable of China in her darkest hour of defeat and despair but a morality play about the insuperable difficulties facing Everyman walking the path of charity.

Autumn is Pa Chin's best novel in the mode of indignation; *Cold Nights*, his best in the mode of love. Insofar as love transcends anger and represents a more comprehensive awareness, the latter is the finer and more mature achievement. With the publication of this novel at the age of forty-three, Pa Chin could have looked forward to decades of creative felicity. He was no longer the hasty and automatic writer of supposed daemonic possession, no longer the revolutionary propagandist of unreasoned hate; instead, he had become a meticulous craftsman and compassionate realist, and although he still valued truth as something of infinitely greater consequence than art he knew now that, as an artist, he could serve truth only by telling the truth about life, by exploring the dark recesses of the human heart and illuminating its path of love. But it was quite inevitable that, when the Communists ushered in an unprecedented era of intellectual and artistic conformity in 1949, Pa Chin would no longer be able to write in accordance with his new conviction.

Despite his many unwitting contributions to the Communist cause, Pa Chin was in Commuist eyes a very incorrect writer. His revolutionary enthusiasm never conformed to the requirements of the party line; his humanitarian feelings catered to the petty-bourgeois sensibility. He was therefore twice sent to Korea to recondition his outlook and to learn at first hand the "peace-loving heroism" of the Communist party and the Chinese people. In subsequent records of Korean impressions, the remolded author seemed determined to stay correct at all costs, to endow Chinese and North Korean soldiers with superhuman strength and endurance, to vilify the United States in the blackest color possible. The following, for example, is supposedly Pa Chin's personal testimony to the American perpetration of germ warfare:

> We have seen small disease-carrying flies propagating their kind on a snow-covered ground at seventeen degrees below zero; we have seen heaps of dead fish dumped on the high hills; we have seen thousands of live fleas transported from snow-covered regions; we have seen dead rats infected with the plague; we have also seen germ containers of various sizes and shapes thrown from American airplanes . . . not to mention the myriad moldy leaves, chicken feathers wrapped in gauze, the disease-carrying crows and magpies, the germ-carrying flies, mosquitoes, pork, foxes, and other hard-to-name, strange things.[24]

It is sad to think that a writer once dedicated to truth could have fabricated such implausible lies as seeing flies propagating at a temperature below zero, but it is perhaps even sadder that the Communist Government could have demanded, and accepted, this type of fantasy as valid anti-American propaganda.[25]

CHAPTER 15

Eileen Chang

The Rice-sprout Song, Eileen Chang's own translation of her Chinese novel, was greeted with favorable to excellent reviews in this country upon its publication in spring 1955. Understandably, however, as a severe work of art, it could not compete in sales with other recent fiction about China which has more sentimental appeal: Han Suyin's *A Many-splendored Thing* and Pearl S. Buck's *Imperial Woman.* Nor could the generosity of the press, which enthusiastically welcomes many novels each season, be of much help in enforcing public recognition of its positive merits. Little serious discussion of the novel has followed the initial reviews, and its author remains only a name, with her life and literary career practically unexplored. Yet to the discerning student of modern Chinese literature, Eileen Chang is not only the best and most important writer in Chinese today; her short stories alone invite valid comparisons with, and in some respects claim superiority over, the work of serious modern women writers in English: Katherine Mansfield, Katherine Anne Porter, Eudora Welty, and Carson McCullers. *The Rice-sprout Song* is already to be placed among the classics of Chinese fiction.

To those whose knowledge of the author is confined to the English version of the novel it will probably come as a surprise that little in Eileen Chang's literary career has apparently prepared for that searching study of village life under Communism. For years she was best known for *Romances,* a collection of her stories depicting, in the main, bourgeois life in Shanghai and Hong Kong. Nor was there any biographical evidence to suggest that she was intimate with rural life prior to the Communist conquest of the mainland. For, unlike most modern Chinese writers, she was born into an official family boasting traditional opulence as well as an active early interest in Western culture. From her autobiographical essays, "Whispered Words" and "The Guileless Words of a Child," one gathers that her father was the scion of a distinguished family in close touch with the Manchu court. He must also have had some superficial contact with Western literature (one day Eileen discovers one of his books, Shaw's *Heartbreak House,* with his name and address and the date of purchase inscribed in English on the flyleaf), though he seems to have stubbornly adhered to the rights and vices of old-style gentry. Her mother must have been one of the most privileged women of her time, for she and her sister went to France to study when Eileen was still a small child. One reason for this decision must have been her disgust with her husband, who had taken a concubine and become a morphine and opium addict. In her mother's absence, Eileen bore her existence rather cheerfully and watched with absorbing interest the gaily dressed courtesans periodically called upon to decorate her father's parties. But her one-year-younger brother early showed symptoms of a weak character in the environment of a decadent household.

When her mother returned from abroad, Eileen was eight years old and had moved with her father from Tientsin to Shanghai. In a fit of remorse, he had dismissed his concubine and broken his nearly fatal addiction to morphine. For a short while, therefore, Eileen lived as a normal child with her reconciled parents. But her father was soon again under the sway of his terrible temper and vicious habits, and her mother finally had to divorce him. She again went to France. Then a middle school student, Eileen sought maternal solace in the company of her aunt, who had remained in Shanghai.

Not long afterward her father remarried. "My stepmother also smoked opium," she records in "Whispered Words."

> Soon after the wedding we moved to an old Western-style house built in the early years of the Republic. It was our property and I was bòrn there. For me it retained too many memories of our family, like a photograph which has been developed from a film exposed to many a different scene. The whole atmosphere was blurred: where the sunlight could visit, one felt drowsy and where it was dismally dark, one sensed the cold desolation of an ancient grave. But wrapped in its bluish dark colors, the house itself was soberly awake in its strange world. In the intersections of light and darkness, one could see the sunlight, hear the bells of trolleys, and the tune "Susan, Don't Cry" insistently broadcast from the nearby cotton goods store promoting its sales. One could only doze away in this sunlight.[1]

To dispel her gloom, Eileen studied hard at school and dreamed of literary fame. In the year of her graduation (1937), her mother returned from France. Eileen went to see her frequently and her father and stepmother became frightfully angry and jealous. Finally, after a bitter quarrel with her stepmother over her two-week visit with her mother, Eileen was brutally beaten by her father and confined in the house with the doors closely guarded. She aged many years during the first weeks of her confinement. She had some intimation of what madness is like and indulged in dreams of escape, such as she had read in *The Three Musketeers, The Count of Monte Cristo,* and Chinese romances. Her father gave her absolutely no medical attention when Eileen finally fell sick with dysentery. For a whole autumn and winter she lay in her bed brooding; then, at about the time of the Chinese New Year, she escaped. She took a ricksha to her mother's place and never again returned to her father's house.

After a period of hard study Eileen Chang won admission to the University of London, but because of the war she could not go there and settled for the University of Hong Kong instead. In Hong Kong she met with the cosmopolitan set: the Eurasian students as well as the sons and daughters of British, Indian, and overseas Chinese merchants, who appear in some of her stories. In her junior year Hong Kong fell into Japanese hands, and for a while she was interned in her dormitory with her fellow students. Soon afterward she returned to Shanghai, to begin her literary career at the inopportune time of Japanese occupation. But in the absence of browbeating Communist critics, Miss Chang enjoyed almost unimpeded freedom for the cultivation of her individual art. For the remainder of the war period she was the outstanding writer in Shanghai, her essays and stories being eagerly awaited by readers of such leading literary magazines as *Heaven and Earth* (edited by Miss Su Ch'ing, an early protégée of Lin Yutang's). These essays and stories were respectively collected in *Gossip* and *Romances* (1943). *The Collected Stories of Eileen Chang*, first published in Hong Kong in 1954, substantially reproduces the augmented second edition (1947) of the latter volume.

Eileen Chang could not have made significant contributions to Chinese literature if she had broken down under her severe trials as a child and adolescent. Partly because of her keen appetite for life and partly because of her precocious interest in human passions, which intrigued and amused her even when under great sorrow or anguish, one can discern in her writings only the slightest trace of neurotic self-pity with which young women writers are often afflicted. She can be as gay and satiric as Jane Austen, but behind her comic surface is a profound impersonal sorrow over the perversity and pettiness of all passions. It is this astonishing combination—a

Chaucerian gusto for life and all its little enjoyments plus an adult and tragic awareness of the human condition—that marks the young author of *Romances* as a well-nigh unique figure in modern Chinese literature.

As early as she could hold a pen, Eileen Chang was either drawing pictures or writing stories. By her own account, she composed at the age of seven a historical romance set in the period of Sui and T'ang. As her taste changed with the years, she tried her hand at all varieties of popular fiction, ranging from sentimental romance to the proletarian story of social protest. Meanwhile she continued to draw and sketch the people around her. One has little doubt that Miss Chang would have developed into an artist of some distinction if she had received some formal training; as it is, her sketches of many types of people seen in Shanghai and Hong Kong, included in *Gossip,* show a deft touch and an eye for the essential detail.

Since childhood, then, Eileen Chang had registered her delight in the visible world through words and pictures; as a frustrated artist she was eventually to develop a prose fraught with the richest visual imagery of any modern Chinese writer. But her imagination was equally nourished on the other senses. The following passage from her essay "On Music" is a good example of her prodigious appreciation of smells:

> It is the same with smells. I am fond of many odors which people dislike: the slight mustiness of fog, the smell of dust after rain, leek, garlic, cheap perfume. Some people get a headache from inhaling gasoline, but I make a special point of sitting next to the car driver or staying behind the car and waiting there until the exhaust ejects the fumes. Every year when I use gasoline to clean my clothes, the whole room will be filled with a clean, strong, and bright smell; my mother never lets me help her because I would deliberately take it easy and let gasoline evaporate in large quantity.
>
> When milk is overboiled and when firewood is burned

black, their charred fragrance makes me feel hungry. The odor of new paint, because of its newness, is invigorating; it is as if you were spending the new-year holidays in a new house, clean and cool and suggestive of prosperity. Ham, bacon, and peanut oil beget a "greasy" smell when they are stored for too long and have changed from their proper texture of taste. This I like too, because the smell of oil there is more oily, riper and richer, and suggests "the rotten rice and stale granaries" of the old days. At the time when Hong Kong was in a state of war, we had to cook our dishes in coconut oil; at first I would retch because I was not used to its strong, soap-like tang but later I discovered that even the soapy smell has its distinctive cool fragrance. During the war when tooth paste could not be had, I didn't even mind brushing teeth with coarse-grained laundry soap.[2]

Because of the inherent sadness, for her, of music, Eileen Chang professes to like it less, but precisely for this reason it is also an integral part of her world. (The reader of *The Rice-sprout Song* will surely remember the sad clang of gongs accompanying the straggling peasant dancers in the last chapter.) From her mother, a trained musician, she early learned to play the piano and appreciate Western music, and in the same essay "On Music" she shows excellent taste in preferring Bach and Mozart to the romantic composers. But Miss Chang is far from a cloistered product of missionary education, a squeamish young lady turning up her nose at indigenous popular art and music. Fond of Peking Opera and Chinese movies, she went out of her way to watch the shrill-voiced and heavily painted actors of many varieties of regional drama in cheap theaters. To her the monotonous cadence of the insistent music and the crude enactment of the so-called feudalist morality on a bare stage reveals the essence of life underlying the more refined manners of the contemporary world. In a sense her own fiction tries to capture what the Chinese stage presents crudely and unself-consciously: the sense of desolation inherent in all human hunger and frustration. "Desolate" (*ch'i-liang* or *ts'ang-liang*) is her favorite word.

Her childhood education ideally complemented her keen and receptive sensibility. From her stern and old-fashioned father she received training in classical Chinese poetry and prose, without which discipline it is hardly conceivable that a writer in her early twenties, as Miss Chang was when she began to publish, could have explored the resources of the Chinese language with such assurance and skill. During her first years in Shanghai her mother initiated her into the world of Western art, music, and literature. Miss Chang is, of course, no erudite scholar like Ch'ien Chung-shu; at the time when her college education was disrupted by the war, her knowledge of Western culture was in all probability not superior to that commanded by any brilliant graduate from an Eastern girls' college in this country. But to a writer education is more than formal learning; it is what the mind is able to assimilate and retain in the business of everyday living. In that sense, jazz music and Hollywood are of as much importance as Bach and Shakespeare; the tawdry passions of Shanghai Opera as useful as the exquisite sentiments of Chinese poetry. Miss Chang attends at once to vulgarity and refinement; her fiction is the richer for its range of sensibilities.

It is not an accident, therefore, that with her capacity for sensuous knowledge and comprehensive education, her fiction should boast the richest imagery of any contemporary Chinese writer. The intellectual similes of Ch'ien Chung-shu and the pastoral landscape of Shen Ts'ung-wen equal it in distinction, but they represent more restricted modes of observation. Stretching in time from the downfall of the Ch'ing dynasty to the period of the Sino-Japanese conflict (in both style and imagery *The Rice-sprout Song* represents some departures from *Romances*, and shall be treated separately), the world of Eileen Chang is, first of all, a richly appointed world of mansions and flats, complete with the kinds of furniture and clothing to which their inhabitants are accustomed. The author's visual imagination, which rises on occasion to a Keatsian opulence, is always impressive in the detailed description of the clothes of her female characters. Very possibly nothing like this intimate boudoir realism has appeared in Chinese fiction since the great novel *Dream of the Red Chamber*. But in contrast to the world of stable moral standards and feminine fashions of the latter novel, Eileen Chang deals with a society in transition, where the only constants are the egoism in every bosom and the complementary flicker of love and compassion. Her imagery, therefore, not only embraces a wider range of elegance and sordidness but has to suggest the persistence of the past in the present, the continuity of Chinese modes of behavior in apparently changing material circumstances. In that respect her imagery has a strong historical awareness.

Eileen Chang's world is also rich in nature imagery. Its metropolitan character does not preclude the sun and moon, the wind and rain, and that extensive part of vegetation still easily within the reach of a city-dweller's eye. Red azaleas in the arms of a bus passenger; a creeping plant, placed in a pot on the sky terrace of an apartment building, trying vainly to climb upward; summer breeze fluttering like a flock of white pigeons inside the silk blouse and trousers of a rejected lover—touches like these not only enrich the narrative but also define the scene or character under description. Because of her habitual importation of nature, whether as setting or metaphor, into her world of manners, Eileen Chang is also the foremost symbolist among Chinese writers of fiction. And her predominant symbol is the moon, which looks down upon the world of love with cold detachment, hazy sympathy, or benign irony. It is possible to write a monograph to illustrate the uses of the moon symbol in her fiction.

Along with her shrewd use of imagery and symbolism, Miss Chang evinces a powerful grasp of the complexities and subtleties to be observed in social intercourse. Just as she is absolutely uninfluenced by the leftist modes of Chinese fiction, she is little tempted to follow the dazzling fashions of present-day Western fiction—to pursue, for example, stream of consciousness to the neglect of weightier moral concerns. She knows with the instinctive sagacity of a born storyteller that the truth of the human heart is best told within the framework of manners, which condition the expression of emotions in the first place. Understandably, therefore, while she is deeply indebted to Freud and Western novelists for the psychological sophistication and metaphorical enrichment of her stories, she is even more of a dedicated student of traditional Chinese fiction. There is simply no other school that could enable her to make the best fictive use of her personal observations of Chinese society. Along with several stylistic devices—such as prefixing reported speeches with the simple verb *tao* [3] —Eileen Chang gains from her study of Chinese fiction principally a mastery of dialogue and a corroboration of her insight into peculiarly Chinese behavior. The characters in *Romances* are solidly and in some instances frighteningly Chinese; they are therefore solidly and frighteningly real. While she is primarily concerned with the world of her contemporaries, her study of Chinese fiction has led her to stress the strong persistence of traditional sensibility even in an apparently uprooted and cosmopolitan set. Sensibility evolves slowly; old manners die hard even during a period of unprecedented technological and economic change. Each character in *Romances* is sharply defined against his social and economic background, against his parents, and by extension against a culture in decadence.

Examples are necessary to support our description of Eileen Chang as a short-story writer. In many of the *Romances* the basic situation is a courtship, flirtation, or affair, but what is involved is more than the expected comedy or pathos of the love game: it is the condition of a soul unpropped by its usual stays of vanity and desire. Miss Chang professes not to abide by the classical formula of tragedy because it is her belief that the sheer weight of habit and animalism precludes the possibility of any prolonged flights of sublimity or passion. For her as for most story-writers since Chekhov, tragic revelation comes only at the moment when the protagonist, temporarily outside the shell of his ego, surveys the desolation of his triumph or failure. Even in her satirical tales tragic knowledge is always implicit in the temporary disarray of the hero's composure or sudden disappointment of his expectations. But a few of her longer and more ambitious stories fall nothing short of the full tragic commitment, and one of these we shall now examine in some detail in order to appreciate her art at its highest level of intensity.

The Golden Cangue, a long story of over 28,000 words, is in my opinion the greatest novelette in the history of Chinese literature. It is a new type of Chinese fiction bearing happy witness to its author's skillful appropriation of the elements of both the native and the Western tradition. In method and style it is clearly indebted to the great Chinese domestic novels, while for its psychological and moral sophistication it apparently owes more to Western fiction. But the whole work is undeniably the creation of a highly distinctive and individual talent.

The Golden Cangue traces the life of a woman from her frustrated and unhappy youth to her malevolent and mad age. When the story opens, the saucy and shrewd Ch'i-ch'iao, whose family owns a cooking-oils store, has been married for five years to the paralytic second son of a wealthy official family. The marriage was possible because no daughter from a family of equal wealth and position would consent to a match with a puny invalid and because Ch'i-ch'iao's elder brother was avaricious enough to sacrifice his sister's happiness. Ch'i-ch'iao accepts her intolerable situation with courage, parrying with occasional material assistance her brother's greed and defying petulantly but with self-possession the snobbery of her husband's family. Her one consolation is that, in the event of her husband's death, she will become a rich and independent woman. But still normal and healthy despite the opium habit she has acquired while nursing her husband, she craves love. The sight of her two weakling children only reminds her of the travesty of sexual attention her husband pays her on rare occasions. In her frustration she fancies herself to be in love with the third son of the family.

This third son, Chiang Chi-tsê, has been married only a month. A good-looking wastrel, he regularly visits brothels and flirts with maidservants. But he draws a firm line in regard to Ch'i-ch'iao's attentions. He rightly reasons that it will be very imprudent to form a liaison with a sister-in-law under the same roof; besides, with her bad temper, he would have a most difficult time extricating himself from this affair once he got tired of her. When Ch'i-ch'iao supplicates for his love and feels his legs with her hands, he only squeezes her foot once and tells her to desist.

Ten years later, with the death of her husband and mother-in-law, Ch'i-ch'iao is finally in a position to enjoy the reward of her patience. (The author introduces at this juncture a powerful scene of a family quarrel over the division of property.) Chi-tsê, who has squandered most of his fortune even before he has inherited it, now pays Ch'i-ch'iao a visit and protests undying love to her.

> Ch'i-ch'iao bowed her head, basking in glory, in the soft music of his voice and the delicate pleasure of this occasion . . . All these years she had been playing blindman's buff with him and could not near his person; who could have expected today! To be sure, half her life had gone—the flower-years of her youth. Life was always like that, devious and unreasonable. Why had she to marry into the Chiang family in the first place? For money? No, it was so that she could meet Chi-tsê and fulfill her preordained love for him. She lifted her head slightly and saw Chi-tsê standing close to her, his hands clasping her

fan and his cheek nestling against it. He had also grown
ten years older, but after all he was the same person. Is
he deceiving her now? Can it be possible that he is only
thinking of her money—the money for which she has
sold her life? This very thought made her suddenly very
angry. Even if she has misconstrued his intentions, can
the suffering he has undergone for her make up for the
suffering she has undergone for him? It has not been
very easy for her heart to die; now he is again tempting
her. She hates him. He is still looking at her. His eyes—in
spite of the ten years, he is still the same person! Even if
he is deceiving her now, would it not be better to post-
pone this discovery till some later time? Yes, even if she
knows he is deceiving her, can't she accept his love for
real, since he is such a good actor? [4]

Her weakness, however, is only momentary. The golden
cangue in which she had locked herself during all these years
of waiting and scheming has incapacitated her for love, real
or spurious. (A cangue is a large board frame used to confine
the neck and hands of criminals in the old days in China.)
With a business-like air Ch'i-ch'iao proceeds to discuss money
matters with Chi-tsê and detects him in a lie. Angry beyond
herself, she flings her fan in the direction of his head but up-
sets instead the glass of sour plum drink on the table, which
splashes all over his silk gown. She shows him the door.

Chi-tsê had gone. The maidservants and amahs also
hurriedly left the room after being scolded by Ch'i-ch'iao.
Drop by drop, the sour plum drink trickles down the
table, keeping time like a water clock at night—one drip,
another drip—the first hour, the second hour—one year,
a hundred years. So long, this one moment of solitude.
Ch'i-ch'iao stood there, her hands cupping her head. In
another second she had turned around and was hurrying
upstairs. Lifting her skirt, she half climbed and half
stumbled her way up, continually bumping against the

dingy wall of green plaster. Her Buddha-blue blouse was smudged with large patches of dust. She wanted to look at him once more from her window upstairs. After all she had loved him once and that love had given her no end of pain. This consideration alone should entitle him to some affectionate regard. How many times, to repress herself, she had to steady her body until all her muscles, bones, and the roots of her teeth ached with sharp pain. Today it was all her fault. She acted as if she hadn't known all along that he was no good! If she wants him, then she has to pretend to be stupid and tolerate his badness. Why has she had to unmask him? But isn't life always like that? When one comes down to the heart of a matter, how can one tell what is true and what is false?

She approached the window and pulled open the foreign-style dark-green curtains fringed with velvet pompons. Chi-tsê was walking in the lane toward the street, his gown folded against his arm. Like a flock of white pigeons, the wind on that sunny day fluttered inside his pongee blouse and trousers. It penetrated everywhere, flapping its wings.[5]

Many a story-writer would feel justified in ending the tale at this point: the study of a woman torn between her passion for money and her love for an unworthy man has constituted an interesting theme for much good fiction. The first half of *The Golden Cangue,* moreover, is unlike anything by any other modern Chinese writer: one scarcely encounters elsewhere the vivid recall of upper-class family life of an earlier period (about the time of the downfall of the Ch'ing dynasty), the effortless rendition of dialogue, and the powerful fusion of feeling with imagery that is apparent in the passage just quoted. Yet for Eileen Chang the romantic episode is only the beginning; in the second half of her story she unfolds the lonely madness of Ch'i-ch'iao's later life in all its terror.

Ch'i-ch'iao's two children grow up under the dominance of

her malevolent will. A completely docile weakling, the son Ch'ang-pai has little schooling and early indulges in the vices of his class. Ch'i-ch'iao gives him a wife when he begins to frequent brothels. Then, with the insane jealousy of a frustrated woman unable to abide normal sexual life around her, she induces her son by taunts to leave his wife's bed and to serve her opium. Reclining on the opium couch in the small hours of the night, mother and son joke about the scorned woman. To further humiliate her, Ch'i-ch'iao buys her son a concubine. Years later both wife and concubine break down under the insufferable strain and commit suicide.

But it is in her delineation of the subtle clashes between Ch'i-ch'iao and her daughter Ch'ang-an that Eileen Chang gives the most astonishing evidence of her dramatic power. At her own insistence Ch'ang-an once attended school, but she soon quit because she could no longer endure the shame her mother continually brought upon her in the eyes of her teachers and schoolmates. A sensitive girl, "she felt that her sacrifice was a beautiful and desolate gesture." [6] While her mother is alive, this gesture remains her only self-defense.

Ch'i-ch'iao is obliged by custom to choose a husband for her daughter, but she approaches the task with the greatest reluctance. The better families are not interested because of her own notoriety and Ch'ang-an's plain features, while the poorer familes can always be dismissed for their supposed mercenary interest. The real trouble, of course, lies in Ch'i-ch'iao's unwillingness to relinquish her hold on her daughter. As the years go by, Ch'ang-an becomes a confirmed opium-smoker with a temper as peevish as her mother's.

When she is approaching thirty, a girl cousin takes pity on Ch'ang-an and introduces her to T'ung Shih-fang, a German-returned student in his late thirties. After his eight lonely years abroad and some unhappy love experiences in his early youth, this man has developed a nostalgic longing for the demure type of Chinese girl and finds Ch'ang-an quite to his liking. After several quiet and furtive dates they become formally engaged. To be worthy of her fiancé, Ch'ang-an even summons enough will power to stop smoking opium.

But Ch'i-ch'iao keeps postponing the wedding and scolding her daughter for her shameless impatience. Rather than stand the taunts further, Ch'ang-an finally decides to break off her engagement to Shih-fang. "It would be safe if he could never see her mother, but sooner or later, he had to face Ch'i-ch'iao. Marriage is a lifelong affair; it is possible to remain a thief for a thousand years, but impossible to guard against a thief for a thousand years—how could she know what her mother would not do? Sooner or later there would be trouble; sooner or later there would be an end. This was the most beautiful episode in her life; rather than let other people spoil it in the end, she would terminate it herself." [7]

After she has called off her engagement, Ch'ang-an still goes out with Shih-fang. To their own surprise, they begin to experience real love in each other's company. But this fragile love, of course, cannot hope to circumvent Ch'i-ch'iao's evil genius. The reader is now introduced to the climactic scene in the story, a scene of sheer dramatic surprise in which, quite appropriately, Ch'i-ch'iao is fully visualized for the first time as a prematurely old woman of evil cunning:

> The rumor, however, was heard by Ch'i-ch'iao. Behind Ch'ang-an's back, she asked Ch'ang-pai to invite T'ung Shih-fang over for an informal dinner. Shih-fang thought that the Chiang family was perhaps trying to warn him against his persisting in a delicate relationship with its young mistress. But while he was talking with Ch'ang-pai over two cups of wine about the weather, the world situation, and other sundry matters in that somber and spacious dining hall, he noticed that nothing was mentioned of Ch'ang-an. Then the cold plates were cleared away and Ch'ang-pai suddenly leaned his hands against the table and stood up. Shih-fang turned his head and saw standing against the light on the doorsill a diminu-

tive old woman in a bluish-gray brocade dress embroidered with a dragon design in accordance with the palace style. Her face was blurred and her hands were clasping a big red hot-water bag; two tall and big women servants stood close against her. Beyond the door the sunlight was dark-yellow, and the staircase, carpeted with a checkered oilcloth of lake-green color, led up through the flight of steps to a place where no light was visible. Instinctively Shih-fang felt that this was a mad person—he unaccountably shivered. Ch'ang-pai introduced her, "This is mother."

Pushing his chair backward, Shih-fang stood up and made a bow. Ch'i-ch'iao slowly walked in, her hand holding on to a woman servant's arm. After a brief exchange of greetings, she sat down to help the guest to food and wine. Ch'ang-pai asked, "Where is sister? We have company here and she didn't even come down to help." Ch'i-ch'iao replied, "She'll come down after a couple of pipes more." Shih-fang was greatly shocked and stared intently at her. Ch'i-ch'iao hurriedly explained, "It's such a pity this child didn't have proper prenatal care. I had to puff smoke at her as soon as she was born. Later, after a bout of illness, she acquired this habit of smoking. How very inconvenient for a *hsiao-chieh!* It isn't that she hasn't tried to break it, but her health is so very delicate and she has had her way in everything for so long it's easier said than done. Off and on, it has been ten years now." Shih-fang couldn't help changing color. Ch'i-ch'iao had the prudence and cunning of a mad person. From long and painful experience she knew that, if she wasn't too careful, people would regard her kind of talk with ridicule and mistrust. If she talked too much, her lie would be exposed. So she stopped in time and busied herself with laying out more wine and food on the table. After a while, when the name of Ch'ang-an was again mentioned, she only casually repeated what she had said earlier. Her flat, narrow, and shrill voice cut the people around her like a razor blade.

Quietly Ch'ang-an was coming downstairs, her black embroidered shoes and white silk stockings pausing on the staircase yellowed with sunlight. After a while, she was again going up. Step by step, going up to the place where no light was visible.[8]

Unlike her old self some fifteen years ago, when she was still capable of genuine anger over Chi-tsê's last visit, Ch'i-ch'iao is now the supreme actor, casually demolishing Ch'ang-an's marital chances with a lie. At the complete success of her strategy she evinces no guilt or pleasure because, in the degree she has successfully stamped out normal human impulses in herself and in those around her, she has ceased to be human. In the haunting image of a diminutive, old woman with a blurred face, as well as in her subsequent conversation at the dinner table, complete moral degradation is registered.

Yet in surveying the desolation of her triumph in the small hours of the night, might not Ch'i-ch'iao still feel a flicker of self-pity, a sorrow and regret over her wasted years? With dramatic propriety Eileen Chang concludes her story with a reverie that lays bare the ruin of Ch'i-ch'iao's whole life:

She was lying flat on her opium couch, in a state between sleep and wakefulness. For thirty years now she had been wearing the golden cangue. With the heavy corners of that cangue she had killed several people; those who survived were only half alive. She knew that her son and daughter hated her to the death, that the relatives on her husband's side hated her and that her own kinsfolk also hated her. She felt for the green-jade bracelet on her wrist and slowly pushed it up her thin-as-straw arm until it reached the armpit. Even she herself couldn't believe that in her prime she had had round and full arms. Even during the first few years of her marriage she could barely squeeze a handkerchief of imported crepe inside her bracelet. As a maiden of eighteen or nineteen, she would roll high the lavishly laced sleeves of her blue linen blouse, revealing a pair of snow-white arms, and go to the streets to buy groceries. Among those who liked her were the butcher at the meat store; the sworn brothers of her elder brother, Ting Yü-ken and Chang Shao-ch'üan; and also the son of Tailor Shen. To say that they liked her perhaps only means that they liked to fool around with her; but if she had chosen one of these, it was very likely that her man would have shown her some real love as years went by and children were born. Ch'i-ch'iao adjusted the position of the small, foreign-style pillow with curved fringes under her head and rubbed her face against it. On her other cheek a teardrop stayed on until it dried by itself: she was too tired to brush it away.[9]

By virtue of its powerful symbolism and concrete evocation of two states of being, this passage stands as a supreme example of novelistic intelligence and skill. Ch'i-ch'iao is presented as she is, a shriveled old woman lying on her opium couch, and as she once was, a carefree girl with plump bare arms walking down the streets and joking with her admirers. And this dramatic contrast comes about through her contemplation of her green-jade bracelet. Once the perfect complement of her round and youthful arm, it now loosely encircles the withered flesh only to remind its wearer of her wasted life, her irrevocable innocence. Surely not even the fly hovering over the dead body of Nastasya in *The Idiot* is a more ironic or tragic symbol of mortality. As Ch'i-ch'iao pushes the bracelet all the way up to her armpit, the reader experiences a shivering sensation of terror which only the most moving passages in literature can generate.

In *The Golden Cangue* Eileen Chang has drawn the complete portrait of a woman situated in a particular civilization. A brash young woman of lower social station, thrown against her will amid the proprieties and vices of the official class, ends only as its most corrupt representative. Her warped life, her peculiar cruelty and meanness, cannot be explained except in terms of the society in which she moves. But to say merely that Ch'i-ch'iao is the product of her environment, just as to say that she is the victim of her evil passions, is to give a grossly inadequate account of the tragedy. True, Eileen Chang has evinced an unerring knowledge of the manners and mores of the decadent upper class throughout the story and has studied the heroine's life in terms of an unflinching psychological realism; but what elevates this perception and this realism into the realm of tragedy is the personal emotion behind the creation, the attitude of mingled fascination and horror with which the author habitually contemplates her own childhood environment. In *The Golden Cangue* Eileen Chang has found a perfect fable to serve as the dramatic correlative of her emotion, and the result is an overpowering tragedy embodying an acute moral vision, uniquely her own.

In *The Golden Cangue* the clashes between Ch'i-ch'iao and Ch'ang-an are particularly memorable. Possibly because of her unhappy youth, Eileen Chang is especially drawn to troubled adolescents in a traditional Chinese household, with all its perverse manifestations of love and hatred. A Freudian emphasis is noticeable in several of her stories about a parent-child relationship, particularly "Jasmine Tea" and "The Heart Sutra." [10]

In "Jasmine Tea," a gripping tale suggestive of the case history of her weakling brother, Eileen Chang tackles a theme which has challenged many an important modern novelist: a young man in search of his real father. A physically underdeveloped youth of twenty, Nieh Ch'uan-ch'ing looks much older than his age. He attends a college in Hong Kong, having moved there from Shanghai, after the outbreak of the Sino-Japanese War, with his severe opium-smoking father and stepmother. Yen Tan-chu, an attractive classmate and daughter of the Chinese professor at the college, befriends him because he seems to her so aloof and shy, so unlike the average college boy. Ch'uan-ch'ing, however, is highly envious of her beauty and happiness and chafes under her attention.

Talking to her on the bus one afternoon, Ch'uan-ch'ing learns of her father's full name, Yen Tzu-yeh, which strikes him as being rather familiar. Upon reaching home, he is more than usually irritated with his father's and stepmother's conversation and he soon shuts himself up in his room to search his memory. He distinctly recalls that, as a young boy, he once clumsily tried to decipher the inscription on the flyleaf of a magazine: "To the lady scholar Pi-lo, for her unalloyed enjoyment. Presented by Yen Tzu-yeh." [11] Pi-lo was his mother's name.

As he rummages futilely for this old magazine, Ch'uan-ch'ing begins to read new meaning into the wistful face of his mother as it appears on her only extant photograph, which was taken before her wedding. He has little personal recollection of his mother because she died when he was only four, but piecing together the gossip he has heard at various times from the servants and his stepmother, he now perceives the tragic pattern of her life. As a private tutor at her home, Yen Tzu-yeh and she had fallen in love and he had formally asked for her hand in marriage. But his suit was rejected because his family, though well off, was of the commercial and not of the mandarin class, as hers was. Soon afterward Yen Tzu-yeh went abroad to study and Pi-lo was married into the Nieh family.

> Ch'uan-ch'ing did not dare even guess what Pi-lo's married life had been like. She had not been a bird in the cage. The caged bird, once the cage was open, could still fly away. She had been the bird sewn on a door-screen—a white bird encircled among embroidered golden clouds on a melancholy door-screen of purple brocade. As the months and years went by, her feathers became darkened, then mildewed, then moth-eaten.

When it was time for her to die, she died on the door-screen.

She was dead, she was finished, but what about Ch'uan-ch'ing? Why had he also to suffer? When Pi-lo was married into the Nieh family, she was quite aware of the sacrifice she was making. But when Ch'uan-ch'ing was born into the Nieh family, he was not given the right of choice. Only another bird was sewn onto the door-screen; even if he were beaten to death, he could not fly off that screen. Twenty years with his father had made him a mental cripple. Even if given his freedom, he could not fly away.

No escape! No escape! If there had been absolutely no alternative, it wouldn't have mattered. But now that he had pieced together all the items of hearsay and conjecture and made a story out of them, he for the first time realized that over twenty years ago, before he had been born, he had had the chance for escape. There had been the possibility of his mother marrying Yen Tzu-yeh. He could have been Yen Tzu-yeh's son, Yen Tan-chu's brother. Probably he would have been Yen Tan-chu. If there were he, there could not have been she.[12]

Ch'uan-ch'ing sits in the same class with Tan-chu for her father's course in Chinese literature. The more he worships her father, the more he hates her. The last day before Christmas vacation he is overwhelmed with confusion and finally reduced to tears as he stammers for an answer to Professor Yen's question. Tan-chu joins the class in first tittering, and then laughing at his expense. Angry over his effeminacy, Yen Tzu-yeh dismisses him from class.

That evening a formal Christmas dance is to be held on the campus. Ch'uan-ch'ing has to attend because his father has already bought the ticket for him. But instead of going to the dance he spends the evening pacing up and down the hill upon which the college is located. When the dance is about to end, he walks toward the campus and meets with Tan-chu and her friends. Tan-chu asks him to escort her home. In the cold and wintry night she is particularly beautiful as she apologizes for her father's rude behavior.

What follows should be quoted in full. As Ch'uan-ch'ing walks downhill with Tan-chu, he unleashes all his pent-up fury and behaves in a cruel manner reminiscent of the hero of Dostoevsky's *Notes from the Underground* as he repudiates the loving and kind prostitute Liza. Ch'uan-ch'ing does not want Tan-chu's kind of sympathy, nor does he want her kind of normal and wholesome love if she is willing to grant him that. Torn between hate and jealousy, he wants revenge, a totally unreasoned kind of revenge for her arrogating the father that should have been his and depriving him of his due happiness. Or failing that, he wants the kind of love that would mean the abolition of his name and past history and his complete surrender at the feet of his beloved. Tan-chu's alternate teasing and sympathy finally prompt Ch'uan-ch'ing to blurt out a startling confession: "If you are in love with someone else, to him you will be merely his sweetheart. But to me, you are not only a sweetheart; you are a creator, a father and mother, a new environment, a new heaven and earth. You are the past and the future. You are god." [13]

Stunned but nonetheless flattered by this incomprehensible declaration of love, Tan-chu tries to be of comfort and help to him, which only exasperates him further. As he walks rapidly along the path downhill, she tries to overtake him:

> His selfishness, his rudeness, his perversity she could now forgive because he loved her. Even such an eccentric person was in love with her—that satisfied her vanity. Tan-chu was a good woman, but after all a woman.
>
> He had gone a long distance, but she finally overtook him. She had shouted all the way, "Ch'uan-ch'ing! Wait for me, wait for me!" But Ch'uan-ch'ing had pretended not to hear. Now that she was nearing him, she was for

the moment so confused that she didn't know where to begin. Panting hard, she said, "Tell me all . . . tell me all . . ." Ch'uan-ch'ing forced these words out of his clenched teeth: "I'll tell you. I want you to die. If there were you, there shouldn't be me. If there were I, there shouldn't be you. Understand?"

He clasped tightly both of her shoulders with one arm, and with the other hand he pushed her head down so hard that it seemed as though he wanted to shove it back into her neck. She should have never been born into this world; he wanted her to leave it now. He didn't know how he had got hold of his brutal strength, but his hands and feet were still rather clumsy. She didn't cry out, but struggling, they both rolled down several steps along the path. As soon as he got up, Ch'uan-ch'ing kicked away at the prostrate woman and uttered at the same time a volley of invectives. He talked so fast that even he couldn't follow well what he was saying. Probably something like this: "You took it for granted I am a softy, and so you dare stay alone with me in the hill at the middle of the night . . . I suppose if somebody else were in my place, you wouldn't be quite so sure. You took it for granted that I won't kiss you, beat you, or kill you, isn't that right? Nieh Ch'uan-ch'ing—he won't hurt me! 'Don't worry, Ch'uan-ch'ing will see me home!' . . . You just took me for granted!"

She uttered a soft moan after the first kick and then there was no more sound from her. He couldn't help kicking her savagely a few times more for fear that she might be still alive, but to continue kicking he was afraid. He kicked until his legs became weak and numb. Under the pressure of double fear he finally left her and ran down the hill. He ran as if he were in a nightmare; his feet scarcely touched ground as if sustained on cloud and mist; he only saw flight after flight of the stone path gleaming and dancing under moonlight before his eyes.

Having run a long distance, he suddenly stopped. In the dark hill there was not a single soul except him and Tan-chu. There was a distance of seventy or eighty yards between them now, but he could vaguely hear her spasmodic and difficult breathing. In that second his and her heart were in communion. He knew she didn't die. But so what? Could he still have the courage to go back and finish her?

He stood quietly for two or three seconds, but to him it seemed like two or three hours. He again started to run. This time he didn't stop until he had reached the thoroughfare at the foot of the hill, where there was still traffic.

His home was very cold; the white plastered walls had turned blue as if frozen. There was no stove in Ch'uan-ch'ing's room and the cold air pinched his nose. But the windows weren't open; they had remained shut for so long that the room smelled of dust and hair grease.

Ch'uan-ch'ing prostrated himself on the bed. He overheard his father talking to his stepmother in the next room: "This child is getting wild. Returning from the dance at this late hour!" His stepmother said, "It's about time we gave him a wife."

Tears coursed down Ch'uan-ch'ing's face. His mouth twitched slightly as if he wished to smile but couldn't. His face was frozen as if under an ice mask. His body, too, was frozen inside an ice shell.

Tan-chu didn't die. When school opened two days later, he would still have to face her. He couldn't escape.[14]

The story ends here. In his violent abuse of the girl Ch'uan-ch'ing lays bare the ruin of his life. In his quest for self-identity, in his impotent rage against home and father, and in his envy and detestation of bourgeois happiness the morose and perverse hero is reminiscent of such familiar adolescent heroes of modern Western fiction as Tonio Kröger and Stephen Dedalus. But he is much sicker because the forces binding him are more inexorable. Eileen Chang has placed her hero against a peculiar Chinese decadence. The characteristically Chinese symbol of an embroidered bird mildewing and moth-eaten on a door-screen clinches the difference: with all his morbidity, the arrogant Stephen Dedalus thinks of himself as a man with wings who can fly away at will. Carrying the cross of his deceased mother, Ch'uan-ch'ing immerses himself in self-pity and strives for no liberation. Even his final outburst of violent energy only reveals the abject stance of his soul as it desperately attempts to recover self-importance. Later, as he lies frozen in bed, he is resigned to the fact that his father and stepmother are already plotting his future for him. "He couldn't escape."

In "Jasmine Tea" as in *The Golden Cangue*, Eileen Chang is primarily a writer of tragic insight. Actually, in the bulk of her short fiction, she is more apparently drawn to the vulgarities and ironies of everyday life, the compromises one makes in order to preserve sanity and stave off the pressure of reality. By virtue of her logical consistency Ch'i-ch'iao is almost a unique character in the author's world. Most of her other characters make puny efforts to steer a middle path between romance and tragedy. If their world is still sad, it is not only because life allows so few unalloyed joys, but because the very process of adjustment implies cowardice and disillusion.

In the story "Blockade," an accountant strikes up an acquaintance with a college instructor in the halted trolley—in occupied Shanghai the Japanese police frequently would shut off sections of the city for their own convenience, and all vehicles in the area would have to stop—and confides in her that he is a very unhappy family man with a stupid wife and many children to support. For a moment the college instructor expects some romantic excitement to change the tenor of her hitherto uneventful life. But after the blockade is lifted, the accountant leaves her promptly and mixes himself in the standing crowd. "The lights were again on in the trolley, and she spied him sitting in his old seat some distance away. She was shocked—so he hadn't left the car after all. She knew what he meant by this act: all that took place during the period of blockade should be consigned to oblivion. The whole city of Shanghai had dozed away, had had a preposterous dream." [15]

In "Love in a Fallen City," a long story of courtship told with consummate skill, a wealthy playboy and a divorcée from an old-fashioned home find each other indispensable under the trial of war and settle down to married life. "He is only a selfish man and she is only a selfish woman. In times of war and trouble the egoist has no place in the sun, but there is always a place for a commonplace married couple." [16] Typically, Miss Chang places the couple at the end in a state of genuine if subdued happiness. True affection no matter how arrived at is infinitely to be preferred to dreams impossible of fulfillment: it is only childishness to chafe under the biological and social limitations of life.

Eileen Chang evinces, then, an infinite tolerance for foibles and pretenses, a habit of sympathy catholic in its range and untouched by any degree of moral puritanism. In many good satirists one detects a note of savagery stemming from their abhorrence of their fellow men; with the majority of modern Chinese writers, on the other hand, satire is often a form of hysteria, an indulgence in spite and hatred in the absence of firsthand moral observation. Miss Chang does not profess high-minded ideals, but this does not mean that her moral passion is in any way less intense than that of the professed didacticist. On the contrary, her registration of the inescapable pettiness and sadness of human endeavor is nearly always morally disturbing precisely because, given the human condition, she refrains from overt gestures of indignation or protest. A profound pessimist, she can afford at the same time to be a gay satirist, a good-natured critic of urban manners.

As with Jane Austen, her uncynical detachment and comic brilliance are possible only because of her serious and tragic view of life.

However, few of Eileen Chang's stories are unalloyed comedy: she has neither that intellectual contempt for humanity nor that zestful fondness for idiosyncrasy which distinguishes the heartier laughter of Ch'ien Chung-shu. Only in her contemplation of the sexual mores of city-bred youth—in such stories as "Happy Matrimony," "Glazed Tiles," and, more recently, "Stale Mates" [17]—does she cultivate a lighter mode. But even there her characteristic preoccupation is with the larger ironies implicit in the recalcitrance of the human animal to comply with social habit or convention. Brilliant studies of a transitional generation, these matrimonial tales are nevertheless primarily essays in vanity—in the unpredictable manifestations of pride or malice in the most unlikely circumstances.

With Eileen Chang, then, satire is not an exhortation to good conduct but an adjunct to tragic understanding. It thrives on the spectacle of human folly, but at the same time it tolerates and even honors the normal impulse to achieve some measure of happiness, respectability, and success. Nearly always satire means an enrichment of the Chekhovian drama. In such stories as "Lingering Love," "Waiting," and "Indian Summer: A-hsiao's Autumnal Lament," the blending of delicate satire and subdued pathos is especially felicitous in evoking a sense of loneliness and frustration. The last-named story chronicles a typical day of a maidservant in the employ of a foreign resident in Shanghai. Eileen Chang ably contrasts A-hsiao's moral fastidiousness and strong attachment to her family with the coarse sensibility and heartless philandering of her stingy master, and achieves a haunting portrait of an unspoiled country woman with all her pride and helpless servitude.

The postwar period in Shanghai saw the return from the interior of the Communist and leftist writers, who lost no time in re-orientating literary publication to suit their aims. The hireling writers who had sung the praises of Japan were now either imprisoned or effectively silenced. While Eileen Chang had rigorously eschewed politics, her imprudence in having published her writings during the occupation was not something to be easily condoned by the writers in power. She was apparently not punished, but finding the new literary climate positively hostile, she abstained from writing more fiction. She became a screen playwright and wrote the scripts for some of the better postwar movies.

Little is known of her life from the fall of Shanghai in 1949 to her arrival in Hong Kong in 1952. Unlike such well-known anti-Communist writers as Shen Ts'ung-wen and Chu Kuang-ch'ien, she was apparently not molested, because she was not taken seriously as a reactionary influence. Subject to regimentation but enjoying the advantages of relative anonymity, she observed at first hand Communist life in the cities and villages and stored away impressions that would enlarge her tragic view of the Chinese people. She also examined a good quantity of magazines, plays, and movies to enable her to see the discrepancies between her understanding of the truth and the official lie.

Since her escape to Hong Kong, Eileen Chang has turned out two novels: *The Rice-sprout Song*—published as a book in July 1954 following its serialization in the weekly *The World Today*—and *Love in Redland,* published three months later and subsequently translated by the author into English as *Naked Earth.* As novels about Communism, both are truly impressive performances in that they have retained in admirable balance the dual concern of the traditional novel with both society and the self: they neither overstate in propagandist terms nor sacrifice ordinary reality for the kind of ideological debate that is a staple in Western anti-Communist fiction. Novelists like Koestler and Orwell began as Communist intellectuals; in their subsequent anti-Communist fables they were principally concerned with the dialectic of evil and, for all their brilliance, could not improve upon the insights embodied in the allegory of the Grand Inquisitor. Miss Chang, on the contrary, was no student of Communism; it caught her by surprise. In her novels, therefore, she is able to present the Communist horror in humane rather than dialectical terms, to focus her attention on ordinary humanity as it struggles helplessly to maintain its loyalties and affections under the crushing weight of an alien system.

In keeping with its rural subject matter, *The Rice-sprout Song* is much sparer in style than the author's earlier fiction. Its sentences and paragraphs are shorter, its imagery is less lavish, and in general traditional Chinese narrative devices are discarded in conformity with a Western mode of story-telling. But it would be a mistake to conclude that Miss Chang has chosen to repudiate her earlier achievement and embark upon a new path. On the contrary, the more chastened style of the novel retains the essential metaphorical strength of her language, and a striking imagery and symbolism are in evidence here as in the best of the *Romances*. The vision and sensibility have remained unchanged: they have only become more sharpened in the contemplation of a more urgent subject. Even the historical awareness has remained intact: the novel studies Communism primarily in terms of its impingement upon traditional values and manners. The result is an unforgettable picture of outraged humanity.

The Rice-sprout Song tells of a simple peasant family in a village near Shanghai. In the early section of the novel the hero, a so-called model farmer named Gold Root, has just married his sister Gold Flower to a farmer at a neighboring village and is now expecting the return of his wife from the big city. Moon Scent has been for the past three years a maid-servant in Shanghai and consequently has had no personal knowledge of the vast changes that have taken place in the village under Communism. But immediately upon her return she suspects the worst, even though her elder relatives,

Big Uncle and Aunt T'an, reassure her with their jocular talk about Communist benevolence and her husband proudly un-rolls before her the title deed to his land. Deeply attached to him and their little daughter Beckon, Moon Scent never-theless regrets having returned home and feels that she could contribute more to the support of her family by staying in Shanghai. For one thing, Beckon is perpetually hungry, and for another, within a short time of her return a stream of visitors has come to her to borrow money. She notices further that her husband secretly suspects that she has given her sav-ings to her destitute and aged mother. On her first day home, while they are having a meal of thicker-than-usual gruel, Comrade Wong, the local Communist officer, suddenly pays them a visit and remarks on their food. Gold Root becomes consequently greatly upset and angry. All these little events indicate to Moon Scent the great poverty and tension under which the village now cowers. Life goes on at a tolerable rate for a while, however. A literary cadre, Comrade Ku, is as-signed to live in the village; he, too, suffers from the pangs of hunger.

As the Chinese New Year draws near, the unremitting hunger and oppression begin to tell on every villager. Big Aunt T'an, tearing off her mask of cheerful obedience, is the first to break down. Comrade Wong, meanwhile, goes pa-tiently from hut to hut to persuade each family to donate half a pig and forty catties of New Year cakes, or their equivalent in money, for the relief and comfort of the families of Com-munist soldiers. Gold Root refuses to contribute his share because he cannot afford to; he becomes maddened with anger when Moon Scent finally produces her savings to pla-cate Comrade Wong. On the day when the donations are being collected, the more spirited villagers, Gold Root among them, ask Comrade Wong for a loan to tide them over the new year. On being refused, they attempt to rob the granary guarded by the militia. In the ensuing riot, Beckon is tram-pled to death and Gold Root severely wounded.

Moon Scent helps Gold Root to a nearby bamboo grove. In desperation she seeks succor from Gold Flower, whom her brother loves deeply. But even she dare not harbor a dying criminal. Moon Scent returns to the grove only to find her husband no longer at the spot where she has placed him: she correctly guesses that, in his desire to see her escape into safety, he has drowned himself in the nearby river.[18] Moon Scent, however, returns that night to her village to set fire to the granary. She dies in the conflagration, but the fire is soon quenched. Not too long after, celebrations are again in order as the gift-bearing villagers dance to the rhythm of the Rice-sprout Song on their way to the soldiers' families.

As one reads the novel—the preceding synopsis has been given to facilitate discussion—one is astonished that, while tragically aware of the evil of Communism, the author is almost incapable of malice. Nearly all the characters, including Comrade Wong, are rooted in a piety characteristic of a civilization molded upon the teachings of the sages: Comrade Ku alone is subject to some caricature, because, as a city intellectual, he has lost touch with traditional culture and behaves mainly in obedience to the dictates of hunger, concupiscence, and fear. Miss Chang, who has drawn in A-hsiao a peasant character of compelling interest, extends her sure touch to half a dozen portraits of memorable villagers. By primarily attending to their feelings and manners, she restores to them a sense of humanity missing in works designed to ennoble or sentimentalize them, as in nearly all Communist peasant fiction. Her delineation of the deep affection between Gold Root and his sister is especially moving: it is an achievement worthy to stand beside George Eliot's *Mill on the Floss*. For her dowry Gold Root gives his sister a handsome standing mirror, one of the principal spoils of land reform allotted to him as a model farmer: for this gesture of generosity he is willing to incur the criticism of his relatives and the resentment of his wife. Much later in the novel, when Gold Flower comes to borrow money and is gently told off

419

by his wife, he recalls the childhood pleasures and privations he shared with his sister:

> Gold Root listened and said nothing. He could not expect his wife to part with what little was left of her savings. But his bowels turned with anguish when he thought of the time when he and his sister were children together. Whenever he caught a good cricket he gave it to her. And on the third of the third moon when the townfolk came out to the country to visit their ancestral graves, he ran from grave to grave and hovered around waiting for the give-away rice-flour balls. He was very good at collecting those cakes so that there was always plenty for both of them.
>
> In summer he caught grasshoppers in the fields, tied them up with a blade of grass, and asked his mother to fry them in oil, the whole string of them, till they were half-burned and crispy and tasty.
>
> They had always been poor. He remembered lying in bed in the morning when his mother was taking rice out of the great earthen jar, and he could hear the dipper scrape against the bottom of the jar. At that dreaded scratchy sound he felt a chilly, acidy sadness seep into his bones.
>
> And one day he knew there was nothing to eat in the house. As lunchtime approached he called out to his sister, "Come out and play, Sister Gold Flower." Gold Flower, being much younger than he, had no sense of time. They played and played in the fields. Then he heard his mother calling them, "Gold Root! Gold Flower! Come have your lunch!" He was astonished. They went home and he found she had boiled some beans which she had meant to keep for seeds. The beans were very nice. His mother sat watching them with a smile as they ate.
>
> Now he was fully grown and an owner of land, and

yet it seemed he was just as helpless as before against the force of circumstances. His sister came to him weeping and he had to send her away empty-handed.[19]

When Gold Flower stays for lunch during the same visit, Moon Scent serves "the same thin gruel as they had always, with some stringy wild vegetables floating in it." [20] She has to do this to strike home the fact that her family is as destitute as Gold Flower's. Yet this incident so disturbs the habitually hard-working Gold Root that he wishes to pawn his belongings and get drunk on the proceeds so as to live down his shame. The whole episode registers the exasperation of the human spirit as it submits to the dictates of necessity.

Toward the end of the novel, as Moon Scent implores Gold Flower to hide her wounded brother, the latter recalls her own childhood with a stab of pang: "Her brother himself would never have asked her to do a thing like that. He would understand. The memory of how good he had been to her suddenly flooded over her. And she remembered all that they had meant to each other throughout the years. She felt desolate, as if they were again left with nobody to turn to except each other." [21] But prudence dictates that she should not incriminate her husband and ruin her own future by harboring her brother: necessity precludes love. In the presence of Moon Scent, who has always been resentful of Gold Root's love for his sister and doubtful if she loves him to the same extent, Gold Flower's shamefaced attempts to justify her own cowardice and to refer the whole matter to her mother-in-law elicit the finest tragic irony in modern Chinese literature.

The Rice-sprout Song, then, is a tragic record of the trials of the human body and spirit under a brutal system. Sooner or later, every character has to face the crucial test as the reality around him becomes finally unendurable. Even to Comrade Wong, despite his methodical efficiency in carrying out the orders of his party, comes a moment of despair when his indiscriminate shooting of the peasants convinces him that "We have failed." This kindly and pathetic Communist, insofar as he is human, is at once bigger and smaller than the party. But with all his apparent paternal benevolence his humanity has withered in him since the disappearance of his wife many years ago; what remains is the ghost of a man blindly loyal to the party because he has no other loyalties to fall back on. With profound irony Eileen Chang extricates him from the slough of despond by having him reach the preposterous conclusion that enemy agents must have been responsible for the peasant uprising. It is the only conclusion possible for a man who hugs an illusion in order to maintain a semblance of life. In writing a screen play about an enemy agent attempting to blow up a dam, Comrade Ku, who is more of an opportunist, further reduces Comrade Wong's misinterpretation of this tragic uprising into a standard cliché.

The sense of outrage is present not only in the violation of the emotional integrity of the characters but in the altered texture of everyday village life when traditional behavior is perforce replaced. In chapters 3 and 4 Miss Chang expertly views the village through the eyes of Moon Scent, who, as a newcomer, ponders every departure from custom in the life around her. It has been the peasants' ancient privilege to vent their discontent over the weather, but now, it seems to her, under the benevolent rule of Chairman Mao, even the weather must be praised. Is this genuine gratitude or a hollow ritual? Moon Scent has no doubt in her mind as she goes on to discover further instances of shocking conformity.

Indeed, the whole novel is built upon a violent contrast between hollow ritual and painful reality, between the theatrical artificiality of the Communist regimen and its ultimate horror. The title itself underscores the Communist exploitation of an age-old folk dance for propaganda purposes, the degeneration of a genuine ritual into a government-sponsored mass activity. The peasants are fond of their old ritual: witness the single-minded devotion with which, even under the greatest mental strain, Gold Root prepares his New Year cakes: "With both hands Gold Root deftly kneaded a big white ball of rice flour, the size of a watermelon and burning hot. Bending over the table, he kept rolling it very fast, with a curious little smile on his lips and the intense concentration of one who was fashioning something out of burning rock at the beginning of the world." [22] The newfangled Communist ways are to the peasants a silly ritual at best, tedious and meaningless, amusing at times perhaps, but only tolerated to avoid trouble. The songs and slogans, the classes and meetings, and the dance of the Rice-sprout Song (*yang-ko*)—all this is so much alien theater. But this theater ceases to be a game when bloodshed and fighting, which properly belong to the stage, become an unavoidable part of village life. During the riot, as Moon Scent hurries toward the temple, the headquarters of Comrade Wong, in search of her husband and child, she is confronted with an appalling vision: "But suddenly a militiaman dashed out of the eastern wing with an arm outstretched, holding an archaic lance, the tuft of red hair under the blade fluffed out by the wind. It was a dream-like, fantastic sight hauled down off the stage and thrust into the noonday sun. Moon Scent stood rooted to the spot while he charged past her and disappeared through the gate." [23] This note of frightening reality in the guise of theatrical unreality is ably maintained in the closing scene. As old people like the T'ans wriggle their way to join the thinned ranks of the procession, the yang-ko dance becomes virtually a medieval tableau of the *danse macabre*. The glaring rouge on the emaciated cheeks of the regular troupe and the muffled clang of the gongs and cymbals under an immense sky accentuate the bleak desolation.

In the same manner that she depicts Communist life in terms of the theater, Eileen Chang regularly visualizes her bleak village as an eerie other world, a nightmare, a ghost-haunted landscape. Fragments of Chinese mythology and familiar scenes from popular ghost stories are superimposed upon a hard world of famine and death. In describing a village street in the very first two pages of the novel, she invests the expected squalor and desolation with a touch of the theatrical and eerie:

> On the other side of the pebble-paved street the ground dropped away into a deep ravine. A stone parapet ran the whole length of the road. A woman came out of one of the shops with a red enamel basin full of dirty water, crossed the street, and dashed the water over the parapet. The action was somehow shocking, like pouring slops off the end of the world.
>
> Almost every shop was presided over by a thin, fierce-looking dark yellow woman with shoulder-length straight hair and a knitted cap of mauve wool pulled down square over the eyebrows, a big peacock-blue pompon sticking out at the left ear. It was difficult to tell where the fashion had originated. It bore a strong and disturbing resemblance to the headgear of highwaymen in Chinese operas . . .
>
> Another shop displayed tidy stacks of coarse yellow toilet paper. In a glass showcase standing near the door there were tooth pastes and bags of tooth powder, all with colored photographs of Chinese film stars on them. The pictures of those charmers smiling brightly into the empty street somehow added to the feeling of desolation.[24]

Such touches are nearly always present in the key descriptive passages in the novels.

Toward the end of the novel, especially, the decrepit temple, the headquarters of Comrade Wong, has emerged as an infernal court. The night following the riot, Comrade Ku is temporarily living at the temple and he listens with riveted attention to the shrieks of peasants under torture issuing from the main court:

This could not be true, Ku thought. It was like a traveler in one of those ghost stories taking shelter in the porches of a temple at night and being awakened by the sound of gods holding court over the dead. Peeking at the brightly lit scene, the man in the story recognized a dead relative undergoing cruel tortures. He screamed. And everything went black and all was quiet in the temple.[25]

That same night the T'ans cannot sleep because the door of Gold Root's hut has been left open and it slams in the wind.

> The door banged on with shattering savagery.
> Big Aunt lay awake for a long time listening to it. Then she whispered to her husband, "I do not think it is the wind. It sounds like those two coming back."
> "Don't talk nonsense!" said Big Uncle, who was thinking the same.
> Then Big Aunt realized with a shock that she had spoken of those two as if they were already ghosts. They might still be alive and it would bring them bad luck like a curse. In her contrition she thought of all their goodness, and their youth. And her tears fell onto her hard, flat old pillow of blue cloth stuffed with the white plumes of reeds.[26]

The supernatural machinery is no mere device for enhancing terror. Miss Chang uses it primarily as a portion of the ancient and timeless China, readily comprehensible to the imagination of the peasants, for effective contrast and comparison with the inhuman world of Communism. Thus Gold Root remembers Moon Scent on her wedding night as "some obscure goddess in a broken-down little temple. He remembered seeing an idol like that sitting daintily behind the tattered and begrimed yellow curtains in a neglected shrine." [27] In his youth Comrade Wong has courted his wife at another old temple used by Communists as their headquarters: "invariably she came at night and left at dawn, like a ghost mistress in those old stories." [28] And during these nocturnal meetings, "an old nun who stayed on was 'doing her lessons' at the back of the temple, beating a wooden *mu yu*. It went on and on, an even flow of 'toc toc toc toc,' like water dripping from an ancient water clock, marking time for a dead world." [29] Despite its eerie setting, this romance is infinitely more real to Comrade Wong than his latter-day work at the village; it is the only real thing he has ever possessed.

It is a tribute to her creative intelligence that Miss Chang refuses to be bound by mere contemporaneity. Whereas other novelists, in writing about Communist China, will be solely engrossed in the atrocities perpetrated by the regime, she sees steadily before her eyes the culture of a whole nation. *The Rice-sprout Song*, though a short novel, actually incorporates several worlds. Properly receiving major attention is the world of simple villagers whose loves and loyalties and whose very survival are tested by the alien power of Communism. The Communist world itself is represented by two imperfect, because fallible and human, agents, Wong and Ku, but its brutal power and insidious logic are triumphantly operative in the crushing of the abortive uprising, and in the rationalizations of these two henchmen as they make cowardly reconciliation of reality with theory. But Communism affects not only the economic and moral but also the imaginative life of the people. With a metaphorical power rarely observed in other Chinese novelists, Miss Chang therefore imposes upon the bleak setting of her village the worlds of fantasy and the theater, beloved alike by the literati and peasants. It is because, in the perspective of the humane tradition, Communism is so monstrously unreal, so much of an evil to be exorcised, that fables and myths enjoy such an ironic relevance in the scheme of the novel. Gods and ghosts in the Chinese tradition are mostly beneficent, and unlike Comrade

Wong torturing innocent peasants, even the infernal judges mete out punishments in a most scrupulous fashion. But Communism exceeds in cruelty the most sanguinary melodrama, confirms the worst fears about Hell. In investing the Communist world with an eerie kind of unreality so as to render with full justice the kind of reality insupportable to the human imagination, Eileen Chang has fashioned not merely a tale of suffering but a tragedy instinct with all the human aspirations and dreams against which Communism has always marshaled all its diabolic resources.

More ambitious in scope, *Love in Redland* falls short of the formal perfection of *The Rice-sprout Song* mainly because it attempts the almost possible: to render with full justice the manifold aspects of Communist tyranny. At times the author falls into documentary naiveté in her compulsive eagerness to tell the world what she has seen and heard in Communist China; none of this information is irrelevant to the novel, but to give it proper dramatic attention the novel would need to be much longer than its 280 pages. There is, consequently, especially in the middle portion of the work, an unwarrantably large amount of exposition. But despite these faults there is no doubt about the compassionate quality of the novel, the purity of its language, and the metaphorical richness of its imagery: especially in its first hundred pages, the grim drama of land reform set in a barren and spectral landscape is fully as memorable and profound as anything in *The Rice-sprout Song*.

Following the checkered fortunes of her hero Liu Ch'üan, Eileen Chang tells of the momentous events in the early years of the Communist regime, from the initial land reform through the Three-anti Drive to the Korean Armistice. All these events exemplify the theme of betrayal: the Communist betrayal of the peasant population, of the eagerly cooperative students and intellectuals, of the rank and file of the party faithfuls. Properly "brainwashed," Liu Ch'üan and a group of fellow graduates from Peking colleges are assigned to participate in land-reform work in a Northern village under the guidance of a cynical party functionary. The subsequent brutal mutilation and killing of the middle farmers (because there are no landlords to speak of in that village) constitute a Communist betrayal of the peasants as well as the students, who have hoped to see the accomplishment of genuine land reform. Completely disillusioned, Liu Ch'üan falls in love with Huang Chüan, a co-worker. Impotent to succor the helpless around him and redeem the miscarriage of justice, he snatches brief moments of mutual solace in her company, to sustain his sanity in a world which, to quote Arnold, "hath really neither joy, nor love, nor light/ Nor certitude, nor peace, nor help for pain." Perhaps seldom in the chronicle of fiction has the melancholy mood of "Dover Beach" been so tragically heightened as in this section of the novel.

After his land-reform stint, Liu Ch'üan is assigned to Shanghai to serve as a propagandist for the Resist America–Aid Korea Drive. Here he sees many types of once-idealistic Communists who have lost their zeal: Ko Shan, a tubercular nymphomaniac vainly seeking excitement to drug the painful knowledge of having given her youth and health to the wrong cause; Chao Ch'u and Ts'ui P'ing, typical bourgeois officials who were once the Damon and Pythias of the Red Army performing legendary feats to save each other's lives in the far leaner years of Communist struggle. But now, when the Three-anti Drive has made every Communist official of medium rank fearful for his security and life, Ts'ui P'ing has little compunction in sending his friend to his death in order to establish his own clean record. In response to the Three-anti Drive, Chao Ch'u has somewhat naively written an unsigned letter exposing Ch'en I, the mayor of Shanghai; Ts'ui P'ing gets hold of this letter and turns it in to the mayor. He reasons as follows:

For the Three-anti Drive he didn't have any parents or brothers to inform against, but at least he could afford to offer his devoted friend as a noble sacrifice.

This could probably tide him over the Three-anti ordeal, he thought, and guarantee his promotion.

Of course, his real objective was not this. Yesterday he had to turn in that letter to Ch'en I out of sheer necessity. He had thought of concealing it, but how could a document of this nature be concealed? When its contents gradually leaked out, everybody, knowing his friendship with Chao Ch'u, would impute they were conspirators, and they both would perish.

He was not afraid of death, he told himself. To fall in the battlefield would be honorable, but to fall in the Three-anti campaign would be to negate one's total revolutionary record.

Paradoxically, he wished he could once more save Chao Ch'u's life under enemy fire so as to establish his innocence.[30]

This personal betrayal, of course, is the logical extension of the betrayal of the rank and file by the Communist leadership, which imposes upon them the necessity of treachery.

Liu Ch'üan himself is soon implicated in Chao Ch'u's crime and sent to prison to await execution. Here Eileen Chang borrows, but completely reverses, the plot of *Measure for Measure* to underscore the persistence of love and loyalty in an age of perfidy. Huang Chüan appeals to a powerful bureaucrat for help; he agrees only on the condition that she lose her chastity to become his mistress. She consents to this arrangement, and then in one of the most moving scenes in the book, she sees Liu Ch'üan once more in prison and leaves him forever.

After he has regained his freedom, Liu Ch'üan immediately volunteers for the Korean front so as to numb his pain in the embrace of death. Lying wounded for days in a deserted ditch, he finally receives succor from a fellow soldier Yeh Ching-k'uei, whose career parallels his in the respect that they both have suffered unwarranted mistrust and punishment in the hands of the Communists in spite of their ardor and devotion. The knowledge that Communism has betrayed them both makes them fast friends, especially during the months when they are both interned in the UN compound for prisoners of war. Later, they are to be repatriated, and Yeh Ching-k'uei naturally chooses Taiwan for his destination. But Liu Ch'üan decides to go back to the mainland; he knows his action will grievously disappoint his friend and he is sorry he cannot possibly acquit himself in the latter's eyes:

> Yeh Ching-k'uei was his last friend on earth. To lose such a friend made him sad, but he had lost so many things in life that it didn't matter to harden his heart to accept this final loss.
>
> He wanted to go back to the mainland, to leave his fellow prisoners of war here and to return among the other captives. So long as there was a person like him in their midst, the Communist party could never feel secure.
>
> He didn't expect to see Huang Chüan again, but she had exchanged her happiness for his life and he felt duty-bound to make good use of his life. He couldn't think of any better use for his life.[31]

To merely rehearse the plot may give one the impression that *Love in Redland* is a "corny" novel with its continual emphasis on love, friendship, and sacrifice. But whatever its other faults, the novel is never sentimental. Both heroism and villainy are understated by virtue of the author's habitual employment of irony (as in Ts'ui P'ing's self-justification for his treachery). Liu Ch'üan and Huang Chüan are average human beings with their usual share of fear and cowardice; their actions attain nobility only in the extremely cruel and cynical context of Communism. It is only because Communism is so contemptuous of human lives and disdainful of human feelings that, by default, those who have been lucky enough to retain their normal sensibility appear heroic in stature. Everywhere Miss Chang emphasizes the fact that the only successful Communists are those who have accepted the fact of Communist betrayal and accordingly surrendered their own humanity. Her paradoxical observation that so many Communist officials are corruptly bourgeois in their outlook and behavior should actually cause no surprise: with the surrender of their humanity they can only parade their petty achievements in sexual conquest, material comfort, and personal power as visible symbols of their distinction. There has been the birth of a new class dedicated to the enslavement of the people, but there has been no revolution.

After the detailed critique of *The Rice-sprout Song*, it will be perhaps pointless to examine the imagery of *Love in Redland*, which is often arrestingly beautiful and continues to exhibit an eerie quality. There is perhaps one difference. Whereas in the earlier novel the landscape is a bleak confirmation of human cruelty, the nature imagery in the latter as often mocks that cruelty. The sun and moon shine on regardless of what crimes are being perpetrated on earth: they become fit symbols of normal humanity in the degree the earthlings have relinquished their human attributes. Liu Ch'üan and Huang Chüan appear constantly surprised at the serene beauty of nature, as if, because of their guilty involvement in Communist crimes, they were no longer its fit spectators. And this capability for astonishment confirms the hopeful note of the novel that humanity cannot be completely dehumanized, that the hero's voluntary return to the mainland at the end is not a futile gesture of despair but a necessary act of self-sacrifice. One could fittingly apply the epigraph for *The Brothers Karamazov* to Eileen Chang's novel:

> Verily, verily, I say unto you, Except a corn of wheat fall into the ground and die, it abideth alone: but if it die, it bringeth forth much fruit.

CHAPTER 16

Ch'ien Chung-shu

CH'IEN CHUNG-SHU'S wit and learning had long daz-
zled his friends and students before the publication of *The
Besieged City* called public attention to his importance as a
novelist. His English essays in *T'ien Hsia Monthly* and in
Philobiblon, a postwar quarterly review of Chinese publications, may also have impressed Western sinologists for some
time.[1] Son of the noted historian and scholar Ch'ien Chi-po,
Ch'ien Chung-shu was reared in the rigorous tradition of Chinese scholarship. Gifted with a prodigious memory, he mastered this discipline at an early age and went on to explore
Western culture and literature with an aptitude and zest
unequaled among his Chinese contemporaries. A few years
after his graduation from the Western Languages Department
of Tsing Hua University, he went with his wife, Miss Yang
Chiang (later, also a noted playwright and story-writer), to
study for the B. Litt. degree at Oxford University on a Boxer
Indemnity Scholarship.[2] He returned to China in 1937, a
proficient scholar in English as well as Latin, French, German, and Italian literature. He taught for a short period at
the Southwest Associated University in Kunming and then
returned to Shanghai for the remainder of the war period to

teach at a girls' college and to devote himself to writing.

While still a student at Tsing Hua, Ch'ien Chung-shu had contributed a number of essays to *Crescent Moon;* later in England he wrote a few more for *Wen-hsüeh Tsa-chih* and other journals. In 1941 these essays were published under the title *On the Margin of Life.* From a brilliant conversationalist, they represent only a small fraction of that wit and erudition which habitually delighted and overawed his circle of learned friends. In 1948 Ch'ien Chung-shu published another sampling of his learning, called *On the Art of Poetry.* Composed in an elegant wen-yen style, this book is a minute study in the style and diction of dozens of Chinese poets within the traditional framework of poetic criticism. Despite its sure taste, its astounding range, and the impressive wealth of its references to Western poetics from Plato to the Abbé Bremond, it fails to lay the groundwork for a much-needed revaluation of Chinese poetry.

When the Communists overran China, therefore, Ch'ien Chung-shu's scholarly publications had barely begun to tap his erudition. Contemptuous of his fellow scholars, he had been much too proud to undertake sorely needed tasks of scholarship and criticism, which would appear to him rather elementary. And living under Communism, he could not for years publish any scholarly work of real consequence, even though both he and his wife, like many other Western-trained literary scholars whose services as professors and creative writers were no longer welcome, have been retained in the Literary Research Institute of the Academy of Sciences (the director of the Academy is Kuo Mo-jo). In 1958, however, Ch'ien Chung-shu did manage to publish an anthology, entitled *Selected Sung Poetry with Annotations.* The book could have been much better if the compiler had not been under the obligation to cite Mao Tse-tung as a literary authority in the preface and to include so many poems descriptive of the social conditions during the Sung dynasty. But the preface remains a masterpiece of critical analysis, and the

433

judicious and illuminating comments on the individual poets, little dictated by ideological considerations, prove beyond a doubt that Ch'ien Chung-shu remains the most sensitive and informed reader of Chinese poetry writing today.

Ch'ien Chung-shu will probably continue to make scholarly contributions under the Communists, but it is highly unlikely that he will write in a creative capacity again. This surely is a pity, for what little fiction he has published has already made literary history. In 1946 Ch'ien Chung-shu brought out a volume of stories called *Men, Beasts, Ghosts,* and the next year saw the publication of *The Besieged City,* following its serialization in *Literary Renaissance.* These two books, which represent painstaking work during the war years, are decidedly distinguished. *The Besieged City* especially is superior to any classical Chinese novel in the satiric tradition. It is a safe bet that future generations of Chinese readers will return to this book more frequently than to any other novel of the Republican period for its delightful portrayal of contemporary manners, its comic exuberance, and its tragic insight.

A measure of Ch'ien Chung-shu's distance from the popular writers of his time may be obtained from his satiric fantasy "Inspiration," one of the four stories in *Men, Beasts, Ghosts.* Its subject is the writing profession itself, and with the author's conversance with English poetry, one is not surprised that it owes an obvious debt to Dryden's *Mac Flecknoe,* Pope's *The Dunciad,* and Byron's *The Vision of Judgment.* The hero is a dunce, simply called the Writer because of his wide renown, who suddenly falls sick over his failure to receive the coveted Nobel Prize for Literature. Bitter and unhappy, he now lies helpless in bed, surrounded by a tearful throng of admirers. (One is reminded here of the homage the dying Lu Hsün receives; but the Writer seems more of a composite of Chiang Kuang-tz'u, Ts'ao Yü, and the early Pa Chin.) As the Writer dies, his soul is precipitated, under the sheer weight of his published works, into the Chinese Branch Office of Hell.

This office is presided over by a bearded Judge of apparently urbane manners, and for a while he and the Writer chat pleasantly. Soon, however, a crowd of indistinct shapes press upon the scene, crying faintly in unison, "Give my life back!" The Writer, at first startled, is immediately relieved to know that they are but characters from his novels and plays. He listens sympathetically as they continue airing their grievances: "We demand life from you. Your books depict us as dull and dead, completely lifeless. Our every gesture and speech are like the puppets'; we cannot be reckoned as living people. You have written about us but haven't given us life; so you ought to repay our lives." [3]

What follows is perhaps the happiest piece of criticism of the general run of contemporary Chinese fiction and drama. Ch'ien Chung-shu lets each character come up and accuse the Writer. In doing so, the siren who ruins every man she associates with, the old roué condemned to a life of unflagging libertinage among his concubines, the tough proletarian with always the same oaths on his lips, the young man who advocates the abolition of the family system, another who goes rhapsodic over mother love—they all reveal themselves as the stereotypes that they are. And since these stereotypes are so common, the satire becomes almost pure fun.

While the Writer is parrying his accusers, another figure, the ghost of a lately deceased cultural entrepreneur, emerges from the host of shades and makes a loud protest. He declares that his death is entirely due to that article by the Writer in honor of his fiftieth birthday: it is so fulsomely eulogistic that his life has been cut short as a consequence. This news startles the Writer into thinking. In anticipation of the Nobel Prize, he has just completed his autobiography; could it be that not the disappointment over his failure to receive the award but the writing about himself with his deadly pen, has dispatched him to Hell?

The Judge finally metes out due punishment for the Writer. A young author has been for three years waiting for inspiration to begin work on "an unprecedented piece of composite writing, a novel in five acts and ten scenes, employing the idiom of the familiar essay and table talk and the rhythm and form of modern poetry." [4] It is only fitting that the Writer should resume life as the hero of that future masterpiece so as to experience the limbo-like existence of so many of his own characters. The Writer is ordered to enter the brain of that young author.

Escorted back to earth, the Writer sees the young author engaged in fornication with his landlord's daughter as a desperate experiment to find inspiration. To avoid his unpleasant fate, the Writer enters the girl's ear and causes her to become pregnant.[5] The young author now has to marry her and give up his great novel. A boy is born in due time. "Up to now, we cannot guess whether this boy will become a writer when he grows up." [6]

In reading this delightful satiric fantasy, one notices Ch'ien Chung-shu's genuine affinity with the poets he has imitated. Like Dryden, Pope, and Byron, he shows in the story an aristocratic contempt for the dunces of his age who crowd the literary stage and set the standards of criticism. He is very much an Augustan, self-consciously defending and exemplifying in his prose the virtues of good sense, rational judgment, and a perspicuous style, and castigating with mingled amusement and malice the low breeding of contemporary letters and scholarship. In modern Chinese literature satire is usually a mode of protest against the evils of society; Ch'ien Chung-shu turns the tables on the writers and exhibits them as one of the major components of social and cultural decadence. In *Men, Beasts, Ghosts,* therefore, one is not surprised to find a number of satiric portraits modeled upon well-known writers and professors; apparently in reference to these portraits, Ch'ien Chung-shu writes in the preface:

> As is customary, I have to warn my readers that the characters and incidents in this book are entirely fictitious. Not only are the men law-abiding citizens and the beasts domesticated animals, but even the ghosts are not wild unfettered spirits: they live only within the confines of this book and will positively not stray outside. If any person identifies himself with some man, beast, or ghost in this collection, it amounts to saying that a character in my book, which I have imagined, has walked away, taken on blood and flesh, mind and body, assumed his shape, and now freely moves about in the real world. Since man was first molded of clay, I am afraid there has not been another such miracle of creation. I dare not dream that my art could be so successful; therefore I have to disclaim this possibility beforehand and respectfully thank whoever will so honor me.[7]

Even the most unwary reader, naturally, will be intrigued by this preface to guess the real identity of many a character in the book.

These portraits, of course, are not just a lampoon; they enjoy a degree of universality as exempla of folly and pretension. Ch'ien Chung-shu shares with Pope a clairvoyant ability to detect stupidity in whatever guise; but unburdened with an optimistic and deistic faith he also shows a psychological interest in behavior which is characteristically pessimistic and modern. For to lampoon intellectuals and writers is not Ch'ien Chung-shu's central creative concern: it is rather to unfold the perennial drama of ordinary human beings in desperation, vainly seeking escape or attachment.

The story "Cat" serves as an excellent showcase of Ch'ien Chung-shu's talent for intellectual satire and psychological drama. The heroine Ai-mo is a celebrated hostess for the intellectual and artistic circles in Peiping during the prewar years. The first half of the story depicts a typical tea party of hers, at which her guests admire her charm and exercise their wit, often at the expense of her husband, Li Chien-hou. The Lis and their guests are all satirized at some length. At the same time, the party prepares for the domestic drama of husband and wife, which comes to a head in the second half of the story.

During the ten years of their married life, Chien-hou has been playing second fiddle to Ai-mo, whose sole concern is to maintain her reputation as beauty, wit, and hostess. To reassert his self-importance, Chien-hou tries to find something useful to do and finally hits upon the idea of writing his memoirs. He hires a teen-age boy, I-ku, as his clerical assistant. At the tea party, however, Ai-mo triumphantly produces I-ku as her new protégé, just like her cat Darkie, which every guest is obliged to praise. Accustomed to taking away everything that her husband can call his own, Ai-mo has, furthermore, no compunction in ordering the boy around in the days following the party. She knows that I-ku adores her like a goddess and she won't even give her husband a chance to maintain the illusion that he is seriously working. Outraged, Chien-hou finally quarrels with his wife. A few weeks later, he leaves for Shanghai to look for an apartment; Peiping is then in danger of falling into Japanese hands.

A mutual friend, Ch'en Hsia-chün, informs Ai-mo that her husband has been seen boarding the train with a teen-age girl. Like any other woman informed of her husband's infidelity, Ai-mo is surprised, hurt, and angry; she even sheds tears. To bolster her vanity, she coaxes I-ku to avow his passion for her. Shy and inexperienced, I-ku is not equal to the occasion; besides, Ai-mo's tear-stained face is not particularly pretty. In great anger, she orders him to leave the house.

> Seeing I-ku withdraw in haste, Mrs. Li regretted her own rudeness, surprised that she could have lost her usual poise in such a manner and become so angry on account of Chien-hou. Suddenly she felt old, totteringly

old, and too tired to shoulder the heavy burdens of her reputation, position, and social obligations. She only wanted to escape to a place where she could forget her pride, avoid her present friends, and afford to neglect her appearance and social style. A place where she wouldn't have to look beautiful and young for anybody.

Meanwhile, the train that had started yesterday from Peiping was entering Shantung province. Li Chien-hou looked out the window and his heart felt as arid and shrunken as the yellow dust fleeting behind him. Yesterday's excitement, like the feeling of elation following many drinks, was succeeded only by remorse. He thought that Ch'en Hsia-chün would surely inform Ai-mo of what he had seen and that he couldn't acquit himself if the affair turned serious. It was not worth it to break up a family for the girl beside him, so plain and uneducated! He blamed his lack of circumspection, his inability to control his anger, which had led to this impasse. All these thoughts, of course, completely escaped the girl, who was holding hands with him and gazing out the window at the passing scene. She felt only that life's future, like the interminable journey of the train, unfolded before her infinitely.[8]

The appearance of the plain girl at the end, with all her hope and ignorance, adds a further touch of irony to the story of Ai-mo and her husband.

"Souvenir," the best story in *Men, Beasts, Ghosts,* completely eschews topical satire and reveals with even greater clarity the psychological finesse of the author. As a study of seduction and adultery, it has in its own way the restraint and power of Benjamin Constant's *Adolphe.* Still romantically unattached in her senior year at college, Man-ch'ien finds the new transfer student, Ts'ai-shu, a godsend. He is the son of an old friend of her father's and lives at her home on week ends and holidays. In time, he and Man-ch'ien become very intimate friends, and while he is neither rich nor very bright, the opposition of her family to the match only cements the bond. Upon the outbreak of the Sino-Japanese War, they hurriedly get married and move to the interior. Ts'ai-shu works in a government bureau in a small city.

As the couple have few friends, Man-ch'ien is quite lonely during the day: the local cinemas are atrocious and new books are hard to get. The city becomes somewhat more lively with the arrival of a detachment of the air force to guard it against air raids. One of the pilots, T'ien-chien, is a cousin of Ts'ai-shu's, but Man-ch'ien is not eager to have him over for dinner, ashamed of her plain style of entertainment. After the initial visit, however, the pilot comes more often, usually in the afternoons when she is alone. T'ien-chien fills a need in her life, though she repels his advances. But, after a long absence, she is pained to see him on the street in the company of another girl. Finally he has his will with her.

The story opens with Man-ch'ien returning home from her first and only assignation with the pilot on a languid spring day. She is worried, guilty, and rather disappointed. "If she had known that T'ien-chien could be so rude, she would not have gone out today; at least she would have changed her underwear before going. Thinking of her old underwear, which she still had on and which she should have laundered, she felt even at this moment red to her ears. She was more ashamed and angry over this than over what had happened." [9]

Several weeks later, T'ien-chien dies in action. By that time Man-ch'ien is already pregnant with his seed. Without irony, because he is completely in the dark about the illicit relationship, Ts'ai-shu suggests that, if the child be a boy, he should be named T'ien-chien to commemorate the dead hero. Manch'ien's thoughts, meanwhile, wander along other tracks:

> For the first time Man-ch'ien felt sorry for T'ien-chien as parents feel sorry for their mischievous child as they watch him in a state of sound sleep. T'ien-chien's good

looks, his smartness, his willfulness and slickness—so terribly tempting to women while he was still alive—were now reduced, softened and exposed by death, and appeared but as a child's tricks which couldn't be taken seriously. At the same time Man-ch'ien also felt the comfort that came with liberation. And what about the secret between the two? The incident which she didn't wish to recall and wanted to hide even from herself now suddenly appeared less hateful; it became a private souvenir worth cherishing, like a maple leaf or a petal of the lotus flower pressed in a book. Time will gradually fade its color, but whenever you open the book, it will be there. She shivered, as if her body were tainted with a portion of death or as if a portion of her body had died with T'ien-chien. Luckily, this portion of her body was now a distant stranger to herself; like peeled-off skin or clipped-off hair or nail, it no longer mattered.[10]

The summary and the two excerpts hardly do justice to a story of over thirty-five pages, but they suggest the adult level of narration and the fine quality of perception, both moral and psychological. In Man-ch'ien, Ch'ien Chung-shu has defined the state of a woman who, toying with the idea of a delicate and noncommittal extramarital relationship, is finally caught in a kind of physical reality she detests. Her indifference, fascination, revulsion, and final relief are all rendered with precision.

Ch'ien Chung-shu has written too few stories to call for a rounded judgment. But except for "God's Dream," which is a flippant parable in the manner of Anatole France, the remaining titles in *Men, Beasts, Ghosts*—"Inspiration," "Cat," and "Souvenir"—contribute significantly, each in its own way, to the developing tradition of the Chinese short story.

The Besieged City is the most delightful and carefully wrought novel in modern Chinese literature; it is perhaps also its greatest novel. As a satire, it recalls such famous

Chinese novels as *The Unofficial History of the Literati,* but it is superior to them in possessing greater comic exuberance and a structural unity. Unlike *The Unofficial History,* with its flimsily related episodes involving a great number of characters, *The Besieged City* is a comic odyssey with a continuous picaresque action. Its hero, a good and impractical man, returns from abroad, stays in Shanghai during the first year of the war, undertakes a long journey to the interior, and then again returns to Shanghai. Along the way he meets with all sorts of fools, impostors, and hypocrites, but he does not survive his misadventures a triumphant Tom Jones vindicated in his moral goodness. Rather he is a disappointed and defeated man. As a matter of fact, he loses track of his Sophia Western quite early in the book and later marries another woman who brings him only an increasing awareness of his isolation. In this respect he is more like the heroes of Waugh's early novels: Paul Pennyfeather, Adam Fenwick-Symes, Tony Last.

Having idled for a few years in Europe, Fang Hung-chien returns to China with a spurious diploma from a nonexistent American university. He is a good and intelligent man but also, as he later realizes, a moral coward. He knows where he stands with other people, but he cannot extricate himself from a bad situation, either out of laziness or out of fear that he may hurt others by doing so. While still in college, he was engaged to a girl of his native city (unnamed in the novel, but it can be no other than Wusih, Kiangsu, the author's birthplace) at his father's insistence. Though he knew very little about the girl, he consented to the engagement after only a mild protest. Luckily for him, the girl soon died and her father, to commemorate his only daughter, financed him for his advanced education abroad with the money that should have been her dowry. Fang Hung-chien doesn't care for a degree, but he feels he has to buy one in order to meet the expectations of his father and the father of his late fiancée. Even though he does this to please others at the price of personal mortification, he is made an impostor among impostors. This trait of moral cowardice he exemplifies throughout the novel.

On his return voyage Hung-chien yields to the temptation of the flesh in the form of a vulgar Miss Pao, an overseas Chinese. He becomes quite disgusted when he sees her walking off with aplomb into the arms of her fiancé upon reaching her port of destination. Miss Su Wen-wan, a lady scholar with a doctorate in literature from a French university, also ingratiates herself into his company. He has the greatest difficulty in avoiding her kind offices.

After a brief stay in his native city, Hung-chien moves to Shanghai to live at his late fiancée's home and work in her father's bank. Soon afterward the Sino-Japanese War breaks out and his father and brothers also move to Shanghai. Hung-chien resumes his acquaintance with Miss Su and through her comes to know her cousin T'ang Hsiao-fu, a very sweet and unpretentious girl. While courting the latter in a rather furtive fashion, he can never summon enough courage to break with Miss Su, who lives on the daily expectation that he will propose to her. When he finally serves her notice, it is too late. The furious girl maliciously depicts him to her cousin as a sham and blackguard. Hung-chien comes to see Hsiao-fu when she is still angry with the news; he listens to her sarcasm and reproaches in unprotesting silence. After he has left, she immediately tries to repair her error but is frustrated by a combination of ironic circumstances. Both Hung-chien and Hsiao-fu are heart-broken; but she is sent on a rest cure and marries another man several months later.

The family of his late fiancée adopts an increasingly cold attitude toward Hung-chien because of his romantic entanglements. His own family is also becoming every day more distasteful to him. A disappointed suitor for Miss Su's hand, Chao Hsin-mei, becomes in time his close friend, and they both now decide to accept offers from a newly opened college in the interior. By boat and bus and foot they start on an exhausting journey; with them are three appointees at the same college: two crafty and mean-spirited professors, Li Mei-t'ing and Ku Erh-ch'ien, and one English assistant, Miss Sun Jou-chia.

"Miss Sun had a long face; there were a few freckles on her cheeks which were of the color of old ivory; her eyes were set so wide apart that she wore frequently an expression of surprise. Dressed in a very plain and neat style, she was so shy that she dared not speak one word in company; waves of crimson rolled over her face incessantly." [11] With these words Ch'ien Chung-shu introduces us to his heroine, surely one of the most finished creations in modern Chinese fiction. Jou-chia is an unmistakable product of Chinese culture; behind her shy reticence will in time be seen an imperious will and an oversensitive faculty for suspicion and jealousy, a trait which Chinese women have developed to cope with their age-old subjection to domestic intrigue and misery. Hung-chien is at first indifferent to Jou-chia, but it seems quite plain to Chao Hsin-mei that she is out to trap his unsuspecting friend.

Once settled at the college, Hung-chien is unwittingly drawn into school politics compounded of personal malice and provincial narrow-mindedness. Several faculty members are against him, and his growing intimacy with Jou-chia constitutes another source of their envy. Chao Hsin-mei quits the college after one term to go into business; meanwhile Hung-chien doesn't get his appointment for next year. Ostracized on the campus, he and Jou-chia find love and courage in each other's company and become engaged. They decide to go back to Shanghai. On their way, they get married in Hong Kong, where they also see Chao and the affluent and newly married Miss Su. To Jou-chia it seems incomprehensible that Hung-chien should have preferred herself to that fine and rich lady.

Once back in Shanghai, the relations between Hung-chien and Jou-chia become worsened as their respective families enter into the picture. Jou-chia doesn't like his family at all, especially the old-style officiousness of his father Tun-weng and the ill-disguised malice of his sisters-in-law. On his part, Hung-chien detests her aunt Mrs. Lu, a vulgar missionary type of woman who exercises a preponderent influence over his wife. Finally Hung-chien quits his newspaper job and decides to join Chao Hsin-mei again in the interior. Jou-chia, who has never liked Chao, wishes that her husband would stay on in Shanghai and accept a position from her aunt. This situation precipitates a series of quarrels leading to the inevitable separation of the couple.

The foregoing synopsis leaves out all the satiric material that makes the novel so consistently amusing. The eccentric avant-garde intellectuals in Miss Su's circle, the provincial professors and instructors at the college, the big businessmen and old-style squires in Shanghai, the petty officials, officers, innkeepers, and prostitutes in the interior—all are here in the book, parading in absurd postures of vanity and fraud. Ch'ien Chung-shu does not invite the reader to cherish the foibles of these characters in the manner of Dickens, nor does he affect the didactic tone of classical satire. He knows only too well that, under whatever circumstances, stupidity and selfishness will always flourish and that the satiric task is simply to illuminate these with the light of superior intelligence and culture. Except for Li Mei-t'ing, who, as a transparent type of miser and academic charlatan, does not deserve the large space devoted to him, nearly all the satiric portraits in the novel are immensely comic.

Aside from satire, *The Besieged City* has also the exploratory gusto of a picaresque novel. Its resemblance here to the eighteenth-century English novel is not accidental. During the war the educated Chinese, most of them for the first time, journeyed to the interior and encountered on the road and at the inns the same kind of dismay, fatigue, and mishap that befell English squires of 200 years ago as they set off from London or Bath. Of all the wartime and postwar novels, *The Besieged City* has captured best the comedy and tribulation of travel. As a small example, one may quote the scene in-

volving Hung-chien and his companions examining a piece
of cured meat at a typical inn of the inland provinces:

> The waiter unhooked from the wall a greasy thing of
> black color and submitted it to their inspection. At the
> same time he was repeatedly saying "How delicious!" in
> such a drooling manner as to suggest his fear that the
> greedy eyes of the guests might reduce the size of the fat
> meat. Awakened from its greasy slumber, a maggot on
> the meat began to wriggle. Li Mei-t'ing was the first to
> spot it and he became quite disgusted. From a distance
> he puckered his mouth in the direction of the maggot
> and said, "This won't do!" The waiter hurriedly placed
> his finger on the tender, fat, and white worm and pressed
> it lightly, leaving on the dusty and dirty surface of the
> meat a track as lustrously black as a newly asphalted road.
> At the same time he said, "There's nothing there!" In-
> furiated, Ku Erh-ch'ien asked if he thought all their eyes
> were blind. The rest also exclaimed, "What impu-
> dence!" . . .
>
> This furor prompted the innkeeper to come out, and
> hearing the noise, two maggots in the meat also stuck
> their heads out to look. This time the waiter didn't try
> to wipe out the evidence, only saying repeatedly, "If you
> don't like it, there are people who do—I'll eat it and you
> just look on—" Taking the long pipe from his mouth,
> the innkeeper advised, "These are not worms; they
> won't harm you; they're called 'meat sprout'—'meat'
> —'sprout.' " [12]

Both the satire and the picaresque action add to the meaning and scope of the novel, but its central theme is embedded
almost entirely in the individual drama of the hero. Hung-
chien is the man forever seeking attachment and forever finding that each new attachment is but the same bondage. The
"besieged city," which is discussed quite a few times in the
novel, symbolizes this human condition. In the following pas-

sage, a pseudo-philosopher who prides himself on his personal acquaintance with such eminent men as Bertrand Russell is talking with Miss Su about marriage and divorce:

> Shen-ming said: "I also had a talk with Bertie about his divorces. He quoted an old saying to the effect that marriage is like a gilded cage. The birds outside the cage want to nestle in there and the birds inside want to fly out: so divorce follows marriage and marriage follows divorce and there can be no end to that."
>
> Miss Su said: "In France there is a similar saying. Only it's not about a bird cage, but about a *forteresse assiègee:* people outside the fortress want to rush in and people inside want to get out. Hung-chien, isn't that right?" Hung-chien shook his head to indicate that he hadn't heard the saying before.[13]

This analogy, though applying with especial force to the marriage of Hung-chien and Jou-chia, applies to his other attachments as well. When he is leaving the college, Hung-chien recalls vividly this scrap of conversation; he cannot help contrasting the enthusiasm with which he undertook the journey to the interior with his present feeling of desolation. Except for a few students, no one takes the trouble to say good-by to him:

> A few students whom he had tutored were free in the evening, as they had completed their examinations on that day, and they came to his room to say good-by. He was happy with gratitude and began to understand the psychology of the corrupt mayor who, when leaving his post, insisted that the local population make proper gestures of urging him to stay on, present him the Umbrella of Ten Thousand People, and erect a stone tablet in memory of his virtuous government. To leave a place is like suffering death; you know you have to die but you still hope to see people express the desire that you live

on. You are very much concerned about the good or bad name you leave behind in a place, just as about your posthumous reputation, but you have no means of knowing and you are deeply afraid that after your departure, as after your death, you leave behind only a bad odor such as the candle gives after its flame is snuffed out. When people come to bid you good-by, it is therefore like having filial sons and docile grandsons watch your deathbed; you feel you can die with your eyes contentedly closed.[14]

Each departure from a place, or for that matter, each estrangement from a person you know is like a death. By the time Hung-chien marries Jou-chia, he has almost completely shed his old self that loved Hsiao-fu so hectically. The news of her marriage only brings him a wistful sadness over his inability to recall, with any personal conviction, the delirium and sorrow of only a few months ago. Hung-chien's successive estrangements from Miss Pao, Miss Su, Hsiao-fu, the family of his late fiancée, his own family, his colleagues at the college, and finally his wife dramatize the progressive shrinkage of his spirit to arrive at a state of utter nakedness. *The Besieged City* is a study of man's isolation and his impotence to communicate.

A novel, of course, is not primarily judged by the shallowness or profundity of its theme, the prior question being always to determine how well that theme is embodied. The concluding section of the last chapter of *The Besieged City* is therefore appended here, in a necessarily inadequate translation, to enable the reader to see how the theme is inseparable from the psychological drama and how the drama, among other things, is inseparable from the cowardice of the hero earlier defined. This section chronicles the incidents leading to the final marital rupture. The day before, Hung-chien had quit his newspaper job and decided to go to the interior; Jou-chia had gone to his parents' home with him for a dinner, at which she was offended. The old clock mentioned in the last paragraph of this selection is a wedding gift from Hung-chien's father; it is always several hours behind time.

Downcast and unhappy, Hung-chien was loath to visit his parents, but Tun-weng telephoned him to hurry over. He went there and listened to Tun-weng talk for a long while without getting any concrete suggestion or help. He finally left and went to the moving company to see its manager about the traveling expenses. The manager wasn't there and an appointment was made for the next day. He went next to Mr. Wang's home, and he wasn't there either. At that time the trolley cars were filled with people from their offices; he couldn't get in and proceeded to walk home, thinking at the same time how to melt Jou-chia's resentment. On reaching the residential terrace, he saw a car, the family car of the Lus, and his heart stiffened inside him. He opened the back door and walked through the kitchen, which was used in common with the landlord family. Li Ma wasn't there and the kettle on the stove was singing away. He walked up half of the stairs; the door to the small living room was slightly open and Mrs. Lu was talking loudly. His heart swelled with anger. He was unwilling to go in, and his feet stood pinned there. She was saying: "I also know that Hung-chien has no abilities but quite a big temper; I don't have to listen to Li Ma. Jou-chia, a man is like a baby and you shouldn't *spoil* * him; you are too submissive." Blood rushed to his face; he wished he could shout out loud and rush into the room. But suddenly he heard Li Ma's footsteps coming down the stairs; afraid to be seen by her and caught in an embarrassing situation, he quietly walked out of the door. Anger made him forget about the piercing cold. Not knowing when that disgusting woman would leave, he decided not to return home

* English in the original.

for supper; after all he was unemployed and ready to turn
beggar; there was no sense in saving so trifling an amount
of money. His anger gradually subsided after he had
walked several streets. He passed by a foreign bakery;
inside its window dazzling electric lights illuminated all
kinds of cakes and desserts. Outside the window stood an
old man in a tattered short coat staring at the things inside; on his arm was a basket containing coarse and
clumsy earthen dolls and windmills made of wax paper
pasted together. Hung-chien thought that children in the
cities nowadays wouldn't care for these primitive toys,
since they could have their pick of nice foreign-made
ones; this old man didn't know how to do business. Suddenly in his mind he linked himself with the toys in the
basket; he was not wanted in a time like this; that's why
he had difficulty in getting jobs. He sighed and took out
the wallet which Jou-chia had given him and handed the
old man two dollar-bills. Two little beggars, who had been
waiting outside the door of the bakery to beg from the
outgoing customers, now turned to him and followed him
for a distance. He became hungry after so much walking.
No sooner had he chosen a cheap Russian restaurant and
intended to walk in than he put his hand in his pocket
and found that his wallet was missing. He was so worried
that he perspired a little in the cold wind. So impercepti-
ble was the sweat, however, that it constituted only a kind
of vapory relief for the emotions. Today really was a bad
day! Now he had to go home and he didn't even have the
fare for the trolley. He turned all his bitter resentment
against Jou-chia. If Mrs. Lu hadn't come, he wouldn't be
out in the streets in the cold wind, and if he weren't in
the streets, he wouldn't have lost his wallet. Mrs. Lu was
Jou-chia's aunt and Jou-chia had invited her over; even
if she hadn't, he had still to blame her. Moreover he used
to put his money rather unmethodically in all his pockets,
back and front, left and right; the pickpocket could at

best empty one pocket; now that he had a wallet, all the money was in it and it made everything so convenient for the pickpocket. It was all Jou-chia's idea.

When he came home, Li Ma was washing dishes in the kitchen and asked, "Have you had supper yet?" He pretended not to hear. Li Ma had never seen him coming home with such a straight face and her anxious eyes followed him out of the kitchen. Seeing him, Jou-chia put down the newspaper, stood up and said: "You have come home! Was it cold outside? Where did you have your supper? We waited and waited for you and then ate."

Hung-chien had hurried home for supper; now that he knew supper had been served, he got a kind of satisfaction from his disappointment. He felt as if his anger were now built on a solid foundation. Today he could have a real loud quarrel. He said with a grave face: "I don't have relatives where I can go and have meals. Of course I haven't eaten."

Jou-chia was surprised: "Then let Li Ma hurry and buy you something. Where have you been? We had a long wait. Aunt came especially to see you. I waited and waited for you and then I detained her for supper."

Like a drowning man who has grasped the end of a rope and held on to it with all his might, Hung-chien said: "Oh! She came! That's why! Somebody ate my meal and I have nothing to eat. I appreciate her visit but I didn't ask her! I never go to her place; why should she come to my place? Aunt should stay for supper and husband should go hungry. Good, to make you happy, I'll stay hungry for the night and don't ask Li Ma to buy me anything."

Jou-chia sat down and took up her newspaper and said: "I am sorry I talked to you. Stupid! You can't appreciate kindness. If you want to stay hungry, it serves you right and it's not my business. You have quit your newspaper job and what kind of important national duties are you dealing with out there, my upright and patriotic *ta-lao-yeh?* You came home so late! I shoulder half the expenses at home and I have the right to invite guests. You have no right to interfere. Moreover, the dishes Li Ma makes are all poisonous; you'd better leave them alone."

Anger so aggravated Hung-chien's hunger that his stomach felt a piercing pang. There was not a single penny on him and he couldn't draw money from the bank until tomorrow. But he disdained to ask money from Jou-chia at this moment, and said only: "After all you'll be happier if I die of hunger. Your good aunt will find you a better husband."

Jou-chia smiled coldly: *"Ts'ui!* I think you are mad. You won't die of hunger; being hungry gives you a clearer head."

Another tide of anger surged up inside Hung-chien. He said: "Isn't this the sly trick your good aunt has taught you about? 'Jou-chia, never *spoil* a man too much. Famish him, freeze him, maltreat him.' "

Jou-chia studied her husband's face closely and said: "Oh, so the landlord's maidservant did say that she saw you come home once earlier. Why didn't you walk up the stairs with a clear conscience? You were furtive like a thief, hiding there in the middle of a stairway and listening to people talk. Such things are only fit for your younger brothers' wives and you call yourself a man! Shouldn't you be ashamed?"

Hung-chien said: "I wanted to listen in; otherwise I would be like one hidden inside a drum and wouldn't know how people were maligning me behind my back."

"How did we malign you? Why don't you speak out?"

Hung-chien assumed a knowing air and said: "You know yourself and I don't have to talk."

Jou-chia had really told her aunt what happened the day before; the two women had laughed and reviled in unison. Thinking that all this had been overheard by

Hung-chien, she became a little nervous and said: "All this was not intended for your ear; who told you to eavesdrop? Let me ask you, Aunt said that she was going to get you a job in the factory; did you hear that also?"

Hung-chien startled up and shouted: "Who wants her to get me a job? Even if I turn beggar, I'll not beg from her! She's got Bobby [her pet dog] and you; aren't two running dogs enough? You can tell her that Fang Hung-chien has 'no abilities but quite a big temper'; he won't serve as the running dog of the running dog of the capitalist."

The two stood face to face. In her anger Jou-chia's eyes were strangely bright. She said: "Which of her words has she said wrong! People pity you and if you don't want a rice bowl, the rice bowl won't get moldy. All right, your father will 'get you a place!' But, to depend on the old man is nothing to be proud of; if you can, get a place for yourself."

"I don't depend on anybody. Let me tell you, today I sent a telegram to Chao Hsin-mei and made arrangements with the people at the moving company. After I have left, you can enjoy your quiet. You can not only ask Aunt for supper but also press her to stay overnight. Or, to make things simpler, you can move to her place and let her feed you, like Bobby."

Parting her lips and opening her eyes wide, Jou-chia listened to the finish and then she said with set teeth: "Good, it looks as though we are through. Your luggage and clothes you can take care of yourself; don't come and bother me again. Last year you were loafing in Shanghai without a job. Then you followed Chao Hsin-mei to the interior. When you lost your job in the interior, you again counted on Chao Hsin-mei's help to come to Shanghai. Now that you have lost your job in Shanghai, you are again going to the interior to join Chao Hsin-mei. Think it over yourself: you follow him wherever he goes

and hold fast to his coattails with your teeth. If you are
not a dog, what are you? You have not only no abilities
but no ambition, not to say integrity and rectitude. Take
care you don't incur his dislike lest he kick you away
with his foot. If at that time you again return to Shanghai, I don't see how you can face people. I don't care at
all if you leave or stay."

Hung-chien couldn't stand this any more; he said,
"Then, shut up," and pushed at her chest with his right
hand. She staggered backward, colliding with the edge
of the table; her arm brushed a glass onto the floor and
the broken pieces of the glass stayed in the pool of water.
She panted: "You dare strike me? You dare strike me!"
Li Ma burst in like a bullet, crying: "*Ku-yeh,* how could
you raise your hand and strike her? If you strike me, I'll
cry and let the people downstairs hear— *Hsiao-chieh,*
where did he strike you? Are you hurt? Don't be afraid,
I'm ready to risk my old life to fight him— You're a
man and you beat a woman!— *Lao-yeh* and *t'ai-t'ai* have
never beaten you; I have given you suck since you were
that little and I didn't even pat you with a heavy hand,
and he raised his hand and struck you!" Saying so, she let
her tears roll down. Jou-chia also threw herself on the
sofa and wept bitterly. Seeing her crying piteously, Hung-
chien was unwilling to show pity and hated her even
more. Li Ma protected and comforted Jou-chia near the
sofa, saying: "*Hsiao-chieh,* you don't cry! If you cry, I'll
cry too"—she rubbed away her tears with her apron—
"See, you have beaten her so! *Hsiao-chieh,* I'm thinking
of telling this to *ku-t'ai-t'ai* [meaning her aunt]; only I
am afraid that he will beat you again while I'm away."

Hung-chien said harshly: "You ask your *hsiao-chieh* if
I've beaten her. You hurry and invite *ku-t'ai-t'ai* over and
I won't beat your *hsiao-chieh*." He half pulled and half
pushed her out of the room; but after a minute, she
rushed in again, saying: "*Hsiao-chieh,* I've asked the

landlord's elder *hsiao-chieh* to make a phone call to *ku-t'ai-t'ai*. She will be here soon; we needn't fear him any more." Both Hung-chien and Jou-chia hadn't expected that she would be so serious; but still hostile toward each other, they couldn't stand together and reprove her for her superfluous office. Jou-chia forgot to cry and Hung-chien stared at Li Ma in wonderment like a child who sees a strange animal in a zoo. Having kept quiet for a while, Hung-chien said finally: "Okay, she comes and I go. It's not enough that you two women band against me but you want a third. You will be saying that I, a man, have maltreated you. I'll return when she leaves." He went to the clothes tree to take down his coat.

Jou-chia was unwilling to have her aunt come to aggravate the quarrel; but seeing her husband retreating so, she felt so contemptuous of him that she no longer felt sorry. She hissed: "You are a *coward! Coward! COWARD! * I don't ever want to see a *coward* like you again!" She intended her each word to fall like a whip and to lash up some courage from her husband; not content with this, she grabbed an ivory comb on the table and threw it toward him with all her strength. Hung-chien was on the point of turning his head and making an answer and didn't have the time to dodge. The comb hit him heavily on his lcft cheek and it bounced back to the floor, broken into two pieces. Jou-chia only heard him crying out in pain *"Aya"*; then she looked at the place where the comb had hit and saw that it was red and swollen with blood visible beneath the skin. She regretted she had acted so harshly but at the same time she was afraid he would strike back again. Li Ma hurriedly intervened between the two. Shocked that she could be so cruel, Hung-chien watched her standing there rigidly, supported by the table, her tear-stained face looking like dead ashes, her eyes red, her nostrils quivering, her mouth swallowing

---

* English in the original.

saliva, at once pitiful and frightening. But at the same time he heard footsteps coming upstairs; he couldn't care less and said: "So you are cruel! You want to raise hell so that not only your folks will know it but all the neighbors too. At this very moment the landlord's family has heard it. You have just learned how to be vindictive and brazen-faced, but I still want to live among people and I still want my face. I am leaving; when your teacher comes, learn some more new tricks; you are really an apt pupil and can apply whatever you've learned! Give her my warning, though, that I forgive her this time. If she comes again to corrupt you, I'll go to her house to find her; don't think that I am afraid of her. Li Ma, when *ku-t'ai-t'ai* comes, don't just say bad words about me; you have seen with your own eyes who was striking whom." Approaching the door, he said aloud, "I'm going," and then slowly turned the doorknob so that the eavesdroppers could get the hint and walk away. With wide-opened eyes Jou-chia watched him leaving the room; then she prostrated herself on the sofa, buried her head in her hands, and cried uncontrollably. This shower didn't seem to come from her eyes alone; her heart and all her body seemed to have secreted hot tears. They converged and came out together.

Hung-chien left the house and his nerves were so benumbed as not to feel the cold. Consciously he could only feel that his left cheek was burning hot. His brain fluttered with all kinds of ideas and feelings, dense and confused, like snowflakes driven by the north wind on a wintry day. He walked as his feet dictated. The street lamps, keeping a vigilant night watch, forwarded his shadow from one to another. Another self inside him, as it were, was saying: "It's finished! It's finished!" But his random and confused thoughts became at once collected under the onset of anguish. There was a sudden spasmodic pain on his left cheek; he touched it and it was clammy. He thought it was blood; his heart calmed down under this shock and his legs felt weak. Walking toward the lamp post, he saw that there were no stains on his fingers and then he knew that it was only tears. At the same time he felt fatigue all over his body and hunger inside his stomach. Instinctively Hung-chien put his hand into his pocket, to look for a hawker and buy some bread; then he recalled that there was no money on him. Hunger puts one on fire, but this fire feeds only on paper and cannot last. As he had no place to go, he thought it would be better to go home and sleep; even if he encountered Mrs. Lu, he wouldn't be afraid of her. Granted that he struck her first, her retaliation was so cruel that both scores should be canceled. Looking at his watch, he saw it was past ten; he couldn't be sure at what time he left home and maybe Mrs. Lu had already left. There was no car in the terrace and he felt reassured. As soon as he stepped inside the door, the landlady heard the noise and came forth, saying: "Mr. Fang, so it's you! Your *shao-nai-nai* feels unwell and has left for the Lus' home with Li Ma. She won't be back tonight. Here is the key to your room; she left it in my care and asked me to give it to you. Tomorrow morning you come down and have breakfast with us; Li Ma has told me so." Hung-chien felt his heart was sinking straight down and it would never rise again. He mechanically took the key and thanked her. The landlady looked as if she had something more to say, but he escaped upstairs by big strides. He opened the bedroom and turned on the light. The broken glass and broken comb were still in the same places; on the pile of trunks one was missing. He stood there vacantly and felt so dull in body and mind that he could feel neither worried nor angry. Jou-chia had gone, but her angry face was still in the room and her cries and words stayed in the air, undispelled. He saw there was a card on the table; he walked nearer to have a look and it was Mrs. Lu's. Suddenly mad, he tore it to pieces and said vindictively: "All right, you are certainly free and can leave me like that! Get gone, your mother's egg, get gone and all of you get gone from me!" This brief show of anger used up all his remaining energy; he felt so weak that he could weep disconsolately without end. He reclined on his bed, with his clothes on, and felt that the room was whirling around him. He felt that he shouldn't think any more; he couldn't afford to get sick by any chance; tomorrow he had to see that manager and after that interview he still had to raise money somehow or other to meet the traveling expenses; possibly he could make the Chinese New Year in Chungking. Hope again rose in his heart, like wet firewood which can't get started but has begun to smoke. Everything seemed to be all right. Imperceptibly the black sky and the dark earth began to close in on him, to clamp him tight; he went asleep like the night after all the lights are extinguished. At first his sleep was very thin and brittle; like a pair of forceps, hunger tried to pry open his stupor and he subconsciously had to stave it off. But gradually the forceps became loosened and blunt and his sleep became so sound that it could no longer be nipped, without dreams and without sensations, humanity's primordial sleep, and also a sample of death.

The ancient clock began to chime, as if it had stored up half a day's time and now during the stillness of the night it released it and counted it up: "One, two, three, four, five, six." Six o'clock, that was five hours ago. At that time Hung-chien was on his way home, prepared to treat Jou-chia kindly and to entreat her not to quarrel over what happened yesterday and cause any rift between husband and wife; at that time, Jou-chia was at home, waiting for Hung-chien to return home and have supper, hoping that he would be reconciled to her aunt and agree to work in her factory. This timepiece, which lagged behind time, contained an unintended irony to-ward, and disappointment with, humanity which was more profound than any language, than any tears or laughter.[15]

In the English translation the reader may not be impressed by the straightforward narrative style, which seems to take into account every detail with little discrimination; actually it exemplifies the most rigorous discipline in economy. The bad novelist is often one who works up a big emotional scene by ignoring all the attendant circumstances which seemingly contribute little to or distract from that emotion; the good novelist, on the contrary, is unafraid to view an emotional conflict in the round and dissects it in terms of its petty psychological and even physiological components. Hung-chien is hungry and has lost his wallet; if he can buy himself a supper in a restaurant, he may return home the second time in a considerably better mood and carry out his resolve to settle his differences with his wife. For all one knows, he may even consent to work in her aunt's factory and give up the idea of going to the interior. The quarrel ironically takes its un-alterable course when Hung-chien is ready to concede victory to his wife. Jou-chia flares up because she hates this easy victory, this cowardice in her husband, which is willing to accept defeat rather than come to grips with reality. In this concluding section of the novel the tragic defect in the hero's character receives its climactic illumination.

Ch'ien Chung-shu is a stylist of unusual distinction. In the translation we do not have the epigrams and puns which invariably enliven his comic passages, but we have a specimen of his perspicuous and elegant prose, with its attentiveness to concrete detail and its carefully wrought imagery. Especially is the author a master of similes: several from the selection could be cited for their aptness and precision. Ch'ien Chung-shu is also a symbolist, as is every novelist who is not content to choose his details merely for their dramatic propriety but makes them comment obliquely on the total action. Thus the old man with his basket of primitive toys peering into the window of a foreign bakery is as assuredly a symbol of the hero's fate as is the blind beggar in *Madame Bovary* a symbol of Emma's. And the grotesque clock, with which Ch'ien Chung-shu winds up his narrative, stays in the reader's memory with all its intended irony.

CHAPTER 17

Shih T'o

LESS BRILLIANT than either Ch'ien Chung-shu or
Eileen Chang, Shih T'o (Wang Ch'ang-chien; alternate pen
name: Lu Fen) * was like them a resident of Shanghai under
Japanese occupation. His progress as a writer was rather slow:
though he had become a noted member of the Peking school
in the prewar years and had won the coveted Ta Kung Pao
Literary Prize in 1936 for his first book of stories, *The Valley*,
it was not until the publication of *Marriage* in 1947 that he
claimed serious attention as a novelist.

Like Shen Ts'ung-wen, who helped launch his career, Shih
T'o had little formal education and early showed a predilection for the rural subject matter. For his early sketches and
stories about village and small-town life in his native province
of Honan, he used an ornate and poetic style which seemed
to be in fashion among the younger writers in Peking at that
time: Li Ni, Ho Ch'i-fang, Li Kuang-t'ien, and Lu Li. Because of this cultivation of preciosity, the genres of the short

* According to Yuan Chia-hua and Robert Payne, *Contemporary
Chinese Short Stories*, Shih T'o was born in 1908 (see "Biographical
Notes," following p. 169). But this information may not be reliable, for
on the same page the editors tell us that Lu Hsün died in 1935.

story and the essay tend to overlap in Shih T'o's early publications: *The Valley, Gleanings from My Home Town, Huang Hua T'ai, Wild Birds, The Declining Sun*.

Upon the outbreak of the Sino-Japanese War, he moved from the North to Shanghai. He continued to write, but he was no Japanese collaborator. To cash in on the wartime theater boom, he turned playwright and adopted his present pen name to signify the change. His big hit, *The Big Circus*, adapted from Andreyev's *He Who Gets Slapped*, was thoroughly enjoyable theater as played by its original distinguished cast; the same perhaps could be said of *The Night Inn*, which he and K'o Ling adapted from Gorky's *The Lower Depths*. At the same time, however, Shih T'o published in Hong Kong and the interior a series of studies on small-town life, later collected under the title *The Orchard Town*, and prepared two novels, *Ma Lan* and *Marriage*, which saw publication soon after the victory.

The Declining Sun (1937) is a typical product of Shih T'o's early pastoral period. The title piece, a story about a wanderer's return to his native home, is full of sentimental pastiches; perhaps in even worse taste are two tales in the same vein, "The Pastoral Song" and "A Patch of Land." But the collection also contains a promising satire called "Father and Son." In form it is a fragmentary diary kept by a high school teacher during the span of 1917–37. A typical daring individual of the May Fourth period, this man defied his parents and deserted his country wife to marry the girl of his choice; but as time rolls by he becomes increasingly embittered over the failure of his career and the alarming radicalism of his grown children moving in a different political climate. He is aware that, in the eyes of his elder son, a leftist student leader, he is nothing but a harmless reactionary. In this satirical study of a frustrated life Shih T'o poses a serious question about the whirligig of intellectual fashions in modern China: will not the elder son, now so smart and self-assured, be in time superseded by a new generation and eat the bitter fruit of disillusion? To the perennial theme of father versus son the author adds a biting commentary on the relativism of folly and wisdom in the abeyance of tradition.

The same spirit of inquiry and wonder is apparent in *The Orchard Town* (1946). According to the preface, Shih T'o was moving from Peking to Shanghai in the summer of 1936 and stopped at a small railroad junction to visit an old friend. The strangely stagnant atmosphere of that place enkindled in him the idea of a book tracing the history of a small town since the downfall of the Ch'ing dynasty. While lacking in tragic power, the resulting eighteen sketches share somewhat the irony and compassion of Lu Hsün's *Outcry* and *Hesitation*.

Like several of Lu Hsün's stories, *The Orchard Town* has its point of departure in a self-exiled intellectual's temporary return to his home town. He visits his old friends and inquires after those he used to know. Among the latter are an old maid in her late twenties, sewing away at a bridal wardrobe she will never use; an unhappy squire who used to beat his wives but who lost his nerve following the Communist occupation of the town in 1927; the degenerate and impoverished scions of once locally prominent families. Of particular poignancy are the careers of several once ardent reformers whose advocacy of modern ideas has only brought them poverty, calumny, and death. Understandably, all these characters have appeared elsewhere in modern Chinese fiction: Shih T'o has deliberately chosen a typical set to underscore the persistence of stagnation in a time of apparent change. The real central character is the town itself, which has survived reformers, Communists, and Kuomintang bureaucrats only to continue in its ways of indolence, cowardice, and cruelty.

Frankly despairing over the future of China, Shih T'o, however, was not one to embrace Communism or any other pat solution. As early as 1936 he wrote a satire on Chinese Communist intellectuals called "Ma Lan." In this story a Marxist translator goes to the country and comes back to the city with Ma Lan, a peasant girl, whom he has supposedly rescued from parental oppression. He lives with her and introduces her to his circle of intellectual friends, but Ma Lan is, as one would expect, disgusted with them. Still groping for a satiric style, Shih T'o is quite unable to contrast effectively the girl's innocence and candor with the brutish and artificial life around her. But intrigued with the basic situation, Shih T'o later expanded his story into a novel. *Ma Lan* was completed in 1942 and first published in 1948.

The novel is still clumsy satire; worse than that, it degenerates toward the end into an improbable adventure-romance. But it is noteworthy for its use of certain techniques. *Ma Lan* is divided into four sections, of which the first two and the last are narrated by the first-person observer, one of the heroine's many admirers. The third section, however, is Ma Lan's own record of the events already described in the first two sections. Though Shih T'o doesn't fully explore the possibilities of this method, the use of double perspective indicates a technical and dramatic virtuosity, which is amply revealed in his next novel.

Profiting from his years with the theater and his earlier attempts at satiric fiction, Shih T'o effects in *Marriage* a complete break with the ruminative and elegiac mood and the village and small-town material. The style is now dramatic and swift, and the scene is laid against occupied Shanghai in 1941, before and after Pearl Harbor. The war, however, is merely in the background, imparting meaning and urgency to that relentless struggle for survival in which nearly every one of the characters in the novel is involved. In view of the unevenness of the author's earlier work and his virtual silence under the Communist regime, it is hard to tell whether *Marriage* is just a happy accident or the proof of an important talent. But for sheer narrative skill and excitement, it has few equals in modern Chinese fiction.

The trouble with most satiric fiction is that it is static: the characters reveal themselves at their first appearance and

464

remain unchanged in the course of the story. *Marriage,* however, has suspense. Chapter follows chapter with always a store of surprises in regard to plot and character; though subject to satire, the characters become more rounded with each appearance and more fascinating to watch. This excitement stems in large measure from Shih T'o's expert use of the point of view. Part I of the novel consists of a series of six letters written by Hu Ch'ü-o to his girl Lin P'ei-fang, now living in a small town with her father. Part II is a straightforward third-person narrative carrying on where the last letter stops. The transition is masterly because it takes place at the moment when the hero, buoyed upon new dreams of prosperity and happiness, has ceased to care about the girl whom he has intended to marry. He just doesn't write to her any more.

In the letters the hero, perhaps unconsciously at first, sees himself in the best possible light in order to justify his decision to borrow money and engage in speculation. The first letter recounts the antecedents. Hu Ch'ü-o reminds P'ei-fang that he was a most unfortunate child brought up under the dominance of his hateful father, who contributed practically nothing toward his high school and college education. He tells her further how grateful and lucky he is, a struggling high school teacher stranded in Shanghai, to have won her love and enjoyed the warm hospitality of her family. There is no doubt that her father, who refused to teach school under the Japanese and has retired to a small town to run a grocery store, is a man of patriotic integrity and that P'ei-fang herself, in sacrificing her college education so as to be near him, is a girl of exemplary virtue. But since they left Shanghai, Hu continues, he has been very lonely and is now determined to make some quick money in order to marry her soon and help support her family. He reassures P'ei-fang that he will be most astute in his new role as a speculator.

In the next two or three letters, Hu Ch'ü-o appears the shrewd observer of his new associates, but inevitably his attitude of critical disapproval slackens. While holding on precariously to his rectitude, he is in spite of himself drawn into a new world of evil peopled by such characters as: (1) T'ien Kuo-pao, Hu's college classmate, a pretender to connoisseurship and a timid speculator; (2) his sister T'ien Kuo-hsiu, a frivolous girl of expensive habits, whom Hu—her eventual victim—views at first with abhorrence; (3) their cousin Ch'ien Heng, Kuo-hsiu's accepted suitor, a playboy and shrewd speculator, from whom Hu borrows ten thousand dollars and to whom he entrusts the same for lucrative investment; (4) Dr. America Huang, a blind syphilitic, cheat, and braggart who lives on speculation, blackmail, and delusions of glory; (5) his mistress and later bride, Miss Chang, known as the Old Maid. Each of these characters represents a type of corruption, and Part I records Hu's inevitable immersion in that element.

Hu's deterioration is signalized by his mounting infatuation for Kuo-hsiu: it is not so much love as a passion for vanity, possession, and economic security which comes with marrying a rich girl. By the time he dispatches his last letter to P'ei-fang, his head has been completely turned, in giddy expectation of a wonderful future. Kuo-hsiu, on her part, is going along with him because she has had a quarrel with Ch'ien Heng. But once Hu has consummated his passion with her, she turns away in revulsion from the prospect of marrying a poverty-stricken teacher and returns to the arms of her old suitor.

Meanwhile Hu has used up all his savings and gone heavily in debt because of his expensive dates with Kuo-hsiu and the monthly interest payments on his loan. He goes to see Ch'ien Heng about his investment. By that time Ch'ien Heng hates him thoroughly and the Pearl Harbor incident gives him the easy excuse that the ten thousand dollars has been converted into shares of a foreign stock, which is now completely worthless. (As a matter of fact, Ch'ien Heng has made a handsome profit on this money.) Completely undone, Hu finds to his further consternation that Kuo-hsiu now refuses him the door and that Kuo-pao, to whom he has earlier entrusted two manuscript textbooks, has published them in his own name. Hu again goes to see Ch'ien Heng; they have a fight, from which our hero emerges bloody and beaten. Thoroughly aroused and desperate, Hu later waylays Ch'ien Heng in a dark alley and kills him. He himself is immediately shot down by the police.

Like the heroes of several important modern Chinese novels, Hu Ch'ü-o is a dupe. But unlike them, he is a dupe by lack of worldly experience rather than by reason of his innate goodness. Even in his first letters, there is that element of smug superiority and self-righteousness which doesn't sort well with his vaunted purity. Given the chance to cheat and rob, he will in time become as ruthlessly efficient as Ch'ien Heng. One may argue that the trap into which Hu falls is nothing more than a huge hoax, but it is precisely this element of blindness which the author wishes to emphasize in his hero. In his first letter to P'ei-fang Hu sees himself as an underprivileged child maltreated by society. After he has failed to make good in the world of cutthroat competition, he again falls back upon this idea of social injustice to exculpate his own folly. It is only after he has killed Ch'ien Heng that he comes to know himself for what he is in a moment of extreme mental lucidity. But his passions will be soon cleansed by death.

It is because of Shih T'o's ironic concept of his hero that *Marriage* falls into the pattern of a tragic satire. The career of Hu Ch'ü-o is not contrasted with, but rather parallels, the careers of his associates. Each pursues something he believes to be profoundly good. In this respect Dr. America Huang emerges as the most grotesque and terrifying of the lot because he exemplifies the indestructible will to live. By sheer rapacity and ambition and in spite of his manifest handicaps he succeeds where the hero fails in the struggle for survival. One is almost tempted to regard him as the amoral life force in the allegorical scheme of the novel.

Dr. America Huang is certainly the most hauntingly memorable minor character in a modern Chinese novel. We first see him in a café, in the company of the Old Maid and the other characters. He is neatly dressed in a rather threadbare serge suit and covers his blindness with a pair of dark glasses. His face is completely smooth; not even the eyebrows are observable. He is talking about politics and the stock market with complete self-possession. For a violent contrast, we see him next with the Old Maid in his squalid flat, quarreling at the top of his voice with his landlord, who is trying to evict him. Dr. America Huang was once a teaching assistant at his alma mater in Peiping, handsome in appearance, married to a pretty girl, and ready to go to America for advanced study. Then syphilis, probably hereditary, strikes, and in the process of curing it, he goes blind and his wife deserts him for his doctor. He has been suing her ever since. When she finally settles the suit with a sum of thirty thousand dollars, he marries the Old Maid.

As one reads the first twenty pages of the novel, one naturally suspects that its title has something to do with the future union of Hu Ch'ü-o and P'ei-fang. But instead the novel ends with the wedding of Dr. America Huang and the Old Maid. The blind groom and the haggard bride, who have cohabited for years, constitute assuredly a mockery of the marriage institution. But in their grotesque way the couple triumphantly assert that will to live which has prompted all the folly in the novel.

The mock ceremony therefore concludes the novel with neat irony. The drive for security, pleasure, and power so conditions human existence that each person seems to be a player in a gigantic farce which is not so much pathetic as terrifying. Because Shih T'o is able to inject into his exciting narrative this element of fear, he has written in *Marriage* a novel of genuine distinction.

CHAPTER 18

Communist Fiction, II

PRIOR to the outbreak of the war, literary activities in Communist areas were confined to the most rudimentary types of propaganda: songs, story recitals, and "newspaper plays" designed for the edification of the troops and the local populace. Engaged in a desperate struggle for survival, the Communist leaders could not afford to promote literature and the arts. But the situation radically changed after the Sian Incident of 1936. The Communist Government now enjoyed virtual autonomy in the Shensi-Kansu-Ningsia region; and with the establishment of the Lu Hsün Institute of Arts at Yenan and the influx of a good number of seasoned Communist and leftist writers and intellectuals, it was in a position to build a positive Communist culture. At about the same time Mao Tse-tung began to turn out a series of highly influential books and pamphlets to instruct his now enlarged corps of cultural workers about their duties and tasks in relation to the Communist struggle against the Japanese and the National Government. Even though nearly all the more prominent Communist writers like Kuo Mo-jo, Mao Tun, and Hsia Yen were stationed in Nationalist areas during the war, the sheer industry of writers under Mao Tse-tung and his trusted literary taskmaster Chou Yang soon set in motion a re-orientation of Communist literature.

This literature can be properly divided into two periods: before and after 1949. Though writers since 1942 have undeviatingly turned to Mao's *Talks* for guidance, there is a perceptible difference in spirit between the two periods. During the earlier period, the myth of New Democracy still reigned and writers were under less fear of criticism: consequently they wrote with greater naive spontaneity and apparent eagerness to please the party. Especially during the interim years 1945–49, the collapse of the National Government and the land reforms already being carried out in "liberated" areas promised great excitement. A number of big novels were then produced to provide the illusion that the new Communist literature would have a future of unprecedented greatness.

With the rigid organization of writers into arbitrary regional units in 1949 and the imposition upon them of harsh discipline almost immediately afterward, enthusiasm waned. The reigning critics began to complain about the quantity and quality of the literature produced. The quandary was openly aired: why, with the country making big strides forward in almost every department of endeavor and the corps of writers many times the size of pre-liberation days,[1] could literary production not keep pace with the general national enthusiasm, and why, in comparison with the earlier period, did so few titles merit official endorsement? The situation, actually, should not have caused much puzzlement. It seems plain that, so long as the National Government was in power, it was relatively easy for writers to look forward to a great future and to submit willingly to the stringent requirements of the party line. With the removal of the hated Government, however, the Communist regime itself stood exposed in the eyes of the invincibly petty-bourgeois writers as the enemy. The party leaders tried their best to provide enemies toward which to channel the animosity of the writers and the people

470

at large—the American imperialists, Chiang Kai-shek, the landlords and the well-to-do, and other recalcitrant and saboteur elements in the nation. But these hate campaigns could not disguise the stark poverty and unremitting toil endured by the masses. Writers could only turn into hypocrites if they were to maintain their stand as eulogists of the new China, and hypocrisy was a state of mind completely inimical even to the creation of propaganda art.

If we ignore the rudimentary product of the early Yenan period, the new era of literature began with Mao's *Talks.* Almost immediately literary and art workers began to look for new ways of expressing themselves, to make use of native art forms of popular appeal. *Yang-ko,* a primitive form of peasant dance indigenous to the Shensi region, had been annexed as a potent instrument of propaganda since Mao Tse-tung's pronouncement on the importance of "national forms" in 1938. Now the cultural workers spoke excitedly of the yang-ko opera: by staging peasant dances and songs around a story, the propaganda potential of yang-ko could be realized much more effectively. After such early experimental skits as *Brother and Sister Tilling Virgin Soil,* there finally appeared a yang-ko opera with tremendous appeal: Ho Ching-chih and Ting I's *The White-haired Girl.* Supposedly based on a real story, the opera tells of a servant girl who was raped, and whose father was killed, by an evil landlord. To escape from his further villainy she lived in hiding and fear among the sunless caves (hence her hair turned white) until, with the liberation of the village, punishment was meted out to the landlord and she herself restored to civilized community. Another attempt, following the Yenan literary conference, was to add to the repertoire of the Peking Opera. Two plays based on episodes from *Water Margin* with supposedly revolutionary significance were produced. (After 1949, however, the cultural cadres re-examined the Peking Opera and proscribed the great majority of the plays for their feudalist morality.) Like dance and opera, songs and ballads are readily intelligible forms of propaganda and they were duly encouraged after 1942. Adapted to popular airs, songs in praise of Mao Tse-tung and the Communist party and in denigration of the old ways were produced in abundance; they were mostly crude jingles. Ballads were somewhat fewer; the most praised work in this genre was Li Chi's long narrative *Wang Kuei and Li Hsiang-hsiang* (1945), which, like *The White-haired Girl,* is an exaggerated account of landlord tyranny. In addition, it tells of a checkered romance of the title hero and heroine. They are happily united after the liberation of their village.

In view of the illiteracy of the Communist region, fiction was less stressed than poetry and drama. Before the Yenan literary conference there was little fiction produced besides two slim story collections by Ting Ling. After the conference, however, Chou Yang and the other critics began to look for some new writer fully committed to the Maoist line in literature. They found him in Chao Shu-li, an obscure cadre working with a newspaper, who had barely finished junior high school. But he had learned from his father, a Shansi farmer dabbling in herb medicine, fortunetelling, and balladry, the knack of telling stories and singing songs, and in 1943 he turned this talent to advantage in such stories as "The Marriage of Hsiao Erh-hei" and "The Verses of Li Yu-ts'ai." Chou Yang immediately hailed him as the people's new artist, in command of a new language and new subject matter.[2]

The interim period of 1945–49, as has been noted, witnessed heightened productivity among Communist-area authors, especially novelists. Notwithstanding the success of Chao Shu-li, these earnest novelists seemed to have turned for guidance to such popular Soviet novels as were then available in Chinese translation: Sholokhov's *Virgin Soil Upturned,* Fedor Gladkov's *Cement,* Nicholas Ostrovsky's *The Tempering of the Steel,* Vassily Grossman's *People Are Immortal;* they celebrated the transformation of land and people under Communism in the standard socialist-realist

manner rather than in a manner suggestive of a return to
"national forms." (There were, of course, stories and novels
cast in the popular style, such as Ma Feng and Hsi Jung's
Heroes of the Lü-liang Mountain, but even in Communist
eyes these works, mostly about the war of liberation, cannot
compare in merit with the more methodical novels.) Nearly
all these novels are about rural economy: Liu Ch'ing's *Sowing*
depicts the struggle of peasants against the richer farmers for
the implementation of cooperative farming; Ou-yang Shan's
Uncle Kao traces the success of a rural cooperative store; Ting
Ling's *Sun over the Sangkan River*, Chou Li-po's *The Hurricane*, and Ma Chia's *Ten Days in Chiang-shan Village* all
celebrate land reform in the Northeast. Ts'ao Ming's *Motive
Power* was the lone novel about industrial workers: it tells of
the restoration of a Manchurian power plant by heroic
workers under the guidance of the party. Though all very
dull and mechanical, these novels of national reconstruction
nevertheless mark the height of Communist literary achievement.

After 1949 literary zeal was deadened with the increasing
party insistence on purges and authorial reform. It is not without reason that the Communist literary historians often survey
the period in terms not of actual achievement but of the major
ideological struggles. In fiction the worker, peasant, soldier
line was still rigidly followed. In spite of the Government's
stress on heavy industry, worker fiction continued to lag behind peasant fiction, which dutifully justifies Communist
schemes toward further collectivization of farming.[3] Soldier
fiction naturally turned to the Korean War for its material,
in addition to the staple themes of the anti-Japanese and
liberations wars. As of 1957 very few reputable novelists had
turned out a novel since the establishment of the People's
Republic (though Ai Wu was to publish in 1958 a highly acclaimed novel called *Steeled and Tempered*). The novels
which have received official approval are all by relatively new
writers: Liu Ch'ing's *Walls of Brass and Iron*, Ch'en Teng-
k'o's *Buried Alive* and *Children by the Hwai River*, Ma Chia's

The War Period and After

Flowers Ever in Bloom, Yang Shuo's *A Thousand Miles of Lovely Land,* Chao Shu-li's *San-li Wan,* Tu P'eng-ch'eng's *In Defense of Yenan.*

Because of the uniformity of Communist fiction, it is almost profitless to discuss individual authors. Plots and characters follow certain stereotypes, and the note of propaganda is always prominent. Communist art is by definition optimistic: the celebration of past and present Communist glories and the promise of an even greater future. Tragedy is automatically ruled out because no individual is entitled to his own version of truth. Insofar as it has been traditionally preoccupied with social manners, comedy is also undesirable. The manners of bourgeoisie and gentry are too reprehensible to deserve comic attention; the behavior of the Communist cadres and the worker, peasant, soldier classes is or should be always exemplary. There are, of course, a few still permissible subjects for comedy—the old-style peasant fearful of change but basically good enough to merit improvement, or the haughty or fumbling cadre who has not committed serious errors—but even with these the satiric force is deadened, because the author can never be in league with the individual to defy society. Moreover, these comic characters are tolerated only when there are more important characters to uphold the party line and exemplify party conduct. Even in a short story there should be no faintest suspicion of satire against the positive characters. Thus Hsiao Yeh-mu was severely censured for "Between Us Husband and Wife" and his other fiction—after the film based upon the story had attracted party attention in 1952—on the ground of his supposed bourgeois levity. The story tells of a city intellectual and his peasant wife who have led a compatible life together in impoverished Communist areas. Upon their transfer to Peking following the Communist seizure of the mainland, they begin to experience an estranged relationship. The wife's rustic manners and her eagerness to find fault with the wicked ways of the capital shock her husband, and she, in turn, resents his easy resumption of city manners. The wife's excessive zeal finally brings upon her head the displeasure of party superiors, who ask her to exercise self-criticism. Later, as she confesses her error to her husband, he re-experiences the emotion of love and discerns more clearly her good qualities behind her boorishness. Insofar as Communists are also human, this story constitutes unexceptional domestic drama: after all, even a Communist couple could have differing dispositions and manners, could have quarreled and made up afterward. But the party critics were taken aback by the story's disclosure of conflict and tension between a Communist couple and by its supposed malicious caricature of the proletarian wife. The inference is that any Communist couple, by virtue of their being Communists, should be and are harmonious.

The positive characters should not only behave properly but manifest correct ideology at all times. The heinous fault of the movie *The Life of Wu Hsün*—and the case has its less famous duplications also in fiction—is that the makers of the film have misconstrued Wu Hsün to be a proletarian hero whereas from the Marxist point of view he was but an abject knave. Granted that this legendary beggar, this founder of charity schools for the poor, did have all the accessory proletarian virtues of courage, zeal, and self-denial, did he not beg all his life from the rich rather than start a revolution against them? Wasn't he, therefore, a docile slave of his betters in gladly accepting their philanthropy? The irony of the case is that all critics were praising the movie until the Central Committee of the party pointed out its complete perversity.

Not only the positive characters but the negative should wear their ideology on their sleeves at all times. The landlords, the Kuomintang agents, the Japanese soldiers must always be bad; their ingrained badness prevents them from entertaining one good thought, doing one good deed. For an author to ascribe to these any traits of humanity is to be automatically convicted of petty-bourgeois sentimentality. Thus

Fight Till Tomorrow, a routine war novel in celebration of Communist heroism, was condemned upon its appearance in 1951 (Part I of a radically revised version was published in 1958) because, among his many faults, its author Pai Jen had dared to allow a Japanese officer, Watanabe, a moment of remorse over his course of villainy. He had just ordered his troops to set fire to a Communist military base:

> "Fire, atrocious fire, big fires and small fires, all perpetrated by my own hand!" Watanabe pondered remorsefully and then with heavy steps trudged downhill. He thought to himself that it was not yet a month since the present campaign had started, and already forty-seven of his troops had perished. Every campaign added to the number of widows and orphans in his own country. Suddenly he recalled the scene of his departure: his young wife and his sickly daughter were standing on the pier, tearfully bidding him farewell. "Ah, time went so fast, it has been five years already! Very likely someday I, too, will die like my troops; I will be burned down to ashes and my ashes will be shipped back in a small urn. When my wife and daughter suddenly receive that urn, how grief-stricken they will be!" [4]

Parroting the more authoritative criticism earlier published in the *Literary Gazette,* the critic Pa Jen commented on this passage:

> This is to portray a Fascist bandit as a good man. In doing so, is not the author relinquishing the standpoint of his class and his nation? Whoever he is, a character in a piece of writing is always shouldering the tasks and duties appropriate to his class, he lives, works, and fights for their fulfillment. Therefore the author should give him the features, thoughts, and feelings appropriate to his class. Just think: how could a Fascist engaged in mad aggression, and a commanding officer to boot, have

harbored the thoughts and feelings depicted in this passage? [5]

As is made abundantly clear by the foregoing example, a Communist author can ind·ilge in psychological delineation only at his own risk. Since every character, good or bad, thinks the thoughts, feels the emotions, and dreams the dreams—not that dreams ever occur in recent mainland fiction—appropriate to his own class, psychological portrayal as we understand the term can only be completely irrelevant. Moreover, it is extremely dangerous to reveal the subjective weaknesses and strengths of a character not in full accord with his class status. One may be amused by Chou Yang's summary and critique of a story whose main fault, apparently, is to redeem boredom by adding some psychological twist to the propaganda routine:

> Some writers, in describing positive characters, not only fail to emphasize their new and noble qualities but frequently strive to seek out certain weak spots and dingy corners in the recesses of their soul. A very recent story by Ting K'o-hsin, "Old Worker Kuo Fu-shan" [*People's Literature, 4*, No. 1], may serve as an example. In this story the author depicts Kuo Chan-hsiang, the son of Kuo Fu-shan, as an exemplary character in every respect: a leader among railroad workers, the secretary of the local labor organization of the Party, "capable, inspiring confidence, and enjoying the support of all local party members." Yet, when enemy planes bomb our territory following the American imperialist invasion of Korea, this character suddenly becomes scared of the planes and turns into a "coward in fear of the planes, bombing, and death." Formerly he had been conscripted as a coolie in North Manchuria by the Japanese. One night he escaped from the heap of the dead when the Japanese machine-gunned over two hundred workers. Since then he has become afraid of the sound of the machine guns. His non-

Communist old father now demands that the local party branch expel his unworthy son from the Party, but the secretary of the branch takes a more lenient view of the case and only strips Kuo Chan-hsiang of his secretaryship. In the end, however, under the influence of his father, he overcomes his fear of the planes, and "both father and son become heroes." It is very apparent that the author not only caricatures the behavior of a model Communist member but disregards completely the function of Communist education and leadership. It looks as though a model Communist worker were inferior to a common old worker; as though at the critical moment the decisive factor for a man's behavior were not the degree of his political awakening but the physiological and psychological disturbance and abnormality due to certain causes; as though the atrocities of the imperialists could scare a Chinese worker; as though the reformation of a Communist member were due not to party education but to paternal education. In the whole incident, the decisive factors are physiological and psychological and not political, are in the nature of a family relationship and not of a party relationship. Politically and ideologically, this kind of writing is completely wrongheaded.[6]

With the exclusion of tragedy and comedy, and with the abolition of individual differentiation in psychological and moral terms, the domain of fiction—and of poetry and drama —is very small indeed. What is permissible are the simplest types of pastoral and melodrama. The pastoral mode stresses the idyllic happiness of the people—and it is the predominant mode in Communist pictorial art. But since it is far easier for artists to do group portraits of healthy peasants beaming with happiness and gratitude than for writers to embody this happiness in words, the pastoral mode in fiction is invariably subordinate to the melodramatic, though fabrications of idyllic serenity are useful as prophetic intimations of the socialist future which China will surely enjoy. But so far, by official admission, life in Communist China has been one long incessant struggle against enemies human and natural, and melodrama is the proper literary form for embodying that struggle. Engaged in it are four types of people—the enlightened and therefore incorruptible (the majority of cadres and the leaders among the worker, peasant, and soldier masses), the apparently good but oftentimes deluded (the masses and some cadres), the apparently bad but capable of reform (the middle farmers and citizens, the petty-bourgeois intellectuals and cadres), and the absolutely bad and completely irredeemable (the landlords, the Kuomintang agents, and all other masked or declared enemies of the people). The job of the novelist is to affirm the might of the enlightened, to attest to the reform of the middle groups, to expose and punish the wicked. For the obstruction of Communist programs the saboteur and reactionary elements must be responsible; for the success of these programs the Communist leadership must be given credit. Thus every story and novel observe the melodramatic formula of achievement, reform, and punishment.

In their more sober moments writers and critics alike despaired of the tyranny of formulism. How could writings transcend dullness if plots must conform to the optimistic pattern of struggle and achievement and characters to the national stereotype of good, bad, and reformable? The problem of creating interesting yet typical characters, especially, seemed to occupy the critics.[7] Patiently they demonstrated the techniques employed by Lu Hsün and classical Chinese novelists, by Gogol, Gorky, and Soviet novelists to achieve vivid characterization. Surely if these writers could create memorable characters of definite class physiognomy, our novelists should easily duplicate their success. But in their insistence on the typical traits of characters, these critics have ignored completely the sage advice of F. Scott Fitzgerald: "Begin with an individual, and before you know it you find

479

that you have created a type; begin with a type, and you find that you have created—nothing." Precisely because all novelists under Mao Tse-tung begin with types, they have created nothing.

When less inclined to be cooperative, the critics could always retort that the failure of recent fiction was the failure of the writers themselves to study Marxism-Leninism, to implement Mao Tse-tung's platform, to participate in the lives of the people. As a matter of policy, of course, writers have been regularly assigned to farms, factories, and war fronts to study real life. But the terrible irony here is that, should they honestly report what they saw, they would be immediately deprived of their rights and privileges as literary workers. However conscientiously they have participated in the lives of the people, they can only forgo that living knowledge to fabricate optimistic propaganda in confirmation of Communist success. In her portrayal of Comrade Ku—the literary cadre who witnesses a tragedy but has to report it as a conventional melodrama—Eileen Chang has defined the farcical plight of all writers in China today.

One possible advantage of living among the people is that writers have shown some success in manipulating the folk idiom as it is actually spoken. In comparison with the early revolutionary fiction, which is almost completely divorced from reality, Maoist fiction at least imitates speech and observes the superficies of life with something of documentary exactness. Debarred from matters of moral, psychological, and philosophical interest, writers who still care to some extent about literary art have little choice but to embark upon a path of regional specialization. Compare Ting Ling's *Water* with her more recent *Sun over the Sangkan River* and one is immediately struck by the more disciplined prose of the latter work and its much greater success in handling peasant dialogue. In this connection, perhaps *Uncle Kao* is even more remarkable. A Cantonese writer notorious for his Europeanized style in the thirties, Ou-yang Shan has managed to reproduce the idiom of Shensi with remarkable accuracy. But his novel remains extremely childish nevertheless. Regionalism, when unaccompanied by a personal and comprehensive vision of life, proves at best a self-defeating goal for the writer. One renders the minute particulars of a place and a society so as to reveal their essence; when that essence is preconceived in terms of a cliché, these particulars become, as it were, the dead albatross on the neck of the ancient mariner: the burdensome reminder of a murdered imagination. At their best, the recent novelists have rendered a superficial documentary realism, which is a fake realism because the deep-seated feelings and thoughts of the people have been systematically distorted to allow for the joyous note of the optimistic formula. Even the language of the peasants degenerates into an inert mass of billingsgate and jargon because it can no longer serve true sentiments. The poetic accent of peasant speech under strong emotion is inevitably lacking. The cultivation of specialized idioms, moreover, contradicts the cherished Communist objective of making literature more popular or better understood; it actually vitiates the norm of national or common speech (*kuo-yü*), to which earlier pai-hua writers have nearly always conformed.

Although the foregoing account may be sufficient to characterize Communist fiction since 1942, to be more specific I shall examine a few of its prized exhibits: the works of Chao Shu-li (1903–) and Ting Ling's *Sun over the Sangkan River*. Prevalent Communist opinion takes Chao Shu-li to be a worthy successor to such giants of fiction as Lu Hsün and Mao Tun; as for Ting Ling, even though she herself has been purged, her novel still deserves critical attention because it stood for years as one of the proudest monuments of the Maoist era of literature.[*]

[*] Chao Shu-li, too, has beeen purged since the Cultural Revolution. In the perspective of that revolution, there would seem to have been no recent novelists worthy of praise.

It is almost impossible to discover any merit in Chao Shu-li's early stories, unless one takes as positive virtues their facetious tone (which passes for humor) and their colloquial style (which makes the stories somewhat more enjoyable when read aloud). As a matter of fact, "The Marriage of Hsiao Erh-hei" and "The Verses of Li Yu-ts'ai," which first prompted Chou Yang's glowing praise of their author, are about two of the feeblest stories ever to have been thrust upon public attention: much worse frauds than Bret Harte's supposed classics of frontier realism, "The Luck of Roaring Camp" and "The Outcasts of Poker Flat," ever were for their time. Chao Shu-li's clumsy and clownish style is utterly incompetent to serve the purposes of narration, and his so-called new subject matter is merely a rehash of the familiar themes of antifeudal-ism and Communist benevolence. "The Marriage of Hsiao Erh-hei" is a simple tale designed to discredit superstition and praise the new marital freedom under Communism. Son of a crabbed peasant with an invincible weakness for prognostica-tion, Hsiao Erh-hei is in love with Hsiao Ch'in, the pretty daughter of a village flirt who earns her living as a medium. This young couple, planning to get married, meets with op-position from the hero's father, who believes that their union will spell misfortune, and from the heroine's mother, who wants to inveigle Hsiao Erh-hei for herself. With the interven-tion of the village cadre, this set of complications is easily solved. The father forswears fortunetelling and the mother gives up necromancy and flirting. They become productive farm workers, and their children are happily united. The story reflects the somewhat gentler pace of the Yenan days when it was still possible for writers to provide illusions of idyllic happiness. But instead of being a precursor of new fiction, the story is rather a throwback to the sentimental anti-feudal fiction perpetrated by bad writers of the May Fourth period. Because of the extremely backward conditions in the Communist region, the battle against feudalism, which had been fought and won, had to be restaged.

In "The Verses of Li Yu-ts'ai" the hero is a balladist who enjoys the hobby of making satiric or facetious rhymes out of the passing events of his village. Largely a self-portrait of the author, Li Yu-ts'ai is instrumental in enabling the villagers to see the corruption of their local government and in bringing about a new Communist order. Like "Hsiao Erh-hei," the story is a fumbling attempt at folk humor. It has been especially praised for the rhymes interspersed in the prose narrative. The use of this hoary device means, for the Communists, a successful incorporation of "national forms" into new writing.

In spite of the inanities of these two tales, Chou Yang is perhaps justified in regarding them as a new departure in Communist literature because of their complete dissociation from the Western-slanted leftist tradition and their gleeful naiveté as propaganda. In their attempt to implement the Maoist line in literature, the better-educated writers often had to resort to hypocritical condescension to ensure correctness. But the early Chao Shu-li displayed a childish and gullible delight in the blessings of the Communist regime that is free of irony. In the cult of Chao Shu-li one sees not so much the emergence of a new literature as the promotion of a new mentality ideally conditioned to abet Communist power.

Following his early successes, Chao Shu-li wrote a short novel called *The Changes in Li Village* (1945), which has remained the most readable of his works. Dispensing with his clownishness and making able use of the style of traditional fiction, the author achieves in this work of 200 pages a remarkable feat of narration, especially in view of his limited education. The first half of the novel especially attains a dignity of sorts as it unfolds a picturesque and often arresting panorama of backward northern Shansi. Drawing upon personal experience, Chao Shu-li tells with apparent honesty the tribulations of the peasant hero T'ieh-so and the callous egotism of the opium-smoking landlords and officials of the Yen Hsi-shan provincial government from the year 1928 onward. Gradually but inevitably, however, the fairy-tale quality of naive candor yields to an increasingly assertive propaganda note until the novel becomes a routine piece about the benevolence of the Communist cadres, the awakening and liberation of the peasants, and the punishment of the wicked landlords.

The Changes in Li Village is atypical of recent Communist fiction in that it makes extensive use of the author's intimate knowledge of pre-Communist Shansi without benefit of research. On the whole, the new fiction dispenses with personal reminiscence and embodies the fruit of actual field work. In preparing *Sun over the Sangkan River,* Ting Ling tells us, she participated in the work of the land-reform corps at Hwai-lai and Cholu in Chahar province for the summer of 1946, and in the process of writing the novel she had to observe land-reform work being carried out in various parts of Central Hopei for a four-month period in 1947. Hence this most praised of recent Communist novels—in 1951 it won a Stalin Second Prize for Literature—tackles a definite subject supposedly in the spirit of documentary realism.

The story takes place in Nuanshui Village near the city Cholu, along the Sangkan River. There used to be eight big landowners at the village, but since its liberation by the Communist forces four of them have either met punishment at public trials or successfully escaped to the nearby cities. Panic seizes the remaining four when a new detachment of the Land Reform Corps arrives in the village to complete the unfinished task. The shrewdest of the lot, Ch'ien Wen-kuei, puts up a tough fight to save his life and property. He has already married his daughter to a party member and enlisted his son in the Red Army; now he uses his niece, Hei-ni, as a bait for Ch'eng Jen, once a hired man on his farm and now chairman of the local Peasants' Association. For a brief period, while the land and property of the other three landlords are being seized and redistributed, Ch'ien stands unassailable, relying on his old prestige with the villagers and his new official connections with the party to stave off his inevitable doom. Then, at the combat meeting, Ch'eng Jen, who has hesitated to denounce Ch'ien because of his love for Hei-ni, finally turns against him and whips up a mob fury:

"Friends!" said Ch'eng. "Look at him and me, look how pampered he is; it's not cold yet but he's wearing a lined gown. Then look at me, look at yourselves. Do we look like human beings! Hah, when our mothers bore us, we were all alike! We've poured our blood and sweat to feed him. He's been living on our blood and sweat, oppressing us all these years; but today we want him to give back money for money, life for life, isn't that right?"

"Right! Give back money for money, life for life!" . . .

"All peasants are brothers!" "Support Chairman Mao!" "Follow Chairman Mao to the end!" Such shouts sounded from the stage and from the crowd.

Then people rushed up to the stage, stumbling over each other to confront Ch'ien. Ch'ien's wife with tear-stained cheeks stood before her husband, pleading with them all: "Good people, have pity on my old man! Good people!" Her hair was disheveled, there were no longer flowers in it, the traces of black varnish could still be seen. She was just like a female clown in the theater, making a fine couple with her husband. She had echoed him all her life, and now she still clung to him, unwilling to separate their fates . . .

People surged up to the stage, shouting wildly: "Kill him!" "A life for our lives!"

A group of villagers rushed to beat him. It was not clear who started, but one struck the first blow and the others fought to get at him, while those behind who could not reach him shouted: "Throw him down! Throw him down! Let's all beat him!"

One feeling animated them all—vengeance! They wanted vengeance! They wanted to give vent to their

hatred, the sufferings of the oppressed since their ancestors' times, the hatred and loathing of thousands of
years; all this resentment they directed against him.
They would have liked to tear him with their teeth.

The cadres could not stop everyone jumping onto the
stage. With blows and curses the crowd succeeded in
dragging him down from the stage and then more people swarmed toward him. Some crawled over across the
heads and shoulders of those in front.

Ch'ien's silk gown was torn. His shoes had fallen off;
the white paper hat had been trampled into pieces un-
derfoot. All semblance of order was gone and Ch'ien was
going to be beaten to death, when Yü-min [the village
Party secretary] remembered Pin's last instructions and
pushed his way into the crowd. Having no other way of
stopping them, he shielded Ch'ien with his body, and
shouted: "Don't be in such a hurry to beat him to death!
We've got to ask the county authorities!" And then the
militiamen hastily checked the people . . .

[After the fury had subsided] Ch'ien raised himself
again and kneeled to kowtow to the crowd. His right eye
was swollen after his beating so that the eye looked even
smaller. His lip was split and mud was mixed with the
blood. His bedraggled mustaches drooped disconsolately.
He was a fearful sight, and as he thanked the villagers
his voice was no longer clear and strong, but he stam-
mered out: "Good people! I'm kowtowing to you good
folks. I was quite wrong in the past. Thank you for your
mercy . . ."

A group of children softly aped his voice: "Good people! . . ." [8]

This climactic lynching scene, from which only a few excerpts have been given, ends with Ch'ien writing a statement
which reads: "I, Ch'ien Wen-kuei, a local despot, committed
crimes in the village, oppressing good people, and I deserve

to die a hundred times over; but thanks to the mercy of the liberated gentlemen, my dog life has been spared. In future I must completely change my former evil ways. If I transgress in the slightest or oppose the masses, I shall be put to death. This statement is made by the local despot Ch'ien Wen-kuei, and signed in the presence of the masses. August 3d." [9]

One should note that, while sparing no details in giving a picture of the villagers' maddened hatred for the despot, Ting Ling shrewdly attributes leniency and a respect for order to the cadres, contrary to authenticated reports of their inhumanity with regard to the punishment of the landlords. In all Communist novels about land reform, it is always the people who are after blood and the cadres gratify this desire only to the extent prescribed by legal justice. Unlike journalistic and sociological reports, a novel is of course not subject to factual verification; the reader can judge its truth or falsehood only with reference to his own expectations about the area of experience touched upon, the total tone of the work, and the general ability and intention of the author. There is no doubt that, in the lynching scene as in the rest of the novel, Ting Ling is aiming at a kind of truth, the superficial truth which it is to the advantage of the party to propagate, which every Communist author must propagate if he is to survive. Ting Ling records the fury and the hatred and the brutal beating, all commonplace facts at public trials of landlords; but what the cadres must have done to generate this fury and hatred, what the peasants actually feel while parading their violence, how the landlords themselves feel, not so much over their gross physical punishment as over its monstrous injustice—with all these deeper truths Ting Ling is not concerned, and cannot be concerned. The incomparable superiority of Eileen Chang's *Love in Redland*—whose first hundred pages deal with land reform—to *Sun over the Sangkan River* is precisely due to its author's concern with these deeper truths, her ability to project normal human feelings and attitudes under abnormal circumstances, her evocation of the sense of outrageous crime, implicating alike the cadres and their fear-ridden and hectored peasant accomplices.

A conscientious attempt to tell the party truth, *Sun over the Sangkan River* is for the most part a very dull book. A novel of about 460 pages, it has actually fifty-eight chapters, most of which are short sketches of the villagers and of the cadres who come to work among them. As sociological case histories, however, some of these sketches contain a surprising amount of material for the documentation of fear. Whether out of her mistaken zeal to grasp the dialectic of history in all its complexities or out of her latent hostility toward the Communist regime—even in 1942 Ting Ling was voicing her discontent with the Yenan bureaucrats—we cannot know; but she did devote space to the disquiet and suffering of the persecuted minority, though always careful to establish beforehand their reactionary or feudalist character. The novel therefore does have some interesting moments in its depiction of a village cowering under the fear of land reform.

Among the more touching portraits is that of a devout Buddhist, Hou Chung-ch'üan. He used to be a worker on the farm of his uncle Hou Tien-k'uei, a bad landlord. After the redistribution of the latter's land, however, he refuses to take any part of it, keeping to himself the skeptical knowledge of the vanity of any human reform:

> At the trial of Hou that spring many people urged Chung-ch'üan to settle old scores, but he refused. He said he must have owed his uncle's family something from a former existence, and if he took back what he had paid, in his next existence he would become a horse or an ox. Thus later he insisted on returning to Hou that one and a half *mou* of land given him. Now his outlook was unchanged. The Eighth Route Army talked very well, but he knew from all he had read and heard that never once in thousands of years had the poor been

masters. Chu Hung-wu was born poor, and set himself up as champion of the poor. But after he became emperor, although he was all right for the first few years, he changed. He became champion of his own gang while the common people remained as before. Chung-ch'üan saw that many youngsters in the village took a short view, thinking only of the immediate future and echoing the Eighth Route Army; hence he feared for them. He did not allow his son to mix with such people. If his family was required to participate in any activities, he attended himself, thinking it would not matter if anything happened to him. An old man over sixty, who had never injured anyone in his life, need not fear the Judge of the Dead. But he kept his thoughts to himself. When others expressed approval he simply tugged his beard and smiled. He knew of course one hand could not stop the flood destroying the bank, but he had no idea that the flood would reach his threshold and that he himself would be carried away by it.[10]

Chung-ch'üan is supposed to be a pathetic and rather foolish old man, and his cogitations merely serve to expose his superstitious attitude of resignation. Yet his passive resistance to Communism suggests courage, and his implied comparison of Mao Tse-tung with the founder of the Ming dynasty is ironically apt, though most probably Ting Ling had not intended any irony in the first place.

Another interesting malcontent is the schoolteacher Jen Kuo-chung, who is contemptuous of his colleagues and highly doubtful of the eventual Communist victory. Believing that Chiang Kai-shek will still win, he spreads rumors on the sly to undermine the villagers' confidence in the Communists and often visits Ch'ien Wen-kuei to vent his anger:

Humph, the Communists always say they are working for the poor, for the people, but that's just so much fine talk. Mr. Ch'ien, you should go to Kalgan to see. Hah!

Who live in the best houses? Who ride in cars? Who are always coming in and out of the best restaurants? Aren't they the ones who've grown fat? Mr. Ch'ien, nobody wearing an old-fashioned long gown can get anywhere nowadays.[11]

Such words, even if spoken by a rather disreputable character, carry a surprising weight in a novel designed to glorify Communists as friends of the people.

Sun over the Sangkan River is at its best when it delineates the shifting social alliances following the intrusion of the cadres upon the placid village. Communism abolishes the old privileged class but creates in its place a new one. Tact, snobbery, and diplomacy play about the same roles in human relations as in the old regime. Occasionally Ting Ling forgets about her land reform to probe this social drama. Thus Ch'eng Jen, who is in love with Hei-ni, dare not visit her because she is a member of a landlord family; Ch'ien Wen-kuei and his wife, on the other hand, are solicitous of his company because of his position in the Peasants' Association:

By liberating the village the Eighth Route Army also liberated Hei-ni. Her uncle dropped his match-making and changed his attitude to her, and appeared much more kindly. The increased respect with which Ch'eng was regarded in the village delighted her, for although they were seeing less of each other she did not think he was fickle. She failed to realize Ch'eng's new dilemma. As a matter of fact he was deliberately keeping his distance. He knew all the villagers hated Ch'ien, that although the latter had escaped mass trial twice he was nonetheless the worst enemy of the poor. Now as Chairman of the Peasants' Association Ch'eng ought to identify himself with the masses and not go marrying Ch'ien's niece, while an affair with her would be even worse. He feared this connection might damage his position and set tongues wagging, the more so since the marriage of

Ch'ien's daughter Ta-ni to village Security Officer Chang had caused general displeasure. Hence he must harden his heart. Although his deliberate coldness to Hei-ni was very painful to him, and he felt not a little ashamed of it, still he was a man, he could set his teeth and stick it out.[12]

In any pre-Mao fiction this passage would be unexceptional indeed; but with the Communist discouragement of psychological writing Ch'eng's deliberations constitute one of the rare bright spots in a lackluster novel.

Within the requirements of Communist propaganda, Ting Ling portrays conscientiously many types of village people and party functionaries, including among the latter such undesirable characters as the avaricious Chao Ch'üan-kung; Wen Ts'ai of the Land Reform Corps, who is haughty, pedantic, and inept; and Chang Cheng-tien, whose allegiance to his father-in-law—Ch'ien Wen-kuei—clashes with his party loyalty. The novelist also reproduces adequately the peasant idiom of the Northeast. But this realism is at best superficial because its criticism of the cadres falls safely in line with the *cheng-feng* objectives and never for a moment touches the basic evil of Communism, and because its language, however colloquial, cannot disclose the human heart without at the same time calling in question the Communist concept of happiness and justice. One recalls with nostalgia the more disturbing realism of Mao Tun's *Vacillation,* which depicts the party reformers and the scheming reactionaries of an earlier generation in an entirely different fashion.

Of the post-1949 fiction I am content to give one example only—Chao Shu-li's *San-li Wan.* As the work of the most acclaimed people's novelist it should be as respectable as any other recent novel; moreover, it can be taken as a sequel to *Sun over the Sangkan River.* Ting Ling's novel celebrates land reform; Chao Shu-li's celebrates collective farming. Serialized in *People's Literature* (January–April 1955) and published in book form soon afterward, *San-li Wan* was designed as a major propaganda effort to coincide with Mao Tse-tung's decree on the nation-wide conversion of all arable land into agricultural production cooperatives. Like Ting Ling, Chao Shu-li did intensive field work. In the spring of 1951 he was sent to his native province of Shansi to study a model village that had been liberated in the early forties. The landlords there had long been liquidated and a provisional form of collective farming—mutual aid teams—had been in operation for some time. The novelist arrived at the time when all peasants were required to relinquish their land, cattle, and tools to make the cooperative a going concern. In the next year Chao Shu-li again went back to see how the experiment was working out. The novel supposedly embodies his findings.[13]

Land reform had been carried out on the supposition that the peasants would be better off once the big holdings of the landlords were parceled out among them. Under the policy of collective farming, however, the same peasants were asked to turn over practically everything they owned, not merely the land and goods they had recently acquired. Resentment was inevitable, especially among the industrious middle farmers who were averse to sharing their wealth with the destitute. They naturally became the principal villains in Chao Shu-li's novel.

In San-li Wan Village the middle farmers most strongly opposed to joining the cooperative are Fan Teng-kao, village leader and captain of the mutual aid teams, and Ma To-shou, who, dominated by a scheming, old-fashioned wife and plagued by a discordant large family, won't even give up a portion of his land for a proposed canal to go through. While the latter represents the dogged persistence of feudalist thinking, the former is the much more interesting case of capitalist mentality. A muleteer in the employ of a landlord in the pre-Communist days, Fan Teng-kao has risen to the top mainly by dint of his progressive showing at the time of the land reform. He is now not only the most prosperous farmer but also the village's only small trader, selling more attractive household goods than those sold in the local cooperative store. As captain of the mutual aid teams, he is also in a position to argue with the cadres against his joining the farm cooperative. He is finally subjected to concerted attack at party meetings, however, and always prudent he immediately reverses his position, eloquently repudiating his capitalist selfishness. With Fan's example before them and thanks also to the earnest efforts of the cadres and the more progressive members of their own families, the other recalcitrant farmers also fall in line. On the eve of the national holiday—October 1—the whole village has agreed to join the collective venture and begin work on the canal, to bring about greater productivity in the area.

As a combat novel, *San-li Wan* is much less violent than *Sun over the Sangkan River:* after all, the middle farmers are merely greedy of private gain and have not committed the heinous crimes of the landlords. Chao Shu-li is also much more determined to paint an idyllic picture of the village: evidence of Communist success must be shown if the nation at large is to accept further sacrifices for the implementation of Mao's new agricultural policy. In the novel the resident artist Lao Liang paints three panoramic pictures of the village: San-li Wan today; San-li Wan next year, when the canal will help irrigate the fields; and San-li Wan many years hence, when every household in the cooperative will be prosperous enough to own an automobile. (In reality, of course, the people's communes will soon replace the small-scale cooperatives.) In accordance with the pastoral scheme, Chao Shu-li draws a happy picture of village youth completely docile to the will of the party: Wang Yü-sheng, though handicapped by the lack of a formal education, is a sort of youthful Edison forever designing new tools and machines for the facilitation of large-scale farming, and his elder brother Wang Chin-sheng, the local party secretary, devotes his days and nights to the welfare of the village. As if to compensate for the extreme dullness of large portions of the book devoted to party meetings and a scrupulous geographical survey of the village, the author also concerns himself with romantic entanglements involving six young people. He tries hard to be lively and comic in these romantic scenes but, as might be expected, with no success. In Communist China one evaluates one's mate solely by ideology and capacity for work; subjective romantic feelings are positively discouraged. Under these circumstances the most complicated romance Chao Shu-li is able to manage concerns Fan Ling-chih, daughter of Fan Teng-kao. She is attracted to Ma Yu-i, son of Ma To-shou, because they both have "culture," that is, they both have been to junior high school and are now teachers at the local night school. By the time Ma is proven an irresolute coward completely tied to his mother's apron strings (with his culture, of course, he is too good to remain a negative character; he, too, progresses in the end), Fan has been drawn to Wang Yü-sheng, the village Edison. But she broods over the fact that Wang hasn't been to junior high school: "This youth, so sincere and earnest, so unselfish and clever, so capable and handsome—what a pity he doesn't have culture!" [14] Eventually she dismisses her scruples and is ready to marry him. The prevalence of snobbery among Chinese youth today should prove a matter of positive interest to the novelist, but Chao Shu-li handles it ineptly: the drama of Fan Ling-chih's self-debate, admittedly the romantic high light of the novel, stands convicted as unintentional comedy.[15]

In discussing the works of Ting Ling and Chao Shu-li, I have not touched on worker fiction and soldier fiction, which, because the better writers have preferred to specialize in peasant fiction, seem to merit even less critical attention. The incredible heroism of Stakhanovite workers toiling day and night to "overfulfill" production goals and of Communist troops and volunteers triumphantly battling Kuomintang fascism and American imperialism is to be expected; the formula of achievement, reform, and punishment is rehearsed with even greater monotony. No branch of fiction—of literature—can hope to circumvent the stringent propaganda requirements.

In the early fifties the leading Communist critics—Mao Tun, Ting Ling, Feng Hsüeh-feng, and even Chou Yang—generally deplored the current literary product. But after Hu Feng's withering exposure of its sheer inanity, the literary establishment began to sing a different tune, to maintain that the post-1949 literature was indeed excellent. It could do little to change the inherent formulism of this literature, of course; but it could at least spur production. In the wake of the anti-Hu Feng campaign, therefore, the "prosperity" (*fan-jung*) of literature and art became the new theme: even the slogan "Let a Hundred Flowers Bloom" was primarily designed to promote this prosperity. But the rightist movement soon confirmed its illusory nature.

By the end of 1957 the rightist movement had been quashed and the literary hierarchy was again determined to spur production. Scores of writers and theatrical workers were sent to farms, factories, mines, barracks, and border regions to study Communist life at first hand.[16] By early 1958 the whole nation was straining its every muscle to make the Big Leap Forward to increase production, and literary workers were no exception. Writers in Shanghai alone pledged to deliver 3,000 pieces of work within two years.[17] A much larger quantity of new literature was indeed published in 1958, promising an era of greater freedom for the writers. But unless the Communist leadership is truly unafraid to commit itself to a program of liberalization—which is unlikely—the present phase of literary "prosperity" will again be short-lived.

CHAPTER 19

Conclusion

THE SUCCESS of Communism in China has imposed upon the public a Communist view of modern Chinese literature which is well-nigh unchallenged. Even recent anti-Communist critics on Taiwan and in Hong Kong could only decry or disparage a body of creative and critical writing that represents substantially the Communist idea of modern Chinese achievement in literature: in their eagerness to expose Communist propaganda, past and present, they have not taken the trouble to look for an alternative tradition of possibly greater literary significance.[1] Earlier, in the years immediately preceding the Communist conquest of the mainland, a few European Catholic missionary educators, appalled by the rebellious and atheistic temper of modern Chinese literature, had taken it severely to task. But handicapped by a narrow moralism and an inadequate command of the language, these educators are careless and naive critics given to denouncing the whole contemporary product, with the exception of a few Catholic writers, as the work of the Devil. Their investigations and compilations, based largely on secondary sources, have only a sociological and bibliographical interest.[2]

Yet a literary history, to be meaningful, has to be an essay in discrimination and not a biased survey to satisfy extrinsic political or religious standards. Present-day Communist literary historians are vitiated at the outset by their obligatory allegiance to the ruling power. It is not surprising that in their surveys of the modern period only the names of the literary legislators—Mao Tse-tung, Ch'ü Ch'iu-pai, Chou Yang—are sacrosanct: even the high praise accorded to such leading writers as Kuo Mo-jo and Mao Tun is more an official tribute to their past services in behalf of the Communist party and their present political eminence than a critical recognition of their literary merits. That, in their heyday, Mao Tun was a much better writer than Kuo Mo-jo makes little difference to these historians; in fact, Kuo Mo-jo is invariably assigned a greater literary importance than Mao Tun not only because his official prestige is higher but because his political record has been less checkered with known instances of dissidence. For the Communist historians, therefore, literary excellence is equated with political orthodoxy, and an author's reputation finally depends upon his official status in the literary and political establishment and his continuing maintenance of a spotless record of party loyalty. The downfall of Ting Ling and Feng Hsüeh-feng has made all pre-1957 manuals of modern Chinese literature out of date because their authors could not have detected the antiparty character of these prominent writers (even if they had the necessary political prescience, they could not have denounced these writers when they were still enjoying official favor).

If we discount such political figures as Mao Tse-tung and Ch'ü Ch'iu-pai, Lu Hsün is the only modern author who has been accorded a fully classical stature. But in view of his diminishing use for the present regime and his positively disruptive influence among writers, his official status will be eventually radically revised: it is only because the Communist propaganda machine has been fully in support of the Lu Hsün myth for over twenty years that the displacement of this myth is at present unlikely. For whatever services he may have rendered in the past, an author has eventually to be judged by his usefulness to the present moment. All standards are relative, except this pragmatic test of immediate service-ableness. Even Kuo Mo-jo and Mao Tun can only adopt, as they actually did on many occasions, an apologetic attitude toward their pre-1949 writings because, despite their obvious historic function, they are, in the light of present literary and government policies, embarrassingly incorrect in the degree they are ridden by a revolutionary ideology not in complete accord with Maoism or a bourgeois literary elegance too re-fined for proletarian consumption. A Communist literary his-tory, therefore, is not only subject to continual revision so as to accommodate itself to the latest official caprice; it is per-force a chronicle of writers and their works that have fulfilled and partially outlived their function.[3] They are to be ad-mired as museum pieces are admired, but they no longer constitute a living tradition still able to mold and influence present-day writing. In its insistence that writers observe the political and literary decrees of the day, Communist criticism has nullified tradition and voided the meaning of literary history.

In my survey of modern Chinese fiction, I have been prin-cipally guided by considerations of literary significance. While I have discussed representative Communist authors and examined at some length the prepotent Communist in-fluence, my main intention has been to contradict rather than affirm the Communist view of modern Chinese fiction. The writers toward whom I have shown critical approval or en-thusiasm share by and large the same set of techniques, at-titudes, and fantasies with the other writers of their period, but by virtue of their talent and integrity, they have resisted and in some notable cases transformed the crude reformist and propagandist energies to arrive at a tradition that pre-sents a different literary physiognomy from the tradition com-posed principally of leftist and Communist writers. In his *Studies in Classic American Literature,* D. H. Lawrence gives utterance to one of the profoundest maxims to the imaginative writer: "Lose no time with ideals; serve the Holy Ghost; never serve mankind." [4] In the searching light of this remark, the generally mediocre level of modern Chinese literature is surely due to its preoccupation with ideals, its distracting and overinsistent concern with mankind. In view of the cultural milieu of the modern Chinese writer, this was perhaps as it should be: until social justice, scientific and technological competence, and a measure of national strength were achieved, he had little choice but to serve his ideals. In fact, his ideals came to him in the insidious shape of the Holy Ghost. Not merely in the literary context, the success of Communism was mainly due to its dazzling ability to identify itself with these ideals. It can be said categorically that, with two or three exceptions, no modern Chinese writer possessed enough compelling genius and imagination to carve his own path in defiance of the Zeitgeist; but the writers of talent and integrity, while espousing those ideals, also serve in their fashion, often reluctantly and in spite of themselves, the Holy Ghost. The work of these writers does not evince great imaginative power or technical brilliance; the intrusive presence of utilitarian ideals precludes the disinterested search for excellence; but it does have the quality of honesty, disturbing and illuminating enough in its depiction of the contemporary Chinese scene to deserve the attention of posterity.

In the short-story writers and novelists we have studied, from Lu Hsün to Eileen Chang, there is observable an impressive note of realistic integrity, little adorned with the rhetoric of propaganda. It should offer no surprise that few of these writers were doctrinaire Communists at the time they were producing significant work. (Of the large quantity of leftist and proletarian fiction produced in the United States during the thirties, how very little is remembered today.) The best writers of the first period were not Communists mainly because the Communist current had not yet usurped the mainstream of the May Fourth Movement. In the second period Mao Tun and Chang T'ien-i tower above their fellow Communist writers, but in their best work there is a substratum of deep personal emotion, a ground of reality, which the thin layer of Marxist rhetoric cannot disguise. In the best stories of Chang T'ien-i especially, the emotion of hatred or disgust is completely objectified in dramatic situations, leaving little room for sentimental leftist gestures. In the pair of independent writers of the period, Shen Ts'ung-wen and Lao Shê, we have an affirmation of China grounded upon an intimate knowledge of the land and the people; this affirmation does not exclude the prevalent attitude of repudiation; rather it is included in the modes of pastoral and comedy. Both writers are distinguished for their historical awareness of the Chinese character: its heroic endurance, its present decadence, and its hope for rejuvenation. It may be said that this "character" interpretation is as partial and fanciful as the Marxist economic interpretation, but it at least enabled the novelists to tackle the contemporary scene concretely, with minimal distortion of the kind which is conspicuous in Communist fiction: the "class" physiognomy of the characters arrived at by caricature and idealization.

In the Nationalist interior as well as the Communist areas the war period marks the sad decline of realism, the general contentment with the formulas of patriotic propaganda. This setback is tied in not only with the conditions of poverty and cultural stagnancy but with the establishment of an astringent Communist criticism and censorship, under the sponsorship of Mao Tse-tung himself. Fiction in Communist areas, consequently, becomes completely sterile, even though Communist writers in the Nationalist interior, such as Mao Tun and Sha T'ing, are still able to maintain a semblance of honesty by resort to satire. The most significant literature of the war period is produced neither in the Nationalist nor in the Communist interior; it is turned out by a woman writer in occupied Shanghai, Eileen Chang. Her stories of modern as well as traditional Chinese life are civilized, profound, and often relentlessly tragic. The postwar period, increasingly dominated by Communist letters, nevertheless strives for a short while to equal or even surpass the prewar level of excellence. Several fine novels contribute to that impression: Ch'ien Chung-shu's *The Besieged City,* Pa Chin's *Cold Nights,* Shih T'o's *Marriage.* None of these works heed the literary principles of Mao Tse-tung, but with the rapid disintegration of the National Government they are only isolated examples of creative integrity, utterly impotent to generate any salutary influence to oppose the rising tide of a new Communist literature.

The finer modern Chinese fiction, quite clearly, yields a pattern of meaning and preoccupations different from the general run of fiction of the period. Its first characteristic is its sober examination of contemporary life in China. This realism is accompanied by a sense of pity, considerable satire, and some serious attempt toward an imaginative understanding of Chinese society as a whole. Against the sentimental and overtly didactic approach to the problems of national decadence and backwardness, the best recourse, in keeping with the realistic temper, is satire: Lu Hsün, Lao Shê, Chang T'ien-i, Ch'ien Chung-shu, and nearly all the other good writers are satirists by choice or necessity, to air their disgust with the ugliness of reality as well as to stave off the strong humanitarian pressures. The reverse of satire is self-pity: the admission of one's failure in a world of corruption and decadence. Ubiquitous among the early writers, this narcissistic mode, nevertheless, still represents a desperate means for maintaining honesty and holding out against overt didacticism. In Yeh Shao-chün both satire and self-pity assume muted forms, though his only novel, *Ni Huan-chih,* comes close to being a cry of despondency. In Mao Tun self-pity takes the form of revulsion against the bourgeois way of life. But both satire and self-pity are easily perverted under the ideological compulsion for social reform. In the hands of doctrinaire Communist writers satire is nothing but stereotyped caricature, while self-pity becomes a sentimental posture of social protest with such romantic-revolutionary writers as the early Pa Chin. In the long perspective satire has emerged as the most stable and fructifying feature of modern Chinese fiction, though it is never quite separable from the self-pitying mode.

Whether satirical or humanitarian, the finer fiction commands an adequate personal knowledge of the manners and morals of its times. The shabbiness of most proletarian and romantic-revolutionary fiction of the period is surely due to its almost complete disregard for manners. The situations it depicts are altogether too crude and ideal to be plausible. Whatever their personal attitude toward contemporary behavior, the abler writers all know the impossibility of reaching the higher truth without first attending to the observable reality of social intercourse. Their strong antifeudal passion does not deter the early writers from deeply scrutinizing traditional manners. In Lu Hsün's classical studies of the gentry and peasantry, "Soap" and "Divorce," the exploration of a complex system of traditional manners and morals takes on a quality of horror. In a similar spirit Yeh Shao-chün defines the small gray world of teachers, clerks, and peasants. Ping Hsin and Ling Shu-hua etch with elegant precision a small section of the genteel and shabby-genteel world.

The same fidelity to observable reality characterizes the subsequent good writers. Chang T'ien-i's supreme talent as satirist is his powerful realization of the ugly manners of the village, gentry, and bureaucracy. Although prone to naturalistic exaggeration, Mao Tun is adept at portraying the manners of the big city, so full of contradictions between traditional and modern commercial ways of life. From Lao Shê, Shen Ts'ung-wen, and Wu Tsu-hsiang to Eileen Chang, Ch'ien Chung-shu, and Shih T'o the significant departures and developments in fiction are all solidly grounded in a realistic knowledge of Chinese society.

Despite this achievement in external realism, however, only a very small number of writers have evinced a strong exploratory interest in the realm of the mind. The strivings of an average protagonist are directed toward the change of his environment, so that he rarely attains to the more interesting philosophical or psychological dimension. Of the early writers, Yü Ta-fu alone has the courage to seize the essence of modern life in terms of his subjective sexual fantasies. Shih Chih-ts'un probes the unconscious and obtains some interesting results in a few of his historical tales, but typically, in his contemporary stories, he records the triviality and frustration of city life without capturing any deeper significance. By and large Freud, whose influence permeates modern Western fiction, has had little impact on the Chinese writer. With most of them the task of exposing and reforming glaring national ills assumes such importance that by contrast the exploration of the deeper reaches of the mind can appear only an idle game. To understand is to sympathize and forgive: and the Chinese writer deliberately satirizes or caricatures the bad national types so as to forfeit our sympathy and forgiveness. The psychological dilemma in leftist fiction usually involves the hero's hesitancy before accepting his revolutionary duty, his subsequent recoil from it when the insidious bourgeois influence overpowers his will, and his final self-conquest and renewed dedication. Such conflicts only adorn a thesis whose urgency and importance is never for a moment held in doubt: the hero's advance from doubt or nihilism to a positive faith is a dialectical rather than a psychological progression. In avoiding this pseudo-drama the more overtly satiric fiction actually makes a virtue out of minimal psychological representation. But it is the good writers of the forties who evince a degree of sophistication and subtlety in their psychological portrayal. *Cold Nights* and *The Besieged City* possess the requisite psychological richness of tragedy. In many of Eileen Chang's short stories we find a probing of passion that goes underneath the cloak of custom and habit.

The psychological poverty of modern Chinese fiction can be profitably analyzed against the religious background. The

Confucian intellectual has always been something of a rationalist, though his rationalism is traditionally held in check by a religious awareness, whether Taoist, Buddhist, animistic, or of the mystical Confucian variety, of the folly of human presumption. In discarding the traditional religious safeguards and in feeding upon Western positivism, the modern Chinese mind has become increasingly rationalist and increasingly coarsened. The fathers of the Literary Revolution, Hu Shih and Ch'en Tu-hsiu, represent two types of rationalists. With the exception of Lo Hua-sheng, Shen Ts'ung-wen, and Eileen Chang, modern Chinese writers, whether Marxist or not, have all been rationalists, though it is only fair to add that some retain an instinctive or ingrained pessimism as against their overt optimistic trust in human reason. Reforms and revolutions are rationalistic enterprises, and most satire implies a rationalistic understanding of evil. The superficiality of modern Chinese literature is ultimately seen in its intellectual unawareness of Original Sin or some comparable religious interpretation of evil. When evil is seen as something that can be overcome by sheer human effort and determination, one is no longer able to encompass the domain of tragic experience. In view of the absence of tragedy in traditional Chinese drama and of the strong satiric tradition in Ming and Ch'ing fiction (the distinguished exception is the tragic novel *Dream of the Red Chamber*), one may legitimately wonder whether the study of Western literature has in any significant manner enriched the spiritual life of the Chinese.

In appropriating the Western tradition, it is only to be expected that Chinese writers should accept and make use of what they find most congenial and meaningful. Modern Chinese fiction stems from the realistic and naturalistic traditions of the nineteenth and the early twentieth century, and its mentors are principally Dickens, Turgenev, Tolstoy, Maupassant, Zola, Romain Rolland, Chekhov, Gorky, and the lesser Russians who were writing before or after the October

Revolution. This constitutes an impressive heritage, even though the other giants of the period, such as Flaubert,[5] Dostoevsky, and Henry James, seem to have exerted little influence. But preoccupied with national and social problems, Chinese writers seek from the Western novelists primarily intellectual sympathy and support; they devour their ideological message but pay scant attention to the technical aspects of their art. The kind of problems which seems to have engrossed the serious Western novelists since Henry James would appear very remote indeed to the Chinese. In fact the modern symbolist movement in literature, except for a belated response in poetry and criticism in select academic circles, seems to have had no visible influence on contemporary Chinese expression.

The symbolist movement was launched in conscious protest against naturalistic and scientific positivism, which had cheapened life as well as art in the West; the Literary Revolution in China, on the contrary, pinned its hopes on the nineteenth-century absolutes of democracy, science, and liberalism, to which the symbolists had disavowed allegiance. Seeking intellectual and moral sanction from Western thinkers and writers for their attack on tradition, modern Chinese writers were altogether too sanguine and self-assured to have any affinity with the symbolist writer, with his contempt for mass communication and utilitarian art, his erection of a private world of symbols, his defiant or anxious search for religious certitude or personal integrity as man and artist. Lack of adequate intercultural communication as well as Communist denigration of symbolist literature as a symptom of capitalist decadence, of course, retarded interest in such writers as Eliot, Joyce, and Proust; but even if the works of these authors were sufficiently well-known, it is still inconceivable that they would have impinged on modern Chinese writing to any appreciable degree. Sharing with an eager and receptive public the same aspirations and dilemmas, the modern Chinese writer draws upon and in turn disseminates a public store of ideas; he would see little need for the devices and sophistications by means of which the modern symbolist arrests the general deterioration of language and feeling and sharpens and clarifies his personal vision of truth. To the Chinese writer, truth is well defined and his job is to proclaim it with the language at his disposal.

It is far from my intention to suggest that modern Chinese writers should have gone to school to the symbolists, though exposure to the latter would have enabled them to appreciate the other vital elements of the Western tradition that they have largely ignored. In view of the trend of present-day English and American writers to turn their back on the generation of Eliot and Joyce, it is perhaps even plausible to argue that, as men and women engaged in action and committed to a cause, modern Chinese writers are after all in the central tradition of twentieth-century literature. But a literature is to be judged not by its intentions but by its actual performance: its intelligence and wisdom, its sensibility and style. And by this test the majority of modern Chinese writers, like *engagé* writers everywhere, are seen to suffer from a moral obtuseness, a lack of style and ambition, a conformity of vision and opinion, which are the obvious debilities of too much cultural uniformity or literary cliquism. When one thinks of the great Western novelists of the century, one immediately visualizes for each an imaginary world of sharply defined scenery and people, a world burdened with its specific passions and moral problems. By virtue of its creator's integrity and genius, each world is qualitatively different from any of the others. Of the modern Chinese writers of fiction, possibly four have created worlds stamped with their distinctive personality and moral passion: Eileen Chang, Chang T'ien-i, Ch'ien Chung-shu, Shen Ts'ung-wen. The rest of the good writers, while possessing indisputable individual merits and entitled to distinction for their contributions to the corpus of serious fiction, seem to have contemplated China in much the same fashion, to have drawn upon the same reality for their creation. They are all satiric and humanitarian realists.

As has been said earlier, this satiric and humanitarian realism is not to be lightly scorned; it represents a considerable achievement, especially in view of the heavy odds with which it has to contend: the inescapable immaturities attendant upon a literary re-orientation; the national conditions of instability and turmoil; the climate of patriotic utilitarianism; and, most important, the highhanded and eventually triumphant Communist plot to subvert literature into a mechanical form of propaganda. That the brilliance of the thirties could not be later sustained on a large scale is directly traceable to Communist obscurantism, but in their very aloofness from politics and literary politics and in their lonely pursuit of their craft, the few serious writers of the forties testify to the continuing maturity of modern Chinese fiction and promise its eventual liberation from the narrow philosophical premises of the Literary Revolution. But on the mainland this developing tradition has of course come to a dead standstill with the establishment of the Communist regime. While a few recent works like Eileen Chang's *The Rice-sprout Song* and *Love in Redland* and the Taiwan novelist Chiang Kuei's *The Whirlwind** give evidence of its intermittent vigor among the free Chinese, it is surely futile to speculate when this splendid tradition will again exercise its fructifying function on the mainland, in the shaping of new generations of writers.

* For a discussion of this work see Appendix 2.

Communist Literature Since 1958

EVER SINCE the launching of the Great Cultural Revolution in 1966, nearly all those hitherto responsible for the creation and supervision of literature and the arts in Communist China have ceased to function in their professional capacities. A great many leading writers, playwrights, actors, and directors have been purged, and several have reportedly met death in the process,[1] but even those spared public humiliation and punishment have been effectively silenced. So far as we know, except for *PLA Literature (Chieh-fang-chün Wen-i)*, all literary journals intended for domestic consumption have suspended publication. Even Western observers well informed of the repeated purge of intellectuals since 1949 were at the time unprepared for this massive demonstration of the Communist leadership's total distrust of that class. In any meaningful assessment of mainland literature since 1958, this phenomenon should surely first claim our attention.

While in this epilogue I shall examine this literature primarily with reference to fiction, it must be remembered that the enforcers of the Cultural Revolution have repudiated not only a large number of novels and stories produced between the late fifties and the early sixties, but an even greater number of plays and screenplays of the same period. With all their past contributions to Communism, the authors of these works are now anathema to the regime principally because they have refused to sever their ties with the modern tradition of Chinese culture. That tradition, I need not repeat, first crystallized in the May Fourth Movement of 1919, with its dual concern with the self and the nation. Modern Chinese literature, then, with all its linguistic and formal departures from the traditional literature, differed from it in essence in its advocacy of the claims of the individual and its patriotic concern with China as a land of darkness paralyzed by its inhumanity and impotence. Romantic or sentimental in his demand for love and freedom, the modern Chinese writer was at the same time a satiric and humanitarian realist in his passion to expose the ills of the Chinese society and depict the sufferings of the Chinese people. Though his initial hospitality to diverse Western ideologies eventually hardened into a leftism endorsing in the main the Communist prescriptions for China's cure, he never lost sight of his twin goals of personal emancipation and national rejuvenation. It is precisely because Communism was believed to endorse these goals that a dominant group of writers and nearly all the progressive elements in the theater and cinema embraced the Marxist faith in the late twenties and early thirties. Immediately before and during the war of resistance against Japan, the Chinese Communist Party won further recruits among writers and intellectuals because it seemed to speak for an unqualified patriotism that promised a bright future for the nation.

By adopting leftism, of course, Chinese writers cut themselves off from a great portion of the Western heritage that could have deepened their understanding of man and society. But they availed themselves of the Western literature since the Romantic Movement, especially the classics of the so-called critical realism ranging from Balzac to Gorky—writers of liberal and humanitarian faith who have maintained their high positions in the Soviet canon. This reading could only confirm Chinese writers in their belief in the necessity of realism, in the universality of love and sympathy that transcend classes, and in their prerogative to combat the dark forces in society. Thus, even in the thirties, one could observe their potential rift with the Communist Party, which could not tolerate these intellectual luxuries once it assumed power over a sizable territory. As we have seen, at the Yenan Forum on Literature and Art in 1942, Mao Tse-tung explicitly warned his corps of writers and artists against their partiality to such luxuries; in a sense, he eventually had to launch a cultural revolution because his warnings had borne no fruit.

Even before the forum, many writers in pre-war Shanghai or wartime Chungking and Yenan had felt the sting of official Communist criticism for their maintenance of a leftism deemed subversive of the aims of the party. When some 650 delegates attended the first National Congress of Literary and Art Workers in Peking in July 1949, a sizable number among the writers and the theatrical and cinema workers—the group constituting the predominant majority at the congress—probably had few illusions about a genuine cultural renascence. They had already undergone self-criticism and self-remolding and seen the purge of a few of their comrades, notably Wang Shih-wei in 1942 and Hsiao Chün in 1948. The prominent non-Communist artists invited to attend the conference, such as the painters Ch'i Pai-shih and Hsü Pei-hung, the opera singers Mei Lan-fang and Chou Hsin-fang, and the musician Ma Ssu-ts'ung, would seem to have better cause for rejoicing in their innocence of politics.[2]

But whatever their personal causes for dissatisfaction or complaint, the writers and artists at the congress had no alternative but to avow their allegiance to the Communist regime. During the years of the civil war they could have left for Hong Kong, Taiwan, or some other place, but none did. It would seem that even the disillusioned among them were willing to compromise their artistic integrity and abide by Communist discipline in exchange for tangible gains: a stronger China and a happier proletariat. They were soon to learn, of course, that the same kind of repression that stifled the voice of intellectual freedom would crush the strivings of the people. But at the congress everything went smoothly. Kuo Mo-jo and Mao Tun, senior leftist authors enjoying the highest national prestige, served as chairman and first vice-chairman, but everyone there knew that it was the second vice-chairman, Chou Yang, who was going to supervise the production of culture. Soon after the congress he enlarged his network of control by filling key bureaucratic positions in the literary and art sphere with his Yenan colleagues as well as old friends lately stationed in the Nationalist interior, Shanghai, or Hong Kong.

During the fifties Chou Yang appeared such an implacable persecutor of his fellow intellectuals and artists that it was difficult for Western observers not to detest him. For those harboring illusions about Mao's benevolence, it was especially tempting to believe that Chou Yang had gone beyond his superior's wishes in his excessive harshness. But now, thanks to the wealth of information disclosed during the fall of Chou Yang himself,[3] we know that all the purges and rectification campaigns of the fifties were initiated at the instance of the party's Central Committee with Mao's concurrence. Chou Yang had merely obeyed orders.

It is true that Chou Yang owed his rapid rise in the party hierarchy to his unquestioning obedience to the Communist leadership and his determination to carry out its every whim. It could also be true, as has been repeatedly charged by scholars, that in the fifties Chou Yang regarded Hu Feng, Ting Ling, and Feng Hsüeh-feng as rivals who could challenge his power position and persecuted them with personal vindictiveness. But from the immense output of denunciation at the wake of every purge, it is unfair to single out Chou Yang for our disapprobation when it is the duty of every unscathed writer to excoriate the victims. Lao Shê, a non-Communist author noted for his humor and personal warmth, was no less vehement in his abuse of Hu Feng or Ting Ling, although his simulated zeal did not save him from the wrath of the Red Guards in 1966. It is only because it was Chou Yang's duty to write a long and prominently publicized summary toward the conclusion of every purge or rectification campaign that his role as persecutor appeared especially conspicuous. Whatever his personal failings, we know for certain that he was extremely loyal to his associates and protégés and would go out of his way to help such discredited writers of the Republican era as Chou Tso-jen and provide them with work and income. We also know that even in his Yenan days he would act upon his own literary convictions whenever it was opportune to do so. And as he grew more powerful in Peking, he became emboldened to encourage the production of a literature and art to his own liking, despite his public adulation of Mao. There is also evidence that by the late fifties he cared increasingly for traditional Chinese culture and provided the best editorial guidance to the publication of literary classics, source materials, and textbooks that would enable the student to understand China's past with little ideological distortion.

It is therefore not a paradox to assert that, upon the conclusion of the anti-rightist campaign in 1958, Chou Yang and his group were compelled as much by political circumstances as by their personal convictions to assume an anti-Maoist position, by whatever subtle means. Like their purged colleagues, the Chou Yang group had the left-slanted modern tradition in their bones, and they could not long tolerate Mao's gross violation of that tradition. During the anti-Hu Feng campaign, critics young and old attacked him for his anti-Maoist crimes. Yet, in a matter of years, one by one all these critics —Ting Ling, Feng Hsüeh-feng, Ch'in Chao-yang, Pa Jen, Ho

Ch'i-fang, and Shao Ch'üan-lin (the last two holding high posts in the literary establishment as Chou Yang's closest associates)—were exposed and attacked for making almost the identical demands. They sought a certain degree of freedom for the writer and his right to depict the truth as he sees it, to affirm a classless human nature and portray real characters divested of their straitjackets of heroism and villainy. When Shao Ch'üan-lin and several veteran playwrights who had been close to Chou Yang in the thirties came under attack in 1964, Chou was doomed. Two years later he was purged, and his establishment crashed with him.

Mao Tse-tung had never been a Communist intellectual in the sense that most leftist writers are. Brought up on Chinese classics and history, he had delighted in traditional Chinese novels as a youth, but in his ignorance of foreign tongues he had never developed a fondness for Western literature. Of all modern Chinese writers, Lu Hsün held the greatest appeal for men of traditional tastes. I suppose Mao did enjoy his miscellaneous essays and classical poems, even though his public praise of Lu Hsün in 1940 was mainly dictated by political reasons. But Mao could not have found the Western-slanted literature of the leftist tradition to his liking, and as early as 1938 he called upon cultural workers to utilize the "national forms" of literature and art in explicit repudiation of that tradition. The *Talks at the Yenan Forum on Literature and Art* further confirmed his intense distaste for the leftist product.

The *Talks* appears to pay the highest compliment to the people—the worker, peasant, soldier masses—since only by living among them can the writer or artist alter his petty-bourgeois outlook and discover the real essence of Communist life. But it is an ambivalent compliment, since Mao makes no bones about the real mission of literature and art, which is to instruct and educate the people. Admittedly they are backward, illiterate, and unenlightened. But in the same breath Mao declares that, by virtue of their class status, they are inherently filled with the proper revolutionary spirit and socialist zeal; and it is the duty of the writers and artists, with their disadvantaged higher education and class status, to imbibe that spirit and zeal from them. However, while it is possible for Mao to maintain two contradictory views of the people, the writer is faced with a real dilemma. The convenient solution, as we have seen described in Chapter 18, is to single out a few among the people and cadres as the Communist vanguard—noble, selfless, filled with immense hatred for the old society and infinite gratitude to the party—and depict the rest as in need of varying degrees of ideological reform. Those beyond reform—landlords, reactionaries, Koumintang agents, and saboteurs—are invariably described as villains comitting evil deeds or harboring evil designs to disrupt socialist construction.

The earliest leftist literature also has its stereotyped heroes and villains. But in the absence of stringent party discipline, the revolutionary hero, usually drawn from the petty-bourgeois rather than the proletarian class, can fall passionately in love, kill a personal enemy, and embark on many other kinds of adventure denied his present-day Communist counterpart. He is also free to ponder a wide range of thoughts and experience a wide range of emotions. Even if he is often too idealized or romanticized to be real, the hostile society against which he contends is usually recognizable with its contrasting scenes of capitalist depravity and proletarian squalor, and it is invariably in the depiction of this dark society under warlord or Kuomintang rule that the gifted leftist writer compels our admiration for his satiric power or humanitarian passion. The same writer, now much older, still sees darkness about him; however, not only is he denied the right to expose the kind of evil that will discredit the Communist Party, but he is not even allowed to depict the elemental passions of man in their true colors. Except for his love of labor and

Epilogue

his adoration of Mao, the Communist hero in recent literature is virtually passionless.

While Western scholars are understandably concerned
about the fate of writers who have made their reputations
before the thirties—such as Kuo Mo-jo, Mao Tun, Pa Chin,
and T'ien Han—because their names are more familiar, it
seems to me that far more tragic have been the stunted
careers of those who began to attract notice in the thirties
and contributed significantly to the literature of the forties.
Among novelists one could name Ai Wu, Lu Ling (purged
during the anti-Hu Feng campaign), Sha T'ing, Shih T'o,
and Tuan-mu Hung-liang; among playwrights there are an
even greater number who enlivened the wartime stage in
Chungking or occupied Shanghai. For all these authors,
their thin volume of publications since 1949 contrasts sadly
with their prolific output of greater artistic integrity before
that date.

Ai Wu is luckier than most in that before the Cultural
Revolution he had been little victimized by the rectification
campaigns and maintained a modest pace of productivity. A
talented author showing great signs of maturity in his postwar
novels, he has specialized in worker fiction since 1949 and
written some of the most technically competent stories among
the approved literature, collected in the volume *Homeward
Journey* (1958).[4] The themes of his fiction, however, are
predictably trite, and their contrast with his narrative skill is
especially pronounced in his major work of the Communist
period, *Steeled and Tempered* (1958; English translation,
1961), generally regarded as the best novel about industrial
life ever published in Communist China.

Ai Wu sets his story in a factory town in the northeast and
builds up quite ably the tensions existing among three steel
workers on the one hand and between the party secretary at
the factory and its manager on the other. The principal hero,
Ch'in Tê-kuei, is a selfless worker who has repeatedly made
steel in record time. Of his two co-workers in charge of the

same furnace on different shifts, the elder one, also a labor
hero, is resentful of the upstart and unwilling to share his
hard-earned experience with others. The other rival simply
wants to get by without over-exerting himself, and he also
fancies a girl worker in a neighboring factory, who, need-
less to say, is in love with Ch'in. As for the feud on the higher
level, the manager wants to speed up production at all costs
and has nothing but contempt for the party secretary's indirect and time-consuming approach to the problem by trying
to raise the morale of the workers individually and collec-
tively. Both sets of circumstances help precipitate a crisis at
the factory, during which Ch'in Tê-kuei has to risk his life to
save it from being blown to pieces. Severely burned and in
a coma for days, he could have died, and his self-sacrifice
would at least have taught a lesson to the reckless manager
and spurred the other furnace chiefs to a greater zeal for
production. But Ai Wu prefers to end his novel on a false
note: we are supposed to believe that neither the lazy furnace
chief nor the manager is ultimately responsible for the accident—it is solely the handiwork of a Kuomintang saboteur
in the employ of the factory. This cheap surprise ending is
apparently designed to prove that no serious conflicts could
have arisen among builders of socialism, despite their varying
attitudes toward work: only an enemy agent could have
wanted to wreck the new China—symbolized by the factory.

Steeled and Tempered is a novel written to formula in that
it upholds the Communist vanguard (Ch'in Tê-kuei and the
party secretary), attests to the self-improvement of the less
enlightened (Ch'in's co-workers and the manager), and ex-
poses the enemy (the saboteur). But since Ai Wu actually
lived among steel workers for years, he does tell us a great
deal about their life at home and in the factory and about
the process of steel-making. In all the best post-1957 novels
we find this type of conscientious realism seriously compromised by the formulaic requirements of Maoist propaganda.

Epilogue

Great Changes in A Mountain Village (1958; English translation, 1961), a peasant novel of exceptional distinction, further proves the point. Like Ai Wu, its author Chou Li-po was schooled in the leftist tradition in the thirties, but he went to Yenan during the war and became one of Mao's most obedient students in trying to learn peasant life at first hand. *The Hurricane* (1948), his Stalin Prize–winning novel about land reform in the northeast, brought him fame. Although he could not report all the cruel truth about the persecution of a landlord in that novel, he described the cadres' persistent attempts to whip up mob fury among the peasants in great detail. And like other conscientious novelists of that time, he also tried his hardest to reproduce the dialect of the region. In the mid-fifties Chou Li-po was assigned to his home region in Hunan to observe the launching of an agricultural production cooperative. *Great Changes in A Mountain Village*, which embodies his findings, gives further proof of his astonishing ability to render dialect.

The same kind of realism informs his descriptions of the village. In Chapter 3, for example, Chou Li-po gives a vivid account of a meeting of party cadres and village leaders. It begins at 9 P.M. and, after a break during which the participants amuse themselves with card games and other forms of relaxation, resumes at eleven:

> People came in again, sitting informally round the table. The director of women's work, who always arrived late, had only just come. She put her baby, not yet weaned, on the table, and let him crawl all over it. The little creature had on a pair of padded trousers, split in the middle, exposing his fat little white bottom, with a blue birth-mark. As soon as he saw the clock, he tried to get hold of it. The director of women's work shouted at him so loudly to stop him that he was frightened and cried. She had to take him into her arms, opened her dress and stuffed a nipple into the little yelling mouth.[5]

Unlike the American reader, who would never associate breast-feeding with a business meeting, the witnesses around the table are too inured to such scenes to be shocked. The novelist has, furthermore, sided with them in chiding the woman for being chronically late, and yet what is truly shocking is that she has no choice but to carry her baby with her at this late hour to attend the compulsory meeting, however perfunctorily. Incidentally, the phrase "not yet weaned" implies that the baby is old enough to be weaned; the Chinese text carries no such connotation.

In his conscientious fashion, therefore, Chou Li-po gives enough real scenes of the village to make a non-Communist reader want to sympathize with all those reluctant peasants forced to give up their own holdings to join the cooperative. Even with respect to members of the vanguard, one feels that they pay too high a price for their selfless dedication. Because of his almost total neglect of his home in attending to his duties, Liu Yü-sheng, the head of a mutual-aid team, is divorced by his incomprehending wife, whom he evidently loves very much. Though he is eventually matched to a more public-spirited widow, the plight of the tradition-bound woman in going through with the divorce and the pain and suffering endured by Liu are depicted with genuine feeling.

Before the cadres succeed in urging the villagers to join the agricultural cooperative, a rumor has spread among them that the trees on the hills will be expropriated. In the words of the late Tsi-an Hsia, who was the first Western reader to emphasize the merits of the novel:

> A panic sets in on a night when they go out in mass, including the very old and the very young, to protect their trees from expropriation. They succeed in denuding the hills, as more than one thousand trees are cut down. Thus they suffer losses, but at least the trees won't go to the collective. Then, on page 270, only fifteen pages later, the co-operative is established. As a pure propagandist,

Chou Li-po is hardly convincing with his hurried account of the transformation of the peasants' "political awareness," while he describes their resistance at greater length and with far more precision. But as a propagandist at war with the artist in him, he perhaps can do no more. An anti-Communist novelist would be tempted to put in a melodramatic scene of armed revolt; but the cruel fact of submission, so poignantly rendered by Chou Li-po, is a more powerful accusation of the terrible reality in Communist China.[6]

Like Ai Wu, Chou Li-po asserts the might of the Communist vanguard and the reformability of the less enlightened. But since he ends his novel in a far less contrived manner (although still a very clumsy one), it leaves us with a much stronger impression of "the terrible reality in Communist China." Without imputing to the author any conscious desire to criticize or embarrass the regime, it would seem that his very endeavor to experience the life of the people has made him less effective as a propagandist. It would have made things far easier for all concerned if, at the Yenan Forum, Mao had told his writers and artists to be simple propagandists exempted from the necessity of learning from the people. But in 1942 and for many years afterward, perhaps Mao seriously believed that any true depiction of the life of the people would inevitably confirm their joy in Communism and their love for socialist construction. In any event, he was then too much influenced by the Soviet doctrine of socialist realism to do otherwise. As long as feudalism and imperialism were rampant, one could agree with Mao that it was possible for writers to depict the actual reality without compromising their faith in Communism. But if the people remained unhappy, even after the presumed obstacles to Communist success—Japanese aggression, Kuomintang misrule, landlord and bourgeois domination of the national economy, American imperialism in the form of the Korean war—had been removed one by one, the Communist government itself would stand exposed as the cause of China's continuing misery. Under the circumstances, to exhort writers and artists to observe reality would not be in the best interests of the party and government. Consequently, a new cultural policy was launched in 1958—the year of the Great Leap Forward.

The anti-rightist campaign of the previous year had confirmed the continuing dissidence of a great many writers, and the practice of socialist realism by even the most loyal supporters of the regime tended to affirm the Communist cause only at the cost of disclosing serious conflicts in society. It would be far better, the planners of the Great Leap must have thought, for writers to ignore such conflicts and to spur the people to greater heights of zeal and productivity by emphasizing the past achievements of the party and its even more glorious future. Whereas Mao's *Talks* remained an oracle and a great many writers continued to be assigned to villages, factories, and barracks to observe reality, the new literary formula adopted for the Great Leap Forward period was "the Combination of Revolutionary Realism and Revolutionary Romanticism." It stressed, on the one hand, the larger cultural role of the masses themselves spontaneously singing their zeal for production and their faith in the future without benefit of literary middlemen (the "mass poetry" movement); on the other, it emphasized the greater freedom allowed professional writers in choice of subject matter so that, instead of being bound to contemporary reality, they could now depict the whole history of modern China in order to praise more effectively the heroic record of the Communist Party in bringing about the nation's rejuvenation. It must be noted, however, that while both policies embraced revolutionary romanticism in their praise of past and future Communist achievements, in fact they led to contrary trends: one encouraging literary production that was still further removed from the leftist tradition in its unprofessional naiveté and undisguised eulogistic intent, and the other fostering a literature closer in spirit to the earlier leftist product if for no other reason than that of thematic affinity—the depiction of a China in the clutches of feudalism and imperialism.

Chou Yang bestowed equal blessings on both trends, apparently with Mao's approval. Yet in retrospect it becomes clear that, although it was consistent with his deep-seated distrust of the intellectuals to attempt to turn millions of workers, peasants, and soldiers into part-time singers and poets, Mao must later have come to regret the policy of granting writers greater freedom, even if this was in the good cause of generating enthusiasm for the party by depicting its heroic past. The Chou Yang group, on the other hand, had to uphold professional standards and could not have sponsored the mass poetry movement with much real enthusiasm. And with their commitment to the leftist tradition, they must have welcomed the opportunity to promote a literature which, if still superficial in its obligatory praise of Communism, would have the richer appeal of that tradition. Even if they did not seriously intend to revive leftism, they would still have wanted a literature of greater audience potential. As the nation's cultural director, Chou Yang had to ponder the appeal of new books, movies, plays, concerts, and displays at museums. Their educational value would have been little if they had attracted few people. The Hundred Flowers Movement of 1956 was launched partly to combat audience indifference to Communist literature and art, but the situation was no better after the anti-rightist campaign of the following year. It would do no harm, Chou Yang could have reasoned, to let the people escape into a bygone world of more varied and colorful humanity so that they could return to their tasks refreshed in spirit.

Consequently, 1958 was a year of vigorous literary activity. In addition to such workmanlike novels of socialist realism as *Steeled and Tempered* and *Great Changes in A Mountain Village*, it saw the publication of several very popular novels which signalized the start of the new romantic genre, notably Liang Pin's *Keep the Red Flag Flying* and Miss Yang Mo's *The Song of Youth*.[7] This trend continued with vigor for a few years. And although Yang Mo's novel is a self-contained work about the autobiographical heroine's political awakening in the thirties, most other novels recalling the late Ch'ing and Republican periods were conceived by their authors as multi-volume projects that should have ended with the Communist victory in 1949 and after. But with the subsequent shift in cultural policy, none of these projects was even completed.

The Three-Family Lane (1959) is perhaps the finest work of this nostalgic genre. Its author, Ou-yang Shan, planned it as Part I of an ambitious pentalogy entitled *A Generation of Heroes*. In 1962 he completed the second part, *Bitter Struggle*, but two years later he was purged. A veteran leftist novelist who had published his first book in 1927, he went to Yenan in 1941 and subsequently established himself as the ranking author of his home province when he became chairman of the Kwangtung branch of the Writers' Union. An earlier novel of his, *Uncle Kao*, is briefly discussed in Chapter 18.

The Three-Family Lane traces the fortunes of three families related by marriage from the last years of the Ch'ing dynasty to the revolutionary debacle of 1927. It is reminiscent of such family chronicles with regional settings as Pa Chin's *Torrent Trilogy*, but it is finer than they in its rich evocation of place (Canton) and period. In fact, the author seems to have patterned his work after China's supreme domestic novel, *Dream of the Red Chamber*.[8] Its handsome hero, Chou Ping, is by design a Chia Pao-yü of the proletarian class, ingenuous and candid to the point of idiocy and adored to distraction by two beautiful cousins. The proletarian cousin, Ch'ü T'ao, deserves the intended comparison with Bright Cloud, but whereas the guileless maid of the classic novel dies a victim of feudalist oppression, her modern counterpart is felled by an imperialist bullet as she marches with her comrades in the forefront of a workers' demonstration. Just as Pao-yü loses his gaiety after the death of Bright Cloud and increasingly meditates on his religious vocation, the grief-stricken Chou Ping, too, becomes a changed person and decides to turn Communist to avenge his cousin's martyrdom. The bourgeois cousin, Ch'en Wen-t'ing, is in some ways suggestive of Pao-yü's maid Pervading Fragrance, although she may be intended to embody the qualities popularly attributed to Precious Clasp. She, too, avows selfless love, but after the hero has gone into hiding as a Communist worker she loses courage, yields to family pressure, and marries a rising member of the Kuomintang. Chou Ping steels himself under this double deprivation of love and embarks for Shanghai for a more active revolutionary career.

The Communist viewpoint, while pervading the whole novel, becomes prominent only in the second half where, in depicting the Communist setbacks in Kwangtung in 1925–27, the author consistently caricatures the historic reality of the bourgeoisie and the official-gentry class by not allowing one of their members to become a Communist. In the first half, however, he has not only depicted the youth of the May Fourth period with sympathy and understanding but invested its manners and aspirations with a nostalgic reality of rare charm. Despite all his romanticized goodness and purity, Chou Ping is one of the truly noble characters in modern Chinese fiction, though his eventual conformity to Communist discipline in *Bitter Struggle* diminishes his archetypal significance as a proletarian Chia Pao-yü.

The popularity of revolutionary chronicles (and the plays and movies based on them) soon brought about the recrudescence of historical drama. During the early sixties plays and operas celebrating defiers of tyranny became the rage, even though very few novelists and screen playwrights appropriated historical topics beyond the late Ch'ing period. The Peking opera, of course, had always drawn its stories from history, and during the fifties there had been a few historical plays (notably Ts'ao Yü's *The Gall Bladder and the Sword*) designed to arouse fervor for national construction. But the systematic creation of new historical plays and operas with satiric or critical references to the present regime was certainly a bold gesture toward cultural independence. Just as during the war years in Chungking the leftist playwrights had staged historical plays to stimulate patriotism and satirize the National Government, the historian Wu Han[9] and several veteran writers like T'ien Han and Meng Ch'ao were again exploiting history and legend for the stage to make veiled attacks on Mao at the precise time when the consequences of his blunders in economic policy had made him most vulnerable to criticism.

Whether the Chou Yang group had shifted its allegiance to Chief of State Liu Shao-ch'i during this period of cultural liberalization is for our purposes immaterial. What is of decided interest is that, given the conditions of more relaxed control, professional writers should have returned to the kind of sentiments prevalent in prewar Shanghai and wartime Chungking and reasserted the kind of humanitarianism and satire expicitly repudiated in Mao's *Talks*. During the same period the Chou Yang group also sponsored publications affirming the leftist achievement in literature, cinema, and theater and thus making possible a better understanding of current literature and art in the broader perspective of the modern tradition.

In June 1964, Mao Tse-tung, who a year earlier had indicated his displeasure with the current cultural products, issued a directive accusing nearly all members of literary and art organizations of being aloof bureaucrats in danger of falling into revisionism and decrying their failure to implement the policies of the party over the past fifteen years.[10] Chou Yang again had to fall in line and start a rectification campaign. Although, according to his later accusers, he did this with perfunctory enthusiasm, he still had to sacrifice two of his closest allies, Shao Ch'üan-lin and Hsia Yen, as well as Ou-yang Shan, among other important writers.

Mao's 1964 directive amounted to a confession of his almost total failure since 1949 to remold writers and artists through their study of his *Talks*. His distrust of the Chou Yang group would seem to have taken shape as early as 1960. In that year he ordered Defense Minister Lin Piao to reeducate the armed forces so that they might become a model for the whole nation. Although in 1942 Mao had decreed a worker, peasant, soldier line for literature and art, by 1960 he seems to have preferred the soldier to the worker and peasant because of his greater docility and political reliability. In remolding the PLA, Lin Piao deified Mao to the point where his writings have apparently come to replace the classics of Marxism-Leninism as the sole repository of truth. In particular, three of Mao's short essays which are innocent of Marxist philosophy but highly inspirational in their stress on altruistic love of country and party and readiness to embrace martyrdom were made the objects of unremitting study.[11] The soldiers of the PLA were urged to grasp Mao's thought through their study of these pieces and to use it in every conceivable situation to enhance their zeal, productivity, and intelligence. In short, just as Mao had earlier abandoned the Soviet model of socialist realism for literature and art through his promotion of the mass poetry movement, by 1960 he had also realized the irrelevance of Soviet-style Communist ideology for the remaking of man. Man could be remolded only with the aid of Mao's own thought. Chinese culture of the feudal and Republican past was also totally irrelevant: it sufficed for the soldiers (and the population at large) to recall at regularly scheduled meetings the "bitterness" of the preliberation years in order to reinforce the myth that, with all its shortcomings, the present was infinitely preferable.

The literature and art produced under the auspices of the PLA, far more than that sponsored by Chou Yang, is designed to supplement the study of Mao's thought. It consists mainly of biographies, novels, movies, and plays about model soldiers who have sacrificed their lives for country and party, and it includes selections from their diaries. In 1963, an utterly selfless soldier named Lei Feng, who had died in an accident a year earlier, was made an object of national emulation. Since then a long succession of young martyrs (plus a few living heroes) have been similarly glorified. Their diaries and biographies are hardly literature, but there has been virtually no other literature produced in China since the Cultural Revolution.

The most ambitious literary work sponsored by the PLA has been Chin Ching-mai's *The Song of Ou-yang Hai,* a novel about the life and self-sacrifice of the title hero. First serialized in magazines in 1965, the book was launched with great fanfare, and by the time of its second edition, April 1966, a million copies were in print.[12] (An abridged English translation is available in *Chinese Literature* [1966], nos. 7-11.) Like other such biographical novels, *The Song of Ou-yang Hai* begins with a chapter of unbelievable sentimentality which stresses the stark destitution of the Ou-yang family at the time of the hero's birth and during his early youth. Having thus emphasized his ideal proletarian background, the novel nevertheless goes on for the remaining nine chapters to concern itself almost exclusively with his steady spiritual improvement under the guidance of the party and the thought of Mao Tse-tung.

In tracing the evolution of Chinese Communist literature from the early Yenan period to *The Song of Ou-yang Hai,* one is struck by the complete reversal of the roles of the party and the individual hero. In the opera *The White-haired Girl* (1946), the heroine is passive throughout. Much abused, she goes into hiding until she happily rejoins humanity with the liberation of her village by the Red Army. Nothing is expected of her; she is entitled to her share of the blessings of Communism simply by virtue of her past sufferings as a member of the oppressed class. (It is interesting to note that in a subsequent revised version of the opera, the heroine, along with her fellow villagers, has become far more militantly class conscious, and she volunteers for army service at the end![13]) In all the novels about land reform, the peasants are given land, and all they have to do is to obey the cadres and muster up enough courage to denounce the landlords.

But in subsequent years, in proportion to the government's growing inability to bestow many tangible benefits upon the people in return for their strenuous participation in various programs of socialization, the stress has been increasingly upon the people's own political awakening and voluntary enthusiasm for building socialism. To have gained an education under the guidance of the cadres and the thought of Mao is their sufficient and only reward. In *The Song of Ou-yang Hai*, the party's expectations for the hero are so high that he cannot even enjoy himself while doing good, since such complacency would promote vanity or pride. Whereas his prototype, Lei Feng, has a wonderful time doing good deeds and is constantly getting recognition and praise, Ou-yang Hai is repeatedly misjudged by his fellow soldiers and superiors. The author makes it quite explicit that the hero's very desire to excel has to be crushed before he can transform himself into a worthy pupil of Mao doing the bidding of the party and anonymously performing good deeds on his own without the least trace of self-importance. Ou-yang Hai achieves the true humility of a saint at the end, but it is almost a relief to see him sacrifice his life to prevent a train wreck, because his constant struggle to match his conduct against the word of Mao and the demands of the party is finally brought to an end.

The Song of Ou-yang Hai is not a psychological novel in the Western sense. The hero, though a young bachelor of sturdy health, is incapable of a single frivolous or wayward thought, or even of a momentary interest in the opposite sex. But it is definitely a novel of moral instrospection in its strikingly neo-Confucian obsession with disinterested virtuous conduct. The problem of how to become a good Communist has almost replaced the problem of how to achieve a Communist society as the overriding concern of the Mao-Lin leadership.

No new novels have been published during the frenzy of the Cultural Revolution: the constant study of Mao's works has apparently displaced the need for any other kind of literature. A few ballets and modern-dress Peking operas produced at the request of the PLA under the personal supervision of Mao's wife, Chiang Ch'ing, have been given immense publicity as evidence of a new theater liberated from all bad influences, traditional Chinese as well as modern Western. A group of clay sculptures known as "The Rent Collection Compound," portraying the oppression and revolutionary fervor of poor peasants under Kuomintang rule, has been proudly hailed as an example of the art inspired by Mao's thought. But few other art projects have received similar attention from the press.

In the present lull of cultural activity, it may be instructive to ponder the prospects for literature and art in Communist China, especially in the light of the Cultural Revolution. The purge of the Chou Yang group and the repudiation of nearly all professional writers and artists certainly seems to indicate that the Mao-Lin leadership has been disenchanted with culture. The intent of the Cultural Revolution, when viewed in detachment from the political struggles that have occasioned it, is to destroy all culture incompatible with Mao's thought—not only the feudal culture of the past, but the modern and leftist traditions upon which Communist culture itself was built.

The need for such drastic action is quite obvious. To the extent that culture implies a respect for man's past and a curiosity about what is going on in other parts of the world, it will be antithetical to the requirements of a political system which intends to remold man from scratch, uninfluenced by the past or by contemporary cultural modes elsewhere. The repeated purges and rectification campaigns prompted by the loyalty of writers and artists to the leftist tradition and their awareness of growing intellectual freedom in the Soviet bloc have demonstrated the impossibility of building a new culture tailored to Maoist requirements as long as such loyalty and awareness remain unextinguished. Mao's growing reliance on spare-time writers and artists from the ranks of the people for the manufacture of a culture compatible with his thought would indicate his belief that, precisely because these amateurs are culturally disadvantaged, they will be the more reliable. While Mao had earlier intended to rescue the Chinese people from their poverty and backwardness, by 1958 he appeared to delight in their material poverty and cultural "blankness" as the necessary condition for their total remolding. But no people of China's antiquity, however poor and illiterate, could be culturally blank: hence the necessity to obliterate all signs of historical culture that could remind them of their past.

While cultural orthodoxy is at present maintained by the intense propagation of Mao's thought and the decorative efforts of part-time writers and artists to affirm that thought, one wonders if professionalism—in both the creation and supervision of culture—will not revive with the gradual stabilization of the present regime. As long as there is need for culture to embellish Mao's thought and occupy people's minds when they are not engaged in productive activity, culture in that sense will remain a vast enterprise requiring planning and control. Of the cultural leaders who have effectively replaced the Chou Yang group, Chiang Ch'ing is Mao's wife and Yao Wen-yüan reportedly is his son-in-law,[14] and they can be counted on to do his bidding as long as the Chairman remains alive. But, like the Chou Yang group, the new establishment will in time acquire a degree of autonomy in implementing the cultural line and train a large corps of subordinates to oversee the production of literature and art. And insofar as their obligatory allegiance to the Mao-Lin leadership could not totally extinguish their genuine liking for literature and art, could we not predict that at least some members of the new establishment, like the dissident literary bureaucrats of the fifties, will want to preserve certain values antithetical to the regime and clamor for a more truthful cultural product incompatible with the aims of Communist education?

But in the foreseeable future the quality of culture can only continue to deteriorate. For the past twenty years the making of literature and art has been mainly the responsibility of those who received their training in pre-Communist days. Prior to the Cultural Revolution, nearly all the important singers in the Peking opera had been stars before 1949. Among stage and screen actors victimized by the Cultural Revolution, all the prominent ones had achieved great popularity in wartime Chungking or postwar Shanghai. Even most of the writers who had not published before 1949 received their education in the thirties and forties. Since the last twenty years have not produced an abundance of young talent, with the removal of these old professionals the prospects for literature and art look bleak indeed.

When addressing a group of textbook editors in 1951, Chou Yang warned that in breadth of knowledge and culture his own generation was inferior to that of Liang Ch'i-ch'ao and Hu Shih. And it looked as if "each generation will be inferior to the preceding one if you are even less learned than we."[15] He was, of course, speaking the truth. The men he was addressing were presumably in their thirties and forties, but those who have received all their education under the Communist regime will be even worse prepared. Recent visitors to China like K. S. Karol and Alberto Moravia have revealed the incredible ignorance of the younger writers and artists. Karol met theatrical workers who had never heard of Brecht, Satre, Ibsen, and Shaw.[16] Totally untrained in

Western literature, the younger writers are only slightly better acquainted with their own literary heritage. During the early sixties, writers were encouraged by Chou Yang to study the approved national classics, but this policy was soon reversed. Today a writer, like everyone else, has very little to read except the works of Mao and a few national newspapers and magazines. Even if he has access to a well-stocked library, he will probably be too busy or too prudent to make much use of it. And even a potential literary genius cannot thrive on a steady diet of Mao and jargon-filled journalism.

In view of the cultural isolationism that deprives young people of their proper intellectual nourishment, the steady deterioration of educational standards, and the probable maintenance of the cult of Mao even if Mao himself passes from the scene, the future health of literature and art on the mainland seems likely to depend solely on the continuing resilience of the human spirit to maintain its sanity, skepticism, and creativity under the most deadening circumstances. But, on the other hand, it would be cruel of us in the West to continue to expect the emergence of dissident writers and artists to demonstrate the survival of that spirit, when the punishment visited upon them and upon all those implicated in their crime will only crush them without alleviating in the last the suffering of their fellow countrymen. Actually, since literature and art in Communist China are designed as a means of education to fill the vacant hours of the people and to reconcile them to the regime, the disappearance of such literature and art or their further deterioration until nobody pays them any attention is, after all, not such a tragedy as some scholars would suppose. It is only when people can freely express their real feelings and thoughts again that it would be realistic to expect the rebirth of a genuine literature and art. As conditions now stand, such a prospect is totally unlikely.

Obsession With China:
The Moral Burden
of Modern Chinese Literature

WITH THE establishment of the People's Republic on the mainland in 1949, a distinctive period of Chinese literature which began with the Literary Revolution of 1917 has come to a close. While this period is readily distinguishable from the earlier periods by its systematic use of the vernacular and its adoption of Western literary forms and techniques, one cannot apply the same criteria to define its immense difference from the succeeding period of Communist literature, since the more recent writers on the mainland have not departed to an appreciable extent from the linguistic and literary conventions of the immediate past. What distinguishes this "modern" phase of Chinese literature alike from the traditional and Communist phases is rather its burden of moral contemplation: its obsessive concern with China as a nation afflicted with a spiritual disease and therefore unable to strengthen itself or change its set ways of inhumanity. All the major writers of the period—novelists, playwrights, poets, essayists—are enkindled with this patriotic passion, though in this essay I shall confine my examples to quotations from fiction.

Traditionally the Chinese have regarded themselves as the inheritors of a human civilization, guided by the Confucian precepts for moral self-discipline and benevolent government and by the Buddhist ideal of compassion. Their modern obsession with China's impotence represents historically a new self-awareness brought about by the long series of defeats and humiliations they have suffered since the mid-nineteenth century. But for the writers, as for all other members of the awakened elite, this obsession does not merely register alarm over the government's failure to cope with internal turmoil and foreign aggression: the shame that has been visited upon China also reflects its moral bankruptcy, its callous unconcern with human dignity and human suffering, irrespective of its power position in the world. Thus while one may say that the truculent swagger of the Peking government has remade the national image abroad and freed the writers from their obsession with their country's shameful past, their other obsession with human suffering and degradation must have persisted, though denied creative expression, in view of the much worsened condition of the people under the Communist rule. As a propaganda product designed to celebrate the achievements of the party in power, the literature actually produced in Communist China shares nothing of the fiery critical temper of the twenties and thirties and is justifiably designated a new phase of Chinese writing. But the periodic spectacle of writers and critics braving persecution to speak out for a humanitarian literature of realistic integrity testifies to their continuing obsession with the welfare of the Chinese people.

In the international context modern Chinese literature also appears to be of peculiar interest for its obsessive patriotism. On the surface I may seem to have overemphasized the negative connotations of this patriotism, since there is a sense in which modern Chinese literature is modern because it stands for progress and modernization. The late Ch'ing intellectuals were eager to adapt Western governmental institutions for Chinese use and to introduce the study of Western science and technology. Professor Benjamin Schwartz's study of one such intellectual, Yen Fu, is aptly titled *In Search of Wealth and Power,* in reference to his conscious quest for these national goals.[1] In 1919 Ch'en Tu-hsiu defended the new culture movement in the names of Mr. Science and Mr. Democracy. The modern Chinese writer has certainly shared the same passion for a wealthy, strong, democratic, and technologically armed China. Insofar as its advocates regard Communism as a step beyond democracy, the democratic ideal would seem to be implicit in their vision of a classless society. During the Sino-Japanese war Mao Tse-tung persuaded a great many Chinese to accept his version of Communism by writing a book beguilingly titled *The New Democracy.*

These same ideals have certainly informed modern Western civilization, and yet its most significant literature betrays little joy in those positive achievements that have been the envy of every Chinese patriot. If anything, the concern of modern Western literature with the individual psyche has betrayed its rebellious stance against the modern environment. In his challenging essay "On the Modern Element in Modern Literature," Lionel Trilling has identified that element with "the disenchantment of our culture with culture itself—it seems to me that the characteristic element of modern literature, or at least of the most highly developed modern literature, is the bitter line of hostility to civilization which runs through it."[2] By citing such spiritual progenitors of modern literature as Nietzsche, Frazer, and Freud, as well as such representative works as "Notes from Underground," "The Death of Ivan Ilytch," "Heart of Darkness," and "Death in Venice," Trilling is able to define the intensely spiritual but subversive character of modern literature, with its celebration of the primal, nonethical energies and its distrust or repudiation of the pieties and assumptions under-lying Western civilization. Trilling has not dwelt upon the further point, but he would certainly agree that it is precisely the impersonal environment of modern man that has made possible this modern literature of nihilism and irrationality.

Insofar as modern Chinese literature implicitly endorses the rational ideals of democracy and science, it would seem to have little in common with modern Western literature as Trilling defines it. There has been no modern Chinese writer consumed with the passion of Dostoevsky or Tolstoy, of Conrad or Mann, to probe the illness of modern civiliza-tion. But at the same time every important modern Chinese writer is obsessed with China and spares no pains to depict its squalor and corruption. It would seem that he is equally concerned with spiritual sickness, but whereas every modern writer of England, America, France, and Germany (and the rule also applies to a few exceptional writers of Soviet Rus-sia) [3] automatically identifies the sick state of his country with the state of man in the modern world, the Chinese writer sees the conditions of China as peculiarly Chinese and not ap-plicable elsewhere. He shares with the modern Western writer a vision of disgust if not despair, but since his vision does not extend beyond China, at the same time he leaves the door open for hope, for the importation of modern Western or Soviet ideas and systems that would transform his country from its present state of decadence. If he had the courage or insight to equate the Chinese scene with the condition of modern man, he would have been in the mainstream of modern literature. But he dared not do so, since to do so would have blotted out hope for the betterment of life, for the restoration of human dignity. The price he pays for his obsession with China is therefore a certain patriotic provinci-ality and a naiveté of faith with regard to better conditions elsewhere. But so long as he is at his proper task—the impas-sioned depiction of China as a land of darkness—he is pro-ducing a literature which shares a spiritual affinity with the

most significant modern Western literature, despite its explicit denial of universality.

Up to the Opium war of 1842 the Chinese were sustained by a sense of their unchallenged cultural superiority,
even when they were living under foreign rule. During the
collapse of an indigenous dynasty and the initial period of
foreign conquest, patriotic sentiment would run high among
Confucian statesmen and scholars, but their detestation of the
barbarous aggressor implies an inflation of their cultural
pride rather than the reverse. But once a foreign dynasty
became more firmly established, patriotism would subside
and scholars would again seek government service without
feeling ashamed. In the view of traditional Chinese historiog-
raphy, the downfall of a dynasty is ultimately due to its
failure to live up to the Confucian ideal of a responsible
and benevolent government. That ideal, therefore, as distinct
from the treacherous ministers and weak emperors held responsible for the fall of a dynasty, was never the object of
satiric contemplation. By the extension of the same logic, a
foreign dynastic house could as well serve the Confucian ideal
as a native house. In traditional Chinese satire as in the
classical Western variety, therefore, only those persons and
customs are castigated that flout the guiding principles of
their society.

As a major example of satire written before the Opium
War we may cite the early nineteenth-century novel *Flowers
in the Mirror (Ching-hua yuan)*.[4] Justly celebrated for his
shrewd observations on Chinese society, the author Li Ju-
chen (1763–ca. 1830) places his heroes through a voyage to
many imaginary countries with manners and customs amus-
ingly suggestive or corrective of those prevailing in China.
Thus in the Country of Gentlemen sellers would keep lower-
ing the price of their goods while buyers would insist on paying more—a caricature of commercial transactions in China
or any other land. After witnessing one such scene, the

537

voyagers pay a vist to the elderly brothers, Wu Chih-ho and Wu Chih-hsiang, who question them about many absurd customs in China. Among these is foot-binding:

> "I have heard that your country has a practice known as foot-binding," Wu Chih-ho said. "I understand that it is most painful at the beginning and causes a girl to cry day and night. Sometimes the skin is broken and the flesh exposed. During the worst period the victim can neither sleep nor eat because of the excruciating pain. I used to think that it was a form of cruel punishment inflicted on disobedient daughters, but later I found that it was all done in the name of beauty. Now does one shave off pieces of the nose to make it smaller or level off a high forehead? Why should crippled feet be regarded as beautiful? Did Hsi Shih and Wang Ch'iang, two of the most beautiful women of their time, cut off half their feet to make themselves beautiful? To my mind to cater to this perverted taste is no different from trafficking in obscene articles."[5]

Many chapters later, while in the Country of Women, one of the voyagers will be abducted for service in its ruler's male harem. The excruciating pain he undergoes while his feet are being made smaller further dramatizes Wu Chih-ho's disapproving comment.

But even in castigating this most inhumane of Chinese customs, Li Ju-chen maintains his self-possession as an educated Chinese who regards such customs as aberrations from an ideal state of Chinese culture. We are informed that the Wu brothers are descendants of T'ai-po, uncle of King Wen of the Chou dynasty and a sage in his own right, who yielded his throne to his younger brother and fled to the then barbarous region of Wu to serve as a civilizing influence. As the home of the Wu brothers, the Country of Gentlemen can be seen as a land where the virtues governing the pristine Chou culture are still practiced with assiduity. Wu Chih-ho actu-

ally employs Confucian and Taoist arguments against foot-
binding. The rhetorical question, "Now does one shave off
pieces of the nose to make it smaller or level off a high fore-
head?" could have been asked by Chuang Tzu.

By the turn of the century, when the Manchu dynasty is
about to collapse, we come upon another major novel of
satiric intent, *The Travels of Lao Ts'an* (*Lao-ts'an yu-chi*).
Its author, Liu È (1857–1909), was, like Li Ju-chen, an un-
conventional scholar of intellectual curiosity, but as a man of
the late Ch'ing he was far more open to the Western influence
and promoted without success various schemes of modernization. In the novel he indicts the harsh and incompetent officials of his time from the viewpoint of a sensible and benevolent Confucian somewhat fearful of the drastic consequences of the impending revolution, but in his commiseration with the poor and the wrongly persecuted one detects a
pronounced note of humanitarianism which, while entirely
consonant with Confucian teaching, suggests the Western influence. Especially, *The Travels of Lao Ts'an* betrays its late-
Ch'ing character (and its satiric distance from *Flowers in the
Mirror*) in its allegorization of China as a foundering and
leaking ship torn by dissension and mutiny. Chapter 1 records a dream in which Lao Ts'an and two of his friends spy
such a ship near the Shantung coast:

> The ship was very heavily loaded; the hold must have
> contained many kinds of cargo. Countless people, men
> and women, were sitting on the deck without any awning
> or other covering to protect them from the weather—
> just like the people in third-class cars on the railway from
> Tientsin to Peking. The north wind blew in their faces;
> foam splashed over them; they were wet and cold, hungry
> and afraid. They all had the appearance of people with
> no means of livelihood. Beside each of the eight masts
> were two men to look after the rigging. At the prow and
> on the deck were a number of men dressed like sailors.

It was a great ship, twenty-three or twenty-four chang long, but there were many places in which it was damaged. On the east side was a gash about three chang long, into which the waves were pouring with nothing to stop them. Farther to the east was another bad place about a chang long through which the water was seeping more gradually. No part of the ship was free from scars. The eight men looking after the sails were doing their duty faithfully, but each one looked after his own sail as though each of the eight was on a separate boat: they were not working together at all. The other seamen were running about aimlessly among the groups of men and women; it was impossible at first to tell what they were trying to do. Looking carefully through the telescope, you discovered that they were searching the men and women for any food they might be carrying and also stripping them of the clothes that they wore.[6]

The entire dream sequence is of immense interest as a political allegory, but the short excerpt should serve to establish its note of satiric urgency. According to the notes provided by Professor Harold Shadick in his excellent translation, "the twenty-three or twenty-four chang represent the twenty-three or twenty-four provinces into which China was divided before the revolution of 1911," "the gash three chang long represents Manchuria ... [then] already threatened by Japan and Russia," and the "bad place to the east" is "Shantung, already threatened by Germany and Great Britain."[7] Later in the dream, the captain (the emperor) and his helmsmen (chief ministers of state) are challenged by mutineers (revolutionaries), who are themselves motivated by greed and opportunism and incapable of steering the ship out of danger and providing for the hungry and cold passengers (the people) aboard. Lao Ts'an and his two friends eventually get into a small boat and sail toward the ship, bringing with them "a reliable compass, a sextant, and several other nautical instru-

ments."[8] Once aboard the ship, however, they are denounced
by the crew and passengers alike as "traitors sent by the
foreign devils."[9] No sooner have they returned to their boat
than it sinks under the weight of missiles hurled from the
ship.

Though Lao Ts'an wants to offer Western nautical instru-
ments to save the ship of China, he in no way repudiates the
Chinese tradition and appears in the novel as an autobiographical hero of Quixotic temper, a benevolent Confucian
drawn to the mystic teachings of the Taoist-Buddhist variety.
But he is convinced that moral virtues alone cannot save an
endangered ship: while a more benevolent captain and crew
would have better cared for the passengers and forestalled the
rise of mutineers, they would have to repair the leaks, steer
clear of the storm, and know where they were heading. Liu Ê
is typical of the elite of his generation in believing with the
reformer-statesman Chang Chih-tung that while it is vital to
preserve the essence of Chinese civilization in all matters relating to moral and political conduct, there is also an urgent
need to apply Western learning in all practical matters beyond the prescription of the Confucian classics.[10] In the novel
the relevance of practical knowledge is emphasized in the
hero's concern with the Yellow River, whose waywardness
over the centuries has been the despair of the Chinese government.

Only twenty-four years younger than Liu E, Lu Hsün
decidedly belonged to a new generation much less sanguine
about the essential soundness of Chinese culture. While his
small output as a pioneer story-writer in the Western style
does not justify his reputation as the greatest of modern
Chinese authors, what had arrested the attention of discriminating readers even before his name had been exploited by the
Communists was precisely his modernity, which in the
Chinese context means a hypersensitive awareness of the
rottenness of all strata of Chinese society. In Lu Hsün's stories,
if the scholar-gentry class bears greater responsibility for

China's shame, the illiterate masses are no more hopeful in their state of stupor and superstition. With luck the Chinese youth might be spared the fate of their elders, but he is not too sure.[11]

In contrast, despite his repeated personal frustrations and failures, Liu Ê is much more hopeful. He depicts his hero as a savior in his several roles. Though the distrust of officials has prevented him from executing his plan for safeguarding the Yellow River from flooding its banks, he is a traveling doctor skilled in the cure of diseases and a knight-errant without arms intent on rectifying injustice wherever he encounters it. The young Lu Hsün was apparently equally hopeful when he embarked for Japan to study medicine. But once exposed to Western thought and literature through a course of self-study, he saw the futility of medicine in coping with the spiritual sickness of a people almost certainly doomed to extinction if they did not gird themselves for a tough struggle. While scholars of Liu Ê's generation were already exposed to the theory of the survival of the fittest through Yen Fu's influential translation of T. H. Huxley's *Evolution and Ethics*,[12] Lu Hsün's additional study of Nietzsche drove him to the conclusion that all the moral wisdom of the Chinese tradition, upon which both Li Ju-chen and Liu Ê had drawn to castigate the malpractices of the Chinese society and government, was but a form of hypocrisy sanctioning the cruelty of what would eventually be known in Communist jargon as the feudal system. In his first story, "The Diary of a Madman" (1918), Lu Hsün depicts China as the land of man-eaters who cover up their historical record of inhumanity with high-sounding words like benevolence and righteousness. The indictment is put in the mouth of a madman to minimize the shock of a radical critique of Chinese civilization, but there is no doubt that it is the author himself speaking in the following Nietzschean exhortation by the madman:

"You should change, change from the bottom of your hearts!" I said. "You must know that in future there will be no place for man-eaters in the world.

"If you don't change, you may all be eaten by each other. Although so many are born, they will be wiped out by the real men, just like wolves killed by the hunters. Just like reptiles!"[18]

It matters little whether this gloomy prediction is warranted by the facts of Chinese history. What matters is that, under the paralytic condition of China during the last years of the Ch'ing and the early years of the Republic, the Chinese imagination was finally released from its obligation of self-flattery to enter upon a phase of relentless and ruthless self-examination. A sense of China's shame, impotence, and ugliness informs nearly all the serious literature produced during the period 1918–37. As has been suggested earlier, this new awareness also served to enkindle the passion for human dignity and freedom. Young people should defy their parents to marry whomever they please; peasants, coolies, and factory workers should receive fair treatment and get adequate compensation for their labor. Much of this literature designed to secure our sympathy for the young and the poor would today appear unabashedly sentimental—what is of historical interest and lends it a degree of poignancy is its enveloping awareness of the Chinese context. It would seem that ultimately China gets blamed for all its problems. Thus, in imitation of Thomas Hood's "The Song of the Shirt," Wen I-to wrote a predictably bad poem about the Chinese laundrymen in America, but typically he sees their humiliation as an extension of China's shame.[14] In the story "Sinking," Yü Ta-fu writes of a Chinese youth in Japan suffering from homesickness and a high-strung nervous condition traceable to sexual deprivation. But even he, when driven to suicide, blames all his subjective troubles on China: "O my country, my mother country, you are the cause of my death! I wish you could become rich and strong soon! Many, many of your children are still suffering!"[15]

Such sentimentalities notwithstanding, the predominant mode of modern Chinese fiction is realism. To ensure complete realistic integrity, a few novelists of the late twenties and early thirties would adopt the mode of satiric fantasy and inspect China as if it were an alien land explored for the first time. Shen Ts'ung-wen's *Alice in China* (1928) and Lao Shê's *City of Cats* (1932) are among the best-known works of this category. Both continue the allegoric-satiric tradition of Li Ju-chen and Liu Ê, but as works by major writers of their time their obsession with China is characteristically modern and betrays a savagery surpassing Lu Hsün's.

In Chapter 6 of Shen Ts'ung-wen's fantasy, Alice and the Rabbit (he is described as a Scottish gentleman with the name of John Nash) are driving around in a Chinese city. They are stopped by a starveling who makes an unconvincing attempt at a hold-up so that he may be punished with death. Upon interrogation, he becomes more friendly and tells his life story. Having begged for a number of years, he has just the day before picked up a discarded newspaper and read an article addressed to the poor, which has fortified his wish to end his life. This article, entitled "A Proposal for an Easy Way Out for All Our Chinese Compatriots Suffering from Poverty," contains the following passage:

I have therefore submitted this earnest and fool-proof plan with the same kind of sincerity that motivated the Dean to write "A Modest Proposal" in behalf of the Irish people. Actually, if all the children of starving parents are killed according to my proposal when they have completed two years of life and then properly cured like hams and seasoned with salt and pepper, within one or two months they will become quite edible and could be sold at a reasonable price to upper-class Chinese as well as foreigners professing a friendly interest in China.

Wouldn't this be a nice plan? If we dispose of poor Chinese children in this fashion, I dare say that all the yellow-skinned people now clamoring for "co-existence and co-prosperity" with China, and the white people too, will be only too happy to spend a little money to buy the meat of Chinese children, provided that it be dressed and salted with due regard for cleanliness and for the preservation of its proper texture. However, if we are going to adopt this plan, before the market is fully developed (since at first the supply will exceed the demand for this exotic food), we should reserve a certain number of supernumerary infants for child labor: in this manner the upper-class Chinese will be assured of their supply of concubines, slave girls, and prostitutes, and the foreigners will have no lack of boy-servants. Ay, this is indeed a most economical plan."[16]

In his ultimate development as a story-writer, Shen Ts'ung-wen is as unlike Swift as possible with his serene faith in humanity, but when composing *Alice in China* (in many respects an immature work) to vent his disgust with all aspects of Chinese society, the young author finds the savage irony of "A Modest Proposal" quite to his purpose. In a way, of course, his scheme for the wholesale slaughter of Chinese infants, while obviously echoing Swift, continues Lu Hsün's indictment of China as a cannibalistic society. At the end of *Alice in China*, the British heroine is transported to a market place in Hunan where the Miao aborigines repair every five days to sell their young daughters to Chinese buyers as future prostitutes and slave girls. A three-year-old lies about her age and sings songs to enhance her monetary value. Her father finally sells her for ten Chinese dollars. With all the logical bent of her precocious mind, Alice knows as yet nothing about prostitution and cannot figure out why people want to buy young girls:

All this struck Alice as most odd. The buying and

selling of children as if they were goods was not as puzzling, however, as the question to what end they were bought. Everyone has to eat; so you buy someone just to feed her? A little girl can only cry and do nothing else: could it be possible that some people, bothered by the lack of noise in their homes, buy a little girl just to beat her and torment her so that her incessant crying will make their home life more interesting?[17]

By this time, however, Alice has seen enough of China and decides to go home.

In *City of Cats* a Chinese pilot who has crashed his plane on a Martian country known as Catland finds himself a captive-guest of one of its prominent citizens, Big Scorpion. Eventually the pilot accompanies his host to the capital of Catland, observes its strange governmental and educational systems, watches its invasion by a neighboring country and the quick extinction of its race when the last two surviving cats, so cowardly before their enemy, fight each other to the death. Lao Shê models the cats after his countrymen. They grow and live on a kind of narcotic leaf known as *mi-yeh*, just as the Chinese used to smoke opium. They are lazy, cunning, greedy, sensual, filthy, cowardly, afraid of foreigners but imitative of their bad fashions. The invading enemy, characterized by their short stature, are the Japanese, who in the early thirties were already planning their conquest of China. Lao Shê apparently wrote *City of Cats* to impress upon his countrymen the imminence of their doom, and the result is the most savage indictment of China ever penned by a Chinese.

In many places in the novel the satire is too insistent and obvious, which perhaps justifies the author's eventual dismissal of it as an artistic failure.[18] But at its best *City of Cats* is anything but broad burlesque or crude caricature. Especially magnificent is Chapter 5, a devastating study of a traditional Chinese woman in all her meanness and servitude. She is the widow of an ambassador who had retained all the vices of an upper-class Chinese gentleman except addiction to narcotics, and she has in her charge eight of his concubines. As the chapter opens, their house has just crumbled, and the widow has alone survived the wreckage. Surrounded by the corpses, she vents her suppressed fury before the Chinese pilot and curses them one by one, beginning with the earliest victim of the ambassador's lechery:

"This one," she pinched the skin on the face of one of the dead girls, "this dead fox—when she was only ten years old she was gotten by the Ambassador. Ten years old! Her flesh and bones had not yet got their full growth, and she was used by the Ambassador! The first month she didn't want it to get dark. As soon as darkness came she—this little dead fox—she would cry out—call for father and mother—clutch my hand and wouldn't let it go. She called me Mother—called me Ancestor— wouldn't let me leave her. But I'm a virtuous wife. I couldn't compete with a ten-year-old slave girl for the Ambassador's favors. If the Ambassador wanted his pleasure, I couldn't interfere. I was his wife and I had to maintain my wifely dignity. This little fox—as soon as the Ambassador started toward her, she would scream to heaven and earth, yell with an inhuman sound. When the Ambassador was taking his pleasure—oh, how she screamed. 'Dear Madam Ambassador! Good Ancestor! Come, save me!' When the thing was done, she would lie motionless. Pretending to be dead? Really in a faint? I didn't know, nor did I investigate much. I gave her medicine, gave her food—this dead thing—and she thanked me not at all for my kindness! Later, when she had grown up—oh, what an ingrate—she was only sorry that she couldn't swallow the Ambassador whole. And when the Ambassador bought another one, this one cried from dawn to dark, blaming me because the Ambassador bought women. I was the Ambassador's wife—a virtuous and proper wife—but this little fox blamed me for not controlling the Ambassador. Worthless, stinking vixen!"[19]

In reading this passage, one may become too shocked by the ambassador's treatment of the slave girl to notice even weightier ironies. While it is part of Lao Shê's intention to depict the bestial ways of the ambassador—of any man in China wealthy enough to buy concubines and slave girls—the ultimate horror of the passage lies in the speaker's total acceptance of her role as the ambassador's wife and total un-awareness of her own plight. However pitiable, the dead woman is after all not a Dostoevsky heroine of sheer passive suffering. At first the hapless victim of the ambassador's lust who cries for succor in sheer physical pain, she just as natu-rally craves for sex once she has outgrown her fear. Resigned to her status as a plaything, this brutalized creature at least knows what she wants and cries from dawn to dark when someone has supplanted her as the ambassador's favorite. The principal wife, however, is warped by her upper-class educa-tion and cannot react as naturally. Though vindictive and cruel in her age, she was once not without sympathy in her willingness to give the slave girl medicine and food. It is in her refusal to interfere with her husband's debauchery and total indifference to her conjugal rights that she reveals her abject and deliberate martyrdom. She is above all in her own conceit and in the eyes of her society "a virtuous and proper wife," and her martyrdom begins with her determina-tion to live up to that role. It may be presumed that, as a girl from a proper family, she has not consulted her own wishes when marrying. While she presumably enjoys sex (her spite-ful recital of the second phase of the slave girl's career betrays this), she has been taught to regard sexual pleasure as primar-ily a man's prerogative, and it will be beneath her dignity to demand sexual attention herself or to compete with her husband's growing harem. She does not intercede for the ten-year-old before her husband because she is afraid of being stigmatized as a jealous wife lacking in magnanimity. More-over, as is made clear in other passages of her monologue, it actually redounds to her honor and glory to share her husband with his concubines. She abides by the perverse logic that the more concubines he has, the richer and more powerful he ap-parently is, and therefore the more she herself is to be con-gratulated for her good fortune to be married to such wealth and position.

Her self-abnegation is of course compensated for by her socially sanctioned pleasure in maltreating the concubines in her own right and in enjoying their misery as, one by one, each favorite is supplanted by the ambassador's latest acquisi-tion. But her dominion over them is not complex until her husband dies, and in this respect she is not unlike Moon Lady, the principal wife of the profligate Hsi-men Ch'ing in the classic novel *Chin P'ing Mei*.[20] Moon Lady, however, is much less cruel: she permits a few concubines to remarry and sells the rest, whereas the ambassador's widow keeps vigilant watch over the eight women to ensure their maintenance of a state of joyless chastity. Morever, while her husband is alive, Moon Lady is depicted as a frustrated and unhappy woman: she complains, seeks Buddhist consolation, and occasionally quarrels with his favorite, Golden Lotus. The ambassador's wife, however, is totally uncomplaining and therefore the more abject of the two women. Through a few pages of her monologue, Lao Shê has captured the ambassador's wife in the essential horror of her existence.

The eight-year war against Japan began in July 1937. About a year earlier the slogan "Literature for National De-fense" had already created a big stir. It was a catch phrase coined by the Communist-controlled united front to woo all patriotic elements in the writing profession, but even without this propagandist drive most writers would of themselves have wanted to support the war of resistance, to glorify Chinese heroism, and to build the morale of the people. Thus, to the great impairment of his creative integrity, the author of *City of Cats* accepted the role of propagandist with enthusiasm, turning out several plays, a novel, and much poetry that could not compare in quality with his best early novels. Most leftist and independent writers of stature, who had earlier probed the Chinese psyche in a negative fashion, now reaffirmed the Chinese moral tradition of loyalty and courage and chose for their satiric targets only those elements felt to be endangering or sabotaging the war effort. But in the last years of the war, when conditions in the Nationalist interior had deteriorated, the tendency toward total satire was again noticeable among writers who saw in the physical exhaustion of a war-torn country the alarming resurgence of the forces of corruption and injustice. They again expressed great sympathy for the poor and downtrodden, though marital freedom appeared to be no longer an issue.

By that period, however, the writers in Yenan had long forsaken total satire to subserve the aims of the Communist Party. While the so-called fascists and traitors were denounced, among those working for the Communist cause only the petty-bourgeois intellectuals were safe targets of criticism and ridicule. In other words, writers under Mao Tse-tung, if they wanted to be satirists, could only satirize themselves and all those others who had retained the spirit of liberalism and freedom. Heralding the Literary Revolution in 1917, Ch'en Tu-hsiu had wanted to "overthrow the painted, powdered, and obsequious literature of the aristocratic few."[21] Now, once again, writers were turned into obsequious eulogists of the party in power. But in traditional China the obsequious courtiers are very often the same people responsible for the creation of a "literature of the hermit and recluse," which, if it appears "pedantic, unintelligible, and obscurantist" to Ch'en Tu-hsiu's prejudiced eye, is at least highly individualistic. In contrast, the new eulogists are now denied the freedom to roam in the mountains or lead a hermit-like existence. Far more than the literature produced in the Nationalist interior in the same period, the Communist literature of the war years and immediately after suffers from its emasculation of satire and the shrinkage of its range of fantasy and realism. It has forfeited its modern character.

The literary picture has further darkened since 1949. During the early years of the Communist regime one could detect among the writers perhaps a genuine willingness to support all kinds of mass programs designed to rebuild China and test its strength. So far as I know there was not a single writer who did not greet Chinese participation in the Korean war with a public avowal of personal enthusiasm. But the modern Chinese writer has been characteristically far more obsessed with the quality of life in his country than with its power position in the world. If, living under Communism, he could rejoice in the refurbished national image as a great power, he at the same time became increasingly unhappy about the loss of his freedom and the tribulations of the people. Hence what Mao Tse-tung had denounced in his *Talks at the Yenan Forum on Literature and Art* as the petty-bourgeois attitude of the modern writer—his demand for realism and for his satiric right to expose the darkness of society and his championship of human dignity and human love—has continued to manifest itself, if not in creative writing to a perceptible extent, at least in the voluminous literature of critical dissent. Since the launching of the Great Cultural Revolution in 1966, even Chou Yang, the chief guardian of Mao Tse-tung's literary policy for over twenty years, has been purged as a counterrevolutionary revisionist.

The story of the Chinese writers' continuing dissent and defiance has been told often, and even the small amount of literature produced since 1949 that exhibits the modern characteristics of critical realism and humanitarian pity has been analyzed to some extent.[22] For the purposes of my essay I am more concerned with the imaginative quality of the approved literary product written during the early years of the regime when writers appeared more cooperative. As my specimen I shall quote a passage from Yang Shuo's *A Thousand Miles of Lovely Land* (1953), a novel about Chinese participation in the Korean war which was highly acclaimed at the time of its publication. Except for one minor Chinese officer who betrays his petty-bourgeois upbringing, all the volunteers are selfless patriots displaying the greatest fraternal feeling for the Koreans and the greatest contempt for the American imperialists. Like most novels published in the fifties, however, the work has retained a residual personal quality and would be regarded today as highly subversive by the enforcers of the Cultural Revolution. If need be, the author could be denounced for his lingering desire to carve out an "independent kingdom" of happiness beyond the control of the Communist Party.

In the novel, the young railway engineer Wu T'ien-pao and his fiancée, a nurse, are volunteers on the Korean front, though they are both too busy and unselfish to want to see each other. However, before the hero dies, a victim of American bombing, he is allowed a moment of lassitude during which he dreams of his future. Extremely tired, he thinks of the day when he will be discharged from service decorated with honors. He also thinks of his fiancée:

> After victory they would immediately get married. From then on they would be always together and never apart. Everyday, after the day's work is done, they would eat at the same table and study under the same lamp. But on Sundays he wouldn't allow her burying her head among books. They would go out and take a stroll together, with their children. Yes, they would then have children, a girl and a boy. He would take the girl by hand and she would take the boy. They would take a big bus of the Soviet model and in no time they would arrive at a Soviet movie called "The Happy Life."

Could this be only a dream? In the future who wouldn't be living this kind of life?[23]

The passage is completely antiquated by the Sino-Soviet rift, among other momentous events. No right-thinking Chinese youth of today would think of riding in a Soviet-style bus (presumably it is bigger, faster, and more comfortable than the Chinese model) to see a Soviet movie, and no Soviet movies have been shown in China for years. Nor could he entertain the hope that he and his fiancée, if they were given the permission to marry, would stay home evening after evening—this would be pure wishful thinking. Even if by sheer luck they were stationed in the same locality, they would have to attend mass activities of one sort or another in the evenings. It is also unlikely that they could have personally cared for their family in the American fashion. But the supreme irony of the hero's fantasy lies in the title of the movie he will take his family to see—even with the cozy and idyllic existence he fancies for himself six or seven years from hence, "The Happy Life" is nevertheless a synthetic product manufactured in a Soviet studio. For the Chinese, it is happiness enough to watch such a movie on a Sunday afternoon with his family.

But my point is not to dissect the petty-bourgeois and revisionist daydream of a Communist hero in a novel of the early fifties; it is, rather, to underscore its poignancy as a plea for a minimal personal life. In the novels of the twenties and thirties defense of human dignity often appears in the guise of a deliberate cultivation of moral nihilism, just as patriotic concern with China's future takes the form of devastating satire of its present ills. The modern writer can afford to be grandiose and extravagant. Outwardly a selfless advocate of the heroic life, the writer under Communism actually equates a bright socialist future with whatever little dreams of personal happiness still lurk in his heart. He has abdicated his responsibility as a fearless critic of society, but he cannot submit himself to total dehumanization. The petty-bourgeois daydream of the dying engineer will appear tame and dreary beside Lu Hsün's sweeping condemnation of cannibalism, Shen Ts'ung-wen's ironic proposal to slaughter two-year-old infants, or Lao Shê's grim portrayal of a virtuous and proper wife in the traditional mold. But insofar as the intentional savagery of the latter writers stems from their burning desire to assert human dignity in a land of darkness, Yang Shuo's deliberate or perhaps unselfconscious importation of a bit of fantasy in favor of domestic and individual happiness in a novel designed to glorify other-directed Communist heroism can also be seen to partake of the modern spirit of his predecessors. Unless one remembers the Communist writer's compulsory parroting of the official line on all matters touching China's fate, his surreptitious concern with happiness would look pathetic indeed.

The Whirlwind

ONE OF THE greatest works of modern Chinese fiction, Chiang Kuei's *The Whirlwind* easily ranks with Eileen Chang's *The Rice-sprout Song* and *Love in Redland* as a searching study of Chinese Communism, as the critic Kao Yang has maintained in his long article "Comments and Reflections on *The Whirlwind*" (the *Literary Review*, August 1959). What is perhaps less obvious is that the novel represents also the latest flowering of the satiric tradition in China—from the classical novelists to Lao Shê, Chang T'ien-i, and Ch'ien Chung-shu. In her short stories Eileen Chang has utilized only the domestic tradition in Chinese fiction; though little trained in the craft of Western fiction, Chiang Kuei appears to be more ambitious in having appropriated the techniques of both the domestic and the picaresque novel. The trend is surely salutary that, among serious Japanese and Chinese novelists today, their eagerness to contribute to world literature has impelled them to explore with increasing success the resources of their native traditions.

Completed early in 1952, *The Whirlwind* first saw publication in late 1957 as a private edition of 500 copies. It immediately aroused great interest in Taiwan, partly because, after reading through his complimentary copy, Hu Shih promptly wrote the author a letter of strong endorsement, which was duly publicized. Hu Shih's enthusiasm is understandable: among the host of cliché-ridden anti-Communist novels published in Taiwan, Chiang Kuei's work stands out as a gripping chronicle of the rise of Communism, masterly told against the complex background of Chinese life—with all its corruption and horror—from the May Fourth period to the early years of the Sino-Japanese War. There is no other novel so fascinatingly detailed in its coverage of the manifold aspects of modern China.

In the first sixty pages Chiang Kuei depicts the organizational activities of the early Communists in the Shantung city T (Tsinan); for the remaining 460 pages he focuses his attention mainly on Fang Chen, the home town of the Fang clan, among whose members are at once Communist conspirators and decadent scions of hereditary opulence. The hero is Fang Hsiang-ch'ien, a gentleman-scholar turned Communist, who is genuinely concerned about China's welfare and devotes himself to the task of building Communist strength in his local region. His principal comrade is his nephew Fang P'ei-lan, a bandit-hero of the old school, generous to a fault and beloved by his plebeian followers. Quite fairly, therefore, the author embodies in his heroes the two strands of the Chinese tradition that are least decadent: Confucian intellectualism and the type of underworld chivalry (*hsia*) so celebrated in popular fiction. Yet even these two leaders are no bulwark against the forces of corruption inside and outside the Communist ranks: the novel ends with the permanent establishment of the Communist forces in Shantung, the chaos of the regions under their control, and the betrayal and downfall of the two early organizers.

These two leaders fail because, in Chiang Kuei's scheme, their quarrel with Chinese society is fundamentally an expression of disgust not so much toward the glaring national evils as toward the human condition itself, and no revolution can succeed at the price of abolishing the unique and at times intolerable burden and responsibility of being human. In advocating Communism, Fang Hsiang-ch'ien, like K'ang Yu-wei, Sun Yat-sen, and many other late Ch'ing intellectuals before him, stands convicted of utopianism, the folly of attempting to replace the natural familial and social bonds with an abstract, and supposedly far happier and more equitable, human order. In persuading Fang P'ei-lan to join him, Fang Hsiang-ch'ien plays on the domestic misery of his nephew, only to reveal the pathetic stupidity of his socialist vision:

> "Since the October Revolution Russia has achieved socialist reconstruction. Everybody works, everybody tills the field, everybody is fed, everybody is equal, and everybody is free. Free to marry and free to divorce. If you are not happy with your wife, you can immediately divorce her and marry another. The state provides nurseries: once a child is born, send him to the nursery. You don't have to take care of him and he won't bother you from then on. If sick, you get free treatment in state hospitals; when you get old, you are taken care of in the state asylum until you die. In a word, the Russians have made it."
>
> "My, where in heaven and on earth could there be such a blessed place?"
>
> "This is the Confucian vision of harmony. 'When the great Tao prevailed, the world was a common state . . .'" [p. 105]

Fang Hsiang-ch'ien's speech is an appeal to pure irresponsible selfishness: get rid of your wife if she no longer pleases you; get rid of your children since they are so many unwanted by-products of your sexual activity. That the Russian scheme of dehumanization could be seriously interpreted as the attainment of Confucian harmony indicates that, even among the more enlightened Chinese of the Republican era, a bankruptcy of human values has taken place. (Though passages in some Confucian classics support the utopian vision, the unmistakable Confucian emphasis on *li* indicates, finally, a realistic acceptance of the condition of man as a social being: the alternative to moral and aesthetic refinement of behavior is anarchy.) If the appeal of Communism to its more or less disinterested leaders lies in its amoral welfarism, little wonder that its acceptance by the more selfish elements of society would mean the unchaining of the forces of anarchy and rapacity. In this regard, *The Whirlwind* provides a sardonic spectacle of raw sensuality, greed, and deceit.

In his letter to the author, now serving as a foreword to the book, Hu Shih has praised merely the fluency of its style, the vigor of many of its scenes, and the subtle analysis of the success of Communism. Kao Yang, in his critique, has called further attention to its indebtedness to the traditional Chinese novel and has explained in Freudian terms the abnormal sexual behavior of many of its characters. But though a careful reader, he fails to see that descriptions of aberrant behavior very often serve a satiric purpose and that, as a matter of fact, the novel is largely comic (some scenes are maliciously and uproariously funny)—the kind of absurd comedy which modern Chinese novelists have done so well.

To borrow a phrase that Irving Howe applies to *The Possessed* (*Politics and the Novel*, Meridian Books, p. 57), *The Whirlwind* is "drenched in buffoonery." It lays no claim, of course, to being a profound philosophical novel, as is *The Possessed* with its powerful evocation of nihilistic and totalitarian nightmares and snatches of beatific Christian vision, and its author is not a student of Dostoevsky. But in contemplating a humanity relentlessly selfish and relentlessly bent toward self-destruction, Chiang Kuei can only adopt, as did the Russian novelist, the pose of derisive laughter to drive home the lesson of anarchy and help assert the claims of sanity. Few characters in *The Whirlwind* are spared the author's ridicule because, Communists and non-Communists alike, they are nearly all immersed in corruption.

First of all, even if the Communists served worthy ends, the methods they adopt to achieve these ends would only strengthen the forces of evil. Though on the whole a man of moral rectitude, even Fang Hsiang-ch'ien has to compromise early in his career as an underground Communist worker. To avoid detection and strengthen his movement, he cannot afford the luxury of moral scruples. The early Communists, therefore, see little wrong in resorting to blackmail and murder, in encouraging the traffic of vice and narcotics, in collaborating with the Japanese military and any other evil forces that may further their strength. The extreme deference and power enjoyed by the two prostitutes P'ang Yüeh-mei and P'ang Chin-lien (mother and daughter) among the Communists—at once liaison officers and carnal solace— are only a grotesque reminder of the lengths the Communists would go in order to better their position.

Secondly, as individuals, the Communists are no better than their nonrevolutionary, self-seeking compatriots. Early in the novel the author gives a deft caricature of a Communist representative from Shanghai who resorts to extortion and terrorism not to advance the fortunes of his party but to maintain an expensive affair with a local actress. He is soon decapitated: the first of the many macabre comedies in the book, which ends with the grotesque satire of two successful Communists: Hsü Ta-hai, the ruthless man who is not above selling his loving master and immediate superior Fang P'ei-lan (and Fang Hsiang-ch'ien) for self-advancement; and Fang T'ien-ai, Fang Hsiang-ch'ien's earliest disciple and protégé, who feels no qualms in repudiating his illustrious family name to become the adopted son of the elder prostitute. These two events symbolize the complete displacement of the cornerstone of traditional Chinese social structure—

loyalty and filial piety—by unashamed treachery and opportunism. In a way, these young Communists are what their elders, Fang Hsiang-ch'ien and Fang P'ei-lan, would have become if they had been completely divorced from the traditional code of honor and inured to the environment of deceit.

The novel moves relentlessly toward anarchy. Yet the author is saying at the same time that Communism could not have come to power if the seeds of anarchy had not been already planted in the consciousness of the nonrevolutionary Chinese. Hence the ample space devoted to tracing the fortunes of the major Fang households—their unplanned self-destruction, in a way, serves as an ironic parallel to the systematic bringing about of social upheaval by the Communists. The sensualists, like the revolutionaries, are impatient with the human condition, and demand unlimited scope for their appetites. The landlord Fang Jan-wu, perhaps the most asinine wastrel in modern Chinese fiction, squanders his fortune with reckless abandon merely to install cheap prostitutes at his house. On the other hand, the old lady Fang, who treats the concubine Hsi-men with unspeakable sadism because for a number of years the latter had usurped her late husband's affections, is a prime example of the thirst for revenge. And revenge, like sensuality, is the sure harbinger of anarchy.

Despite the great critical success of *The Whirlwind,* Chiang Kuei was for some unknown reason ignored by the Taiwan literary world and lived for years in dire poverty. He has since written two novels—*Double Ninth* (*Ch'ung-yang,* 1961) and *The Green Sea and the Blue Sky: A Nocturne* (*Pi-hai ch'ing-t'ien yeh-yeh-hsin,* 1964)—which, he believes, are comparable to *The Whirlwind* in seriousness, but the rest of his recent writings are by his own admission pot-boilers. Since the mid-sixties his fortunes have improved somewhat, although he still lives alone in a dingy hotel room and receives only a nominal salary for his work as a scenarist at a movie studio. At a time when Taiwan is seriously promoting a "Cultural Renaissance," that one of its greatest writers, and an anti-Communist to boot, should suffer gross neglect and receive no financial support whatever for his serious writing projects remains a puzzling case of irony indeed.

Notes

WHEREAS IN THE main text I have in most cases merely translated the titles of Chinese publications into English, all such titles are transliterated in the notes, which are primarily intended for the specialists. When a title appears for the first time, its English meaning is given in parentheses; subsequently it is recorded only in its transliterated form. To avoid confusion, no abbreviations have been adopted for titles of books and periodicals. When the date and place of publication are not given for a book, the information is available in the Bibliography. Occasionally, however, I have entered in the Bibliography a more authoritative edition of a book than the one actually used in the preparation of this study; in that case, the pertinent data concerning the latter edition will be found in the notes.

1. THE LITERARY REVOLUTION

1. Two sections of Ch'en Tu-hsiu's editorial, from one of which these phrases are taken, have been translated in Huang Sung-k'ang, *Lu Hsün and the New Culture Movement of Modern China*, pp. 13–14.

2. *Chien-shê li-lun chi* (Toward a Constructive Literary Theory), Vol. 1 of *Chung-kuo hsin-wen-hsüeh ta-hsi* (A Comprehensive Anthology of Modern Chinese Literature), pp. 46–47. "Wen-hsüeh kai-liang ch'u-i" (Suggestions for a Reform of Literature), "Wen-hsüeh ko-ming lun" (For a Literary Revolution), and all the subsequent important discussions about pai-hua and the crea-

tion of a pai-hua literature are to be found in that volume and Vol. 2 of the same anthology, *Wen-hsüeh lun-cheng chi* (Literary Debates). I am naturally indebted to these for the historical information in this chapter.

3. In "Notes on Translation," *The Atlantic Monthly* (November 1958), Arthur Waley gives high praise to Lin Shu as a translator, especially of Dickens. "Dickens, inevitably, becomes a rather different and to my mind a better writer. All the overelaboration, the overstatement and uncurbed garrulity disappear" (p. 111). Granted that Lin Shu's "precise, economical style" makes better reading than Dickens' "uncontrolled exuberance," shouldn't a translator's primary duty be fidelity to the spirit and style of the original?

4. In *The Chinese Renaissance* Hu Shih gives a concise exposition of his theory of Chinese literature.

5. Hu Shih, "Chien-shê ti wen-hsüeh ko-ming lun" (For a Constructive Literary Revolution), *Chien-shê li-lun chi*, p. 136.

6. Ch'ien Hsüan-t'ung, "Chung-kuo chin-hou ti wen-tzu wen-t'i" (The Language Problem in China: Its Prospects), ibid., pp. 142–44. A thorough materialist who shared with Ch'ien a contempt for Chinese culture and a desire to abolish the Chinese language at that time was Wu Chih-hui, who unaccountably was held in high esteem by such liberal critics as Hu Shih and Ch'en Yüan. For a survey of the cultural debates of the period see Wing-tsit Chan, *Religious Trends in Modern China* (New York, 1953), chap. 6, "The Religion of the Intellectual."

7. Fu Ssu-nien, "Han-yü kai-yung p'ing-yin wen-tzu ti ch'u-pu t'an" (Preliminary Remarks on the Latinization of Chinese), *Chien-shê li-lun chi*, p. 149.

8. Recent literary historians (Wang Yao, Ts'ao Chü-jen, Liu Shou-sung, et al.—see Bibliography, I) have all perpetuated the error that the *Critical Review* was launched in 1921. The first issue of the journal appeared in January 1922.

9. Dewey and his wife arrived in China on May 1, 1919, on the eve of the May Fourth Movement, and didn't leave until July 1921. For an account of Dewey's lecture tour and his influence in China, see Hsia Tao-p'ing's translation of Hu Shih's address given at the University of Hawaii in the summer of 1959, "Dewey tsai chung-kuo" (John Dewey in China), *Tzu-yu Chung-kuo*

(Free China), *21*, 4 (August 1959). For a brief account of the visits of the other celebrities in the early twenties, see the chapter on Dewey and Tagore in Ts'ao Chü-jen, *Wen-t'an wu-shih-nien* (Fifty Years of Chinese Literature), *1*, 180–81. It is a sad thing to notice that Dewey and Russell have persisted as oracles of truth, the last word in Western scientific enlightenment, to a large segment of intellectuals on Taiwan, most of whom have probably never followed the anti-Dewey reaction in recent American educational thought, nor apparently read the more recent writings of Russell. The chief organ of these intellectuals is the aforementioned Taipei fortnightly, *Tzu-yu Chung-kuo*.

10. Mei Kuang-ti, "P'ing t'i-ch'ang hsin-wen-hua che" (The Promoters of New Culture), *Wen-hsüeh lun-cheng chi*, pp. 127–32. This essay first appeared in *Hsüeh Heng* (Critical Review), *1*, 1.

11. While it is not certain whether the initial May 30 demonstration was spontaneous or organized by the Communists, scholars are agreed that the Communist party directed and exploited the subsequent antiforeign demonstrations and boycotts to its immense advantage. This unanimity of opinion can be shown in passages taken from two representative recent studies in Chinese Communism by American scholars:

> The tremendous surge of mass energies kindled by the May Thirtieth incident of 1925 was, it is true, somewhat in the nature of a spontaneous outburst. . . . The Communist Party was, however, quick to take advantage of this popular surge and the young enthusiasts of the Communist Party soon stole a march on the non-Communist elements of the Kuomintang in the matter of mass organization, for in spite of Sun Yat-sen's lectures the non-Communist elements in the Kuomintang failed, even at this early date, to show a proper appreciation of the potentialities of mass power.
> Benjamin I. Schwartz, *Chinese Communism and the Rise of Mao* (Cambridge, Harvard Univ. Press, 1952), p. 52.

> The May 30 and [subsequent] Shakee-Shameen shootings made truth out of Soviet propaganda against the "foreign imperialist," and, by inflaming latent Nationalist militancy,

strengthened the Communist position within the Kuomin-tang. Bolshevik leaders boasted that in several labor or-ganizations Chinese Communist agitators jumped overnight from labor union assistants to leaders. Workers who had formerly distrusted or even hated the Communists now con-sidered them as friends, and numbers joined the party. Com-munists gained similar strength within organs of the Kuo-mintang itself.

> Robert C. North, *Moscow and Chinese Communists* (Stan-ford University Press, 1953), p. 82.

An examination of Chinese fiction dealing with the May Thirti-eth Movement, however, tends to support the impression that Communists were instigators of the initial May 30 demonstrations (see my discussion of the novel *Rainbow* in Chap. 6, pp. 148–55). The students of Shanghai College, a Communist training center, were especially active in the movement; see Ting Miao, *Chung-kung wen-i tsung-p'i-p'an* (A Comprehensive Critique of Chinese Communist Literature), pp. 30–31.

12. Liang Shih-ch'iu, "Hsien-tai chung-kuo wen-hsüeh chih lang-man ti ch'ü-shih," *Lang-man-ti yü ku-tien-ti* (Romantic and Classic), pp. 1–39.

13. The June 1918 number of *New Youth* was devoted to Ibsen. In addition to Hu Shih's essay on Ibsenism, it featured the com-plete translated text of *A Doll's House* (by Hu Shih and Lo Chia-lun) and the first installments of two other plays in translation. For an enumeration of the many early translations of Ibsen's works, see A Ying (Ch'ien Hsing-ts'un), "Ibsen ti tso-p'in tsai chung-kuo" (Ibsen in China), *Wen-i Pao* (The Literary Gazette), No. 17, September 1956.

14. *Shih-liao so-yin* (Source Materials and Indices), Vol. 10 of *Chung-kuo hsin-wen-hsüeh ta-hsi,* reprints the tables of contents of *New Youth* from *1,* No. 1 to *9,* No. 6 (September 1915 – October 1921). An examination of this material effectively destroys the theses that the new culture movement was the creation of Marxist intellectuals and that early in its career *New Youth* went Marxist. (Parroting Mao Tse-tung, Chinese Communist historians reached these conclusions by minimizing the importance of Hu Shih and magnifying the contributions of Ch'en Tu-hsiu and especially

of Li Ta-chao.) While the May 1919 number of the magazine was devoted to Marxism, it is equally significant that the October 1920 number focused its attention on Russell, welcoming his arrival in China from Soviet Russia, where he had toured. I append here a substantial list of Western authors and thinkers either translated or discussed at length in the pages of *New Youth* during the period 1915–20 (from 1921 on, the journal became pronouncedly Marxist in emphasis): Turgenev, Wilde, T. H. Huxley, Schopenhauer, Benjamin Franklin, the Goncourt Bros., Maupassant, Dostoevsky, Bergson, J. S. Mill, Nietzsche, Ibsen, Strindberg, Sienkiewcz, Tolstoy, Andersen, Herbert Spencer, Marx, Bakunin, Austin Dobson, Andreyev, Kuprin, Dewey, Malthus, Russell, Björnson, Korolenko, Gorky, Artzybashev. This list shows quite clearly the diverse intellectual preoccupations of the journal's editors and contributors.

15. For the views of scientific positivists and religionists during a famous debate in 1923, see *K'o-hsüeh yü jen-sheng-kuan* (Science and Philosophy of Life), 2 vols. Shanghai, 1923. Both Hu Shih and Ch'en Tu-hsiu wrote introductions for this compilation.

16. For the January 1918 number of *New Youth* Chou Tso-jen wrote "Dostoevsky ti hsiao-shuo" (The Novels of Dostoevsky); for another early journal *Shao-nien Chung-kuo* (Young China), *1*, No. 8 (1920?) he wrote "Ying-kuo shih-jen Blake ti ssu-hsiang" (The Thought of the English Poet Blake). *Shih-liao so-yin,* which lists the contents of all the important journals of the period, mentions no earlier articles exclusively devoted to these two authors. It is a pity that because Chou Tso-jen eventually turned Japanese collaborator, his splendid and varied contributions to the Literary Revolution and the new culture movement have never been given due recognition.

17. See Achilles Fang, "From Imagism to Whitmanism in Recent Chinese Poetry: A Search for Poetics That Failed," *Indiana University Conference on Oriental-Western Literary Relations,* ed. Horst Frenz and G. L. Anderson. Hu Shih's reliance on the Imagist credos for his proposed literary reforms was first pointed out by the *Critical Review* group; see especially Mei Kuang-ti's article referred to in n. 10 above.

18. The most remarkable of these is perhaps Chang Hen-shui, who has turned out over the decades a staggering number of best-

selling novels. Joseph Schyns et al., *1500 Modern Chinese Novels and Plays*, listed in 1948 55 novels by the author, but even this list cannot be complete. Having successfully weathered the war years (1937–45) as a patriotic novelist, Chang Hen-shui is today an accepted literary worker in Communist China.

19. For a critical account of the early pai-hua poetry see Chu Tzu-ch'ing, "Tao-yen" (Foreword), *Shih chi* (Poetry), Vol. 8 of *Chung-kuo hsin-wen-hsüeh ta-hsi*. Read also Yeh Kung-ch'ao, "Lun hsin-shih" (On Modern Poetry), *Wen-hsüeh Tsa-chih* (Literary Magazine), *1*, No. 1 (Peiping, 1937), and articles by Mao Tun, Chu Tzu-ch'ing, et al. in the modern poetry number of *Wenhsüeh* (Literature), *8*, No. 1 (Shanghai, 1937), for representative critical opinions in the thirties. The best discussions on pai-hua poetry and its future, however, are all quite recent in date: Yü Huai (pen name of Stephen C. Soong), "Lun hsin-shih ti hsingshih" (The Form of Modern Poetry), "Tsai-lun hsin-shih ti hsingshih" (Further Remarks on the Form of Modern Poetry), respectively in Nos. 15 and 18 of *Jen-jen Wen-hsüeh* (Everyman's Literature), Hong Kong, 1953; Liang Wen-hsin (pen name of Wu Hsing-hua), "Hsien-tsai ti hsin-shih" (Modern Poetry Today), *Wen-hsüeh Tsa-chih* (Literary Review), *1*, No. 4 (Taipei, 1956); Hsia Tsi-an, "Pai-hua-wen yü hsin-shih" (Pai-hua and Modern Poetry), ibid., *2*, No. 1 (March 1957); "Tui-yü hsin-shih ti i-tien i-chien" (My Views on Modern Poetry), *Tzu-yu Chungkuo, 16*, No. 9 (Taipei, 1957).

20. In spite of the uniform mediocrity of the early drama, there was, of course, a great deal of theatrical activities during this period. See Hung Shen, "Tao-yen" (Foreword), *Hsi-chü chi* (Plays), Vol. 9 of *Chung-kuo hsin-wen-hsüeh ta-hsi;* also Ts'ao Chü-jen, *Wen-t'an wu-shih-nien, 2,* 21–26.

2. Lu Hsün

1. For a list of useful biographies and memoirs by Cheng Hsüeh-chia, Chou Tso-jen, Feng Hsüeh-feng, Hsü Kuang-p'ing, Ts'ao Chü-jen, and Wang Shih-ching, see Bibliography, V, 1. Unlike the others, Cheng Hsüeh-chia's biography is written from the anti-Communist point of view and is harshly critical of his subject.

2. *Mao Tse-tung hsüan-chi* (The Selected Works of Mao Tse-tung), *2* (Peking, 1952), 668–69.

3. In his 1923 survey of "Wu-shih-nien lai chung-kuo chih wen-hsüeh" (Chinese Literature of the Last Fifty Years), Hu Shih specifically cites the writings of Lu Hsün and Chou Tso-jen as examples of the best new literature. In spite of his personal animosity toward Lu Hsün, Ch'en Yüan lists *Na han* (The Outcry) among "Hsin-wen-hua-yün-tung i-lai ti shih-pu chu-tso" (The Ten Outstanding Publications since the New Culture Movement). The essay is included in *Hsi-ying hsien-hua* (The Causeries of Hsi-ying).

On the contrary, Ch'eng Fang-wu's unfavorable review of *Na han* in *Creation Quarterly*, *2*, No. 2 (subsequently included in Li Ho-lin, ed., *Lu Hsün lun*), is typical of the group who later became Communist writers. Kuo Mo-jo's hostility toward Lu Hsün was especially notorious: he professed not being able to finish reading *Na han*, a small book. It is only since Lu Hsün's death that he has been compelled to adopt an adulatory attitude toward him.

4. Preface to *Na han*, *Lu Hsün ch'üan-chi* (The Complete Works of Lu Hsün), *1*, 271.

5. Ibid., p. 281. In translating this and the subsequent passages from Lu Hsün's short stories (with the exception of the passage from "Medicine"), I have consulted Chi-chen Wang, *Ah Q and Others: Selected Stories of Lusin*, New York, Columbia University Press, 1941.

6. Ibid., p. 291.

7. Ibid., p. 277.

8. Lu Hsün, "Tao-yen" (Foreword), *Hsiao-shuo erh-chi* (Fiction, Second Series), Vol. 4 of *Chung-kuo hsin-wen-hsüeh ta-hsi*, p. 2.

9. *Lu Hsün ch'üan-chi*, *1*, 309.

10. Ibid., p. 357.

11. *Hsiao-shuo erh-chi*, p. 2.

12. *Lu Hsün ch'üan-chi*, *2*, 159.

13. Ibid., p. 170.

14. Ibid., p. 196.

15. Ibid., pp. 199–200.

16. Ibid., p. 204.

17. Ibid., pp. 31–32.

18. See Feng Hsüeh-feng, *Hui-i Lu Hsün* (Lu Hsün: A Memoir), pp. 86–88.

19. One may cite here a petty quarrel from which Lu Hsün emerged clearly beaten. In 1933, at the request of the editor of *Huo-chü* (The Torch), a literary section of the Shanghai *Ta Wan Pao*, the noted author and editor Shih Chih-ts'un recommended *Chuang Tzu* and *Wen Hsüan* as most suitable reading for aspiring young writers. Lu Hsün, who could not abide classical Chinese literature, promptly attacked Shih for his "infatuation with the skeleton." Since both *Chuang Tzu* and *Wen Hsüan* are among the most esteemed titles in Chinese literature, Shih had little difficulty in defending his choice and ridiculing his opponent mercilessly. But Lu Hsün must have the last word, in private if not in public. In a letter to Yao K'o, dated November 5, 1933, Lu Hsün unintentionally convicts himself of unpardonable snobbery in suggesting that Shih's lower social origins must have been responsible for his sudden enthusiasm for *Chuang Tzu* and *Wen Hsüan:* "This man came from a family engaged in trade; when he came across ancient classics, quite expectedly he would regard them as the rarest treasure, just as a nouveau riche is particularly fond of affecting the manners of a genteel scholar. Just try to read his writings; where can you find in these a trace of the spirit of *Chuang Tzu* and *Wen Hsüan?*" See *Lu Hsün shu-chien* (The Letters of Lu Hsün), p. 411.

20. *Lu Hsün shu-chien* throws merciless light on the author's daily life in Shanghai and fully substantiates the truth of my portrait. To many of his correspondents at that time he reveals his dissatisfaction with his perpetually harassed and busy life, affording absolutely no leisure for sustained creative and research activity, and his disgust with his servitude to the League of Left-wing Writers. In a particularly revealing letter to his good friend Hu Feng, dated September 12, 1935, he writes:

> I feel it would be better to have a few new writers appear among the people who do not belong [to the League]; they may show something fresh. Once a man has joined, he will be forever involved in petty squabbles and cannot make his voice heard. Take me as an example. I always feel that I am

bound in an iron chain while a foreman is whipping me on the back. No matter how hard I work, the whip will fall. When I turn my head and ask what are really my faults, the man will clasp his hands and politely shake them and say that I am doing an extremely fine job; that he and I are surely the best of friends; and what a fine day ha, ha, ha . . . That so often disconcerts me. I dare not speak to the outsiders about ourselves; to the foreigners, I simply avoid the subject. If I have to speak, I only lie. You see what a predicament I am in [p. 947].

In contrast to the polemic essays of the same period, the letters at times show an endearing honesty, a strain of loneliness, and a desire for friendship and personal warmth. Yet with all his actual distaste for "squabbles" and "lying," Lu Hsün knew then of his failing creative powers and took no active steps toward changing his mode of existence. For an excellent study of Lu Hsün's personal and polemic life in the middle thirties, see the chapter on "Lu Hsün and the Dissolution of the League of Leftist Writers" in Tsi-an Hsia, *The Gate of Darkness: Studies on the Leftist Literary Movement in China.*

21. *Lu Hsün ch'üan-chi, 2, 252.*

22. Ibid., *4, 107.*

3. THE LITERARY ASSOCIATION

1. "Wen-hsüeh Yen-chiu Hui" has been variously translated as the "Literary Research Society" or "Society for Literary Studies." However, in every issue of *The Short Story* one finds on its masthead the English equivalent for the name of the society: the Literary Association.

2. For a listing of the contents of *The Short Story* up to December 1926, see *Shih-liao so-yin.* A good recent article on the history of the magazine is Hsü T'iao-fu, "Hsiao-shuo Yüeh-pao hua-chiu" (A Reminiscent Chat on *The Short Story*), *Wen-i Pao,* No. 15, August 1956.

3. Ku Chieh-kang studied under Hu Shih at Peking University and later made important contributions to the study of ancient

Notes

Chinese history. His *Autobiography of a Chinese Historian, Being the Preface to a Symposium in Ancient Chinese History,* trans. A. W. Hummel (Leyden, 1931), offers valuable insights into the mind of Chinese intellectuals and scholars following the Literary Revolution.

4. *Yeh Sheng-t'ao hsüan-chi* (The Selected Works of Yeh Sheng-t'ao), p. 8.

5. Ibid., p. 11.

6. Ibid., p. 47.

7. Ibid., pp. 51–52.

8. Ibid., p. 54.

9. *Yeh Sheng-t'ao wen-chi* (The Works of Yeh Sheng-t'ao) (Peking, 1958), *3*, 404. Until the reappearance of *Ni Huan-chih* in this standard edition, for a number of years the novel was available in Communist China only in a truncated version put out by the Jen-min Wen-hsüeh Ch'u-pan-shê in 1953: it removed the last third of the work so as to expunge its note of despondency. For a detailed exposé see T'ang Wen-ping (Stephen C. Soong), "Ni Huan-chih: shui huan chih?" (*Ni Huan-chih:* Who Altered It?), in *Chin-jih Shih-chieh* (The World Today), No. 44, Hong Kong, January 1, 1954.

10. "Ying-wen chiao-shou" (The English Professor), *Shih-nien* (A Decade), ed. Hsia Mien-tsun, pp. 316, 333.

11. *Yeh Sheng-t'ao wen-chi* (The Selected Writings of Yeh Sheng-t'ao) (Shanghai, 1948), p. 52.

12. Ibid., pp. 56–57.

13. Ibid., p. 77.

14. Ibid., p. 78.

15. *Ping Hsin hsiao-shuo chi* (The Collected Stories of Ping Hsin) (Shanghai, Kaiming Press, 1943), p. 178.

16. Ibid., pp. 234–36.

17. In 1945, however, Su Hsüeh-lin turned out a volume of stories entitled *Shan-shui chi* (The Cicada's Shell) which, while predominantly patriotic in tone, shows a deep appreciation of the Confucian virtues and makes expert use of the traditional narrative style. Published by the Commercial Press, this volume contains seven stories, mainly about Ming loyalists fighting the Manchu invasion.

18. *Hua chih ssu* (The Temple of Flowers), pp. 78–79.

19. Ibid., pp. 79–80.

20. Ibid., p. 87.

21. *Nü-jen* (Women), p. 40.

22. Entitled *Wei-ch'ao chui-chien* (Letters From an Endangered Home), this volume was edited with a preface by Cheng Chen-to for the Commercial Press in 1947.

23. *Hsiao-shuo i-chi* (Fiction, First Series), Vol. 3 of *Chung-kuo hsin-wen-hsüeh ta-hsi,* p. 200.

24. Ibid., pp. 201–2.

25. Ibid., p. 202.

26. *Wei-ch'ao chui-chien,* p. 226.

27. Allen Tate, "The Man of Letters in the Modern World," in *The Forlorn Demon* (Chicago, Henry Regnery, 1953), pp. 3, 12.

4. THE CREATION SOCIETY

1. Mistranslations, of course, were equally notorious in the pages of *Creation Quarterly* and the succeeding Creationist journals. The poet Wen I-to early pointed out the errors in Kuo Mo-jo's translation of Fitzgerald's *Rubáiyát;* see his article "Omar Khayyám chih chüeh-chü" (The Four-line Poetry of Omar), reprinted from *Creation Quarterly, 2,* No. 1, in *Wen I-to ch'üan-chi* (The Complete Works of Wen I-to), *3* (Shanghai, Kaiming, 1948), 203–21. In comparison with the Literary Association, the most reprehensible stylistic fault of the Creationists, however, is their pedantic habit of transliterating long foreign terms when corresponding Chinese terms are available or could be readily coined, e.g. *i-tê-wo-lo-chi* for "ideology" and *yin-t'ieh-li-ken-chui-ya* for "intelligentsia." In reading Creationist writings, I was long puzzled by the term *ao-fu-ho-pien,* which turned out to be a transliteration of the German "aufheben." All these terms can be found in the famous article "From Literary Revolution to a Revolutionary Literature"; its author, Ch'eng Fang-wu, was perhaps the worst pedant among the Creationists.

2. For a listing of the contents of these publications up to December 1926, see *Shih-liao so-yin.* Cheng Po-ch'i's "Tao-yen" (Foreword) to *Hsiao-shuo san-chi* (Fiction, Third Series), Vol. 5 of *Chung-kuo hsin-wen-hsüeh ta-hsi,* contains a good summary of the early history of the Creation Society.

3. By the time he completed his translation of *Faust,* Pt. II, Kuo Mo-jo had become completely disenchanted with Goethe, one of his early heroes. It is rather unusual for a translator to disparage the work he has just translated, but Kuo did precisely that in his introduction to his completed translation. This introduction is included in *T'ien-ti hsüan-huang* (Heaven and Earth).

4. Kuo Mo-jo's literary and scholarly writings, exclusive of translations, are being gathered in a standard edition of *Mo-jo wen-chi* (The Works of Kuo Mo-jo), eleven volumes of which have already been published by the Jen-min Wen-hsüeh Ch'u-pan-shê, Peking, since 1956.

5. Notably, the songs in *T'ang-ti chih hua* (The Devoted Siblings), which is Kuo Mo-jo's best play; *Hu fu;* and *Ch'ü Yüan.*

6. Lest I be accused of being unduly severe on Kuo Mo-jo, the curious reader is advised to consult the early criticism of the author, written long before his recent establishment as the foremost modern Chinese poet and a cultural hero worthy to stand beside Lu Hsün. Upon the appearance of *Three Rebellious Women,* Hsiang P'ei-liang, a noted early playwright and story-writer, wrote a devastating review called "So-wei li-shih-chü" (The So-called Historical Drama), which contains the following: "The characters he has created are all characterless and lifeless things . . . His villains are reduced to a state of disgusting and ridiculous buffoonery. . . . The author's didactic appetite is so huge that it beggars comparison." In "Kuo Mo-jo lun" (Kuo Mo-jo Appraised), perhaps the best critical essay on the author, Shen Ts'ung-wen describes Kuo's poetry as "the outcry of a naive person" and goes on to evaluate his fiction: "His prose is suitable for the writing of an official proclamation, a manifesto, a telegraphic dispatch, but not suitable for the writing of fiction." These early criticisms are included in Li Lin, comp. *Kuo Mo-jo p'ing-chuan* (Kuo Mo-jo: Critical and Biographical Studies).

7. "Chih Ch'eng Fang-wu shu" (A Letter to Ch'eng Fang-wu), *San-wen i-chi* (Essays, First Series), Vol. 6 of *Chung-kuo hsin-wen-hsüeh ta-hsi,* pp. 219–20, 227–28.

8. "Wu-liu-nien lai ch'uang-tso sheng-huo ti hui-ku" (In Retrospect: My Writing Career during the Past Five or Six Years), ibid., pp. 165–66.

9. "Ch'en lun" (Sinking), *Hsiao-shuo san-chi,* pp. 70–71.

10. "Ku-ch'ü" (The Past), *Yü Ta-fu wen-chi* (The Selected Writings of Yü Ta-fu), p. 80.

11. Ibid., p. 81.

12. With characteristic irony, Yü Ta-fu confided to a reporter his reasons for leaving the League:

> People are now forming a clearer view of the League of Left-wing Writers. At first, people thought that the terms "a left-wing writer" and "a Communist member" are synonymous. Those who think so are in the wrong. We should know that left-wing writers are left-wing writers and Communist members are Communist members, though a portion of the left-wing writers did join the Communist party.
>
> Yes, I was one of the inaugurators of the League of Left-wing Writers. But the Communist headquarters were dissatisfied with me, saying that my writings are individualistic. I admit to this charge because I am of petty-bourgeois origins and cannot avoid being so. But this thing called society, is it not composed of innumerable "individuals"? If this is so, then I believe that to expose the lives of individuals is also to expose the life of a certain class in society . . .
>
> Later, the Communist headquarters assigned me field work. I told them that to distribute pamphlets and to engage in chores of a similar nature are rather beyond my ability; so they became even more dissatisfied with me. Just recently I voluntarily crossed off the name of Yü Ta-fu from the League of Left-wing Writers.
>
> It is very difficult for a person of petty-bourgeois origins to engage in field work. If he is reluctantly compelled to do so, he can only hurt the cause of the masses. As the saying goes, "he is incompetent to help accomplish something, but more than able to ruin something." There seems to be only one path open to the petty bourgeoisie: to become teachers and civil servants.

This passage is from Tsou Hsiao, comp. *Yü Ta-fu lun* (Yü Ta-fu: Critiques), pp. 186–87.

13. In "Tsai-lun Yü Ta-fu" (More about Yü Ta-fu), *T'ien-ti hsüan-huang*, Kuo Mo-jo, apparently feeling guilty, tries to depict himself as the indirect cause of his long-estranged friend's death.

Other writers have offered other solutions as to why the Japanese police wanted to track down and kill Yü Ta-fu. See especially [Hsü] Tsu-cheng, "Yü Ta-fu chui-i" (Yü Ta-fu Remembered), *Wen-i Shih-tai* (Literary Times), *1*, No. 3, Peiping, August 1946.

5. Leftists and Independents

1. In *Soviet Russia in China* (New York, 1957) Chiang Kai-shek admits (p. 215) that "we lacked initiative in propaganda and substance in ideology."

2. Huang Jen-ying, ed., *Ch'uang-tsao-shê lun* (Critiques of the Creation Society) reprints Wang Tu-ch'ing's article as well as rejoinders by Kuo Mo-jo and Chang Tzu-p'ing, entitled respectively "Ch'uang-tsao-shê ti tzu-wo p'i-p'an" (My Appraisal of the Creation Society) and "Tu Ch'uang-tsao-shê lun" (On Reading Wang Tu-ch'ing's "The Creation Society").

3. *Yü Ssu* started publication in 1924 and folded in 1931. For a detailed account of its history see Ch'uan Tao, "I Lu Hsün hsien-sheng ho *Yü Ssu*" (My Reminiscences about Lu Hsün and *Yü Ssu*), *Wen-i Pao*, No. 16, August 1956. This article corrects some errors in Lu Hsün, "Wo ho Yü Ssu ti shih-chung" (My Relationship with Yü Ssu), *Lu Hsün ch'üan-chi*, Vol. 4.

4. Upton Sinclair was immensely popular in China during the second half of the twenties. His *Mammonart* (1925) was an important tract to the revolutionary writers.

5. Entitled "Ko-ming shih-tai ti wen-hsüeh" (Literature of the Revolutionary Times), this address is included in *Erh-i chi, Lu Hsün ch'üan-chi, 3*, 402–10.

6. *Wen Hsüeh* was not a League-sponsored magazine, and it is perhaps not even strictly accurate to call it leftist. In his 1937 essay "Shih-nien-lai ti chung-kuo wen-hsüeh" (Chinese Literature of the Last Ten Years), in Fan Chung-yün, ed. *Shih-nien-lai ti chung-kuo* (China: The Last Ten Years), its editor and publisher Fu Tung-hua explicitly dissociates *Wen Hsüeh* from the leftist literary movement and sees it as a continuation of *The Short Story*, carrying forward the realistic tradition first enunciated in Chou Tso-jen's "Humane Literature." In view of the fact that both Fu and his succeeding editor, Wang T'ung-chao, were former members of the Literary Association, one cannot very well

doubt Fu's sincerity when he asserted *Wen Hsüeh's* nonleftist character. (A translator of Homer, Milton, and other Western classics, Fu scored his greatest commercial success with his translation of *Gone with the Wind* during the war years: a leftist author would have scorned to translate that notorious American best-seller.) But a perusal of the contents of *Wen Hsüeh* confirms the general contemporary impression that it was indeed the "star" magazine of its time, and its stars—Lu Hsün, Kuo Mo-jo, Mao Tun, Hsia Yen, Chang T'ien-i, et al.—were invariably the prominent leftist and Communist authors of the day. Moreover, like many other leftist and Communist journals of the middle thirties, it was released through the Sheng-huo Shu-tien (the Life Book Co.). In spite of Fu Tung-hua's disclaimer, therefore, the leftist character of the magazine seems to me quite obvious.

Precisely because it pursued a more flexible leftist policy and attracted a great many eminent writers, *Wen Hsüeh* was without doubt the most durable and influential leftist magazine of its time. In contrast, the League-sponsored journals were limited in appeal and often specialized in character. Some other leftist magazines of the middle thirties were: *I Wen* (Translations), edited by Huang Yüan with the support of Lu Hsün and devoted to the translation of Soviet literature; *Tso-chia Yüeh-k'an* (The Writers' Monthly), edited by Meng Shih-huan and supported by Feng Hsüeh-feng and Hu Feng; *Wen-hsüeh Chieh* (The Literary World), edited by Chou Yüan—a collective pseudonym—and supported by Chou Yang. The two last-named magazines represented two opposed groups of leftist and Communist writers following the dissolution of the Left-wing League in spring 1936. For more information see chap. 13.

7. Feng Hsüeh-feng, *Hui-i Lu Hsün,* p. 126.

8. The Chinese sources I used agree with the statement in Huang Sung-k'ang, *Lu Hsün and the New Culture Movement of Modern China* (p. 141), that Ch'ü Ch'iu-pai was put to death on June 18, 1935. In *Moscow and Chinese Communists,* however, Robert C. North records January 18, 1935, as the date of his execution. In spite of this possible error, the story of Ch'ü's death as retold by Dr. North (p. 165) is worth quoting for the light it throws on the Communist martyr as a petty-bourgeois revolutionary with his typical romantic bravado:

Ch'ü Ch'iu-pai, plagued by tuberculosis, was left behind when the [Long March] began—by Mao's personal order, Li Ang [author of *Hung-sê wu-t'ai,* The Red Stage] records. Captured forthwith by Nationalist troops, Ch'ü remained in prison until his execution on January 18, 1935. On that day, according to a story then current, he was brought from prison to the place of execution on a stretcher. There he drained a glass of whisky, asked for brush and paper, and wrote down [a poem.] . . . Then, according to the story, he met his death singing the "Internationale" in Russian, a cigarette drooping languidly from his fingers.

9. According to Liu Shou-sung, *Chung-kuo hsin-wen-hsüeh shih ch'u-kao* (History of Modern Chinese Literature: A Preliminary Draft), Vol. 1, *Luan-t'an chi ch'i-t'a* (Random Plunking and Other Essays) was first published in 1938 by Hsia Shê, Shanghai. The enlarged edition, which I used, was put out by the same Shanghai publisher in 1949; simply titled *Luan-t'an,* it includes nearly all of Ch'ü's polemic prose.

10. See Chang Pi-lai, "I-chiu-erh-san-nien *Chung-kuo Ch'ing-nien* chi-ko tso-che ti wen-hsüeh chu-chang" (The Literary Opinions of Several Contributors to *Chinese Youth* in 1923), in Li Ho-lin et al., *Chung-kuo hsin-wen-hsüeh shih yen-chiu* (Studies in Modern Chinese Literary History). Chang Pi-lai has subsequently reaffirmed the importance of the *Chinese Youth* group in his own *Hsin-wen-hsüeh shih-kang* (A Short History of Modern Chinese Literature), Vol. 1.

11. Sung Yang (Ch'ü ch'iu-pai), "Ta-chung wen-i ti weň-t'i" (The Problem of the Literature for the Masses), *Wen-hsüeh Yüeh-pao* (Literature Monthly), *1,* No. 1 (Shanghai, June 1932), 5.

12. See John De Francis, *Nationalism and Language Reform in China* (Princeton, 1950), chap. 5: "The Influence of the Soviet Union."

13. Quoted in Li Ho-lin, *Chin-erh-shih-nien chung-kuo wen-i-ssu-ch'ao lun* (Chinese Literary Thought of the Past Twenty Years), p. 285.

14. In *Wen-t'an wu-shih-nien, 2, 70,* Ts'ao Chü-jen states that the ta-chung-yü movement was the direct result of a discussion among Ch'en Tzu-chan, Ch'en Wang-tao, Hsia Mien-tsun, Hsü

Mou-yung, Yeh Shao-chün, Yüeh Ssu-ping, and himself in the summer of 1934, and ridicules the Communist literary historians who attributed the movement to the leadership of Lu Hsün or Ch'ü Ch'iu-pai. While Ts'ao is entirely right in stating the actual origin of the movement, he fails to see the connections between this and the earlier ta-chung wen-i movement. If one examines the writings of Ch'ü Ch'iu-pai, one is inclined to agree with the Communist historians that Ch'ü decidedly prepared for the ta-chung-yü and Latinxua movements, even though he never actually employed the term ta-chung-yü as a slogan.

15. For the simplification of Chinese characters and other language reforms adopted since 1955 see Hsia Tao-t'ai, *China's Language Reforms* (New Haven, 1956), and Harriet C. Mills, "Language Reform in China: Some Recent Developments," *Far Eastern Quarterly, 15*, No. 4, August 1956.

16. Edited by Ch'en Wang-tao with the assistance of Mao Tun, Ch'en Tzu-chan, Hsü Mou-yung, and Ts'ao Chü-jen, *T'ai Pai* published mainly tsa-wen, reportage, and popular scientific articles. The Liberty Page (*Tzu-yu T'an*) of *Shen Pao*, of course, had been for some years a bastion of left-wing tsa-wen writers, prominently Lu Hsün.

17. Chou Tso-jen's theory that the modern literary movement meant a return to self-expression is expounded in his lectures on *Chung-kuo hsin-wen-hsüeh ti yüan-liu* (The Origins of Modern Chinese Literature).

18. *Wen-hsüeh Tsa-chih* soon ceased publication—upon the outbreak of the war in July 1937. Chu Kuang-ch'ien revived it during the postwar years 1947–48. This magazine should not be confused with *Wen-hsüeh Tsa-chih* or *Literary Review*, which began publication in Taipei in 1956 under the editorship of Hsia Tsi-an.

19. Chu Kuang-ch'ien, "Wo tui-yü pen-k'an ti hsi-wang" (My Hopes for This Magazine), *Wen-hsüeh Tsa-chih, 1*, No. 1 (Shanghai, 1937), 9-10.

6. MAO TUN

1. For a summary of his literary education up to the early thirties see Mao Tun, "T'an wo-ti yen-chiu" (About My Studies),

Yin-hsiang kan-hsiang hui-i (Impressions, Reflections, and Reminiscences). The author's "Wo-ti hsiao chuan" (An Autobiographical Sketch), *Wen-i Yüeh-pao, 1,* No. 1, gives a succinct account of his childhood and youth.

2. In May and June of 1957 a group of writers, translators, and critics who were not party members held several meetings to discuss the bureaucratism and cliquism of the Writers' Association. Mao Tun attended these meetings as a nonparty member. Commenting on the arrogance of Communist authors, Lü Chien observed: "I have known many party-member writers who don't even respect Mao Tun and Kuo Mo-jo, saying that the latter can talk only about technique. If even these two authors are slighted, it is easy to imagine the psychological condition of other [non-Communist] writers." For the opinions of other non-Communist writers at these meetings see *Wen-i Pao,* No. 11 (June 1957), pp. 2–3.

3. *Tung yao* (Vacillation), Pt. II of *Shih* (The Eclipse), pp. 151–52.

4. *Hung* (Rainbow), pp. 69–70.

5. Ibid., pp. 75–76.

6. Ibid., p. 160.

7. *Tzu yeh* (The Twilight: A Romance of China in 1930), p. 529.

8. Mao Tun's essays on Lo Hua-sheng, Ping Hsin, and Wang Lu-yen are included in Mao Tun et al., *Tso-chia lun* (On Writers). See also his "Tao-yen" (Foreword) to *Hsiao-shuo i-chi* for his evaluation of the achievement of the Literary Association in fiction.

9. Mao Tun, "Ch'iu shou" (Autumn Harvest), in *Ch-uang-tso hsiao-shuo ti-i-chi* (Stories, First Series) (Shanghai, Shen Pao Yüeh-k'an shê, 1933), p. 42.

7. LAO SHÊ

1. For Lao Shê's observations on the intellectual climate in Singapore see his *Lao-niu p'o-ch'ê* (The Rickety Ox-cart), pp. 32–35.

2. *Chao Tzu-yüeh,* p. 308.

3. Ibid., p. 104.

4. Ibid., p. 62.

5. In the Chinese the clergyman is simply called Yi, and the widow, Mrs. Wen-tu. The names Evans and Wendell have been arbitrarily adopted here for their approximation to Chinese sounds.

6. *Erh Ma* (The Two Mas), p. 167.

7. *Li hun* (Divorce) has two English versions: *The Quest for Love of Lao Lee,* by Helena Kuo, and *Divorce,* by Evan King.

8. *Li hun* (Shanghai postwar edition, 1947), p. 278.

9. Ibid., p. 279.

10. Ibid., p. 281.

11. Ibid., p. 283.

12. *Niu T'ien-tz'u chuan* (The Biography of Niu T'ien-tz'u) has been translated into English as *Heavensent.*

13. *Niu T'ien-tz'u chuan,* p. 306.

14. Ibid., pp. 272–73.

15. A faithful translation in the main, *Rickshaw Boy* (New York, Reynal and Hitchcock, 1945) ends with the happy reunion of Hsiang-tzu and Hsiao Fu-tzu. By omitting crucial passages descriptive of the hero as a dastardly loafer and informer, the translator, Evan King, creates the final image of Hsiang-tzu as a happy man reinstalled in the family of Professor Ts'ao and successfully rescuing Hsiao Fu-tzu from her cruel fate as a third-class prostitute. The altered ending is typical of the optimistic sentimentality of the new material: "In the mild coolness of summer evening the burden in his arms stirred slightly, nestling closer to his body as he ran. She was alive. He was alive. They were free" (p. 384). It is a pity that, in view of the scarcity of good English translations of modern Chinese fiction, *Rickshaw Boy* should be so distorted in text and spirit from the original.

16. *Lo-t'o Hsiang-tzu* (Camel Hsiang-tzu) (Shanghai, 1946), p. 308.

17. Ibid., p. 122.

18. Ibid., p. 285.

19. Ibid., p. 186. In translating this and the preceding passage from *Lo-t'o Hsiang-tzu,* I have consulted *Rickshaw Boy.* The corresponding passages in the English version are to be found respectively on pp. 372, 230.

Notes

8. SHEN TS'UNG-WEN

1. "Shen chih tsai-hsien" (The Reappearance of Gods), chap. 10 of *Feng Tzu*, first printed in *Wen-hsüeh Tsa-chih, 1,* No. 3 (Peiping, 1937), 143–44.

2. "Hsi-t'i" (Exercise), *A-chin* (Kaiming Press, 1949), pp. 3–4. This essay originally served as the preface to *Ts'ung-wen hsiao-shuo hsi-tso hsüan* (Selections from Ts'ung-wen's Fiction and Other Writings).

3. *Ts'ung-wen tzu-chuan* (The Autobiography of Shen Ts'ung-wen) (rev. ed. Kaiming, 1943), p. 21.

4. Both stories, "Three Men and A Girl" and "Ta Wang," are included in Ching Ti (Chin T'i) and Robert Payne, trans., *The Chinese Earth.*

5. Ting Ling, "I-ko chen-shih-jen ti i-sheng—chi Hu Yeh-p'in" (The Life of an Upright Man—Hu Yeh-p'in), being the preface to *Hu Yeh-p'in hsüan-chi* (Selected Works of Hu Yeh-p'in) (Peking, 1951), p. 17.

6. Shen Ts'ung-wen, "Ch'en-mo" (Silence), *Wen-chi Yüeh-k'an, 1,* No. 6 (November 1936), 1132.

7. Su Hsüeh-lin, "Shen Ts'ung-wen lun" (Shen Ts'ung-wen: A Critique), being the preface to *Shen Ts'ung-wen hsüan-chi* (Selected Stories of Shen Ts'ung-wen), p. 15. This essay is also included in Mao Tun et al., *Tso-chia lun.*

8. "Lung Chu," *Shen Ts'ung-wen hsüan-chi,* p. 146. The revised version is included in *Ch'un* (Spring), Kaiming, 1947.

9. Shen Ts'ung-wen, "Hui Ming," *Hei yeh* (Black Night) (Kaiming, 1949), p. 16.

10. Shen Ts'ung-wen, "Hsiao-hsiao," *Hsin yü chiu* (New and Old), pp. 27–28. Two translations of this story are available; see Bibliography, V, 9.

11. "Sheng" (Living), *Shen Ts'ung-wen hsüan-chi,* p. 50.

12. Translation adapted from Chi-chen Wang, *Contemporary Chinese Stories* (New York, Columbia University Press, 1944), pp. 106–7. Professor Wang translated "Yeh" (Night) under the title "Night March."

13. "Hsi-t'i," *A-chin,* p. 5.

14. Shen Ts'ung-wen "Ching," (Quiet), *Hei-feng chi* (Black Phoenix) (Kaiming, 1943), p. 40.

15. Ibid., p. 46.

9. Chang T'ien-i

1. For a good biography by a close friend see Chiang Mu-liang, "Chi Chang T'ien-i" (About Chang T'ien-i), in Ssu-ma Wen-sen, ed., *Tso-chia yin-hsiang chi* (Impressions of Authors).

2. See the essay on Chang T'ien-i in Hu Feng, *Wen-i pi-t'an* (Literary Essays), pp. 38–87.

,3. "Ti-chu" (The Bulwark), in *Chui* (Pursuit), pp. 14–16.

4. "Lü-t'u chung" (On the Journey), ibid., pp. 118–19.

5. "Chung-ch'iu" (The Mid-Autumn Festival), ibid., p. 179.

6. "Lu Pao-t'ien," in *T'ung-hsiang-men* (Fellow Villagers), p. 179.

7. "Ch'un-feng" (Spring Breeze), in *Wen Hsüeh, 6,* No. 2 (February 1936), 229–230.

8. *Hsiao Pi-tê* (Little Peter), p. 24.

9. "Ch'u-tsou i-hou" (After Her Departure), in *Chang T'ien-i wen-chi* (The Selected Writings of Chang T'ien-i) (Shanghai, 1948), pp. 52–53.

10. *Yang-ching-peng ch'i-hsia* (The Strange Knight of Shanghai), pp. 93–94. For other humorous examples of Chinese advertising see Lin Yutang, *A History of the Press and Public Opinion in China,* Chicago, 1936.

11. In an autobiographical sketch written specially for Edgar Snow, *Living China,* Chang T'ien-i lists the authors who have exerted the greatest influence on him. It is not surprising that Dickens heads the list, followed by Maupassant, Zola, Barbusse, Tolstoy, Chekhov, Gorky, and Lu Hsün.

12. Two of the sketches, "Hua Wei hsien-sheng" (Mr. Hua Wei) and "Hsin-sheng" (New Life), had their first periodical publication in 1938, and the third, "T'an Chiu hsien-sheng ti kung-tso" (Mr. T'an Chiu's Job) , was written in November 1937. The edition I have used, however, supplies the information that *Su-hsieh san-p'ien* (Three Sketches) was first published in Chungking in January 1943.

Notes

13. Three stories and a one-act play about children are available in English in a slim volume entitled *Stories of Young Chinese Pioneers*.

10. PA CHIN

1. Pa Chin, *Sheng chih ch'an-hui* (Life's Penitence), p. 58.
2. Ibid., pp. 13–14.
3. Pa Chin, *I* (Remembrances), p. 25.
4. Ibid., pp. 40–41.
5. *Sheng chih ch'an-hui*, p. 126. This passage is also quoted in Wang Chi-wen's translation of Jean Monsterleet, *Pa Chin ti sheng-huo ho chu-tso* (Pa Chin's Life and Works), p. 24.
6. *Mi-wang* (Destruction) (Shanghai, Kaiming, 1939), p. 118.
7. Ibid., pp. 39–40.
8. Ibid., p. 119.
9. Ibid., p. 213.
10. Ibid., pp. 81–82.
11. Ibid., p. 227.
12. Artzybashev's *Sanin* was highly popular in China in the twenties and thirties. There were three translations of the novel, including one by Cheng Chen-to and one by Pa Chin himself.
13. *Ai-ch'ing ti san-pu-ch'ü* (The Love Trilogy), p. 232.
14. Ibid., p. 178.
15. Ibid., p. 295.
16. Ibid., p. 395.
17. Ibid., p. 396.
18. *Ch'iu* (Autumn), pp. 1–2.

11. COMMUNIST FICTION, I

1. Ch'ien Hsing-ts'un, *Hsien-tai chung-kuo wen-hsüeh-tso-chia* (Contemporary Chinese Writers), *1*, 166. In spite of his notorious partisan criticism, Ch'ien Hsing-ts'un is a remarkable man of letters. During the war he stayed in Shanghai until Pearl Harbor and wrote, under the pen name of Wei Ju-hui, about a dozen popular plays, mostly historical. Under the name of A Ying he has written many books and articles on the vernacular literature

of the Ming and Ch'ing period; he is also a most diligent bibliographer of modern Chinese literature.

2. See the chapter on Chiang Kuang-tz'u in Tsi-an Hsia, *The Gate of Darkness.*

3. See Ch'ü Ch'iu-pai, "Hsüeh-fa wan-sui" (Long Live the Literary Dictators!), in *Luan-t'an.* In this bold article, written in June 1931 and supposedly sent from New York, Ch'ü Ch'iu-pai dismisses all existing contemporary literature as of little value; Chiang Kuan-tz'u is merely a practitioner of "minor reactionary literature." What Ch'ü wants is *ta-fan-tung wen-hsüeh* or major reactionary literature, i.e. a literature that truly supports Communist objectives. He prophetically states that the aim of this literature is to show that "the majority oppress the minority"— "let the hundred millions of people kill thousands or ten thousands of people, arrest hundreds of thousands, and confiscate the property and land of a couple of millions" (p. 134).

4. *Ch'ung-ch'u yün-wei ti yüeh-liang* (The Moon Emerging from the Clouds), p. 119.

5. See Shen Ts'ung-wen, *Chi Ting Ling* (About Ting Ling), p. 29.

6. Ting Ling, "I-ko chen-shih-jen ti i-sheng," in *Hu Yeh-p'in hsüan-chi*, p. 21.

7. *Chi Ting Ling hsü-chi* (More about Ting Ling), pp. 11–13.

8. Ibid., pp. 14–15.

9. Han Shih-heng, "Wen-t'an shang ti hsin-jen" (New Personalities on the Literary Stage), in *Hsien Tai* (Les Contemporains), *4*, No. 6 (April 1934), 970–71. Han Shih-heng is now a generally forgotten name, but his critical essays in *Yü Ssu* and *Les Contemporains* attest to a serious concern with modern Chinese literature.

10. Ting Ling, "Shui" (Water), 3d and final installment in *Pei Tou* (The Big Dipper), *1*, No. 3 (November 1931), 68–69.

11. Ibid., p. 71.

12. Philip Rahv, "Proletarian Literature: A Political Autopsy," *The Southern Review, 4*, No. 3 (winter 1939), 620.

13. In *Wen-t'an wu-shih-nien* Ts'ao Chü-jen highly endorses *Jen chien* (The Human Condition), a novel by Li Hui-ying recently published in Hong Kong. Ts'ao calls it "a realistic novel,"

"a novel truly reflective of the actual life during the war of resistance" (2, 131). I have not seen this work, but Ts'ao's opinion merits attention.

14. The speeches are to be found respectively in Hsiao Chün, *Pa-yüeh ti hsiang-ts'un* (Dairen, 1946), p. 166, and T'ien Chün, *Village in August* (New York, Smith and Durrell, 1942), p. 168.

15. *Pa-yüeh ti hsiang-ts'un*, p. 242.

16. In his preface to the novel Lu Hsün compares it to Fadeyev's *The Nineteen*. Other popular Soviet novels already translated into Chinese by the middle thirties were Sholokhov's *And Quiet Flows the Don,* Dimitry Furmanov's *Chapayev,* and Alexander Serafimovich's *The Iron Stream.*

17. In 1941 Ting Ling wrote another story called "Wo tsai hsia-ts'un ti shih-hou" (When I Was at Hsia Village), subsequently collected in a volume under the same title. This story also shows the author's great sympathy for a maligned and scorned Communist-area girl, but it was not subject to attack until 1957.

18. This editorial is excerpted in Wang Yao, *Chung-kuo hsinwen-hsüeh shih kao* (A Draft History of Modern Chinese Literature), 2, 245.

19. Yen Hsüeh and Chou P'ei-t'ung, "Hsiao Chün ti *Wu-yüeh ti k'uang-shan* wei-shih-mo shih yu-tu ti?" (Why Is Hsiao Chün's *Coal Mines in May* Poisonous?), *Wen-i Pao,* No. 24 (December 1955), 43.

20. Lin Yutang, who knew Wang Shih-wei as a contributor to one of his literary magazines in the thirties, has recorded in *The Secret Name* (New York, Farrar, Straus, and Cudahy, 1958) a rare reappearance of this author since 1942:

About the time of my visit in Chungking [in 1944], a group of foreign newspaper correspondents had asked and been given permission to visit Yenan and the Chinese journalists took advantage of this occasion to go along. One of the mysteries they wanted to solve was the whereabouts of this man Wang. The Chinese reporters inquired and the Communists of Yenan replied that he was well and alive. They asked to see him, and the request was rejected, but the Chinese journalists insisted. Finally the Communists agreed to show them Wang. He came along, thin and quiet, and took his position on a bench. To every question the Chinese reporters put to him, he answered in the correct manner. Everything was fine and wonderful in Yenan. Finally there was a slip. One of the Chinese reporters asked him what he was doing and his reply was that he was now occupied in pasting matchboxes [pp. 227–28].

12. WU TSU-HSIANG

1. "Kuan-kuan ti pu-p'in" (Kuan-kuan's Tonic), in *Hsi liu chi* (West Willow), pp. 135–36.

2. Ibid., p. 161.

3. Wang Yao, *Chung-kuo hsin-wen-hsüeh shih kao,* *1,* 244–45. Wang Yao's book, of course, has been found sadly wanting, following the downfall of many a prominent literary figure since 1955, but its treatment of Wu Tsu-hsiang has not been vulnerable to criticism.

4. *Shih-nien* (A Decade), one-volume edition, 1938, is a short-story anthology of unusual comprehensiveness and high quality. It was prepared by Hsia Mien-tsun to commemorate the tenth anniversary of the founding of the Kaiming Press, a publishing company much devoted to the promotion of contemporary literature. In addition to most fiction writers discussed in Parts I and II of the present study, *Shih-nien* includes a story each of such authors as Ai Wu, Chiang Mu-liang, Chin I, Hsiao Ch'ien, Sha T'ing, Shih Chih-ts'un, Tuan-mu Hung-liang, Wang Lu-yen, Wang T'ung-chao, and Chou Wen, whose entry "Ai" (Love) is a most remarkable story. This anthology therefore serves as an impressive tribute to the range and achievement of the many short-story writers immediately prior to the outbreak of the war. Besides the Kaiming Press, the other important publishers of contemporary literature in the middle thirties were Wen-hua Sheng-huo Ch'u-pan-shê (the Culture and Life Press), Liang-yu T'u-shu Kung-ssu (the Good Friend Publishing Co.), the Communist-dominated Sheng-huo Shu-tien, and the Commercial Press.

5. For a representative opinion see Yü Kuan-ying's review of the novel in *Wen-i Fu-hsing* (Literary Renaissance), *1,* No. 5 (June 1946), 633–36.

13. Conformity, Defiance, and Achievement

1. Feng Hsüeh-feng, *Hui-i Lu Hsün*, p. 147.
2. *Lu Hsün ch'üan-chi, 6*, 529.
3. Ibid., pp. 529–30.
4. Ibid., pp. 530–31.
5. Ibid., p. 534.
6. Quoted from Lü K'o-yü (Feng Hsüeh-feng), "Tui-yü wen-hsüeh-yün-tung chi-ko wen-t'i ti i-chien" (My Views on Several Problems Pertaining to the Literary Movement), in Li Ho-lin, *Chin erh-shih-nien chung-kuo wen-i-ssu-ch'ao lun*, p. 565. In calling Chou Yang "a junior Ch'ien Hsing-ts'un," Feng was merely echoing Mao Tun, who, though among the original signers of the manifesto for a "Literature for National Defense," soon changed to Lu Hsün's side and attacked Chou Yang harshly in two articles: "Kuan-yü yin-ch'i chiu-fen ti liang-ko k'ou-hao" (About the Two Controversial Slogans) and "Tsai-shuo chi-chü" (A Few Additional Remarks).

7. The *People's Daily* supplied a biographical headnote for "Kuan-yü Hu Feng fan-ko-ming chi-t'uan ti ti-san-p'i ts'ai-liao" (The Third Compilation: Materials Concerning the Counterrevolutionary Hu Feng Clique), reprinted in *Wen-i Pao*, No. 11 (June 1955), 4. In 1954 and 1955 *Wen-i Pao* carried scores of articles on Hu Feng; to these I am mainly indebted for the report on Hu Feng in this chapter.

In her paper "Hu Feng's Conflict with the Communist Literary Authorities," Merle Goldman has supplied a brief sketch of the author's life based on the autobiographical note in Hu Feng, *Chien wen-i jen-min* (Sword, Literature, and People), Shanghai, 1950. The most detailed study of the Hu Feng case by an American scholar, Goldman's paper appears in *Papers on China*, Vol. 11 (1957), mimeographed for private distribution by the Center for East Asian Studies, Harvard University.

The best-informed biographical sketch of Hu Feng I have seen, however, is in Yang Yen-nan, *Chung-kung tui Hu Feng ti tou-cheng* (The Persecution of Hu Feng by Chinese Communists), pp. 78–85. Yang is positive about Hu Feng's early Communist affiliations and describes in some detail his repatriation from

Japan as an unwanted alien in active support of the Japanese Communist movement: "In 1933 the Japanese Communist party was outlawed. Because Hu Feng's name was on the blacklist, he was imprisoned, along with twenty-odd important Japanese Communists. [Following the execution of the Japanese party leader] Hu Feng was forcibly expelled and sent back to his own country" (p. 79). Possibly,without this hero's feather in his cap, Hu Feng could not have won immediate recognition in Shanghai literary circles in 1934.

8. *Lu Hsün ch'üan-chi, 6,* 540–42. During the persecution of Feng Hsüeh-feng in 1957, Chou Yang and his colleagues maintained that Lu Hsün's long letter was really drafted by Feng. In 1966, following the downfall of Chou Yang himself, his group's perpetration of this official lie was exposed. See the article on Feng Hsüeh-feng in Ting Wang, *Wen-hua ta-ko-ming p'ing-lun-chi* (Comments on the Great Cultural Revolution) (Hong Kong, Tang-tai Chung-kuo Yen-chiu-so, 1967), pp. 129-31.

9. In *Wen-hsüeh lun-kao* (A Tentative Treatise on Literature), Vol. 2, the Communist critic Pa Jen prefaces his exposition of the Maoist term "national forms" with a discussion of Stalin's role toward the formulation of this concept:

> In his writings on the Chinese Revolution, Stalin especially stressed the characteristics of the Chinese nation. Stalin taught us that the promotion of revolutionary enterprises in any country must depend on the fusion of the general principles of Marxism-Leninism with the national characteristics of that country: "The principal task of the leadership is to discover and grasp the national characteristics inherent in the [Communist] movement of each country and ably fuse these with the general principles of the Communist International so that the principal objective of the Communist movement become easily realizable and actually realized" [p. 644].

In a footnote Pa Jen supplies the information that the quotation is taken from Stalin, "Shih-shih wen-t'i chien-p'ing" (Brief Comments on Current Affairs) in *Stalin ch'üan-chi* (The Complete Works of Stalin), *9,* 299.

10. *Mao Tse-tung hsüan-chi*, 2, 496–97.

11. Quoted from Hu Feng, *Tsai hun-luan li-mien* (In a Muddle), in Ts'ai I, "P'i-p'an Hu Feng ti tzu-ch'an-chieh-chi wei-hsin-lun wen-i-ssu-hsiang" (A Critical Appraisal of Hu Feng's Capitalist, Idealistic Literary Thought), *Wen-i Pao*, No. 3 (February 1955), 8.

12. Quoted from *Tsai hun-luan li-mien*, in Wei Pi-chia, "Hu Feng fan-ko-ming li-lun ti ch'ien-ch'ien hou-hou" (Hu Feng's Counterrevolutionary Theories: A Chronological Survey), 2d installment, *Wen-i Pao*, No. 15 (August 1955), 10–11. Of all the articles published in *Wen-i Pao* in 1955, Wei Pi-chia's gives the most detailed account of the evolution of Hu Feng's literary thought.

13. "Tsai Yenan wen-i-tsu-t'an-hui shang ti chiang-hua" (Talks at the Yenan Literary Conference), in *Mao Tse-tung hsüan-chi*, 3, 897.

14. Ibid., p. 874.

15. Ibid., p. 884.

16. Ibid., p. 891.

17. See above, p. 620, n. 10.

18. Quoted in Wang Yao, *Chung-kuo hsin-wen-hsüeh shih kao*, 1, 54.

19. Among the resolutions adopted at the Ku-t'ien Conference of 1929 was Mao Tse-tung's proposal for increased propaganda activity by the Red Army in the form of preparing simple educational and propaganda texts, initiating theatrical activities, collecting and revising popular ballads, etc. See Ting I, *Chung-kuo hsien-tai wen-hsüeh shih lüeh* (A Brief History of Modern Chinese Literature), p. 89. For an account of Ch'ü Ch'iu-pai's activities as Minister of Education and head of the Bureau of Arts (*i-shu chü*), see chap. 5 in Liu Shou-sung, *Chung-kuo hsin-wen-hsüeh shih ch'u-kao, 1,* 306–18.

20. See the title essay in Chou Yang, *Chien-chüeh kuan-ch'ê Mao Tse-tung wen-i lu-hsien* (Resolutely Implement the Mao Tse-tung Line in Literature), p. 72.

21. Of course, by the middle thirties the clamor for democracy was already inseparable from the agitation for united resistance. The phrase "freedom of speech" in the Literary Workers' Manifesto on the United Resistance and on Freedom of Speech is

significant for its democratic connotations. There were many democratic groups, not necessarily Communist-directed, operating in Shanghai during the time of the Sian Incident.

22. However, at the time of its founding, the Anti-aggression Association boasted 45 executive members (*li-shih*), among them such prominent Communist writers as Kuo Mo-jo, Mao Tun, Feng Hsüeh-feng, Ting Ling, Hsia Yen, and T'ien Han. Chou En-lai served as one of its honorary executive members. I am indebted for this information to Ting I, *Chung-kuo hsien-tai wen-hsüeh shih lüeh*, p. 116.

23. I might also mention here Li Chieh-jen on the strength of the superlative praise accorded him in Ts'ao Chü-jen, *Wen-t'an wu-shih-nien*, 2, 44–45. A French-returned student, Li Chieh-jen was primarily known in the twenties and thirties for his translation of French fiction: *Madame Bovary* and *Salammbô*, Maupassant, Daudet, Marcel Prévost, Edmond de Goncourt. From 1935 to 1937, however, Li applied himself to the composition of a naturalistic trilogy about Chengtu, Szechwan, from the Boxers' Uprising to the Republican Revolution of 1911: *Ssu-shui wei-lan* (Ripples on Dead Water), *Pao-feng-yü ch'ien* (Before the Storm) and the three-volume *Ta po* (The Great Wave). Ts'ao Chü-jen regards these novels as "superior in achievement to the works of Mao Tun and Pa Chin." *Ta po*, especially, is "a great work . . . with which Mao Tun's *The Twilight* could hardly hope to compare." Since Ts'ao has the highest respect for Mao Tun, this would make Li Chieh-jen virtually the greatest modern Chinese novelist. However, no other literary historian that I know of has devoted any attention to his fiction. All three works have been recently reprinted by the Tso-chia Ch'u-pan-shê, Peking: *Ssu-shui wei-lan*, 1955; *Pao-feng-yü ch'ien*, 1956; *Ta po*, 2 vols., 1958. But, unfortunately, according to the author's postscripts to the new editions, while *Ssu-shui wei-lan* has undergone only slight revision, *Pao-feng-yü ch'ien* has been extensively revised, and *Ta po* rewritten from scratch, and much reduced in size.

24. Ai Wu's better-known works all fall within the period 1938–49. Among these are story collections: *Ch'iu hsiu* (Autumn Harvest), *Huang-ti* (The Waste Land); autobiographies: *Wo-ti yu-nien shih-tai* (My Childhood), *Wo-ti ch'ing-nien shih-tai* (My Youth); novels: *Feng-jao ti yüan-yeh* (The Fertile Plain), *Chiang-*

shang hsing (On the River), *Ku-hsiang* (My Native Place), *Shan-yeh* (Mountain Wilderness), *I-ko nü-jen ti pei-chü* (A Woman's Tragedy).

25. In *Wen-i Fu-hsing*, 2, No. 1 (August 1946), the leading impressionistic critic Liu Hsi-wei (Li Chien-wu) praises *The Hungry Kuo Su-o* very highly in his review of "San-ko chung-p'ien" (Three Novelettes). In the same journal, *3*, No. 5 (July 1947), Lu Hung warmly endorses Lu Ling's short-story collection, *Ch'ing-ch'un ti chu-fu* (The Blessings of Youth), in his review of Sha T'ing's *K'un-shou chi* (Beasts at Bay). Since *Wen-i Fu-hsing* was the most respected postwar literary magazine, its opinion should be taken as representative.

26. For a typical view of wartime literature, and especially of drama, see D. L. Phelps, "Letters and Arts in the War Years," in H. F. MacNair, ed., *China*.

27. All included in *Chü-hsüan* (Selected Plays), Vol. 2 of *Kuo Mo-jo hsüan-chi* (Selected Works of Kuo Mo-jo), Peking, 1951.

28. Most of their poetry was published in the postwar magazines, such as *Wen-i Fu-hsing*. Several poems by Tu Yün-hsieh are available in English in the special number on contemporary Chinese literature of *Life and Letters & the London Mercury*, *60*, No. 137.

29. During the war Wu Hsing-hua published a translation of Rilke's *Das Buch der Bilder*. In 1946 many of his poems were published in the Peking journal *Wen-i Shih-tai*. His good friend Stephen C. Soong has subsequently reprinted his poetry over the pen name Liang Wen-hsin in the Hong Kong journal *Jen-jen Wen-hsüeh* and the Taipei *Wen-hsüeh Tsa-chih*. Wu Hsing-hua received a grateful mention by his former teacher at Yenching University, Professor Harold Shadick, in the preface to his translation of *The Travels of Lao Ts'an*. In 1957 Wu Hsing-hua was a professor at Peking University.

30. Wang Yao, *Chung-kuo hsin-wen-hsüeh shih kao*, 2, 208–9.

31. Hu Feng referred to this incident in a letter (dated July 22, 1944) to Shu Wu, excerpted in "Kuan-yü Hu Feng fan-tang chi-t'uan ti i-hsieh ts'ai-liao" (Some Materials Concerning the Hu Feng Anti-Party Clique), *Wen-i Pao*, joint issue of Nos. 9–10 (May 1955), 29.

32. Quoted in Wei Pi-chia, "Hu Feng fan-ko-ming li-lun ti ch'ien-ch'ien hou-hou," *Wen-i Pao*, No. 15 (1955), 13.

33. Quoted in "Kuan-yü Hu Feng fan-tang chi-t'uan ti i-hsieh ts'ai-liao," *Wen-i Pao*, Nos. 9–10 (1955), 30.

34. From the letter to Niu Han, dated January 16, 1951, excerpted in "Kuan-yü Hu Feng fan-ko-ming chi-t'uan ti ti-erh-p'i ts'ai-liao" (The Second Compilation: Materials Concerning the Hu Feng Counterrevolutionary Clique), *Wen-i Pao*, No. 11 (1955), 19.

35. "Wa-ti shang ti chan-yü" (The Battle on the Marsh) was published in *Jen-min Wen-hsüeh* (People's Literature), March 1954. Subject to censure with that story were two earlier stories by Lu Ling: "Ni ti yung-yüan chung-shih ti t'ung-chih" (Your Ever Faithful Comrade) and "Chan-shih ti hsin" (A Soldier's Heart). They appeared respectively in *Chieh-fang-chün Wen-i* (Literature of the Liberation Army), February 1954, and *Jen-min Wen-hsüeh*, December 1953.

36. I have translated, with minor omissions, a series of quotations in Li Shao-ch'in, "Ts'ung Gide shuo-ch'i" (To Start with Gide), *Wen-i Pao*, No. 5 (1955), 26. Distributed as a supplement to *Wen-i Pao*, Nos. 1–2 (1955), Hu Feng's memorandum was not sent to foreign subscribers to the journal.

37. I heartily agree with the criticism leveled at Yü P'ing-po by Lin Yutang in "P'ing-hsin lun Kao O" (Re-opening the Question of Authorship of "Red Chamber Dream"). This is one of the *Studies Presented to Yuen Ren Chao on his Sixty-fifth Birthday*, Taipei, 1958.

38. "Hu Feng's Conflict with the Communist Literary Authorities," *Papers on China*, *11*, 178.

39. During his speech Hu Feng remarked sarcastically, "Perhaps the presidents and vice presidents of the Federation of Literary and Art Workers and the Writers' Association [Kuo Mo-jo, Mao Tun, Chou Yang, et al.] have regular access to [this secret publication], but it is certainly not available to us committee members or executive members." See *Wen-i Pao*, No. 22 (November 1954), 14.

40. These two items appear in ". . . ti-san-p'i ts'ai-liao," *Wen-i Pao*, No. 11 (1955), pp. 5, 6. However, new evidence has been un-

earthed since 1955 to prove Hu Feng's counterrevolutionary character. In Chou Yang's address delivered at the Third National Conference of Delegates of the Writers' Association of 1956, he reports that "judging from our most recently discovered material, this apostate had already written, during the bloody reign of white terror in the years 1927–29, 'Fan-kung ti chin-t'ien ho ming-t'ien' (Anti-Communism Today and Tomorrow) and several other articles frantically slandering and insulting the Communist party and inciting people to maintain 'the iron will of anti-Communism' and rise as one man to 'crush' the Communist party" (*Wen-i Pao*, joint issue of Nos. 5–6, March 1956, 6). However, Hu Feng was presumably at that time a propagandist in the employ of the Kuomintang; there is still no proof of his cooperation with the Kuomintang since he joined the Left-wing League in 1934.

41. See Liu Pai-yü, "Wei fan-jung wen-hsüeh ch'uang-tso erh fen-tou" (To Strive for the Abundant Creation of Literature), *Wen-i Pao*, Nos. 5–6 (1956), 30.

42. Shen Yen-ping (Mao Tun), "Wen-hsüeh i-shu kung-tso chung ti kuan-chien-hsing wen-t'i" (The Key Problem Concerning Literary and Art Work), *Wen-i Pao*, No. 12 (June 1956), 3.

43. Quoted in [Shao] Ch'üan-lin, "Hsiu-cheng chu-i wen-i ssu-hsiang i-li" (An Example of Revisionist Literary Thought), *Wen-i Pao*, No. 1 (January 1958), 13. Huang Ch'iu-yün's article, "Pu-yao tsai jen-min chi-k'u ch'ien-mien pi-shang yen-ching" (Don't Shut Our Eyes before the Sufferings of the People) appeared in *Jen-min Wen-hsüeh*, September 1956.

44. See Theodore Hsi-en Chen, "The Thought Reform of Intellectuals," *Annals of the American Academy of Political and Social Science* (January 1959), p. 86. This article is a good summary of the Communist attempts to reform intellectuals since 1949.

45. *Wen-i Pao*, which was a weekly in 1957, first responded to the antirightist movement only in the June 23 number; the preceding June issues contain predominantly rightist and revisionist articles. It was only by the July 7th issue that the journal became fully committed to the antirightist cause.

46. See Tung-fang Chi-pai, "Tsai yin-an mao-tun chung yen-pien ti ta-lu wen-i," 1st installment, *Tzu-yu Chung-kuo, 20*, No. 7 (April 1959), 216. Tung-fang Chi-pai's long article is an ex-

cellent survey of the antirightist movement, though to appreciate the magnitude of the literary persecution one should read *Wen-i Pao* and other major mainland journals for 1957 and 1958.

47. See *Wen-i Pao*, No. 25 (September 1957), which reprints the speeches by Shao Ch'üan-lin, Kuo Mo-jo, Mao Tun, Pa Chin and Chin I, Lao Shê, and Ch'ien Chün-jui, and summarizes the speeches by Lu Ting-i and Chou Yang in the lead article.

48. Following her downfall, Ting Ling served for some time as a charwoman in the Peking headquarters of the Writers' Association. In "Writers in China Today" (*The Atlantic*, December 1959), Peggy Durdin reports (p. 107) that Ting Ling "has been subjected to two years of reform through labor at a desolate spot on the northern fringe of Manchuria." Mrs. Durdin does not specify on what date Ting Ling began her penal servitude.

49. For a summary of the crimes of the Ting-Ch'en clique see Chou Yang, "Wen-i chan-hsien shang ti i-ch'ang ta-pien-lun" (The Great Debate on the Literary Front), *Wen-i Pao*, No. 5 (March 1958), 2–14.

50. Mao Tun was not a party member. Though he was the president of the Writers' Association, Chou Yang and his clique —Shao Ch'üan-lin, Liu Pai-yü, Lin Mo-han, Ho Ch'i-fang—were in virtual control of the organization. Mao Tun joined the dissident voices in attacking the bureaucratism of the Association; in the *People's Daily*, May 23, 1957, he wrote: "The Writers' Association is like a *yamen;* the few leaders of the Association have become rulers over writers, and its members have become their 'author-subjects.'" The veteran writer Chien Hsien-ai quoted this statement in an article in *Wen-i Pao*, No. 12 (June 1957), 6.

51. *Wen-i Pao*, No. 5 (March 1958), 4.

14. THE VETERAN WRITERS

1. Mao Tun lived quite an unsettled life during most of the war years. Upon the fall of Shanghai he trekked via Hong Kong to Changsha and then Wuhan, where he and his friends launched a literary magazine called *Wen-i Chen-ti*. When they decided to move the magazine to Canton, Mao Tun went down there in February 1938, but immediately afterward he moved to Hong

Kong, where he edited concurrently the literary page of *Li Pao*. At the end of that year he was invited to serve as dean of a college in Sinkiang, and he stayed there for over a year. Soon after he left, in May 1940, he lectured for a short period in Yenan at the Lu Hsün Institute. By the following October he had gone from Yenan to Chungking. In the spring of 1941, following the New Fourth Army Incident, he left the wartime capital for Hong Kong, when he stayed until after Pearl Harbor. In the spring of 1942 he escaped to Kweilin; nine months later he settled down in Chungking. For a reliable account of Mao Tun's life during the war years see Yeh Tzu-ming, *Lun Mao Tun ssu-shih-nien ti wen-hsüeh-tao-lu* (Mao Tun: His Literary Journey through Forty Years), pp. 136–58.

Story of the First Stage was written during Mao Tun's first stay in Hong Kong and serialized in *Li Pao* in 1938; it was first published in book form in Chungking in 1945. *Putrefaction* was composed in the summer of 1941 during the author's second stay in Hong Kong and serialized in the same year in the Hong Kong magazine *Ta-chung Sheng-huo*. *Maple Leaves* was written in Kweilin in 1942 to pay for the author's traveling expenses to Chungking and was published in book form by the Kweilin publisher, the Hua-hua Book Co., in 1943. The above information is gathered from the author's bibliographical and biographical notes to the new editions of the three novels in *Mao Tun wen-chi* (The Works of Mao Tun), Vols. 4–6, Peking, 1958. Until the republication of these novels in this standard edition, there had been no authoritative information concerning the dates of their composition and first publication; recent literary historians (Wang Yao, Liu Shou-sung, Ts'ao Chü-jen, et al.) had all assumed that *Maple Leaves* was composed before *Putrefaction*.

2. *Ti-i chieh-tuan ti ku-shih* (Story of the First Stage of the War) (Shanghai, 1948).

3. *Fu shih* (Putrefaction) (Dairen, 1946), pp. 170–71.

4. The title of the novel is *Shuang-yeh hung-ssu erh-yüeh-hua;* Tu Mu's line runs *Shuang-yeh hung-yü erh-yüeh-hua.*

5. See "Hsin-pan hou-chi" (Postscript to the New Edition), *Mao Tun wen-chi, 6,* 255–59.

6. *Shuang-yeh hung-ssu erh-yüeh-hua* (Shanghai, 1947), p. 214.

7. *Ch'ang ho* (The Long River) (Kaiming, 1949), p. i.

8. Ibid., pp. 20–22.

9. So far as I know, four chapters of this work have received periodical publication: "Ch'ih-yen" (The Red Incubus), "Hsüeh-ch'ing" (Snow and Sunshine), "Ch'iao-hsiu yü Tung-sheng" (Ch'iao-hsiu and Tung-sheng), and "Chuan-ch'i pu-ch'i" (A Romance Quite Ordinary). The two last-named chapters appeared respectively in *Wen-hsüeh Tsa-chih*, 2, Nos. 1 and 6, Peiping, 1947.

10. See Ma Feng-hua, "Hui-i Shen Ts'ung-wen chiao-shou" (My Recollections of Professor Shen Ts'ung-wen), *Tzu-yu Chung-kuo, 16*, No. 3 (February 1957), 97–101. This article is a moving account of Shen Ts'ung-wen's life during the early years of the Communist regime.

11. In his short biography of Lao Shê, Chao Yen-sheng writes, "When the 'National Writers' Anti-Aggression Association' was organized [in Hankow] on March 27, 1938, he became the president, and by repeated re-election has retained that position" (*1500 Modern Chinese Novels and Plays*, p. 85). Actually, though Lao Shê served as the administrative head of the organization for the remaining war years, he had relinquished the title of president after he moved to Chungking from Hankow. In a speech given on August 7, 1957, at the anti-Ting-Ch'en meetings, he boasts of his past record:

> At first, when the Writers' Association was established in Chungking, we were fearful that Chang Tao-fan [a leading Kuomintang propagandist who served as Minister of Information, 1942–43, and chairman of the Kuomintang Cultural Movement Committee, 1940–48] might wangle for himself the position of president, and so we abolished the presidency and only appointed several department chairmen to manage the affairs of the Association. But I was actually in charge. It was I who had to deal with Chang Tao-fan and it was I who united the writers.
>
> *Wen-i Pao*, No. 20 (August 1957), 7

12. *Huo-tsang* (Cremation), p. vi.

13. Ibid., p. iii.

14. Ibid., p. 77.

15. *T'ou-sheng* (Ignominy), p. 458.

16. Ibid., pp. 107–8.
17. Ibid., pp. 353–54.
18. *Huo* (Fire), *1*, 250.
19. Ibid., *2*, 290.
20. Ibid., *3* (Kaiming, 1951), 343.
21. Ibid., p. 286.
22. *Ti-ssu ping-shih* (Ward No. 4), p. 356.
23. *Han-yeh* (Cold Nights), p. 299.
24. Pa Chin, *Sheng-huo tsai ying-hsiung-men ti chung-chien* (Living among Heroes), p. 8. Primarily intended for foreign consumption, the English version *Living amongst Heroes* has understandably removed the article from which I have translated.
25. Yet, with all his prudence, Pa Chin was eventually subject to persecution. In April 1958 he wrote a routine article for *Wen-i Pao* denouncing Howard Fast, but unlike other Chinese writers attacking the ex-Communist writer at that time, Pa Chin showed a greater degree of sympathy and regret than was deemed proper. Even though he immediately apologized for his indiscretion, he became increasingly the target of attack until, by October 1958, a new movement was under way to denounce his pre-1949 writings as an expression of anarchism. But because many readers wrote in defense of their favorite author, this anti-Pa Chin campaign was eventually discontinued. For a brief summary of this campaign up to December 1958 see Yo Ch'ien, "Chung-kung tou-cheng pu-tao Pa Chin" (Chinese Communists Couldn't Knock Out Pa Chin), *Lien-ho P'ing-lun* (United Voice Weekly), Hong Kong, December 26, 1958.

15. EILEEN CHANG

1. *Liu-yen* (Gossip), pp. 159–60.
2. Ibid., pp. 209–10.
3. Though the characters *shuo* and *tao* have about the same meaning as "said" in the expression "John said" and are often used in conjunction, as *shuo-tao*, Eileen Chang, in *Chuan-ch'i* (Romances), though not in her subsequent novels, invariably uses the more traditional form *tao* to introduce reported speeches, whereas most contemporary writers use the more colloquial *shuo*.

Moreover, in *Romances,* again unlike her contemporaries, she does not allow herself the liberty of Western syntax in such varied ways of recording dialogue as

"I hate him," John said. "He is mean."

"I hate him. He is mean," John said.

She uses only the traditional form:

John said, "I hate him. He is mean."

4. *Chang Ai-ling tuan-p'ien hsiao-shuo chi* (The Collected Stories of Eileen Chang), pp. 114–15.

5. Ibid., p. 116.

6. Ibid., p. 119.

7. Ibid., p. 129.

8. Ibid., pp. 130–31.

9. Ibid., pp. 132–33.

10. "Hsin ching" (The Heart Sutra) is the title of a most popular Buddhist sutra. Eileen Chang is fond of appropriating popular titles for her stories: *The Golden Cangue* itself is the title of a well-known Peking opera, *Chin-so chi.* One of the most regrettable omissions from the *Collected Stories* is the long story *Lien-huan t'ao,* which the author discusses with much gusto in "Tzu-chi ti wen-chang" (My Own Writings), one of the essays in *Gossip.* This story also borrows its title from a popular Peking opera. Set in Hong Kong in the late Ch'ing period and cast in the style of the novel *Chin p'ing mei, Lien-huan t'ao* should prove to be an even more ambitious piece of fiction than *The Golden Cangue.* But probably it was never completed.

11. *Chang Ai-ling tuan-p'ien hsiao-shuo chi,* p. 172.

12. Ibid., pp. 174–75.

13. Ibid., p. 182.

14. Ibid., pp. 183–84.

15. Ibid., p. 331.

16. Ibid., p. 164.

17. "Stale Mates" first appeared in *The Reporter, 15,* No. 4, September 1956. Under the title of "Wu-ssu i-shih" (A Nostalgic Tale of the May Fourth Period), its Chinese version was published in *Wen-hsüeh Tsa-chih, 1,* No. 5, January 1957.

18. In chap. 17 of the English version Gold Flower later identifies her brother's corpse and wishes to adopt a son to perpetuate

his family. This episode has no counterpart in the Chinese.

19. Eileen Chang, *The Rice-sprout Song* (New York, Scribner's, 1955), pp. 111–12.

20. Ibid., p. 113.

21. Ibid., p. 154.

22. Ibid., p. 122. At times, for the sake of greater intelligibility, Eileen Chang blunts somewhat the metaphorical edge of her prose in the English version. The Chinese counterpart of this passage specifically refers to the goddess Nü Kua smelting the rock, a Chinese myth about the creation (*Yang-ko*, pp. 140–41).

23. Ibid., p. 143.

24. Ibid., pp. 1–2.

25. Ibid., p. 166.

26. Ibid., pp. 163–64.

27. Ibid., pp. 31–32.

28. Ibid., p. 69.

29. Ibid., p. 69.

30. *Ch'ih-ti chih lien* (Love in Redland), pp. 205–6.

31. Ibid., pp. 280–81.

16. CH'IEN CHUNG-SHU

1. Ch'ien Chung-shu was contributing to English journals even in the early thirties. I accidentally ran into an article of his in *The China Critic, 6,* No. 50 (Shanghai, December 14, 1933), entitled "On 'Old Chinese Poetry.'"

2. Ch'ien Chung-shu's B. Litt. thesis was published as two separate papers in *Quarterly Bulletin of Chinese Bibliography:* "China in the English Literature of the Seventeenth Century," *1,* No. 4, December 1940; "China in the English Literature of the Eighteenth Century," *2,* Nos. 1–4, 1941.

3. *Jen shou kuei* (Men, Beasts, Ghosts), p. 108.

4. Ibid., p. 117.

5. This incident may serve as an example of Ch'ien Chung-shu's erudition. He informs the reader that, according to some medieval theologians, women's auditory canals are "quae per aurem concepisti" (ibid., p. 119).

6. Ibid., p. 119.

7. Ibid., p. 1.
8. Ibid., pp. 87–88.
9. Ibid., pp. 122–23.
10. Ibid., pp. 154–55.
11. *Wei-ch'eng* (The Besieged City), p. 174.
12. Ibid., pp. 223–24.
13. Ibid., p. 127.
14. Ibid., p. 382.
15. Ibid., pp. 470–79.

18. COMMUNIST FICTION, II

1. As of 1956, the Chinese Writers' Association boasted 946 members, though only one-fifth of that number were active writers. See Liu Pai-yü, "Wei fan-jung wen-hsüeh ch'uang-tso erh fen-tou," *Wen-i Pao,* joint issue of Nos. 5–6 (March 1956), 29.

2. See Chou Yang, "Lun Chao Shu-li ti ch'uang-tso" (On the Writings of Chao Shu-li), quoted in Wang Yao, *Chung-kuo hsin-wen-hsüeh shih kao, 2,* 313, 316.

3. In his address delivered at the Third National Conference of Delegates of the Writers' Association of 1956, Chou Yang admits that "industrial construction and the workers' struggles are, relatively speaking, still poorly and inadequately reflected in literature." See Chou Yang, "Chien-shê shê-hui-chu-i-wen-hsüeh ti jen-wu" (The Task of Building a Socialist Literature), *Wen-i Pao,* joint issue of Nos. 5–6 (March 1956), 11.

4. Quoted in Pa Jen, *Wen-hsüeh lun kao, 2,* 469.

5. Ibid., pp. 469–70. In a note Pa Jen acknowledges his indebtedness to earlier criticism of the story published in *Wen-i Pao* (January 1952) and *Chieh-fang-chün Wen-i* (April 1952).

6. From the title essay in *Chien-chüeh kuan-ch'ê Mao Tse-tung wen-i lu-hsien,* pp. 83–84.

7. Mao Tun, Ting Ling, Feng Hsüeh-feng, and all the other important critics have written on this problem. For a more systematic discussion see Pa Jen, *Wen-i lun kao, 2* (Pt. III, On Literary Creation).

8. "Sun over the Sangkan River," *Chinese Literature,* spring 1953 (Peking, Foreign Languages Press), pp. 259–61. In this as

in the following excerpts from the English translation, I have silently modified the spelling of a few words and of the names of the characters.

9. Ibid., pp. 262–63.

10. Ibid., pp. 107–8. I have deleted some interpolated material from the translation.

11. Ibid., p. 42.

12. Ibid., p. 40.

13. See Chao Shu-li, "*San-li Wan* hsieh-tso ch'ien-hou" (*San-li Wan:* An Account of Its Composition), *Wen-i Pao,* No. 19, October 1955.

14. "San-li Wan," 4th installment in *Jen-min Wen-hsüeh* (April 1955), p. 57.

15. Even Communist critics were somewhat distressed by the colorless descriptions of love in the novel; Lu Ta ventured some disparaging remarks in "Ch'üeh-fa ai-ch'ing ti ai-ch'ing miao-hsieh" (Love Descriptions Which Failed to Embody the Sentiment of Love), *Wen-i Pao,* No. 2 (January 1956), 22–25. However, immediately afterward, in his address to delegates of the Writers' Association (see above, n. 3), Chou Yang reaffirmed the importance of the novel.

16. *Wen-i Pao,* No. 34 (December 1957), 2–3, carries two interviews with authors and playwrights who are going among the masses. Among the thirty-five nontheatrical writers listed by name who have already gone or are about to go among the masses are nearly all the active Communist authors of today: Ts'ao Ming, Liu Ch'ing, Chao Shu-li, Ma Feng, Chang T'ien-i, T'ien Chien, Kang Ch'o, Yang Shuo, Li Chi, Liu Pai-yü, Wei Wei, Lu Chu-kuo, et al.

17. *Wen-i Pao,* No. 6 (March 1958) carries a series of articles about the Big Leap Forward among literary and art workers. The news article on Shanghai appears on p. 19.

19. CONCLUSION

1. For the more notable books by anti-Communist critics see titles by Ting Miao, Cheng Hsüeh-chia, Shih Chien in the Bibliography, above.

2. The most considerable publication of this group is Joseph

Schyns et al., *1500 Modern Chinese Novels and Plays*. Despite a good introduction by Miss Su Hsüeh-lin and a very useful biographical dictionary of authors by Chao Yen-sheng, the book is in the main an uncritical compilaton of extremely unreliable synopses of and comments on popular literary works—mostly contemporary but some traditional. Other members of this group are O. Brière, author of critical articles on contemporary authors for the *Bulletin de l'Université l'Aurore;* H. Van Boven, whose *Histoire de la littérature chinoise moderne* uses mainly secondary sources. Jean Monsterleet, who has written a slim volume called *Sommets de la littérature chinoise contemporaine* in addition to some monographs on modern authors, probably also belonged to this group.

3. The most ambitious histories of modern Chinese literature published so far in Communist China are Wang Yao, *Chung-kuo hsin-wen-hsüeh shih kao,* 1951–53, and Liu Shou-sung, *Chung-kuo hsin-wen-hsüeh shih ch'u-kao,* 1956. Although the former study precedes the latter by only a few years, to compare the two is to discover the much greater space devoted to insignificant Communist authors and the shocking omission of a great many standard authors by the latter volume. Wang Yao discusses, though disapprovingly, the works of Shen Ts'ung-wen, Chou Tso-jen, Lin Yutang, and Shih T'o; Liu Shou-sung scarcely refers to them. Writing in the early fifties, Wang Yao regards Hu Feng almost as much of a critical authority on contemporary Chinese literature as Chou Yang and Feng Hsüeh-feng and quotes all three with equal frequency; Liu Shou-sung cites Chou Yang and Feng Hsüeh-feng constantly but treats Hu Feng as a most insidious and villainous counterrevolutionary. But in view of the downfall of Feng Hsüeh-feng and many other once respected Communist authors since 1957, even Liu Shou-sung's book itself is in need of extensive revision to maintain even temporarily its orthodoxy. It should be noted that both Wang and Liu regard their histories as *kao* or drafts—Liu is even more modest in calling his work a *ch'u-kao* or preliminary draft—so as to ensure for themselves the right to revise their books in the light of changing circumstances.

4. *Studies in Classic American Literature,* Anchor Books, p. 27.

5. I agree with such critics as F. R. Leavis, Martin Turnell, and

Vivian Mercier in assigning Flaubert a much smaller body of achievement than he used to be credited with. In invoking Flaubert's name here, however, I am primarily calling attention to the kind of dedication to art for which the French novelist was famous. Similarly, when I refer to the generation of Eliot and Joyce later in the chapter, I am using these names as the most conspicuous examples of artistic dedication in twentieth-century English and American literature, and I do not want it to be imputed to me that I admire everything Eliot and Joyce wrote with indiscriminate enthusiasm. Personally, I think that Eliot's recent plays are inferior and that Joyce's impulse toward composing *Finnegans Wake* was completely wrongheaded.

EPILOGUE

1. Of the fiction writers receiving individual attention in this book, Ping Hsin and Shen Ts'ung-wen have reportedly killed themselves since the Cultural Revolution, though we have no way of knowing whether such unconfirmed news circulating in Hong Kong and Taipei is true or not. But the suicide of Lao Shê is certain. D. W. Fokkema, a specialist in Chinese Communist literature serving in the Dutch consulate in Peking in 1966, writes in his informative article "Chinese Literature under the Cultural Revolution" that "one has learned, however, of the tragic death of Lao She, who committed suicide under red guard pressure in September 1966" (*Literature East & West, 13,* Nos. 3-4 [December 1969], p. 341). To my great regret, Dr. Fokkema's article was not published until after I had completed the epilogue.

2. Ch'i Pai-shih, Hsü Pei-hung, and Mei Lan-fang all died before 1966 and hence were spared the humiliations visited upon their younger colleagues. In the early sixties Chou Hsin-fang played the upright Ming official Hai Jui in a newly written opera called *Hai Jui shang-shu* (Hai Jui Memorializes the Emperor), which was subsequently construed as an oblique attack on Mao Tse-tung. Consequently, he was assaulted by the Red Guards in 1966. He reportedly met death as a result, but according to a news story in the *New York Times,* December 19, 1969, he was

subjected to renewed attack by the press in that month and so must have been alive. Ma Ssu-ts'ung (Ma Sitson) is the only major cultural figure to have escaped from China during the Cultural Revolution. His ordeal under that revolution is described in a series of articles he wrote for *Life* Magazine (June 2, July 14, 1967).

3. See especially *Wu-ch'an chieh-chi wen-hua ta-ko-ming tzu-liao-hsüan: ti-erh-chi* (Documents Pertaining to the Great Proletarian Cultural Revolution: The Second Compilation) (Hong Kong, San-lien shu-tien, 1966). This collection is a mine of information about Chou Yang, since it reprints only articles culled from the mainland press exposing his crimes.

4. Three of these stories are discussed in my "Residual Femininity: Women in Chinese Communist Fiction," *The China Quarterly*, No. 13 (January–March 1963). This article, which examines stories by many other authors as well, is also available in Cyril Birch, ed., *Chinese Communist Literature.*

5. Derek Bryan, trans., *Great Changes in A Mountain Village* (Peking, Foreign Languages Press, 1961), p. 39. The corresponding Chinese passage appears in *Shan-hsiang chü-pien* (Peking, Tso-chia ch'u-pan-she, 1958), pp. 33–34.

6. T. A. Hsia, "Heroes and Hero-Worship in Chinese Communist Fiction," *The China Quarterly*, No. 13, pp. 117–18. This article is also reprinted in Birch's *Chinese Communist Literature.*

7. *The Song of Youth* is discussed at length in Hsia, "Heroes and Hero-Worship in Chinese Communist Fiction."

8. Cf. C. T. Hsia, *The Classic Chinese Novel: A Critical Introduction* (New York, Columbia University Press, 1968), chap. 7. The major characters of *Dream of the Red Chamber*, including Chia Pao-yü, Bright Cloud, and Pervading Fragrance, are all discussed therein.

9. The attack on Wu Han and his opera *Hai Jui pa-kuan* (Hai Jui Dismissed from Office) in 1965 signaled the start of the Cultural Revolution.

10. These directives or "instructions," given by Mao in December 1963 and June 1964, were not made public until 1966. They are translated in "Raising High the Great Red Banner of Mao Tse-tung's Thought and Wrathfully Denouncing Chou Yang, Ringleader of the Sinister Gang in Literary and Art Circles,"

Peking Review, No. 32 (August 5, 1966), p. 36. This article enumerates the charges against Chou Yang made by the Propaganda Department of the Chinese Communist Party's Central Committee.

11. The English texts of these three pieces—"Serve the People," "In Memory of Norman Bethune," "The Foolish Old Man Who Removed the Mountains"—appear, among other places, in K. H. Fan, ed., *The Chinese Cultural Revolution: Selected Documents* (New York, Grove Press, 1968), pp.300–06.

12. In the article cited in n. 1, D. W. Fokkema states that "Chin Ching-mai's widely acclaimed novel *Song of Ouyang Hai (Ou-yang Hai chih ko,* 1965) was repeatedly rewritten and apparently no final text yet has been published" (p. 339). Dr. Fokkema rightly notes that the emphasis on "the non-final nature of the literary text" was a new principle governing literary criticism during the Cultural Revolution, and he makes a careful study of the textual discrepancies among the several versions of *The Song of Ou-yang Hai.* My own comments on the novel are based on an examination of the second edition, published by Jen-min wen-hsüeh ch'u-pan-she, Peking, in 1966.

13. *The White-haired Girl* assumes many theatrical forms and has been periodically revised. According to D. W. Fokkema, "In November 1967 Chiang Ch'ing also was led by the idea that a work of art is never finished, when she explained that the famous ballet *The White-Haired Girl (Pai mao nü),* although countless times revised, has to be changed again" (p. 339). The particular instance of revision referred to in my text is discussed in K. S. Karol, *China: The Other Communism* (New York, Hill and Wang, 1967), pp. 257–58. Mr. Karol visited Communist China in 1965.

14. A key member of the Cultural Revolution group, Yao Wen-yuan led the attack on the major victims of the revolution in the intellectual and literary circles. In April 1969 he was elected as a member of the Politburo at the Ninth Congress of the Chinese Communist Party. I see no reason to doubt his status as Mao's son-in-law, though the mainland press has never confirmed it.

15. *Wu-ch'an chieh-chi wen-hua ta-ko-ming tzu-liao- hsüan: ti erh-chi*, p. 148.

16. Karol, p. 291.

APPENDIX 1

1. *In Search of Wealth and Power: Yen Fu and the West* (Cambridge, Mass., Harvard University Press, 1964).

2. Lionel Trilling, "On the Modern Element in Modern Literature," *Partisan Review, 28,* No. 1 (January–February 1961), p. 10.

3. I have in mind especially Boris Pasternak and Evgeni Zamyatin, the latter best known for his grim fantasy, *We.*

4. Lin Tai-yi, trans., *Flowers in the Mirror* (London, Peter Owen, 1965), is an abridged version of the whole novel.

5. George Kao, ed., *Chinese Wit and Humor* (New York, Coward-McCann, 1946), p. 187. The translation is by Chi-chen Wang.

6. Harold Shadick, trans., *The Travels of Lao Ts'an* (Ithaca, Cornell University Press, 1952), p. 8.

7. Ibid., pp. 238–39.

8. Ibid., p. 9.

9. Ibid., p. 11.

10. For a brief exposition of Chang Chih-tung's thought, see Joseph R. Levenson, *Liang Chi'i-ch'ao and the Mind of Modern China* (Cambridge, Mass., Harvard University Press, 1965), pp. 6–7.

11. In addition to Chap. 2, I have studied Lu Hsün's obsession with China in my "On the 'Scientific' Study of Modern Chinese Literature," *T'oung Pao, 50,* Nos. 4–5 (1963). See also the illuminating essay "Aspects of the Power of Darkness in Lu Hsün" in Tsi-an Hsia, *The Gate of Darkness: Studies on the Leftist Literary Movement in China.*

12. Cf. Schwartz, *In Search of Wealth and Power,* Chap. 4, "Western Wisdom at Its Source: *Evolution and Ethics.*" Liu Ê's awareness of Darwinian biology (cf. "Translator's Introduction" to *The Travels of Lao Ts'an,* p. xviii) must have been due to his

reading of Yen Fu's translation of Huxley's work, entitled *T'ien-yen lun.*

13. *Selected Works of Lu Hsun, 1,* p. 19.

14. Wen I-to, "The Laundry Song," in Kai-yu Hsu, trans., *Twentieth Century Chinese Poetry* (New York, Doubleday, 1963), pp. 51–52.

15. Translated from Yü Ta-fu, *Ch'en-lun,* 10th ptg. (Shanghai, T'ai-tung t'u-shu-chü, 1928), "Ch'en-lun," p. 72. Each of the three stories in this collection has its own separate pagination.

16. *A-li-ssu Chung-kuo yu-chi, 1* (Shanghai, Hsin-yüeh shu-tien, 1928), pp. 135–36. The "yellow-skinned people now clamoring for 'co-existence and co-prosperity' " refers to the Japanese.

17. Ibid., 2, p. 233.

18. Lao Shê disparages *City of Cats* on literary grounds in *Lao-niu p'o-ch'e* (Shanghai, Jen-chien shu-wu, 1937), pp. 43–49. But his real motive for doing so, I suspect, lies in his attempt to dissociate his name from a work notorious for its virulent attack on the Chinese Communist Party and its supporters and sympathizers. By the middle thirties the leftist and Communist writers had clearly dominated the Chinese literary scene, and Lao Shê would not have wanted to be identified as a staunch anti-Communist.

19. James E. Dew, trans., *City of Cats* (Ann Arbor, 1964), p. 20. This constitutes *Occasional Paper No. 3,* edited by James I. Crump, Jr. for the Center for Chinese Studies of the University of Michigan. I have slightly revised the translation. The corresponding passage in Chinese appears in *Mao-ch'eng chi* (Shanghai, Hsien-tai shu-chü, 1933), pp. 126–27.

20. For a discussion of *Chin P'ing Mei* and its major characters, see C. T. Hsia, *The Classic Chinese Novel: A Critical Introduction,* Chap. 5.

21. In the February 1917 number of *Hsin Ch'ing-nien,* Ch'en Tu-hsiu launched the Literary Revolution by declaring his intent "to overthrow the painted, powdered, and obsequious literature for the aristocratic few ... the stereotyped and over-ornamental literature of classicism . . . the pedantic, unintelligible, and obscurantist literature of the hermit and recluse" (Chow Tse-tsung, *The May Fourth Movement,* p. 276). I have translated

Ch'en's three labels for traditional Chinese literature myself in Chap. 1.

22. Examples of this literature are examined in T. A. Hsia, "Heroes and Hero-Worship in Chinese Communist Fiction," and C. T. Hsia, "Residual Femininity: Women in Chinese Communist Fiction." Both articles appeared in *The China Quarterly*, No. 13 (January–March 1963).

23. Translated from Yang Shuo, *San-ch'ien-li chiang-shan* (Peking, Jen-min wen-hsüeh ch'u-pan-she, 1953), p. 190. In view of its subversive character, it is not surprising that the passage has been drastically revised in the official English version. I quote the corresponding passage from Yuan Ko-chia, trans., *A Thousand Miles of Lovely Land* (Peking, Foreign Languages Press, 1957), pp. 209–10:

> When victory is won, we shall live together as man and wife and never part again. After the day's work, we'll have supper at the same table and study by the same lamp. She is a great lover of flowers. She used to plant balsam under the window and rouged her fingernails with the petals. We'll surround our house with all sorts of flowers so that we can pass every day among them.

Glossary

THIS glossary of Chinese names, titles, and terms is divided into four sections. Section I lists the twenty fiction writers (Bibliography, sec. V) as well as twelve other authors who have received important mention. The titles of works by these authors (with the exception of those already cited in the Bibliography) and all the fictitious characters in their works actually mentioned in the text are recorded in Chinese. Section II lists the names of all other Chinese persons mentioned in the text and notes (with the exception of those whose publications are in English) and the titles of works by these Chinese which are mentioned in the text but not entered in the Bibliography. Because titles of magazine and newspaper articles by Chinese authors referred to in the notes are transliterated there, they are omitted from this section, but historical personages, including those who are mentioned in the text as characters in fiction, are entered.

Section III lists all titles of Chinese periodicals and newspapers mentioned in the text and notes, with the exception of those already entered in the Bibliography, sec. III. It also includes all titles of Chinese works excluded from sections I and II, mostly titles of familiar classics and fiction. In section IV are entered all Chinese forms of address, and other special terms and phrases given in transliterated forms in the text. Even though the meanings of these terms are either explained in the text or self-evident in the contexts in which they appear, it seems to me useful to record them in Chinese for readers who cannot readily identify them.

Since names of many authors and a great many titles are recorded in Chinese only in the Bibliography, the latter should be regarded as an integral part of the Glossary.

I

1. Ai Wu 艾蕪

    Autumn Harvest 秋收

    The Waste Land 荒地

    My Childhood 我的幼年時代

    My Youth 我的青年時代

    The Fertile Plain 豐饒的原野

    On the River 江上行

    My Native Place 故鄉

    Mountain Wilderness 山野

    A Woman's Tragedy 一個女人的悲劇

    The Tempering of Steel 百錬成鋼

2. Eileen Chang

    Romances 傳奇

    "Whispered Words" 私語

    "The Guileless Words of a Child" 童言無忌

    "On Music" 談音樂

    "The Golden Cangue" 金鎖記

      Ch'i-ch'iao 七巧; Chiang Chi-tsê 姜季澤;

      Ch'ang-pai 長白; Ch'ang-an 長安;

      T'ung Shih-fang 童世舫; Ting Yü-ken 丁玉根;

      Chang Shao-ch'üan 張少泉; Tailor Shen 沈裁縫.

    "Jasmine Tea" 茉莉香片

      Nieh Ch'uan-ch'ing 聶傳慶; Yen Tan-chu 言丹朱;

      Yen Tzu-yeh 言子夜; Feng Pi-lo 馮碧落.

"Blockade" 封鎖

"Love in a Fallen City" 傾城之戀

"Happy Matrimony" 鴻鸞禧

"Glazed Tiles" 琉璃瓦

"Indian Summer: A-hsiao's Autumnal Lament" 桂花蒸:

阿小悲秋

"Lingering Love" 留情

"Waiting" 等

"The Heart Sutra" 心經

"Lien-huan T'ao" 連環套

The Rice-sprout Song

Gold Root 金根; Gold Flower 金花; Moon Scent 月香;

Beckon 阿招; Big Uncle T'an 譚老大;

Big Aunt T'an 譚大娘; Comrade Wong 王霖; Comrade

Ku 顧岡.

Love in Redland

Liu Ch'üan 劉荃; Huang Chüan 黄絹;

Yeh Ching-k'uei 葉景奎; Ts'ui P'ing 崔平;

Chao Ch'u 趙楚; Ko Shan 戈珊; Ch'en I.

3. Chang T'ien-i

"A Dream of Three and a Half Days" 三天半的夢

"Twenty-one" 二十一個

"The Bread Line" 麵包綫

"The Failure of Lord Snake" 蛇太爺的失敗

"Mr. Ching-yeh" 荆野先生

"Mutation" 移行

"The Bulwark" 砥柱

   Huang Yi-an 黃宜庵 ; Chen Mei-tzu 貞妹子 .

"On the Journey" 旅途中

   Chi San-tsuan-tzu 計三鑽子

"The Mid-Autumn Festival" 中秋

   K'uei Ta-yeh 葵大爺

"Lu Pao-t'ien" 陸寶田

"Spring Breeze" 春風

   Principal T'ung 佟校長 ; Teacher Chin 金老師 ;

   Teacher Ting 丁老師 ; Teacher Ch'iu 邱老師 ;

   Yu Fu-lin 尤福林 ; Liao Wen-pin 廖文彬 ;

   Lin Wen-hou 林文侯 ; Chiang Jih-hsin 江日新 .

"After Her Departure" 出走以後

   Mrs. Ho Po-chün 何伯俊太太 ; Wang Ma 王媽

In the City

   T'ang Lao-erh 唐老二

The Strange Knight of Shanghai

   Shih Po-hsiang 史伯襄 ; Shih Chao-ch'ang 史兆昌 ;

   Shih Chao-wu 史兆武 ; Hu Ken-pao 胡根寶 ;

   Half Dust 半塵子 ; T'ai-chi Chen-jen 太極真人 ;

   Mary Ho 何曼麗 .

Three Sketches

   "Mr. Hua Wei" 華威先生

   "New Life" 新生

"Mr. T'an Chiu's Job" 譚九先生的工作

"A Strange Place" 奇怪的地方

"The Kingdom of the Golden Duck" 金鴨帝國

4. Chao Shu-li

"The Marriage of Hsiao Erh-hei" 小二黑結婚

Hsiao Ch'in 小芹

"The Verses of Li Yu-ts'ai" 李有才板話

The Changes in Li Village

T'ieh-so 鐵鎖

San-li Wan

Fan Teng-kao 范登高; Fan Ling-chih 范靈芝;

Ma To-shou 馬多壽; Ma Yu-i 馬有翼;

Wang Chin-sheng 王金生; Wang Yü-sheng 王玉生;

Lao Liang 老梁.

5. Chiang Kuang-tz'u

"Proletarian Revolution and Culture"

無產階級革命與文化

"The Present-day Chinese Society and Revolutionary Literature"

現代中國社會與革命文學

The Youthful Tramp

Wang Chung 汪中; Lin Hsiang-ch'ien.

The Moon Emerging from the Clouds

Wang Man-ying 王曼英; A-lien 阿蓮;

Li Shang-chih 李尚志.

6. Chiang Kuei

    The Whirlwind

    Fang Hsiang-ch'ien 方祥千 ; Fang P'ei-lan 方培蘭 ;

    P'ang Yüeh-mei 龐月梅 ; P'ang Chin-lien 龐錦蓮 ;

    Hsü Ta-hai 許大海 ; Fang T'ien-ai 方天艾 ;

    Fang Jan-wu 方冉武 ; Lady Fang 方老太太 ;

    Mistress Hsi-men 西門氏 .

7. Ch'ien Chung-shu

    "Inspiration" 靈感

    "Cat" 貓

    Li Chien-hou 李健侯 ; Ai-mo 愛黙 ; I-ku 頤谷 ;

    Ch'en Hsia-chün 陳俠君 .

    "Souvenir" 紀念

    Man-ch'ien 曼倩 ; Ts'ai-shu 才叔 ; T'ien-chien 天健

    "God's Dream" 上帝的夢

    The Besieged City

    Fang Hung-chien 方鴻漸 ; Sun Jou-chia 孫柔嘉 ;

    Su Wen-wan 蘇文紈 ; Miss Pao 鮑小姐 ;

    T'ang Hsiao-fu 唐曉芙 ; Chao Hsin-mei 趙辛楣 ;

    Li Mei-t'ing 李梅亭 ; Ku Erh-ch'ien 顧爾謙 ;

    Fang Tun-weng 方遯翁 ; Mrs. Lu 陸太太 ; Li Ma 李媽 .

8. Chou Yang (Chou Ch'i-ying 周起應)

    "Literature at the Present Juncture" 現階段的文學

    "We Must Fight" 我們必須戰鬥

"The Great Debate on the Literary Front"

文藝戰線上的一場大辯論

9. Hsiao Chün

" 'Love' and 'Patience' among Comrades"

論同志之'愛'與'耐'

Village in August

Hsiao Ming 蕭明; Anna 安娜; Ch'en Chu 陳柱;

Wang Lao-san 王老三 ·

10. Hu Feng (Chang Ku-fei 張谷非)

"What Do the Masses Want from Literature?"

人民大眾向文學要求什麼?

"The Cultural Movement Under a Protracted War"

論持久戰中的文化運動

"Realism Today" 現實主義在今天

"Time Has Now Begun!" 時間開始了!

"Anti-Communism Today and Tomorrow"

反共的今天和明天

11. Hu Shih

"Suggestions for a Reform of Literature"

文學改良芻議

"For a Constructive Literary Revolution"

建設的文學革命論

A History of Pai-hua Literature 白話文學史

Experiments 嘗試集

12. Kuo Mo-jo

    "Revolution and Literature" 革命與文學

    Goddesses 女神

    "The Hound of Heaven" 天狗

    "The Nirvana of the Phoenixes" 鳳凰涅槃

    "Earth, My Mother" 地球，我的母親

    Three Rebellious Women 三個叛逆的女性

    The Devoted Siblings 棠棣之花

    Ch'ü Yüan 屈原

    Hu Fu 虎符

    Odes to New China 新華頌

13. Lao Shê

    Ta-ming Lake 大明湖

    Chao Tzu-yüeh

      Miss Wang 王靈石 ; Ou-yang T'ien-feng 歐陽天風 ;
      Mo Ta-nien 莫大年 ; Wu Tuan 武端 ;
      Chou Shao-lien 周少濂 ; Li Ching-shun 李景純 .

    The Two Mas

      Ma Tsê-jen 馬則仁 ; Ma Wei 馬威 ;
      Mrs. Wendell 溫都太太 ; Mary 瑪力 ; Evans 伊牧師 ;
      Catherine 凱薩林 ; Paul 保羅 ; Alexander 亞力山大 ;
      Li Tzu-jung 李子榮 ; Mao 茅 ; Washington 華盛頓 .

    Divorce

      Lao Li 老李 ; Ting Erh-yeh 丁二爺 ; Hsiao Chao 小趙 ;
      T'ien-chen 天真 ; Old Brother Chang 張大哥 ;

Ma K'o-t'ung 馬克同 ; Mrs. Ma 馬太太 ·

The Biography of Niu T'ien-tz'u

Ssu Hu-tzu 四虎子

Camel Hsiang-tzu

Liu Ssu-yeh 劉四爺 ; Tiger 虎妞 ;

Professor Ts'ao 曹先生 ; Hsiao Fu-tzu 小福子 ;

Yüan Ming 阮明.

North of Chienmenkwan 劍北篇

Cremation

Mayor Wang 王舉人 ; Liu Erh-kou 劉二狗 ;

Meng-lien 夢蓮 ; Ting I-shan 丁一山 ;

Captain Shih 石隊長 ; Uncle Sung 松叔叔.

Four Generations Under One Roof

Old Man Ch'i 祁老人 ; Ch'i T'ien-yu 祁天佑 ;

Jui-hsüan 瑞宣 ; Jui-feng 瑞豐 ; Jui-ch'üan 瑞全 ;

Chrysanthemum 菊子 ; Kuan Hsiao-ho 冠曉荷 ;

Big Red Melon 大赤包 ; Kao-ti 高弟 ; Chao-ti 招弟 ;

Ch'ien Mo-yin 錢默吟 ; Lan Tung-yang 藍東陽.

14. Li Chieh-jen 李劼人
    Ripples on Dead Water 死水微瀾
    Before the Storm 暴風雨前
    The Great Wave 大波

15. Ling Shu-hua
    "The Tea Party" 吃茶
    "The Second Encounter" 再見

"After the Tea Party" 茶會以後

"Embroidered Pillows" 繡枕

"The Eve of the Mid-Autumn Festival" 中秋晚

Ching-jen 敬仁

"Little Liu" 小劉

"Schoolmistress Li" 李先生

"Akiko" 晶子

"Chiyoko" 千代子

"On a Journey" 旅途

16. Lo Hua-sheng

   A History of Taoism 道教史

   "The Vain Labors of a Spider" 綴網勞蛛

   Shang-chieh 尚潔

   "Ch'un-t'ao" 春桃

   "Mr. Tung Yeh" 東野先生

   "Yü-kuan" 玉官

   Ch'en Lien 陳廉; Hsing-kuan 杏官.

17. Lu Hsün

   The Outcry 吶喊

   "The Diary of a Madman" 狂人日記

   "K'ung I-chi" 孔乙己

   "Medicine" 藥

   Hsia Yü 夏瑜; Hua Hsiao-shuan 華小栓.

   "My Native Place" 故鄉

   Jun-t'u 閏土

"The Country Theater" 社戲

"A Little Incident" 一件小事

"The Story of Hair" 頭髮的故事

"The True Story of Ah Q" 阿 Q 正傳

Hesitation 彷徨

"Benediction" 祝福

   Hsiang-lin Sao 祥林嫂

"In the Restaurant" 在酒樓上

   Lü Wei-fu 呂緯甫

"Soap" 肥皂

   Ssu-ming 四銘; Hsüeh-ch'eng 學程.

"Divorce" 離婚

   Ai-ku 愛姑; Ch'i Ta-jen 七大人.

"The Happy Family" 幸福的家庭

"The Solitary" 孤獨者

"Remorse" 傷逝

Wild Grass 野草

Morning Flowers Picked in Evening 朝華夕拾

Old Legends Retold 故事新編

Tomb 墳

Hot Wind 熱風

Erh-i Chi 而已集

Triple Leisure 三閒集

"Replies to an Interviewer during Illness"

   病中答客問

18. Lu Ling 路翎

The Hungry Kuo Su-o 饑餓的郭素娥

The Children of the Rich 財主底兒女們

Chiang Shun-tsu 蔣純祖

The Blessings of Youth 青春的祝福

"The Battle on the Marsh" 窪地上的戰役

19. Mao Tse-tung

"The Position of the Chinese Communist Party in the National Struggle" 中國共產黨在民族戰爭中的地位

"On the Correct Handling of Contradictions among the People" 關于正確處理人民內部矛盾的問題

20. Mao Tun

Disillusion

Ching 靜; Hui 慧; Pao-su 抱素; Ch'iang Meng 強猛

Vacillation

Hu Kuo-kuang 胡國光; Fang Lo-lan 方羅蘭;

Sun Wu-yang 孫舞陽; Mei-li 梅麗.

Pursuit

Chang Ch'iu-liu 章秋柳; Shih Hsün 史循;

Chang Man-ch'ing 張曼青; Chu Chin-ju 朱近如;

Wang Chung-chao 王仲昭.

Rainbow

Miss Mei 梅女士; Dr. Mei 梅老醫生; Wei-yü 韋玉;

Liang Yü-ch'un 梁遇春; Liang Kang-fu 梁剛夫.

The Twilight

Wu Sun-fu 吳蓀甫; Chao Po-t'ao 趙伯韜;

Tu Tso-chai 杜竹齋；Li Yü-t'ing 李玉亭；

Fan Po-wen 范博文；Tu Hsin-t'o 杜新籜；

Chang Su-su 張素素；Tseng Ts'ang-hai 曾滄海；

Feng Yün-ch'ing 馮雲卿；Wu Hui-fang 吳蕙芳．

Story of the First Stage of the War

P'an Hsüeh-li 潘雪莉

Putrefaction

Chao Hui-ming 趙惠明

Maple Leaves as Red as February Flowers

Chao Shou-i 趙守義；Wang Po-shen 王伯申；

Chang Hsün-ju 張恂如；Hsü Ching-ying 許靜英；

Huang Ho-kuang 黃和光；Wan-ch'ing 婉卿；

Ch'ien Liang-ts'ai 錢良材．

Discipline 鍛鍊

"Creation" 創造

"Suicide" 自殺

"A Girl" 一個女性

"Lin's Store" 林家舖子

"Spring Silkworms" 春蠶；"Autumn Harvest" 秋收

Lao T'ung-pao 老通寶；To-to-t'ou 多多頭．

"From Kuling to Tokyo" 從牯嶺到東京

"On Reading *Ni Huan-chih*" 讀倪煥之

21. Pa Chin

Destruction

Tu Ta-hsin 杜大心；Li Leng 李冷；

Glossary

Li Ching-shu 李靜淑 ·

The Love Trilogy: Fog 霧 ; *Rain* 雨 ; *Thunder* 雷 ;

Lightning 電

Chou Ju-shui 周如水 ; Ch'en Chen 陳真 ;

Wu Jen-min 吳仁民 ; Chang Jo-lan 張若蘭 ;

Li P'ei-chu 李佩珠 ; Kao Chih-yüan 高志元 ·

The Torrent

Kao Chüeh-hsin 高覺新 ; Chüeh-min 覺民 ;

Chüeh-hui 覺慧 ; Ch'in 琴 ; Shu-hua 淑華 ;

Shu-ying 淑英 ; Mei 梅 ; Hai-ch'en 海臣 ; Ming-feng 鳴鳳 ;

Hui 蕙 ; Grandmother Chou 周老太太 ;

Chou Po-t'ao 周伯濤 ; Young Squire Mei 枚少爺 ;

Mistress Ch'en 陳姨太 ; Ch'ien-erh 倩兒 ;

Ts'ui-huan 翠環 ·

Fire

Feng Wen-shu 馮文淑 ; Chu Su-chen 朱素貞 ;

Liu Po 劉波 ; T'ien Hui-shih 田惠世 ·

Leisure Garden

Mr. Yao 姚國棟 ; Mr. Yang 楊三老爺 ·

Ward No. 4

Dr. Yang 楊大夫

Cold Nights

Wang Wen-hsüan 汪文宣 ; Shu-sheng 樹生 ·

"Dog" 狗

624

"Ghost" 鬼

"Chickens and a Pig" 豬與雞

22. Ping Hsin

Letters to My Little Readers 寄小讀者

"The Superman" 超人

"Awakening" 悟

"Loneliness" 寂寞

Hsiao-hsiao 小小; Mei-mei 妹妹; Hsüan-ko 萱哥.

"A Year Away From Home" 離家的一年

"Since Her Departure" 別後

Yung-ming 永明; Wang Ma 王媽.

"The West Wind" 西風

23. Sha T'ing 沙汀

Voyage Beyond the Law 法律外的航線

The Sowers 播種者

Storming the Gate 闖關

Prospecting for Gold 淘金記

Beasts at Bay 困獸記

The Return of the Native 還鄉記

24. Shen Ts'ung-wen

Feng Tzu 鳳子

Alice in China 阿麗思中國遊記

The Border Town

Ts'ui-ts'ui 翠翠

Watching Clouds in Yunnan 雲南看雲集

Winter Scene in Kunming 昆明冬景

The Long River

    T'eng Ch'ang-shun 滕長順; Yao-yao 夭夭;

    The Old Sailor 老水手.

"Three Men and a Girl" 三個男子和一個女人

"Ta Wang" 大王

"Under the Moonlight" 月下小景

"Lung Chu" 龍朱

"The White Kid" 小白羊

"Hui Ming" 會明

"Hsiao-hsiao" 蕭蕭

    Ox Boy 牛兒; Yüeh Mao-mao 月毛毛.

"San-san" 三三

"Living" 生

    Wang Chiu 王九; Chao Ssu 趙四.

"Night" 夜

"Big and Small Yüan" 大小阮

"The Housewife" 主婦

"The Day before He Ran Away" 逃的前一天

"On the Mountain Path" 山道中

"Quiet" 靜

    Yo-min 岳珉; Pei-sheng 北生.

"Daytime" 白日

Four chapters of an unfinished romance:

"The Red Incubus" 赤魘

"Snow and Sunshine" 雪晴

"Ch'iao-hsiu and Tung-sheng" 巧秀和冬生

"A Romance Quite Ordinary" 傳奇不奇

25. Shih Chih-ts'un 施蟄存

"The General's Head" 將軍底頭

"Shih Hsiu" 石秀

26. Shih T'o

Wild Birds 野鳥集

"The Pastoral Song" 牧歌

"A Patch of Land" 一片土

"Father and Son" 父與子

Marriage

Hu Ch'ü-o 胡去惡 ; Lin P'ei-fang 林佩芳 ;

T'ien Kuo-pao 田國寶 ; T'ien Kuo-hsiu 田國秀 ;

Ch'ien Heng 錢亨 ; Dr. America Huang 黃美洲 ;

The Old Maid 老處女 .

27. Ting Ling

'Meng K'o" 夢珂

"The Diary of Miss Sophia" 莎菲女士的日記

"Shanghai, Spring 1930," I and II 一九三〇年春上海

"The T'ien Village" 田家沖

"In the Hospital" 在醫院中

Lu P'ing 陸萍

"Thoughts on March 8" 三八節有感

"The Life of an Upright Man—Hu Yeh-p'in" 一個真實人

的一生 —— 記胡也頻

Sun over the Sangkan River

Ch'ien Wen-kuei 錢文貴; Hei-ni 黑妮;

Ch'eng Jen 程仁; Chang Yü-min 張裕民;

Hou Chung-ch'üan 侯忠全; Hou Tien-k'uei 侯殿魁;

Jen Kuo-chung 任國忠; Chao Ch'üan-kung 趙全功;

Wen Ts'ai 文采; Chang Cheng-tien 張正典.

28. Ts'ao Yü 曹禺

The Thunderstorm 雷雨

Sunrise 日出

The Wilderness 原野

Peking Man 北京人

Metamorphosis 蛻變

Dr. Ting 丁大夫

Romeo and Juliet 柔密歐與幽麗葉

Family 家

29. Tuan-mu Hung-liang 端木蕻良

The Khorchin Grasslands 科爾沁旗草原

The Sea of Earth 大地的海

The Great River 大江

30. Wu Tsu-hsiang

"Kuan-kuan's Tonic" 官官的補品

"Eighteen Hundred Piculs" 一千八百担

Sung Po-t'ang 宋柏堂; Sung Yüeh-chai 宋月齋.

"The Fan Village" 樊家舖

Hsien-tzu Sao 線子嫂

"A Certain Day" 某日

31. Yeh Shao-chün

"Rice" 飯

Mr. Wu 吳先生

"One Lesson" 一課

"Yi-erh" 義兒

"The Little Coppersmith" 小銅匠

"The Principal" 校長

"Struggle" 抗爭

"The English Professor" 英文教授

Tung Wu-kou 董無垢

"Solitude" 孤獨

"Autumn" 秋

"Richer by Three or Five Pecks" 多收了三五斗

"The Emperor's New Clothes" 皇帝的新衣

"Two Buddhist Priests" 兩法師

Abbot Hung I; Abbot Yin Kuang.

32. Yü Ta-fu

"Sinking" 沉淪

"Moving South" 南遷

"Silver-gray Death" 銀灰色的死

"Ts'ai Shih Chi" 采石磯

    Huang Chung-tsê; Tai Tung-yüan.

"One Intoxicating Spring Evening" 春風沉醉的晚上

"Late-blooming Cassia" 遲桂花

"The Past" 過去

    Lao San 老三

"A Trip Home" 還鄉記

"Smoke Silhouettes" 烟影

"In the Cold Wind" 在寒風裏

II

A Lung 阿瓏 (I Men 亦門)

Ai Ch'ing 艾青

  "The Second Time He Died" 他死在第二次

  "Understand Authors, Respect Authors" 了解作家，尊重作家

Ai Ssu-ch'i 艾思奇

Chang Chih-tung 張之洞

Chang Hen-shui 張恨水

Chang Hsien-chung 張獻忠

Chang Po-chün 章伯鈞

Chang Shih-chao 章士釗

Chang Tao-fan 張道藩

Chang Tzu-p'ing 張資平

Chao P'ing-fu 趙平復

  (Jou Shih 柔石)

Ch'en Ch'i-hsia 陳企霞

Ch'en Chiung-ming 陳烱明

Ch'en Ch'o 陳焯

Ch'en Heng-chê 陳衡哲

Ch'en I 陳毅

Ch'en Li-fu 陳立夫

Ch'en Meng-chia 陳夢家

Ch'en Ming 陳明

Ch'en Shih-hsiang 陳世驤

Ch'en Teng-k'o 陳登科

   Buried Alive 活人塘

   Children by the Hwai River

淮河邊上的兒女

Ch'en Tu-hsiu 陳獨秀

   "For a Literary Revolution"

文學革命論

Ch'en Tzu-chan 陳子展

Ch'en Wang-tao 陳望道

Ch'en Yüan 陳源

Ch'en Yung 陳涌

Cheng Chen-to 鄭振鐸

Ch'eng Fang-wu 成仿吾

   "From Literary Revolution to a

   Revolutionary Literature"

從文學革命到革命文學

Chia Chi-fang 賈冀汸

Chiang Ching-kuo 蔣經國

Chiang Feng 江豐

Chiang Kai-shek 蔣中正

Chiang Mu-liang 蔣牧良

Ch'iao Kuan-hua 喬冠華

Chien Hsien-ai 蹇先艾

Ch'ien Chi-po 錢基博

Ch'ien Chün-jui 錢俊瑞

Ch'ien Hsing-ts'un 錢杏邨

   "The Age of Ah Q Is Dead"

死去了的阿Q時代

Ch'ien Hsüan-t'ung 錢玄同

Chin I 靳以

Chin Sheng-t'ai 金聖嘆

Chin T'i 金隄 (Ching Ti)

Ch'in Chao-yang 秦兆陽

   "Realism—the Broad Path"

現實主義—廣闊的道

路

Chou En-lai 周恩來

Chou Fo-hai 周佛海

Chou Li-po 周立波

   The Hurricane 暴風驟雨

Chou P'ei-t'ung 周培桐

Chou Tso-jen 周作人

"Humane Literature"

人的文學

Chou Wen 周文

"Love" 愛

Chou Yüan 周淵

Chu Ching-wo 朱鏡我

Chu Hung-wu 朱洪武 (Chu Yüan-chang 朱元璋)

Chu Kuang-ch'ien 朱光潛

"My Hopes for This Magazine"

我對於本刊的希望

Chu Teh 朱德

Chu Tzu-ch'ing 朱自清

Ch'ü Ch'iu-pai 瞿秋白

"Long Live the Literary Dictators!" 學閥萬歲

Ch'ü Yüan 屈原

Nine Songs 九歌

Ch'uan Tao 川島

Chung T'ien-fei 鍾惦棐

Fang Jan 方然

Feng Chih 馮至

Sonnets 十四行集

Feng K'eng 馮鏗

Feng Nai-ch'ao 馮乃超

Feng Tzu-k'ai 豐子愷

Feng Yu-lan 馮友蘭

Feng Yü-hsiang 馮玉祥

Feng Yüan-chün 馮沅君

Fu Ssu-nien 傅斯年

Fu Tung-hua 傅東華

Han Shih-heng 韓侍桁

Ho Ch'i-fang 何其芳

Ho Ching-chih 賀敬之, Ting I 丁毅

The White-haired Girl

白毛女

Hou Chin-ching 侯金鏡

Hsia Mien-tsun 夏丏尊

Hsia Tao-p'ing 夏道平

Hsia Yen 夏衍

The Fascist Bacillus

法西斯細菌

Hsiang P'ei-liang 向培良

Hsiao Ch'ien 蕭乾

Hsiao Hung 蕭紅

Hsiao Yeh-mu 蕭也牧

"Between Us Husband and Wife" 我們夫婦之間

Hsü Chieh 許傑

Hsü Chih-mo 徐志摩

Hsü Mou-yung 徐懋庸

Hsü T'iao-fu 徐調孚

Hsü Tsu-cheng 徐祖正

Hsüan Hsien 璇僊

"Autumn in the Hua-yüeh Villa" 華月廬的秋天

Hu Ch'iao-mu 胡喬木

Hu Ch'iu-yüan 胡秋原

Hu Hsien-su 胡先驌

Hu Sheng 胡繩

Hu Tsung-nan 胡宗南

Hu Yeh-p'in 胡也頻

A Bright Future Lies Ahead of Us 光明在我們前面

Huang Ch'iu-yün 黃秋耘

Huang Chung-tsê 黃仲則

Huang Lu-yin 黃廬隱

Huang Yao-mien 黃藥眠

Huang Yüan 黃源

Hung I 弘一

Hung Shen 洪深

K'ang Cho 康濯

K'ang Yu-wei 康有為

Kao Ch'ang-hung 高長虹

Kao Yang 高陽

Keng Chi-chih 耿濟之

Ko Ch'in 葛琴

"Total Retreat" 總退卻

K'o Ling 柯靈

The Night Inn 夜店

Ku Chieh-kang 顧頡剛

Lao Nai-hsüan 勞乃宣

Li Ang 李昂

The Red Stage 紅色舞台

Li Chi 李季

Wang Kuei and Li Hsiang-hsiang 王貴與李香香

Li Ch'u-li 李初梨

Li Hui-ying 李輝英

The Human Condition 人間

Li Kuang-t'ien 李廣田

Li Ni 麗尼

Li Po 李白

Li Shao-ch'in 黎少芩

Li Ta 李達

Li Ta-chao 李大釗

Li Tzu-ch'eng 李自成

Li Wei-sen 李偉森

Li Yu-jan 李又然

Liang Ch'i-ch'ao 梁啟超

Liang Shih-ch'iu 梁實秋

"The Romantic Tendencies in Modern Chinese Literature" 現代中國文學之浪漫的趨勢

Liang Shu-ming 梁漱溟

Lin Hsiang-ch'ien 林祥謙

Lin Mo-han 林默涵

Lin Shu 林紓

Lin Yutang 林語堂

Liu Ch'ing 柳青

Sowing 種穀記

Walls of Brass and Iron 銅牆鐵壁

Liu Fu 劉復

Liu Hsüeh-wei 劉雪葦

Liu Pai-yü 劉白羽

Liu Pin-yen 劉賓雁

Liu Shao-t'ang 劉紹棠

"The Development of Realism in the Socialist Age" 現實主義在社會主義時代的發展

"My Views on the Current Literary Problem" 我對當前文藝問題的一些意見

Lo Chia-lun 羅家倫

Lo Feng 羅烽

"This Is Still the Age for *Tsa-wen*" 還是雜文的時代

Lo Lung-chi 羅隆基

Lu Chu-kuo 陸柱國

Lu Hung 蘆葓

Lu Li 陸蠡

Lu Ta 魯達

Lu Tien 蘆甸

Lu Ting-i 陸定一

Lü Yüan 綠原

Lü Chien 呂劍

Lü K'o-yü 呂克玉 (Feng　Pa Jen 巴人 (Wang Jen-shu 王
Hsüeh-feng)　任叔)

Pai Jen 白刃

Ma Chia 馬加　*Fight Till Tomorow*
Ten Days in Chiang-shan Vil-　戰鬥到明天
lage 江山村十日
Flowers Ever in Bloom　Pai Lang 白朗
開不敗的花朵　*For a Happier Tomorrow*
為了幸福的明天

Ma Feng 馬烽, Hsi Jung 西戎
Heroes of the Lü-liang Moun-　P'eng K'ang 彭康
tain 呂梁英雄傳　P'eng Tê-huai 彭德懷
Mei Kuang-ti 梅光迪　Pien Chih-lin 卞之琳
Meng Shih-huan 孟十還
Mu Mu-t'ien 穆木天
Mu Tan 穆旦　Shao Ch'üan-lin 邵荃麟
Shao Li-tzu 邵力子
Shu Ch'ün 舒羣
Nieh Cheng 聶政　Shu Wu 舒蕪
Nieh Jung 聶嫈　"On the Subjective" 論主觀
Niu Han 牛漢　"I Must Study Anew the *Talks*
at the Yenan Literary Confer-
ence" 從頭學習'在延安
Ou-yang Shan 歐陽山　文藝座談會上的講話'
Uncle Kao 高乾大
Soong, Stephen C. 宋奇

Su Hsüeh-lin 蘇雪林

   The Bitter Heart 棘心

   Shan-shui Chi 蟬蛻集

Su Wen 蘇汶 (Tu Heng 杜衡)

Sun Ta-yü 孫大雨

Sun Yat-sen 孫文

   San Min Chu I 三民主義

Sung Chih-ti 宋之的

Tai Tung-yüan 戴東原

Tai Wang-shu 戴望舒

Teng Chung-hsia 鄧中夏

T'ien Chien 田間

T'ien Han 田漢

Ting Hsi-lin 丁西林

Ting K'o-hsin 丁克辛

   "Old Worker Kuo Fu-shan"

   老工人郭福山

Ts'ai Yüan-p'ei 蔡元培

Tsang K'o-chia 臧克家

Ts'ao Hsüeh-ch'in 曹雪芹

   Dream of the Red Chamber

   紅樓夢

Ts'ao Ming 草明

Motive Power 原動力

Tseng Kuo-fan 曾國藩

Tu Mu 杜牧

Tu P'eng-ch'eng 杜鵬程

   In Defense of Yenan 保衛延安

Tu Yün-hsieh 杜運燮

Wang Chao 王照

Wang Ching-wei 汪精衛

Wang Jo-wang 王若望

Wang Lu-yen 王魯彥

Wang Mou-tsu 汪懋祖

Wang Shih-wei 王實味

   "The Wild Lily" 野百合花

Wang Tu-ch'ing 王獨清

   The Death of Yang Kuei-fei

   楊貴妃之死

   "The Creation Society: A Final Appraisal and an Account of My Role in Its History"

   創造社：我和牠的始終與牠底總賬

Wang T'ung-chao 王統照

Wei Pi-chia 魏璧佳

Wei Wei 巍巍

Wen I-to 聞一多

Wu Chih-hui 吳稚暉

Wu Hsing-hua 吳興華 (Liang Wen-hsin 梁文星)

Wu Mi 吳宓

Wu P'ei-fu 吳佩孚

Wu Tsu-kuang 吳祖光
The Song of Righteousness 正氣歌

Wu Wen-tsao 吳文藻

Yang Chiang 楊絳

Yang Shuo 楊朔
A Thousand Miles of Lovely Land 三千里 江山

Yang Ts'un-jen 楊邨人

Yao Hsüeh-yin 姚雪垠

Yao P'eng-tzu 姚蓬子

Yeh Kung-ch'ao 葉公超

Yeh T'ing 葉挺

Yen Fu 嚴復

Yen Hsi-shan 閻錫山

Yen Hsüeh 晏學

Yin Fu 殷夫 (Pai Mang 白莽)

Yin Kuang 印光

Yü Kuan-ying 余冠英

Yü P'ing-po 俞平伯
Studies in Dream of the Red Chamber 紅樓夢研究

Yüan Shui-p'o 袁水拍
Mountain Ballads of Ma Fan-t'o 馬凡陀的山歌

Yüeh Ssu-ping 樂嗣炳

Yün Tai-ying 惲代英

III

Awakening 覺悟

Big Dipper 北斗

Book of Changes 易經

Book of Poetry 詩經

Brother and Sister Tilling Virgin Soil 兄妹開荒

Bureaucracy Exposed
官場現形記

Chan K'ai 展開

Chieh-fang-chün Wen-i
解放軍文藝

Chin P'ing Mei 金瓶梅

Chinese Youth 中國青年

Chuang Tzu 莊子

   "Autumn Floods" 秋水

   "Horses' Hoofs" 馬蹄

Creation Daily 創造日

Cultural Critique 文化批判

Cultural Gazette (Harbin)
文化報

Deluge 洪水

Hope 希望

Hsin Min Pao (Chengtu)
新民報

I Wen 譯文

Jen Ch'ien 人間月刊

Jen-jen Wen-hsüeh 人人文學

Journey to the West 西遊記

July 七月

K'o-hsüeh yü Jen-sheng-kuan
科學與人生觀

Li Pao (Hong Kong) 立報

Liberation Daily (Yenan)
解放日報

Lien-ho P'ing-lun (Hong Kong)
聯合評論

Life of Wu Hsün 武訓傳

Literary News 文藝新聞

Literary Study 文藝學習

Miscellany of Mass Literature
大眾文藝叢刊

Mass Literature 大眾文藝

Middle School Student 中學生

Modern Fiction 現代小說

National Daily, The (Hankow)
民國日報

New Current 新流月報

New Life 新生

Pathfinder 拓荒者

Peking Ch'en Pao 北京晨報

Peking Literature 北京文藝

Pen Liu 奔流

People's Daily, The (Peking)
人民日報

Realistic Literature
現實文學

Red and Black 紅黑月刊

Shao-nien Chung-kuo
少年中國

Shen Pao (Shanghai) 申報
　Tzu-yu T'an 自由談

Shih-wu Kuan 十五貫

Social Daily, The (Shanghai)
社會日報

Sprout 萌芽

Starting Point 起點

Ta-chung Sheng-huo 大眾生活

Ta Kung Pao (Tientsin and Shanghai) 大公報

Ta Wan Pao (Shanghai)
大晚報

　Huo-chü 火炬

T'ai Pai 太白

T'ai-shang Kan-ying P'ien
太上感應篇

Travels of Lao Ts'an
老殘遊記

Tso-chia Yüeh-k'an 作家月刊

Tzu-yu Chung-kuo 自由中國

Tz'u Yüan 辭源

Unofficial History of the Literati
儒林外史

Water Margin 水滸傳

Wen Hsüan 文選

Wen-hsüeh Chieh 文學界

Wen-hsüeh Yüeh-pao (Literature
Monthly) 文學月報

Wen Hui Pao (Shanghai)
文匯報

Women's Magazine
婦女雜誌

Wen-i Shih-tai
文藝時代

World Culture 世界文化

World Today 今日世界

IV

cheng-feng 整風

ch'i-liang 凄涼

ch'i-tzu chen 七子針

chü-jen 舉人

chüeh-fa jen-hsin 掘發人心

chuang-yüan 狀元

fan-jung 繁榮

fu-yen 敷衍

hsia 俠

hsiao-chieh 小姐

hsing-ling 性靈

hua-hsia 華夏

ku-yeh 姑爺

ku-t'ai-t'ai 姑太太

k'un-ch'ü 崑曲

kuo-yü 國語

lao-hao-jen 老好人

lao-yeh 老爺

latinxua 拉丁化

li 禮

li-shih 理事

liu-tzu lien 六子連

mou 畝

pa-kua-ch'üan 八卦拳

pai-hua 白話

p'u-t'ung-hua 普通話

shao-nai-nai 少奶奶

shih-k'uai 市儈

sin wenz 新文字

ta-chung wen-i 大眾文藝

ta-chung-yü 大眾語

t'ai-t'ai 太太

ta-ku 大鼓

tang-tsu 黨組

tsa-kan 雜感

tsa-wen 雜文

tsai-tao 載道

ts'ang-liang 蒼涼

ts'u-pao 粗暴

wen-yen 文言

yamen 衙門

yen-chih 言志

Bibliography

UNLESS otherwise noted, all Chinese publications in this bibliography are understood to have been published in Shanghai. I have not given the names of Chinese publishers; specialists, with access to large Chinese collections in libraries, can easily obtain this information if interested. For Chinese books I have recorded the publication dates of first editions whenever this information was available. When it was not available, the publication dates of the editions actually consulted by me are entered.

I. Modern Chinese Literature: Surveys and Studies

A

Ayers, William. "The Society for Literary Studies, 1921–1930," *Papers on China* (mimeo.), *8*. Harvard University, Center for East Asian Studies, 1953.

Birch, Cyril. "Fiction of the Yenan Period," *The China Quarterly*, No. 4 (October–December 1960).

————, ed. *Chinese Communist Literature*. New York, 1963.

Borowitz, Albert. *Fiction in Communist China 1949–1953* (mimeo.). Massachusettes Institute of Technology, Center for International Studies, 1954.

Chao Chung. *The Communist Program for Literature and Art in China*. Hong Kong, 1955.

Chow Tse-tsung. *The May Fourth Movement: Intellectual Revolution in Modern China*. Cambridge, Mass., 1960.

Chu, Fu-sung. "Wartime Chinese Literature," in *China: After Seven Years of War*, ed. Hollington K. Tong. New York, 1945.

Bibliography

Fokkema, D. W. "Chinese Literature Under the Cultural Revolution," *Literature East and West, 13,* Nos. 3-4 (December 1969).

————. *Literary Doctrine in China and Soviet Influence, 1956–60.* The Hague, 1965.

Frenz, Horst, ed. *Asia and the Humanities.* Bloomington, 1959. Contains Chun-Jo Liu, "People, Places, and Time in Five Modern Chinese Novels," and David Y. Chen, "The Trilogy of Ts'ao Yü and Western Drama."

Giles, Herbert A. *A History of Chinese Literature.* With a continuation by Liu Wu-chi. New York, 1966.

Goldman, Merle. "Hu Feng's Conflict with the Communist Literary Authorities," *Papers on China* (mimeo.), *11.* Harvard University, Center for East Asian Studies, 1957.

————. *Literary Dissent in Communist China.* Cambridge, Mass., 1967.

————. "The Fall of Chou Yang," *The China Quarterly,* No. 27 (July–September 1966).

Hightower, James R. "The Literary Revolution," chapter 17 in *Topics in Chinese Literature.* Rev. ed. Cambridge, Mass., 1953.

Hsia, C. T. "On the 'Scientific' Study of Modern Chinese Literature," *T'oung Pao, 50,* Nos. 4-5 (1963).

Hsia, Tsi-an. *The Gate of Darkness: Studies on the Leftist Literary Movement in China.* Seattle and London, 1968.

Hsiao Ch'ien. *Etching of a Tormented Age: A Glimpse of Contemporary Chinese Literature.* London, 1942.

Hu Shih. *The Chinese Renaissance.* Chicago, 1934.

Huang Sung-k'ang. *Lu Hsün and the New Culture Movement of Modern China.* Amsterdam, 1957.

Li, Tien-yi. "Continuity and Change in Modern Chinese Literature," *Annals of the American Academy of Political and Social Science, 321,* January 1959.

Liu, Chun-jo. "The Heroes and Heroines of Modern Chinese Fiction: From Ah Q to Wu Tzu-hsü," *Journal of Asian Studies, 16,* No. 2 (February 1957).

Mei, Yi-tsi. "Tradition and Experiment in Modern Chinese Literature," in *Indiana University Conference on Oriental-Western*

Literary Relations, ed. Horst Frenz and G. L. Anderson. Chapel Hill, 1955.

Monsterleet, Jean. *Sommets de la littérature chinoise contemporaine.* Paris. Translated into Chinese by Chu Yü-jen 朱煜仁 as *Hsin-wen-hsüeh chien-shih* 新文學簡史 . Hong Kong, 1953.

———— "Contemporary Chinese Letters," *Books Abroad, 28,* summer 1954.

Moy, Clarence. "Kuo Mo-jo and the Creation Society," *Papers on China* (mimeo.), *4.* Harvard University, Center for East Asian Studies, 1950.

Phelps, D. L. "Letters and Arts in the War Years," chapter 27 in *China,* ed. H. F. MacNair. Berkeley and Los Angeles, 1946.

Pollard, D. E. "Chou Tso-jen and Cultivating One's Own Garden," *Asia Major,* n.s. *11,* Pt. 2 (1965).

Prüšek, Jaroslav. *Die Literatur des befreiten China and ihre Volks-traditionen.* Prague, 1955.

————. "Subjectivism and Individualism in Modern Chinese Literature," *Archiv Orientálini, 25* (1957).

————, ed. *Studies in Modern Chinese Literature.* Berlin, 1964. Some articles in German.

Schyns, Jos., et al., ed. *1500 Modern Chinese Novels and Plays.* Peiping, 1948. Contains Su Hsüeh-lin, "Present Day Fiction and Drama in China," and Chao Yen-sheng 趙燕聲 , "Short Biographies of Authors."

Scott, A. C. *Literature and the Arts in Twentieth Century China.* New York, 1963.

Tagore, Amitendranath. *Literary Debates in Modern China,* 1918–1937. Tokyo, 1967.

van Boven, Henri. *Histoire de la littérature chinoise moderne.* Peiping, 1946.

Wales, Nym. "The Modern Literary Movement," appendix A in *Living China: Modern Chinese Short Stories,* ed. Edgar Snow. New York, 1936.

Yang I-fan. *The Case of Hu Feng.* Hong Kong, 1956.

B

Chang Pi-lai 張畢來. 新文學史綱 第一卷(A Short History of Modern Chinese Literature. Vol. 1: The First Period). Peking, 1956.

Cheng Hsüeh-chia 鄭學稼. 由文學革命到革文學的命 (From Literary Revolution to Literary Strangulation). Hong Kong, 1953.

Chu Kuang-ch'ien 朱光潛. 現代中國文學 (Contemporary Chinese Literature), *Wen-hsüeh Tsa-chih*, 2, No. 8 (Peiping, 1948).

Fu Tung-hua 傅東華. 十年來的中國文學 (Chinese Literature of the Last Ten Years), in 十年來的中國 (China: The Last Ten Years), ed. Fan Chung-yün 樊仲雲. 1937.

Kuo Chen-i 郭箴一. 中國小說史 下冊 (A History of Chinese Fiction, Vol. 2). Changsha, 1939.

Lan Hai 藍海. 中國抗戰文藝史(A History of Chinese Literature during the War of Resistance). 1947.

Li Ho-lin 李何林. 近二十年中國文藝思潮論(Chinese Literary Thought of the Past Twenty Years). Chungking and Shanghai, 1939.

Li Ho-lin et al. 中國新文學史研究 (Studies in Modern Chinese Literary History). Peking, 1951.

Liu Shou-sung 劉綬松. 中國新文學史初稿 (History of Modern Chinese Literature: A Preliminary Draft). 2 vols. Peking, 1956.

Ting Miao 丁淼. 評中共文藝代表作 (Representative Chinese Communist Works Examined). Hong Kong, 1953.

—— 中共文藝總批判 (A Comprehensive Critique of Chinese Communist Literature). Hong Kong, 1954.

—— 中共統戰戲劇 (Chinese Communist Drama of the Coalition Period). Hong Kong, 1954.

Ting I 丁易. 中國現代文學史略 (A Brief History of Modern Chinese Literature). Peking, 1957.

Ts'ai I 蔡儀. 中國新文學史講話 (Lectures on Modern Chinese Literary History). 1952.

Ts'ao Chü-jen 曹聚仁. 文壇五十年 (Fifty Years of Chinese Literature). 2 vols. Hong Kong, 1955–56.

Tung-fang Chi-pai 東方既白. 在陰黯矛盾中演變的大陸文藝 (The Dismal and Contradiction-filled Pattern of the Changing Literature on the Mainland), *Tzu-yu chung-kuo, 20*, Nos. 7–9 (Taipei, 1959).

Wang Chê-fu 王哲甫. 中國新文學運動史 (A History of the New Literary Movement in China). Peiping, 1933.

Wang Yao 王瑶. 中國新文學史稿 (A Draft History of Modern Chinese Literature). 2 vols. 1951–53.

Wu Ch'i-yüan 伍啟元. 中國新文化運動概觀 (A Guide through the New Culture Movement in China). 1934.

II. ANTHOLOGIES AND REFERENCE WORKS

A

Acton, Harold and Ch'en Shih-hsiang, trans. *Modern Chinese Poetry*. London, 1936.

Boorman, Howard L., ed. *Biographical Dictionary of Republican China*. 4 vols. New York, 1967–70.

Chai, Ch'u, and Winberg Chai, trans. and eds. *A Treasury of Chinese Literature*. New York, 1965.

Davidson, Martha, comp. *A List of Published Translations from Chinese into English, French, and German*. Part I: Literature, Exclusive of Poetry; Ann Arbor, 1952. Part II: Poetry; New Haven, 1957.

Fairbank, J. K., and K. C. Liu. *Modern China: A Bibliographical Guide to Chinese Works*. Cambridge, Mass., 1950.

Hsu, Kai-yu, trans. *Twentieth Century Chinese Poetry*. New York, 1963.

Kao, George, trans. and ed. *Chinese Wit and Humor*. New York, 1946. Pages 267–344 contain translations from the modern period.

Kyn Yn Yu. *The Tragedy of Ah Qui and Other Modern Chinese Stories*. Trans. from the French into English by E. H. F. Mills. London, 1930.

Life and Letters & the London Mercury, 60, No. 137 (January 1949). Special number on contemporary Chinese literature.

Payne, Robert, ed. *Contemporary Chinese Poetry*. London, 1947.

Perleberg, Max. *Who's Who in Modern China, from the Beginning of the Chinese Republic to the End of 1953*. Hong Kong, 1954.

Snow, Edgar. *Living China: Modern Chinese Short Stories*. New York, 1936.

Wang, Chi-chen, trans. *Contemporary Chinese Stories*. New York, 1944.
———, ed. *Stories of China at War*. New York, 1946.

Wu, Eugene. *Leaders of Twentieth-century China*. An Annotated Bibliography of Selected Chinese Biographical Works in the Hoover Library. Stanford, 1956.

Yeh, Chun-chan, trans. *Three Seasons and Other Stories.* London, 1946.

Yuan Chia-hua and Robert Payne, trans. *Contemporary Chinese Short Stories.* London, 1946.

Yuan, Tung-Li, comp. *China in Western Literature: A Continuation of Cordier's Bibliotheca Sinica.* New Haven, 1958. Contains an exhaustive bibliography of English, French, and German book-length studies in and translations of Chinese literature published during the period 1921–57. Recent titles published by the Foreign Languages Press, Peking, are included in its listing of modern Chinese fiction in translation.

B

Chang Ching-lu 張靜廬, ed. 中國近代出版史料 (Bibliographical and Historical Materials Concerning Chinese Publications of the Recent Past). Vol. 1, 1953. Vol. 2, Peking, 1957. Covers the period 1862–1918.

———, ed. 中國現代出版史料 (Bibliographical and Historical Materials Concerning Contemporary Chinese Publications) Peking, 1954–57. Vol. 1: 1919–27; Vol. 2: 1927–37; Vol. 3: 1937–49.

———, ed. 中國出版史料補編 (Addenda to Bibliographical and Historical Materials Concerning Chinese Publications). Peking, 1957. These six volumes by Chang Ching-lu constitute an invaluable bibliographical guide to Chinese publications 1862–1949, with especially full coverage of leftist and Communist publications.

Chang Jo-ying 張若英 (錢杏邨). 中國新文學運動史資料 (Source Materials on the History of the Modern Literary Movement in China). 1934.

Bibliography

Chao Chia-pi 趙家壁, ed. 中國新文學大系 (A Comprehensive Anthology of Modern Chinese Literature: 1917–27. 10 vols. 1935–36.

1. 建設理論集 (Toward a Constructive Literary Theory), ed. Hu Shih.

2. 文學論爭集 (Literary Debates), ed. Cheng Chen-to 鄭振鐸.

3. 小說一集 (Fiction, 1st Series), ed. Mao Tun.

4. 小說二集 (Fiction, 2d Series), ed. Lu Hsün.

5. 小說三集 (Fiction, 3d Series), ed. Cheng Po-ch'i 鄭伯奇.

6. 散文一集 (Essays, 1st Series), ed. Chou Tso-jen.

7. 散文二集 (Essays, 2d Series), ed. Yü Ta-fu.

8. 詩集 (Poetry), ed. Chu Tzu-ch'ing 朱自清.

9. 戲劇集 (Plays), ed. Hung Shen 洪深.

10. 史料索引 (Source Materials and Indices), ed. A Ying 阿英 (錢杏邨). Contains selections from Hu Shih, 五十年來中國之文學 (Chinese Literature during the Last Fifty Years), and Ch'en Tzu-chan, 陳子展, 最近三十年來中國文學史 (Chinese Literature during the Last Thirty Years).

Chao Ch'ing-ko 趙清閣, ed. 無題集 (Without a Title: Stories by Contemporary Chinese Women Writers). 1947.

Hsia Mien-tsun 夏丏尊, ed. 十年 (A Decade). One-vol. ed. 1938.

Mao Tun, Pa Chin, et al. 創作小説第一集 (Stories, First Series). Shen Pao Yüeh-k'an shê, 1933.

III. INFLUENTIAL MAGAZINES (listed in chronological order)

新青年 (La Jeunesse, or New Youth). During its most influential period, 1915–21, its prominent editor was Ch'en Tu-hsiu.

新潮 (The Renaissance). Ed. Fu Ssu-nien 傅斯年 and Lo Chia-lun 羅家倫. Peking, 1919–21.

小説月報 (The Short Story Magazine). The chief organ of the Literary Association for the period 1921–32. Edited, in succession, by Shen Yen-ping, Cheng Chen-to, and Yeh Shao-chün.

學衡 (The Critical Review). The chief members of the Hsüeh Heng Shê were Mei Kuang-ti 梅光廸, Wu Mi 吳宓, and Hu Hsien-su 胡先驌. Nanking, then Peiping, 1922–33.

創造季刊 (Creation Quarterly). An organ of the Creation Society. 1922–24.

創造週報 (Creation Weekly). An organ of the Creation Society. 1923–24.

語絲 (Yü Ssu Weekly). The prominent members of the Yü Ssu Shê were Lu Hsün and Chou Tso-jen. 1924–31.

現代評論 (Contemporary Review). Ed. Ch'en Yüan. 1924–28.

創造月刊 (Creation Monthly). An organ of the Creation Society. 1926–28.

新月 (The Crescent Moon Monthly). The chief members of the

Crescent Moon Society were Hsü Chih-mo, Liang Shih-ch'iu, Hu Shih. 1928–33.

太陽月刊 (The Sun Monthly). The chief members of the Sun Society were Chiang Kuang-tz'u and Ch'ien Hsing-ts'un. 1928.

現代 (Les Contemporains). A monthly edited by Shih Chih-ts'un and Tu Heng (Su Wen). 1932–34.

論語 (The Analects Fortnightly). Founder, Lin Yutang. 1932–37; revived, 1946–48.

文學 (Literature). A prominent leftist magazine edited by Fu Tung-hua 博東華 and later, Wang T'ung-chao 王統照. 1933–37.

大公報星期文藝 (*Ta Kung Pao* Sunday Literary Supplement). Edited, in succession, by Shen Ts'ung-wen and Hsiao Ch'ien for the period 1934–37. The postwar editor was Chin I 靳以.

人間世 (This Human World, a fortnightly). Founder, Lin Yutang. 1934–35.

文學季刊 (Literature Quarterly). Ed. Cheng Chen-to and Chin I. Peiping, 1934–35.

文季月刊 (Wen-chi Yüeh-k'an). A monthly edited by Pa Chin and Chin I. Peiping, 1935–37.

宇宙風 (The Cosmic Wind, a fortnightly). Founder, Lin Yutang. 1935–47.

T'ien Hsia Monthly (天下). The best English journal launched by Chinese intellectuals. Among its contributors were John C. H. Wu 吳經熊, Wen Yüan-ning 溫源寧, Yao K'o 姚克, Ch'ien

Chung-shu. Translation of modern Chinese fiction, drama, and poetry. 1935–41.

文學雜誌(Wen-hsüeh Tsa-chih). A monthly edited by Chu Kuang-ch'ien in 1937 and then revived by him for the period 1947–48.

文藝陣地(Wen-i Chen-ti). A wartime literary journal published at first in Hankow in 1938, then in Canton, Hong Kong, and Chung-king. Edited by Mao Tun and others.

抗戰文藝(K'ang-chan Wen-i). The chief organ of the Chinese Writers' Anti-aggression Association. First published in Changsha in 1938 with Tsang K'o-chia 臧克家 as editor, and then moved to Chungking under the editorship of Lao Shê and Yao P'eng-tzu 姚蓬子.

大眾文藝(Ta-chung Wen-i). The most important journal of the wartime Communist-area writers. Edited in Yenan by Ho Ch'i-fang 何其芳, Chou Wen 周文, Ting Ling, and Liu Pai-yü 劉白羽.

文藝雜誌(Wen-i Tsa-chih). A wartime journal in Kweilin edited until his death in 1945 by Wang Lu-yen 王魯彥.

天地(T'ien Ti Fortnightly). The best literary journal in occupied Shanghai. Edited by Su Ch'ing 蘇青 (pen name of Feng Ho-i 馮和儀).

文藝生活(Wen-i Sheng-huo). Edited by Ssu-ma Wen-sen 司馬

文森 . First published in Kweilin during the war; then banned; then re-published after the war in Canton and Hong Kong. An important Communist journal.

Philobiblon. A quarterly review of Chinese publications edited by Chiang Fu-ts'ung 蔣復璁 and Ch'ien Chung-shu. Published by the National Central Library, Nanking, for the period 1946–48.

文藝復興 (Literary Renaissance). The outstanding postwar monthly. 1946–48. Edited by Cheng Chen-to and Li Chien-wu 李健吾 .

小説月刊 (Fiction Monthly). A postwar journal edited by Mao Tun and others. Hong Kong and Shanghai, 1948–1951(?).

人民文學 (People's Literature). The most important literary monthly in Communist China. Edited by Mao Tun with many assistants, 1949–53; since July 1953, Shao Ch'üan-lin 邵荃麟 , Yen Wen-ching 嚴文井 , and Chang T'ien-i have served, in succession, as chief editors.

文藝報 (The Literary Gazette). The most important critical review in Communist China. Among its early editors were Ting Ling and Feng Hsüeh-feng. Editor-in-chief, as of 1958: Chang Kuang-nien 張光年 .

文學雜誌 (Literary Review). The most vital literary journal for its time in Taipei, 1956–60. Edited by Hsia Tsi-an 夏濟安. In 1959 Hou Chien 侯健 became co-editor.

IV. WORKS BY CHINESE CRITICS:
DISCUSSIONS OF MODERN CHINESE CULTURE AND LITERATURE,
STUDIES IN CONTEMPORARY AUTHORS,
AND LITERARY THEORIES AND POLEMICS

Chao Ching-shen 趙景深. 文人剪影 (Silhouettes of Authors).
1936.

Ch'en Hsi-ying (Ch'en Yüan) 陳源. 西瀅閒話 (The Causeries of
Hsi-ying). 1928. Brilliant essays on contemporary Chinese culture,
politics, and literature.

Ch'en Tu-hsiu 陳獨秀. 獨秀文存 (Collected Essays of Tu-hsiu)
4 vols. in 2. 1927.

Ch'en Tuan-chih 陳端志. 五四運動之史的評價 (A His-
torical Evaluation of the May Fourth Movement). 1935. Uses the
Marxist approach.

Cheng Chen-to 鄭振鐸. 疴僂集 (The Hunchback). 1934.

Ch'ien Hsing-ts'un 錢杏邨. 現代中國文學作家 (Con-
temporary Chinese Writers). 2 vols. 1929–30. Appraisals of Lu
Hsün, Kuo Mo-jo. Chiang Kuang-tz'u, Yü Ta-fu, Chang Tzu-p'ing,
Mao Tun, and Hsü Chih-mo.

Chou Tso-jen. 周作人. 中國新文學的源流 (The Origins of
Modern Chinese Literature). Peiping, 1932. The author has also
written pertinent criticism on contemporary Chinese and Japanese
literature in his many collections of essays.

Chou Yang 周揚 · 馬克斯主義與文藝 (Marxism and Literature). Dairen, 1946.

—— 表現新的群眾的時代(To Express the New Age of the Masses). Chiamussú, 1948.

—— 堅決貫澈毛澤東文藝路線(Resolutely Implement the Mao Tse-tung Line in Literature). Peking, 1952.

—— *China's New Literature and Art.* Peking, 1954.

Chu Kuang-ch'ien. 孟實文鈔 (The Essays of Meng-shih). 1935.

—— 文藝心理學(The Psychology of Art). 1936. An influential manual of aesthetics.

Ch'ü Ch'iu-pai 瞿秋白 · 亂彈 (Random Plunking). 1949. A collection of the author's critical and polemic writings.

—— 瞿秋白文集 (Collected Writings and Translations of Ch'ü Ch'iu-pai). 8 vols. in 4. Peking, 1953–54.

Feng Hsüeh-feng 馮雪峯 · 論民主革命的文藝運動 (The Literary Movement of the Democratic Revolution). 1949.

—— 馮雪峯論文集 (Collected Essays of Feng Hsüeh-feng). Peking, 1953.

Fu Tung-hua. 山胡桃集 (Walnuts). 1935. A collection of essays, some critical in nature.

Han Shih-heng 韓侍桁 · 文學評論集 (Essays in Literary Criticism). 1934.

Han Shih-heng. 參差集 (Unequal Essays). 1935.

Ho Yü-po 賀玉波. 現代中國作家論 (Studies in Modern Chinese Writers). 2 vols. 1932. Appraisals of Mao Tun, Chang Tzu-p'ing, Yeh Shao-chün, Pa Chin, Shen Ts'ung-wen, and others. Very plodding criticism.

Hsia Cheng-nung 夏征農. 新形勢下的文藝與文藝工作者 (Literature and Literary Workers in a New Age). Harbin, 1948.

Hsü Chih-mo 徐志摩. 落葉 (Fallen Leaves). 1926. Essays and addresses by a distinguished early poet.

Hu Feng 胡風. 文藝筆談 (Literary Essays). 1936.

—— 密雲期風習小記 (The Gathering Clouds: the Manners of a Period). 1938.

—— 論民族形式問題 (On the Problem of National Forms). Chungking, 1940.

—— 民族戰爭與文藝性格 (The National Struggle and Literature). Chungking, 1945.

—— 在混亂裏面 (In a Muddle). Chungking, 1945.

—— 逆流的日子 (Stemming the Adverse Current). 1947.

—— 論現實主義的路 (On the Path of Realism). 1948.

—— 劍，文藝，人民 (Sword, Literature, and People). 1950.

—— 胡風對文藝問題的意見 (Hu Feng's Literary Opinions). A Supplement to the January 1955 number of *Wen-i Pao*.

Hu Shih 胡適. 胡適文存 (Collected Essays of Hu Shih). 1st ser.

657

2 vols. 1921; 2d ser. 2 vols. 1924; 3d ser. 2 vols. 1930. Of monumental importance toward an understanding of modern Chinese literature and thought.

Huang Jen-ying 黃人影, comp. 創造社論 (Critiques of the Creation Society). 1932.

Huang Ying (Huang Lu-yin) 黃英 (黃廬隱). 現代中國女作家 (Contemporary Chinese Women Writers). 1931. On Ping Hsin, Huang Lu-yin, Ling Shu-hua, and Ting Ling.

Kuo Mo-jo 郭沫若. 沫若文集 (The Works of Kuo Mo-jo). In progress. Peking, 1956– . Vol. 11, 1959.

—— 文藝論集 (Studies in Literature). 1925.

—— 天地玄黃 (Heaven and Earth). Dairen, 1948.

—— 今昔蒲劍 (Chin-hsi P'u-chien). 1949.

Li Ch'ang-chih 李長之. 迎中國的文藝復興 (Welcome the Literary Renaissance in China). Chungking, 1944.

Li Ho-lin, comp. 中國文藝論戰 (Literary Polemics in China). 3d printing 1930.

Li Kuang-t'ien 李廣田. 詩的藝術 (The Art of Poetry). 1944.

—— 灌木集 (Shrubs). 1946.

—— 文學枝葉 (The Leaves and Branches of Literature). 1948. Poet, essayist, and novelist, the author was early associated with Pien Chih-lin and Ho Ch'i-fang.

Li Lin 李霖, comp. 郭沫若評傳 (Kuo Mo-jo: Critical and Biographical Studies). 1932.

Li Nan-cho 李南桌 · 文藝論文集 (Literary Essays). Includes a preface by Mao Tun, entitled 悼李南桌 (Li Nan-cho: In Memoriam). Chungking and Hong Kong, 1939.

Liang Shih-ch'iu 梁實秋 · 浪漫的與古典的(Romantic and Classic). 1927.

—— 文學的紀律(The Literary Discipline). 1928.

—— 偏見集(Prejudices). 1934.

Liang Tsung-tai 梁宗岱 · 詩與真 (Poetry and Truth). 1935. Essays on poetry by a follower of Goethe and Valéry.

Lin Huan-p'ing 林煥平 · 抗戰文藝評論集 (Critical Essays on Wartime Literature). Hong Kong, 1939.

Liu Hsi-wei 劉西渭 (pen name of Li Chien-wu 李健吾). 咀華集 (Chü-hua Chi). 1936.

—— 咀華二集 (Chü-hua Erh-chi). 1941. Although rated as an important critic, Li Chien-wu is too impressionistic and generous in his appraisal of his contemporaries to merit serious attention, though his two volumes of criticism are admittedly superior to most Marxist-orientated studies. A French-returned student and author of a critical biography on Flaubert, Li Chien-wu was also a popular playwright during the war.

Mao Tse-tung 毛澤東 · 在延安文藝座談會上的講話 (Talks at the Yenan Literary Conference), in 毛澤東選集第三卷 (The Selected Works of Mao Tse-tung, 3). Peking, 1953. The author's other writings, especially 新民主主義 (The

New Democracy), are also helpful toward an understanding of the Communist concept of modern Chinese literature, and of the present state of Communist writing.

Mao Tun et al. 作家論 (On Writers). 1936. Includes Mao Tun's essays on Lo Hua-sheng, Ping Hsin, Wang Lu-yen, and Hsü Chih-mo; Hu Feng's essays on Lin Yutang and Chang T'ien-i; and Su Hsüeh-lin's essay on Shen Ts'ung-wen.

Pa Jen 巴人 · 文學論稿(A Tentative Treatise on Literature). 2 vols. 1954. Perhaps the most coherent and detailed presentation of the Marxist theory of literature by a Chinese critic, drawing upon a wealth of traditional and contemporary Chinese literature for illustrations.

Shao Ch'üan-lin 邵荃麟, Hu Sheng 胡繩, et al. 大衆文藝叢刊批評論文選集 (Selected Critical Essays from *Miscellany of Mass Literature*). Peking. 1949. Includes articles by Mao Tun, Ting Ling, and Feng Nai-ch'ao 馮乃超 ·

Shen Ts'ung-wen and Hsiao Ch'ien. 廢郵存底 (Letters Saved from Oblivion). 1937. A sampling of letters by the editors of the *Ta Kung Pao* Literary Supplement in reply to their readers, this volume contains some trenchant criticism on the state of Chinese writing in the thirties.

Shih Chien 史劍 · 郭沫若批判 (Kuo Mo-jo: A Critique). Hong Kong, 1954.

Bibliography

Shih Chih-ts'un 施蟄存 · 燈下集 (Under the Lamp). 1937. A volume of essays by a distinguished story-writer and editor.

Ssu-ma Wen-sen 司馬文森 , ed. 作家印象記 (Impressions of Authors). Hong Kong, 1950.

—— ed. 創作經驗 (Writers on Their Craft). Hong Kong, 1948. Both volumes are selections from *Wen-i Sheng-huo*, edited by Ssu-ma Wen-sen.

Su Hsüeh-lin 蘇雪林 · 青鳥集 (The Blue Bird). 1938. Contains valuable articles on Chou Tso-jen and Hsü Chih-mo.

Su Wen 蘇汶 (pen name of Tai K'o-ch'ung 戴克崇), ed. 文藝自由論辯集 (Debates on the Freedom of Writers). 1933.

Ta K'ai 達凱 · 論中共文藝政策及其活動 (On the Chinese Communist Literary Policy and Its Implementation). Hong Kong, 1952.

Wang P'ing-ling 王平陵 · 新狂飆時代 (The New Age of Storm and Stress). Chungking, 1943. The author is a veteran Kuomintang writer, still active in Taiwan today.

Yang Yen-nan 楊燕南 · 中共對胡風的鬥爭 (The Persecution of Hu Feng by Chinese Communists). Hong Kong, 1956.

V. NOVELISTS AND STORY-WRITERS

In this section I have attempted to give, among other things, the titles of books by the twenty fiction writers who have received individual attention in the present study. While the coverage of fiction is fairly complete, I have not otherwise aimed at thoroughness: translations and scholarly works by these authors are generally omitted. Many titles listed below are out of print and their publishers have gone out of business, following the successful establishment of the publishing industry as a government monopoly on the mainland in the early fifties. However, a great majority of these titles will be found in the libraries of major American universities.

For years, the Peking Government was wary of reprinting, in any extensive fashion, the pre-1949 modern Chinese literature: up to 1954 the only authors whose complete works were available were Lu Hsün, Wen I-to, and Ch'ü Ch'iu-pai. Since 1956, however, a change of policy has been discernible in the more ambitious publication program of the People's Literature Press (人民文學出版社); by 1958 the latter had brought near completion the collected writings (*wen-chi*) of Kuo Mo-jo (see Bibliography IV), Mao Tun, Pa Chin, and Yeh Shao-chün (see below). But one must use these editions with caution because many of the pre-1949 works of these authors may have been subject to silent revision.

For those who want to read a sampling of the listed fiction writers in the original, two series of anthologies are recommended. In 1948 the Chinese Writers' Association (中華全國文藝協會) published through the Ch'un Ming Book Co. (春明書局), Shanghai, a Library of Contemporary Authors (現代作家文叢). Among the authors chosen are Lu Hsün, Mao Tun, Yü Ta-fu, Yeh Shao-chün, Pa Chin, Ting Ling, and Chang T'ien-i. This set of *wen-chi* (文集) is to be preferred to the better-known Library of Modern Literature (新文學選集), published by the Editorial Committee of the Library of Modern Literature, under the general editorship of Mao Tun, through the Kaiming Press (開明書店). In 1951–52, the Committee published two series of dead and living authors, among them Lu Hsün, Yü Ta-fu, Hsü Ti-shan (Lo Hua-sheng), Chiang Kuang-tz'u, Mao Tun, Yeh Shao-chün, Ting Ling, Pa Chin, Lao Shê, Chang T'ien-i, and Chao Shu-li. However, these *hsüan-chi* (選集) hardly represent each author at his best, as only those items which are least reproachable from the viewpoint of the present government are included.

The best guide to modern Chinese fiction in translation is Martha Davidson, *A List of Published Translations from Chinese*, *1* (see above, Bibliography II). However, even this diligent compilation hasn't tracked down all the translated items of fiction that could be found in obscure journals through the years. The *List,* of course, takes no notice of the many translations of recent Communist as well as earlier modern works turned out by the Foreign Languages Press in Peking in the last few years. The interested reader should consult the recent annual bibliographies prepared by the *Journal of Asian Studies* (formerly the *Far Eastern Quarterly*) for the relevant titles in English or Russian. He is also advised to consult *Chinese Literature,* an English journal published by the Foreign Languages Press and edited by Mao Tun. Since its initial appearance in 1951, it has translated a great deal of contemporary Chinese writing.

For the commonly available anthologies of modern Chinese fiction, I have adopted the following abbreviations:

Kin Yn Yu: Kin Yn Yu, *The Tragedy of Ah Qui and Other Modern Chinese Stories.*

Snow: Edgar Snow, *Living China.*

Wang: Chi-chen Wang, *Contemporary Chinese Stories.*

China at War: Chi-chen Wang, *Stories of China at War.*

Yuan and Payne: Yuan Chia-hua and Robert Payne, *Contemporary Chinese Short Stories.*

1. Lu Hsün 鲁迅 (Chou Shu-jen 周樹人)

A. Works

鲁迅全集 (The Complete Works of Lu Hsün). 20 vols. 1938.

鲁迅全集補遺 (Addenda to the Complete Works of Lu Hsün), ed. T'ang T'ao 唐弢 . 2 vols.: Vol. 1, 1946; Vol. 2, 1952.

鲁迅書簡 (The Letters of Lu Hsün), ed. Hsü Kuang-p'ing 許廣平 . 2 vols. in 1, Peking, 2d ed. 1952.

B. Translations

Wang, Chi-chen. *Ah Q and Others.* New York, 1941.

Yang Hsien-yi and Gladys Yang, trans. *Selected Works of Lu Hsün.*

2 vols. Peking, 1956–57. For other translations of the author's stories see Kin Yn Yu, Snow, Wang, Yuan and Payne.

C. *Critiques and Biographies*

For a more inclusive list of books see Eugene Wu, *Leaders of Twentieth-century China: IV, D.* Huang Sung-k'ang's *Lu Hsün and the New Culture Movement of Modern China,* which adopts the orthodox Communist interpretation of the author with little deviation, also contains a rather full list. However, by far the most exhaustive bibliography is Shen P'eng-nien 沈鵬年, 魯迅研究資料編目 (A Catalogue of Research Materials on Lu Hsün), Peking, 1958.

Brière, O. "Un Écrivain populaire: Lou Sin," *Bulletin de l'Université l'Aurore, 3,* No. 7, Shanghai, 1946.

Cheng Hsüeh-chia 鄭學稼. 魯迅正傳 (The True Story of Lu Hsün). Hong Kong, 1953.

Chinnery, J. D. "The Influence of Western Literature on Lu Xún's 'Diary of A Madman,'" *Bulletins of the School of Oriental and African Studies, 23* (1960).

Chou Hsia-shou 周遐壽 (Chou Tso-jen). 魯迅的故家 (Lu Hsün's Old Home). 1953.

——— 魯迅小說裡的人物(The Characters in Lu Hsün's Fiction). 1954.

Feng Hsüeh-feng. 回憶魯迅 (Lu Hsün: A Memoir). Peking, 1952.

Hsü Chieh 許傑. 魯迅小說講話 (Lectures on the Stories of Lu Hsün). 1951.

Hsü Kuang-p'ing. 欣慰的紀念 (In Grateful Memory), ed. Wang Shih-ching. Peking, 1953. A collection of essays by the author's widow.

Li Ho-lin, ed. 魯迅論 (Lu Hsün: Critiques). 1930.

Mills, Harriet C. "Lu Hsün and the Communist Party," *The China Quarterly*, No. 4 (October–December 1960).

Ts'ao Chü-jen. 魯迅評傳 (Lu Hsün: A Critical Biography). Hong Kong, 1957.

Wang Shih-ching 王士菁 . 魯迅傳 (The Life of Lu Hsün). 1948.

Wang Tso-liang. "Lu Hsün," *Life and Letters & the London Mercury, 61*, No. 142, June 1949.

2. Yeh Shao-chün 葉紹鈞 (Yeh Sheng-t'ao 葉聖陶)

A. Works

葉聖陶文集 (The Works of Yeh Sheng-t'ao). 3 vols. Peking, 1958. In progress.

Short Stories

隔膜 (The Barrier). 1922.

火災 (Fire). 1923.

線下 (Under the Line). 1925.

城中 (In the City). 1926.

未厭集 (Without Satiety). 1928.

四三集 (At Forty-three). 1936.

Novel

倪焕之 (Ni Huan-chih). 1930.

Children's Tales

稻草人 (The Scarecrow). 4th printing 1927.

古代英雄的石像 (The Statue of an Ancient Hero). 2d ed. 1941.

Essays

With Yü P'ing-po 俞平伯. 劍鞘 (The Scabbard). Peiping, 1924.

未厭居習作 (Writings from the Studio of No Satiety). 1935.

西川集 (West of Szechwan). Chungking. 1945.

B. *Translations*

"Mrs. Li's Hair" and "Neighbors," in Wang.

Jen, Richard L. "A Man Must Have a Son," *T'ien Hsia, 6*, No. 4, April 1938.

Chow, T. S. "A Bumper Crop—A Story," *China Today*, new ser. *1*, No. 2, 1934. (A translation of "Richer by Three or Five Pecks").

Barnes, A. C. *Schoolmaster Ni Huan-chih*. Peking, 1958.

3. Ping Hsin 冰心 (Hsieh Wan-ying 謝婉瑩)

A. *Works*

冰心小說集 (The Short Stories of Ping Hsin).

冰心詩集 (The Poems of Ping Hsin).

冰心散文集 (The Prose Writings of Ping Hsin).

These three volumes were originally published by Pei Hsin Book Co. (北新書局), Shanghai, in 1932–33. Later they were reprinted by the Kaiming Press.

關於女人 (About Women). Chungking, 1943.

B. Translations

"Boredom," in Kyn Yn Yu.

Jen, Richard L. "The First Home Party," *T'ien Hsia, 4*, No. 3, March

1937.

C. Critiques

Li Hsi-t'ung 李希同 , comp. 冰心論 (Ping Hsin: Critiques).

1932.

See also Mao Tun et al., *On Writers;* Huang Ying, *Contemporary*

Chinese Women Writers.

4. Ling Shu-hua 凌叔華

A. Works

花之寺 (The Temple of Flowers). 1928.

女人 (Women). 1930.

小哥兒倆 (Little Brothers). 1935.

Ancient Melodies. With an introduction by V. Sackville-West. Lon-

don, 1953. Author's name given as Su Hua.

B. Translations

"The Helpmate," in Wang.

Ling Shu-hua and Julien Bell. "What's the Point of It?" *T'ien Hsia,*

3, No. 1, August 1936.

———. "A Poet Goes Mad," ibid., *4*, No. 4, April 1937.

Ling Shu-hua. "Writing a Letter," ibid., *5*, No. 5, December 1937.

C. Critiques

Huang Ying, op. cit.

5. Lo Hua-sheng 落華生 (Hsü Ti-shan 許地山)

A. Works

綴網勞蛛(The Vain Labors of a Spider). 1925.

無法投遞之郵件(Letters That Couldn't Be Sent Anywhere). Peiping, 1928.

解放者 (The Liberator). Peiping, 1933.

危巢墜簡(Letters from an Endangered Home). Commercial Press, 1947.

B. Translations

"After Dark," in Kyn Yn Yu.

C. Critiques

Mao Tun et al., op. cit.

6. Yü Ta-fu 郁達夫

A. Works

達夫全集(The Collected Works of Yü Ta-fu). 7 vols. 1928–31.

This edition was published by Pei Hsin Book Co. and consists of the following titles:

寒灰集 (Cold Ashes). Mainly fiction, some prose.

雞肋集 (Chicken Ribs). Fiction, including "Sinking."

過去集 (The Past). Fiction and prose.

奇零集 (Fugitive Pieces). Prose.

敝帚集 (Battered Brooms). Prose.

蕨薇集 (Ferns). Fiction.

斷殘集 (Miscellaneous Pieces). Prose and translations.

The edition does not include the following:

日記九種 (Nine Diaries). 1927.

668

迷 羊　　　(The Stray Sheep). 1928.

她是一個弱女子　　　(She Was a Weak Woman; or, Forgive
　　　　　Her! 饒了她). 1932.

屐 痕 處 處　(Footprints Here and There). 1934.

閑 書　(Books for Idle Hours). 1936.

B. *Translations*

"Disillusioned," in Kyn Yn Yu.

"Wistaria and Dodder," in Snow.

C. *Critiques*

Su Ya 素雅 , comp. 郁達夫評傳 (Yü Ta-fu: Critical and Biographical Studies). 1932.

Tsou Hsiao 鄒嘯 , comp. 郁達夫論 (Yü Ta-fu: Critiques).
1933.

　　　7. Mao Tun 茅盾 (Shen Yen-ping 沈雁冰)

A. *Works*

茅盾文集 (The Works of Mao Tun). 8 vols. Peking, 1958. In
progress.

Novels and Novelettes

蝕 　 (The Eclipse). 1930. Comprises 幻滅 (Disillusion), 動搖
(Vacillation), and 追求 　 (Pursuit).

虹 　 (Rainbow). 1930.

三人行 (Three Men). 1931.

路 (The Road). 1932.

子夜 (The Twilight: A Romance of China in 1930). 1933.

多角關係 (Polygonal Relations). 1936.

第一階段的故事 (Story of the First Stage of the War).
Chungking, 1945.

腐蝕 (Putrefaction). 1941.

霜葉紅似二月花 (Maple Leaves as Red as February Flowers).
Kweilin, 1943.

Short Stories

野薔薇 (The Wild Roses). 1929.

茅盾短篇小說集 (The Collected Short Stories of Mao Tun).
1934.

委屈 (Grievances). 1945.

Plays

清明前後 (Before and after the Spring Festival). 1947.

Essays

話匣子 (Chatterbox). 1934.

速寫與隨筆 (Sketches and Notes). 1935.

印象感想回憶 (Impressions, Reflections, and Reminiscences).
1936.

蘇聯見聞錄 (What I Saw and Heard in Soviet Russia). 1947.

B. *Translations*

Kuhn, Franz. *Schanghai im Zwielicht*. Dresden, 1938. A translation of
The Twilight.

Hsü Meng-hsiung. *Midnight*. Peking, 1957. A translation of *The
Twilight* as revised by A. C. Barnes.

Shapiro, Sidney. *Spring Silkworms and Other Stories*. Peking, 1956.

Yeh, Chun-chan. *Three Seasons and Other Stories*. Includes Mao

Tun's "Spring Silkworms," "Autumn Harvest," "Winter Fantasies."

"Suicide" and "Mud" in Snow; "Spring Silkworms" and "A True Chinese" in Wang; "Heaven Has Eyes" in *China at War*.

C. *Critiques*

Brière, O. "Un Peintre de son temps: Mao T'oen," *Bulletin de l'Université l'Aurore, 3*, No. 4, 1943.

Fu Chih-ying 伏志英 , comp. 茅盾評傳 (Mao Tun: Critical and Biographical Studies). 1931.

Huang Jen-ying 黃人影 , comp. 茅盾論 (Mao Tun: Critiques). 1933.

Yeh Tzu-ming 葉子銘 · 論茅盾四十年的文學道路 (Mao Tun: his Literary Journey through Forty Years). 1959.

8. Lao Shê 老舍 (Shu Ch'ing-ch'un 舒慶春)

A. *Works*

Novels

老張的哲學 (The Philosophy of Lao Chang). 1928.

趙子曰 (Chao Tzu-yüeh). 1928.

二馬 (The Two Mas). Postwar ed. 1948.

小坡的生日 (Hsiao P'o's Birthday). 1934.

貓城記 (The City of Cats). 1933.

離婚 (Divorce). 1933.

牛天賜傳 (The Biography of Niu T'ien-tz'u). 1936.

駱駝祥子 (Camel Hsiang-tzu). 1938.

火　葬　　　　(Cremation). First postwar ed. 1946.

四世同堂　　(Four Generations under One Roof). A novel in
　　　　three parts:

　　　　惶惑　　(Bewilderment). 1946.

　　　　偷生　　(Ignominy). One-vol. ed. 1948.

　　　　饑荒　　(Famine). Serialized in *Fiction Monthly*, 1950–51.

Short Stories

趕　集　　　　(Kan Chi). 1934.

櫻海集　　　　(Ying Hai Chi). 1935.

蛤藻集　　　　(Clams and Seaweeds). 1936.

東海巴山集　(Tung-hai Pa-shan Chi). 1946.

In the postwar period the Ch'eng Kuang Press (晨光出版公司　)
reprinted the stories in the first three collections in 微神集 (Wei
Shen Chi) and 月牙集　(The Crescent Moon) and also put out
most of Lao Shê's novels in a uniform series.

Plays

The author's wartime plays include 殘霧 (Dispersed Fog), 面子
問題 (The Problem of Face), 張自忠 (Chang Tzu-chung), 國
家至上 (The State Above All). Under the Communist regime he
has written such plays as 方珍珠 (Fang Chun-chu), 1950; 春華
秋實 (Spring Flowers and Autumn Fruit), Peking, 1953; 龍鬚溝
(Dragon-beard Ditch), Peking, 1953; 西望長安 (Look Westward
to Ch'ang-an), Peking, 1956.

Other Works

老牛破車 (The Rickety Ox-cart). 1937.

B. *Translations*

King, Evan. *Rickshaw Boy*. New York, 1945.

———— *Divorce*. St. Petersburg, 1948.

Kuo, Helena. *The Quest for Love of Lao Lee*. New York, 1948.

Heavensent. London, 1951.

Pruitt, Ida. *The Yellow Storm*. New York, 1951. An abridged version
of *Four Generations under One Roof*.

Kuo, Helena. *The Drum Singers*. New York, 1952. The Chinese version of this novel, written during Lao Shê's postwar stay in New
York, has never been published.

Liao Hung-ying. *Dragon Beard Ditch*. Peking, 1956.

Short Stories

"Black Li and White Li," "The Glasses," "Grandma Takes Charge,"
"The Philanthropist," "Liu's Court" in Wang; "They Take Heart
Again," "Portrait of a Traitor," "The Letter from Home" in *China
at War;* "The Last Train" in Yuan and Payne; "Dr. Mao" and "Talking Pictures" in George Kao, *Chinese Wit and Humor*.

C. *Studies*

Birch, Cyril. "Lao Shê: the Humourist in His Humour," *The
China Quarterly*, No. 8 (October–December 1961).

9. Shen Ts'ung-wen 沈從文

A. *Works*

In the postwar period the Kaiming Press published a uniform set
of Shen Ts'ung-wen's works, comprising:

Short Stories

阿金 (A-chin), 黑夜 (Black Night), 春 (Spring), 春燈集

(Ch'un Tun Chi), 黑鳳集 (Black Phoenix), 月下小景 (Under Moonlight).

Novelettes

邊城 (The Border Town), 神巫之戀 (The Witch Doctor's Love).

Novel

長河 (The Long River).

Other Writings

從文自傳 (The Autobiography of Ts'ung-wen), 湘行散記 (Random Sketches on a Trip to Hunan), 湘西 (West Hunan), and 廢郵存底 (Letters Saved from Oblivion).

However, these titles preserve only a small portion of the author's published writings; it is advisable, therefore, to list the more significant titles among his numerous early story collections:

十四夜間	(Night of the Fourteenth). 1929.
如蕤集	(Ju Jui Chi). 1934.
浮世輯	(The Floating World). 1935.
八駿圖	(Eight Steeds). 1935.
新與舊	(New and Old). 1936.
主婦集	(The Housewife). 1939.

Biographies

記胡也頻	(About Hu Yeh-p'in). 1932.
記丁玲	(About Ting Ling). 1934.
記丁玲續集	(More about Ting Ling). 1939.

Selections

從文小說習作選 (Selections from Ts'ung-wen's Fiction and Other Writings). 1935.

674

沈從文選集 (The Selected Stories of Shen Ts'ung-wen). 1936.

B. Translations

Ching Ti and Robert Payne. *The Chinese Earth*. London, 1947. Fourteen stories, including *The Frontier City* (*The Border Town*).

"Pai Tzu" in Snow; "Night March" in Wang; "The Lamp" and "Under Cover of Darkness" in Yuan and Payne.

Lee Yi-hsieh, "Hsiao-hsiao," *T'ien Hsia*, *3*, No. 3, October 1938; also translated as "Little Flute" by Li Ru-mien in *Life and Letters Today*, *60*, No. 137.

C. Critiques and Memoirs

Ma Feng-hua 馬逢華. 回憶沈從文教授 (My Recollections of Professor Shen Ts'ung-wen), *Tzu-yu Chung-kuo*, *16*, No. 3, February 1957.

Mao Tun et al., op. cit.

10. Chang T'ien-i 張天翼

A. Works

Short Stories

從空虛到充實 (From Vacuity to Fullness). 1931.

小 彼 得 (Little Peter). 1931.

蜜 蜂 (The Honeybee). 1933.

移 行 (Moving About). 1934.

反 攻 (Counterattack). 1934.

團 圓 (Reunion). 1935.

清 明 時 節 (Spring Festival). 1936.

追   (Pursuit). 1936.

同 鄉 們   (Fellow Villagers). 1939.

速 寫 三 篇   (Three Sketches). Chungking, 1943.

Novels

鬼 土 日 記   (A Journal of Hell). 1931.

一   年   (One Year). 1933.

洋 涇 浜 奇 俠   (The Strange Knight of Shanghai). 1936.

在 城 市 裏   (In the City). 1937.

B. *Translations*

Yang, Gladys. *Big Lin and Little Lin*. Peking, 1958. Translation of a prewar tale for children entitled 大林和小林.

Stories of Young Chinese Pioneers. Peking, 1954.

"Mutation," in Snow; "The Road," "The Inside Story," "Smile," and "Reunion," in Wang; "A New Life," in *China at War*; "The Breasts of a Girl," in Yuan and Payne; "Mr. Hua Wei," in Yeh, *Three Seasons and Other Stories*.

C. *Critiques and Memoirs*

Hu Feng, *Literary Essays*.

Chiang Mu-liang, "About Chang T'ien-i" (記張天翼), in Ssu-ma Wen-sen, ed., *Impressions of Authors*.

11. Pa Chin 巴金 (Li Fei-kan 李芾甘)

A. *Works*

For a fuller list of Pa Chin's published writings and translations see the bibliography in Monsterleet, *Pa Chin,* cited below.

Bibliography

巴金文集 (The Works of Pa Chin). 9 vols. Peking, 1959. In progress.

Novels and Novelettes

滅亡 (La Pareo; or, Destruction). 1929.

新生 (New Life). 1932.

春天裏的秋天 (Autumn in Spring). 1932.

砂丁 (The Antimony Miners). 1932.

愛情的三部曲 (The Love Trilogy). 1936.

激流三部曲 (The Torrent: A Trilogy)

　　家 (Family), 1933; 春 (Spring), 1938; 秋 (Autumn), 1940.

火 (Fire). Chungking. Part I, 1940; Part II, 1941; Part III, 1945.

憩園 (Leisure Garden). Chungking, 1944.

第四病室 (Ward No. 4). 1946.

寒夜 (Cold Nights). 1947.

Short Stories

巴金短篇小說集 (The Collected Short Stories of Pa Chin). 2 vols. 1936.

光明 (Light) 4th ed. 1935.

髮的故事 (The Story of Hair). 1936.

長生塔 (The Longevity Pagoda). 1936.

小人小事 (Little People and Little Events). 1945.

Other Works

憶 (Reminiscences). 1936.

生之懺悔 (Life's Penitence). 1936.

夢與醉 (Dreams and Drunkenness). 1938.

靜夜的悲劇 (Tragedy in a Silent Night). 1948.

生活在英雄們的中間 (Living among Heroes). Peking, 1953.

保衛和平的人們 (Defenders of Peace). Peking, 1954.

B. *Translations*

Living amongst Heroes. Peking, 1954.

Jen, Richard L. "Star," *T'ien Hsia*, 5, Nos. 1–4, 1937.

"Dog," in Snow; "The Puppet Dead," in Wang.

C. *Critiques*

Brière, O. "Un Romancier chinois contemporain: Pa Kin," *Bulletin de l'Université l'Aurore, 3,* No. 3, 1942.

Lang, Olga. *Pa Chin and His Writings: Chinese Youth Between the Two Revolutions.* Cambridge, Mass., 1967.

Monsterleet, Jean. 巴金的生活和著作 (Pa Chin's Life and Works). Translated from the French by Wang Chi-wen 王繼文. 1950.

12. Chiang Kuang-tz'u 蔣光慈 (Chiang Kuang-ch'ih 蔣光赤)

A. *Works*

Poetry

新夢 (The New Dream). 1925.

哀中國 (Lament for China). 1925.

鄉情 (Nostalgia). 1928.

哭訴 (Lament). 1929.

Novels and Novelettes

少年飄泊者 (The Youthful Tramp). 1925.

野祭 (Sacrifice in the Wilderness). 1927.

菊芬 (Chü-feng). 1927.

短　袴　黨　(Sans-culotte). 1928.

麗莎的哀怨　(Lisa's Sorrows). 1929.

衝出雲圍的月亮　(The Moon Emerging from the Clouds).
1930.

田　野　的　風　(Wind in the Fields). 1932.

Short Stories

鴨綠江上 (On the Yalu River). 1927.

B. *Critiques*

Ch'ien Hsing-ts'un. *Contemporary Chinese Writers, I.*

13. Ting Ling 丁玲 (Chiang Ping-chih 蔣冰之)

A. *Works*

Novels and Novelettes

韋　護　(Wei Hu). 1930.

水　(Water). 1933.

母　親　(Mother). 1933.

太陽照在桑乾河上 (Sun over the Sangkan River). Peking, 1952.

Short Stories

在　黑　暗　中 (In the Darkness). 1928.

自　殺　日　記 (A Suicide's Diary). 1929.

一　個　女　人 (A Woman). 1930.

法　網　(Dragnet). 1931.

夜　會　(Night Meeting). 1933.

意　外　集 (Unexpected). 1936.

我在霞村的時候 (When I Was at Hsia Village). 1st Peiping
ed. 1946.

Selections

丁玲傑作選 (The Choice Works of Ting Ling). 3d printing 1937.

延 安 集 (Selected Writings of the Yenan Period). Peking, 1954.

B. *Translations*

Yang Hsien-yi and Gladys Yang. *The Sun Shines over the Sangkan River*. Peking, 1953. Earlier published in *Chinese Literature* (spring 1953) as *Sun over the Sangkan River*.

"The Flood" (an incomplete translation of *Water*) and "News," in Snow.

C. *Critiques*

Chang Wei-fu 張惟夫, comp. 關於丁玲(About Ting Ling). 1933.

Chang Pai-hsüeh 張白雪, comp. 丁玲評論(Ting Ling: Critiques). 1934.

Chu Chieh-fan 朱介凡. 論丁玲'太陽照在桑乾河上' (Ting Ling's *Sun over the Sangkan River*: A Critique), *Wen-hsüeh Tsa-chih*, 5, No. 2, October 1958.

Huang Ying, op. cit.; see also Shen Ts'ung-wen's biographies of Ting Ling and Hu Yeh-p'in.

14. Hsiao Chün 蕭軍 (T'ien Chün 田軍)

A. *Works*

Novels

八月的鄉村 (Village in August). 1936.

第 三 代 (The Third Generation). 1937.

五 月 的 礦 山 (Coal Mines in May). Peking, 1954.

Short Stories

羊 (Sheep). 1935.

江 上 (On the River). 1936.

B. *Translations*

King, Evan. *Village in August.* New York, 1942.

"Aboard the S.S. 'Dairen Maru' " and "The Third Gun," in Snow.

C. *Critiques*

Liu Chih-ming 劉芝明, Chang Ju-hsin 張如心, et al. 蕭

軍思想批判(A Critical Analysis of Hsiao Chün's Thought).

Dairen, 1949.

15. Wu Tsu-hsiang 吳組緗

A. *Works*

西柳集 (West Willow). 1934.

飯餘集(After-dinner Pieces). 1935.

鴨嘴澇 (Duck Bill Fall; later retitled 山洪 Mountain Torrent).

Chungking, 1943.

16. Eileen Chang 張愛玲

A. *Works*

張愛玲短篇小說集 (The Collected Stories of Eileen

Chang). Hong Kong, 1954

流言 (Gossip). Hong Kong. A pirated edition, no publication date

秧歌(The Rice-sprout Song). Hong Kong, 1954.

赤地之戀 (Love in Redland). Hong Kong, 1954.

The Rice-sprout Song. New York, 1955.

Naked Earth. Hong Kong, 1956. An English version of *Love in Redland.*

"Stale Mates," *The Reporter, 15,* No. 4, September 1956. A Chinese version of the story, entitled 五 四 遺 事 (A Nostalgic Tale of the May Fourth Period), appeared in *Wen-hsüeh Tsa-chih, 1,* No. 5, January 1957.

B. *Critiques*

The bulk of my chapter on Eileen Chang has appeared in Chinese as 張愛玲的短篇小說 (Eileen Chang's Short Stories), *Wen-hsüeh Tsa-chih, 2,* No. 4, June 1957, and 評秧歌 (*The Rice-sprout Song:* A Critique), ibid., 2, No. 6, August 1957.

17. Ch'ien Chung-shu 錢鍾書

A. *Works*

寫在人生邊上　(On the Margin of Life). 1941.

人　獸　鬼　(Men, Beasts, Ghosts). 1946.

圍　城　(The Besieged City). 1947.

談　藝　錄　(On the Art of Poetry). 1948.

宋　詩　選　註　(Selected Sung Poetry, with Annotations). Peking, 1958.

18. Shih T'o 師 陀 (Wang Ch'ang-chien 王長簡)

A. *Works*

Short Stories

谷　(The Valley). 1936.

里門拾記 (Li Men Shih Chi). 1937.

落 日 光 (The Declining Sun). 1937.

果園城記(The Orchard Town). 1946.

Novels

結　婚 (Marriage). 1947.

馬　蘭 (Ma Lan). 1948.

Essays

黃花苔 (Huang Hua T'ai). 1937.

江湖集 (Rivers and Lakes). 1938.

看人集 (Watching People). 1939.

Plays

大馬戲團 (The Big Circus). Adapted from Andreyev's *He Who Gets Slapped*.

K'o Ling 柯靈 , co-author, 夜店 (Night Inn). Adapted from Gorky's *The Lower Depths*.

19. Chao Shu-li 趙 樹 理

A. Works

李家莊的變遷 (The Changes in Li Village). Peking, 1949.

趙樹理選集 (The Selected Works of Chao Shu-li). Peking, 1952. Includes all his acclaimed stories.

三　里　灣 (San-li Wan). Peking, 1956.

B. Translations

Yang, Gladys. *Changes in Li Village*. Peking, 1953.

—— *Sanliwan Village*. Peking, 1957.

C. Critiques

Kuo Mo-jo, Chou Yang, et al. 論趙樹理的創作 (On the Writings of Chao Shu-li). Hupeh, 1949.

20. Chiang Kuei 姜 貴

A. Works

旋風 (The Whirlwind). Taipei, 1959. A limited private edition of the novel was published in 1957, under the title 今檮杌傳 (Chin T'ao-wu Chuan).

B. Critiques

Kao Yang 高陽. 關於'旋風'的研究 (Comments and Reflections on *The Whirlwind*), *Wen-hsüeh Tsa-chih, 6,* No. 6, August 1959.

Index

Index

Index

Index

Index

Index

Date Due
